A Thirteenth-Century Preacher's Handbook
Studies in MS Laud Misc. 511

MARY E. O'CARROLL, SND

The papal approval of two religious orders, the Order of Preachers and the Order of Friars Minor, that followed the decrees of the Fourth Lateran Council of 1215 gave a powerful impetus to the work of preaching within the medieval Church, producing a veritable sermon industry relating to *pastoralia* of every kind. Together with the *summae* of virtues and vices, the *artes praedicandi*, and compilations of *exempla*, the sermon collection proved one of the commonest aids to preachers. Despite all the problems of manuscript survival in Britain, collections of sermons are among the more numerous groups of manuscripts to have survived. MS Laud Miscellaneous 511 is but one among them. This study aims to show that the manuscript is not only a characteristic example of the late medieval literary-pastoral genre of the sermon collection, but also a preacher's handbook of some significance, for within its slightly larger-than-pocket-book size it contains a collection of unusual exempla, *florilegia*, and numerous other aids to preaching.

The first part of this book contains a palaeographical description of the manuscript (some three hundred and fifty manuscripts were consulted to provide a comprehensive yet detailed context for the study of MS Laud Misc. 511). Careful analysis of the provenance, date, sources, and liturgical character suggests that the manuscript was a compilation, both English and Dominican, made in the central Midlands, very probably in Oxford, between 1256 and 1275.

Subsequent chapters study the audience of some of the sermons, namely the nuns at Elstow, reconstructing the life of the community around the time. The wide-ranging exploration of various other aspects of the collection (from the use of secular and scriptural authorities, distinctions, and *exempla* to the liturgical context) attempts to show the manuscript's rich treatment of doctrinal and pastoral themes.

The volume is rounded out by several appendices. These include a complete catalogue of the manuscript; an alphabetical list of sermon theme, *incipit*, and thema; a detailed analysis of sermon authorities; and a survey of the liturgical context, which synthesizes research on an important but neglected topic. Together they provide valuable resources that should do much to further research in sermon studies.

STUDIES AND TEXTS 128

A Thirteenth-Century Preacher's Handbook:
Studies in MS Laud Misc. 511

by

Mary E. O'Carroll, SND

PONTIFICAL INSTITUTE OF MEDIAEVAL STUDIES

CANADIAN CATALOGUING IN PUBLICATION DATA

O'Carroll, Mary E. (Mary Elizabeth), 1932-
    A thirteenth-century preacher's handbook : studies in MS
Laud Misc. 511

(Studies and texts, ISSN 0082-5328 ; 128)
Includes bibliographical references and index.
ISBN 0-88844-128-2

1. Bodleian Library. Manuscripts. Laud Misc. 511.   2. Sermons,
English (Middle) - History and criticism.   3. Preaching -
England - History - Middle Ages, 600-1500.   I. Pontifical Institute
of Mediaeval Studies.   II. Title.   III. Series: Studies and texts
(Pontifical Institute of Mediaeval Studies) ; 128.

BV4208.G7O22 1997   252'.00942'09022   C97-930663-9

© 1997 by
Pontifical Institute of Mediaeval Studies
59 Queen's Park Crescent East
Toronto, Ontario, Canada M5S 2C4

Printed in Canada

To my father
Edward Cecil O'Carroll (1906-1988)

His interest and encouragement were constant and
unremitting, enabling me to complete the task

Contents

Acknowlegements   ix
Foreword   xi

1. Background   1
    A. Preaching Revival and Practice Before 1215 2   B.
    Conciliar Decrees of 1215 and Diocesan Statues in Ecclesia
    Anglicana 8   C. Assistance of the Friars 15   D. The
    Medieval Sermon: Theory... 21   E. ...and Practice 24   F.
    Preaching Aids 30   G. Conclusion 34

2. The Training of Dominican Preachers   35
    A. ...in their Constitutions 35   B. ...in the Chapter Acts 39
        C. The System 43   D. The Curriculum and Books 51   E.
    ...in the English Province 58

3. MS Laud Miscellaneous 511   75
    A. Palaeographic Description 75   B. Contents 84   C. The
    Source Books Used 85   D. Named Sermons 88   E. Other
    Identified Sermons 92   F. Some Links Between the
    Identified Sermons and Some of the Source Books Named in
    MS Laud Misc. 511 96   G. A "Dominican" Book? 101   H.
    The Dating of MS Laud Miscellaneous 511 108

4. The Provenance of MS Laud Miscellaneous 511   117
    A. Liturgical Evidence 117   B. Local References 124   C.
    Palaeographic Evidence 126   D. Conclusion 128

5. An Audience for the Sermons   130
    A. Does the Audience Matter? 130   B. The Elstow
    Community 133   C. The Sermons Preached at Elstow 143
        D. The Time-and-Place-Dated Sermons as One Group 161
        E. Some Catechetical Elements in the Dated Sermons 168
    F. Conclusion 174

6. Sermon Aids in the Handbook   175
    A. Sermon Summaries or Distinctions in the Marginalia 175
    B. The *Exempla* in MS Laud Miscellaneous 511 191   C. MS
    Laud Misc. 511 as a Miscellaneous Sermon Aid 201   D.
    Conclusion 212

7. Paschal Preaching   213
    A. The Authorities in the Paschaltide Sermons 215   B. The
    Sermons for Easter Sunday: a Codicological Significance 221
    C. The Catechetical Content of Nine Sermons for Easter
    Sunday 225   D. Background to the Sermons for the Second
    Sunday after Easter 230   E. The Sermons for the Second
    Sunday after Easter: Catechetical Content 242   F.
    Conclusion 254

8. Advent Sermons on Liturgical Themes   255
    A. Some Specific Characteristics of These Advent Sermons 256
    B. The Authorities in the Advent Sermons 258   C. The
    Liturgical Links of the Six Advent Sermons 260   D. The
    Catechetical Content of the Six Advent Sermons 263   E. To
    Whom Were These Sermons Preached? 271

    Afterword   273

Appendix 1. A Catalogue of MS Laud Misc. 511   275
Appendix 2. The Rejected Folios   321
Appendix 3. The "Missing" Sermons   322
Appendix 4. Concordance: Schneyer-O'Carroll   323
Appendix 5. Sermon Theme, Incipit, and Thema   329
Appendix 6. The Source-Books   340
Appendix 7. The *Exempla*   342
Appendix 8. The Liturgical Context of the Manuscript   355
Appendix 9. Selected Texts   382
Appendix 10. An Analysis of Sermon Authorities   398
Appendix 11. Summaries of Selected Sermons   406
Appendix 12. Index of Manuscripts   430

    Bibliography   436
    Index   457

Acknowledgements

As the research and work for this book have lasted twenty years, and as both have been accomplished not in the context of the teaching which, despite the upheavals and demands of education since 1988, provides the natural locus for scholarly interaction and exchange, but in tandem with my responsibilities for reorganisation and administration in higher education, the list of acknowledgements is correspondingly lengthy.

None of my work could have been accomplished without the generous support of my Sisters in Notre Dame communities, especially those of Childwall, Oxford, Brixton, Southwark and Parbold. To my supervisor, colleague and friend, Professor C.H. Lawrence, I owe deepest thanks for help so willingly and unstintingly given me over eighteen years. Without the interest of my father, together with the practical aid and constant encouragement of Père Louis Jacques Bataillon of the Leonine Commission, the original thesis would not have been completed. As those who have studied in Duke Humfrey in the 1970s know, the wealth of learning and wisdom of the late Dr R.W. Hunt was bestowed on all seekers after manuscript knowledge. He did much to open the mysteries of MS Laud Misc. 511 to me. The capacity of scholarly sharing so splendidly shown by Dr Hunt has been further exemplified by many scholars on my way. I am grateful particularly to David d'Avray and the late Osmund Lewry OP. The staffs of the Bodleian Library, the British Library, and the Institute of Historical Research in the University of London have been invariably helpful. But I could not have completed the original research without the active help of Tom Hurley, my Vice-Principal in Notre Dame, Mount Pleasant in the summer of 1979, and a sabbatical term in 1982 facilitated by Dr James Burke, Rector of the Liverpool Institute of Higher Education, now Liverpool Hope University College. During those years in Liverpool the librarians of Notre Dame and later, of Christ's and Notre Dame, gave me much help.

The revision of my thesis for publication has been aided by a grant from the Leverhulme Foundation. The task has been totally supported by Heythrop College in the University of London. I owe a great debt of gratitude to Brendan Callaghan SJ, Principal, to Michael Walsh, Heythrop's librarian, and Michael Morgan, deputy librarian, to Dr Joe Laishley SJ for the time and resources so freely made available. Dr David Howlett of the Medieval Latin Dictionary, Hugh Lawrence and above all, Monica

Kilshaw SND, helped me with my Latin corrections. Hugh Lawrence, Mary O'Brien SND and Mary Christine Vaughan SND have been my readers, while the late Ignatius Gompertz SND and Mary Kathleen Brennan SND have put their linguistic skills in French to good use for the book. Kay Gwilt, sometime cataloguer in Heythrop Library, has helped me with the bibliography.

All my initial typing, word-processing and computer input was aided by Tim Curtis SJ, and advice on its computer progress by my brothers-in-law, Peter Gilbert and John Reynolds. To John I owe a special debt of gratitude for rescuing nine years' work on this book by a self-invented process from a crashed computer and with my sister's agreement and support, re-formatting and desk-topping its contents.

The publication of this book has been assited by a grant from the Scouloudi Foundation in association with the Institute of Historical Research, University of London; by a publication subvention from the British Academy; by a financial gift from Liverpool Hope University College; by gifts from three other sources who prefer to be anonymous and by a generous grant from the Isobel Thornley Bequest asministered by the History Faculty in the University of London.

I owe an immense debt of gratitude to both my editors at the Pontifical Institute of Mediaeval Studies, Ron B. Thomson and Fred Unwalla. Without their friendly help and undoubted expertise this work could not have been transformed from manuscript to book. None, however, of the legion mentioned above are responsible for any of its errors.

Finally, I owe a debt of thanks to two superb G.P.'s, Dr D. Bennet and Dr W. Marson, and to the doctors and nurses of St. Thomas's Hospital, London, who under Providence have twice restored some measure of health to me in recent years. I am grateful to all the persons mentioned and to many anonymous others who, in their several ways, have enabled this book to appear.

Foreword

The particular manuscript belonging to the Bodleian Library, MS Laud Miscellaneous 511, was brought to public notice by Father Pelster in his article on the manuscript in the *Bodleian Quarterly Record* in 1930.[1] In his article he made a number of comments including an expression of hope that the books of sermons of Richard Fishacre OP and Simon of Hinton OP might be identified from this manuscript.[2] This hope has not been realised. Nevertheless, the manuscript was such that in 1958 Dr Daniel Callus OP recommended it to me as worthy of deeper study.

At that time I was hoping to study sermons as source material throwing light on the history of the thirteenth century. The tentative study begun in 1958, however, was shelved in favour of classroom teaching and educational administration. In 1976 I was offered the opportunity to study for a higher degree. The first and second topics chosen proved impracticable but the third, work on MS Laud Misc. 511, was possible. In the light of my teaching of religion in the previous sixteen years the object of the study of the manuscript shifted from historical information in itself to an historical enquiry about sermons themselves. The chapters and appendices that follow contain some of the fruits of that enquiry. This initial study was completed in 1983.

During my revision work of the past ten years, medieval sermon studies have multiplied in number and extent; while studies in the thirteenth century have abounded, particularly in the areas of the history of ideas, of women in history, and in the detailed study, in England, of baronial households. This last area has demonstrated a significant change in historical methodology which has occurred in the past decade, namely the use of the computer as a tool of historical research. For example, the assembling of a card index of Dominican friars 1221-1348 which gave me material for describing their educational organisation in the English province took over six months to gather. If I were to repeat the enquiry now, the use of a computer data base would lead to quicker, richer and more varied results. Nevertheless, these changes and developments have not required

---

[1] F. Pelster SJ, "An Oxford Collection of Sermons of the end of the Thirteenth Century (MS Laud Misc. 511, S.C. 969)", *BQR*, vol 6 (1930) 168-172.

[2] Ibid., p. 170.

any significant modification of the original studies I made in MS Laud Misc. 511. If anything my longer acquaintance with the manuscript has increased my respect both for the knowledge and the skill of the friar-compiler of this preacher's handbook.

Feast of S. Thomas Aquinas,
28 January, 1995.

1

Background

Towards the end of Chapter 14 in Jane Austen's *Pride and Prejudice*, Mr Collins, to the consternation of the youngest of Mrs Bennet's five daughters, proposes to read aloud from *Fordyce's Sermons*. In 1766 Rev. Dr Fordyce had published a collection of sermons for his own use and that of others.[1] The Rev. Dr J. Fordyce's action was not so very different from the action four centuries previously of the compiler of MS Laud Misc. 511, who was an anonymous English Dominican, probably a member of the Oxford Blackfriars community. In the tradition of his order of preachers, the compiler of MS Laud Misc. 511 gathered sermons from a variety of sources and ordered them according to the Temporal cycle of the Sunday liturgy. Most attention in chapters 2 to 4 of this book is focussed on the Dominican preaching tradition and then on the actual manuscript, establishing its content, codicology, provenance and dating; while in chapters 5 to 8 attention moves to detailed examination of some of the catechetical contents of the manuscript.

Before plunging into the actuality of our manuscript, however, it is necessary to provide some context. Various elements in its background are identified in concentric circles. The first and widest circle is a very wide view, but a snapshot, of developments in preaching from the twelfth to the early thirteenth century. The next circle takes a brief look at the Fourth Lateran Council's decrees on preaching and hearing confessions, and on one part only of the Lateran reforms, namely the attempts of the bishops of the Church in England, Ecclesia Anglicana, to implement the pastoral concerns of the Fourth Lateran Council within their own dioceses. From here we enter the smaller circle of the diocese of Lincoln under Bishop Grosseteste and, as it were in close-up, find how he implemented the Lateran decrees about preaching and hearing confessions. In this pastoral task he continuously sought the help of the Dominican and Franciscan friars. The smallest and last circle is a brief look at the theory and practice of preaching as exemplified in St. Augustine, Robert Basevorn, Humbert of Romans, and Thomas Waleys OP. Thus it is hoped a framework for the detailed studies of MS Laud Misc. 511 is established. It is

---

[1] Jane Austen, *Pride and Prejudice*, originally published in 1813. This edition, with Introduction and notes by Brigid Brophy, (London: Pan Classics, 1967), 51, 300-301.

hoped too that those who read the following pages will gain more profit than did the Misses Bennet from hearing *Fordyce's Sermons.*

A. PREACHING REVIVAL AND PRACTICE BEFORE 1215

Preaching is an essential function of the Christian Church. The gospel was originally proclaimed by the Word through the word. The parable of the Sower (Matt. 13:3-23) with its explanation can be seen as the prototype of all Christian preaching. From apostolic times, the "Good News," the kerygma or message, has been communicated through preaching. The bishop of the local church was ordained to break the bread of the eucharist and the bread of the scriptures for his flock, the latter by preaching. These have been essential episcopal functions exclusive to the bishop in the early Church, increasingly shared with abbots in their monasteries as time went on. The Lateran Council of 1215 marked a significant modification of the earlier tradition through its formal injunction to bishops to share with others the responsibility of preaching, and so make preaching to the laity more available.

The art of preaching is homely and practical. It has indeed many affinities with the art of cooking, especially bread-making. The produce of both preacher's art and cook's art is transient. Sometimes the raw materials are imperfectly baked. The results are best sampled immediately. On the other hand, the formula or recipe by which preacher and cook operate changes little, the basic ingredients remain. Tradition is important in both arts. A sermon or homily is a mutable part of a religious occasion, which by its very mutability helps to make that specific occasion unique. A second function of a homily or sermon is the Christian marking of a special occasion for a community or a group or an individual: a church consecration, a new academic year, a burial. For preaching to be effective it must meet the needs and experiences of the times.

The practice of preaching in the Church—though in the early middle ages honoured more in the breach than in the observance—has been recognised from apostolic times. While in patristic and post-Vatican II times, the bread of the scriptures and the bread of the eucharist were and are broken within the one celebration, in the later middle ages the two were more often separated, although a liturgical connection in the theme or text of the sermon could be retained. Moreover, the preaching revival of the twelfth and thirteenth centuries was more often than not an outdoor activity. Only from the mid-thirteenth century, for example, did the Dominicans and other mendicant orders build specific preaching churches such as can still be seen in many European cities.

The changes in preaching practices of the twelfth century, the consequences of which emerged in the thirteenth century, were a complex process, stemming from many related developments: the Gregorian church reform movement, monastic reform, the ideal of the apostolical and evangelical life, the emergence of the canons regular, the growth of theology as an academic discipline, the ideas and activities of non-clerical—sometimes non-orthodox—religious groups, the impetus of the crusading ideal. All these in one way or another involved preaching.[2]

Preaching played a vital role in the long process of the Gregorian church reform, both by outlining the perceived necessary changes in practice—celibacy, elimination of simony—and establishing in theory at least a greater independence by the Church from the imperial, or regal or

---

[2] The following books proved helpful in writing the introductory part of this chapter: David d'Avray, *The Preaching of the Friars* (Oxford: Clarendon Press, 1985); John W. Baldwin, *Masters Princes and Merchants: the social views of Peter the Chanter and his circle*, 2 vols (Princeton: University Press, 1970); Geoffrey Barraclough, *The Medieval Papacy* (London: Thames and Hudson 1968); Robert Bartlett, *The Making of Europe: conquest, colonization and cultural change 950-1350* (London: Penguin/BCA, 1993); Hans-George Beck, Karl August Fink, Josef Glazik, Erwin Iserloh and Hans Wolter, *From the High Middle Ages to the Eve of the Reformation*, vol 4 in *The History of the Church*, ed. Hubert Jedin, trans. Anselm Biggs (London: Burns Oates, 1980); Rosalind and Christopher Brooke, *Popular Religion in the Middle Ages, 1000-1300* (London: Thames and Hudson, 1984); M.D. Chenu, *La Théologie au douzième siècle* (Paris, 1957), trans. J. Taylor and L.K. Little as *Nature, Man and Society in the Twelfth Century* (Chicago: University Press, 1968); Georges Duby, ed., *A History of Private Life*, Vol 2, *Revelations of the Mediaeval World*, trans. Arthur Goldhammer (Cambridge Mass. and London: Belknap HUP, 1988); C.H. Haskins, *The Renaissance of the Twelfth Century* (London, 1927); Friedrich Heer, *The Medieval World: Europe 1100-1350* (London: Weidenfeld, 1962); C.H. Lawrence, *Medieval Monasticism*, 2nd ed. (London: Longman, 1989); idem, *The Friars: the impact of the early Mendicant movement on Western Society* (London: Longman, 1994); Jacques Le Goff, *The Medieval World* (London, 1990), trans. by Lydia G. Cochrane from *L'Uomo Medievale* (Rome, Bari, 1987); Emmanuel Le Roy Ladurie, *Montaillou*, trans. Barbara Bray, (London: Scolar Press, 1978); E.W. McDonnell, *The Beguines and Beghards in Medieval Culture with special emphasis on the Belgian scene* (New Brunswick, NJ, 1954); Michel Mollat, *The Poor in the Middle Ages*, trans. Arthur Goldhammer (New Haven and London: Yale UP, 1986); Colin Morris, *The Papal Monarchy: the Western Church from 1050-1250* (Oxford: Clarendon Press, 1989); Jonathan Riley-Smith, *What were the Crusades?* 2nd ed. (London: Macmillan, 1992); Beryl Smalley, *The Study of the Bible in the Middle Ages*, 3rd ed. (Oxford: Blackwell, 1983); idem, *The Gospels in the Schools c. 1100-c.1280* (London and Ronceverte: Hambledon Press, 1985); idem, *The Beckett Conflict and the Schools: a study of the Intellectual in Politics* (Oxford: Blackwell, 1973).

princely power in the appointment of bishops. This movement, as organised by the papacy, sought popular support through preaching. The sermons themselves, while appealing in religious terms for religious reforms,
can also be interpreted with much validity as propaganda for a different
pattern of church organisation. This not only gave more power to the
papacy over the Church as such, but modified its relationships with rulers,
particularly with the German emperors, so as to give it more control over
the lands in disputed possession by Pope and by emperor. The potential
in this situation, for political trouble in general and for war in particular,
was great. The alliance between the papacy and a popular movement for
Church reform opened the way for future popular lay reform movements
in the twelfth century, some of which were less susceptible to control by
ecclesiastical authority.

Some of the monastic reforms owed much to the powerful call to live
the *vita apostolica*, the ideal life of the early Church as described in the
Acts of the Apostles (2:42-47). It was a call particularly to evangelical
poverty, and as such provided not only strong motivation for the attack
on simony in the Church, but also for opposition to the money-requiring
institutions emerging in the reformed Church itself. Further, the *vita apostolica* was seen as a call to imitate the life of Christ, and the apostles and
their preaching as seen in the gospels. The very term, imitation of Christ,
contains ambiguities and the potential for bitter division among the imita-
tors. In modern terms the twelfth-century perception of the *vita apostolica*
is akin to religious myth in the profundity of its grip on the religious
consciousness and practices of the time. Preaching was an important activity propagating this call, especially popular preaching by itinerants such
as St. Romuald, Peter the Hermit, St. John Gualbert, Arnold of Brescia,
Robert of Arbrissel.[3] The universality of this call to the apostolic life took
varied forms, with equally varied effects.

One result was the movement of the Canons Regular, which harnes-
sed the spiritual energy of the ideal of apostolic life to the clerical life.
While initially aimed at reforming cathedral chapters, introducing communal life according to the Rule of St. Augustine, the Augustinian canons
regular were soon establishing houses independent of any cathedral link

---

[3] Jedin, *History*, 4: 98-112; see also F.L. Cross and E.A. Livingstone, edd., *The
Oxford Dictionary of the Christian Church*, 2nd ed. (Oxford: OUP, 1964); for Romuald,
ODCC 1201 and Morris, *Papal Monarchy*, 70-75; Peter the Hermit, *ODCC* 1072 and
Morris, *Papal Monarchy* 73; St.John Gualbert, *ODCC* 749 and Morris, *Papal Monarchy*
70-72; Arnold of Brescia, *ODCC* 92 and Morris, *Papal Monarchy* 404-408; Robert of
Arbrissel, Morris, *Papal Monarchy* 71-73.

but claiming canonical status. St. Norbert, founder of the Premontratensi-
ans, the White Canons, is an example of still another type of the *vita apostolica*. Norbert and his companions lived a contemplative life after the
Cistercian manner, and were engaged in preaching missions. Later, Norbert was consecrated archbishop of Magdeburg. His White Canon followers established many priories in desolate or newly-settled places, such as
Blancheland in the uncertain English and Scottish borderlands and in the
expanding Christian frontiers in eastern Germanic and Slavic lands.

The growth of schools, not necessarily of monastic origin, is a significant development in the twelfth century. Many of these were cathedral
schools, such as those at Chartres, Laon, Paris and Hereford. At some of
these were gifted teachers like Peter Abelard, Anselm of Laon, Richard and
Andrew of St. Victor, Peter Lombard, Peters of Poitiers and Peter the
Chanter. In the mid-twelfth century, the success—existence even—of a
school was related directly to the skill and popularity of the master. Only
towards the end of the century and in the first years of the thirteenth
century did masters and scholars settle more permanently in places such
as Bologna, Paris or Oxford, thus enabling the academic communitities
and institutions which became universities to emerge.

Many of the twelfth-century theologians, of whom Peter the Chanter
is an outstanding example, saw their function as moral as well as intellectual. Reform of the Church was part of their agenda; preaching was one
of its means. According to Peter the Chanter, in the scholastic discipline
of theology careful reading of Scripture—*lectio*—was seen as the foundation; disputing the questions raised by lectio—*disputatio*—was the walls;
while preaching—*praedicatio*—was the roof. Thus was the building—theology—raised.[4] It was no accident either, that one of Peter the Chanter's
pupils, Stephen Langton, was a significant reformer in Church and society
in England, or that another mature student of Peter's, Fulk of Neuilly, was
a powerful popular preacher in Paris and its environs, or yet another was
influential at the papal court, later becoming Pope as Innocent III.[5]

The burgeoning of new life in the twelfth century in culture, society,
the Church, the towns, the economy, is a well-attested fact. One of its
manifestations is the emergence of lay preachers. The Gregorian reform
movement had mobilised popular support for its implementation. Yet some
elements of organisation in the reformed institutions were themselves contradictory. For example, so that clerics should gain a theological education
in the schools, the practice grew of giving the lucky ones a benefice, some-

[4] Baldwin, *MPM*, vol 1, 90-91.
[5] Baldwin, *MPM*, vol 1, Chapter 2; also Part 2, "Masters," 63-157.

times several, as economic support during their time of study. The churches granted as benefices were themselves left without a pastor unless a vicar was appointed. In the complexities of land-holding in a feudal society, dioceses, churches and monasteries had an economic value to their lord, whether emperor, king, prince, baron or local landowner, and at times of changeover following the death of a bishop or abbot or abbess, could be retained by the lord for his financial profit. These kinds of situation contributed to uneven, often inadequate, pastoral care in villages and in rapidly growing towns. There was a spiritual vacuum which traditional parish priests—present or absent—and vicars were ill-equipped to fill. Such elements, together with the strong religious appeal of the *vita apostolica*, not only to those laity who joined the new monastic and canonical orders but also to those who remained lay, stimulated lay people to be active themselves in preaching the gospel and following Christ in poverty. Both men and women were found in these lay groups. This lay activity is exemplified by followers of people like Arnold of Brescia, Robert of Arbrissel, Waldo, and lay movements like the Waldensians—and their orthodox part, the poor Men of Lyons—the Humiliati, the first Franciscans and the Beguines. When these popular movements are taken in conjunction with another popular religious activity, namely going on pilgrimage which meant a variety of mobile lay groups, then the rich potential of difficulties for the status quo of the Church of the time is seen.

The very subject of popular preaching, the gospels and especially the poverty of Christ and his apostles, was a criticism of many aspects of the twelfth-century Church, and a direct challenge to the increasing clerical control characteristic of the Gregorian reform. The contrast between some of the theory of Christian living and its practice, or lack thereof, was increasingly obvious. The biggest problem, however, was the fact that the institutional Church had no category for active lay apostolic life. Initially, a common response of the Church to popular preaching which criticised existing practice in Church and society was condemnation. Agreement on the nature of punishment following condemnation was less clear: whether the Church could punish, should punish, or whether the condemned person should be regarded as outside Church and society and handed over to the civil or royal power for punishment? Another common reaction rather than response was confusion: those in authority in the Church did not know what to do. While the Waldensians were pushed into an heretical situation by Church decisions, the Humiliati, through the perceptive action of Innocent III, were enabled to remain as lay preachers within the Church. To the radical new group of lay preachers led by the charismatic Francis of Assisi, Innocent III gave his blessing.

The ambivalent nature of some aspects of twelfth-century popular preaching is seen in the growth of the Catharist heresy. This non-Catholic religion flourished in many of the towns of northern and central Italy and in urban and rural parts of Provence. Its leaders, both men and women, known as the Perfecti, lived lives of great self-discipline and austerity—a marked contrast both to its own adherents and to many Christian leaders of the time. The chief means of spreading the new Manichaeism was preaching. In response, Christian preaching missions were organised. St. Bernard undertook one, the main effect of which was the involvement of the Cistercian Order in preaching work among the Cathars or Albigensians for the next few decades. Later, the bishop of Osma, with one of his canons, Dominic Guzman, was similarly engaged, with equal lack of success. Eventually, however, Dominic's experience in Provence elicited the need for theologically-trained preachers who lived the apostolic life. This experience, together with the support of Innocent III, resulted in the foundation of the Order of Preachers.

Lastly there is the part played by the Crusades in stimulating a preaching revival. From the standpoint of the twentieth century it is difficult to understand the idealism, enthusiasm and commitment to going on crusade to the Holy Land that swept men and women of all sorts and conditions, and even children, into the movement. It is a measure of the influence of the idea of the *vita apostolica* that so many people felt so passionately about the Holy Land, the place where Jesus Christ lived and died, that they were willing to raise funds, leave home and family, take the cross and, certain of their salvation if they died in the attempt, venture eastwards. But, as many scholars have indicated, other strong motives, probably not consciously acknowledged in twelfth-century terms, fostered the crusading ideal. Social and economic pressures such as population growth, shortage of land and holdings for younger sons, together with the traditional desire of Church leaders to curb local wars and so encourage the use of military skills and aggression further east, played their part.

A crusade was called by the Pope. He was willing to grant jealously-guarded ecclesiastical finance to aid those rulers willing to take the cross. The raising of a military host to follow the leader was largely the work of popular preachers who were commissioned for the task by the Pope. St. Bernard yet again was the best-known, though only one of an army of crusade preachers. A crusade was preached, successfully or unsuccessfully, several times in the twelfth century. After 1204, however, some of the crusade participants and supporters were beginning to recognise some of the flaws in the more barbarian West's attack on a more sophisticated East. In the early thirteenth century a decisive modification of "crusade" occurred. Instead of reserving the preaching and mobilising of a crusade to freeing

the Holy Land from the infidel, the idea of using a crusade against any in-
fidels emerged. So it was that the crusade against the Cathars led by Simon de Montfort was authorised, and set the precedent for later crusades
such as the Baltic crusade against the Lithuanians from 1236 onwards.

Throughout all aspects of the life of the Church in the twelfth century, the revival of preaching is a fact. In many ways it was a positive encouragement to the spiritual growth of groups and of individuals. But
popular preaching also posed a threat to both social and ecclesiastical
structures. It aroused strong expectations among the listeners, including
a desire for further reform in the Church. On the whole, the twelfth-century Church had little control over the preaching revival of the times. It
was not unexpected, therefore, that preaching should be part of the agenda of the Fourth Lateran Council. It is to this Council, and in particular,
to its effects on the development of the Church in England, Ecclesia Anglicana, we now turn.

B. CONCILIAR DECREES OF 1215 AND DIOCESAN STATUTES IN ECCLESIA ANGLICANA

In 1215 Pope Innocent III summoned an ecumenical council to meet in
Rome. Representing England were the archbishop of Canterbury, Stephen
Langton, the bishops of Chichester (Richard Poore, later of Salisbury and
Durham), Coventry and Lichfield, Exeter, Lincoln (the revered Hugh of
Wells), Rochester, and Worcester. The bishops-elect of Ely and Norwich
were also present, together with several abbots, priors and monk-proctors
of some English monasteries. The bishops of Bath and Wells, London,
Salisbury, and Winchester stayed at home; while the sees of Durham, Carlisle and Hereford, being vacant, had no representatives. The king's proctor was Richard Marsh—later bishop of Durham.[6] The sermons, discussions and debates were crystallised in seventy canons.[7] Just as the Council
of Trent, 1545-1563, set the pattern of the Church for nearly four centuries,
so the Fourth Lateran Council indicated the lines of ecclesial development
for over two centuries at least. The central aim of the council was to

---

[6] F.M. Powicke and C.R. Cheney, *Councils and Synods With Other Documents Relating to the English Church 1205-1313*, 2 vols. (Oxford: Clarendon Press, 1964) 1: 47.

[7] J. D. Mansi, ed., *Sacrorum conciliorum nova et amplissima collectio*, 31 vols. (Flo-
rence, 1759-1798), vol. 22, col. 953-1086. See also Norman Tanner, ed., *Decrees of the
Ecumenical Councils*, 2 vols (London and Georgetown: Sheed and Ward and
Georgetown UP, 1990), 1: 229-271.

promote reforming activity, particularly to raise the standards of behaviour and learning amongst the clergy.[8]

In some of its canons, notably 10 and 21, the Fourth Lateran Council not only stimulated much pastoral activity in the thirteenth century, but has strongly influenced pastoral life in the Church even to the twentieth century. Canon 10, *De predicatoribus instituendis*, was of great significance for preaching:

> We therefore decree by this general constitution that bishops are to appoint suitable men to carry out with profit this duty of sacred preaching, men who are powerful in word and deed and who will visit with care the peoples entrusted to them in place of the bishops, since these by themselves are unable to do it, and will build them up by word and example. The bishops shall suitably furnish them with what is necessary, when they are in need of it, lest for want of necessities they are forced to abandon what they have begun. We therefore order that there be appointed in both cathedral and other conventual churches suitable men whom the bishops can have as coadjutors and cooperators not only in the office of preaching but also in hearing confessions and enjoining penances and in other matters which are conducive to the salvation of souls. If anyone neglects to do this, let him be subject to severe punishment.[9]

Canon 21, usually known as *Utriusque sexus*[10] is equally significant. This canon made confession at least once a year to one's own parish priest obligatory, but required too that confessors be discreet, cautious and compassionate. This further emphasised the requirement of the annual confession at Easter or thereabouts. Moreover, for good or for ill, the reception of the sacrament of penance became linked in pastoral practice with the reception of holy communion at Mass.

The implications of these two canons alone for the education and work of priests were not only far-reaching but profound. It is hardly surprising that, despite canon 13 of the same council forbidding the foundation of new religious orders, Innocent III and his successor, Honorius III, gave whole-hearted support to the inspiration of Francis Bernardone, an Italian layman, for his evangelical preaching Order of Friars Minor, and equally to the plan of the canon, Dominic Guzman of Calruega, for found-

---

[8] For example, Canons 11, 14-19, 27-31.

[9] Mansi, col. 997-1000. English trans. taken from Tanner, *EC*, 239-240; see also H. J. Schroeder, *Disciplinary Decrees of the General Councils* (St. Louis, 1937), 251-252.

[10] Mansi, col. 1007-1010; Tanner, *EC*, 245.

ing a religious family totally dedicated to preaching: the Order of Preachers.[11]

It is significant for the implementation in England of the decrees of the Fourth Lateran Council that at least seven of the bishops of Ecclesia Anglicana in the thirteenth century were scholar-bishops who were mainly theologians. Three, two theologians and one canonist, were raised to the altars of the Church: Edmund of Abingdon, archbishop of Canterbury,[12] Richard de Wyche, bishop of Chichester,[13] and Thomas de Cantilupe, bishop of Hereford.[14] For another two, Walter de Cantilupe, bishop of Worcester,[15] and his friend, Robert Grosseteste, bishop of Lincoln, canonisation processes were seriously considered.[16] The spiritual quality of episcopal leadership in the thirteenth century was a significant factor in effective Church reform. Circumstances also conspired to give the English bishops of this time a freer hand than was customary. The raising of the Interdict meant a fresh spiritual opportunity, while the accession of the child-king, Henry III, with the support of the bishops, gave to the English Church for a time at least more freedom of action than had been available for many decades. The possibilities for implementing the decrees of a reforming council were good. Many of the English bishops did this through diocesan synods, with their resulting statutes.

Cheney's work on English diocesan synods has shown the relationships between the many sets of diocesan statutes of the thirteenth century, while Powicke and Cheney have made it possible to study with ease the actual texts of these statutes.[17] All the diocesan statutes except Langton's

[11] M.H. Vicaire, *Histoire de Saint Dominique* (Paris, 1957); idem, *St. Dominic: His Life and Times*, trans. Kathleen Pond (London, 1964), Chapter 11.

[12] C.H. Lawrence, *St. Edmund of Abingdon* (Oxford: Clarendon Press, 1960) for documentation. See also *ODCC*, 445.

[13] C.H. Lawrence, "St. Richard of Chichester," in *Studies in Sussex Church History*, ed. M.J. Kitch (1981), 35-55; *ODCC*, 1185.

[14] Eric Kemp, *Canonization and Authority in the Western Church* (Oxford: OUP, 1948), 176; *ODCC*, 236.

[15] *ODCC*, 236.

[16] Eric Kemp, "The Attempted Canonization of Robert Grosseteste," in *Robert Grosseteste, Scholar and Bishop*, ed. D.A. Callus (Oxford: Clarendon Press, 1955) 241-6; *ODCC*, 603-604.

[17] M. Gibbs and G. Lang, *Bishops and Reform, 1215-1272* (Oxford, 1934). The conclusions are largely replaced by C.R. Cheney, *English Synodalia of the Thirteenth Century* (Oxford, 1941), 2nd imp. with new introduction (Oxford, 1968).

Canterbury Statutes I, 1213-1214[18] draw in greater or lesser detail from the canons of the Fourth Lateran Council. They also incorporate relevant parts of specific legislation of Ecclesia Anglicana and especially that of the Council of Oxford in 1222.[19]

This is not the place to discuss in length or detail the relationship between theory and practice of synodal statutes. It is probably as complex as the relationship between the theory of the medieval *artes predicandi* and actual sermons. The repetition of synodal statutes may indicate breach of observance; it may, as Hamilton Thompson remarked, indicate the diligence of bishops' clerks in copying episcopal registers.[20] Nevertheless, the synodal statutes do give an indication of what English diocesan bishops of the early and mid-thirteenth centuries thought were important pastoral matters. High on the list come instruction of the faithful, sacramental practice, and the conduct and education of the clergy. Here, three matters only will be examined: the "syllabus" for religious instruction including teaching about emergency baptism; directives about preaching; directives about the sacrament of penance.

The first of the three elements for elucidation was what bishops expected lay people to know as a minimum and how they were to learn it. In his statutes 3, 4, 5, under the titles *De agnitione fidei, De trinitate credendis, De symbolo docendo*,[21] Richard Poore established a catechetical pattern which most other diocesan statutes took over in whole or in part. Lay persons must believe in the Trinity and must know the articles of faith as set out in the Apostles' Creed. They should know by heart the Creed, the Our Father, and the Hail Mary. Parents should teach their children, but the parish priest was also expected to ensure that this knowledge was passed on. From some of the statutes it seems that this teaching was to be given at the time of confession.[22] The Winchester statutes declare:

[18] Baldwin, *MPM* 1, 109-110, 192, 200, 266. Langton's statutes, which precede Lateran IV, reflect in several places the teaching of his master, Peter the Chanter. See Phyllis Barzillay Roberts, "The Pope and the Preachers: Perceptions of the Religious Role of the Papacy in the Preaching Tradition of the Thirteenth-Century English Church," in *The Religious Roles of the Papacy: Ideals and Realities 1150-1300*, ed. C.J. Ryan (Toronto: PIMS, 1989), 277-297, on the relationship between the English synodal statutes and the Fourth Lateran Council.

[19] Powicke and Cheney, 1: 100-125.

[20] A.H. Thompson quoted in C.R. Cheney, *Episcopal Visitation of Monasteries in the Thirteenth Century* (Manchester, 1931) 4.

[21] Powicke and Cheney, 1: 61.

[22] Powicke and Cheney, 1: Winchester 134; Worcester 172; Lincoln 269.

> In giving penance the priests shall diligently instruct parishioners con-
> cerning faith in the Trinity, the Passion and Incarnation; and wisely
> provide that their people are not ignorant of the Lord's prayer and the
> Apostles' Creed in their mother tongue.

Most diocesan statutes have variants of this statute. Worcester II[23] includes instruction on the seven vices, and the sevenfold daily praying of the Our Father and the Creed, together with an Our Father at the crucifix in the graveyard. Coventry and Lichfield[24] adds the Hail Mary to the above sevenfold repetition. Exeter[25] has the same prayers, but not the repetition. The only statutes containing nothing about the knowledge required of the laity are those of York I.

Two sets of statutes, Salisbury and Coventry and Lichfield, mention schools.[26] Those of Salisbury, however, are for teaching grammar to poor scholars; while Alexander of Stavensby of Coventry and Lichfield, having declared that there should be no division between pastoral work and teaching, continues:

> Therefore we command that those concerned should see that in every
> place where there is directing of schools, there should be men such as
> know how to instruct others in doctrine and who wish to educate
> them by the example of a good life.

In his statutes Grosseteste declares:

> Let the rectors of churches and parish priests carefully see that the
> children of their parish are taught with care, and that they know the
> Our Father, Creed, and the Hail Mary, and know how to sign them-
> selves correctly with the Sign of the Cross. And because, as we have
> heard, even some adults do not know these prayers, we ordain that
> when lay people come to confession they be carefully examined to see
> whether they know the above—and to see to what extent it is neces-
> sary that they be instructed in them by the priests.[27]

All diocesan statutes make provision for other elementary information to be given to the laity, namely the administration of baptism in case of necessity. The main provision is for a new-born child whose life is endangered. Some statutes add interesting bits, indicating that the formula can be said in English or French:

---

[23] Powicke and Cheney, 1: 172.
[24] Powicke and Cheney, 1: 213.
[25] Powicke and Cheney, 1: 228.
[26] Powicke and Cheney, 1: Salisbury 94; Coventry and Lichfield 211.
[27] Powicke and Cheney, 1: 269.

> The form of baptizing children in time of necessity should be as fol-
> lows: "I baptize you N. in the name of the Father and of the Son and
> of the Holy Ghost. Amen." English or French or any other language
> can be used, for they have equal power, and afterwards the child will
> not be baptized again with due solemnity. But if there is doubt about
> the form of baptism, let it be thus: "If you are not already baptized, I
> baptize you" etc.[28]

From the brief accounts above it is clear that the practical problems
of giving people even very simple religious instruction were immense and
not specific to the thirteenth century. Of all the diocesan statutes, those of
Lincoln are the most straightforward. In these thirteenth-century decrees
the agents of instruction are the priests, except in the case of children's
prayers where it is the parents' duty. In some of the statutes the place and
opportunity of instruction seem to be the place and time of confession.[29]
If confession was obligatory once a year, then the question of the effectiveness of the implementation of the requirement for instruction is raised.
Once-yearly instruction is plainly insufficient. Given the rush for confessions before Easter, the giving of instruction to each penitent as required
by statute would be impractical. If confession was becoming a more frequent practice, then opportunity for instruction increased. In the early
Church the initiation and instruction of the catechumens was carried out
through the celebration of the first part of the Mass, especially the Scripture readings and the homily associated with them. This, however, was
catechesis for mainly literate laity. In the thirteenth century, apart from the
people increasingly educated for commerce in the new towns and some
of the upper classes, the problem of catechesis was how to educate the
illiterate in their religion.

Many of the statutes mention preaching, specifically in connection
with the condemnation of fornication. Salisbury I, for example, has a
standard expression:

> In confessions and sermons especially on the greater feasts, it should
> very often be impressed upon lay folk, that any intercourse of man
> and woman, except in marriage, is a mortal sin.[30]

---

[28] Powicke and Cheney, 1: 180, Winchester—this exemplifies the others: 68-69,
Exeter; 115, Oxford; 136, Winchester; 180, Worcester II; 214, Coventry and Lichfield.

[29] Powicke and Cheney, 1: 134, Winchester; 172, Worcester notes "before confession"; and Lincoln, 276, recommends instructing "subjects" in the Lord's Prayer and
the Creed.

[30] Powicke and Cheney, 1: 72.

Only Robert Grosseteste and Richard de Wyche, in their respective statutes, suggest other topics than this for preaching. Grosseteste[31] requires that parish priests preach on the ten commandments, on the seven deadly sins, the seven sacraments of the Church. Richard de Wyche[32] requires frequent preaching on the Trinity, and on the incarnation, birth, passion, resurrection and ascension of Christ, and on the general resurrection from the dead. It is not clear, however, whether Robert Grosseteste and Richard de Wyche have made explicit what was common practice in all English dioceses, or whether they have articulated the exception. When, however, the requirements of religious education, as seen in the above statutes, are linked with the pastoral policy of Grosseteste, as seen below, it seems very likely that the missing link between means and practice was the friars' preaching to the people.

With regard to canon 21 of the Fourth Lateran Council, *Utriusque sexus*, most diocesan statutes have a variant of the one found in the Worcester statutes:

> Before the penitent's confession, the priest should give advice with comfort and exhortation: comfort not to despair about the magnitude or enormity of the sin, or about the number of sins; exhortation to confess the circumstances of the sin, pouring out his heart before the Lord like water.[33]

Such comment is not only spiritually sensitive, but morally searching. Four different dioceses, one of which—Winchester—repeats the recommendation thrice, strongly recommend to parish priests the use of the pastoral services of members of the Order of Preachers and of the Order of Friars Minor in hearing confessions.[34] The Salisbury statutes declare:

> Because of the religious spirit of the Friars Preachers and Friars Minor, and for the salvation of souls, we have decided that the faithful be allowed to approach them for confession whenever they wish outside Lent if they have received permission from their own priest—after having paid the customary offerings to their own church.

---

[31] Powicke and Cheney, 1: 268

[32] Powicke and Cheney, 1: 455.

[33] Powicke and Cheney, 1: Worcester 172; see also Salisbury 73.

[34] Powicke and Cheney, 1: Winchester I 1224, 133; Winchester III, 1237?, 415; Winchester IV, 1262-5, 706; Salisbury II, 1238-44, 386; Lincoln, 1235-53, 480; Wells 1258?, 595.

The Wells statutes[35] permitted "the hearing of confessions in Lent and outside the parish" by the friars because of "the holy fruit of their lives and preaching." The dioceses of Lincoln and Chichester equally welcomed the pastoral services of the friars in hearing confessions, although bishop Gilbert of St. Leofard in the statutes of Chichester II, 1241-1255, forbade the reception of and preaching by unauthorised orders of friars.[36] This hints at a problem that became more acute throughout the thirteenth century, and that the Salisbury statutes tried to solve; namely, hostility between diocesan priests and friars over the offerings of the faithful, especially if these seemed to be diminishing lawful parish dues. It is in describing the function of the friars in diocesan work that the link between preaching and hearing confessions as two elements in one pastoral service is explicitly made in some diocesan statutes in Ecclesia Anglicana. It is necessary now to make some enquiry about the co-operation of the friars with the English bishops in their attempts to implement the pastoral decrees of the Fourth Lateran Council about preaching and the hearing of confessions.

C. Assistance of the Friars

It has been observed above that accurate information about parochial clergy in the twelfth and early thirteenth centuries is sparse.[37] The nature of the pastoral care of the time is difficult to establish. Given the growth of the lay preaching movements which were meeting some of the spiritual needs of the hungry sheep, it is likely that paucity of information reflects paucity of pastoral care. There is a further question about the way in which pastoral care was perceived in those times. The comments of the bishop of Senlis in 1180 are interesting:

> For it is most unworthy that a person who in the cathedral church has been assigned to the holy altar in his due turn according to his dignity as a canon, should be tied to a parochial cure. It is foreign to the dignity of a canon to bless marriage beds, purify women after childbirth, refer to the bishop the brawls and contentions of the people and be subject to the rural dean; and that he should be counted among local and lower-class priests who, because of the dignity of his office,

[35] Powicke and Cheney, 1: 595.
[36] Powicke and Cheney, 1: 1088-1089.
[37] See, Phyllis B. Roberts, "The Pope and the Preachers," 285-286; also see 294-295 for a bibliographical note on this problem.

is entered in the roll of the church among those who are great in the church.[38]

The bishop regards the pastoral matters of a parish as clearly inappropriate for a canon of a cathedral. This is one viewpoint. The moral concerns and their pastoral implications of Peter the Chanter in his teaching in Paris provide a contrasting perspective.[39] Nevertheless as Morris notes, attitudes towards priestly ministry were changing, changes confirmed by the canons of the Fourth Lateran Council:

> The most striking feature was the advance from the older ideals of cultic purity of the clergy to a demand for an active pastorate directed towards the faithful as a whole.[40]

The information available about the education parish clergy received in the twelfth century is even sparser than the information about their perception and practice of pastoral care.[41] Perhaps in the days before the Gregorian reform, and in those parts of the Church where Gregorian directives about celibacy were still unpractised, parish priests who were themselves sons of priests gained a certain basic knowledge and practice from serving, as it were, apprenticeships to their fathers, passing this experience on in turn to their own sons. As far as England is concerned, it is necessary to take into account the negative pastoral effects of the depredations of Richard I and his brother, John, on the Church, as well as the pastoral deprivations of the Interdict in John's reign. The need for assistance to priests both in some form of education and in training for pastoral ministry was great indeed.

Thirteenth-century synodal statutes exist for most dioceses of the Ecclesia Anglicana. There seem relatively few records showing how these statutes were practised. Lincoln under its energetic and pastoral bishop, Robert Grosseteste, is easier to examine, as more material is to hand concerning the pastoral implementation of the Fourth Lateran Council and of the diocesan statutes, and also concerning the use of the friars. It is worth noting that, by the end of the thirteenth century the Dominicans had established priories in every diocese of England and Wales except Rochester. Moreover, each cathedral city except Rochester, had its Blackfriars. The Franciscans were even more ubiquitous, with sixty friaries by the end of

---

[38] Morris, *Papal Monarchy*, 289.

[39] Baldwin, *MPM*, Chapter 1.

[40] Morris, *Papal Monarchy*, 438.

[41] d'Avray, *Friars*, 19-21, 49-50.

the same century. These facts, taken in conjunction with the support of at least five dioceses for the efforts of the friars in pastoral care, shows that what we know was certainly occurring in the Lincoln diocese was probably happening in other dioceses of the Ecclesia Anglicana as well.[42]

In 1235, at about the age of sixty-seven, Robert Grosseteste was appointed Bishop of Lincoln.[43] Lincoln was the largest diocese in England and Wales, stretching from the borders of Yorkshire in the north to the Thames in the south, and including at least eight shires. Grosseteste immediately sought the help of the Friars Preachers in his new pastoral responsibilities. He wrote begging letters, some of them very moving, to Alard, prior provincial of the Dominicans,[44] to the provincial chapter,[45] and to the man from whom he most wanted help, his old friend John of St. Giles.[46] To John he wrote:

> Unless I am much mistaken, this, "the building of a heavenly house," can be more adequately done by you in your native land, rather than elsewhere.... I also firmly believe that your presence has never been so much desired by other men as it is by us and by your beloved friends, now staying with us; nor is there any bishop who requires your help so much in preaching the word of salvation as I do, who, more than other bishops I know, am weighed down by the heavy burden of pastoral care.

That care Grosseteste outlined to Jordan, master-general of the Dominicans, when he was begging for the continued help of the friars:

> It does not escape the wisdom of your loving concern that my diocese is much more extensive than any other in the kingdom of England; and has a greater number of people to fill it.... There is more need for help, efficacious help in proclaiming the word of God, hearing confessions and imposing penances.[47]

---

[42] Morris, *Papal Monarchy*, 489-496.

[43] D.A. Callus, ed., *Robert Grosseteste, Scholar and Bishop* (Oxford, 1955), 1-7, 146 seq.; Emden, *BRUO*, 2: 830-833. See R.W. Southern, *Robert Grosseteste: The Growth of an English Mind in Medieval Europe* (Oxford: Clarendon Press, 1986), for a new assessment of Grosseteste's early education, experience in the schools, scientific knowledge, theology and pastoral work. See also James McEvoy, *The Philosophy of Robert Grosseteste* (Oxford: Clarendon Press, 1982), 3-48.

[44] H.R. Luard, ed., *Roberti Grosseteste Episcopi quondam Lincolniensis Epistolae RS* 25 (London, 1862), Letter XIV, 1235: 59-60, to Alard OP.

[45] Ibid., Letter XV, 1235: 61 to Alard and the Provincial Chapter.

[46] Ibid., Letter XVI, 1235: 61-62 to John of St. Giles OP.

[47] Ibid., Letter XL, 1237: 131-133.

Further letters of his, for example, to prior provincial Matthew in 1242[48] and to Hugh of St. Cher in 1245,[49] emphasised not only his personal continuing need, but that of the whole Ecclesia Anglicana for generous help from the Dominican friars. Grosseteste received equally generous help from the Franciscans; indeed, for many years he was given the permanent help of another great friend, Adam Marsh OFM.

In a letter he wrote to "the lord Pope and cardinals" in 1250,[50] Grosseteste gave a thumbnail sketch of the manner in which he used the pastoral skills of the friars:

> Listen kindly, please, to a few words about a new, unusual practice. After my appointment as bishop, I considered myself as both bishop and shepherd of souls; and I considered it necessary not to require the blood of my sheep in strict censuring at my hands, but to visit, with all diligence, the sheep committed to me, as Scripture explains and teaches. Hence I began my episcopate by travelling around each of the rural districts, ordaining priests for each, calling them to assemble on certain days, and in certain places, making sure that the people be forewarned to be present on the same day and in the same place, with their children for confirmation, to hear the word of God, and to go to confession. When the clergy and people were assembled together, I myself, as often before, explained the word of God to the clergy, and some friar preacher or friar minor did the same for the people. Four friars subsequently heard confessions and imposed penances. And when the children had been confirmed, on the same day and the following day I, together with my priests, applied ourselves to investigations, corrections, and reforms, according to all that is involved in the duty of inquisition.

The friars in Grosseteste's plan were engaged in preaching to the people and in hearing confessions; while Grosseteste carried out the task of visitation, especially with the priests, following as it were a foundation course in pastoral care. Grosseteste's vigorous new work of reform, together with the tough reprimands he handed out, caused much upset throughout his huge diocese, sometimes in religious houses.[51] His inquisitional style, most likely modelled on the royal courts of justice, could encourage people to report on one another rather than look to their own faults. Moreover, a process as new as this, however worthy, and involving a long

[48] Ibid., Letter C 1242?: 304-305 to Matthew OP, Provincial.
[49] Ibid., Letter CXV, 1245: 335-336 to Cardinal Hugh of St. Cher.
[50] Powicke and Cheney, 1, 265.
[51] Southern, *Grosseteste*, 257-260; Morris, *Papal Monarchy*, 533.

and strong use of the friars, would not necessarily commend itself to existing vested interests whether temporal or spiritual. Perhaps Grosseteste's practice was a necessary step towards a greater interiorisation of the moral responsibility of the individual, and towards the necessary distinction between sin as being in the internal forum, and crime as belonging to the public forum. Nevertheless, the good intentions of Grosseteste were patent and, in his inimitable way, many of the requirements of the Fourth Lateran Council's reforming canons were implemented.

As well as organising pastoral occasions of the kind just described, Grosseteste also wrote many works for the education of his priests, to help them in their cure of souls. Some English bishops, like Alexander of Stavensby of Coventry and Lichfield, had attached small treatises on the vices and on confession to their synodal statutes;[52] while others, like Walter de Cantilupe,[53] had made the synodal statutes themselves an exercise in applied moral theology. The scholar-bishop, Grosseteste, wrote books. Here, however, only one of Grosseteste's many treatises, his *Templum Dei*,[54] will be considered. If survival and numbers of manuscripts are any indication, this treatise was one of the best-sellers in manuals for parish priests to the end of the middle ages. Written partly in continuous prose, partly in note-form, this little book is a handy summary—a catechism, later ages would say—of applied Christianity. God's temple, which is both bodily and spiritual, is adorned with virtues, six "ornaments." Grosseteste puts together the three theological virtues and three only of the cardinal virtues, omitting Justice. Then he treats of the articles of the Creed. linking them to the six virtues noted, and weaves in the gospel commandments of love and the decalogue. Next come the seven deadly sins, linked in thirteenth-century manner with the petitions of the Our Father, the "mercies" of the gospel, the gifts of the Holy Spirit, the virtues and the beatitudes. The seven sacraments, and relevant canon law (excommunications, reserved sins), are also treated. In all, much instruction, solidly grounded in Scripture, is compressed into a small space. The use and well-deserved popularity of this little manual made it one of the most important pastoral aids, not only of the thirteenth, but also of succeeding centuries, It stands as a sign of Grosseteste's care of his priests and people.

Despite his complaint to prior provincial Matthew about the frequent

---

[52] Powicke and Cheney, 1: 214-220, treatise on the seven deadly sins; 220-226, treatise on confession and penance.

[53] Powicke and Cheney, 1: 295-325.

[54] Robert Grosseteste, *Templum Dei*, edd. J.Goering and F.A.C. Mantello, Toronto Medieval Latin Texts, 14 (Toronto, 1984).

change of friars,[55] Grosseteste probably had Dominicans with him for his eighteen years of episcopate. A number of Dominicans would have gained valuable pastoral experience from temporary membership in Grosseteste's *familia*. Is it too fanciful to suggest that Simon of Hinton could for part of his pastoral time have been a member of Grosseteste's, or some other, episcopal *familia*? Similarly, could not active diocesan pastoral work with priests and people have been some of the context for the composition between 1250 and 1260 of Simon's treatise, *Summa Juniorum*?[56] The *Summa Juniorum* begins with an exposition of the articles of the Creed, then of the ten commandments, of the seven petitions of the Our Father, the seven gifts of the Holy Spirit, the eight beatitudes and the seven deadly sins. The emphasis in the text is on the positive side of good living rather than on the negative side of sinfulness, an emphasis shared with Grosseteste in contradistinction to some of the other episcopal statutes. The approach to the holy eucharist leans more to worship and adoration and presence at Mass, with less emphasis on the reception of holy communion. There is no external evidence to link the writing of Simon of Hinton's *Summa Juniorum*, a manual for priests,[57] with Grosseteste's work of education for priests of his own diocese, yet there is nothing in Simon's treatise that would make it impossible for it to have been associated with Grosseteste's pastoral practice. In fact, it does confirm the involvement of the friars with the reforming activity of the English bishops after the Fourth Lateran Council.

The Ecclesia Anglicana in the thirteenth century was lively and active. Led by some remarkable bishops, the gospel challenge of the *vita apostolica* was once more being given to clergy and laity alike. In cooperation with the hierarchy of the time, as exemplified by the partnerships of John of St. Giles OP and Adam Marsh OFM with their old friend Bishop Robert of Lincoln, the English Dominicans and Franciscans made their contribution of hearing confessions and preaching. Before either establishing an historical context for, or making any specific analysis of, the contents and function of MS Laud Misc. 511, it is necessary to look at the theory and practice of preaching in the thirteenth century.

---

[55] See n. 48.

[56] Oxford, Bodleian Library, MS Laud Misc. 397, fol. 106-152. Other MSS are listed in the Index of Manuscripts. See also L.E. Boyle, "Three English Pastoral Summae," *Studia Gratiana* 11 (1967) 133-144.

[57] L.E. Boyle, "Aspects of Clerical Education in fourteenth-century England," *The Fourteenth Century*, Acta Vol 4 (1977) 19-32, especially 20.

D. THE MEDIEVAL SERMON: THEORY...

The medieval sermon has been much studied in the past century. After the foundation works of Lecoy de la Marche[58] and Cruel,[59] the significant studies were those of Gilson.[60] Gilson saw the sermon as a key to the understanding of medieval thought and culture. Many valuable studies of the medieval sermon followed hard on Gilson's plea, for example, the monographs of Davy,[61] and Charland,[62] with their editions of original material. In recent decades, the mammoth achievement of J.B. Schneyer in producing a *Repertorium* of Latin sermons, 1150-1350, has facilitated the comparative study of sermons.[63] Another contributor to the understanding of the sermon, through historical studies of ancient and medieval rhetoric, is Harry Caplan.[64] In the past twenty years there has been a major increase in sermon studies, much of it focussed on manuscript sermons in Latin and various vernaculars.[65]

[58] A. Lecoy de la Marche, *La Chaire Française au Moyen Age*, 2nd ed. (Paris, 1886).

[59] R. Cruel, *Geschichte der Deutschen Predigt im Mittelalter* (Detmold, 1879). A most useful account of Cruel's work is found in David d'Avray's thesis, "The Transformation of the Medieval Sermon," Bodleian Library, MS D.Phil. c 2088, Oxford, 1976.

[60] E. Gilson, "Michel Menot et la technique du sermon médiéval," *Revue d'Histoire Franciscaine* 2 (1925) 301-350; later reprinted as chapter V in *Les Idées et les Lettres* (Paris, 1932). This article has been very influential in setting the agenda for sermon studies.

[61] M.M. Davy, *Les sermons universitaires parisiens de 1230-1231* (Paris: Vrin, 1931).

[62] Th.M. Charland, *Artes Praedicandi. Contribution à l'histoire de la rhétorique au Moyen Âge* (Paris and Ottawa, 1936).

[63] J.B. Schneyer, *Wegweiser zu Lateinischen Predigtreihen des Mittelalters* (Munchen, 1965); ibid., *Repertorium der Lateinischen Sermones des Mittelalters für die Zeit von 1150-1350*, 11 vols. (Munster, 1969-1990).

[64] H. Caplan: see "Bibliography of the Writings of Harry Caplan," 271-276 in *Of Eloquence*, edd. A. King and H. North (Ithaca and London, 1970).

[65] d'Avray, *Friars*; L.J. Bataillon, *La prédication au xiiie siècle en France et Italie*, Variorum Collected Series CS 402, (Aldershot UK and Brookfield Vermont, 1993); Nicole Bériou, *La Prédication au béguinage de Paris pendant l'année liturgique 1272-1273* (Paris: Etudes Augustiniennes, 1978); idem, *Sermons aux clercs et sermons aux 'simple gens': la prédication de Ranulph de la Houblonnière à Paris au xiiie siècle* (Paris: Etudes Augustiniennes, 1980); Carlo Delcorno, *Giordano da Pisa e l'antica predicazione volgere* (Florence: L. Olschki, 1975); Jean Longère, *Oeuvres oratoires de maîtres parisiens au xiie siècle*, 2 vols. (Paris, 1975); idem, *La Prédication médiévale* (Paris: Etudes Augustiniennes, 1983); Phyllis B. Roberts, *Stephanus de Lingua-Tonante: Studies in the Sermons of Stephen Langton* (Toronto: PIMS, 1968); Richard H. and Mary A. Rouse, *Preachers, Florilegia and Sermons: Studies on the 'Manipulus Florum' of Thomas of Ireland*

The first context for the medieval sermon is Christian tradition. The greatest exponent among the Latin Fathers of this continuity of tradition was St. Augustine; firstly in his actual preaching, and secondly with his analysis of Christian preaching in *De Doctrina Christiana*.[66]

In the first three books Augustine indicates the principles to be followed in studying, translating, reading and interpreting the Scriptures. In Book I he approaches their study as a believer seeking a deepening of his faith; in Book II he discusses signs; in Book III he analyses ambiguous signs. In Book IV he describes the methodology of the above teaching, analysing passages from the Epistles of St Paul and from the prophet Amos[67] to show the distinctive nature of Christian eloquence, the subordination of the medium to the message:

> He who seeks to teach in speech what is good, spurning none of these three things, that is to teach, to delight, and to persuade, should pray and strive that he be heard intelligently, willingly and obediently. When he does this well and properly, he can justly be called eloquent, even though he fails to win the assent of his audience.[68]

"To teach in speech what is good," the preacher according to Augustine needs a thorough knowledge of the Scriptures.[69] Augustine also commends the use of Roman eloquence. But he equally recommends the subordination of the principles of eloquence to clarity of expression, so that the understanding of the hearers is facilitated.[70] Because of his towering stature as a Christian thinker and as a theologian, Augustine's influence on the following centuries was paramount.[71]

As Gilson indicated, a valuable key to understanding the medieval sermon is the *ars predicandi* or handbook on preaching. This literary genre flourished from the late twelfth century to the fourteenth century; while

---

(Toronto: PIMS, 1979); Michel Zink, *La prédication en langue romane avant 1300* (Paris: Nouvelle bibliothèque du moyen âge, 1976). The activities of the *International Medieval Sermon Symposium* founded by Gloria Cigman in 1979 have fostered and facilitated communication in sermon studies.

[66] St Augustine of Hippo, *De Doctrina Christiana* PL 34, cols. 15-122; translations used here from D.W. Robertson, *On Christian Doctrine* (New York: Bobbs-Merrill, 1958).

[67] Robertson, *DDC* IV, iv, 120-121; IV, vii, 124-132; IV, xx, 146-152.

[68] Robertson, *DDC* IV, xvii, 142-143.

[69] Robertson, *DDC* IV, v, 121-122.

[70] Robertson, *DDC* IV, x, 133-135.

[71] C.S. Baldwin, *Mediaeval Rhetoric and Poetic to 1400* (New York, 1929), 51.

the requirement of the Fourth Lateran Council that bishops should take their preaching responsibilities seriously, or delegate others to do so on their behalf, stimulated an increasing production of preaching-aids. The *artes predicandi* offer a method for selecting the content of the sermon, based primarily on Scripture, while using other kinds of material in a subordinate manner as well. They give methods of elaborating the distinctions according to the four senses of Scripture; or by asking how? what? why? and when? about each part of the distinctions; or by using etymologies which enable the allegorical interpretation to be further developed; or by giving methods of division-making. They define the structure of the sermon, namely the theme, the protheme or antitheme, prayer, divisions confirmed by authorities, and conclusion. Finally they suggest methods for holding and sustaining the attention of the hearers; and offer advice about voice, posture and gesture, and anything of use in helping a preacher to perform successfully in the pulpit. The image of the sermon-tree from the *Aquinas Text* summarises the approach to sermons of an *ars predicandi*.

> Preaching is like a real tree. As a real tree develops from root to trunk and the trunk puts forth main branches and the main branches multiply into other branches, so in preaching the theme develops into the protheme or prelocution as root into trunk. Then the prelocution or protheme grows into the principal divisions of the theme as the trunk into the main branches. And the principal branches beyond multiply into secondary divisions, that is, subdivisions and subdistinctions, and finally expand.... Its theme is divided into three parts; each part is divided into three members; each member can be amplified by several of the nine methods described.[72]

As a method of self-help, or an exemplar of a 'teach yourself' book, the *artes predicandi* came in a variety of lengths, different levels of complexity and varying styles from formal to colloquial.[73] But as well as contain-

---

[72] Caplan, *Of Eloquence*, 78.

[73] Jennifer Sweet researched the *artes predicandi* of Alexander of Ashby, Richard of Thetford and Hugh Sneyth in "English Preaching 1221-1293," unpublished thesis in the Bodleian Library MS B.Litt d.109*; Harry Caplan, "The 'Aquinas Text', A Late Mediaeval Tractate on Preaching," in Caplan, *Of Eloquence*, 40-78; ibid., "'Henry of Hesse' on the Art of Preaching", in Caplan, *Of Eloquence*, 135-159; M. de la Bigne, ed., *Maxima Bibliothece Veterum Patrum* (Lyons, 1677), vol. 25, Humbert of Romans, *De Eruditione Religiosorum Praedicatorum*; see also Simon Tugwell, *Early Dominicans: Selected Writings*, The Classics of Western Spirituality (London: SPCK, 1982), 181-384; trans. W.M. Conlon, *Treatise on Preaching* (Westminster Md., 1951); ed. Th.M. Charland, *Robert Basevorn Forma Praedicandi*, 233-323 [this was translated

ing theoretical analyses of preaching, *artes predicandi* could also by the nature of their content be a practical source of sermons and thus an active sermon-aid. Undoubtedly the changes in preaching practice of the late twelfth to the early thirteenth century were strong enough to last several centuries. By the mid-fourteenth century, however, the scholastic style of preaching was commonplace, and the need for the *artes predicandi* in their earlier profusion diminished.

E. ...AND PRACTICE

The manuscript Laud Misc. 511, which is the subject of this study, belongs to the category of literature that we call "sermon-aids." It is not, however, a theoretical treatise like the *artes praedicandi*. Its compiler designed it as a practical help in preaching. It contains a large number of sermons. If we consult it on the question of sermon method, we can find plenty of practical examples to illustrate the sermon theory noted above.

The key to any specific sermon was a text from Scripture. On this rule the *artes predicandi* are unanimous. The technical name for this key text in a sermon is "theme." Waleys emphasises that the Scripture quotation must not be wrested out of context,[74] while Robert Basevorn argues that to take an unknown non-scriptural text as a theme could lead to error of doctrine.[75] MS Laud Misc. 511 has 138 themes for 243 pieces, the majority being sermons, which illustrate fidelity to the tradition that sermons should be preached on the Scripture readings of the Mass. One hundred and seventy sermons are directly related to the pericopes, while a further ten sermons[76] are preached on Scripture texts directly related to the feast being celebrated. Only thirty-two sermons in the collection are not directly related to the Mass of the day. To summarise briefly: of these thirty-two, four themes (22, 32, 119 and 167) are taken from the Introit or Office of the Mass; nine themes (33, 78, 104, 111, 118, 122, 159, 161, 227) are mainly Old Testament texts, all except 118 and 122 fitting into the liturgical meaning

---

by J.J. Murphy as "The Form of Preaching" in *Three Medieval Rhetorical Arts* (Berkeley and London, 1971), 114-215]; Charland also edited Thomas Waleys *De Modo Componendi Sermones* in his *Artes Praedicandi*, 328-403.

[74] Charland, 341.

[75] Charland, 251; *TMRA*, 134-135.

[76] See Appendix 1, "A Catalogue of MS Laud Misc. 511." Numbers 21, 22, 23 (for Christmas), 99 (for Passion Sunday), 114, 115, 116, 120, 121 (all five for Easter Sunday), 158 (for the Ascension).

of the day through concordance. Thus, for instance, for the Ascension the themes use the word "ascendere." Finally there are the themes which are taken from the Divine Office. Again, these honour the spirit of the liturgy in celebrating the feast of the day.

The theme was followed by the protheme or what our manuscript, following what seems to be English terminology, calls the "antitheme." The antitheme ends with a prayer. The aim of the antitheme was to establish rapport with the congregation. Humbert of Romans, the Dominican who wrote many practical works on preaching for his brethren, declares it useful for permitting latecomers to settle in before the sermon proper starts.[77] On occasions which had two liturgical celebrations, for example, a feastday coinciding with a Sunday, the preacher had to decide which took precedence. If he chose the Sunday then he would devote the body of the sermon to that, but use the antitheme for the superseded feast, and vice-versa. There are no examples of this in the manuscript. Basevorn defines the antitheme as "winning over the audience," and recommends either the telling of suitable stories or giving an explanation of the preacher's function.[78] Humbert recommends that when a preacher is unknown, he should use this time to introduce himself, reassuring his hearers that he is not seeking their money![79] Alternatively, the preacher could quote Scripture which reflected the meaning of his theme, but using different words, synonyms, or words of the same root as the theme, i.e., verbal concordances. So the possibilities of the sermon were opened, and the preacher could gracefully combine the repetition of the theme with a call to prayer. Sometimes the prayer used was the *Veni Sancte Spiritus,* or an *Ave Maria,* or the *Pater Noster.*[80] In our manuscript an example of a lengthy antitheme ending with the *Pater Noster* is found in a Lenten sermon.[81]

---

[77] Humbert, *Treatise,* 156.

[78] Charland, 260-262; *TMRA,* 145-148.

[79] Humbert, *Treatise,* 157-160.

[80] Charland, 262; *TMRA,* 148; Charland, 349; see also references to MS Laud Misc. 511.

MS Laud Misc. 511, Sermon 167, fol. 150b, ll. 1-5: Invocemus Spiritum Sanctum in principio sermonis nostri, ut descendat super nos et inflammet dono scientie sue, ad verbum suum pronuntiandum et audiendum ad honorem sui et commodum nostri et dicat quilibet "Veni Creator Spiritus."

[81] Sermon 56, fol. 59b, ll. 1-43: Hec verba scripta sunt MT 4 in quibus tanguntur hec tria que predicatoribus sunt necessaria, scilicet, eminentia vite, sapientia sive scientia doctrine, et collatio gratie...cum ergo hec tria sint predicatori necessaria, et sunt a Spiritu Sancto ut hic patet, rogemus etc.

The preacher calls the religious life the desert into which those present have been led, but the secret desert of the mind is prayer. Having developed these points, the preacher asks that all present invite the Lord Jesus to lead them into this desert, and to this end to pray "Our Father." A homely antitheme is found in sermon 72 about people flocking to Bedford to see St Peter.[82] Another describes the sorrow and pride of going to war.[83] A few, like the antithemes to sermons 47 and 206, describe the task of the preacher.[84] At least three "spare" antithemes are recorded but, unlike MS Bodley 25, there is no section devoted to alternative antithemes.[85] Most of the sermons in our manuscript have no antithemes, just a statement of divisions or members of the theme.[86] A few sermons start with "preacher's instructions" to himself, for example, "Tell the gospel story and make the prayer."[87]

The technical term for the expository part of the sermon was the development of the "divisions" or "members." In the Parisian method to which Basevorn alludes, the divisions are treated equally. An example of this is the sermon of Richard Fishacre in our manuscript. It is interesting to note that another version of this sermon from MS Ipswich 6 has only four divisions—and unequal at that—compared to the Laud version of five more or less equal divisions.[88] In the English method, the divisions could

---

[82] Sermon 72, fol. 83vb. See n. 82 in chapter 5 on the Elstow preaching.

[83] Sermon 89, fol. 100va, ll. 1-8: Scitis quoniam reges et principes terrarum, qui etiam iusti et misericordes et liberales existunt et etiam subditos diligunt, et qui a subditis diliguntur, cum ad bella contra inimicos procedunt, ploratus et ululatus fit multus [sic] in omni provincia et per omnem circumquamque regionem.

[84] Sermon 47, fol. 49va, ll. 9-17: Tria, ut frequencius solent attendere sermocinantes, scilicet modo delectabilitatem et eiusdem securitatem et audiencium utilitatem; hinc est quod omnes fere tractatores in prologis suis per hec tria auditores suos attentos et benivolos nituntur reddere ad audiendum; ideo ego, quantum in me fuit, assumpsi mihi materiam in se delectabilem, curam et securam ad tractandum utilem insuper et audiendum.

Sermon 206, fol. 169a, ll. 1-5. has similar phrasing to n. 81.

[85] Sermon 52, fol. 54v., five lines across the bottom margin: Antithema aliud "Non in solo pane vivit homo...."

Sermon 174b, fol. 154r., four lines across the bottom margin: Antithema Humiliamini etc. Verba sunt beati Petri....

Sermon 162, fol. 148a, line 42: Antithema quando volueris.

[86] See Appendix 1, "A Catalogue of MS Laud Misc. 511." "Thema" is recorded in the sermon entries.

[87] Sermon 219, fol. 184va, line 37: Narretur hystoria evangelii, et fiat oratio....

[88] MS Laud Misc. 511, fol. 96va-99va; Ipswich Public Library MS 6, fol. 76r.

be equally treated, or emphasis given to some rather than all. Certainly there are many sermons in MS Laud Misc. 511 which start with a threefold division, but give content for less than three. The compiler of our manuscript deliberately treats two of his source sermons in this way.[89]

In so far as methods of development of the divisions go, our sermon collection is very ordinary, relying mostly on distinctions. This usage, both as content and style, is discussed in detail in chapter 6. There is little conscious use of the senses of Scripture in most of the sermons, though there is an occasional reference to such use.[90] There is certainly no deliberate use throughout a sermon, as seen in a sermon of Robert Kilwardby,[91] of literal exposition separated from mystical or moral. With regard to the use of etymologies in the manuscript, there is little beyond standard interpretations. The actual content of the sermon is constantly illustrated mostly by references to the Scriptures. The technical name for this illustrative mode is "authority." Authorities are abundant, often constituting the greater part of the actual sermon text. Overall, the New Testament provides—but only just—the greater part of scriptural authorities with the Old Testament being source for the lesser part. There are also references to the Fathers and Doctors of the Church. Nearly half come from just two people, St. Augustine and St. Bernard. This proportion reflects the pervasiveness of the influence of St. Augustine and the popularity of St. Bernard in the church of the thirteenth century. St. Gregory is the third main provider, but well behind! Preachers used authorities from other than scriptural or religious writings. In our sermons, allusions to classical literature and poetry are few, as are quotations from philosophers. A fuller discussion and analysis of authorities used in many sermons in our collection is found in Appendix 10.[92] As well as authorities preachers also used stories, real and fictional, to illustrate the content of their sermons. The technical term for this interesting, and often amusing, usage is *exemplum*. Over four hundred *exempla* are found in our manuscript, some in full some only in title.

[89] For example, Sermon 10 by Peraldus and sermon 165 by Petris de Remis have been edited by the compiler of the manuscript in the "English method."

[90] Sermon 27, fol. 24a, ll.1-2: Narretur evangelium mistice....

Sermon 103, fol. 108vb, ll. 20-21: quid intelligere de sensu spirituali....

[91] Cambridge, Trinity College MS 15.38 (373), fol. 212v: Hec verba litteraliter sunt intelligenda et moraliter.... This sermon has been edited by P. Osmund Lewry, "A Passiontide sermon of Robert Kilwardby OP," *AFP* 52, (1982) 89-113.

[92] Appendix 10, "An Analysis of Sermon Authorities."

The conclusion of a sermon is often abrupt, as can be seen in Base-vorn's final paragraphs.[93] Several things, however, are clear: that the end must in some way reflect the theme, that it moves into a prayer or a blessing, that the prayer is eschatological. This enshrines much of the sacramental approach often found in medieval theology which represents historical events in the here-and-now under signs which look to a future fulfilment. Several of the sermons in our manuscript have this kind of ending.[94]

In the context of the theory of the *artes predicandi*, of the stress placed by these same *artes* on the freedom of the preacher to adapt his material, and of the variety of preaching that this method made possible, it seems that our manuscript is not an easily identifiable example of any *ars predicandi*. Rather our manuscript is a tribute to the flexibility in sermon-making. The theory which made the composition, revision and committal to memory of a sermon much simpler also facilitated itinerant preachers giving many diverse sermons in a multiplicity of places.

The *ars predicandi* had a two-fold task: the first, which has already been discussed, the elucidation of the theory of sermon-making with examples; the second, the giving of practical advice on the actual delivery of a sermon.

Waleys stands for most composers of *artes predicandi*. When the rules of Rhetoric were skilfully followed in the spirit of Augustine's *De Doctrina Christiana*, the sermon benefited as an aural and an oral event, for the listeners' attention was caught and the use of rhetorical colours and constructions helped sustain that attention. Because it was a sophisticated technique, the medieval preacher could be tempted to devote too much energy to the rhetoric and not enough to the content. Thomas Waleys was concerned about this problem.[95] In so far as pulpit behaviour is concerned, the author of the *Aquinas Tract* best summarises it.[96] He condemns seven faults in sermons: "the preacher's ignorance, lack of fluency, excessive noisiness, sleepy delivery, finger pointings, tossing of the head, and remote digression."[97] He defines twelve precautions the "fore-sighted preacher" should maintain in the pulpit.[98] Among these recommenda-

---

[93] Charland, 323; *TMRA*, 213.

[94] See Appendix 9, "Selected Texts"; see also in Appendix 1, "A Catalogue of MS Laud Misc. 511," the explicits of sermons 5, 6, 14, 19, 30, 37, 70, 74, 99, 135.

[95] Charland, 335-336.

[96] "Aquinas Text," Caplan, *Of Eloquence*, 40-78.

[97] Caplan, *Of Eloquence*, 58.

[98] Caplan, *Of Eloquence*, 72-75.

tions are the following: he should take "proper care to express the last syllable of each utterance as sharply and completely as the first"; "he should speak complete words intelligibly and slowly"; should show "restraint in looking about"; while "in grave matters of correction the preacher should not resort to specific or personal allusion." Basevorn[99] advises that he should at all costs "avoid prolixity in a sermon lest the people begin to weary and henceforth shun other sermons.... Let the preacher watch the hour and when it is over, cease his sermon."

And what was the language of preaching? On this matter the *artes predicandi* are silent. Nevertheless the question arises in each generation of students of sermons.[100] Sermons to the laity were delivered in the mother tongue, if no other could be understood. Certainly for most laity in thirteenth-century England that would be Middle English with its various dialects; for nuns it could be French or Anglo-Norman. Welsh and Cornish were also used by the friars. Probably in England the use of language reflected the class differences imposed at the time of the Conquest. Sermons to clerics and scholars would be in Latin. (It would, however, be interesting to know what language Grosseteste used in preaching to the local priests of his diocese.) While these vernaculars, especially those derived from Anglo-Saxon, namely Middle English and Anglo-Norman, had written expression, their conventions of writing were not as comprehensive or developed as those of Latin. Unlike Anglo-Saxon to Middle English, Latin had a continuity in grammar, usage and vocabulary, and was not only the language of most education, but also the common language of western Europe as it existed at that time. On the whole in the thirteenth century it was easier to use Latin for writing. MS Laud Misc. 511 contains some fragments of Middle English. Their presence strengthens the case for the use of the mother-tongue in actual preaching. While no-one today really doubts that the language of preaching to the people, certainly in the thirteenth century, was the vernacular, there is more debate about the language of preaching to clerics, students and friars. In the fourteenth century when the gap in educational attainment between clerics and laity was narrowing, in some cases disappearing, the language usage was probably more complex than in the thirteenth century. It is

---

[99] Charland, 42.

[100] L.J. Bataillon, "La Predicazione dei religiosi mendicanti del secolo xiii nell' Italia centrale," *MEFRM* 89 (Paris and Rome, 1977) 691-694; Siegfried Wenzel, *Verses in Sermons: 'Fasciculus Morum' and its Middle English Poems* (Cambridge Mass.: Medieval Academy of America, 1978); L.J. Bataillon, "Approaches to the Study of Medieval Sermons," *Leeds Studies in English*, NS 11 (1980) 24-25; d'Avray, *Friars*, 6-7.

possible that a "macaronic" use of language was far more widespread in
non-popular preaching than has been recognised.[101] Just as the choice
of model sermon was the preacher's, so it was his responsibility to use the
appropriate language. If he were to be faithful to his calling, then it was
his task as a pastor to preach the chosen sermon in the language that
would most move his hearers.

F. PREACHING AIDS

i. Correctoria and Concordances

The *artes predicandi*, however, do not stand on their own. There were
other aids to sermon construction of great importance to the preacher.
Some of these, such as collections of *exempla*, of distinctions, and of selections from the Fathers found in florilegia, are discussed in greater length
later. Here only significant Scriptural aids, largely of Dominican inspiration, will be treated.

The most important task was that undertaken by the Dominicans to
produce a standard critical edition of the Bible, by providing as much
information about alternative textual readings from, as far as possible,
original sources. The general chapter of 1236[102] ordered the friars of the
French province to prepare a *Correctorium* of the Bible that could be used
by the whole Order. The Paris Bible of the early thirteenth century was
the edition chosen by Hugh of St. Cher and other brethren at St. Jacques
as a basis for their work of correction. The principles of textual criticism,
as imperfectly understood at the time, were applied to the biblical text. At
least three editions of the *Correctoria*, as these were called, were produced
by the Order of Preachers. The Franciscans too made their contributions,
especially to later editions. The important thing about the task is not the
quality of the work, now long superseded, but the nature of it, the relent-
less search for an accurate text as reverence for the word of God, so that
preaching the gospel could be facilitated. As an aid to detailed use of the
Scriptures and the identification of specific texts, the Dominicans introduced divisions of the "chapters" by sections a-g for longer ones, a-e for

[101] Siegfried Wenzel, "Macaronic Sermons in Medieval England—some observations," paper given at MSS Symposium Oxford, 1982, pp. 3-4; see also, idem, *Macaronic Sermons: bilingualism and preaching in late-medieval England*, (Ann Arbor: University of Michigan Press, 1994).

[102] ACTA I: 9; see also Smalley, *Bible* Chapter 6; Hinnebusch, *Hist.* 2: 104-106;
Lawrence, *Friars*, 138-141.

shorter ones.[103] Thus the detailed Scripture reference was born. Its value for sermon-making is self-evident.

Another related invention, also pioneered by the Dominicans at St. Jacques under the leadership of Hugh of St. Cher,[104] was the biblical concordance. The use of verbal concordance in the new method of sermon-making has been emphasised by most authors of *artes predicandi.* After many years of unremitting effort, Professor R.H. Rouse and Dr M.A. Rouse have shown its genesis and development.[105] It grew from and displaced the collections of biblical distinctions:

> The concordance was a consciously-created solution to the needs of Latin theologians for a device which would enable them to have in one place all the uses of a given word or phrase in the Scriptures.[106]

The first concordance, made by a group of Dominican friars most probably under the academic leadership of Hugh of St. Cher,[107] solved two problems: the formulation of a system of references; the collection and arrangement of words and references. To the former the friars applied the a-g mode first used to divide the chapters of the Bible; to the latter they applied alphabetical order. This last is, in retrospect, such a simple matter. Yet until it was thought of, there was no easily-checked way of keeping listed information. There are two copies of this first concordance in the Bodleian Library: MS Rawl.G 26[108] (19.5 by 13.4 cm), written in five columns, 56-62 lines to a column; and MS Canon Pat. Lat. 7,[109] minute in size, (10.25 by 6.4 cm). Its hand is equally minute. The size of the latter is ideal for the pocket, but its producation cost would put its ownership beyond the pocket either of any but the very rich or of a community which saw the production of such concordances as part of its work. In this edition of the concordance the idea was fruitful, but the execution as yet unskilled. The second concordance—known as the "English Concordance" because Richard Stavensby's name is linked with it—is, as the Rouses have shown, another group effort. Stavensby was the "completer" of several sec-

---

[103] R.H. and M.A. Rouse, "The Verbal Concordances to the Scriptures." *AFP* 44 (1974), 5-30.

[104] See below, Chapter 3, pp. 94-95.

[105] Rouse, "Verbal Concordances," 5-30; see also R.H. and M.A. Rouse, "Biblical Distinctions in the Thirteenth Century," *AHDLMA* vol 41 (1975), 27-37.

[106] Rouse, "Verbal Concordances," 5.

[107] Rouse, "Verbal Concordances," 6-8.

[108] Oxford, Bodleian Library, *Summary Catalogue,* 14759.

[109] Bodleian Library, *Summary Catalogue* 18993.

tions. This edition tried to give too much information with too little ap-
paratus to utilise it. A copy of this, New College MS F 70[110] is lodged
in the Bodleian. The third concordance, a fresh approach to the task, yet
building on the previous two editions, was produced by 1275. It adds
many variants, new entries, and has an improved alphabetical order. This
concordance was available in *peciae* at the Paris stationers.[111] Its recognition as an academic text ensured its use on a large scale. An example of
this version is MS Bodley 275.[112] Compared with the other samples, this
is a huge manuscript, (43 by 28.6 cm), with over 525 folios, three columns
to a page. The capitals which indicate each section are beautifully and
skilfully decorated. One can sympathise with the scribe who ended folio
519 with, "Ffinito libro sit laus et gloria Christo." Without the invention of
the concordance, the rapid development of the scholastic method of sermon-making would have been difficult, for it gave groups of references
which suggested ways of developing a theme, and it helped in the finding
of synonyms. By the end of the thirteenth century it had joined the
Collection of Distinctions as a sermon aid. The significance of Hugh of St.
Cher's leadership in helping to provide aids for preachers cannot be over-
estimated.

ii. Model Sermon Collections
    A last valuable aid to the preacher was collections of sermons. In the
context of providing good preaching St. Augustine commented:

> There are some who can speak well, but who cannot think of any-
> thing to say. If they can take something eloquently and wisely written
> by others, memorise it, and offer it to the people in the person of the
> author, they do not do wickedly. In this way, which is truly useful,
> many preachers of the truth are made.[113]

    According to Humbert of Romans, Pope Innocent III had preached
a sermon from the works of St. Gregory on the feast of St. Mary Magdalene in order to show what could, even should, be done in preaching to

---

[110] H.O. Coxe, *Catalogus Codicum MSS qui in Collegiis Aulisque Oxoniensibus hodie
adseverantur*, 2 vols. (Oxford, 1852).
    [111] H. Denifle and A. Chatelain, *Chartularium Universitatis Parisiensis*, 4 vols
(Paris, 1889-1897), 1: 532-534.
    [112] Bodleian Library, *Summary Catalogue* 2623.
    [113] Robertson, *DDC*, IV ix, 166-168.

the people.[114] As we have seen, when he was on visitation in his diocese Grosseteste would preach to the priests, while the friars preached to the people. Presumably Grossteste was partly ensuring that his priests received an object lesson in preaching, as well as some content for their own sermons. Those who studied theology at the Schools had to attend sermons regularly and on occasion preach; the friars similarly learnt much about preaching not only by receiving systematic training for it, but also by listening to sermons by the brethren.[115] Hence the writing down of sermons, and the gathering of sermons into collections, became standard practices among the friars.

Père Bataillon has clarified much of the uncertainty about the process of putting sermons in writing in the thirteenth century.[116] The origin of the written sermon is either the preacher's own text, or a summary, or an account—a *reportatio*—made by any of the listeners. In this context, Père Bataillon discusses whether the contents of some of the well-known collections, such as those of Peraldus, did not emanate from the preacher's desk rather than from his pulpit.[117] There was, however, no law of copyright to worry about. Unless officially commissioned by the preacher (as Reginald of Piperno was by Thomas Aquinas) to take down a full account, those who were taking notes could take as much or as little as they chose. That which struck one listener as particularly appropriate or felicitous might leave another cold. So unless *reportationes* were officially corrected by the preacher himself, or were specifically linked to a set of sermons by the reporter, or a rubric indicates an identifiable source, there is no way of knowing whether the sermon texts which are recorded in so many manuscripts are the original composition of the preacher to whom they are

[114] Humbert of Romans, *De Vita Regulari*, 2: 397: "I have heard that Pope Innocent III (in whose reign the Lateran Council was held) being a man of letters, when once he was preaching on the feast of M. Magdalene, had near him someone who held Gregory's homily on that feast; and Innocent spoke, word for word, in the common tongue what had been written there in the Latin.... But when, after the sermon, the book-bearer asked Innocent why he had so done, as he could have preached very well from his own knowledge and skill, the latter replied that he had done this to rebuke and instruct those men who did not condescend to repeat what had been said by others."

[115] J.G. Bougerol, "Les Sermons dans les 'studia' des mendiants," in *Le Scuole degli Ordini Mendicanti (secoli XIII-XIV)*, Covegno del Centro di Studi sulla spiritalita medievale 17 (Todi, 1978), 251-280.

[116] Bataillon, "Approaches," 19-35.

[117] Ibid., 19-20.

atrributed, or not. It has been possible to see the link between sermons and *reportationes* through research into the sermons of Peter of Limoges, who wrote his own.[118] In her study on preaching to the Paris Beguines,[119] Nicole Bériou has demonstrated clearly Peter's method, showing his use of a long *reportatio* and a short *reportatio* for the same given sermon. It is very rare to be able to identify methodology and relationship between texts. Yet surely Peter of Limoges is not an isolated example of a preacher's methodology?

Nevertheless, collections of sermons do exist, and many copies of these collections still exist. They were made with the express intention of being available for other preachers to use. Such are the model collections of Peraldus, Peter of Rheims and many others. MS Laud Misc. 511 is, as will be shown later, a model sermon collection, in an edition of one, which was used in later years for preaching to an identified group.

G. CONCLUSION

The foregoing pages have shown the reality of the preaching revival of the twelfth to thirteenth centuries; have demonstrated the level of pastoral concern expressed in the Fourth Lateran Council and later in the synodal statutes of the Church in England; and have shown a little of the involvement of the friars in meeting these recognised pastoral needs. The specific studies in the provision, codicological content and catechetical content of MS Laud Misc. 511 which follow give further illustration of the pastoral work of the friars, and specifically the Dominicans, in the England of the thirteenth century.

---

[118] Bataillon, *Approaches*, 21-22.
[119] Bériou, *La Prédication*, 107-116; d'Avray, *Friars*, 104-131.

2

The Training of Dominican Preachers

Canon Dominic Guzman, later Brother Dominic, founded the Order of Preachers between 1206 and 1221. Before he began this vital work he served two bishops, gaining invaluable experience for his founding mission. First, as companion to his bishop, Diego of Osma, Dominic became involved in the venture of preaching Christianity, "Praedicatio Jesu Christi," to the Cathars of the Midi. Secondly, Fulk, bishop of Toulouse, gave full support to Dominic as the latter established a small group of active preachers in Fulk's diocese. Despite the prohibition by the Fourth Lateran Council of the formation of new religious orders, the practical effectiveness of Dominic's preachers and Francis of Assisi's little brothers convinced Innocent III and Honorius III of the value of supporting the two new orders of friars and harnessing their spiritual energies to the task of preaching as delineated in canon 10 of the same council.

Within five years of the meeting with Innocent III, Dominic had established his Order of Preachers. Observing the rule of St. Augustine, the brethren nevertheless modified the twelfth century pattern of canonical status and organisation in favour of mendicant poverty and a mobile apostolic life.

The very name, Order of Preachers, indicates its function. Dominic's followers were not equivalent to the Humiliati or even to the first Franciscans. While, like these two groups, they were expected to give the example of the gospel by living the apostolic life as well as preaching it, Dominic required further that his preachers should be educated in Scripture and doctrine as fully as was consonant with the abilities of the individual friars and the resources of the priories and the Order as a whole. In fact, the Order of Preachers in its being is a structure or institution or organisation for the education of its members in theology with the purpose of using that theology in preaching.

A. ...IN THEIR CONSTITUTIONS

By the end of the general chapter of 1221, Dominican priories had been founded—among other places—in Paris, Toulouse, Bologna, Rome, and a group of friars sent to Oxford; an organisation for provinces was outlined;

and a system of chapters recognised. On 6 August 1221 Dominic died.

Seven years later, it was possible for the Order to hold an extraordinary general chapter to codify its existing constitutions.[1] The introduction specifically mentions Jordan of Saxony, the young German friar elected to succeed Dominic. He seemed to those who had known the founder, another Dominic.[2] Although scholars think that the chapter of 1216 produced primitive constitutions, those of 1228 were the first officially drawn up and promulgated in writing. The prologue states plainly the aim of the Order:

> The prelate shall have power to dispense the brethren in his priory when it shall seem expedient to him, especially in those things that are seen to impede study, preaching, or the good of souls; and our study ought to tend principally and ardently and with the highest effort so that we might be useful to the souls of ⟨our⟩ neighbours.[3]

The prologue also emphasises that, if the brethren are to have one heart and mind in the Lord, they must observe the constitutions uniformly. There is continuity here with the work of Dominic, combined with flexibility of action conferred through the power of dispensation.

By comparing the 1228 and 1356-63 constitutions,[4] it should be possible to discern aspects of the intervening development. It should be noted also that the work of Raymund of Penaforte on the constitutions from 1238 to 1241 was a tidying-up process, rather than significant modifications of those of 1228.[5]

---

[1] Ed. H. Denifle OP, *Constitutiones antique ordinis fratrum predicatorum* in *Archiv für Litteratur und Kirchen Geschichte des Mittelalters* (Berlin, 1885), 1: 193-227. Two studies are important for the background to and content of this chapter: J.P. Renard, *La Formation et la destination des prédicateurs au début de l'Ordre des Prêcheurs (1215-1237)* (Fribourg: Imprimerie St. Canisius, 1977) and Dieter Berg, *Armut und Wissenschaft. Beitrage zur Geschichte des Studienwesens der Bettelorden im 13. Jahrhundert* in series *Geschichte und Gesellschaft* 15 (Dusseldorf, 1977).

[2] *ALKG* 1: 193: Iste sunt constitutiones prime ordinis fratrum predicatorum, que erant tempore magistri Jordanis beati Dominici immediate successoris, ex quibus formavit et ordinavit constitutiones alias, que nunc habentur, frater Raymundus de penna forti magister ordinis tercius.

[3] *ALKG* 1: 194; translation from W.A. Hinnebusch, *The History of the Dominican Order*, vo.1 2 (New York: Alba House, 1973).

[4] G. R. Galbraith, *The Constitution of the Dominican Order 1216-1360* (Manchester, 1925) Appendix 2, 203-353.

[5] R. Creytens, "Les Constitutions des frères prêcheurs dans la Rédaction de S Raymond de Penafort (1241)," *AFP* 18 (1948) 29-68.

In the 1228 constitutions the sections about education and preaching are found under the following section numbers and titles:[6]
18. De Visitatoribus
20. De idoneis ad praedicandum
28. De magistro studencium
29. De dispensacione studencium
30. De doctore
31. De predicatoribus
32. Ubi non audeant predicare fratres
33. De scandalo predicacionis
34. De itinerantibus fratribus

In the 1356-63 constitutions the relevant chapters are found in the second distinction under the following numbers and titles:[7]
XI. De visitatoribus
XII. De predicatoribus
XIII. De itinerantibus
XIIII. De studentibus

When the 1228 constitutions are compared with those of 1356-1363, it can be concluded that the principles crystallized within seven years of the founder's death in the 1228 constitutions, were still relevant a century and a quarter later.[8]

What then were Dominic's injunctions about preaching and study? It seems clear that both during Dominic's lifetime and in the first years of the order, novices were allowed to preach, as also were friars after studying theology for one year only. This flexibility could reflect the fact that many qualified scholars flocked into the order in the 1220s; but so did many younger men. The ordering of requirements about preaching and

---

[6] *ALKG* 1: 219-225.

[7] Galbraith, *Constitution*, 246-252.

[8] Chapter XI of the 1356-63 constitutions contains Chapter XVIII of the 1228 constitutions. Chapter XII of the later constitutions contains the substance and, in many places, the exact wording of the earlier constitutions, putting in one chapter numbers 31, 32, 33, and parts of 34. Chapter XIII of the later constitutions contains all the relevant matter, in the same phrasing as the 1228 constitutions, including the command "to receive the Friars Minor with all charity and cheerfulness" (*ALKG* 1: 225 and Galbraith, *Constitution*, 248). A similar process is observed in Chapter XIIII of the later constitutions. All the original matter of sections 28, 29, 30 and part of 34 of the 1228 constitutions are included in the 1356-63 set. The extra parts in chapters XI-XIIII of the later constitutions include some of the clarifications made by general chapters in the intervening 128 years. Berg, 43.

study in the constitutions is significant. No friar could preach publicly until he had studied theology for three years, and he must be twenty-five before he could be ordained. He was expected to be a man of integrity, of piety and of good example, a man of God able to communicate the things of God in his preaching. As the work of preaching implies a travelling life, practical regulations were made: a preacher should always have a companion; they should carry their credentials with them; they must not collect money from preaching. As Dominic had demonstrated from his preaching in the Languedoc, effective preaching of the gospel depended on thorough and continually revised knowledge of the scriptures. Other learning was to be subordinated to this end. The degree of subordination, however, was never specified. It is true to say that, while Dominic stated the principle, there were no clearly established regulations about study during his lifetime.[9] The Dominicans, on the whole, never ranged as widely in their topics of study as did the Franciscans, but did develop a tradition of searching biblical scholarship which in its turn gave a coherent direction to the intellectual life of the Order.

The 1228 constitutions are specific about the serious nature of study, establishing a special post—master of students—to supervise and help coordinate their studies. Without permission, the friars were not to study Philosophy or Arts in the schools outside the priories. Any friar who was sent to study was to receive the necessary books, especially the Bible. To those who would benefit, the master of students could assign cells where they could read, write, pray, or sleep. Any student, however, who misused his study time could lose the privilege of a cell. It was possible for the prior to give dispensation from choir, but not from Compline. Moreover, the Office was to be celebrated briskly, "breviter et succinte"[10] and without any additions, so that both prayer and study time would be well used. Three years of studying Theology were required before any Dominican could be appointed as preacher-general. Finally, to ensure that the hard task of study would be faithfully maintained, the visitors were required to assess annually the assiduity of the study and the sincerity of the preaching. The work of the members of the Order of Preachers was to study in order to preach, "contemplata aliis tradere."

This care for preaching and its preparation was reinforced by the legislation concerning the foundation of a house. In the 1228 constitutions this forms part of Chapter 23 in the second distinction. It states four conditions for the establishment of a convent: permission from the general

---

[9] Renard, 113-118.
[10] *ALKG* 1: De horis et de modi dicendi, 197.

chapter, at least twelve friars, a prior, a lector. This injunction is found in the 1356-63 constitutions as part of an extended first chapter, *de domibus concedendis et construendis,* in the second distinction.[11] The chapter of 1228 codified Dominic's specific requirements about preaching, study and teaching. These same rules, including the ordering by Raymund of Penaforte, were incorporated and expanded, but not significantly modified, in the constitutions of 1356-63. It is a mark of their value that many of them are still part of Dominican practice.

The evidence of the constitutions and of the early foundations indicates an organisation that built education-for-preaching into the living Order. The young Order of Preachers would be developing at the same time, under the same influences as and in interaction with, as the young universities.

B. ...IN THE CHAPTER ACTS

The aim and provisions of the constitutions of the Order of Preachers were fostered, developed and modified by the three kinds of chapters: conventual, provincial and general. The operation of the conventual chapter was specified by the constitutions, and preaching formed a regular part of its activities. Information about the provincial chapters is varied: the records of the province of Provence are so extensive that they have been fruitfully studied by many scholars from Douais onwards; those of the Roman province are not as extensive, but useful none the less; in contrast, records of the English province are non-existent.[12] It is an achievement that Galbraith can make a partial list of the places where English provincial chapters were held from 1238 to 1336.[13] The chapter had a three-year pattern. For two of the three years the provincial chapters elected the diffinitors to represent the province at the general chapter; for the third year, provincial priors alone attended the general chapter. The diffinitors brought with them from their provinces decisions, opinions and information which affected the course of the general chapter. General chapters

[11] Galbraith, *Constitution,* 225.

[12] M. E. O'Carroll, SND, "The Educational Organisation of the Dominicans in England and Wales 1221-1348: a multidisciplinary approach," *AFP* 50 (1980): 23-62.

[13] Galbraith, *Constitution,* 261-265.

were omitted only eight times between 1221 and 1348[14] so the records for those years are comprehensive. The magnitude of the enterprise when travel was limited to the friars' own two feet is remarkable. The difficulties of the operation are illustrated by the suffrages at the end of the chapter accounts, where the deaths of fr. N or N on his way to, or home from, the chapter is recorded.

Through the legislation of the general chapters it is possible to follow the development of Dominican theory and practice concerning preaching and education.[15]

Initially general chapter records were brief: in the 1240s a pattern of reporting emerges; in the fourteenth century records become very long, especially with the extended lists of suffrages, although the latter can afford interesting political sidelights. The general chapter had different kinds of work: it could make legislation; it could elect; it could correct; it could depose; it could appoint. While it existed it was the highest authority in the Order. In the thirteenth and fourteenth centuries new matters for Constitutions are called *Inchoaciones*. These functioned rather like the first reading of a bill in parliament, and many *inchoaciones* fell by the wayside. *Confirmaciones* is the name for the process of approving accepted *inchoaciones*. Two confirmations were required in three successive chapters for a change, or for a new topic to be introduced into the constitutions. More ephemeral, but not less interesting topics were introduced under the titles of *Admoniciones* and *Ordinaciones*. In 1261, for example, Simon of Hinton was admonished because the English province had not obeyed the 1248 requirement that Oxford should become a *studium generale*.[16] Through the *ordinaciones* anxieties about lack of observance could be expressed, or a specific aspect of the constitutions re-emphasised. In this section were made the teaching appointments to the *studia* in the Order, and the appointment of vicars general for provinces awaiting election of a new prior-provincial.

[14] Chapters of 1237, 1253, 1284, 1295, 1299, 1332, 1338, 1345. The causes of omission were the death, deposition or elevation of masters-general. See also Galbraith, *Constitution*.

[15] While Hinnebusch, *Hist.* 2 contains a comprehensive account of the Order's organisation of studies, it seemed useful to make my own set of extracts from the chapter Acts. See also Renard, chapters 6-8 for the early years to 1237; Berg for general survey.

[16] Ed. B.M. Reichert, *Acta Capitulorum Generalium Ordinis Praedicatorum*, 9 vols = MOPH, 3-4, 8-14 (Rome, 1898 seq.) Volumes 3 and 4 are relevant, hereinafter referred to as ACTA I and ACTA II. Hinton reference: ACTA I: 110-111.

As preaching was the main work of the Order, the Acts concerning this will be considered first. The Fourth Lateran Council had emphasised preaching and right instructions about the sacrament of penance, so that the tasks of preaching and hearing confessions were closely linked.[17] Between 1249 and 1346, nine chapters devote some comment to preaching. The Chapter of Treves clarified the constitutions on preaching:

> Priors should ensure very carefully that they do not appoint any brother to the office of preaching unless he be of suitable character and proven learning.[18]

This modification, together with its rider, "lest through inadequate preaching the Order is brought into contempt and endangers souls," received its third chapter, its confirmation, by 1251.[19]

By 1249 the function of preacher-general, the genesis of which is still under debate, had been developed.[20] The chapter of Treves defined the qualities required of him:[21] "he must be mature, and discreet in managing the business of the Order in chapter." The office of preacher-general, appointed only from those who had studied Theology for at least three years, was established to place preaching at the centre of the Order's administrative structure and maintain the status of preaching. As members of the provincial chapter preachers-general had full rights in electing diffinitors to the general chapter, though not in electing the prior-provincial. As non-elected members they provided an element of continuity in the province administration. Within their own convents, however, preachers-general could preach only within the priory's preaching limits. As the Order grew, the number of preachers-general expanded. Many general chapters tried to control this growth, with only partial success. The 1276 chapter fixed the number of preachers-general as equal to the number of priories in the province.[22]

The chapter held at Lyons in 1274 gave the preachers some guidelines to help them maintain good relations with local parish priests: preachers were to be careful not to receive alms for preaching; they were not to trespass on the arranged preaching times of others; at intervals they

[17] Renard, 108-109.

[18] ACTA I: 45-46.

[19] ACTA I: 51.

[20] H. C. Scheeben, "Prediger und Generalprediger im Dominikanerorden des 13. Jahrhunderts," *AFP* 21 (1961), 112-141. See also Renard, 80-91.

[21] ACTA I: 46.

[22] ACTA I: 187.

were to encourage their audiences to pay their tithes and proper dues.[23] These requirements were repeated a generation later at the Chapter of Naples in 1311,[24] together with the criteria for character and learning in a preacher.

In 1282, the capitulants meeting at Vienne warned priors-provincial and diffinitors to ensure that those commissioned "to preach and hear confessions" should observe the canons about the sacrament of penance, especially those of the Fourth Council of the Lateran.[25]

The chapter held at Metz in 1313, probably related to the chapter of Naples two years previously, came back to the function of preaching and the importance of theological preparation. It is interesting to note that "insufficiency" of preachers was not ground for relaxing the rule about the length of the study course:

> Because through insufficient preaching and hearing of confessions our Order may be despised and souls endangered, we forbid that anyone be assigned to the office of preaching or hearing confessions unless he has studied Theology for at least three years.[26]

Another generation passed before the general chapter, this time at Brive in 1346, referred again to preaching and hearing confessions. The constitutions as formulated are repeated, but with the significant comment that the aspiring preacher "must have been able to preach before many of the brethren in the vernacular."[27] This requirement was exemplified in England, where some Dominicans were among the few priests who in those years could hear confessions in Welsh and Cornish.

The volume of capitular comment on the functions of preaching and hearing confessions is small compared with that on education. The requirements of the constitutions are frequently repeated.[28] But clarification of the original rulings and reference to correction of abuses can testify, either to a continuous attempt to keep high ideals about the apostolic care of souls in the forefront of the brethren's lives, or to the non-implementation of the recommended changes of the original rulings. In the

---

[23] ACTA I: 176.

[24] ACTA II: 51.

[25] ACTA I: 218.

[26] ACTA II: 64.

[27] ACTA II: 310.

[28] For example, 1274 ACTA I: 176; 1297 ACTA I: 284; 1312 ACTA II: 56 and 1345 ACTA II: 64 are repetitions. The chapter of Toulouse 1258 warned against unsuitable contents of sermons; ACTA I: 92.

thirteenth century the former interpretation is probably nearer the truth.

C. THE SYSTEM

While the aim and function of the Order were kept before the members, the means of achieving the aim and function, namely education and study, were the subjects of a far greater volume of capitular comment and legislation. In the life of Dominic himself; in the 1228 Constitutions, which embodied his ideas; in the edition by Raymund of Penaforte, 1238-1241, together with the 1356-63 constitutions which demonstrated the continuity of those ideas, the central place of education as a means to implement the end of the Order is paramount. Other aspects of religious life, such as worship, prayer, common life, Dominic could take for granted. But hitherto no religious order had taken a specific task. In so far as preaching was concerned, there was the continuous tradition of the Church to draw on; in so far as education as a means for training preachers was concerned, all was new. The only exception is the training of the Schools from the second half of the twelfth century, but that was an individual responsibility. In the communal approach all was novel and untried. Dominic was the innovator. Living experience was therefore significant.[29]

In the years 1221-1348, there were only sixteen general chapters in which no significant reference to preaching and education was made.[30] It is not practicable to examine each chapter relating to education as was possible for preaching. Instead some representative chapters will be looked at in more detail, and the information considered topically. The outstanding general chapters are those of Valenciennes, 1259; the twelve-year series from Besançon in 1301 to Bologna in 1315; London 1335; Brive 1346. The latter was not innovative, but rather repetitive, for its generation of friars.

Prior to Valenciennes several modifications in the regulations for study had been made. The most important was the constitution introduced in 1246,[31] agreed in 1247, and confirmed in Paris 1248, that the provinces

---

[29] Berg, a valuable analysis of education for both mendicant orders, 16-56. See also the discussion in J. P. Torrell, *Initiation à saint Thomas d'Aquin* (Paris: Cerf, 1993) and Michele Mulcahey's recent study, "The Dominican 'Studium' system and the universities of Europe in the thirteenth century: a relationship redefined," in *Manuels, Programmes de cours et techniques d'enseignement dans les universités médiévales* (Louvain-la-Neuve, 1994), 277-324.

[30] The general chapters of 1238, 1239, 1253, 1262, 1268, 1269, 1279, 1296, 1319, 1322, 1323, 1324, 1326, 1237, 1334.

[31] ACTA I: 34-35.

of Germany, England, Provence and Lombardy should establish *studia generalia* for the use of the whole Order. The English province did not obey immediately, but eventually the four *studia*—Cologne, Oxford, Montpellier and Bologna—joined Paris, though none of them gained the eminence of the Paris *studium*. By 1259 the existence of numerous priory schools and of the *studia generalia* required more organisation, for several reasons. First, because of increasing numbers; secondly, because many of the increased numbers were not university students but young men who required education in Grammar and Latin; third, because the university syllabi had changed, particularly in the area of Philosophy. The Order of Preachers had to adapt to these developments. A group of distinguished Dominican masters—Albert the Great, Thomas Aquinas, Peter of Tarentaise, Florence of Hesdin and Bonhomme of Brittany[32]—were commissioned to sort things out. They drew up twenty-four articles which were promulgated at the chapter of 1259.[33]

The articles provided that young friars living in priories which for any reason had no lector were to be sent to priories with lectors. If this was impracticable, private study on the Bible; on the *Summa de Casibus*, possibly the short one by Paul of Hungary,[34] and if available the long one by Raymund of Penaforte;[35] and on the *Historia Scholastica* of Peter Comestor, was to be undertaken. The latter book provided a combination of sacred and secular history from creation to the death of St. Peter which was very useful, both as a summary Bible history and as a potential source of exempla. Each province was to establish a *studium arcium* where preparatory education in Arts and Philosophy would be given. Timetables were suggested; a method of selecting friars for higher education was described and provincial diffinitors were charged with the annual task both of examining the quality of the studies and of reporting on that and on all related matters to the provincial chapter. So it was that Dominic's embryonic plan matured to an organisation of Schools on a local, provincial and general level, with a curriculum directed to Theology.

In 1274, the capitulants meeting at Lyons reaffirmed the importance

[32] Hinnebusch, *Hist.* 1: 7.

[33] ACTA I: 99-100.

[34] Paul of Hungary, *Summa de Casibus Tractatis de Vitiis et Virtutibus*, 2nd ed., Bibliotheca Casinensis, Series 4 (Monte Cassino, 1880), 191-215.

[35] Raymund of Penaforte; the printed version from the work of John of Freiburg is *Summa de Poenitentia et Matrimonio cum glossis Joannis de Friburgo*, (Rome, 1602; photocopy Farnborough, 1967).

of the 1259 legislation.[36] The next major reorganisation of studies came in the first decades of the fourteenth century, starting with Besançon 1303.[37] The work was continued in the Chapter of Genoa 1305,[38] Padua 1308,[39] Saragossa 1309,[40] Metz 1313,[41] London 1314,[42] and concluded at Bologna in 1315.[43] At Besançon the manner of appointing the master of students was clarified. At Genoa, financial support for students at the *studia generalia* was organised through a levy on the Order; the pattern, progress and length of studies were updated; and the ordering of lectures and exercises during the academic year was arranged. At Padua the master General issued a statement reaffirming the function of study and the need for books to be provided. At Saragossa the importance of a thorough theological study of the Bible was emphasised, and the teaching of "our venerable brother and teacher, Thomas of Aquino" was strongly recommended. The chapters of Metz, London and Bologna codified afresh the legislation on study and teaching. They refined further the function of the master of students in maintaining appropriate standards;[44] restated the rights of students, many of them men in their thirties and forties, to maintenance;[45] required the separation of schools of Logic and Philosophy from those of Theology to prevent overloading the provisioning of the priory;[46] and improved the mode of selecting students for higher education so that suitable ones were kept, while unpromising or idle students were returned to their home priories.[47] As at Valenciennes in 1259, the task of these chapters was codification and rationalisation of the capitular legislation of the preceding years. Equally, this was a process of adaptation.

For the rest of the period to 1348 no new legislation or reorganisation in education was carried out by the general chapters. Both London in

---

[36] ACTA I: 174 seq.
[37] ACTA I: 321-325.
[38] ACTA II: 11-14.
[39] ACTA II: 34-35.
[40] ACTA II: 38-40.
[41] ACTA II: 63-66.
[42] ACTA II: 70-72.
[43] ACTA II: 78-84.
[44] ACTA II: 64, 79.
[45] ACTA II: 65, 78, 79, 82.
[46] ACTA II: 79.
[47] ACTA II: 81, 82.

1335[48] and Brives in 1346[49] repeated for new generations of provincials and students the regulations of the early decades of the fourteenth century.

It remains now to summarise the practical implementation of the legislation outlined above. To cope with the rapid increase of numbers from the first half of the thirteenth century, which stabilised in the second half, the Order gradually established a network of schools in each province at three levels: priory, provincial and general.[50]

The foundation stone of this educational edifice was the priory school. This was a school of Theology in which lectures were given daily by the appointed lector. Although most classes were intended for the brethren, students could come to them from outside the priory. All clerical members of the priory had to be present at the daily lectures, unless permission for absence had been given.[51] This continuous education, which diminished in the two big preaching seasons of Advent and Lent,[52] was for the use and benefit of the *fratres communes*.[53] Most Dominican preachers belonged to the *fratres communes*, and they were the men who carried the bulk of the pastoral tasks of preaching and hearing confessions. Another name for them was *juniores*. As Boyle comments, they "were, in fact, the backbone of the Order and vastly outnumbered the Alberts and Thomases, the lectors and the masters."[54] These were the friars about whose suitability and formation for preaching the chapters were so concerned. For them were written pastoral works like Simon of Hinton's *Summa Juniorum*, Raymund of Penaforte's *Summa de Casibus*, and William Peraldus's *Summae Vitiorum et Virtutum*. It has been argued that Thomas Aquinas composed his *Summa Theologiae* for them as he perceived that, in addition to the substantial formation in moral and pastoral theology received by the *fratres communes*, a broader foundation in systematic theology was needed.[55] These Dominican schools were supported by the

---

[48] ACTA II: 229.

[49] ACTA II: 309.

[50] See O'Carroll, "Ed. Org."; Berg 32-43, 58-67, 118-121.

[51] ACTA II: 39, 175, 196, 208, 251.

[52] Humbert, *De Vita* 2: 254.

[53] L.E. Boyle, "Notes on the Education of the 'Fratres Communes' in the Dominican Order in the Thirteenth Century" in *Xenia Medii Aevi Historiam Illustrantia oblata THOMAE KAEPPELI OP*, ed. R. Creytens (Rome: Edizioni di Storia e Letteratura, 1978) 249-267.

[54] Boyle, "Fratres Communes," 254.

[55] L.E. Boyle, *The Setting of the 'Summa Theologiae' of Saint Thomas*," The Etienne Gilson Series 5 (Toronto: PIMS, 1982), 4.

alms of the townsfolk to whom the friars preached and amongst whom they dwelt. If there were a shortage of lectors in the province, the priory schools bore the lack. Hence the chapter ruling about private study of the Bible, Raymund's *Summa* and the Histories replacing the missing lectures.

Initially the schools or *studia* provided at the second or provincial level were schools of Theology where teaching and learning were of a more advanced standard than in the priory school. They tended to be established permanently in the more important priories of the province. In England, Oxford and London had such; in France, Paris; and in Lombardy, Bologna. Later in the thirteenth century as we have seen, the rapid increase of numbers—many of whom were youths of fifteen—prompted the Valenciennes pattern, which required greater differentiation amongst provincial schools. As well as provincial schools of Theology, there were provincial schools of Arts and of Philosophy. Variations in records of different provinces means that information is available only for some.[56] The underlying principle, however, is the same. A school and its number of students exists only in proportion to the economic resources in alms and gifts of the individual priory. To lessen the material burden, specialist schools in Arts and in Philosophy moved from one priory to another in an annual or biennial rotation. It is likely that the courses in the Arts were for younger friars who needed an academic grounding before studying Theology in the priory school, while the courses in Philosophy were advanced courses for lectors in training. Part of the task of the annual visitors was to seek from among the *fratres communes* friars of academic talent and good character who could be further educated as and when places became available in the provincial schools of Theology. Between 1271 and 1275 the general chapters passed legislation to enable provinces to be subdivided into vicariates or visitations or nations for ease of administration, particularly with regard to visitation and correction, but without vitiating the unity of the province.[57] Once these divisions existed they became useful for other purposes. Very soon the vicariate, visitation or nation became a unit in the provincial provision of education.[58] After 1275, provincial schools of Arts, Philosophy, and Theology were established in each visitation.

The third level of schools in the Order of Preachers was that of general schools, available to friars from all provinces. Initially there was only one for the whole of the Order, that of Paris at St. Jacques. The link

[56] For example, the provinces of Provence and Rome, O'Carroll, "Ed. Org.," 27-31.

[57] ACTA I: 158.

[58] O'Carroll, "Ed. Org.," 28-29, 33.

between the Paris *studium* and the University occurred when Roland of Cremona OP incepted as Master of Theology under John of St. Giles.[59] In 1230 the Dominicans gained a second chair when John of St. Giles dramatically entered the Order. One chair remained with the French province, while the second was kept for friars from other provinces—Thomas Aquinas held this second one. Thus Paris gained theological pre-eminence in the Order of Preachers. The pressure for places at the *studium generale* in Paris, where friars could obtain their university-awarded mastership in Theology, was such that, as we have seen, in 1248 the general chapter named four new *studia generalia*: Bologna, Cologne, Montpellier and Oxford. These still did not fully meet the needs, so in 1290 and 1293 the Roman and Spanish provinces respectively were required to establish a *studium generale* in each province. Then in 1304 the general chapter held at Toulouse commanded all provinces except Greece, the Holy Land and Scandinavia, to set up *studia generalia*.[60] Finally there was some Dominican membership of the mobile *studium curie* founded at the papal court by Innocent IV about 1245.[61]

The level of the Dominican *studium generale* was equivalent to the study of theology in the new faculties of Theology in the young universities. In some cases, as in Paris and Oxford, the *studium generale* was directly linked to the faculty of Theology by having a regent master of Theology in the priory. This link, however, was not necessary for the theological education of the friars. There were probably more friars studying theology at a high level in the *studium generale* than there were actual places for gaining the university qualification.

The provision of lectors was a constant need. Friars were selected initially by the visitors in consultation with the master of students and the prior. Selection of students for the bachelorship and mastership in Theology was made by the general chapter. No student could enter any higher level of studies unless he had taught the penultimate course.[62] After many years of study alternating with teaching assignments, a friar could be chosen to go to a university linked *studium generale* to gain a university Theology degree. The experience of fr Miguel de Polo of the Spanish province illustrates the process:[63] student of Logic at Saragossa, 1349; lector of Logic at Pamplona 1351-1353 and at Barcelona in 1354; lector of

[59] Hinnebusch, *Hist.* 2: 38; chapter 3 is helpful background to the *studia generalia*.

[60] ACTA I: 314, 320; ACTA II: 2.

[61] Hinnebusch, *Hist.* 2: 43.

[62] ACTA II: 12-13, 54.

[63] Emden, *BRUO*, 2: 1493.

Philosophy at Ilende 1335, sub-lector in Theology at Saragossa 1358, bachelor of Theology, possibly from the University of Lerida; lector of Sentences, Oxford 1366; master of Theology, Barcelona 1368. It was a long haul of almost twenty years. The uninterrupted pattern was as follows: as a bachelor of Theology the friar had to lecture on the literal text of the Bible for two years; in later years a sub-lector on the Sentences was appointed; then he became lector on the Sentences for at least one year under a regent master of Theology. The gaining of the Oxford qualification in theology could take nine years to complete. When his course was completed to the satisfaction of his master, he was presented by the regent master to the assembled regent masters in Theology for the final exercises of preaching and disputing. If he performed successfully, he was said to have "incepted." As a master of Theology he could begin to teach others and himself present students for degrees in the university. The secular masters, provided that they could make it viable financially, stayed as regent masters as long as they wished. The friars differed. On the whole a friar rarely taught as regent master for more than two years. This enabled more friars to gain a mastership in Theology, and so provide lectors for the provincial schools of Theology. Moreover, once a friar was qualified as master, he was required to take another teaching post before he could be elected or appointed to any other office in the Order.[64]

Initially, the Order of Preachers was probably better organised at providing a theological education for its members than were the universities of Paris and Oxford. As we have seen, the Dominicans used the universities to complete the education of the future lectors of the important schools of Theology within the Order. The nascent universities and the Order of Preachers were equal in their academic standing in Theology.

By the mid-thirteenth century, both in Paris and in Oxford things had changed.[65] The very popularity of the friars with townsfolk meant that economic benefits, formerly enjoyed by seculars and monastic interests, were diminished by being shared with the friars. This led to bad feeling between the masters and the friars. Moreover, at Oxford, the secular masters and students resented the fact that friars who had not studied the Arts course there and incepted as masters in Arts as required by the custom of the university, could join the higher faculty of Theology

[64] ACTA I: 214; see also A.G. Little and F. Pelster, *Oxford Theology and Theologians AD 1282-1302*, OHS 96 (1934): "Oxford University Customs," 25-56.

[65] M. W. Sheehan, "The Religious Orders 1220-1370," in *The Early Oxford Schools*, ed. R.J.A.I. Catto, vol. 1 of *The History of the University of Oxford*, gen. ed. T.H. Aston (Oxford: Clarendon Press, 1984), 204-205.

directly as students and become bachelors and masters therein. In the preceding decades the new university of Oxford had gained not only administrative and corporate experience but also political power. An increasing number of its former students, climbing the ladder of preferment, were serving significantly in the Church and at the court. Henry III consistently favoured and supported the university. Matters came to a head in 1253 when Thomas of York OFM was refused permission to incept as a master of theology because he had not previously incepted in Arts. A friendly compromise was reached whereby friars could request a dispensation or grace from this statute. What had been a standard practice for the friars was now a conferred privilege. The initial equality between the Order of Preachers and the university was breached.

In Paris events were harsher.[66] The masters of Arts, led by William of St. Amour, attacked the friars about the practice of poverty. A pamphlet war, and even more aggressive activities, attended the dispute. Eventually, in 1257, William was banned from the university and retired to St. Amour. Within a short time more serious opposition arose over the increased use of the philosophy of Aristotle in the Order of Preachers, and specifically of the philosophical teaching of Thomas Aquinas, which was much less Augustinian in its stance than the older traditions. Oxford was embroiled on the edges of the controversy. With two friar archbishops of Canterbury, Robert Kilwardby OP and John Pecham OFM, on the side of the Paris masters and only a few Dominicans, of whom Thomas of Sutton was foremost, on the side of Thomas Aquinas, the immediate Oxford result of the dispute was a foregone conclusion. In time, however, Pecham's injunction seems to have been forgotten at Oxford; while Pecham's successor, Archbishop Winchelsey, supported the Thomists.

In early fourteenth-century Oxford, the fragile settlement of 1253 was challenged by the masters of Arts using the muscle of their numbers to attempt to control the decisions of all the faculties in the university, by proposing that they could be made by a majority from two faculties only. Despite the fact that the student friars of all four orders were numerically dominant in the Oxford Theology faculty, the faculty of Arts itself had far greater numbers. This would have given control to the faculty of Arts. The masters of Arts also specifically wished to force the friars to incept in Arts before starting Theology. This would have destroyed the school system within the Order of Preachers by interfering with their stage-training of lectors. Moreover, it would replace the Order's subordination of the teach-

---

[66] Hinnebusch, *Hist.* 2: 71-78; C.H. Lawrence, *Medieval Monasticism*, 2nd ed. (London: Longman, 1989), 261-263.

ing of Philosophy to Theology with the specific courses used at Oxford. This time round the struggle, beginning in 1303, was long drawn out and vindictive in operation. For nearly a decade, no Dominican could incept in Theology. Eventually the same compromise was reached as in 1253: that the Dominicans would have to ask for the grace to incept in Theology without having previously incepted in Arts. This time, however, the statutes protected the friars from ill-focussed and ill-natured opposition. In the wider struggle, the more numerous faculty of Arts did gain an increase of power, but decisions had to be ratified by three out of the four faculties rather than by two only.[67] The Dominicans, hopeful of papal support to modify the 1314 proposals in their favour, dragged their feet, and eventually what they were reluctant to accept in 1314 they were forced to receive in 1320. Thus, after many years, order and clarity were restored to the relationship between the university and the friars, and the academic dominance of the university was finally accepted by the friars.

Between 1221 and 1348, in an international pattern, the Order of Preachers developed an interlocking system of schools which gave an initial education in Theology, and where necessary in Grammar and Arts, to all clerical friars to prepare them for their pastoral tasks of preaching and hearing confessions. This gave continuing theological education to these friars, provided higher theological studies for those capable of it and selected and trained at the highest theological levels a minority of future lectors of the priory, provincial and general schools. In truth, the Order of Preachers was a thirteenth-century open university.

D. THE CURRICULUM AND BOOKS

We have seen the system of education which the Order of Preachers established to fulfil their aim of forming numerous highly-trained preachers. It is necessary now to examine briefly how the system worked.

Those young friars who needed it were given a primary education in Latin and Grammar, probably in their own priory, although in the fourteenth century some Dominican grammar schools were known. Before being licensed to preach, all the friars had to study Theology for three years. This included a thorough grounding in the Bible, the acquisition of the skills of disputation and some practice in preaching. The students were expected to revise their classes weekly. Oversight of the studies was one of the main duties of the conventual prior. He could also give dispensa-

---

[67] Hinnebusch, *Hist.* 2: 78-9; Sheehan, "Religious Orders," 205-7.

tion from the Divine Office if any friar needed more time for study.[68] Leonard Boyle has identified a manuscript of the British Library, Add. MS 30508, as a miscellany completed from 1260 by a lector of an English priory, possibly Pontefract.[69] It contains an abbreviation of the *Summa Juniorum* of Simon of Hinton; sermon notes; a tract on the commandments, the creed and confession; a second tract on confesssion; a synopsis of all four books of Raymund Penaforte's *Summa de Casibus*; a series of 216 problems or "cases," and some riddles. From this text-book it can be seen that the theological education of the friars was, after Scripture study, directed to the growing science of moral and pastoral theology, a theological area of particular interest and use to the friars. In other words, the course was directed towards the practical and continuing formation of good preachers. A late thirteenth-century exemplar of a conscientious priory lector is John of Freiburg.[70] He held office for over thirty years, but did not teach the same course unchanged year in year out. He started with Raymund's *Summa*. Then he combined this with the work by William of Rennes, and indexed both books. Having been a student of some of the great theologians —Ulrich of Strasbourg, possibly of Albert the Great, Thomas Aquinas and Peter of Tarentaise—he made a theological supplement to Raymund. Eventually, in 1297-98, he started work on a *summa* of his own, one which proved popular in the Order for generations to come. In the later thirteenth and fourteenth centuries the teaching in the priory schools, following the developments in the study of Theology at university from the 1240s onwards probably included a basic course in Arts and Philosophy, taught before the three years of Theology.[71]

During the basic course in Theology in the priory school, the lector and prior would be identifying able students who showed promise as future lectors. Selection was made annually by the visitors. Shortage of lectors could be a reality in Dominican life, and if this happened, the priory schools tended to be the first to suffer. Hence the provisions we have already noted about private study of the Bible, Raymund's *Summa* and Peter Comestor's *Histories*.

We know much more about the further and higher education of

[68] Hinnebusch, *Hist.* 2: 21.

[69] Boyle, "Fratres Communes," 259-266.

[70] Boyle, "Fratres Communes," 258.

[71] Hinnebusch, *Hist.* 2: 30; L.E. Boyle, "The *summa confessorum* of John of Freiburg and the Popularization of the Moral Teaching of St. Thomas and Some of his Contemporaries," *St. Thomas Aquinas 1274-1974 Commemorative Studies*, ed. Armand A. Maurer (Toronto: PIMS, 1974) 2: 245-268.

TABLE 1. THE CURRICULUM IN ARTS AND PHILOSOPHY

Grammar (Arts)
    Donatus, *Barbarismus*
    Priscian, *De accentu*
    ——, *In maiore volumine*
    ——, *In minore volumine*
    Gilbertus Porretanus (attrib.), *Liber sex principiorum*

Old Logic (Arts)
    Porphyry, *Isagoge*
    Aristotle, *Categoriae*
    ——, *De interpretatione*
    Boethius, *Liber divisionum*
    ——, *De differentiis topicis*

New Logic (Arts)
    Aristotle, *Topica*
    ——, *Sophisti elenchi*
    ——, *Analytica priora et posteriora*

Natural Philosophy (Philosophy)
    Aristotle, *De physica*
    ——, *De animalibus*
    ——, *De anima*
    ——, *De generatione et corruptione*
    ——, *De sensu et sensatu*
    ——, *De somno et vigilia*
    ——, *De memoria et reminiscentia*
    ——, *De morte et vita*
    —— (attrib.), *De vegetabilibus et plantis*

Astronomy (Philosophy)
    Aristotle, *De caelo*
    ——, *Meteora*

Metaphysics (Philosophy)
    Aristotle, *Metaphysica*
    —— (attrib.), *De causis*

Moral Philosophy (Philosophy)
    Aristotle, *Ethica*

those friars selected for training as lectors. Unless the friar was already a master of Arts before he entered, as was quite common in the first half of the thirteenth century, the Order had to provide for the education of the student in Arts and Philosophy. In Arts the whole range of Aristotle's logical and scientific works, together with traditional works of Grammar by Priscian and Donatus, made up the bulk of the syllabus. Philosophy was the second important subject area. Again the syllabus was based mostly on Aristotle.[72]

Certain branches of study including Alchemy, Medicine and some Philosophy were forbidden.[73] This syllabus, based on that of the university of Paris, was drawn up by the committee of masters and promulgated in 1259. In this way, the Order of Preachers kept control of the Arts and Philosophy taught in the Dominican schools and made these studies subservient to the study of Theology. Such an approach was not necessarily that of the faculty of Arts in either Oxford or Paris.

The Theology course was twofold in content: a study of the Bible and a study of the *Sentences*. The foundation of biblical study was a thorough knowledge of the literal text. This was called the cursory study. Lectures in this course were given by a *bachelor Biblicus* or *cursor Bibliae*. The lectures which expounded the multiple meanings of the Scripture studied cursorily were given by the regent master or a master of theology. Hugh of St. Cher's postils on the scripture reflect this kind of course. The study of Peter Lombard's four books of *Sentences* gave the rudiments of systematic, sacramental and moral Theology.[74] As the *Sentences* contain many authorities from the Latin Fathers, of whom the most quoted was Augustine, as well as later saints and masters, the *Sentences* was also a course in elementary Patristics. The literal text of the *Sentences* was taught cursorily to the students by the *bachelor Sententiarius* or *cursor Sententiarum*. The master gave the lectures which dealt with problems or *quaestiones* on the text, as well as with specific points he chose to lecture on, i.e., *quaestiones disputata*. The weekly disputation was the exercise which enabled students to make this new knowledge their own. It is probably from this exercise that speculative Theology began emerging. As an apprentice work, bachelors in Theology had to produce a commentary on the *Sentences*. Many of the well-known Dominicans of the thirteenth century produced such a work.

[72] Hinnebusch, *Hist.* 2: 25-29, especially 27-28.

[73] ACTA II: 65, 83.

[74] Peter Lombard, *Sententiae in IV Libris Distinctae*, [ed. I. Brady], 3 vols (Grottaferrata, 1971-1980).

From 1278 onwards, the speculative and moral theology of Thomas Aquinas became more appreciated within the Order, despite their uncertain fortunes outside it, and by 1309 were compulsory texts in the Dominican schools.[75] Thomas was one of the first western theologians—Grosseteste was probably the first—since the early centuries of the Church to make extensive use of the Greek Fathers. His theology was popularised in the early fourteenth century by John of Freiburg—the man we have met as a conscientious priory lector—in his *Summa Confessorum*.[76] Thomas' influence on Dante was deep. Nevertheless the realism in philosophy for which Thomas had laboured, and about which he was profoundly original, was increasingly abandoned in all but the Dominican Order, in favour of the nominalist approach which grew readily from the work and influence of William of Ockham.

The method of teaching was common to all subjects. The book or text was in the hands of the lector, who expounded the text: reading the text in small portions and then "glossing" it. He explained its literal meaning, if the course was being taught cursorily; or, if the course were being taught by the master, he expounded the moral and metaphorical meanings, quoting authorities from sources ancient and modern, sacred and secular. The students had to be able to listen, to concentrate and to memorise. If they were fortunate to possess texts, the Bible was one book each friar should have. They could annotate them. If they could afford to buy writing materials, they could make notes on lectures, but this was exceptional. To ensure that the content of the lectures was remembered, the master of the students or his deputy had to test the students regularly, either daily or weekly. In the weekly disputations, students had to learn to perform each function—proponent, respondent, objector—that this method of argument demanded. What had been passively learnt in the lecture was actively practised in the disputation. But, like the lecture, it was a methodology which depended more on aural and oral skills than modern teaching methods, which appeal far more to the eye. The student's day started early, often at 6.00am. The year followed the academic year except that, because of preaching commitments, lecture courses in Lent would be reduced.[77] Later, when the texts of Thomas Aquinas entered the syllabus, the master of students began a course on them after Easter until August 1st.[78]

[75] ACTA I: 204; ACTA II: 38, 65.
[76] L.E. Boyle, unpublished thesis 1, 268, 273-4.
[77] See note 52.
[78] ACTA II: 83, 169.

It must not be imagined that the two kinds of Dominican education just delineated resulted in a cleavage between the *fratres communes* labouring all the hours of the day in the preaching vineyard and the friars in higher education pursuing their studies for long years in cloistered calm. The studies towards university qualifications were long in years, but no potential lector could move from one stage of study to the next in an unbroken sequence. He was sent back, most likely to a priory school, to teach there out of the studies thus far completed. So teaching stints and study stints alternated in priory, provincial and general schools through the twenty or more years it took to turn a promising student in the first Theology course in a priory school into the master of Theology from Oxford or Paris. All the clerical friars of the province were in contact with higher studies through the constant movement of lectors in and out of the priory schools. There must have been theological interaction, though such is impossible to prove.

Although the Dominicans were mendicants with a high regard for poverty and, in theory at least, eschewed grand buildings and superfluous decoration,[79] they never scrupled to spend money on books. In Humbert of Romans' commentary on the rule there is a chapter which is an eloquent description of the librarian's care of books, including cataloguing, retrieving, recalling, repairing selling and buying.[80] The librarian was also responsible for book-making materials, and for deworming and drying out books requiring such treatments. He was encouraged to use all possible honest means of increasing his stock. Students were to be given money to buy books, but had to render a strict account.[81] The prior-provincial was to distribute books to the friars in need of the basic texts—the Bible, the *Sentences*, the *Historia Scholastica* of Peter Comestor.[82] The brethren were forbidden to copy books for sale to others,[83] but they could make and keep their own postils,[84] or have their own notes bound together. They were bidden to write legibly![85] Friars could publish only with permission.[86] When a friar died, his books were supposed to revert to his

---

[79] ACTA I: 11.

[80] ACTA II: 35, 146; Humbert of Romans, *De Vita Regulari*, vol. 2, Chapter 13, *De Officio Librarii*.

[81] ACTA I: 82, 169.

[82] ACTA I: 14; ACTA II: 40.

[83] ACTA I: 154.

[84] ACTA I: 14.

[85] ACTA I: 92.

[86] ACTA II: 65.

province of origin, unless he had been transferred to another province.[87] As mendicants in a society which had little to do with books, the very emphasis on their value, care, and function witnesses to the seriousness with which the Dominicans undertook their education.

From the beginning Dominicans were assiduous writers of books; not, however, on a diffuse variety of topics, but directed to the study of Scripture and to their pastoral mission.[88] At St. Jacques, Hugh of St. Cher led the team which began to develop a concordance of the Bible. He also wrote commentaries on Scripture which went into many printed editions. Albert the Great produced an astonishing variety of monographs; Vincent of Beauvais in his *Speculum* wrote an encyclopaedia of useful illustrations for preaching; Humbert of Romans was a prolific writer on the Dominican way of life, and produced many and varied preaching aids. The renowned preacher, William Peraldus, not only left hundreds of written sermons, but composed treatises on the vices and virtues which proved popular for many centuries; Thomas Aquinas wrote works in theology and philosophy which are still being studied in modern times. These above are just a few of the many friars who placed their disciplined gifts at the service of preaching and the pastoral care of lay people.

The maintenance of this system depended on a balance between the administration on the one hand and the schools on the other. The preachers-general were meant to be a link between the two sectors. The master of students, some of whose functions have already been described, was responsible for the daily care and supervision of the students; he was not only to correct them, he was equally to safeguard their rights.[89] The prior-provincial and the diffinitors were responsible for general oversight of teaching and ensuring selection of candidates for higher education.[90] The visitors independently examined the system and reported on its functioning to the relevant chapter.[91] The general chapter in its turn assigned students for places in Theology at university, legislated when need arose, and indicated the chain of mutual reponsibility. By this process the development of theology in the universities and the *studia generalia* could be assimilated to the rest of the Dominican system. The adaptations to curriculum and teaching methods would follow on in the provincial and priory schools. There must have been weaknesses, especially in coping with re-

---

[87] See n. 82.

[88] Boyle, *Setting*, 2-4.

[89] ACTA I: 65, 324; ACTA II: 64, 65, 81.

[90] For example, ACTA I: 202; ACTA II: 237-238, 280.

[91] ACTA I: 100, 197; ACTA II: 13.

gional and national differences in the general schools, as the frequency of the admonition "to receive all 'externs' with charity" shows.[92] Nevertheless, despite weaknesses and some unscrupulous use of permissions, the various officials and groups responsible within the Order of Preachers enabled education to take place on an international scale. For the first time in the history of the Church, there was provision of a regular supply of trained theologians as popular preachers. This benefited the exchange of ideas, contributed to the making of theology and pastorally cared for the laity.

E. ...IN THE ENGLISH PROVINCE

It now remains to apply the information gathered above about the training of the friar preacher to the English province, 1221-1348.[93] The English province technically included Scotland and Ireland, but there was little actual sharing, so they are omitted here. In practice, our enquiry relates to England and Wales. Scotland became a separate province in 1481.

> At the second general chapter of the Order of Friar Preachers which was held at Bologna under the Blessed Dominic, there were sent into England Friar Preachers, in the number of thirteen, having as their prior fr Gilbert Ash. In the company of the venerable father, Lord Peter des Roches, Bishop of Winchester, they reached Canterbury. After they had presented themselves to Lord Stephen, the archbishop, and after he had understood that they were preachers, he straightway ordered Gilbert to preach before him in a certain church where he was

---

[92] ACTA I: 110, 265.

[93] The standard monograph on Dominicans in England is W.A. Hinnebusch, *The Early English Friars Preachers*, Institutum Fratres Praedicatorum Dissertationes Historicae, Fasciculum XIV (Rome, 1951). Two other key sources come from research by Dr A.B. Emden and are found in A.B. Emden, "Dominican Confessors and Preachers," *AFP* 32 (1962) 180-210; A.B. Emden, *A Survey of Dominicans in England*, Institutum Historicam Fratrum Praedicatorum Dissertationes Historicae, Fasciculum XVII (Rome, 1967). A third valuable source of information is D.M. Knowles and R.N. Hadcock, *Medieval Religious Houses of England and Wales*, 2nd ed. (London, 1971); A.B. Emden, *A Biographical Register of the University of Cambridge to 1500*, (Cambridge, 1963); A.B. Emden, *A Biographical Register of the University of Oxford to 1500*, 3 vols. (Oxford: Clarendon Press, 1957-1959). See also O'Carroll, "Ed. Org.," 23-62; Berg 98-100, 130-131; Joanna Cannon, "Inghilterra" in "Panorama degli studia degli Ordini Mendicant" in *Le Scuole degli Ordini Mendicant secolo xiii-xiv* (Todi, 1978) 93-116.

Bamburgh

0 ⌐————————⌐ 50
miles

———— Roman roads
- - - - Icknield Way (Greenway)
* Town with houses of four
main orders of friars

Underlined priories are noted in
Worcester Cathedral MS Q93

Newcastle

Carlisle

Yarm

Scarborough

ERMINE

Lancaster

YORK

Beverley

Pontefract

STREET

Rhuddlan

Lincoln

Bangor

Chester

Boston

Newcastle-u-Lyme

Derby

Norwich   Yar-
-mouth

Shrewsbury

WATLING

Stamford Kings Lynn

ERMINE

Leicester

Thetford

Dunwich

Warwick

Northampton

CAMBRIDGE

Ipswich

Worcester

STREET

Dunstable

Sudbury

Hereford

Gloucester

OXFORD

Chelmsford

Haverfordwest

Brecon

Cardiff

Bristol

Kings
Langley

Salisbury

LONDON

Guildford

Canterbury

Ilchester

Winchester

Winchelsea

Chichester   Arundel

Exeter

Truro

			1262	Yarm
		1246 Haverfordwest	1263	Ipswich
		Hereford		Warwick
		1248 Sudbury	1265	Bamburgh
		1251 Bangor	1267	Yarmouth
	1235 Winchester	1252 Leicester	1269	Brecon
	1236 Chester	Scarborough	1275	Guildford
1221 Oxford	1237 Canterbury	1253 Arundel	1277	Chelmsford
1224 London	1238 Cambridge	1256 Dunwich		Newcastle u.-Lyme
1226 Norwich	Lincoln	King's Lynn	1280	Chichester
1227 York	1239 Derby	Pontefract	1281	Salisbury
1230 Bristol	Newcastle	1258 Rhuddian	1288	Boston
1232 Exeter	1240 Beverley	1259 Dunstable	1308	Kings Langley
Shrewsbury	1241 Gloucester	Truro	1318	Winchelsea
1233 Carlisle	Stamford	1260 Lancaster	1335	Thetford
Northampton	1242 Cardiff	1261 Ilchester	1347	Worcester

MAP 1. THE SETTLEMENT OF THE ENGLISH PROVINCE
OF THE ORDER OF PREACHERS, 1221-1348

himself that day to have preached. The prelate was so edified by the friar's sermon that henceforth during his episcopate he favoured and promoted the order and its work. Leaving Canterbury, the friars came to London on the feast of St. Lawrence, and finally reached Oxford on the feast of the Assumption of the glorious Virgin to whose honour they built their oratory. They held the Schools, which are now called St. Edward's, and settled in that parish, but finding that they had there no room for expanding, they removed to another site given them by the king, where now outside the city walls they still dwelt.

Thus did Nicholas Trevet, the fourteenth-century chronicler, describe the coming of the Dominicans to England.[94] The number of brethren was thirteen, one more than the number constitutionally required for a foundation. Unlike the Franciscans in 1224, the Dominicans settled neither in Canterbury nor in London, but went straight to Oxford. Despite the uncertainties about the organisation of the Oxford Schools at this time,[95] it is clear that to the Dominicans Oxford was the first place of settlement, the best place for them to establish a *studium*. For three years Oxford was the only foundation. So it was the place for novitiate formation, for a priory *studium*, and for further and higher studies in Theology. When Robert Bacon, a regent master in Theology entered the Order, 1229-1230, probably during Jordan of Saxony's "fishing expedition" to the university, a chair of Theology became attached to the Oxford School.

In this period, 1221 to 1348, the development of the province can be seen in two stages: 1221-1275, when the province was growing fast; 1275-1348, when growth slowed and visitation divisions and organisation gave a clearer pattern to the provincial structure. The written evidence for its history is sparse indeed; hence the need to use methods from other academic disciplines to reconstruct the story of the Friars Preachers in England and Wales in these years.

a. The Physical Context of the English Province

The growth of the province is well revealed by Map 1. By 1348 there were at least fifty-one priories.[96] In the 1220s only four priories were established. This would indicate that foundations were made only when

---

[94] Ed. T. Hog, N. *Trevet: "Annales Sex Regum Anglie"* (London, 1845), 209, trans. in *The English Dominicans* by Bede Jarrett, revised and abridged by Walter Gumbley (London, 1937), 2.

[95] R.W. Southern, "From Schools to University," in *The Early Oxford Schools*, ed. Catto, 1-36.

[96] The uncertain foundations are not included in this number.

the necessary number of friars with relevant experience was available. Growth was fast and extensive over the next four decades, so that by 1269 forty-one out of the fifty-one priories had come into existence. Only six more convents were founded in the rest of the thirteenth century, while in the first half of the fourteenth century four priories only were established. Twelve of the places were cities or towns which supported four of the main mendicant orders.[97] This argues for a large population and rich economic resources. It is noticeable that of these twelve only Bristol, a wealthy seaport, is in the western part of England; Oxford and Northampton are in the midlands, while the remaining nine are found on the rich eastern side of England. It is equally noticeable that the Dominicans settled earlier in poorer parts of Wales and in the Westcountry, and later in richer East Anglia.

The propinquity of the Dominican priories to the existing Roman road system emerges clearly. These roads were still the quickest way to walk through England and Wales, as the volume of wheeled traffic had not yet destroyed the paving. The very existence of these roads had fostered settlement nearby, and the Dominicans were no exception. For the friars, who were required to walk everywhere in the exercise of their pastoral ministry, the presence of good roads was a bonus. The prehistoric trackway, the Icknield Way, running from the undulating plains of East Anglia north of the scarp of the Chilterns to the upper Thames, was much used in medieval times and particularly as a cross country route between Oxford and Cambridge.

When Dominican settlement is studied in relation to the diocesan divisions of Ecclesia Anglicana, found in Map 2, further facts about the Dominicans emerge. Apart from the dioceses of Chichester, Salisbury and Rochester, at least one Dominican priory was established in each diocese by 1261. Perhaps the comparatively late settlement of Chichester in 1280, and Salisbury in 1281, reflects the pre-existence of their good cathedral schools. No settlement was made in the diocese of Rochester. Perhaps its smallness and scattered parts meant that other houses served it. When it is realised that each priory was a school of Theology, open to non-Dominicans, it is seen that the impoverished dioceses in Wales and the huge isolated diocese of Exeter were generously served by the Dominicans.[98] Moreover, the diocesan map indicates the planning implicit in the settle-

---

[97] Cannon, 100.

[98] From 1978 to 1980, during which years I visited most of the Dominican sites in England and Wales, I was given oral information by local people about "the grammar school" in Bangor, and the site of the priory in Truro.

No Diocesan Records for Ordinations or Licensing Preachers and Confessors
 Bangor
 Chichester
 Durham
 Llandaff
 Norwich
 St. Asaph
 St. Davids

No Ordination Records
 Bath and Wells

No Licensing Records
 Rochester

Many diocesan boundaries follow shire boundaries;
these are often rivers, e.g., Avon, Thames, Trent.

MAP 2. THE DIOCESES OF ENGLAND AND WALES IN RELATION TO THE
VISITATIONS AND PRIORIES OF THE ENGLISH PROVINCE 1221-1348

ment pattern. Perhaps these maps record some of the lost written decisions of English provincial chapters.

As we have already seen, between 1271 and 1275 general chapters passed legislation to enable provinces to be divided into "visitations" or "nations" or vicariates for the purposes of visitation and correction. In the English province these divisions were called visitations. Map 3 shows how the priories were assigned to visitations from 1275 onwards.[99] There were four visitations: those of Cambridge, London, Oxford and York. In most cases the visitations follow diocesan boundaries which for many are rivers. For example, the Trent, the Thames, the Avon, and parts of the Severn all mark diocesan divisions. All four visitations, however, are represented in the large diocese of Lincoln. The visitations were used for educational purposes in the English province. Oxford, London and Cambridge each had a provincial school of Theology.[100] There is no direct written evidence about York, but a convergence of different evidence, some gained from study of ordination lists, some from the significance of York as head of the northern province of Ecclesia Anglicana, leads to the conclusion that York also contained a provincial school of Theology.[101] In the latter part of the period, following the legislation of the general chapter, other specialised schools were probably established in each visitation.

It remains to examine the organisation of schools in the province after 1270. Oxford had been declared a *studium generale* in 1248, but the implementation of the general chapter decree was delayed until 1261. In the second half of the century the priory at Cambridge, situated as it was in a university town, became in practice a *studium generale*, although it was recognised as such by the general chapter only in 1320.[102] As we have noted, the head of each visitation also housed a provincial school of Theology. But again the paucity of written records makes it difficult to know where other specialised schools could have been sited. There is one

[99] O'Carroll, "Ed. Org." 33-36. The maps record the partial list of the visitations found by A.G. Little on the fly leaf of MS Q 93 of Worcester Cathedral Library. I have added ascriptions made by Hinnebusch and Knowles assigning non-MS Q 93 listed priories to visitations. I have clarified riverine border towns in relation to diocesan placement, particularly Oxford, London and Bristol which have hinterlands of more than one diocese according to the *Taxatio Ecclesiastica Angliae et Walliae auctoritate P. Nicolai IV, circa 1291*, edd. T. Astle, S. Ayscough and J. Caley (London: Record Commission, 1802).

[100] O'Carroll, "Ed. Org.," 47-49.

[101] O'Carroll, "Ed. Org.," 55-56.

[102] Hinnebusch, *Early English Friars*, 340.

0 |————————| 50
miles

———— Roman roads
- - - - Icknield Way (Greenway)

● Cambridge
■ London   } Visitations
✴ Oxford
▲ York

Bamburgh

Newcastle

Carlisle

Yarm

Scarborough

Lancaster

YORK

Beverley

Pontefract

ERMINE STREET

Rhuddlan
Bangor   Chester

Newcastle-u-Lyme

Derby

Lincoln

Boston

ERMINE

Shrewsbury

WATLING

Stamford   Kings Lynn

Norwich   Yar-mouth

Thetford

Dunwich

Leicester

Warwick

Northampton

CAMBRIDGE

Ipswich

Worcester

Haverfordwest   Brecon

Hereford

Gloucester

Dunstable

Sudbury

FOSS

OXFORD

Chelmsford

WATLING STREET

Cardiff   Bristol

Kings Langley

LONDON

Salisbury

Guildford   Canterbury

Ilchester

Winchester

Winchelsea

Chichester   Arundel

Exeter

Truro

MAP 3. THE PRIORIES AND VISITATIONS IN THE ENGLISH PROVINCE
OF THE ORDER OF PREACHERS AFTER 1275 AND BEFORE 1348

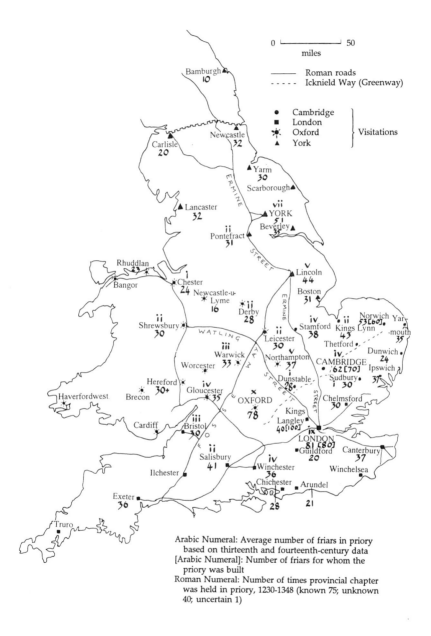

0 └──────────────┘ 50
            miles

────── Roman roads
- - - - - Icknield Way (Greenway)

● Cambridge
■ London   ⎫
☼ Oxford   ⎬ Visitations
▲ York   ⎭

Bamburgh ▲
10

Newcastle ▲
32

Carlisle ▲
20

Yarm ▲
30

Scarborough ▲

Lancaster ▲
32

vii
YORK ▲
51
Beverley ▲
35

ii
Pontefract
31

Rhuddlan
23

i
Chester ☼
24

Bangor

Newcastle-u-
Lyme ☼
16

Lincoln ∨
44

Boston
31

Norwich Yar-
53 [60]
ii

ii
Derby
28

ii
Shrewsbury ☼
30

Stamford
38

ii
Kings Lynn
43

-mouth
35

Leicester
30

Thetford ●

iv
Dunwich ●
24

WATLING

iii
Warwick
33 ☼

∨
Northampton
37

CAMBRIDGE
62 [70]

Ipswich
37

Worcester ☼

i
Sudbury ●
30

Hereford ☼
30+

iv
Gloucester ☼
35

Dunstable
28

Chelmsford
30

Haverfordwest
Brecon

x
OXFORD
78

Kings
Langley
40 [100]

ix
LONDON ■
81 [80]

Cardiff

iii
Bristol ☼
30

Guildford ●
20

Canterbury
37

ii
Salisbury
41

iv
Winchester ■
36

Winchelsea

Ilchester

Chichester
28

Arundel ■
21

Exeter ●
36

Truro

Arabic Numeral: Average number of friars in priory
   based on thirteenth and fourteenth-century data
[Arabic Numeral]: Number of friars for whom the
   priory was built
Roman Numeral: Number of times provincial chapter
   was held in priory, 1230-1348 (known 75; unknown
   40; uncertain 1)

MAP 4. INFORMATION ABOUT THE HOUSING CAPACITY OF
DOMINICAN PRIORIES IN THE ENGLISH PROVINCE 1221-1348

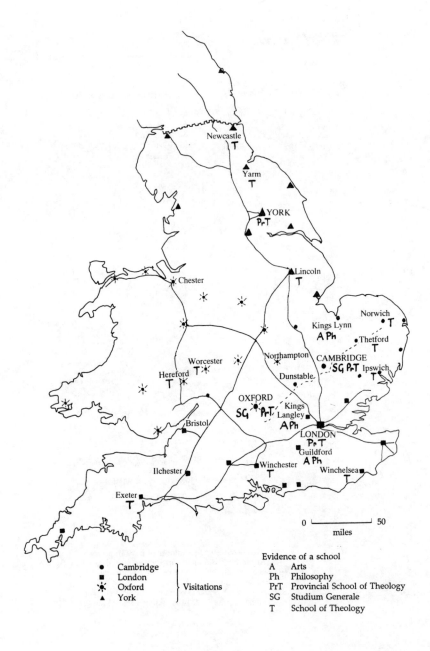

Evidence of a school
A   Arts
Ph   Philosophy
PrT Provincial School of Theology
SG   Studium Generale
T   School of Theology

- Cambridge
- London
※ Oxford   } Visitations
▲ York

MAP 5. INCOMPLETE INFORMATION ABOUT SCHOOLS IN THE
ENGLISH PROVINCE OF THE ORDER OF PREACHERS 1221-1348

clue, however, in the housing capacity of the priories. This is recorded on Map 4.[103] If houses were large enough to house a provincial chapter, then it was equally possible for them to contain a specialised provincial school. In her article, Joanna Cannon lists the references to specific schools.[104] But ascriptions to one date are insufficient evidence for a fixed school. It is known from the provincial records of other provinces within the Order of Preachers that provincial schools of Arts and Philosophy were mobile, rarely staying in one house for more than one or two years at a time. This was a deliberate policy, to spread the economic burden of school provision throughout the province. In the face of little written evidence and in the light of the mobility of schools, I have kept a minimalist approach and recorded only named schools (Map 5). In the latter part of our period, both the Cambridge and the London visitations had a school of Arts and Philosophy, the one at King's Lynn, the other at King's Langley. It is unlikely that the Oxford and York visitations had nothing similar. Several priories, such as Exeter, Hereford, Worcester, Winchester, Winchelsea, Ipswich, Norwich, Thetford, Lincoln, Yarm and Newcastle are recorded as having Theology schools. But could not some of these have been the standard priory school? From its years as a budding university, Northampton could well have been a significant school in the Oxford visitation.[105] Most of the houses named had living space for extra members in the commmunity. Until more evidence, however, is forthcoming, it is not possible to be more specific about the location of actual specialised schools. It is possible, nevertheless, to state that during the years 1221-1348, the English province established an educational system in the Order's tradition, and after 1275 organised it within a visitation structure.

b. The Personnel Context of the English Province

It is now possible to look at the members of the English province of the Order of Preachers, considering their numbers, qualifications and pastoral functions. On the basis of the average numbers in each house recorded on Map 4, a total of 1,453 Dominicans is reached, despite the fact that for several priories no numbers are available.[106] Hinnebusch con-

---

[103] O'Carroll, "Ed. Org.," 52-56.

[104] Cannon, 101, 103-104, 106, 112-116.

[105] C.H. Lawrence, "The University of Oxford and the Chronicle of the Barons' War," *EHR* vol. 95 (1980), 99-113.

[106] Hinnebusch (*Early English Friars*, 271-275, table on page 274, 328-331) gives information about the numbers of friars in this period. These figures were drawn up in the 1930s and 1940s. Since then Knowles and Hadcock have published more

cludes that 1,795 could be taken as a realistic total for Dominicans in England in the first quarter of the fourteenth century. On the evidence available, that seems a fair approximation.

Of these 1,795 friars by no means all would be preaching. As Humbert showed in his De Officiis Ordinis,[107] certain offices in the priory were carried out by lay brothers; for example, porter, refectorian, cook, tailor, custodian of the dormitory. Each priory had at least seven laybrothers, and some of the larger foundations, like Oxford and London, would need more for the maintenance of community life. If 400 of the total is allowed for laybrothers, that leaves 1,395. Of this number a proportion would be novices, or students preparing for the priesthood; others would be engaged in full time study or teaching; others again in the task of preaching. To give body to this theorising, it is possible to quote actual numbers of known ordinations from 1290 onwards.[108] Between 1290 and 1348 there are 373 recorded ordinations of Dominicans to the priesthood;[109] but the diocesan registers for the years 1290 to 1348 are defective (see Map 2). In the registers of twelve dioceses there is no continuity of record. The dioceses of London and Norwich, the most populous areas in England at the time, are two for which no records at all are available. In the twelve dioceses for which some records remain, 373 ordinations are recorded, from 1290 to 1348. In 1979 I made a study of Dominican lists as gathered by Emden and others and, using place-name study and statistics, reached a total of 1,308 Dominicans in preaching and hearing confessions from 1221 to 1348.[110] This is a conservative estimate.

The other source of statistical information is the registers of licences granted to Dominicans to hear confessions.[111] Emden by his careful research has provided much information. In the twelve dioceses for which records are available, 443 licences for hearing confessions are issued to Friars Preachers between 1300 and 1348. Some of these are double, even treble, repetitions of a name, as the same friar can be licensed at different

---

recent information, especially about royal gifts of money at standard rates to provide food and clothing for the brethren. I have used this information and made it into statistics (Map 4). The biggest discrepancy is in the numbers for the Bristol priory.

[107] Humbert of Romans, De Vita Regulari, 2: 179-371.

[108] O'Carroll, "Ed. Org.," 39, graph 2.

[109] Some names are repeated; at least two are discernible as separate friars.

[110] O'Carroll, "Ed. Org.," 58-62, Emden, "Dominican Confessors," and Emden, Survey; also lists from BRUC and BRUO.

[111] Emden, "Dominican Confessors."

times in different dioceses. Robert Holcot is a good example of this.[112] About half of the total, 219 licences in all, is granted in one diocese only, Lincoln. If Dominicans were hearing confessions they were undoubtedly preaching. As a minimum then, over 400 Friars Preachers were preaching and hearing confessions in England and Wales during the first half of the fourteenth century. Presumably these friars were licensed for work outside their priory churches such as preaching in parishes, and to a lesser extent to communities of nuns. But there is so little uniformity in the new episcopal right to license confessors, compared to the ordination ritual, that it is waste of time to try to put more body on the number of 400 confessors. Only one thing is certain about the end of our period, and that is that proportionally more friars died in the Black Death than laity. That speaks for itself.

It is possible to learn from the same database how long it took for a friar to be trained for the priesthood. There was no standard length of course. The clear requirement is the age of twenty-five years. If novices were young men who had already completed the Arts course prior to entry, then ordination could follow fairly soon after some theological study. If novices entered at sixteen, then their progress to the priesthood would be much longer. For example, in the diocese of Lincoln, Bernard of Aylesbur' was ordained subdeacon at High Wycombe on 19 December 1293; deacon at Banbury on 13 March 1294; and priest at Dunstable on 18 September 1294.[113] Thomas of Oxon' took a little longer: he was ordained subdeacon at Banbury with Bernard of Aylesbur'; ordained deacon at Dunstable when Bernard was priested; and ordained priest himself a year later 24 September 1295, at Great Berkhamstead.[114] It is possible that this Thomas of Oxon' is the same Dominican who was licensed to hear confessions in the Lincoln diocese on 17 April 1318.[115] There is no other Thomas of Oxon' despite Thomas being a common name, although there are two John of Oxon's. The latter are distinguished in the confessor licence records by one being listed Jo de Oxon' senior. Hugh Topsfelde illustrates the manner in which some students moved to different priories for train-

---

[112] O'Carroll, "Ed. Org.," 38, graph 1.

[113] Emden, *Survey*, 122.

[114] It must be remembered that ordinations took place normally on Ember days, and in churches or chapels designated by the bishop. Sometimes he used chapels in one or other of his manors; sometimes he would use the chapel of his London house. Information about and from the diocesan Register is a safer guide together with geography than geography alone.

[115] Emden, *Survey*, 195.

ing: he was ordained acolyte on 23 September 1335 in Hereford Cathedral.[116] On 14 June 1337, at Aston in the Coventry and Lichfield diocese, he was ordained subdeacon.[117] On 30 September of the same year, at King's Norton in the diocese of Worcester, Hugh was ordained deacon.[118] He reached the priesthood on 19 September at Colwich in the Coventry and Lichfield diocese.[119] It would require much more detailed study to track down the true relationship between ordination records and registers for licensing confessors. Two examples must suffice. A William Maundeville was ordained deacon on 19 September 1304 at Pagham in the diocese of Canterbury; he was ordained priest three months later on 19 December at West Tarring.[120] On 20 June 1231, a fr Wm Mandeville, with others, was licensed to hear confessions in the Winchester diocese.[121] A fr William of Neuporte, who was licensed at the same time to hear confessions, is found earlier in the ordination lists of the Worcester diocese, when he was ordained deacon in Fulham on 21 December 1308.[122]

One conclusion is indisputable: that from 1221 to 1348, the Order of Preachers educated and put at the active disposal of the Church hundreds of Dominicans who could supplement the work of parish priests, rectors and vicars in preaching and hearing confessions. The Order of Preachers was not the only one doing this work; the Friars Minor were doing as much, probably more in popular preaching, but it made a significant contribution. It is a tribute to the work of the friars that by the second half of the fourteenth century, not only was the standard of religious education among lay people higher than it had been in the thirteenth century, but so had the standard of education among non-university-educated parochial clergy improved.[123]

So far the result of the system of education in the English province has been seen in the provision of numerous priests, preachers, and confessors. We need to ask ourselves whether it is possible to obtain some indication of the quality of their work. First, preachers will be considered, then teachers, and finally some friars of renown.

---

[116] Emden, *Survey*, 105.

[117] Emden, *Survey*, 68.

[118] Emden, *Survey*, 198.

[119] See n. 115.

[120] Emden, *Survey*, 51.

[121] Emden, "Dominican Confessors," 303.

[122] Emden, *Survey*, 197.

[123] W.A. Pantin, *The English Church in the Fourteenth Century* (Cambridge: CUP, 1955), 261-262.

It is difficult to be specific about preachers. Hinnebusch can find matter for only six pages in his monograph.[124] Some preachers were like William of Abingdon, of whom Eccleston relates that he was reproved by Henry III; for whereas formerly he had been an eloquent preacher, all he could say in the present was "Da, da, da."[125] Yet a contemporary of William's was John of St. Giles, some of whose sermons have been published by M.M. Davy, and who rendered such sterling service to Grosseteste in the Lincoln diocese.[126] No English names, however, are found on the fourteenth-century list of eminent preachers of the Order,[127] but numerous volumes of sermons in many English libraries bear mute witness to the past eloquence of industrious preachers. Little work has been done on ascribing the sermons to individuals. For example, the catalogue of the Laud Miscellaneous manuscripts alone contains scores of volumes described simply "sermones." Some ascriptions are made. Only in a piecemeal manner, few names apart from well-known ones are identified. In her thesis, Jennifer Sweet has compiled a valuable list of sermons to be found in manuscript in Oxford libraries, but she can make few ascriptions.[128]

Turning from the preachers to the teachers, we find equally meagre sources of information. Again, Dr Emden's lists are the quarry. A search of the Oxford and Cambridge registers of graduates prior to 1500 yields a total, from 1221 to 1348, of seventy-four masters of theology and thirteen bachelors of theology; six of this latter group were trapped in the disputes between the Order and the university in the early fourteenth century. This total is probably a minimum. The English general schools of Oxford and Cambridge were required to accept foreign students as well as Englishmen and Welshmen.[129] Moreover, it does not include English students who may have been assigned to study in a *studium generale* of another province. The total, nevertheless, gives an average of seven masters of theology qualified in each decade. This number would not be sufficient for the needs of the provincial schools of Theology. They were probably supplemented by lectors who had studied all the stages and done the courses in the general schools, but never had the chance of a place at a university.

[124] Hinnebusch, *Early English Friars*, 313-318.

[125] Thomas of Eccleston, *De Adventu FF Minorum in Angliam*, 46.

[126] M.M. Davy, *Les sermons universitaires parisiens, 1230-1231* (Paris, 1931), 271.

[127] *Laurentii Pignon Catalogi et Chronica*, MOPH 18 (Rome, 1936).

[128] Sweet, *English Preaching*, Appendix 4, 164-172.

[129] W.A. Hinnebusch, "Foreign Dominican Students and Professors at the Oxford Blackfriars," in *Oxford Studies presented to Daniel A. Callus*, OHS NS 16 (Oxford, 1964), 101-134.

The kind of contribution English Dominicans made is best illustrated by some of the friars described in Emden's university registers. I have selected two groups. The smaller set is composed of friars who were drawn into a wider life than that of study and preaching. Hugh of Manchester, a master of Theology, possibly of Oxford, was prior provincial from 1279 to 1282;[130] William of Hotham, an individualist in the Hinton style, who incepted at Paris, was twice provincial;[131] Luke de Wodeford, master of Theology by 1300;[132] and Richard de Winkley, master of Theology in 1331, was prior-provincial from 1336 to 1339.[133] All these men were involved in the royal service, chiefly as confessors, but also in a variety of royal missions. The Plantagenet kings appreciated men of quality like these Dominicans. But such involvement was not without its problems, and did not pass uncriticised. It is, in fact, a good example of Humbert of Romans' comments on the good and less good effects of helping people.[134]

The second and larger group is a selection of English Dominicans, all masters of Theology, mostly of Oxford and Cambridge, whose lives and works illustrate the implementation of Dominic's ideas and ideals in the English province. As with the first group they are listed in historical order. Robert Bacon,[135] Richard Fishacre,[136] Simon of Hinton,[137] Robert Kilwardby,[138] William Rothwell,[139] Richard Knapwell,[140] Hugh Sneyth,[141] Robert Bromyard,[142] Thomas Jorz,[143] Thomas Sutton,[144] William Macclesfield,[145] Nicholas Trevet,[146] John of Cesterlade,[147] Thomas Waleys,[148]

---

[130] Emden, *BRUO*, 2: 1213.

[131] Emden, *BRUO*, 2: 970-971.

[132] Emden, *BRUO*, 3: 2071.

[133] Emden, *BRUO*, 3: 2060.

[134] Humberti de Romanis, *De Eruditione Praedicatorum*, De occupationibus praedicatorum circa negotia saecularia hominum c. xlii, 470, 475.

[135] Beryl Smalley, "Robert Bacon and the early Dominican School at Oxford," *TRHS* 4th Series (1948), 1-19.

[136] Emden, *BRUO*, 2: 685-686.

[137] Emden, *BRUO*, 2: 937; idem, *BRUC*, 306-307.

[138] Emden, *BRUO*, 2: 1051-1052.

[139] Emden, *BRUO*, 3: 1596, xl.

[140] Emden, *BRUO*, 2: 1058; Little and Pelster, 89-91.

[141] Emden, *BRUO*, 3: 1725, xlii; Little and Pelster, 68, 100.

[142] Emden, *BRUO*, 1: 278; Little and Pelster, 75-76.

[143] Emden, *BRUO*, 2: 1023; idem, *BRUO*, 3: xxxiv; Little and Pelster, 187-188.

[144] Emden, *BRUO*, 3: 1824-1825 xliii; Little and Pelster, 101, 281-282.

[145] Emden, *BRUO*, 2: 1200-1201; 3: xxxiv; Little and Pelster, 270-275.

Simon Boraston,[149] Robert Holcot,[150] Thomas de Lisle,[151] Thomas Hopeman,[152] Thomas Ryngestede,[153] and John Bromyard.[154] The very roll recalls eminent scholars. There was Kilwardby, famed as a philosopher before entering the Order, and famed as a theologian who did much to bring Augustine to the thirteenth-century Church, as well as for his opposition to Thomas Aquinas; Archbishop of Canterbury, perhaps sent upstairs to end as Cardinal of Santa Sabina. There were Thomas Sutton and Richard Knapwell, two of the earliest Oxford Thomists, who must have helped dispel the fears of the special commission sent by the general chapter to ensure England's fidelity to Aquinas.[155] Thomas Jorz who, having been prior-provincial, ended as Cardinal of Santa Sabina; and Nicholas Trevet, a chronicler respected for his genuine sense of history, were known beyond the Order. Robert Holcot was one of the best-known preachers of the fourteenth century who introduced his method of "pictures" and who has been identified with Thomas Waleys by Beryl Smalley as one of the "classicising" friars.[156] The last decades of his life were spent in preaching, and he died during the Black Death. Simon Boraston and Thomas Waleys shared a robust independence. Both were influential schoolmen, while the latter saw the inside of a papal prison over several long years for criticising the Pope.[157] Thomas de Lisle, later Bishop of Ely, is one of the few Dominicans some of whose known sermons survive.[158] John Bromyard, Thomas Waleys, Simon Boraston and Robert Holcot all wrote practical treatises of value in preaching. Holcot's *Commentary on the Book of Wisdom* was so popular it survived beyond medieval times into many printed editions. Most of the men on the above list were writers as well

---

[146] Emden, *BRUO*, 3: 1902-1903, xliv; Little and Pelster, 283-285.

[147] Emden, *BRUO*, 1: 379; Little and Pelster, 184-185.

[148] Emden, *BRUO*, 3: 1961-1962; Beryl Smalley, "Thomas Waleys OP," *AFP* 24, (1954), 50-107.

[149] Emden, *BRUO*, 1: 221; idem, *BRUC*, 73.

[150] Emden, *BRUO*, 2: 946-947; idem, *BRUC*, 309-310; Beryl Smalley, "Robert Holcot OP," *AFP* 26, (1956), 5-97.

[151] Emden, *BRUC*, 370.

[152] Emden, *BRUC*, 313, 946-947.

[153] Emden, *BRUC*, 449.

[154] Emden, *BRUO*, 1: 278.

[155] ACTA I: 199.

[156] Beryl Smalley, *English Friars and Antiquity* (Oxford, 1960), 135-136.

[157] Ibid., 76-78.

[158] Schneyer, *Repertorium*, 5: 631-670.

as teachers and preachers. The treatises are mainly biblical commentaries, but there are contributions significant in number and quality to Philosophy, old and new; to Systematic Theology in commentaries on the *Sentences*; and to Moral Theology with pastoral treatises. Many of them rendered service to their brethren by holding office as prior-provincial. Many too were diffinitors. Several were known active preachers. All of them, at one time or another, had been involved in teaching their brethren either as lectors in the priory schools, or in the provincial and general schools of the province and Order. Is it not just and proper to take these known friars as representative of the spirit and learning of the hundreds of anonymous Dominicans who stand behind them?

Despite the paucity of written evidence, it has been possible to show that in the thirteenth century the English province of the Order of Preachers established its convents and its priory, provincial and general schools; educated its men; trained its lectors and preachers, all in the spirit of St. Dominic; and in so doing contributed mightily to the well-being of Ecclesia Anglicana.

3

MS Laud Miscellaneous 511

A. Palaeographic Description

The papal approval of two religious orders, the Order of Preachers and the Order of Friars Minor, which followed hard on the heels of the decrees of the Fourth Lateran Council of 1215, gave a powerful impetus to the work of preaching within the Church. A veritable sermon industry relating to *pastoralia*[1] of every kind developed. Among the *summae* of virtues and vices, of confessors, the *artes praedicandi*, the *exempla* collections etc., the sermon collection proved one of the commonest aids to preachers. Even a cursory examination of the Summary Catalogue in the Bodleian Library shows the large number of thirteenth and fourteenth century manuscripts which are briefly described as "sermones." Despite all the problems of manuscript survival in Britain, collections of sermons are among the more numerous groups of manuscripts to remain. MS Laud Miscellaneous 511[2] is one of this legion of manuscripts. In 1925 Etienne Gilson, in his article "Michel Menot et la technique du sermon médiéval,"[3] made many suggestions for the systematic study of medieval sermons. Many of those suggestions have been followed in recent decades, and the examination of specific sermon collections has proved fruitful.[4] I hope to show that MS Laud Misc. 511 is a good example of the late medieval literary-pastoral genre, the sermon-collection.

---

[1] L.E. Boyle,"Summae confessorum" in *Les Genres litteraires dans les sources théologiques et philosophiques médiévales: définition, critique, et exploitation,* (Louvain, 1982), 227-237—chart of pastoralia, ibid., 231; "The Fourth Lateran Council and Manuals of Popular Theology" in *The Popular Literature of Medieval England,* ed. Thomas J. Heffernan (Knoxville, 1985), 30-43—annotated chart.

[2] Oxford, Bodleian Library, *Summary Catalogue,* 969; H.O. Coxe, *Bodleian Library Quarto Catalogue, 2: Laudian Manuscripts,* rev. R.W. Hunt (Oxford, 1973) col. 370 and Addenda, 567. For discussion of this manuscript see F. Pelster, "An Oxford Collection of Sermons," *BQR* 6 (1929-1930) 168-172; and Sonia Patterson, "Paris and Oxford Manuscripts in the thirteenth century," unpublished thesis deposited in Bodley, MS B.Litt.d 1457; 30-31, 104-105, 128-135.

[3] E. Gilson, "Michel Menot et la technique du sermon médiéval," *Revue d'Histoire Franciscaine* 2 (1925), 301-350, reprt. in *Les Idées et les Lettres* (Paris, 1932), chap V.

[4] See, for example, N. Bériou, *La Prédication au béguinage de Paris pendant l'année liturgique 1272-1273* (Paris, 1978).

MS Laud Misc. 511 contains 204 leaves of writing and two leaves as front end-papers, one of them being a paste-down. The foliation, which is modern, is ii + 204. Folio i contains on the right-hand side some plain-chant written in square, not thin-line, notation. On folio i verso is an inscription in a fourteenth-century secretary hand which runs:

Reverende pater gardiane licenciam vestram unum verbum Reverendi patres et fratres de

There are no end-papers at the back of the manuscript. Folio ii recto has a modern pencil manuscript title and number. Folio ii verso has a seventeenth-century inscription denoting ownership in 1633 by Archbishop Laud, Chancellor of the University of Oxford. On the edge is a shelf mark, "E 46."

The manuscript is written in black ink on parchment. The length of the writing block, a column, is not uniform but varies from 16.5 to 17.9 cm. The ruled width of most columns is 4.8 cm, though the script itself is more often 5.1 cm in width. The page size also varies slightly according to the gatherings, but averages 22 cm length by 15 cm width. In the last two gatherings, the edges have not been cropped in the same way as the other fifteen gatherings. Each page has two columns, with the lines numbered in arabic numerals in fives. The standard line-numbering runs from 5 to 40 on most pages, although a few have thirty-nine or forty-five lines.[5] The lines of script, except in the last two gatherings, generally exceed the numbered lines, averaging forty-two lines to a column. A few pages have line numbers written in red.[6] In the bottom margin, between eight and nine narrower lines have been ruled in pencil. This latter was an academic practice. Each column is also numbered in arabic numerals, beginning with columns 1 and 2 on folio 5r, and ending with 783 and 784 on folio 204v. Folios 155r and 155v have no numbers, but are headed *Nichil*. In a few places column numbers have been omitted or duplicated.[7]

It is likely that the original manuscript contained at least nineteen gatherings of which eighteen remain. The first gathering R i is composed of folios rejected from gathering xi. The differences in rubricating and flourishing were noted first by Mrs Patterson.[8] A detailed examination has

---

[5] MS Laud Misc. 511, fol. 29-37, 40-41v, 115v. Over 45 numbered lines are found on fol. 136-137v, 159-161v, and 163; fol. 104 has over 50 numbered lines.

[6] Ibid., for example, fol. 122v-125, 131v, 180v.

[7] Ibid., for example, column numbers 108-110 have been omitted; on fol. 203v columns 769 and 780 are found next to each other, 770-779 omitted.

[8] Patterson, "Paris and Oxford Manuscripts," 133 fn 2.

shown that the text in folios 1-4 is identical, barring scribal error, with the replacement bifolia. The rejected text seems more accurate in its Latin than the replacement text, but the parchment is of low quality. The reason for the rejection possibly lies more with the inadequacy of the parchment and the resultant visually poor text than in the text itself. Despite some variations in the number of folios within each gathering, gatherings i to xv are consistent in format—the letter of the alphabet is repeated, followed by the appropriate roman numeral, until the thread is reached. Many of the gatherings have copyist's cues in the bottom inner margin of the last format, xvi having an alphabetical pattern and xvii a numerical one. In all the gatherings the bifolia are arranged alternately, one pair facing inwards on the hair side, the next on the flesh side of the parchment. The alternate cream and yellow shades of the openings in the manuscript confirm this. The collation of the gatherings is shown in Table 1.

TABLE 1. THE COLLATION OF MS LAUD MISC. 511

Number	Folios	Thread	Notes
R i 4	1-4	2-3	Reject folios, front bound
i 12	5-16	10-11	5 'a' in Bottom Margin BM 16v 'i' in middle BM
ii 12	17-28	22-23	17 'b' in middle BM pencil
iii 10	29-38	33-34	29 'c' in middle BM pencil
iv 12	39-50	44-45	39 'd' in middle BM pencil
v 12	51-62	56-57	51 'e' in middle BM pencil
vi 12	63-74	68-69	63 'f' in middle BM pencil
vii 12	75-86	80-81	75 'g' in middle BM pencil
viii 12	87-98	92-93	87 'h' in middle BM pencil
ix 8	99-106	102-103	no discernible marks
x 12	107-118	112-113	107 'k' in middle BM pencil
xi 12	119-130	124-125	121 marks, but not clear; folios 120r+v + 129r+v and 119r+v + 130r+v are the two bifolia which have replaced the reject folios, now R i
xii 12	131-142	136-137	131 'm' in middle BM pencil
xiii 12	143-154	148-149	143 'n' in middle BM pencil
xiv 14	155-168	161-162	155 'o' very faint
xv 12	169-180	174-175	169 'p' very faint
xvi 12	181-192	186-187	181-186 'a' to 'f' BM right
xvii 12	193-204	198-199	193-198 'i' to 'vi' BM left

MS Laud Misc. 511 is written in four different book-hands. These and their location within the manuscript are noted in Table 2. Hand A is a beautiful hand that looks professional. The scribe writes "below top line,"[9] and rarely exceeds the line-numbered column pattern. The letters are clearly and carefully formed. The scribe uses standard abbreviations and punctuation. The latter has at least two signs: a dot in the middle of a letter space like the top of a semi-colon; and a sign similar to a "tur" abbreviation placed at the top of the writing line and indicating a question mark. Hand B is the main hand in the manuscript. The scribe writes consistently "above top line." The writing is much less neat, tends to sprawl out of the writing block and often exceeds the standard forty-two line pattern, but not consistently. This scribe uses many more abbreviations. The small "a" is characteristic, formed with two strokes only; the small "d" has two patterns, often used in the same column; the shape of the capital letters is not consistent. Scribe B uses similar punctuation to that of scribe A. He is also careful in writing references: for example the relevant book of Kings or of the Epistles of Peter and Paul is indicated by the number of dots over the capital letter of the reference. Hand C is very like Hand A in general style but is less clear to read. This scribe has many corrections in his text. Hand D is quite different. This scribe writes consistently "below top line," and never exceeds the forty lines in the column. The letters are formed quite differently: the "a" is two-compartment, the "e" is continuous, while the stroke of the "d" is nearer the horizontal than the vertical. He uses the same signs for punctuation as Hands A and B, but his abbreviations are fewer than either. From the letter shapes, and from the variations between the "above top line" of Hand B and the "below top line" of Hands A, C

TABLE 2. THE FOUR MAIN BOOK-HANDS

Hand A	folio 5—folio 50v
Hand B	folio 51—folio 118v
Hand C	folio 119—folio 120v
Hand B	folio 121—folio 128v
Hand C	folio 129—folio 130v
Hand B	folio 131—folio 180v
Hand D	folio 181—folio 204v
(Hand B	folio 1—folio 4v)

[9] N.R. Ker, "From 'above Top Line' to 'below Top Line': a change in scribal practice," *Celtica* 5 (1960) 13-16.

and D, I would date tentatively the hands as mid-thirteenth to second half of the thirteenth century.

A problem of close acquaintance with a manuscript is that one tends to see all variants within a hand as by a different scribe. This was so within Hands A and B in this manuscript. After many lengthy discussions with the late Dr R.W. Hunt, the conclusion was that, allowing for variants arising from mood, speed, pen, weather, etc., Hand A was one scribe and Hand B another.

MS Laud Misc. 511 has rubricated headings and markings throughout. The rubricator has copied the minute black top or bottom marginal—running—headings which contain information about either the liturgical timing or the source book of the piece indicated. Some of these headings have been lost in cropping prior to binding. The running titles are found only up to folio 180v. In a few cases there is a discrepancy between the running black headings and the red headings at the top or by the side of the piece. The information in the black heading has been given greater weight than the red, as it is nearer the source. If, however, the internal evidence of the piece agrees with the red heading, that has been given preference. Many of the red marks on the actual letters are applied clumsily, and in some cases hinder the reading of the text. One characteristic feature of this manuscript is the use of squiggles (with eyes and noses) in the margin. Many of these profile "faces" are rubricated, so they belong to the genesis of the text. Their function is that of emphasis or even bracketing. The sermon no. 158 on fol. 158v-159 is abundantly decorated with little devil faces, some with hoods as well as horns. In general, all the markings are efficient in conveying information and rendering the text easier to analyse.

With regard to Hands A, B and C, the changes of scribe make no significant difference to the content of the manuscript, which comprises sermons and sermon-material in the liturgical order of the *Temporale*. There are, however, significant differences with the change to scribe D. In the major portion of the manuscript, as already noted, not only is information given in the running titles and duplicated in the rubrics, but all contents—apart from two items—are in exact liturgical order. In the last two gatherings written by scribe D, there are neither source books indicated nor running titles inserted, while the liturgical order is far from exact. Out of fifteen items, three are misplaced. Nevertheless there is some continuity in that scribe D takes up at the Tenth Sunday after Trinity, the Sunday at which scribe B finished, and that—except for one item—only sermons from the last part of the Temporal cycle are included.

Our manuscript contains a variety of annotations. In the first part of the manuscript there are marginal summaries, written in a very clear cursive—not book—hand, many of them rubricated.[10] Other annotations, which seem to change when the scribe changes, are side marginal titles relating to the content of the piece.[11] These annotations seem to belong to the original writing of the manuscript. Two types of annotations were made after the manuscript was first written: verbal and non-verbal.

The following comments on the verbal annotations are tentative rather than conclusive. There are marginal and interlinear notes;[12] cross-references;[13] arabic numerals in the side margins indicating the divisions in a sermon;[14] time and place notes made by preachers at Elstow;[15] and abbreviations of emphasis, chiefly "Nota" and "Nota bene."[16] The greater number of the annotations have been written in black ink, with a few in brown ink and yet others in pencil. There are several distinguishable hands; Table 3 gives a brief description of each annotating hand. Finally, there are two individual annotations: one at the bottom of fol. 1 which is a form for a contract of service, possibly a "rough" copy; and one at the bottom of fol. 4v, a short passage about Alexander the Great.

TABLE 3. THE ANNOTATING HANDS IN MS LAUD MISC. 511

Hand E 1   An Elstow preacher.
Hand E 2   Second Elstow preacher.
Hand F   The annotator who uses the axe-shaped paraph, and who writes some margin headings, many of them in boxes.
Hand G   The annotator who liberally scatters "Nota bene." He has also added all the marginal and interlinear content.
Hand H   Writes many non-rubricated margin summaries up to fol. 74v.
Hand K   Writes some summary notes after fol. 51.
Hand L   Writes notes about the "missing sermons."

[10] These are printed in Appendix 1, "A Catalogue of MS Laud Misc. 511."

[11] At least 30 folios, mostly between fol. 39 and 74v have these; also on fol. 150, 172, 178r+v, 179, 180v 186, 203.

[12] Hand G has annotated the following sermons, which are the only ones with extra content: 58, 110, 114, 147, 152, 153, 154, 165, 167, 168, 206, 210, 233, 234.

[13] MS Laud Misc. 511, fol. 8b (col 337.30) with 93vb (col 14.30); fol. 81b (col 636.25) with fol. 170b (col 288.35)

[14] Ibid., for example, fol. 127, 150v (in red), 173v.

[15] Ibid.; see Appendix 1, "A Catalogue of MS Laud Misc. 511."

[16] Ibid.; too numerous to cite, but examples are found on fol. 53v, 141. Many are written in black ink, a few in brown ink, and many—not easily visible—in pencil.

The non-verbal annotations seem to perform the modern grammatical functions of the asterisk, the exclamation mark, the bracket, underlining for emphasis, and a device for indicating a new paragraph. The patterns for these marks are found in Table 4. Styles A 1-6 are common in the manuscript, patterns 1, 3 and 5 being associated with the flamboyant manner of writing "Nota" and with the hand that has added extra content, Hand G. Style 4 and 4a are associated with Hand F.[17] Some marks are less common: for example, the shield occurs once;[18] eyes five times;[19] marks reminiscent of Grosseteste's indexing symbols, a few times;[20] and fingers, about sixteen times.[21] They are drawn in four different ways; some are associated with Hand F.

MS Laud Misc. 511 also has some decoration that is functional, in that in most cases the flourished initial marks the beginning of a new item.[22] The opening initial on folio 5 is gilded and flourished in red and blue. The other initials in gatherings i—xv are bright blue and flourished red. Many of them are painted over or beside an earlier decorated initial which is small, coloured black and decorated in red and black, often in a diamond pattern. In gatherings xvi and xvii the initials are alternately blue letters flourished red, and red initials flourished with a greeny blue. The quality of the flourishing in these last two gatherings is not as professional as that in the first fifteen gatherings, apart from the clumsier patterns of the two replacement bifolia. A full discussion of the flourishing of this manuscript is found in Mrs Patterson's thesis. Her conclusion is that the flourishing of MS Laud Misc. 511 is associated with the second half of the thirteenth century and is of English rather than of French origin.

The last major codicological point to be considered is the binding of the manuscript. The patterns are shown in Table 5. MS Laud Misc. 511 is bound between thick bevel-edged wooden boards, 23 by 16 cm, covered with non-shiny—once white—leather that is now much worn and torn. On the back board is a metal eye for a clasp. There is a little gap between the back board and gathering xvii. This gap, the lack of end papers, toge-ther with the incomplete nature of the sermon on folio 204v, all indicate the loss of at least one gathering from the original book. It does not seem

---

[17] Ibid., for example, fol. 105v, 116v, 146v.

[18] Ibid. Shield: fol. 59a.

[19] Ibid. Eyes: fol. 23a, 31vb, 43b, 48b; 49vb, eye with finger.

[20] Ibid. Indexing symbols: fol. 86vb, 147vb, 177vb.

[21] Ibid. Fingers: fol. 11va, 15b, 20a, 23vb, 33va, 49vb, 51vb, 113a, 116vb, 144va (pencil), 154b, 171a, 195b.

[22] Ibid. Two exceptions: fol. 36vb extra initial, fol. 191vb initial omitted.

TABLE 4. ANNOTATING MARKS IN MS LAUD MISC. 511

A. Common Marks

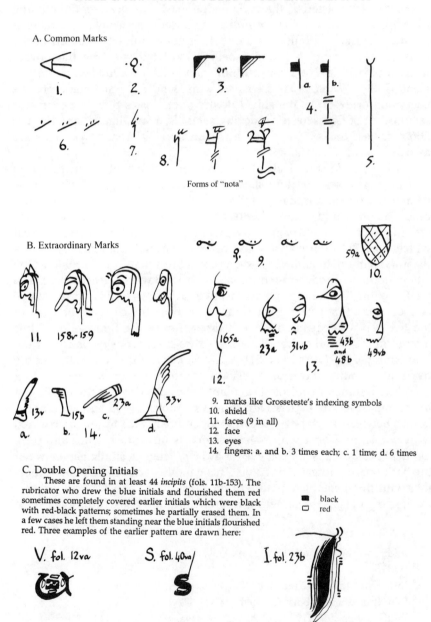

Forms of "nota"

B. Extraordinary Marks

9. marks like Grosseteste's indexing symbols
10. shield
11. faces (9 in all)
12. face
13. eyes
14. fingers: a. and b. 3 times each; c. 1 time; d. 6 times

C. Double Opening Initials

These are found in at least 44 *incipits* (fols. 11b-153). The rubricator who drew the blue initials and flourished them red sometimes completely covered earlier initials which were black with red-black patterns; sometimes he partially erased them. In a few cases he left them standing near the blue initials flourished red. Three examples of the earlier pattern are drawn here:

■ black
□ red

TABLE 5. THIRTEENTH-CENTURY BINDING PATTERNS AND THOSE OF MS LAUD MISC. 511

Patterns of Bindings, According to H.G. Pollard

Similar pattern, mid-13th to 14th centuries ("The Construction of English Twelfth Century Bindings," p. 11, figure 7)

Second half of 13th century: thongs enter by a groove on the outside of the board ("Describing Medieval Bookbindings," p. 57, figure 3)

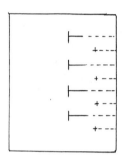
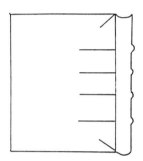

Ms Laud Misc. 511: Pattern of Thonging

Front Board

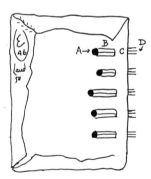

Back Board

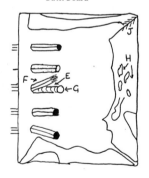

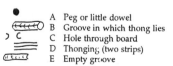

	A	Peg or little dowel		F	Loose thong
	B	Groove in which thong lies	o	G	Empty peg hole
	C	Hole through board		H	Holes in leather
	D	Thonging (two strips)	⇒⇒⇒	J	Stitching
	E	Empty groove			

possible that there could be more than two gatherings in the present space. The gatherings have been bound onto five double thongs of leather. While there is some later stringing by way of repair, there is no evidence of a complete re-stitching. The thongs are fixed to each board by being brought from the spine of the mansucript through a slanting hole from the outside to the inside of the board on its inner edge. Each thong fits in a groove and its end is pegged into the board with a small dowel.

From criteria established by Graham Pollard[23] and by the staff of the Bodleian Library[24] on medieval bindings, it seems clear that the pattern of binding of MS Laud Misc. 511 falls generally into Pollard's second period of medieval book-binding, 1230/50 to 1450. But the pattern of the thonging into the boards in equal parallel, as in our manuscript, is a book-binding practice of the second half of the thirteenth century, which gave way to alternate long and short thong-fitting from about 1300. It seems very likely that the binding of MS Laud Misc. 511 is the original binding, and is either contemporaneous with, or made very soon after, the written contents.

B. CONTENTS

Apart from the repeat contents of the first four folios, folios 5-204v contain 234 pieces. While these are not numbered, the large blue initial flourished red is in the majority of cases a reliable guide to the start of a new item. This is the foundation of the numbering system I have made. Most of the contents are sermons, either in whole, in part, or in summary. Of these most are probably summaries made by listeners, "reportationes." A few pieces I have called "sermon material": some are "florilegia" from the Fathers and Masters; some are useful gobbets. In most cases, the sermon material is related by alphabetical listing to its leading piece, which is numbered. A full list of contents is found in the Appendix 1, "A Catalogue of MS Laud Misc. 511." This appendix has grown so that it now performs at least three functions: it records information about the manuscript's content; it contains analysis of that information, especially of the liturgical pattern of the manuscript, and of its source books; it contains tables which permit a methodology of sermon identification.

[23] H.G. Pollard, "Describing Medieval Bookbindings" in *Essays presented to R.W. Hunt*, 50-65; also "The Construction of English Twelfth Century Bindings," *The Library*, 5th Series, 17 (1962), 1-22.

[24] Bodleian Library, Introduction to the section "The Sequence of Medieval Bookbinding," in *12th Century Manuscripts written in England: an exhibition in honour of N.R. Ker* (catalogue unpublished).

Four of the sermons in the manuscript are duplicated. Numbers 45 and 48 are identical in content. They are taken from the same source book, but they differ in style, 45 being written continuously, and 48 being written in distinction form. Number 124 is identical with the first part of 104 but as the scribe has drawn attention to this repetition, the inclusion of 124 may well be unintentional. Numbers 148 and 156, while drawn from different source books, are in substance the same text with minor differences of conjunctions. The link between 213 and 217 is more complex. It is not exact repetition, but a good example of a substantial part of an antitheme being identical in imagery, development and—to a large extent—vocabulary with that of another sermon. The complication is palaeographical, for 213 belongs to the section of MS Laud Misc. 511 organised by the compiler, and 217 belongs to the last two gatherings.

C. THE SOURCE BOOKS USED

An unusual feature of this sermon collection, compared with many other manuscripts of collected sermons, is that MS Laud Misc. 511 is not a homogeneous book but a compilation, drawn from at least thirteen different source books. This fact applies strictly only to gatherings i to xv, as the compiler of this major part of the manuscript had little to do with gatherings xvi and xvii. It is essential to examine the source books, so that the sermon contents can be seen in perspective.

The red titles above or at the side of the piece name not only the liturgical occasion of the sermon, but the source book from which it was copied. The source books in manuscript order of first appearance are as follows: *Liber Minimus* (8); *Liber Tabulatus* (1); *Liber Niger Minor* (8); *Liber Virginis Gloriose* (1); *Liber Niger Maior* (8); *Liber Proprius* (61); *Parvus Liber Niger* (3); *Parvus Liber Rubeus* (41); *Liber Rubeus Minor* (22); *Liber Rubeus Maior* (26); *Quaternus Oxoniensis* (2); *Liber "Confessiones" Augustini* (7); *Parvus Liber Rubeus Minor* (2). For the last two gatherings, xvi and xvii, the red title contains only liturgical information. So the source book enquiry applies only to a part, albeit a major one, of the manuscript.

I have assigned twelve pieces to books on the links of propinquity and similar characteristics: 52 was assigned to *Liber Proprius* as it is an alternative antitheme to 51, which comes from that book; similarly, 77b and 174b were respectively assigned to 77a and 174a, also from *Liber Proprius*; 205 to *Liber Proprius*; 85 to *Liber Minimus*, according to a margin note; 112 to *Liber Rubeus Minor*; 113 a+b+c were assigned with the sermon material already belonging to *Liber Rubeus Minor*; finally, sermons 81, 117, 134 and 169 were assigned to their respective books by their part reference. Piece

16 has a book, but the interpretation is not clear. The title is *de parvo libro co*. There is no contraction sign over the "o." It could be interpreted as *liber collationum*; but, because of the uncertainty and because it has only one piece, this source book has been omitted. That leaves 16 pieces unplaced: 195 is a reference, so it needs no book; five, including H. de Mordon's, are sermons 2, 8, 50, 124, 166; the remainder are sermon material: 149, 150-151, 175-181 inclusive.

The names of the source books are interesting. *Liber "Confessiones" Augustini* and *Liber Tabulatus* are probably what their names indicate. Perhaps the sermons were copied onto blank pages left when the main work was completed. *Liber Virginis Gloriose* could be a book of miracles of Our Lady, or the liturgical book of the Office of the BVM, or a book of stories and legends similar to those described in the *Catalogue of Romances*.[25] This source book is mentioned in the reference notes to "the missing sermons." *Quaternus Oxoniensis* could be a a student's notes of sermons heard in Oxford, or it could be a gathering copied from a *pecia* of an exemplar which contained sermons. Exemplars were approved by the masters of the university as works that could be hired for copying by masters and students.[26] In the book trade *quaterni* were folios, already written by a professional or amateur scribe, which were prepared by professional bookmakers for a possible future binding. Christopher de Hamel describes the process:[27]

> ...The professional also sewed the book into vellum wrappers.. the transcript was thus presumably returned to the scribes "in quaternis" (as it would be called), finished and sewn but not yet in a proper binding. Some manuscripts remained like this, and others received permanent bindings later.[28]

The other source books are described in terms of colour—red or black—

---

[25] H.L. Ward and J.A. Herbert, *Catalogue of Romances in the Department of Manuscripts of the British Museum*, 3 vols. (London, 1883-1910); also R.W. Southern, "The English Origins of the 'Miracles of the Virgin'," *MARS*, 4: 176-216.

[26] *Statuta Antiqua Universitatis Oxoniensis*, ed. Strickland Gibson (Oxford, 1931), 167-8, 183-7.

[27] Christopher de Hamel, "The Production and Circulation of Glossed Books of the Bible in the Twelfth and early Thirteenth Centuries," unpublished thesis deposited in Bodley, MS D.Phil.c.2678, 232-3.

[28] Bodleian Library, *12th Century Manuscripts*. A number of manuscripts with soft parchment or leather covers were displayed in this exhibition. From observation it seemed clear that a manuscript without full binding between wooden boards had far less chance of survival than a manuscript like MS Laud Misc. 511.

and size—*maior*, *minor* and *parvus*. These books were not necessarily bound in wooden boards, as is MS Laud Misc. 511. In fact, full binding was probably a much rarer practice than in modern times. Many books were kept as *quaterni* in loose covers of parchment or leather, coloured accordingly and of a size appropriate to their folios. The problem of standardising page size, as Pollard has shown[29] is difficult, because the use of any piece of writing parchment depended on the non-standard sizes of the animals providing the original skins. *Liber Minimus* is probably a "pocket book" about 12 by 7 cm. All its contributions, except for one, to MS Laud Misc. 511 are very short. It seems more like a book of jottings or ideas. *Liber Proprius* is the compiler's own book. It is likely that he kept it in chronological order; for probably when he heard a sermon that he liked, or saw one, or composed one he thought worth keeping, he copied it into his own book. This book had contents beyond the Tenth Sunday after Trinity, the liturgical point at which gathering xv ends. Sermon 37, assigned to Trinity XVIII, but liturgically misplaced in the manuscript, is copied from *Liber Proprius*. It seems reasonable to infer that *Liber Proprius* had been in existence for some time, in that sixty sermons from it are included in the manuscript. It is possible that part of the desire of the compiler to have a new book was that the contents of *Liber Proprius* had so accumulated that he was unable to find what he wanted when he needed it.

Confirmation of the non-liturgical order of some of the source books is found in Appendix 6, "The Source Books." A few of the references in the manuscript to the source books give a number reference as well. One minor problem, however, is the correct interpretation of the transcribed numbers. Present convention indicates that the position of a number indicates its value as a unit, a ten, or a hundred. There is no uniformity in thirteenth-century arithmetical conventions. Sometimes when 100 is being written followed by two other digits, e.g., 176, the 100 is identified not just by its placing, 176, but can be written as 1 followed by a dot in mid-space, and then the numbers remaining, 1·76. This convention is not used in every case.

For only three of the source books, *Parvus Liber Rubeus*, *Liber Proprius*, and *Liber Rubeus Minor*, is the evidence sufficient to draw some conclusions about the order of content. From the reconstructions, it is clear that none of the three was made in liturgical order. Perhaps, like *Liber Proprius*, *Parvus Liber Rubeus* and *Liber Rubeus Minor* were made by the individual

---

[29] H.G. Pollard, "Notes on the Size of the Sheet," *The Library*, 22 (1941-1942), 105-137.

in the order in which he heard or read them, that is in chronological order. The numbering systems of the books differ, however. *Liber Proprius* seems to have a folio numbering system, while the other two have a column and line numbering system in arabic numerals. It should also be noted that these two books contain sermons with English vernacular phrases. It is interesting to note that the compiler of our manuscript changed from the folio numbering system of *Liber Proprius* to the arabic numbering of column and line used in *Liber Rubeus Minor* and *Parvus Liber Rubeus*. Five other source books had some kind of numbering system, but the references are neither clear nor numerous enough to do more than show the fact of their usage. So before the making of MS Laud Misc. 511 was begun, the compiler had at his disposal at least thirteen books of sermons. Comment can be made on the sermon contents of a few of these source books and on aspects of their significance within a compilation, but first the number of sermons ascribed to known preachers must be established.

D. Named Sermons

In this compiled collection of sermons, only three are ascribed to an author. No. 82 is a sermon for the Fourth Sunday of Lent by Richard Fishacre OP. No. 66 is a sermon for the Second Sunday of Lent by Simon Hinton OP. No. 166 is a lovely little sermon for Pentecost by fr H. de Mordon. A fourth sermon, No. 182, for the Third Sunday after Trinity has a note "de manu H," but so far nothing has been gleaned about H. Attempts to identify H. de Mordon have been similarly fruitless. Fishacre and Hinton, the latter largely through the study of Beryl Smalley, are better known.[30]

Richard Fishacre[31] was the first Englishman educated in the Dominican Order to incept in Theology at Oxford, about 1244. He incepted under his friend and teacher, Robert Bacon, through whom a chair in the faculty of Theology had come to Blackfriars. The list of Fishacre's writings is long, although not all texts ascribed to him survive.

---

[30] Ed. T. Kaeppeli, *Scriptores Ordinis Praedicatorum medii aevi*, 3 vols. (Rome, 1970-1980), 3: 303-306 has a full bibliography; see also L.E. Boyle, "Three English Pastoral Summae," *Studia Gratiana* 11 (1967) 133-144.

[31] *BRUO* 2, 685-686; 3, xxiii; see also R.J. Long's biographical essay in *Dictionnaire de spiritualité, ascétique et mystique; doctrine et histoire*, publié sous la direction de Marcel Viller SJ assisté de F. Cavallera et J.de Guibert SJ avec le concours d'un grand nombre de collaborateurs (Paris: Beauchesne, 1988) 13, 563-565.

In the past decade R.J. Long has been doing much to identify and edit the works of Fishacre, and has made a beginning in the identification of characteristics of his style.[32] Fishacre's most significant contribution to the study of Theology was his *Commentary on the Sentences*, a commentary of which Thomas Aquinas desired his own copy. So far only the prologue of this very lengthy commentary has been edited.[33] Written probably between 1240 and 1243, this commentary was the first "modern" theological treatise to come from Oxford, as Fishacre adopted the Paris practice, much disliked by Grosseteste, of separating biblical exegesis from speculative Theology in its various branches.[34] Fishacre's theological interests and writings were focussed much more strongly on philosophy than on biblical studies. His constitution was not robust and he died, a comparatively young man, in 1248. He was one of the first of the brethren to be buried in the new Blackfriars cemetery in Paradise on the southern boundary of Oxford. It is probable that Fishacre was teaching in the Oxford *studium* until he died. Although it is unlikely that he was regent all that time. Daniel Callus assessed Fishacre's significance:

> His influence was far-reaching and profound both in Oxford and Paris; in Oxford especially on the Franciscan, Richard Rufus of Cornwall, and on the Dominicans, Simon of Hinton and Robert Kilwardby; in Paris particularly on S Bonaventure.[35]

I have published the Fishacre sermon from our manuscript.[36] There are two points of interest relating this sermon to Fishacre's *Commentary on the Sentences*. First is the link between the theme of the sermon, "Non enim

[32] See R.J. Long, "Richard Fishacre and the Problem of the Soul," *The Modern Schoolman* 52 (1975) 263-70; "Richard Fishacre's 'Quaestio' on the Ascension of Christ: an Edition," *Med.St.* 40 (1978), 30-55; "The Virgin as Olive Tree: a Marian Sermon of Richard Fishacre and Science at Oxford," *AFP* 52 (1982) 77-87.

[33] R.J. Long, "The Science of Theology according to Richard Fishacre," *Med.St.* 34 (1972) 79-98. The project of editing Fishacre's *Commentary on the Sentences* is proceeding under the auspices of the Bavarian Academy of Sciences with the intention of publishing between 1995 and 2005.

[34] Further to Fishacre's method see C.H. Lawrence, "The University in State and Church" in *The Early Oxford Schools* ed. Catto, 101.

[35] D.A. Callus OP, "Introduction of Aristotelian Learning to Oxford," *PBA* 19 (1943), 258-9.

[36] M. E. O'Carroll SND, "Two Versions of a Sermon by Richard Fishacre OP for the Fourth Sunday of Lent on the Theme: 'Non enim heres erit filius ancille cum filio libere'," *AFP* 54 (1984), 113-141.

heres erit filius ancille cum filio libere" (Gal. 4:30) and a passage in the *Prologue* to his *Commentary*. Under the images of Agar the handmaid and Sara the wife, Fishacre discusses the relationship between the study of all the handmaid branches of knowledge or sciences as preparation for the delights of study of the queen science, Theology.[37] The second link is the interdependence in his sermon of two passages wherein he discusses the nature of hell as a place subject to "compression"—almost a black hole—with similar passages in his *Commentary*.[38] It seems most likely that his sermon was composed between the completion of that part of the *Commentary* and his death, perhaps between 1240/3 and 1248. I was able to locate another version of the same sermon in MS 6 of Ipswich Public Library.[39] The texts of the two sermons, on the same theme, while not identical, are so close that they very likely originate from the sermon preached by Fishacre. They are in fact an excellent example of the problem which besets students of sermons in discerning the original text of a given sermon, and, in default of precise information, of analysing the relationships of *reportationes* of sermons to the originals. It would seem to me that the version in MS Laud Misc. 511 is a *reportatio*, but that the version in the Ipswich MS 6 is a different *reportatio*, and that the former is nearer the source. The Laud version contains more *exempla*—which tend to be more ephemeral than the doctrinal parts of a sermon—and preserves a proverb in the orginal French. The Ipswich version has the proverb in Latin. The comparison of the two texts illustrates how the reporter of a sermon selected the content and determined the depth and length of treatment of the divisions of a sermon. Finally, this sermon of Fishacre's demonstrates the close relationship between the study of Theology and preaching described by Peter the Chanter:

> The training of Holy Scripture consists of three exercises: reading (*lectio*), disputing (*disputatio*) and preaching (*predicatio*)... First, reading is laid down like the basement and foundation for what follows... Secondly, the structure or walls of disputation are put in place.. Thirdly, the roof of preaching is erected... After the roof of preaching has been put in place so that we and our neighbours are protected from the heat, rain, hail and wind of vice, the

[37] Long, "Science of Theology," 85-6.

[38] O'Carroll, "Two Versions," 127-128, 131-132.

[39] Kaeppeli, *SOPMA* 3, 305. No. 3472, Ipswich Public Library, MS 6; kept in the library of Ipswich School since 1982. See also M.R. James, "Description of the Ancient Manuscripts in the Ipswich Public Libraries," *Proceedings of the Suffolk Institute of Archaeology and Natural History* 22 (1936), 86-103; and N.R. Ker, *Medieval Manuscripts in British Libraries*, 2, *Abbotsford to Keele* (Oxford, 1977), 990-994.

consistory of the palace of the High King will be completed, in which he distinguishes laws and right.[40]

Richard Fishacre's possible successor in the chair of Theology at Blackfriars, Oxford was Simon of Hinton OP. who is named as the author of sermon No. 66.[41] By 1239, he was a bachelor of theology, so he must have been in his early thirties. It is possible that the Dominican practice of short "regencies" in Theology began with him, as by 1253 Hugh of Mistretune had incepted and completed his Theology teaching and Peter Manners was the then occupant of the chair of Theology. Beryl Smalley has brought Simon of Hinton to life in her studies of his works.[42] Unlike Fishacre, he was no innovator, rather he favoured the older tradition of teaching. He preferred biblical studies to philosophical or theological speculation, and brought common sense and his own experience to bear on interpretation. He used many comparisons from daily life to illustrate his teaching; his *Summa Juniorum* is a good example of his practical interest in applied theology. Simon's writings reflect some of the interests of the Oxford of his time, especially a certain scientific bias. In 1254, he was elected prior provincial and remained in office until he was deposed by the general chapter of 1261, held in Barcelona, for not implementing the chapter decree of 1246-8 to establish the priory school at Oxford as a *studium generale* for the whole Order. Simon was then appointed lector at Cologne. Fortunately his exile only lasted a year, and he returned to England in 1262. Beryl Smalley sums him up:

> Simon cannot be classed as an outstanding theologian or exegete in comparison with the great men of the thirteenth century, but he is lively, fresh, inquisitive.[43]

Simon of Hinton's sermon is found in Appendix 9. The text is unsatisfactory and seems corrupt in many places. Moreover, the sermon as out-

---

[40] J.W. Baldwin, *Masters, Princes and Merchants: The Social Views of Peter the Chanter and his Circle*, (Princeton, 1970), 1: 90-1, 2: 63-4. The original text of Peter the Chanter is *Verbum Abbreviatum*, MS Arras 643 (571), fol. 2vb. See also Smalley, *Bible*, 208-213, especially 209: "The line between *lectio* and *predicatio* is thinly drawn."

[41] *BRUO* 2, 937; *BRUC*, 306-7; Paris General Chapter 1246, ACTA I, 34-5, 40-45.

[42] Smalley, *Bible*, 319-23, 331, 369, 371-2; see also fn 43; Beryl Smalley, "Some more Exegetical Works of Simon of Hinton," *RTAM* 15 (1948) 97-106; "The 'Quaestiones' of Simon of Hinton," in *Studies in Medieval History presented to F.M. Powicke* (Oxford, 1948), 209-222.

[43] Beryl Smalley, "Two Biblical Commentaries of Simon of Hinton," *RTAM* 12 (1946), 80.

lined in the opening phrases is not complete. So far, no comparative text has been identified. There are few discernible *exempla* in the sermon, but the tendency of its imagery is to use comparisons from nature: plants, gardens, fire, the sun, light, vapour, colour. A small portion, column 73a in the Laud manuscript, shares imagery and ideas with Fishacre, expecially the references to *diaphonum* and *tenebrosa*. On the whole, if the sermon had not been ascribed to a known person, it would not demand any detailed study.

Two of the sermons, then, in the manuscript were composed by eminent Dominicans who flourished as teachers of Theology in the University of Oxford, and in the schools of the Order from the 1230s and, in Simon's case, into the third quarter of the thirteenth century.

E. OTHER IDENTIFIED SERMONS

A search through Schneyer's *Repertorium*[44] gave no further possibility of identifying any other sermons of either Richard Fishacre or Simon of Hinton in this manuscript. The concordance between my catalogue of MS Laud Misc. 511 and that of Schneyer is found in Appendix 4. But Schneyer had already identified eight of the sermons in the Laud manuscript. I reject the ascription of sermon 67 (68 Schneyer) to Simon of Hinton as a *collatio* to sermon 66 (67 Schneyer), as there is no textual link between the sermons, as well as the fact that they are taken from different source books, Simon's from *Liber Niger Minor* and 67 from *Liber Rubeus Maior*. But the existence of seven identified sermons required that the possibility of identifying others should be explored.

My method for identifying possible repetitions of sermons has evolved over several years. To obtain a fast retrieval, three alphabetical lists are needed: one with the sermon themes; a second with the sermon *incipits*; and from this second list a third brief list of cues is drawn up. Only items with identical cues need the more detailed comparison against the sermon theme, the *incipit*, and the opening words of the body of the sermon, the *thema*. If there is a direct agreement among these three items, then a more detailed study of the texts of the sermon is indicated.[45]

Schneyer had already identified sermons by William Peraldus OP,

---

[44] Schneyer, *Repertorium*, 9: 56-69.

[45] The lists, but not the cue list, for MS Laud Misc. 511 are found in Appendix 5, "Sermon Theme, Incipit, and Thema," while the *themas* are found in the actual catalogue of the manuscript contents (Appendix 1).

Petrus de Remis OP, and Johannes Halgrinus de Abbatisvilla in MS Laud Misc. 511. Using Schneyer's *Repertorium*, searches were made through his lists of sermons in collections attributed to these three preachers, as well as through the sermons of Richard Fishacre and Simon of Hinton. Then the sources were examined in greater detail, using some of the manuscripts cited by Schneyer. For Peraldus there was a sixteenth-century printed source, but for the others only manuscript sources. Apart from a Cambridge manuscript containing sermons by Richard Fishacre,[46] I have used only manuscripts available in Oxford. Of those I chose the ones which combined early provenance, ease of reading and fullest text.[47] It should be noted at this point that, while there are more standard texts for the sermons of Peraldus and John of Abbeville, the texts of Petrus de Remis exhibit much greater divergence.

Sermon themes similar to some of those in the manuscript were found in sermons by Petrus de Remis, Jordan of Saxony, Peraldus, and Hugh of St. Cher, together with the anonymous late thirteenth-century Dominican collection in MS Bodley 25. The sermons of Richard and Hugh of St. Victor were looked at. A comparison of my three lists with the volume of Schneyer's *Repertorium* containing Franciscan sermons[48] yielded only one match by a friar whom Louis Bataillon has shown to be not a Franciscan.[49] The alphabetical list of sermon themes showed parallels with some of the collections, the most notable being those of Hugh of St. Cher and William de Montibus. There are then from the sermons noted in Schneyer's *Repertorium* some identifications of sermon themes from MS Laud Misc. 511 with Dominican and secular preachers, but not with Franciscan preachers.[50]

---

[46] Cambridge: Trinity College, MS B 15 38 (MS 373).

[47] The manuscripts used for identifying sermons are given below, pp. 97-98, notes 63, 64 and 67.

[48] Schneyer, *Repertorium*, 7: 1-495.

[49] Schneyer, *Repertorium*, vol. 7, no. 654, 422: a sermon of Johannes de Castello, c. 1273. In his researches on Italian friars and preaching, Père L.J. Bataillon has shown that Johannes de Castello is not a Franciscan.

[50] I had assumed that sermon themes were commonplace. In fact for MS Laud Misc. 511 the opposite is truer. For 44 themes, there are no matchings in any of the comparative sources; for 26 themes, there are matchings in only one of the comparative sources; while for 25 themes only are there matchings in five or more of the comparative sources. This process identified an agreement in theme only of three of those in MS Laud Misc. 511 with sermon themes of Stephen Langton. But similarity of theme carries no implication of similarity of sermon content.

As a result of the process described in the preceding paragraphs, eighteen possible identified sermons in the Laud manuscript were located. My criteria for acceptance or rejection of a sermon identification include: substantial verbal match for the identifiable whole and or part of an anti-theme; substantial verbal match for the whole or a significant part of the body of the sermon. Of the initial eighteen, eight sermons were accepted, nine were rejected, one was classed as doubtful. The preachers to whom the eight sermons are attributed are William Peraldus, Petrus de Remis and Hugo de St. Cher, all Dominicans. The one doubtful ascription is 229, which has similarities according to the method with one attributed to Hugh of St. Cher.[51] It is now possible to state that, in addition to the five sermons identified by Schneyer and the three named sermons, a further eight sermons have been identified. MS Laud Misc. 511 contains sixteen identified sermons, most of them by Dominican preachers.[52]

Something has already been said about Richard Fishacre and Simon of Hinton. The other identified makers of sermons are even better known. John of Abbeville was a famous master of Paris in the early years of the thirteenth century, being regent in Theology, 1206-1216.[53] It is possible that he was the master of Robert Bacon.[54] He became archbishop in 1225, and cardinal of Santa Sabina two years later. In 1237 he died.

Hugh of St. Cher was one of the great early preachers and teachers in the Order of Preachers. Before he entered in 1225, he was already a doctor of law and a bachelor of theology.[55] From 1229 to 1233 Hugh was

---

[51] It was not possible to find a comparative source in the United Kingdom. In 1988 Père Bataillon could not locate it in his available sources of Hugh of St. Cher, but did notice considerable use of Book II, De Peccato Linguae in Peraldus, Summae Virtutum ac Vitiorum (Antwerp, 1588.)

[52] The identified sermons in MS Laud Misc. 511 numbered according to Appendix 1, "A Catalogue of MS Laud Misc. 511":

10	Guilelmus Peraldus OP	98	John of Abbeville †1237
33	Petrus de Remis OP †1247	108	Petrus de Remis OP
60	Petrus de Remis OP	117	Petrus de Remis OP
66	Simon of Hinton OP	127	Petrus de Remis OP
77a+b	Guilelmus Peraldus OP	165	Guilelmus Peraldus OP
78	Hugh of St. Cher OP	171	Hugh of St. Cher OP
82	Richard Fishacre OP †1248	198	Guilelmus Peraldus OP
83	Petrus de Remis OP	166	H. de Mordon

[53] P. Glorieux, Répertoire des maîtres en théologie de Paris au xiiie siècle, 2 vols. (Paris, 1933-1934), 1, no.113, 272-3.

[54] Smalley, Bible, 265.

[55] Kaeppeli, SOPMA 2, 269-281; Glorieux, Répertoire 1, no. 2, 43-51.

in Paris, first as lector in the Sentences, then as master of theology. This was followed by a three-year stint as prior of St. Jacques. For two terms, 1227-30 and 1236-1244, he was provincial of the French province. In 1244 he became cardinal of Santa Sabina. Hugh was probably the mastermind behind the start of the corporate work on the Biblical Concordances made at St. Jacques. After a further twenty years of service to the Church, he died in March 1263. It is likely that, although his sermons are not dated, they come from his time in Paris.

William Peraldus,[56] born about 1200, entered the Order of Preachers at Lyons, possibly about 1236.[57] Salimbene records in his Chronicle that Peraldus stayed with the Franciscans at Vienne in 1249 "in order to preach and hear confessions."[58] The only other certain date in his life is his election as prior of Lyons in 1261. He probably died in 1270.[59] All his life Peraldus was an untiring preacher, and his writings reflect his pastoral care. His first great work is the *Summae de Virtutibus et Vitiis*.[60] His second is the sermons for Sundays and feastdays. Dondaine dates the composition of his sermons on the Epistles to 1240-1245.[61] The dating of the composition of his sermons on the Gospels is difficult to pinpoint. It is certain that they preceded the sermons for feast-days, which were known to be in existence by 1259-1260.

Petrus de Remis[62] is less famous than the preceding two. His connection with the Order of Preachers, however, is even earlier, for he was prior provincial of France from 1224 to 1227; prior of St. Jacques, 1227 to 1230; and provincial for a second time, 1230 to 1233. In 1245 he was consecrated bishop of Agen, and he died in 1247. It is very likely that he knew St. Dominic personally.

Three of the identified preachers whose sermons are found in our manuscript were dead by 1248: John of Abbeville, Petrus de Remis, and Richard Fishacre. The only selections of the sermons of Peraldus identified in the manuscript are from his sermons on the Epistles, dated 1240-45. So

---

[56] A. Dondaine OP, "Guillaume Peyraut: vie et oeuvres," *AFP* 18 (1948) 162-236; Kaeppeli, *SOPMA* 2, 133-152.

[57] M. Aron, *Saint Dominic's Successor* (London, 1955) 50 records a vague tradition that Peraldus entered the Order of Preachers as one of Jordan's "catches."

[58] Dondaine, "Peyraut," 172-173.

[59] Ibid., 180.

[60] Ibid., 186-7.

[61] Ibid., 204.

[62] Kaeppeli, *SOPMA* 3, 256-7. The Dominican "provincie Francie" was not the geographical France of today.

twelve of the identified sermons in MS Laud Misc. 511 were in existence by 1250, and eleven of them are by Dominicans.

F. SOME LINKS BETWEEN THE IDENTIFIED SERMONS AND SOME OF THE SOURCE BOOKS NAMED IN MS LAUD MISC. 511

It is now possible to discuss in more detail some of the identified sermons and some of the source books. Thirteen sermons and five source books are linked, although conclusions can be suggested for only eleven sermons between three books. They are as follows:

from

Liber Niger Minor	66	Simon of Hinton OP
Liber Rubeus Maior	82	Richard Fishacre OP †1248
Parvus Liber Rubeus	60	Petrus de Remis OP †1247
	98	John of Abbeville †1237
	133	Petrus de Remis OP
Liber Rubeus Minor	83	Petrus de Remis OP
	108	Petrus de Remis OP
	117	Petrus de Remis OP
	127	Petrus de Remis OP
Liber Proprius	10	Guilelmus Peraldus OP
	77a+b	Guilelmus Peraldus OP
	78	Hugh of St. Cher OP
	165	Guilelmus Peraldus OP
	171	Hugh of St. Cher OP
	198	Guilelmus Peraldus OP

It is clear that, by comparing the sermons listed as belonging to the source books with the very much smaller number of identified sermons within the source books, none of the books named in the Laud manuscript is a model collection as the term is commonly understood. If that were so, then there would be a source book totally devoted to, for example, the sermons of Peraldus or Petrus de Remis. From the evidence of the numbering systems already noted, three of the source books, namely *Parvus Liber Rubeus, Liber Rubeus Minor* and *Liber Proprius*, are books with sermons in chronological rather than liturgical order. The source books may have been made from one preacher's own sermons, perhaps together with *reportationes* from the sermons of others, and sermons copied from a model collection like the sermons of Peraldus and Petrus de Remis. It is not possible on the evidence available to say more about any identity of these source books.

It has been possible, however, from a textual comparison of the sermons found in MS Laud Misc. 511 with other sources for the same sermons, to explore similarities or differences. This is examined first in the sermons themselves in the order of the preachers, John of Abbeville, Peter of Rheims, Hugh of St. Cher and William Peraldus, using manuscripts available in the Bodleian library. The second is to explore whether there are differences between the source books.

For John of Abbeville's sermons there were four manuscripts available,[63] the best of which for meaning and completeness of text together with ease of reading is MS Lyell 6. In the one sermon, number 98, attributed to John of Abbeville there is a complete match only in the antitheme of the sermon as found in MS Lyell.

Secondly to take the sermons of Peter of Rheims—numbers 60, 83, 108, 117, 127 and 133 in the manuscript—there were two manuscripts available, the best of which, on the criteria already noted for the sermons of John of Abbeville, was MS Auct. D.4.12.[64] In sermon 60, 88 out of 112 lines (that is four-fifths) are identical. In sermon 83, there is a shortening of the antitheme with the Laud text ending halfway through the MS Auct. version. Sermon 108, apart from the omission of the Old Testament authorities, has an identical text with the Auct. manuscript except for the final seven lines. Neither sermon 117 nor sermon 127 is exact as a copy, but the relationships between the Laud version and the Auct. source are too close to see them as anything but the same sermon. In sermon 133 two out of three-and-a-quarter columns, that is, nearly three fifths, are identical—Laud with Auct.

For the sermons of Hugh of St. Cher, there were five manuscripts, the best of which proved to be two Laud manuscripts.[65] In sermon 78, only one full division and one-half of Hugh's original sermon is used in the Laud manuscript. But fresh *exempla* are inserted, including the story of the Cistercian monk of Roche Abbey in Yorkshire and the famous fable of the stag.[66] Sermon 171 includes the whole of the second division and half the third division of the Bodley source.

[63] Johannes Halgrinus de Abbatisvilla—Oxford, Bodleian Library, MS Lyell 6., MS Lat.th.e 46, MS Lincoln College 79, MS Merton College 22.

[64] Petrus de Remis OP—Oxford, Bodleian Library, MS Auct. D.4.12, MS Laud Misc. 506.

[65] Hugh of St. Cher OP—Oxford, Bodleian Library, MS Bodley 157, MS Laud Misc. 172 fol. 42-92, MS Laud Misc. 318 fol. 65, MS Laud Misc. 504 fol. 51-111, MS Laud Misc. 506 fol. 108.

[66] See Chapter 6, sections B. and C. on *Exempla* and Sermon Material.

Lastly, there are five manuscripts, the best of which proved to be MS Ashmole 1290, and the printed edition from Lyons of 1576 for Peraldus.[67] The Ashmole versions and the printed book are practically identical. The variants are found in the four sermons in MS Laud Misc. 511. In number 10, the sermon finishes in the middle of the comparative texts. The Ashmole MS treats of *pedes, manus, os, lingua, aures, oculi, capita,* while the Laud takes only the first four. In Sermon 77a+b the antitheme 77b is totally different from MS Ashmole 1290; while in 77a, the body of the sermon, only two sections are similar: the image of the pilgrim going to the Holy Land, and the image of Jerusalem. Sermon 165 from the Laud MS has a different incipit from the Ashmole source but is very close to the body of the sermon, with one exception. The Ashmole version gives only three lines to the topic of prayer. MS Laud Misc. 511 expands this treatment of prayer to twenty-five lines, and then ends the sermon. The comparative text continues with three further topics: fraternal charity, fasting and listening to God's word in sermons. In Sermon 198 again the antitheme differs in the Laud version from MS Ashmole 1290, but the main body of the sermon is identical, except that the Laud text is cut short.

When these identified sermons are taken in relationship to their original authors, it can be seen that the versions in MS Laud Misc. 511, while identifiable, are not identical; rather, they are adapted. Can any of these adaptations be related to any of the source books? It is difficult to say, as in *Parvus Liber Rubeus* and *Liber Rubeus Minor* the differences could arise from existing variants in content, or in different and varied sources for the sermons copied in the usual way.

While the same conditions could exist for the compiler of *Liber Proprius* copying his sermons into his books, nevertheless the relationship between its sermons and the comparative texts is much looser. In many ways it is both editorial and creative. This freedom is found in the compiler's use of the sermons of Peraldus and those of Hugh of St. Cher. It would have been useful if some of the sermons in *Liber Proprius* had been those of Petrus de Remis, as a further clarification of relationships between sources and copies could have been possible. Nevertheless, it does seem that the maker of *Liber Proprius* treated his sources more freely than the makers of *Parvus Liber Rubeus* and *Liber Rubeus Minor*, choosing to put what he thought appropriate into his own book.

---

[67] Guilelmus Peraldus OP—Oxford, Bodleian Library, MS Ashmole 1290, MS Lat.th e 16/17 fol. 30-96, MS Laud Misc 376 fol. 53 seq., MS Laud Misc. 439 fol. 177-252, MS Rawl. A 373 fol. 1-119; *Sermones eximii praestantesque, super Epistolas Dominicales totius anni* (Lyons, 1576).

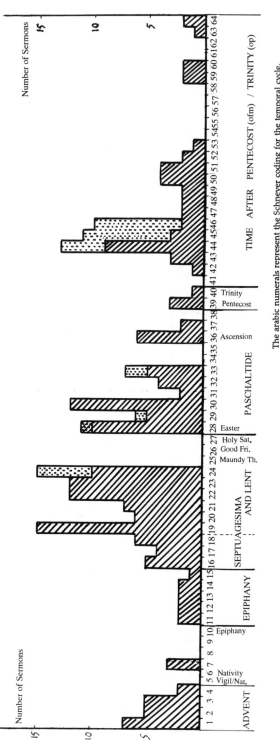

TABLE 6. HISTOGRAM OF THE MANUSCRIPT

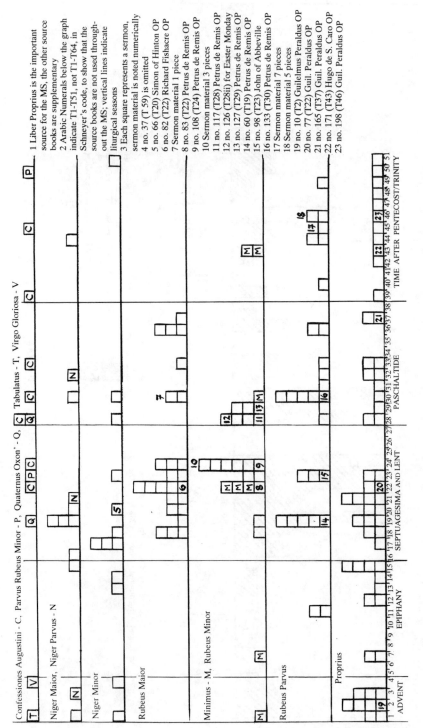

1 Liber Proprius is the important
source for the MS, the other source
books are supplementary

2 Arabic Numerals below the graph
indicate T1-T51, not T1-T64, in
Schneyer's code, to show that the
source books are not used throughout the MS; vertical lines indicate
liturgical seasons

3 Each square represents a sermon,
sermon material is noted numerically

4 no. 37 (T 59) is omitted

5 no. 66 (T20) Simon of Hinton OP

6 no. 82 (T22) Richard Fishacre OP

7 Sermon material 1 piece

8 no. 83 (T22) Petrus de Remis OP

9 no. 108 (T24) Petrus de Remis OP

10 Sermon material 3 pieces

11 no. 117 (T28) Petrus de Remis OP

12 no. 126 (T28ii) for Easter Monday

13 no. 127 (T29) Petrus de Remis OP

14 no. 60 (T19) Petrus de Remis OP

15 no. 98 (T23) John of Abbeville

16 no. 133 (T30) Petrus de Remis OP

17 Sermon material 7 pieces

18 Sermon material 5 pieces

19 no. 10 (T2) Guilelmus Peraldus OP

20 no. 77 (T22) Guil. Peraldus OP

21 no. 165 (T37) Guil. Peraldus OP

22 no. 171 (T43) Hugo de S. Caro OP

23 no. 198 (T46) Guil. Peraldus OP

TABLE 7. HISTOGRAM OF THE SOURCE BOOKS IN THE MANUSCRIPT

The information about the contents of MS Laud Misc. 511 has been set out in the form of histograms in Tables 6 and 7. From these diagrams it will be seen that the information about the manuscript takes many pages, whereas in graph form much information is compressed and some significances emphasised. Table 6 indicates the contents of the Laud manuscript, Table 7 the contents of the source books. Both are made using Schneyer's liturgical numbering for the *Temporale*. The importance of the *Temporale*, with the emphasis placed by the compiler on liturgical seasons and high days, can be seen clearly. If the graph of *Liber Proprius*—presumably the compiler's starting point—is examined, it can be seen how he supplements gaps in his own provision from other books. Several emphases in the compilation can be noted: all the material for Palm Sunday came from other sources; the sermons for the Second Sunday after Easter were gathered from as many different sources as possible; on the other hand, the sermon material came from only three source books; the nature of the sermon material indicates a particular focus on the passion, death and resurrection of the Lord, and on mercy, thanksgiving and prayer. The histogram also shows how individual sermons for Advent were added. Lastly, it shows quite dramatically how the compilation ended abruptly with the Tenth Sunday after Trinity.

The facts of the various source books and the links with the identified sermons indicate that the making of the sermon collection which is now MS Laud Misc. 511 was not as simple or direct as has been thought. In fact MS Laud Misc. 511 suggests some serious questions about the transmission of thirteenth-century sermons.

G. A "DOMINICAN" BOOK?

MS Laud Misc. 511, as we are seeing, is an interesting manuscript about which more questions can be asked than can easily be answered. It is clear that most of the identified content in our manuscript has strong Dominican links, but is it possible to call the manuscript a "Dominican" book? Another area of questioning is the very appearance of the page with its blue initials flourished red, its numbered columns and its numbered lines. The genesis of the following discussion was the need to examine the assumption Pelster made in his article that this manuscript was Dominican. In a thirteenth-century context, the immediate comparison for Dominican is Franciscan.

Even if there is a point of comparison, how can it be said that a manuscript is Dominican or Franciscan? Is it in fact possible to make this assumption a category? For example, in so far as content is concerned, BL

MS Add. 23935 can legitimately be called a Dominican manuscript, as it contains the master general's master-copy of the Dominican liturgical reform. Similarly a copy of Thomas Eccleston's *De Adventu Fratrum* could be called a Franciscan manuscript. A manuscript could be Dominican or Franciscan by annotated ownership, as seen in the the lists included in Ker's *Medieval Libraries*.[68] Thirdly, a manuscript could be Dominican or Franciscan by its place of production and its palaeographic conventions. In the thirteenth century, however, Dominicans and Franciscans alike gave a common apostolic service, being similarly moved by the needs of their times. The content of their manuscripts, especially their theological ones, could only narrowly be labelled Dominican or Franciscan. Some differences could be discerned from their respective traditions, so that a bias towards preaching is expected in the Order of Preachers and a bias towards poverty among the Friars Minor. But in so far as these two Orders interacted, it is also legitimate to seek preaching among the Friars Minor and poverty among the Preachers. Only the first two categories described here give any basis for valid criteria of comparison.

But in the thirteenth century a second locus of comparison for Dominicans is university. The parallels between the scholastic practices of the young universities and those of the various *studia* of the Order of Preachers are many, and similarly for the Friars Minor. Books are the key. So our starting point is *The Medieval Libraries of Great Britain*. Although Mr Ker noted its limitations in respect of the books of the friars,[69] there is no other comparable work of reference.

A list of all manuscripts belonging to the twelfth, thirteenth and fourteenth centuries which Ker ascribed to ownership by Dominican and Franciscan houses was compiled. The time limit was imposed because it seemed that anything before the twelfth century (which could have come to the friars by gift or purchase), and from the fifteenth century, would be too removed from the enquiry. Ownership of books was seen as a specific, identifiable link between the book and the Order which, while not necessarily implying manufacture, reflects in some way the interests and activities of the owners.

In the same manner, two other lists were drawn up: the first of the manuscripts named in Ker's book as having belonged to the libraries of

[68] N.R. Ker, *Medieval Libraries of Great Britain*, 2nd ed. (London: Royal Historical Society, 1964).

[69] N.R. Ker, "Cardinal Cervini's Manuscripts from the Cambridge Friars," in *Xenia Medii Aevi Historiam Illustrantia oblata Thomae Kaeppeli*, ed. R. Creytens (Rome, 1978), 51, footnote 1.

colleges in Oxford and Cambridge during the same time period; the second of manuscripts named as belonging to monastic communitites in and near Oxford. The college and monastic libraries were seen as two ends of an academic spectrum.

A further list was drawn up of books already identified as "English." Bringing together manuscripts in Mrs Patterson's list, shelf 643f in the British Library, and manuscripts associated with Grosseteste's works[70] facilitated a compilation of a base group of manuscripts for discerning English scribal and decorating characteristics. Examination of these manuscripts emphasised the close connection between an "English" identification from other sources with the use solely of blue capitals flourished red as part of decoration. This usage does not preclude the use of alternate red (flourished blue) and blue (flourished red) initials. These decorative practices were confirmed verbally by Mr Ker.

In the course of the above work, four other sets of manuscripts were looked at: the group of Oxford manuscripts selected by Dr R.W. Hunt in 1974 to mount a commemorative exhibition for the 700th anniversary of the arrival of the Franciscans;[71] manuscripts of Commentaries on the Sentences of English scholars;[72] manuscripts of some theological works composed by British scholars in the thirteenth century;[73] and copies of Raymund of Penaforte's *Summa de Casibus* because of its ubiquity. Actual scrutiny of the manuscripts was limited to those held by libraries in Oxford, London and Cambridge.

About 350 manuscripts were examined. The physical signs looked at and recorded included: blue initials flourished red; arabic or roman numbering on folios or pages or sections; arabic or roman numbering or lettering of columns; numbering or lettering of lines in columns. If faces appeared often these were recorded, as was any use noticed of Grosseteste's indexing symbols. The index of manuscripts is annotated with the information gathered.

When the analysis of the manuscripts in the various groups of the

[70] Mrs Patterson gave me a copy of her personal list; Dr Schofield and Dr J. Backhouse of the British Library informed me that Dr E. Millar had classified shelf 643f as "English"; S.H. Thomson, *The Writings of Robert Grosseteste* (Cambridge, 1940). Most of the 350+ manuscripts consulted are listed in Appendix 12.

[71] R.W. Hunt, *The Coming of the Friars*, (1974); Catalogue of Manuscript Exhibition, Bodleian Library, Oxford (*Catalogue*, Duke Humfrey R.6. 141 k).

[72] Ed. F. Stegmuller, *Repertorium Commentariorum in Sententias Petri Lombardi* (Wurzburg, 1947).

[73] List compiled from Ker, *Medieval Libraries*.

sample was combined, certain trends appeared: the comparative absence of numbering systems from the monastic group, the higher proportion of Dominican-owned manuscripts than Franciscan-owned manuscripts that were numbered in some way. But in three of the sub-groups—namely the manuscripts of the Commentaries on the Sentences, the theologians' manuscripts; and the manuscripts displayed in the "Friars Exhibition"—the proportion of manuscripts with some form of numbering was much greater. The initial sample of 350 manuscripts yielded 120 manuscripts having strong links with the friars and with the new universities. Of the 120 manuscripts ninety have some form of numbering. Table 8 shows the detail.

TABLE 8. KINDS AND EXTENT OF NUMBERING SYSTEMS IN 90 MANUSCRIPTS

	Folios	Pages	Columns	Sections	Totals
WHOLE					
Arabic	19	4+	8	20	51+
Roman	1	1+	0	0	2+
Letter	0	0	0	0	0
Sub-total	20	6	8	20	54
PART					
Arabic	21	1	1	8	31
Roman	0	0	0	1	1
Letter	0	0	3	1	4
Sub-total	21	1	4	10	36
TOTALS	41	7	12	30	90

Even a quick scrutiny of Table 8 shows that seventy five per cent of the manuscripts linked with the friars and the universities have a numbering system in whole or in part; and that of the ninety manuscripts, at least eighty-one have an arabic numbering system. This could be a reflection of the rapidly increasing numeracy which the new arabic system fostered. In particular, Oxford had a strong interest in mathematics and science, much of which required efficient arithmetic. Where calculation is important, arabic numerals are far superior to roman numerals. Their use outside mathematics and science can be readily appreciated. It is equally important to note that there was a wide variety in the use of the numbering system; in the ninety manuscripts, numbering of folios and sections is more frequent than numbering of columns. There is no uniformity of numbering conventions in this group of ninety manuscripts. The information from the above group about numbering of lines in fives is of equal interest, and is set out below.

TABLE 9. TABLE TO SHOW MODES OF INDICATING LINES

Whole Manuscripts	Part Manuscripts	Owners
MANUSCRIPTS WITH LINES NUMBERED IN FIVES		
Roy 10 B vii (Fishacre)		OP Cambridge prob
	Camb Ff 6 10 (6 fols.)	Jesus Coll. Oxford
	Bodl 365 (7 fols.)	Merton, Oxford
Balliol 62 (Ric.Rufus)		OFM author
New Coll. E 112 (Fishacre)		OP author
	Roy 5 C vii (1 fol.)	OP London
Roy 6 C ix		OP Warwick
	Hereford P iii 12	OFM Hereford
Roy 1 A viii (400+ fols.)		? Grosseteste link
	Oriel 15	?
TOTALS: 5	5	10
MANUSCRIPTS WITH LINES LETTERED		
	Corpus 225 (Oxf)	OP Beverley
Univ 190 (Oxf)		OP Beverley
	Bodl 745 (fol. 1-74)	OP author
	Roy 11 B iii	Bury St. Edmunds
TOTALS: 1	3	4

While the numbers of the manuscripts are too small, despite the initial size of the samples (350+, 120), to warrant any firm conclusions, some facts can be noted. Of the ten whole manuscripts with line numbering in fives there are, through authorship and ownership, six Dominican links and two Franciscan links; through ownership, two Oxford college links; and through content, one link with Grosseteste. Moreover, two of the manuscripts are of the first Oxford *Commentary on the Sentences* by Richard Fishacre OP; and one is of another commentary, this time by a pupil of Richard Fishacre, Richard Rufus of Cornwall OFM. The focus of these four different kinds of linkage is friars and Oxford. Of the manuscripts with lettering, three have Dominican links, one being a very early Oxford commentary on the Psalter by Robert Bacon.[74]

It would seem that, if records could be kept of manuscripts with line-numbering in fives, it could lead to interesting results concerning the book trade in the thirteenth century. It is clearly an English practice with—as noted above—a usage by the friars and in Oxford. In Paris and other centres on the continent, an alphabetical division of a page was used, either a-e or a-g.[75] On the technical side, it is not clear at what stage in the writing of a manuscript the line numbering is inserted. From some of the manuscripts examined, it would seem that the numbering has been put in at the end. Perhaps the partial input, as noted above, is accounted for by the tediousness of the exercise. But it is also possible for numbers to be put in as part of the page to be written on.[76] Perhaps there is no regular stage at which the numbers are written, but insertion depends on the scribe, the annotator, or even the later user.

It is now time to return to the question with which this section opened: whether there are "Dominican" manuscripts. It would seem that, unless there is a library-ownership ascription or a convergence of different kinds of internal evidence, it is not possible to speak of "Dominican" books, although it is possible to speak of mendicant books.

In looking at and handling over 350 manuscripts in the sample discussed in the previous section, I have gained a number of impressions. Some of the books are big and heavy, beautifully written and decorated, such as large Bibles, library books of Theology and works of the Fathers. The ownership, in the thirteenth century, of the large well-executed manuscripts is likelier to be by a monastic or college library. This does not mean that the friars did not have books like this for their use, but it was unlikely that they either made or paid for such. They could receive them as a gift from a benefactor or from a highly-educated novice, or could acquire them at second hand. Some of the manuscripts in the sample have

[74] Beryl Smalley, "Robert Bacon and the early Dominican School at Oxford," *TRHS* 4th Series (1948) 1-19.

[75] Père L.J. Bataillon and Dr Nicole Bériou drew my attention to an English manuscript bought by Pierre de Limoges, who carefully removed the line-numbering in fives and replaced them with letters of the alphabet.

[76] London BL, MS Roy 6 E v folios 69r, 69v and 135 have column numbers written in without any text; while Oxford, MS New College E 112 has line numbers in fives written in *before* any text was copied.

pecia marks as described by Destrez.[77] These books are very plain. Such decoration as they have is functional, and blue and red only. These were found more often in college libraries and with the mendicants. Another group is of the one-volume Bibles. Some are larger, some smaller, depending on the size of the script, and some can only be read by modern eyes with help. They are written in the two-column style, most often with blue initials flourished red alternating with red initials flourished blue. Sometimes they are illuminated, but sparingly.[78] Many have lists of alphabetical tables at the end. Many Bibles of known Dominican ownership have the list of Hebrew names, and often a table of cues of the epistles and gospels of the Sunday.

A characteristic difference between mendicant books and other academic theology books is size. As more of the friars' books are handled, their portable format becomes clearer, whether they were to fit in a pocket or in a satchel. In the thirteenth century friars mostly walked and carried their books with them, the smaller the lighter. In a fair proportion of mendicant books, the quality of the parchment is less good; often with variations in thickness, sometimes with holes and tears. Probably their poverty, which they shared with most students, dictated their use in personal books of inferior parchment. Many of the friars' books are much annotated: corrections with comments; extra material, often utilising the margins; scripture references; marginal references; interlinear notes; and the use of indexing symbols. Some of the latter are definitely derived from those of Grosseteste.[79]

In reflecting on the comparatively high proportion of books linked with Dominican and Franciscan ownership that have numbering systems, as seen in Table 8, it seems clear that the work of preaching encouraged the practice of speedy retrieval of sermons and cross-referencing of con-

[77] J. Destrez, *La 'Pecia' dans les manuscrits universitaires du xiiie et xive siècles* (Paris, 1935).

[78] Oxford, Bodleian Library, MS Lat. Bibl e 7 [olim Dyson Perrins MS 5]. This was the Bible illuminated for Blackfriars, Oxford by William de Brailles. Mendicants also possessed big Bibles, glossed Bibles and corrected Bibles. See J.C. Schnurman, "Studies in the Medieval Book Trade from the Late 12th to the Middle of the 14th Century with Special Reference to the Copying of Bibles" (Oxford, 1960), Bodl.Lib MS B.Litt d 815.

[79] R.W. Hunt, "Manuscripts Containing the Indexing Symbols of Robert Grosseteste," *BLR* 4 (1953) 241-244. R.W. Southern, *Robert Grosseteste: The Growth of an English Mind in Medieval Europe* (Oxford, 1986), 186-197, and footnotes on pages 43, 179, 211, 247.

tent. The wide variety of numbering and lettering patterns discernible in so many mendicant manuscripts and the lack of uniformity among mendicant manuscripts testify to a strong unity of purpose: the determination to make content and illustration easily available to the preacher.[80]

From the foregoing information it seems clear that, while MS Laud Misc. 511 contains identified sermons of Dominican and mostly French provenance, its Dominican ascription while possible is still not certain. But there is no doubt that the book itself is English in its manufacture, in its technical style, and in some of its sermon content.

H. THE DATING OF MS LAUD MISCELLANEOUS 511

There are at least five factors to be taken into account in trying to date this manuscript: the time-and-place-dated sermons in it; the style of script; the mode of manufacture of the book; the contents of the manuscript known from other sources; the liturgical changes of the mid-thirteenth century, particularly those associated with the friars.

In his article on this manuscript Pelster states:

> The MS was written after 1279, and more probably after 1283 though some of the sources were considerably older. First the writer has added the date to a number of sermons which he himself apparently delivered at Elnestowe.[81]

While one hesitates to contradict a scholar like Pelster, nevertheless so much has been learnt about the dating of manuscripts in the past sixty years that, in the light of fresh information, his statement has to be re-examined. Tables 10 and 11 record the information about the time-and-place-dated sermons in the manuscript. Because of this dating of the sermons, the dating of the manuscript seems simple. But, once questions are asked, the simplicity yields to complexity. Were the Elstow sermons preached before the manuscript came into existence? Were the Elstow sermons preached from this manuscript? Is the compiler of the manuscript a preacher at Elstow? Did the Elstow preachers compose the sermons they delivered there? Such answers as are possible lie in the interplay of literary and palaeographical information.

---

[80] R.H. and M.A. Rouse, *Preachers, Florilegia and Sermons: Studies on the 'Manipulus Florum' of Thomas of Ireland* (Toronto: PIMS 1979), 1-42.

[81] F. Pelster, "An Oxford Collection of Sermons," *BQR* 6 (1929-1930), 168.

TABLE 10. TIME-AND-PLACE-DATED SERMONS IN MS LAUD MISC. 511
ACCORDING TO MANUSCRIPT ORDER

No.	Cat. No.	Theme and Schneyer Ref.	Place and/or Time Annotation
1 1278	50 fol. 53va	Ductus est Jesus [Matt. 4:1] (T 19)	predicatur sermo iste aput Eln' prima Dominica Quadragesime anno Domini m cc lxx viii.
2 1281	53 fol. 55b	Ductus est Jesus [Matt. 4:1] (T 19)	predicatur aput Elnest' anno circuli lunaris ix.
3 1283	64 fol. 69va	Hec est voluntas Dei [1 Thess. 4:3] (T 20)	predicatur sermo anno lunaris xi.
4 1278	72 fol. 83vb	Cum eiecisset Jesus demonium [Luke 11:14] (T 21)	predicatur apud Elnest' anno circuli lunaris vi.
5 1283	77 fol. 93a-b	Illa que sursum est [Gal. 4:26] (T 22)	predicatur sermo iste apud Eln' anno lunaris xi ** (see 7).
6 1275	78 fol. 94a	Erat proxima Pascha [John 6:4] (T 22)	Iste sermo predicatur aput Elnest' anno Domini m cc lxx quinto * (see 10, 12).
7 1282	90 fol. 101ab	Christus per proprium sanguinem [Heb. 11:12] (T 23)	predicatur apud Eln' anno lunaris x ** (see 5).
8 1277	100 fol. 106vb	Noli timere filia Syon [John 12:15] (T 24)	predicatur sermo anno lun' v apud Eln' usque verbum "Cantandum est Domino."
1283		This sermon was used twice	Iterum anno lunaris xi. margin note; fol. 107va huc usque predicatur lunaris v.
9 1279	136 fol. 127ab	Christus passus est [1 Pet. 2:21] (T 30)	Dominica secunda post Pasch' anno circuli lunaris vii predicatur apud Eln'.
10 1275	153 fol. 141a	Si quid petieritis [John 16:23] (T 33)	Iste sermo predicatur aput Elnest' Dominica proxima ante Ascensionem anno domini m cc lxx v * (see 6, 12).

11	207	Misereor super turbam	Dominica hec antithema anno domini
1277	fol. 170vb	[Matt. 5:32] (T 47)	m cc lxx vii.

12	230	Quodcumque solveris	Iste sermo predicatur aput Elnest'
1275	fol. 198vb	[Matt. 16:19] (S 46)	anno domini m cc lxx quinto * (see 6, 10).

13	231	Que est ista	predicatur iste sermo in Assumptione
1279	fol. 200a	[Cant. 6:9] (S 59)	Beate Virginis circuli lunaris vii anno domini m cc lxxix.

The dates of six of the sermons are given in terms of *anno domini*. The other seven sermons are dated according to lunar calculation.[82] Happily, the manuscript gives an equation by the annotation of Sermon 231 with a double entry: year of grace 1279 = *anno circuli lunaris vii*. From this equation the other lunar dates were worked out and checked against Pelster's calculations. So, ten sermons contained in this manuscript were preached on eleven occasions from 1275 to 1283. For the present argument, the three sermons which are only time-dated—64, 207 and 231—but not place-dated, are being ignored, as they fall within the above time scale and their omission neither enhances nor diminishes the argument.

Initially, it seemed that only one person had preached the sermons at Elstow. Closer examination of the annotation, however, showed at least two different styles of hand: the first is an upstanding largish secretary hand using several capitals, a flamboyant abbreviation for "ur" and "er," a looped "d" and an "a" with a tail; the second is a smaller neat hand with a sloping—sometimes hooked—"d," and a smaller simpler way of writing the abbreviations. This second group by the smaller hand had divergences in the manner of letter formation, enough to question, but not enough to posit, a third hand. When the ten inscriptions were examined together in microfilm printouts, the differences between the two hands were clear, but the possible difference within the second hand was less clear.[83] When the content of the inscriptions was analysed in relation to the separate hands, the two different modes of dating emerged, coinciding with the two different annotating hands, as shown in Table 11. The writer of the

---

[82] C.R. Cheney, *Handbook of Dates for Students of English History* (London, 1945), Preface and "Reckonings of Time," 1-11. See also A. Cappelli, *Cronologia, cronografia e calendario perpetuo*, 3rd ed. (Milan, 1969).

[83] I owe much of this palaeographical comment to the late Dr R.W. Hunt, who was so generous with his time in examining this manuscript.

TABLE 11. TIME-AND-PLACE-DATED SERMONS IN MS LAUD MISC. 511
ACCORDING TO SCRIBAL AND CHRONOLOGICAL ORDER

Year	Elstow Preacher E 1	Elstow Preacher E 2	No Place Noted
1275	78, 153, 230 [all AD]* same anno-tating hand		
1276			
1277		100 anno lun' v only a part of it used	207 [AD]
1278	50 [AD]	72 circuli lun' vi	
1279		136 circuli lun' vii	231 [AD] + circ'lun'
1280			
1281		53 anno circ'lun' ix	
1282		90 anno lun' x **	
1283		77 anno lun' xi **100 anno lun' xi	64 anno lun' xi

bold annotation had preached at Elstow in 1275 and 1278, recording the
fact in the year-of-grace dating. I have called him E1.

The other writer, whom I have called E2, had begun preaching at Elstow in 1277 and preached there, probably five more times, until 1283. He
dated his Elstow preaching engagements by the lunar method of dating.
Whether these two preachers alternated during these years or succeeded
one another is not clear, although the available evidence favours the latter
interpretation. The existence of at least two Elstow preachers diminishes
the likelihood of the compiler of the manuscript and one of the Elstow
preachers being the same person. It also makes the suggestion that the
manuscript was made after 1279 or 1283 more difficult to sustain. If the
first Elstow preacher had made this manuscript after he had preached
three sermons in 1275, would he have been very careful to give the source
book for the first two sermons he preached, and yet omit the source book
for the third? Or, if he did not make the manuscript, but the second
Elstow preacher did, how did they eventually collaborate in making the
manuscript? And, if either of them did make the manuscript, why is their
writing not found in other places in the manuscript? Surely the function
of the place-time dating is practical; namely, keeping a record of activities.

I do not think that Pelster's identification of the compiler of MS Laud Misc. 511 with one of the Elstow preachers can stand.

It is necessary also to look at the Elstow sermons to enquire whether the audience was nuns only, or nuns and local laity. The fact that there was never a parish church after the founding of the Norman abbey,[84] and that after the Reformation the nave of the abbey church was retained as the parish church while the rest was quarried and ruined, indicates that the abbey church functioned as the medieval parish church. On the other hand, if the sermons were intended as spiritual conferences for the nuns and linked with opportunity for confession, the laity would have been excluded. The latter possibility is the more likely. That the two preachers preached identified sermons at Elstow neither confirms nor excludes the possibility that the sermons were composed for the occasion. Sermon 72,[85] preached in 1278, which in its antitheme refers to Bedford just a mile-and-a-half away, is not proof that the sermon was composed for the Elstow audience. It could have been, but it could also have been composed at any time in these years for the people of the Bedford archdeaconry. Sermon 100, preached in Elstow in 1277 and again in 1283, has a reference to many who take the cross and go overseas.[86] We know from the annals of Dunstable that in 1275 Master Raymund and Brother John were collecting the crusading tenths in the area.[87] But that still does not prove the sermon was composed for the Elstow congregation. Rather the opposite, for this sermon was used twice at Elstow. It was likely to be a pre-existing text. From a reading of the Elstow sermons, none of them seems to have been specifically composed for the people there. Moreover, there are disparities of style and marked differences in approach to the use of Scripture which cannot be related in any clear way to preacher E1 or preacher E2. The unity of the Elstow sermons lies not in an internal literary and pastoral style, but in an external unity imposed by the liturgical occasion. This discussion of the nature of the Elstow sermons leads to the conclusion that the two preachers wrote in an already existing book their comments about the time and place at which they used these sermons at El-

---

[84] David Baker, *Excavations at Elstow Abbey, 1965-1970* (Bedford, 1970), 7-14.

[85] MS Laud Misc. 511, fol. 83vb, ll. 5-6.

[86] MS Laud Misc. 511, fol. 107va, ll. 6-12.

[87] Ed. H.R. Luard, *Annales Monastici* 3 RS (London, 1866) 267: Eodem anno, in crastino Epiphanie, magister Raymundus et Frater Johannes, principales collectores decimae Terrae Sanctae, noluerunt stare juramento nostro super taxatione bonorum nostrorum, sed per se ipsos taxarunt omnia bona nostra per loca, ad quadringentas marcas annuatim.

stow. That book, which they took with them into the pulpit, was MS Laud Misc. 511. In that case, the manuscript was in existence in more or less its present form by 1275.

A second factor to be examined in the dating of MS Laud Misc. 511 is the style of writing. The observation made by N.R. Ker about the change in scribal practice, from writing "above top line" to writing "below top line," which occurred in the thirteenth century, has already been noted. But Ker also draws attention to the differences between professional scribes, who were likelier to adopt the new practice sooner, and the non-professional scribe who would tend to keep to the older style best known to him.[88] MS Laud Misc. 511 contains both scribal styles—hands A, C, and D who write "below top line" and scribe B who writes "above top line." Such a mixture of styles in one book by different scribes, professional or not, would be commoner in the mid- than in the later thirteenth century although, as Ker shows, this argument would hold less well for a non-professional scribe. Possibly, if a non-professional scribe is involved, a contributory factor would be the age at which he was writing a book. If he were a mature man by 1250, he would have learned writing in the earlier decades of the century. Without re-training, and without the incentive of earning his living, it is unlikely that he would modify significantly writing habits developed in youth. If, however, a non-professional scribe were still a young man by 1250, he might be taught to set out a page "below top line" as a matter of course. If this change of scribal practice noted by Ker is valid for MS Laud Misc. 511, then the mixture of writing styles within it would support an earlier rather than a later date for the making of this manuscript.

From the codicological description and context of MS Laud Misc. 511, it is not a monastically related manuscript. It shares a number of features which characterise works of Theology linked with Oxford, and equally linked with the friars. It has no *pecia* marks. It is a single, "one-off" manuscript rather than a copy of a well-known book. What then is the significance of the four scribes? Are they professional or non-professional? Graham Pollard has made helpful comments on thirteenth-century scribes.[89] He distingushes between on the one hand, academic scholars who copied texts for themselves and impecunious students who earned some cash by copying and, on the other hand, the few highly skilled copyists who made

[88] Ker, "From 'above Top Line'," 14.

[89] H.G. Pollard, "The 'pecia' system in the medieval universities" in *Essays presented to N.R. Ker*, 156. See also Chap III, "Scribes and Script" in de Hamel, "Glossed Books."

a living from writing. Only the latter could be described as professional scribes. Whether Pollard's comments can be applied equally to the writing of books outside university towns and to traditional places of learning like London is uncertain; nevertheless, his remarks are useful in trying to assess the writing of the four scribes of our manuscript. The quality of their work is not equivalent to that of many thirteenth century Bibles; but it is still better than the writing found in some informal texts, especially Hands A and C. There is insufficient evidence to know how scribes functioned in a non-academic context, so a small-town making of the manuscript can neither be proved nor disproved. If, however, it were written in a university town, it could be that scribes A, C and D were hired undergraduates. It is difficult to guess what B would be. If, on the other hand, the manuscript was written in the context of a religious community of mendicants, then the geographical location would be immaterial. The conditions of manpower for writing could be met either from members of the community or, in the case of the Dominicans, by hiring lay scribes. In any case, hand B seems to be the oldest of the four. The four scribes fit better into a religious community context than into a university one, with scribe B as an older member.

The third factor to be considered in the dating of this manuscript is the dating of the binding.[90] In the process of book-making the binding is the last stage, but it is not certain in any medieval book that it follows immediately upon the completion of the writing. Neither is it a certainty that a binding contains one homogenous text. But, if the binding is original it can give an upper time limit for the completion of the manuscript. As we have seen above, the style of the binding of MS Laud Misc. 511 belongs to the thirteenth century, the second stage of medieval binding, 1230 to 1300.

But in the one binding of our manuscript there are substantially two books, one longer, one shorter, but both incomplete. One is identified as gatherings i to xv, the second as gatherings xvi and xvii. The different characteristics have been described earlier. But all seventeen gatherings have been put into one binding. Questions arise. Can the same person be responsible for compiling two such different pieces? If the compiler of the first xv gatherings combined the whole, then why did he not put as good order into the second part as into the first? If this compiler did not complete the making of the book, someone else must have added some sermons for the latter part of the *Temporale* together with a small *Sanctorale*,

---

[90] Many articles by Graham Pollard lie behind this section. They are fully noted in the bibliography.

for the whole manuscript seems to share the same column-numbering hand. Behind the binding of MS Laud Misc. 511 there must have been resources greater than those enjoyed by one person with sole responsibility for making a compilation. This binding must have been completed by 1275, when preacher E1 took this sermon collection, in substantially the same form as it is today, into the pulpit at Elstow and preached sermon 230 from the second part of the book.

A fourth factor influencing the discussion of the dating of this manuscript comes from some of the actual sermons. Of the sixteen sermons identified in this manuscript, twelve were in existence as sermons before 1250. Sermons belong to ephemeral rather than to enduring literature. They are often the more effective for being contemporary or near contemporary with their hearers. The past sermons of a contemporary are often popular if the contemporary is of increasing importance, but if his importance dies with him, then his writings also often diminish, even die. Is it not likely that the compiler of our manuscript would include named sermons of Richard Fishacre and Simon of Hinton, either because he knew them or had been taught by one or both of them? If the manuscript were not written until after 1279 or 1283, one is faced with the problem of why only named sermons by Richard Fishacre and Simon of Hinton were included, but equally famous regent-masters in the Oxford *studium* like Robert Kilwardby, William of Hotham, Richard Knapwell, Hugh Sneyth and Hugh of Manchester were omitted. The emphasis of the dating of the known sermon content, while proportionately small, is on the second quarter of the thirteenth century. The fact that the manuscript is a compilation would put its making later than the actual dates of the composition of the known sermons, but not markedly later. Two Advent sermons have some dating evidence: sermon 13 actually possesses a date, 1251; while sermon 14 has an *exemplum* giving a list of the titles of the king of England. The title, *Dux Normanniae*, is missing. By the Treaty of Paris, 1259, the king of England agreed to drop this title from his list.[91] In fact the *exemplum* could be better evidence towards the dating of the manuscript than is the given date.[92] The evidence of the known sermons would suggest that the making of MS Laud Misc. 511 belongs to the third quarter of the thirteenth century.

The last factor to be considered in the dating of the manuscript is a

---

[91] See Chapter 8 n.6 and n.10, see also the Appendix 9, "Selected Texts," for the full transcript of Sermon 13.

[92] See Chapter 8, pp. 257-258.

liturgical one.[93] For a variety of reasons, but particularly to keep unity of observance in the Order of Preachers, and in the Order of Friars Minor to give some shape to the corporate life of worship, both orders began significant liturgical revisions in the mid-thirteenth century. Neither revision, as is the way with matters liturgical, proceeded with harmony or unanimity, and the highest authority in each order had to impose the changes on their respective orders. In the case of the Franciscans, Haymo of Faversham, elected minister-general in 1240, was the originator. At the chapter at Bologna in 1243, he gave to the Franciscans a revised missal and rubrics, based on the practice of the papal chapel. He died in 1244, leaving the revision of the Divine Office incomplete. Unfortunately John of Parma, as minister-general, not realising the incompleteness of Haymo's work, promulgated it in 1247. This led to much confusion, greatly prolonged. In the case of the Dominicans, the chapter at Bologna in 1244 required a liturgical reform to be carried out. The following year the Commission of the Four Friars was established, but their work was unacceptable. Eventually in 1254 the general chapter commissioned Humbert of Romans, the newly elected master-general, to organise the changes and promulgate them. In 1256 the revision of the liturgy was completed. On the whole, as will be argued later, the liturgical order of our manuscript follows the pattern established by the Order of Preachers in 1256. This gives the earliest possible date for the making of MS Laud Misc. 511.

It remains but to look at the interaction of the five factors delineated. While no single factor can be completely conclusive, the convergence of the evidence is strong: the identified sermons point to the second quarter of the thirteenth century; the liturgical evidence points to the early third quarter of the thirteenth century; the scribal style points to the mid-thirteenth century; the manufacture of the book points to a date from 1250 to 1300; the practical solution to the two Elstow preachers giving their ten sermons at the abbey between 1275 and 1283 points to a date prior to 1275. It seems reasonable to conclude that MS Laud Misc. 511 was compiled, written, flourished, and rubricated in two separate parts which were bound as one book either between 1256, the earliest date of the Dominican revision of the liturgy, or 1259, the year Henry III agreed to renounce the title *Dux Normanniae*, and the Fourth Sunday of Lent, 24 March 1275, when the first Elstow preacher used this manuscript for his sermon there.

---

[93] See Appendix 8, "The Liturgical Context of the Manuscript."

4

The Provenance of MS Laud Miscellaneous 511

In default of a direct statement about the ownership, provision and making of a manuscript, provenance has to be established as far as possible by internal evidence. For MS Laud Misc. 511 this falls into three main groups: liturgical practices, changes and links; local information of various kinds; and a further look at the palaeographic information.

In his article, Pelster declared that this manuscript was a Dominican collection of sermons made in Oxford. It is important to examine this claim. Two points could indicate Franciscan links. The first, comparatively minor, is the inscription in a fourteenth-century hand on folio 1, which begins "Reverende pater gardiane...." "Guardian" is the title of the superior in a Franciscan friary. The second is the identification of line numbering in fives as a specifically Franciscan practice. The possibility that the manuscript was Franciscan in origin, that it could have been made in London or Cambridge or almost anywhere in England, had to be investigated.

It has already been established that MS Laud Misc. 511 is a manuscript made in England before 1275. It is not, however, a simple copy of one collection like that of Peraldus in MS Gray's Inn 20; but a preacher's working collection containing not only sermons but also preaching material. Two of its specific palaeographic features, line numbering in fives and arabic numbering of columns, have been shown to be Mendicant as well as academic practices. The inscription referred to could have been jotted down by a borrower. There is no positive evidence to link this manuscript with the Franciscans, but there are several pieces of evidence to confirm a Dominican link. Taken singly these would not be strong enough, but taken together they present a picture which is best interpreted by positing a Dominican provenance of this manuscript.

A. LITURGICAL EVIDENCE

The bias towards a practising preacher is not in itself uniquely Dominican. Franciscans and secular masters were equally popular preachers, sometimes more so. But the Dominicans are first and foremost an Order of Preachers, and their activity in this area, in the provision of both sermons and sermon aids, has been well attested. This manuscript fits into that tradition. It contains sermons, sermon material, some florilegia and annotated *exempla*. The codicological style is not exclusively Dominican but, as seen in the previous chapter, all the practices found in it are found in other manuscripts whose Dominican links are known. There are only three proper names in the manuscript, but two of them are identified as those well established English Dominicans of the mid-thirteenth century, Richard Fishacre and Simon of Hinton. In his *Repertorium*[1] Schneyer had identified a further five sermons: no. 10, by Peraldus OP; nos. 60, 83 and 117 by Petrus de Remis OP; and no. 98 by John of Abbeville. The Dominican link is strengthened by four of these ascriptions. As shown in the previous chapter, further sermons have been identified:[2] three by Petrus de Remis, three by Peraldus and two by Hugh of St. Cher OP. All these sermons are by Dominicans, some of them not only of international standing but also of the earliest generations of Dominican preachers. As seen in the previous chapter, the one possible Franciscan ascription proved false.[3] Thus our manuscript possesses a strong Dominican element in content and in authorship of all but one of the identified sermons.

Further English Dominican links exist in evidence about preachers at the Benedictine abbey of Elstow. In the Fourth Lateran Council, the Church expressed considerable misgivings about the quality of the spiritual life of the faithful. Among others, two pastoral measures, influential not only in the rest of the century but well beyond it, were recommended. Bishops were directed to preach, either themselves or through licensed preachers; and regularity was introduced into the celebration of the sacrament of penance.[4] In practice, attending sermons and going to confession, the popular term for the sacrament of penance, became closely related. The new Orders of Friars Preachers and Friars Minor were pre-eminent in this pastoral work, and many bishops, like Grosseteste, appreciated their contribution to the pastoral care of the faithful.

Religious women too were encouraged to have friars as confessors. The influence of the Dominicans on religious women, notably their own Second Order, but also on the life of Beguines, was part of their work from the outset and, despite efforts to curtail it, remained in the Domini-

---

[1] Schneyer, *Repertorium*, 9: 58-69 and Appendix 4, "Concordance: Schneyer –O'Carroll."

[2] See Chapter 3, n.52.

[3] See Chapter 3, n.49.

[4] Mansi, col. 22, Decrees X and XXI of the Fourth Council of the Lateran, 998-999, 1007-1010. See also Tanner, *EC*, 239-240, 245.

can tradition.[5] The Franciscans also developed a similar pastorate. A.G. Little comments:

> ...it is worth noting that during the later thirteenth and earlier fourteenth centuries the bishops in many dioceses made a point of insisting that the confessors to nuns should be chosen, not from the secular clergy, but from the Mendicant Orders, especially the Minorites.[6]

Apart from the Council of Oxford, which declared that the confessions of nuns were to be made only to priests deputed by the bishop,[7] there seem to be no references to confessors for nuns in the diocesan statutes. A.G. Little, however, records references to bishops' registers.[8] An example, probably characteristic of such exhortations, is from a letter written by Bishop Thomas de Cantilupe to the nuns of Lyngebrook after his visitation made early in 1277.[9] He directs that they are to have a Franciscan or other religious appointed as confessor, or a secular priest, provided that the latter is well educated and of reputable life. No specific injunctions of this kind have been found for Elstow Abbey in the thirteenth century. There are, however, at least two fourteenth-century records of appointments of actual confessors. On 11 July 1333, John de Newport OP was licensed by the bishop of Lincoln to hear the confessions of the nuns of Elstow Abbey.[10] Again on 9 March 1347 John de Newport OP, Nich. de Langetoft OP and a Franciscan were similarly licensed.[11] Thus a Dominican link of hearing confessions at Elstow existed in the first half

[5] For Dominican pastoral care of religious women see W.A. Hinnebusch, *The History of the Dominican Order*, vol. 1 (New York, 1966), 387-393, which relates the conflicting views in the order from 1221 onwards. By 1257 the matter was resolved through the efforts of Hugh of St. Cher and Humbert of Romans. See also Jordan of Saxony, *Epistulae*, ed. A. Walz OP, MOPH 23 (Rome, 1951) and E.W. McDonnell, *The Beguines and Beghards in Medieval Culture* (New Brunswick, NJ, 1954).

[6] A.G. Little, *Studies in English Franciscan History* (Manchester, 1917), 119.

[7] Powicke and Cheny, 1: 124."Confiteantur autem moniales sacerdotibus ab episcopis sibi deputatis."

[8] Little, *Studies*, 119, n1.

[9] R.G. Griffiths and W.W. Capes, ed., *Registrum Thome de Cantilupo, Episcopi Herefordensis AD MCCLXXV-MCCLXXXII*, Canterbury and York Society 2 (1907), 202. "Item deinceps eligatis vobis confessores de commorantibus in nostra diocesi; videlicet de fratribus Minoribus Conventus Herefordie, aut aliis religiosis vel secularibus viris competentis litterature, boneque conversacionis et vite, in dicta diocesi, ut consuevistis."

[10] Emden, "Dominican Confessors," 197.

[11] Emden, "Dominican Confessors," 198.

of the fourteenth century. In this context, it is very likely that the two preachers who were using MS Laud Misc. 511 to preach sermons at Elstow were hearing the confessions of the nuns as well. It is also likely that they were Dominican friars, and that the men we know to have been appointed in the fourteenth century were continuing a pastoral charge that had been with the Dominicans for many decades.[12]

The last element of evidence in the liturgical field for Dominican provenance of our manuscript is that of the organisation and practice of the liturgy.[13] Through the meticulous work of many scholars and especially that of S.J.P. van Dijk, some of the thirteenth-century changes are understood more clearly. Like the sixteenth and twentieth centuries, the thirteenth century witnessed liturgical changes of such dimensions that a new direction was given to liturgy in the western Church. The Dominican and Franciscan Orders were involved in this change. In the Dominican Order the work of liturgical revision was started by the General Chapter in 1245, but in 1254 the General Chapter authorised the fifth Master General, Humbert of Romans, to complete the revision—which was done by 1256—and promulgate it throughout the Order. In the Franciscan Order the work of liturgical organisation was done between 1240 and 1244 by the Minister General, Haymo of Faversham. Clues to the Dominican provenance of this manuscript are to be found in features that distinguished the Dominican from the Franciscan liturgical practices.

The term "liturgy" covers the organisation of Church worship in the Mass, the Divine Office, the celebration of the sacraments, and occasional celebrations. Only the first two elements are considered here. The Mass has always been seen as the centre of all liturgy. In the western Church there were from the fifth century two main liturgical orders: the Romano-African and the Gallic.[14] In the latter there were four different liturgies: the old Spanish liturgy, later known as the Mozarabic rite; the Gallican of the kingdom of the Franks; the Celtic liturgy of Scotland, Ireland, and Northumbria; and the liturgy of Milan. The Roman rite was brought to

---

[12] The nearness of the Franciscan house at Bedford, and the appointment of more than one confessor in 1347 (one being OFM) means that for Elstow, given the paucity of evidence, the possibility of OFM links remain.

[13] Appendix 8, "The Liturgical Context of the Manuscript," contains a fuller examination of the elements only referred to here.

[14] J.A. Jungmann, *The Mass of the Roman Rite*, 2 vols. (New York, 1951); idem, *The Early Liturgy to the time of Gregory the Great* (London: Darton Longman and Todd, 1960) 227-277, 288-307; S.J.P. van Dijk and J.H. Walker, *The Origins of the Modern Roman Liturgy* (London and Westminster Md., 1960) Chapter 2.

Canterbury by St. Augustine of Canterbury. Despite the differences, mainly in the wording of prayers, they shared much in action and in the words of eucharistic consecration. By the thirteenth century the Roman rite was widespread, but with many local variants depending on the traditions of local areas. At this time Mass was a complex celebration, much of it sung, the rest chanted with many different ministers taking interrelated parts. For such ceremonies many different books were required, such as a gospel book for the deacon; an epistle book for the subdeacon; a book of collects for the main celebrant; chant books such as *Graduales* and *Kyriales* for the singers; rubric books or orders of celebration for the master of ceremonies. Such solemn and lengthy services—some of which remain today as High Mass—were common practice in monasteries, cathedrals, religious houses, and any important household chapel with a number of chaplains, such as the Chapel Royal. How far such ceremony was used in a parish church is difficult to ascertain, as little research seems to have been done. It cannot be assumed that the parish celebration was the same as that in the cathedral.

The monastic influence was paramount in the celebration of the Divine Office, which was complex and time-consuming. The latter was the context for the requirement in the first Dominican constitutions that the Office should be celebrated "breviter et succincte."[15] Like the Mass, the celebration of the Office was a group activity, and the participants used a number of different books: antiphoners, psalters, lectionaries, responsorials and so on.

The Fourth Lateran Council of 1215 showed its interest in the liturgy by several canons, not only those relating to sacramental practice, but also those which established minimum standards for the practical and reverent care of churches, altars, sacred vessels, etc.[16] Behind these provisions was an attempt to meet better the needs of the laity. In the papal household, Innocent III's changes in the Office adapted a largely monastic observance for use in the papal chapel. Here the people who celebrated the Office were also responsible for the business of the papal court and chancery; that is, it was a secular—not monastic—group.[17] The reformed papal Office was taken up by some groups of canons beyond the papal court; in particular, the canons of Assisi cathedral welcomed it and began using

---

[15] I Const., *ALKG* 1: 197.

[16] Tanner, *EC*, Fourth Lateran Council, Canons XVII, XIX, XX, XXVII, 243-244, 248.

[17] Van Dijk and Walker, *Origins*, chapter 4; S.J.P. van Dijk, "The Authentic Missal of the Papal Chapel," *Scriptorium* 14 (1960) 257-314.

it.[18] That the papal chapel could introduce its own changes emphasises the fact already noted that, within a strong tradition of action and word, there was considerable flexibility. Local modifications and liturgies were common and, despite the attempts attributed to the papacy,[19] uniformity was neither sought for, nor imposed on, the Church as a whole. The different ways in which the Order of Preachers and the Order of Friars Minor reorganised their respective liturgies is informative for later, as well as thirteenth-century, developments.

In 1979 I published an article showing the pericopes for the Sunday Mass, the *Temporale*, and the major celebrations of Christmas, Epiphany and Easter, in the Dominican and Franciscan liturgies respectively.[20] The differences here led to further comparisons of two kinds, namely other uses and other areas of liturgy, especially the Divine Office. For the former I have revised my published lists by comparing the uses of Paris, Sarum and York with my existing Dominican and Franciscan lists. As far as the last is concerned a detailed comparison of all the elements in the Divine Office has been made only for the liturgy of Advent in the Dominican, Franciscan, Paris, Sarum and York uses. For other liturgical celebrations in the Office, comparisons have been made only for specific feasts. The discussions and full tables showing these investigations are in Appendix 8, "The Liturgical Context of the Manuscript."[21]

What is noteworthy about the Dominican and Franciscan liturgical revisions of the mid-thirteenth century is that the Dominican retains the pattern of the Roman liturgy, while the Franciscan follows the pattern of the papal chapel, stemming from the revisions made by Innocent III and Honorius III. This papal pattern was adopted by the Franciscans via the canons of Assisi, and became eventually the basis of the missal and the liturgical changes of the Council of Trent. It should also be emphasised that the revolution was not so much in the content of the liturgy as in its organisation. In the former the major difference is in timing, so that in some of the *Temporale* the Franciscan is ahead of the Dominican (sometimes by a week, sometimes by a fortnight). In the latter, the simplification of rubrics led to a single missal (and a single Breviary) instead of the huge variety of books, and ultimately to the mode of celebration known as low

---

[18] Van Dijk and Walker, *Origins*, 182.

[19] W.R. Bonniwell, *A History of the Dominican Liturgy 1215-1945* (New York, 1945) 70-77.

[20] M.E. O'Carroll, "The Lectionary for the Proper of the Year in the Dominican and Franciscan Rites of the Thirteenth Century," *AFP* 49 (1979), 79-103.

[21] See below, pp. 358-381.

Mass. In the thirteenth-century liturgical uses, it has become clearer as my investigations have continued that only variants provide the specific and positive clues for an ascription of any ecclesiastical piece such as a sermon to a particular use.

Appendix 8, Table 1[22] shows that the correlation in MS Laud Misc. 511 between the readings of the day and the sermons preached, in every case follows the Dominican and Sarum use, not the Franciscan. Even if the Franciscans preaching in England did not use their own liturgical readings but those common to dioceses and parishes, one would expect that, in a collection containing not only sermons for the people but some for students and a religious community, at least one or two sermons—if the collection were itself Franciscan—would reflect the Franciscan order of liturgical readings. There is nothing positive to suggest any correlation between our manuscript and the Franciscan lectionary. In the sermons of the manuscript there is one correlation of one sermon, no.26 for the First or Second Sunday after the octave of Epiphany, with the order of the Sarum and York readings. This correlation most likely reflects the English aspect of the compiler's own book, and the sermon is either from a collection prior to the Dominican reform or an example of Humbert's acknowledgment, in his letter about the reform, that patience was needed in making the changes. Number 229 is the only sermon in our manuscript from the Common of Saints. Its theme is "Homo quidam peregre proficiscens" (Matt. 25:14). In Table 6[23] are set out the liturgical sources of this particular pericope. It belongs to the Dominican, Paris, Sarum and York uses, but is not an option in the Franciscan use. Where the Second Sunday of Lent is concerned, again the Dominican, Sarum, York reading is followed.

There are, however, other liturgical elements in the manuscript that are significant for identification and which link with the other uses but not necessarily with the Franciscan. This information is set out in Appendix 8, Tables 2 and 3.[24] Their meaning is wider than just identification. These sections show how the Divine Office can be a source of sermon themes, despite the fidelity of this collection to the general practice of taking the sermon theme from the epistle or gospel of the day.[25] Themes are taken from the Breviary: from hymns, like sermon 89; from antiphons, like

[22] Appendix 8, pp. 360-370.

[23] Appendix 8, pp. 380-381.

[24] Appendix 8, pp. 371-373.

[25] It is worth reiterating that the Divine Office is profoundly scriptural in its content, and that antiphons, versicles, responses, and responsories are often direct quotations from the psalms.

the sermons on Our Lady, nos. 231-234; from the invitatory, as in several Advent sermons.[26] These choices are all found in the Dominican, Paris, Sarum and York uses. All, except the Advent invitatories, are found in the Franciscan use.

If there were no other evidence available about provenance, one would hesitate to say that the sermons in our manuscript were preached on the liturgy of the Dominican use; but, in the context of the liturgical information in the main body of the collection, these sermons based on the Divine Office fit with the Dominican aspect already seen. This is particularly so of the small sanctoral section. Among the six sermons, four are about Our Lady. Devotion to the Mother of God is, and has been from the start, the main sanctoral devotion in the Order of Preachers. One other of these sermons is for the feast of the Exaltation of the Cross, when the English province held its provincial chapter.[27]

There is one more item of liturgical information in the manuscript which fits in a Dominican context, namely the use of the term *Office/Officium* for what the Franciscans and later Roman use call the *Introit/Introitus*. Appendix 8, Table 2[28] illustrates this. The sermon themes, and in a few cases, references within the sermons themselves, all fit exactly with the Dominican use.

The convergence of the different aspects of information about, and contained in, the sermons of this manuscript, whether codicological, literary, historical or liturgical, is the most powerful reason for stating that MS Laud Misc. 511 is a collection of sermons compiled by a Dominican friar. In this context it is possible to be more categorical about the dating of the manuscript and to assert that the lower time limit for the making of this manuscript cannot be before 1256, the year of the revised liturgy of the Order of Preachers.

B. Local References

As we have seen, Pelster made several statements about MS Laud Misc. 511. A more prolonged study shows that his judgement about its dating has to be modified from post-1279 to 1256-1275, but that his statement about its Dominican character is upheld. It is opportune to discuss the third assertion: that this manuscript was made in Oxford.

[26] Appendix 8, pp. 373, 377-379.
[27] Galbraith, *Constitution*, 261-265.
[28] Appendix 8, pp. 371-372.

First it seems clear that this manuscript is English. There are many exempla relating to *rex anglie*, but very few to *rex francie*; a number of real life stories are English.[29] Some of the idiom behind the Latin is English,[30] as in the sermons for Advent. Two of the three named preachers are well known Englishmen. The manuscript contains six examples of Middle English.[31] All these facts point to England as the country of origin.

By 1256, as the map of Dominican settlement shows, there were about thirty Dominican priories in England; and one clue to the place of origin is the use of the manuscript at Elstow. When Pelster's dating was accepted, it seemed that the place of origin and of the visitation structure were linked.[32] The nearest Dominican house to Elstow is Dunstable in the Cambridge visitation. Elstow is more or less equidistant from Oxford and Cambridge, but is not on the Icknield Way, which at that time was one of the main links between these two places. So Cambridge was a genuine contender for the genesis of this manuscript. With the revised dating of the manuscript, however, visitation links while possibly embryonic were not definitive, and so Cambridge was no more significant in this matter than any other priory in the province.

Another factor was examined, namely Elstow's ecclesiastical links. First, Elstow is in the Bedford archdeaconry within the diocese of Lincoln. The bishop had the right to licence confessors, and it was likelier that he would licence friar confessors from priories within the diocese rather than from outside it. Oxford priory is in the Lincoln diocese, but so too are the priories of Dunstable, Stamford, Northampton, Leicester, Boston and Lincoln. There is a further limiting factor in that religious houses often had ecclesiastical links with the areas in which they held lands.[33] Such links were as strong as the links in the locality of the religious house. Many Elstow holdings are found in the east and central Midlands, especially in

[29] MS Laud Misc. 511, sermon 33, fol. 35b line 20; sermon 72, fol. 83vb line 3; sermon 232, fol. 203a line 33. See also the section on sermon material in Chapter 6.

[30] L.J. Bataillon, "Approaches to the study of Medieval Sermons," *Leeds Studies in English*, NS 11 (1980), 22-24.

[31] See Appendix 1: *Serm.* **78, 95, 96, 106a, 130** and **134**.

[32] M.E. O'Carroll, "The Educational Organisation of the Dominicans in England and Wales 1221-1348: a multidisciplinary approach," *AFP* 50 (1980) 23-62.

[33] I owe this information to Dr R.W. Hunt who suggested that an examination of land-holdings of a religious house can indicate the geographical direction of its ecclesiastical links.

Bedfordshire and Oxfordshire, but very few in East Anglia.[34]

If Elstow land interests are correlated with Dominican houses it appears more likely that the Dominican preachers at Elstow came from Dunstable, Northampton or Oxford. It must be noted that the manuscript was not necessarily made in the house to which the Elstow preachers belonged. Dunstable is on the Icknield Way, about ten miles south of Elstow; Northampton and Dunstable are on the Watling Street. There is no easy direct route from Oxford to Elstow. Of the triangle—Oxford, Elstow, Northampton—the journeys of Oxford to Northampton or Elstow to Northampton are easiest.[35] It is also significant that between 1260 and 1265 Northampton had a budding University,[36] fostered partly by a migration of Cambridge students and masters in late 1260, and an addition of Oxford students during the suspension of the Oxford Schools from 1264 to 1265. The Dominicans had been in Northampton since 1233. About the eighth foundation, it was a well-established priory with about thirty-five to forty friars, though not so important as Oxford. The Oxford Blackfriars was the first foundation, in 1221, and had been designated by the general chapters of 1246 to 1248 a *studium generale*, although this was not implemented until after 1260. The Dominican house of second importance was London, for the size of the community and of the school. It would seem that the Dominican link was west of Elstow, and possibly with Dunstable or Northampton or Oxford.

C. PALAEOGRAPHIC EVIDENCE

Further evidence for the place of origin of MS Laud Misc. 511 comes from the codicology of the manuscript. It is an addition to the small group of manuscripts already identified as having arabic-numbered columns and

---

[34] S.R. Wigram, *Chronicles of the Abbey of Elstow* (Oxford, 1885), 12-40.

Bedfordshire	8 holdings	Middlesex	1 holding
Buckinghamshire	4 holdings	Huntingdonshire	1 holding
Hertfordshire	1 holding	Northamptonshire	3 holdings
Leicestershire	1 holding	Oxfordshire	6 holdings
Lincolnshire	2 holdings	Gloucestershire	1 holding
Essex	2 holdings		

Three holdings were geographically unidentified.

[35] Using the existing roads based on the Roman road system, I explored the communication links noted.

[36] C.H. Lawrence, "The University of Oxford and the Chronicle of the Baron's War," *EHR* 95 (1980) 99-113.

line-numbering in fives, and as having a link both with the study of Theology, especially at Oxford, and with Mendicant scholastic practice. There is, however, another manuscript whose written appearance of two column blocks with small running titles—red—in the top margin, the appearance of which forcibly reminded me of our manuscript: MS Add 49999,[37] for many years on permanent exhibition in the King's Library of the British Museum. This manuscript proved to be a psalter, probably written in Oxford, most definitely illuminated in Oxford in the second quarter of the thirteenth century by William de Brailles. In a masterpiece of detection,[38] Graham Pollard reconstructed the life story of William de Brailles, who had his workshop in Catte street—on the present site of All Souls opposite the Radcliffe Camera. We know that William decorated a Bible for the Oxford Blackfriars.[39] So in its first fifteen gatherings our manuscript shares an unusual feature with an identified Oxford manuscript.

At this point it is necessary to return to the unresolved problem of the four scribes of MS Laud Misc. 511. Certainly, the manuscript makes more technical sense now that its ascription to a religious community of Dominicans is clearer. Dominicans were allowed to spend a day a week on copying sermons; but they were also allowed to hire scribes, while priories with *studia generalia* were able to give licences for visiting scribes.[40] In his *Instructiones de Officiis Ordinis*,[41] Humbert of Romans lays down rules about the making of books within the priory by hired scribes. They are to work under the watchful eye of one of the brethren in a place separate from the conventual quarters. Then there is the fact of the contract roughed out on folio 1 of the manuscript.[42] By their choice of poverty,

---

[37] British Library, MS Add 49999 [olim Dyson Perrins MS 4].

[38] H.G. Pollard, "William de Brailles," *BLR* 5 (1954-6), 202-209.

[39] Bodleian Library, MS Lat Bibl. e 7 [olim Dyson Perrins MS 5].

[40] K.W. Humphreys, *The Book Provisions of the Mediaeval Friars 1215-1400* (Amsterdam, 1964), 26; see also W. A. Hinnebusch, *The History of the Dominican Order*, vol. 2 (New York, 1973), 210.

[41] Humbert of Romans, *De Vita Regulari*, 2: 266-267.

[42] MS Laud Misc. 511, folio 1, bottom margin: "Dominica proxima post festum sancti Leodegarii, invenit michi Johannes Gile fideiussores, scilicet, Ricardum Blithe et Johannem le[Go]ode, quod fideliter operabitur et ministrabit tam in absencia quam in presentia, et tam noctibus quam in diebus in cu[ri]a et domo pernoctabit? tam festis quam feriis diebus secundum quod ei precipitur, et recipiet singulis quindenis unum bussellum siliginis, et in toto termine a fest' S Michaelis usque ad annunciationem beate Marie [d]uodecim denarios pro mercede." Coxe, *Laudian*

individual friars were precluded from entering into a contract of service as there outlined. But a lay scribe employed in the priory could practise writing out a specific contract for Johannes Gile on part of one of the rejected bifolia. I could find no names in Salter's *Medieval Oxford* to match the names in the contract,[43] although the surname "Good" (still to be found in some parts of Oxfordshire today) is recorded there a number of times. Of the four hands in MS Laud Misc. 511, hands C and D could be hired scribes. But, bearing in mind the comments of Pollard and de Hamel about the use of scribes both cleric and lay and realising that some of the young friars in the community could have come from the ranks of penniless students, I conclude that MS Laud Misc. 511 was written by a group of scribes, most likely Dominicans; but the possibility that there was some contribution from a hired scribe has to remain open.

Those who wrote the first fifteen gatherings of our manuscript were working from at least thirteen source books. We know that three of the source books, *Liber Proprius, Parvus Liber Rubeus, Liber Rubeus Minor,* containing as they do identified sermons in existence by 1250, were themselves compilations, probably in chronological order. The manuscript is, as it were, a second generation compilation. Although the writing was done in liturgical sequence, many of the source-books must have been readily available, as it were "on reserve." The compiler must have kept a careful check on the task to ensure as successfully as he did the very high standard of accuracy in the liturgical order. The compiler, the friar who used his "own book" as one of the sources, was the inspiration behind the first fifteen gatherings. Someone else took responsibility for binding the first fifteen gatherings, with another unequal and independently produced part-book of at least two gatherings, to produce the manuscript virtually as it exists today. So the manuscript was a corporate effort.

D. Conclusion

When we put the different factors enumerated above together and try to establish a possible place for the making of our manuscript, we can clarify some of the elements we are looking for. They include a Dominican priory which had several sermon collections which could be taken out of general

---

Manuscripts, Addenda, p. 567.

[43] H.E. Salter, *Medieval Oxford*, OHS 100 (Oxford, 1936); *Survey of Oxford* (Oxford, 1960) 19.

use to be available for the copyists, which would have had a good relationship with local scribes and fairly large numbers of cheap employees
to draw on, and which would have received sermon books from the continent rapidly. Despite Northampton's serious claim for consideration,
London and Oxford are the most likely houses to fulfil these conditions.
But London does not have any relationship at all with Elstow. Of the two,
the edge lies with Oxford, the site of the named *studium generale*, the
original foundation of Dominican settlement in England, the home for
some time of both Richard Fishacre and Simon of Hinton. I conclude that
it is highly probable that MS Laud Misc. 511 was made in Oxford, although I do not think there is enough evidence to be as definite about its
place of origin as is Pelster.

5

An Audience for the Sermons

In the last two chapters we have been preoccupied with our manuscript, examining it in minute detail, establishing its date, its possible provenance, its Dominican genesis, and we have gained an overall picture of its chief contents: 234 items, mostly sermons. In the Dominican tradition of "usefulness," the main purpose of such a book as MS Laud Misc. 511 would be actual preaching. One of the problems which has faced students of medieval sermons is the identification of the audience for which the sermon is intended. According to the theory of the *artes praedicandi*, sermons fall into several categories: university sermons or *sermones ad scolares*;[1] sermons to the clergy, *ad clerum*; to the laity, *ad populum*; to specific groups in society, *ad status*. The best known of these model collections is that of Humbert of Romans, fifth master-general of the Dominicans.[2]

A. Does the Audience Matter?

Many modern students of sermons taking seriously the theory of the *artes praedicandi* have expended much time and energy on this question of identifying the audience to whom the sermons they see before them in manuscript or print were preached. In her seminal study of the sermons of Stephen Langton, Phyllis Barzillay Roberts indicates in an appendix a classification of sermons according to audiences.[3] In the case of sermons *ad status*, preachers such as Humbert of Romans in Part II of his *De Eruditione*

---

[1] Regarding the category of university sermons, *sermones ad scolares*, there is a growing consensus that the term "university sermon" should be restricted to formal occasions when a sermon would be preached *coram universitate*, and for those academic exercises when a bachelor of theology became a master. (IMSS discussions at biennial symposium, 1979; also exchanges with Père Bataillon.)

[2] M. de la Bigne, ed., *Maxima Bibliotheca Veterum Patrum* (Lyons, 1677), vol. 25, Humbert of Romans, *De Eruditione Religiosorum Praedicatorum*; Simon Tugwell OP, *Early Dominicans: Selected Writings* (London, 1982) 181-384; W.M. Conlon OP, *Treatise of Preaching* (Westminster Md., 1951).

[3] Phyllis Barzillay Roberts, *Stephanus de Lingua-Tonante: Studies in the Sermons of Stephen Langton* (Toronto: PIMS, 1968) Appendix A, 217.

have the audience in the forefront of their minds. The question about the audience for which the sermon is intended is being asked in the wrong context.

Students of sermons work with written sources, existing in hundreds of thousands of extant manuscripts which bear powerful silent witness both to the creativity and to the busy copying of preachers and scribes. But the written sermon in full or in summary is only the tip of the iceberg, for most mediaeval sermons were never recorded; many remain a jumble of notes as in MS Hatton 107.[4] The medieval sermon is first and foremost an oral and aural form to communicate the word of God in information for the formation of Christians. In this it is part of the traditional task and practice of the Church in handing on the message.[5] Like the teacher in the modern classroom, the medieval preacher was trying to communicate with a group of people in front of him. The good teacher or lecturer selects from the written prepared material what is most effective for the current class. What is said may not tally exactly with the teacher's written text. A similar marriage of knowledge and practical skill characterises the good medieval preacher. The question then of to which audience a sermon was preached is relevant only in the actual communication of the sermon, valid for the first occasion on which the sermon was preached or for the identified specific use of actual sermons later. So for the majority of sermons in writing available to scholars for study, the question of the audience is irrelevant. The preacher using the written sermon had the freedom to adapt his material to the group before him. The written form of the medieval sermon then is secondary in importance to the spoken form and it is, unlike written sermons of later centuries, a purely utilitarian literary form. But if the preacher did give actual information about his use of a written sermon, then it is proper to declare that the audience does matter. It is fair to conclude that in sermon studies the audience only matters if it has been specified by the preacher himself or by the sermon reporter.

We are indeed fortunate that the annotation of thirteen sermons in our manuscript indicates that the book was used for actual preaching, and that ten of these sermons were preached at the Benedictine nunnery at

---

[4] Oxford, Bodleian Library, MS Hatton 107.

[5] International Medieval Sermon Symposium (Oxford, 1982), *Report*, 25-29. The nature of the medieval sermon as an oral/aural event was demonstrated most interestingly when two sermons, one of Thomas Jorz OP and one of a 14c anonymous preacher, were delivered, the first in Latin, the second in Middle English. Both sermons were surprisingly clear to follow. The pattern of divisions, repetitions and rhythmic endings was, in practice, an aid to listening.

Elstow between 1275 and 1283 by at least two, possibly three, Dominicans. They are preacher E1, who preached three sermons in 1275 and one in 1278; preacher E2, who preached three sermons there between 1277 and 1279; and, if the palaeographical differences in annotation are not strong enough to postulate a third friar, a further three sermons between 1281 and 1283. We know from Lincoln episcopal records that two Dominicans were appointed as confessors at Elstow, namely John of Newport and Nicholas of Langetoft, in the first half of the fourteenth century. Many of the dates on which the sermons were preached at Elstow are either in the first week of March or around March 20th, liturgically in Lent, so the thirteenth-century friars could have been confessors as well as preachers to this community. The convent they came from could be Dunstable or Northampton or Oxford.[6] It is possible then to gather information and partially reconstruct the actual audience for these specific sermons: the Benedictine nuns of Elstow.

In Elstow there is a meeting of the monastic and mendicant modes of religious life.[7] Already in the decades prior to 1275 many women had shown interest in and enthusiasm for the *vita apostolica*. In the thirteenth century, however, freedom for women to act in the same manner as men did not exist; and religious women also required pastoral care from the men. This was a particular quandary for the Church authorities. In the first place, it was commonly accepted that women belonged to their fathers; and their fathers gave them into the care of their husbands. For those women, mostly from the upper classes, who did not marry but entered convents, the Church had to exercise this element of masculine control. In the second place, it was commonly assumed that, following the example of Eve, women were an occasion, even a cause, of sin for men. This too required ecclesiastical control. Different solutions had been tried: double monasteries as at Fontevrault and in the Gilbertines; female counterparts of male orders, as in the Cistercian and Premonstratensian nuns. Increasingly, however, the ambiguities of ecclesiastical attitudes to women,

[6] See Chapter 3, pages 109-113, and Chapter 4, pages 119-120, 125-126 for the detailed information about the preachers and sermons at Elstow.

[7] See Felicitas Corrigan, *Benedictine Tapestry* (London: DLT, 1991); C.H. Lawrence, *Medieval Monasticism*, 2nd ed. (London: Longmans, 1989); Le Goff, *Medieval World*; *Medieval Women*, ed. D. Baker, SCH Subsidia 1 (Oxford: Basil Blackwell, 1978), see particularly chapter 1 "Monks" and chapter 8 "Women and the Family"; *Women in the Church*, ed. W.J. Sheils and Diana Wood, SCH 27 (Oxford: Basil Blackwell, 1990); Sally Thompson, *Women Religious: The Founding of English Nunneries after the Norman Conquest* (Oxford: Clarendon Press, 1991).

whether religious or lay, led to very strict legislation for separation in the Gilbertines and, in the Cistercians, abandonment of the cure of feminine souls. The Dominicans, already well-known for their links with the followers of Mary of Oignies and with the beguines of Flanders, took with considerable reluctance the Cistercians' place. They were no less immune to the ecclesiastical ambivalence about the pastoral care of women religious than were the Cistercians. Despite, as we have noted above, many efforts on the part of some of their membership to relinquish this pastoral task, the Dominican Order remained in practice laden with much responsibility for nuns and beguines. Although inspiring, even exemplary, patterns of friendship between men and women religious, such as Benedict and Scholastica, Francis and Clare, Jordan of Saxony and Diana d'Andalo existed, such relationships indicating a genuine human equality betwen men and women, were the exception. In the daily reality of religious life for women in the thirteenth century, it is clear that the way of apostolic life was no more open to them than it was to laymen. Only religious and clerical men possessed that option. In fact, many freedoms religious women had enjoyed in previous centuries were in the thirteenth century eroded in favour of increasing requirements for the confinement of nuns within the monastic enclosure. This is the general background for our enquiry into the Elstow community.

B. THE ELSTOW COMMUNITY

Approached on the road from London, one-and-a-half miles south of Bedford, the village of Elstow appears much as it must have done for many centuries: farmland, clumps of trees, a stream meandering through water meadows. On the left, a church far larger than the usual English parish church stands on a slight rise. Elstow High Street is bordered by many restored brick and timber-framed cottages. A turn to the left by the inn leads to a gravelled road running between the common on the right[8] and a wall to the left, beside which are a field and the present churchyard. It is rare in the late twentieth century to be able to discern so readily the pattern of settlement of a late medieval village. We can reconstruct some of the history of Elstow from what is on the ground, what is in the ground,

---

[8] On the common stands a fifteenth-century building known as the Moot Hall. It has associations with John Bunyan.

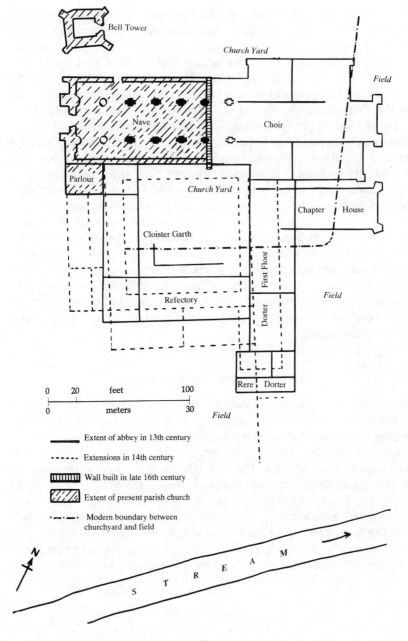

Bell Tower

Church Yard

Field

Nave

Choir

Parlour

Church Yard

Chapter | House

Cloister Garth

First Floor

Refectory

Dorter

Field

Rere | Dorter

Field

| 0 | 20 | feet | 100 |
| 0 | | meters | 30 |

——— Extent of abbey in 13th century

- - - - - Extensions in 14th century

Wall built in late 16th century

Extent of present parish church

—·—·— Modern boundary between
churchyard and field

N

S T R E A M

PLAN OF ELSTOW ABBEY

adapted from David Baker, *Excavations at Elstow Abbey, 1965-1970*

and what is in records.[9]

The church, which looks ill-proportioned, with a height almost equal to the length of the present church (about 100 feet/30 meters), consists of most of the nave of the former abbey church, originally 185 to 200 feet (55 to 60 meters) long. The plan shows that the foundations of the retro-choir and apse are situated beyond the present graveyard, in a field. As the lay-out follows a traditional Benedictine plan of the south-facing kind,[10] it is comparatively simple to reconstruct the position of the main buildings: chapter house, dormitory, refectory and western range. Whether the infirmary existed in the traditional south-eastern position can only be answered by further excavation. The church was the first stone building, raised, as the nave arcading and clerestory show, in the late Romanesque style. The tympanum above the north door, a lovely bas-relief of Christ with the apostles Peter and John, indicates what some of the decoration could have been.[11] By the mid-twelfth century the main conventual buildings, including a chapter house at least sixty feet (eighteen meters) in length, were in existence. At this time the cloisters were probably a lean-to timber construction.

The excavations of 1965 to 1970, described by Baker, show that the abbey underwent several extensive building programmes. In the thirteenth century a new west front extended the church and a monastic parlour—now the vestry—was built, a room with a beautiful groined roof supported by a single slender central pillar. At the eastern end of the church a new apse was built. In the fourteenth century a wholesale rebuilding of the conventual buildings occurred, moving the structures about fifteen feet (4.5 meters) to the west, while the refectory range was extended southwards. The cloisters were rebuilt in stone. How the community functioned on a building site is a real question. Northwest of the abbey church is a free-standing bell tower, dating from the fifteenth to the early sixteenth century. This probably replaced the separate parish church, of which the thirteenth-century records speak. Before the Dissolution the villagers were already sharing the abbey church with the nuns. In the late sixteenth century the people walled up their portion of the nave to make the existing

[9] S.R. Wigram, *Chronicles of the Abbey of Elstow* (Oxford, 1885); a nineteenth-century compilation of records, including charters, pertaining to Elstow. Eileen Power, *Medieval English Nunneries* (Cambridge, 1922); this book has much sporadic information on Elstow. David Baker, *Excavations at Elstow Abbey, 1965-1970* (Bedford, 1970).

[10] Baker, *Excavations*, 9.

[11] It is in a similar tradition, although not as large, as the Romanesque sculpture of Christ and the raising of Lazarus in Chichester Cathedral.

parish church, while the choir, apse and conventual buildings became a useful quarry for the neighbourhood. The structural evidence, both on and in the ground, indicates that Elstow was a rich foundation.

From the written records we can reconstruct a partial history of the community who lived in these splendid buildings. According to Dugdale,[12] Elstow was founded about 1078 by Judith, niece of the Conqueror, after the execution of her Saxon husband, Waltheof, earl of Huntingdon. The foundation was dedicated to the Holy Trinity, Our Lady and St. Helen, and extensively endowed.[13] In economic terms it was a wealthy foundation among women religious in England. By 1160 Elstow had over forty-six land holdings. Some of the land was held by a number of charters. As well Elstow had received from Henry II one charter permitting the nuns free warren on all their lands, and one granting a four-day fair around the feast of the Holy Cross, 3 May.[14] By the mid-fourteenth century, the land holdings numbered seventy-one to seventy-five, while on the eve of the Dissolution, the total was ninety-four.[15] The income of the Abbey in the thirteenth and fourteenth centuries is not known, although Knowles and Hadcock quote a figure of £112 in 1291.[16] Using the financial records from the Dissolution it is possible to work out Elstow's comparative financial position from 1535-1539.[17] Among Benedictine nunneries Elstow was eighth out of the top ten, and eleventh in all women's religious houses (see Table 1). Allowing for inflation rates between the thirteenth and sixteenth centuries, it is unlikely that there was much change in the relative position of the two groups of top ten Benedictine men and women, both in themselves and as male and female. One thing is very clear. Incomes of women's religious communities, even the richest, tended to be three-figure totals, while the equivalent men's religious communities had four-figure incomes. Some of this difference reflects different sizes of community, and some of it reflects the relative poverty of the women's religious houses compared with those of the men.

---

[12] W. Dugdale, *Monasticon Anglicanum* (London, 1655-1673), 3 vols. ed R. Dodsworth (London, 1846), 3: 411: Judith comitissa Waleri comitis sponsa fundavit ecclesiam in villa de Helenestow, tempore Gulielmi primi, et sancti moniales ibi constituit. Testes donationis, Robertus comes de Mellent. Ecclesia dedicata Trinitate, Mariae, et Helenae.

[13] Wigram, 12-14.

[14] Wigram, 42, 43.

[15] Wigram, 207-208.

[16] Knowles and Hadcock, 258.

[17] Knowles and Hadcock, 209-233.

TABLE 1. ANNUAL INCOME OF BENEDICTINE NUNS AND MONKS

from returns at the Dissolution c. 1535

Nuns	£ p.a.	Rank Order	Monks	£ p.a.
Shaftesbury	1166	1	Westminster	3470
Barking	862	2	Glastonbury	3311
Wilton	601	3	St. Albans	2101
Amesbury (Font.)	494	4	Reading	1938
Romsey	393	5	Abingdon	1876
Wherwell	339	6	Ramsey	1761
St. Helens (London)	320	7	Bury St. Edmunds	1656
ELSTOW	284	8	Tewkesbury	1598
Godstow	274	9	St. Augustine's (Cant.)	1413
Nuneaton (Font.)	253	10	Evesham	1183

One other form of income possessed by Elstow came from the giving of "titles," guarantees of a living to an ordinand from amongst the holdings of churches. The exact nature of the financial arrangement reached between the abbey and the ordinand is not known. Twenty-seven of these were made between 1291 and 1297.[18] Some limited profit must have accrued to the abbey. As Eileen Power has shown, religious women were at a disadvantage, rarely being able—unlike the men—to manage their affairs directly. They had to employ business managers, with all the potential for loss that that entailed. One of the problems noted in episcopal visitations proved to be economic weakness and/or mismanagement. Building, of course, is a traditional impoverisher of religious houses, and we have seen that Elstow had building programmes in the thirteenth and fourteenth centuries.[19] In 1387 Bishop John Buckingham left injunctions for the then abbess of Elstow, Anastasia Duyn, about economic management:

> Let the Abbess for the government of the aforesaid monastery have faithful servants in especial for the government and supervision without waste of the husbandry and the manors and stock and woods of the aforesaid house;

---

[18] Rosalind T. Hill, ed., *The Rolls and Register of Bishop Oliver Sutton 1280-99*, 8 vols. (Lincoln Record Society, 1948-1986), 3: xiii-xiv.

[19] Power, *Nunneries*, 161-236, especially 228.

the which the Abbess herself is bound, if she can, to supervise in person, or else let her cause them to be industriously supervised by others; and to look after the external and internal business of the house and to prosecute it outside, let her appoint also some man of proven experience and of mature age.

In practice it was probably very difficult for a group of women living in a religious community to be independent in their finances, in their local management of property or in their accounting. Rather they were dependent in varying degrees on male assistance. This dependence is strongly noted by Sally Thompson in her study of women religious from 1066,[20] confirming the conclusions made seventy years before of Eileen Power. It can be assumed that the economic position of Elstow in the thirteenth century was modest and, in times of building expenditure or weak leadership, precarious.

Lastly, in economic and social terms the abbey lands were held directly of the king. When the abbess died or resigned, the abbey and all its properties fell to the king. Moreover, royal permission to elect a successor had to be sought. The task of asking for this was fulfilled by two proctors, often members—sometimes obedientiaries—of the community, who travelled to court for the purpose. It is this licence-giving which is recorded in the Patent Rolls. From its records, together with references from episcopal registers and sometimes from contemporary chronicles, a list of the abbesses can be gained. Only the thirteenth-century ones are included here:[21]

1222-1233   Mabel[22]
1233-1241   Wymarca[23]
1241-1251   *Agnes of Westbury*,[24] resigned
1251-1258   Albreda de Saunford[25]
1258-1281   Anora de Baskerville,[26] disputed election

[20] Thompson, *Women Religious*, 4.

[21] Italic names indicate proctorship at Court to seek permission to elect.

[22] Wigram, 146; *Calendar of the Patent Rolls, Henry III to Edward III 1216-1292*, prepared by J.G. Black and others under the superintendence of the deputy Keeper of the Records, M.C. Maxwell-Lyte, (London, 1891 proceeding), hereinafter *CPR* and relevant monarch; *CPR, H. III*, 1232-47, 7.

[23] *CPR, H.III*, 1232-47, 8, 13, 154; F.N. Davis, ed., *Dioecesis Lincolniensis, Rotuli Roberti Grosseteste*, Canterbury and York Society 10 (1910-1913), 318.

[24] *CPR, H.III*, 1232-47, 225; *CPR, H.III*, 1247-58, 88.

[25] *CPR, H.III*, 1247-58, 90, 622; Davis, *Dioecesis*, 335-6.

[26] *CPR, H.III*, 1247-58, 630. "In consideration of her weakness she may do her fealty to the said Henry (Bishop of Lincoln) instead of coming in person to the King."

1281-1294   Beatrice de Scoteney[27]
1294-1314   *Clemencia de Balliol,*[28] resigned disputed election

The leadership of the community lay in the hands of these women. Most of them came from aristocratic or landed families, as did the majority of the nuns in the community. In later times, women of newly-wealthy families would be accepted. On the whole, unlike the modern Church, monastic life for women was open only to those of gentle birth.[29] Some of these women chose it from a real sense of vocation, some as a preferable alternative to being unmarried in a parental or fraternal home.

As with all Benedictines, the Divine Office was the chief work of the community. The organisation of the practicalities of community life lay with the abbess and the obedientiaries, so some of the time was spent in administration. The number of persons in the community is not known, although Knowles and Hadcock give a total of nineteen in 1441.[30] Eileen Power judges that in the sixteenth century only four out of 111 women's religious houses had more than thirty members. She places Elstow among eight houses with between twenty and thirty members.[31] A community of about twenty would be barely large enough for all necessary administrative and liturgical functions.

Whether the nuns were learned, like Benedictine nuns in the modern Church, is questionable. The quality of their education is difficult to establish. In the thirteenth century, Latin was essential for a literary education. French was the language of the court and of the aristocracy, as well as some form of Anglo-Norman; English the language of the peasantry and of most townsfolk, although the use of English was moving upwards socially. Both French and English were developing fast; conventions of spelling, pronunciation and grammar were evolving but not standardised. So while they could be used for reading and writing, it was easier to use Latin for all educational functions. The difficulty English nuns had with understanding Latin was noted by several bishops.[32] It is probable that

---

[27] *CPR, Ed.I, 1271-81,* 463; *CPR, Ed.I, 1292-1301,* 86; Wigram, 79-80.

[28] *CPR, Ed.I, 1292-1301,* 87; *CPR, Ed.II, 1313-17,* 200.

[29] Eileen Power, *Medieval Women,* ed. M. M. Postan (Cambridge, 1975), 89-90.

[30] Knowles and Hadcock, 258.

[31] Power, *Nunneries,* 3; the 8 houses are Elstow, the Minories, Nuneaton, Denny, Romsey, Wherwell, Dartford, St Mary's Winchester.

[32] Power, *Nunneries,* 247-9 where she notes that Archbishop Pecham writes to the nuns at Godstow, sometimes in Latin, sometimes in French. See also R.G. Griffiths and W.W. Capes, ed., *Registrum Thome de Cantilupo, Episcopi Herefordensis AD MCCLXXV-MCCLXXXII,* Canterbury and York Society 2 (1907), 202: "Hanc quidem nostram

the Elstow nuns had enough Latin to be able to sing or recite the Divine Office, but whether their Latin was good enough for them to know the meaning of what was sung or said is a separate matter. According to Eileen Power, the level of education among nuns was low, and by no means equivalent to that of the men.[33] For Elstow itself we know very little about any tradition of scholarship. It is possible, however, using the same groups of Benedictine houses studied for income, to look at their respective ownership of books as recorded in Ker's *Medieval Libraries*[34] (see Table 2). Of the thousands of books in their scattered libraries, Ker has identified at least 935 manuscripts and twenty printed books belonging to the top ten houses of Benedictine men before the Dissolution. For the top ten Benedictine nunneries he lists only thirty-seven manuscripts and no printed books. Of these thirty-seven manuscripts only five are neither prayerbooks, psalters, calendars or spiritual writing.

The five manuscripts are:[35] a late twelfth-century copy of Peter Comestor's *Historia Scholastica* and some of Hugh of St. Victor's works commissioned by C. de Chanvil, abbess of Elstow; two works belonging to Nuneaton, a thirteenth-century French version of some of Grosseteste's works, and a thirteenth-to-fourteenth-century copy of Giraldus Cambrensis; a fourteenth-century *Chronicon* belonging to Romsey; and a fifteenth-century work in French of writings of St. Augustine and St. Bernard owned by Barking. So in the thirteenth century Elstow possessed at least one book. It seems clear that education and scholarship were related on the one hand to the clerical status of the Benedictine men, and not to the religious status of Benedictine men and women; and on the other to the

---

epistolam per vestros penitentiarios plures in anno, in lingua Gallica vel Anglica, quam melius noveritis."

[33] Power, *Nunneries*, 237-255. Nicholas Orme, *English Schools in the Middle Ages* (London, 1973), 52-55. See also Power, *Medieval Women*, 76-78.

[34] Ker, *Medieval Libraries*, 2-3, 6, 16-22, 40-47, 77, 80-81, 90-91, 93, 140, 153-154, 154-158, 164-168, 177, 188, 195-197, 198.

[35] Barking: Oxford, Magdalen College, MS lat 41. Romsey: London, BL, MS Lansdowne 436. Nuneaton: Grosseteste—Cambridge, Fitzwilliam Museum, MS McClean 123; G. Cambrensis—Douai, Bibl. mun., MS 887. Elstow: London, BL, MS Roy 7 F iii, fol. 196v: "Scriptus est liber iste anno tertio coronationis Regis Ricardi quem scribere fecit C. de Chanvil, bone memorie Abbatissa beate Maria de Helenstow, in eruditionem et profectum conventus sui et ceterorum inspicientium. Hunc librum scripsit Robertus filius Radulphi discipulus et scriptor ultimus magistri Roberti Bonni de Bedeford' quorum anime...." Although the scribe is identified, Dr R.W. Hunt was of the opinion that it was more likely that the manuscript was actually written in Paris, not Bedford, as had been thought.

TABLE 2. OWNERSHIP OF MANUSCRIPTS AND PRINTED BOOKS

by the top ten houses of Benedictine nuns and monks respectively

Nuns	mss	books	Rank Order	Monks	mss	books
Shaftesbury	6	0	1	Westminster	39	2
Barking	12	0	2	Glastonbury	39	2
Wilton	3	0	3	St. Albans	135	1
Amesbury	5	0	4	Reading	126	1
Romsey	2	0	5	Abingdon	31	4
Wherwell	4	0	6	Ramsey	39	2
St. Helens	0	0	7	Bury St. Edmunds	243	3
ELSTOW	1	0	8	Tewkesbury	10	2
Godstow	2	0	9	St. Augustine's	267	1
Nuneaton	2	0	10	Evesham	26	2
Totals	37	0			955	20

economic wealth of the men in contrast to the economic poverty of the women. It is very unlikely that, just as one swallow does not make a summer, so at Elstow the possible scholarship of Abbess Cicely, as she is named by Knowles and Hadcock, indicates a tradition of learning.

How then did the nuns employ themselves? Perhaps some spun, others would have embroidered church vestments and decorations. Eileen Power has examined the fact that in the fourteenth and fifteenth centuries, as attested by bishops' visitation records, a school for some young girls and little boys was organised at Elstow. Its existence brought episcopal censure and attempts at regulation, but never quite closure.[36] The first mention of a school is in the late twelfth century, when Bishop Hugh of Lincoln sent the five-year-old Robert of Noyon there.[37] For the thirteenth century there are no records of the school, but it is possible that there was continuity between the twelfth and fourteenth centuries. Probably running a school eked out the meagre income of the house and, at the same time, in giving some education similar to that available in the households of married ladies, protected marriage prospects in a hereditary landholding society where marriages were important social and political events. In

[36] Power, *Nunneries*, 261-284, especially 262-3; 568-569.
[37] Power, *Nunneries*, 262, 569.

practical terms it seemed that the children lived with, not separate from, the nuns. It was the disruption of monastic discipline caused by this which, with some reason, disturbed the bishops and contributed, certainly in the fourteenth and fifteenth centuries, to problems within the community.

The late thirteenth century brought to the Elstow community two problems which found their guarded way into episcopal registers. On 25 June 1270 Bishop Gravesend wrote to Walter Giffard, Archbishop of York, that "disorders have taken place in the nunnery of Elvenstowe in which the abbess and your sister are concerned. We will correct them firmly but quietly out of regard to you and your brother."[38] Many of the Giffard family of that generation went into the Church: Walter, the eldest son, died as Archbishop of York; the second son, Godfrey, mentioned in the above letter, was Bishop of Worcester; one daughter, Juliana, was abbess of Wilton by 1275; another, Mabel, was abbess of Shaftesbury in 1291; Agatha, the daughter referred to above, was a nun and later prioress at Elstow. None of the Giffard girls seemed to have been a good influence in their respective religious houses. The nature of the offence was never delineated; but ambition and pride, competition and non-observance of vowed chastity, were not unknown in the cloister. This example, indeed, emphasises the more general problem in women's religious life in medieval times. Once in the cloister, there was no way a woman could leave legitimately. Troublemakers had to be contained, probably at some cost to the quality and harmony of community life. On the death of Anora in 1281, there was a disputed election. A minority supported Prioress Agatha for abbess, and proceeded against the majority who chose Beatrice de Scoteney.[39] The bishop, Oliver Sutton, intervened to settle the election. He reported on it to the king:

> Since, therefore, after hearing and more fully understanding the arguments on either side, we have, by the pontifical authority, and in accordance with the claims of justice, promoted the said Lady Beatrice (against whom, so far as we can learn, no objection can be maintained according to canonical ordinances) to the Abbacy of that house....

It is clear that the majority of the community repudiated Agatha, and by implication Anora. Perhaps they wished for a better kind of leadership, more consonant with a vocation to religious life. There is also the possibi-

---

[38] Power, *Nunneries*, 463-464; W. Brown, ed., *The Register of Walter Giffard, Lord Archbishop of York, 1266-1279*, Surtees Society 109 (1904), 164.

[39] Wigram, 78-79.

lity that Agatha had incurred some kind of impediment to abbatial office according to canon law. Certainly, Agatha did not get her own way as completely as her sisters appeared to.The way in which the second problem was resolved seems to testify to a preference by the Elstow community for a proper living of the monastic life. It is just after the first problem surfaced, and during the course of the second problem, that Dominican friars preached to the nuns at Elstow from our manuscript. In no way was it a learned audience. Many of its concerns, especially that of domestic economy, would have differed little from the generality of women's concerns and anxieties during those decades. But we also know that, despite the problems the nuns encountered, there was a genuine desire for the holiness expected in religious life.

C. The Sermons Preached at Elstow

i. Methodology

When I started work on the manuscript in 1977, there was no understood or accepted pattern for studying sermons in themselves as catechetical events. In 1978 Nicole Bériou published her monograph, *La Prédication au Beguinage de Paris pendant l'année liturgique 1272-1273*, on a Paris manuscript[40] contemporary with MS Laud Misc. 511. In Dr Bériou's work I found many parallels and so adapted her method of presentation as follows.[41] Each sermon studied was given headings concerning liturgical occasion, scriptural reference, source-book, place in the manuscript, and any dating in accordance with Appendix 1, "A Catalogue of MS Laud Misc. 511." This was followed by an English precis of the sermon. Part A is the summary of the antitheme. If there is no antitheme, this is recorded as "none." Part B is the summary of the body of the sermon, complete or incomplete. If the manuscript indicates in the opening words of the sermon the divisions to be treated, but does not fulfil the purpose, that fact is recorded at the end of the summary. These sermon summaries are found in Appendix 11.

Another tool of understanding is the analysis of the "authorities" used in the sermons. Most of these, not unexpectedly, proved to be Scripture, and fell within one of the recognised groupings perceived by medieval exegetes, namely the five books of the Law: Pentateuch; the historical books, which included Tobias, Judith and Esther; the Psalms, which were

---

[40] Paris, BN, MS lat. 16481.

[41] Bériou, *La Prédication*, 123.

often interpreted Christologically; the popular sapiential books, including Job; and finally the prophets. Seasonal liturgical links with Scripture emerged in these different studies. The other groups of authorities included, in thirteenth-century terms, Fathers of the Church and other commentators past and present; philosophers of various persuasions; sometimes classical allusions; and finally the illustrations from experience and daily life known as *exempla*.

The deeper question remained, however. By what criteria was the sermon content to be assessed? There can be a problem of reading post-thirteenth-century theological interpretation into thirteenth-century material. If, however, a predominantly catechetical rather than a strict theological approach is taken, the matter is simplified. All catechetics is theologically based, but focussed on handing on to the current generation the message of the gospel as summarised in the creed. The theologian, on the other hand, is extending theological boundaries through speculation and application of Christian tradition in a variety of fields from Scripture to Systematic Theology to Canon Law to Moral Theology to history of Doctrine, at the same time being prepared for new areas of theological search to develop. One must not deny the necessary interplay between Theology and Catechetics, but one must not confuse the methodology, purposes and content of the two disciplines.

For the Elstow sermons[42] this catechetical approach led to some study of the common topic, the sacrament of penance. But following the structure of the Creed, other topics were looked at such as ideas and images about God, Jesus Christ, Our Lady, the Church, sacraments, sin and the four last things—death, judgement, hell and heaven.

Although only ten sermons are actually both in time-and-place-dated for Elstow, the three time-only dated ones are included in the group.[43] Moreover, sermon 136, which also belongs to the collection of sermons for the second Sunday after Easter, has been assigned there for detailed study.

---

[42] The numbers, according to Appendix 1, of the dated sermons are as follows: 50, 53, 64, 72, 77, 78, 90, 100, 136, 153, 207, 230 and 231.

The sermons were preached at Elstow as follows: Preacher E1, 1275: 78, 153, 230; 1278: 50. Preacher E2, 1277-1279: 100, 72, 136; 1281-1283: 53, 90, 77, 100 repeated.

[43] The time-only-dated sermons 64, 207, 231 were included with the Elstow sermons, following a discussion with Dr R.W. Hunt, who advised that the 13 sermons be studied together.

ii. The First Elstow Preacher

Preacher E1 preached at Elstow four times in all, including twice in Lent, once on the Fourth Sunday of Lent in 1275, 24 March; and another time on the first Sunday of Lent 1278, March 6. In neither Lenten sermon are the given distinctions fully developed.[44] In sermon 78 he deals only with the first two "loaves." The hearers are exhorted to sorrow for sin through the virtue of compunction,[45] the practice of which is like the progress of a storm.[46] He then motivates contrition through remembrance of personal sins, realisation of future judgement, and fear of hell.[47] The latter is illustrated by the *exemplum* of the laybrother of Roche Abbey.[48] In sermon 50, under the image of the "first day of the journey" of the Israelites into the desert, the preacher exhorts his hearers to think of the desert and to practise penance now rather than postpone it. He deals briefly with contrition.[49] The remainder of both sermons delivered by preacher E1 is devoted to instruction on verbal confession. In sermon 78 this is the "second loaf"; in sermon 50 it is "the second day." The necessity

[44] Sermon 78 [fol. 94a, ll. 12-16]: "Isti quinque panes spiritualiter accepti necessarii sunt cuilibet penitenti, videlicet, cordis contritio, oris confessio, et tres partes satisfactionis penitentie, videlicet, ieiunium, elemosina et oratio."
      Sermon 50 [fol. 54a, ll. 8-10]: "Iste tres diete deserti, sunt tres partes penitentie, scilicet, contritio, confessio, satisfactio."

[45] Sermon 78 [fol. 94a, line 38–fol. 94b, line 3]: "Primo, turbatur in anima bona perturbatione pro peccatis. Deinde, veniunt suspiria et gemitus quasi tonitrua pro peccatis, postea, venit pluvia lacrimarum lavans faciem et emundans animam, et tandem, venit sol, scilicet Christus, per gratiam // qui etiam minora peccata sicut sol atthomos facit recognoscere et totum hominem interius illuminat."

[46] Sermon 78 [fol. 94a, ll. 31-36]: "Sicut enim in tempestate, primo, turbatur celum et fit obscurum, deinde, cum magno tumultu veniunt tonitrua, postea, pluvia in magna habundantia, ultimo, venit sol qui totum illuminat."

[47] Sermon 78 [fol. 94b, ll. 3-22]: "Et sunt plura que contritionem peccatorum inducunt; primum, est peccatorum nostrorum recordatio....Item, extremi iudicii expectatio....Item, infernalium penarum precogitatio."

[48] Sermon 78 [fol. 94b, ll. 27-32]: "Sicut patet per exemplum cuiusdam conversi de Rupe, cui, ad mortem languenti, apparuit quidam spiritus ignitus, et dixit ei; 'þus ssal i brenne also hot for alle mine sinnes yat no man ne wot.'"

[49] Sermon 50 [fol. 54a, ll. 10-17]: "Contritionem magnam oportet habere, ut, scilicet, penitens tripliciter doleat; primo, quod unquam diabolo consensit et peccatum perpetravit; secundo, quod peccatum commissum nullo modo iteraret; tertio, quod ex quo commissum est, firmum habeat propositum, per Dei gratiam, numquam ulterius recidivandi nec diabolo consentiendi."

for promptness in confession is urged in both.[50] In 78, the example of the stag is related as an image of forgiveness;[51] showing how the stag, despite its swallowing of the poison of sin, is healed and rejuvenated by drinking from the fountain of life. In sermon 50, the preacher shows that delay in confessing is folly like weeding a half-reaped field, or poulticing a wound in which the knife remains.[52] He urges frequency of confession in the fearful hope that one confession at least will be pleasing to God.[53] He also emphasises that confession is made to God.[54] In sermon 78, drawing on the examples of Mary Magdalene in her determination to live aright, and on Judith who, despite her tears and fears, resolutely slew Holofernes, the preacher declares the need for confession to be resolute.[55] Both sermons conclude by emphasising the need for honesty in confession, using the popular term from the *vita apostolica*, "naked."[56] In sermon 78 this is construed as making no excuses and suppressing nothing;[57] while in sermon 50 it is applied to the image of healing. Only if the wound is shown to the physician can it be healed, similarly for forgiveness sins should be confessed without excuse or pretence.[58] Both

[50] Sermon 78 [fol. 94va, ll. 4-5]: "Et debet confessio esse festina et accelerata."
   Sermon 50 [fol. 54a, line 21]: "Debet enim confessio esse festina."

[51] Sermon 78 [fol. 94va, ll. 15-25]:. "Nota quod cervus, senio pinguatus excrescentibus pilis et cornibus, serpentem flatu narium hauriens de caverna sua, et hausto veneno siti exestuans, ardentissimo cursu, loca hiancia linosa [limosa] atque lutosa transiliens, ad fontem properat ut bibat; quo hausto, omne venenum evomit, cornua et pilos deponit, et sic reiuvenescit." See Sweet, "English Preaching," 102.

[52] Sermon 50 [fol. 54b, ll. 5-11]: "Item, nonne fatuus esset qui purgaret segetes suas postquam medietatem messuerit? Item, tales fatui sunt, quia tunc primo volunt ferrum extrahere a vulnere; quando iam sanatum est vulnus, cum tamen dicat auctoritas quod, dum ferrum est in vulnere, non est malagma apponere [sic]."

[53] Ibid. [ll. 18-20]: "Item, confessio debet esse frequens, si forte, inter multas confessiones, inveniatur una placens Deo."

[54] Ibid. [ll. 32-33] "Deo autem confitetur non homini sicut confitenti."

[55] Sermon 78 [fol. 94vb, line 3 and ll. 5-19]: "Item, debet confessio firma..." then references to Mary Magdalene (Luke 7:36-50) and to Judith (Jth. 13:6-10).

[56] Sermon 78 [fol. 94 vb, ll. 28-30]: "Item, debet <confessio> esse nuda quia non sufficit confiteri per nuntium vel epistolam set viva voce et ore proprio."
   Sermon 50 [fol. 54b, ll. 35-36]: "Item, confessio debet esse nuda non operta."

[57] Sermon 78 [fol. 94vb, ll. 35-39]: "Item, debet esse nuda, ut nude nudam ex omni parte manifestet confitens conscientiam suam, sublato omni velamine defensionis, excusationis, suppressionis, subtractionis."

[58] Sermon 50 [fol. 54b, ll. 36-41]: "Quia non potest sanare medicus, nisi prius fuerit detectum vulnus, et sunt homines multi, qui, cum egra membra medico ostendere deberent spirituali sana tantum ostendunt bona opera narrando tacendo

sermons give practical instruction which is also educating the consciences of the listeners.

In sermon 153, for the Sunday before the Ascension, 19 May 1275, preacher E1 selects a straightforward one on prayer. It is not imaginative in its scriptural examples; but it is practical and positive, stating that prayer is about relationship with God in response to grace.[59] The section giving scriptural examples of prayer ends with the comparison that a little old woman could amass more real treasure in one hour of prayer than a thousand soldiers could gain by thirty years of looting.[60] The sermon also emphasises that prayer is only rightly made through Jesus the saviour.[61] The remaining half of the sermon—completing the distinctions outlined at the start—is devoted to the hindrances to prayer caused by anger, envy, an unforgiving heart, pride and a sinful tongue.[62] This negative teaching on prayer is a further aid to development of conscience. The preacher suitably gives tongue in this section, commending humility, and condemning above all abusiveness, "which is disgraceful in an actor, more disgraceful in a man, and most disgraceful in a woman."[63] Did this outburst reflect an actual situation at Elstow, or is it just an example of one of the ways of expanding a distinction? The sermon ends with advice to have recourse to Our Lady for help in prayer.[64]

---

peccata."

[59] Sermon 153 [fol. 141a, line 42-fol. 141b, line 5]: "Magna est virtus pure orationis, que, quasi quidam persona // ad Deum ingreditur, et ibi mandatum peragit quo caro pervenire nequit propter eiusdem nobilitatem et efficaciam totiens ad orandum monet nos Deus in Scriptura Sacra."

[60] Sermon 153 [fol. 141b, ll. 41-43]: "Unde vetula aliquando, plus terre in celo una hora adquirit orando, quam mille milites armati per xxx triginta annos privando."

[61] Sermon 153 [fol. 141va, ll. 10-18]: "Cum enim salutem anime petimus, in nomine Jesu petimus, et tunc, cum ad salutem petimus quicquid petierimus Patrem impetravit. Cum enim forinseca petimus que ad nostram salutem non pertinent, repellitur oratio, et refutatur, quia in nomine Salvatoris non petimus."

[62] Sermon 153 [fol. 141va, line 21-fol. 141vb, line 39] "Sunt enim multa que impediunt effectum orationis; peccata enim impediunt ne exaudiamur....[line 35] Item, ira et invidia impediunt orationem....[fol. 141vb, line 23] Item, superbus impedit orationem....Item, peccatum lingue impedit orationem, cuiusmodi sunt: mendacium, detractio, diffamatio, accusatio, contentio, convicium, et huiusmodi."

[63] Sermon 153 [fol. 142a, ll. 13-16]: "Turpe est convicium in histrione, turpius in alio homine, sed turpissimum in muliere."

[64] Sermon 153 [fol. 142a, ll. 27-31]: "Si vis impetrare et non deficere, lava a malitia cor tuum, et resolve illud in lacrimas, et constituas nuntium tuum Virginem Gloriosam, sepius cantando 'Ave Maria'."

About six weeks later, preacher E1 was again at Elstow on 30 June 1275. Instead of choosing a sermon for the Third Sunday after Trinity, he took a sermon on St. Peter, whose feast had been celebrated the day before. In sermon 230, the kingship and victory of Christ over sin and Satan are given due honour,[65] illustrated by an interesting *exemplum* about the king of England.[66] That all prelates share the sinful, poverty-stricken human condition is shown, goes the sermon, by the power of the keys being given to the sinner, Peter, and his successors.[67] The ecclesiology implicit in this comment is significant. The compassion of God for our sinfulness is seen in that Christ our brother gives the power of forgiveness to the prelates of the Church.[68] There is also the assumption in the attitude of the medieval Church to heresy that, because of the essential goodness of what is available, those who are turning away can be compelled to enter.[69] It is not clear whether the force of "compel" lies in its primary meaning, to force against an individual's freewill, or whether it is an allusion to the parable of the wedding feast (Luke 14:14-24), which is an

[65] Sermon 230 [fol. 198vb, ll. 27-33]: "Dominus noster Jesus Christus, rex et conditor omnium creaturarum, sine principio Deus in fine seculorum, pro salute hominis factus est homo; cum iam transiret ex hoc mundo ad Patrem, sciens infirmitates nostras neminem posse vivere sine peccato...ait Petro."

[66] Ibid. [fol. 199a, ll. 8-15] "Si enim Rex Anglie coronaret filium suum et pauperes mendicantes constitueret ianitores, constat quia nulli pauperi introitum denegarent, et forte vocarent eos si non gratis venirent. Sic Dominus noster Jesus Christus...."

[67] Sermon 230 [fol. 198vb, line 40-fol. 199a, line 8]: "Istud non tantum Petro dicitur, // immo omnibus in apostolatum Petro succedentibus archiepiscopis et episcopis, similiter aliis prelatis maioribus et minoribus secundum quod vocati sunt in Ecclesia Dei. Unde magna spes tribuitur peccatoribus celum possidendi. Ex quo sibi consimiles, videlicet, peccatores constituit regni celestis ianitores."

[68] Sermon 230 [fol. 199b, ll. 8-12]: "Similiter Deus Pater, princeps orbis terrarum, Christum filium suum verum Deum et hominem, qua propter frater noster est, judicem constituit super omnes gentes."

Ibid. [ll. 14-17]: "Nos ergo qui petimus terram viventium, nobis tribui fiduciam habeamus, frater enim noster sententiabit contra dyabolum quia inimicus eius est."

Ibid. [fol. 199b, line 40-fol. 199va, line 4]: "Ut ergo singulos // a peccatis eripe-ret, potestatem suam contulit prelatis ecclesiarum, et quoscumque solverint super terram a peccatis, sint soluti et immunes in celo."

[69] Sermon 230 [fol. 199va, line 37-fol. 199vb, line 1]: "Claves ecclesie contulit Dominus Petro et ceteris ecclesiarum prelatis, ut et ipsi intrent et subditos suos intrare permittant, et etiam renuentes // intrare compellant, sicut in evangelio servo dixit paterfamilias."

image of the Church. The key given to Peter is penance.[70] We should grapple bravely and at length with this task of penance as schoolboys toil with their books. By perseverance, contemplation and sweetness are reached.[71] In this sermon the sinfulness of the Church and its prelates is not mere rhetoric, but recognition of an ecclesial condition, while the power of the keys in penance is practice of the virtue of penance as well as the sacrament.

Preacher E1 chose to give encouragement to the nuns at Elstow. As we know from the trouble of 1270 and from the later disputed election featuring one of the principal trouble-makers, the nuns did need encouragement in their spiritual life, as well as a reminder of the fallibility of prelates or superiors. The sermons preacher E2 selected emphasise two essentials of religious life—prayer and penance. Would he have so chosen had he not expected to strike a chord in the hearts of his listeners? Moreover, the sermons he picked out had sufficient illustration from Scripture and elsewhere to meet the sensibilities and understanding of an audience of women.

iii. The Second Elstow Preacher

Preacher E2 first preached at Elstow from our manuscript in 1277. Here only sermons 100 and 72 will be discussed, as sermon 136—which belongs to this sub-group—will be studied later. Sermon 100, preached on Palm Sunday, 21 March 1277, is a good example of method by the relation of its divisions to the words and images of the theme. In its totality, it makes less sense than most of the other Elstow sermons. It is based, however, on images related to the entry of Christ into Jerusalem: the implication of kingship, the use of an ass and its foal, the waving of palms, the shouts of the children and people; and each of its seemingly unrelated divisions has lively illustrations. The first part compares Christ as king to

---

[70] Sermon 230 [fol. 199vb, ll. 27-34]: "Clavis ista est penitentia. Qui ergo vult liberaliter intrare, ab illis prelatis clavem accipiat penitentie, et manu gestat, scilicet, opere, et patebit introitus. Sed omnes vellent ire ad celum et nullius ferre clavem secum, quod est impossibile."

[71] Sermon 230 [fol. 200a, ll. 8-20]: "Sic enim est de penitentibus sicut de pueris; primo addiscentibus invite enim vadunt ad scolas, invite repetunt, invite reddunt. Sed cum iam senserunt dulcedinem scientie, gratis in longinquis partibus causa discipline accedunt, et multas penas et inedias patiuntur, ut bene addiscant sic penitentibus non statim occurrit suavitas sed permanentibus delicie reputantur."

earthly kings[72] and exhorts the listeners to honour their heavenly king by living a good and honourable life.[73] In contrast to this and to rouse compassion, the preacher compares Christ as king of men in and through his humility and his suffering.[74] Without any recorded link, the sermon then moves to the second division, the ass.[75] Then follows an allegorical treatment of the ass, and later the colt, to illustrate human sinfulness, and finally an exhortation to avoid sin. Then, once again without a recorded link, the preacher talks about palms. He condemns false palmers,[76] and

[72] Sermon 100 [fol. 106vb, ll. 4-32]: "Scitis enim quod quilibet rex terrenus potestatem habet super unum populum, ut Rex Francie in sua regione, Rex Anglie in sua regione....[line 12] Item, alii reges dominantur in aliquo loco certo et determinato.... [line 14] Item, aliorum regum potestas durat ad tempus quia hodie extollitur et cras non invenietur, hodie, rex, indutus purpura, sedens in solio; cras, indutus cilicio, iacet in sepulcro. Alii reges tantum super corpus accipiunt potestatem sed Deus habet potestatem super corpus et animam hoc est quod dicitur in evangelio....[line 22] Et nota quod duo debentur regi: honor et timor; timor quia potens est, honor quia summus est, set timemus regem terrenum propter eius momentaneam potestatem multo plus ergo timere Dominum eum qui habet potestatem eternam. Sed si esses nunc coram aliquo rege terreno, et diceret tibi 'prohibeo te facere hoc' et statim faceres, signum esset quod parum illum timeres sed Deus prohibet peccatum sicut volumus habere regia celestia et vitare pena inferni."

[73] Sermon 100 [fol. 106vb, ll. 34-38]: "Quia summus debetur ei honor, honorem magnum facit ei quilibet, qui ducit vitam sanctam et honestam, quia cum vulgariter dicitur: 'Honor magnus est domino si familia eius sit honesta in habitu gestu' etc; sicut honor est Domino nostro etc., id est Christus."

[74] Sermon 100 [fol. 106vb, ll. 42-43 and fol. 107a, ll. 4-17]: "Iste rex potentissimus dicitur rex hominum, non angelorum nec aliarum creaturarum....Ille dicitur mansuetus qui pacificus est, et nulli malefacit vel maledicit, sed ille dicitur mansuetior, qui pacificus est, nec, etiam cum malefactum fuerit ei vel maledictum, non malefacit vel maledicit. Sed ille dicitur mansuetissimus qui pacificus est et nulli maledicit vel malefacit, et cum maledictum fuerit ei vel malefactum, econtra bona dicit et bona facit. Istam mansuetudinem pre cunctis habuit Christus qui post dura Iudeorum verba, flagella, alapas, illusionem, suspensionem inter latrones villissimam, benedixit et benefecit eis ad Patrem orando."

[75] Sermon 100 [fol. 107a, ll. 20-33]: "Asinus parvus animal est vile et laboriosum, cum tota die laboraverit, nocte cubat in fimo....[line 26] Item, asinus fortis in parte posteriore et debilis in anteriori....[line 32] Item, asinus non laborat libenter nisi pungatur aculeo et scorpione." Ibid [fol. 107b, ll. 6-7, 12-13]: "Asinus est peccator senex, pullus iuvenis....Asinus vilis est non aptatus non comptus strigili."

[76] Sermon 100 [fol. 107b, line 41-fol. 107va, line 12]: "Palma figurat victoriam inimicorum. Unde consuetudo inolevit in quibusdam partibus, quod victor in bello // coronaretur corona palmarum in signum victorie. Sed multi sunt hodie falsi

compares them to those who either do not make a good confession or who relapse into sin, having made their Easter confession.[77] In 1283 this sermon was again preached at Elstow; but this time the whole of it, including the fourth section about the children singing as the Lord went by in procession.[78] So, the sermon continues, all must sing to the Lord by a good life, a pure conscience, making satisfaction and listening to sermons![79] Christ is our teacher, gentle with us now, but harsh at judgement.[80] Then the allegory of the journey into Jerusalem is continued. Jerusalem, the vision of peace, is our true home. This idea leads to the image of a home being prepared for a guest, and the soul being the home at the door of which Christ stands knocking (Apoc. 3:20).[81] The sermon ends with the praise of Our Lady, who is the real throne of Christ.

This sermon was preached twice at Elstow. Could it have been remembered for its vivid illustrations, and so a repeat requested? What is more interesting is the glimpse the repetition affords into the practical use

---

palmeri qui ferunt palmas in manibus nec tamen adhuc de hostibus triumpharunt, scilicet demone mundo. Multi enim, cruce signati, vadunt ultra mare et ibi morantur ad tempus, et cum repatriaverint, dicunt se fuisse aput Ierusalem, portant palmam, portant sclavinium, qui nunquam forte viderunt mare Grecum nec medietatem itineris sui perfecerunt."

Ibid. [fol. 107va, ll. 19-21]: "Sic nec confessi nec compuncti, ferentes hodie palmam falsam et fictam et vanam, faciunt Deo oblationem."

[77] Sermon 100 [fol. 107va, ll. 23-28]: "Ferunt palmam qui iam de hostibus triumpharunt, omni tempore anni virescere debent, in bonitate et penitentia cepta, et non in Pascha recidivare quoniam nulla est penitentia quam sequens coinquinat culpa."

Ibid. [ll. 30-34]: "Quicumque enim cogitat recidivare post Pascha, et sic accipit corpus Christi, inimicus Dei est, et simulat se amatorem Dei cum non sit, et potest comparari Iude traditori, qui osculo tradidit Filium Dei."

[78] Cf. Matt. 21:15, and the Antiphons for the Palm Sunday procession, which sing about the welcome the Hebrew children gave Christ.

[79] Sermon 100 [fol. 107va, ll. 36-41]: "Cantandum est Deo in corde per mundas cogitationes per dulces meditationes; in ore per secretas et pias orationes. Cantandum est etiam Domino per bonam vitam, mundam conscientiam, placentem operationem libenter audire sermones et huiusmodi."

[80] Ibid. [ll. 4-7]: "Sic magister noster Christus docens nos de laga sacramenta, et huiusmodi; si nesciamus in die iudicii reddere, non solum verberabit virgis sed malleis."

[81] Sermon 100 [fol. 107vb, ll. 14-17]: "Quia, si Rex Anglie tibi mandaret quod tecum hospitaretur et moraretur, non solum domum contra ipsius adventum mundares, sed etiam ornares cortinis, tapetis, et huiusmodi."

of written sermons. Moreover, it illustrates perfectly the freedom of the preacher to adapt his written source to the group of persons before him, and the time at his disposal. If the preacher had not recorded the fact, we would never have known that the whole sermon was not preached at El-stow in 1277.

Sermon 72, preached on the Third Sunday of Lent, 20 March 1278, is on penance. It was probably chosen because its antitheme has a refer-ence to an imaginary visit of St. Peter to nearby Bedford.[82] Taking up the gospel of the day, the sermon shows sin as causing spiritual disorder,[83] spiritual blindness[84] and spiritual dumbness.[85] Christ casts out the de-mon when through grace the sinner repents, gives sight to the blind when the sinner reviews his whole life. The preacher is emphasising the need for examination of conscience and so suggests to the penitent the question of how, why and when sin was committed. Similarly there is an exhor-tation to make confession, using the image of the dumb man gaining speech. Confession is to be free, honest and sincere, made to God and man.[86] The rest of the sermon, with its illustrations, is similar in content and emphasis to sermons 51 and 78.[87] The reference to recidivism in so

[82] Sermon 72 [fol. 83vb, ll. 3-9]: "Si Beatus Petrus Apostolus nunc, sicut olim, in terris ambularet, et denunciasset in ecclesiis circumquamque quod quicumque aput Bedeford' ad verbum suum audiendum accederet, benedictionem suam reciperet, multi sunt qui diligenter accurrerent, et libenter eum audirent."

[83] Ibid. [ll. 34-38]: "Nonne satis demoniacus est qui mavult servire diabolo quam regnare cum Christo? Qui diligit mortem, id est peccata, que eternaliter mori faci-unt, et odit vitam, id est Christum, qui est anime vita, et ad vitam ducit eternam."

[84] Ibid. [fol. 84a, ll. 7-11]: "Nonne cecus diceretur qui scienter malo adhereret, et bonum denegaret, qui posset iter rectum incedere, et in lacum profundum se precipitaret? Talis est peccator."

[85] Ibid. [ll. 13-18]: "Peccator mutus est qui enim habet linguam paratam et doctam in mendaciis, detractionibus, maledictionibus, periuriis, tardia vero et curtam in di-vinis orationibus, proximorum edificationibus, confessionibus revelandis. Nonne satis mutus est?"

[86] Sermon 72 [fol. 84a, ll. 22-26, 32-35]: "Dominus enim demonium eicit cum gratia sua largiente, peccator conteritur, dolet et contremiscit pro peccatis. Cecum illuminat cum, recordatus malorum qui fecerit, recogitat....[line 32] muto reddit loquelam, cum peccator, corde contritus, et peccatis ad memoriam reductis, Deo et homini voluntarie nude et pure confitetur."

[87] Sermon 72 [fol. 84b, ll. 9-11]: "Primo enim debet confitens propria et specialia peccata nominatim exprimere, deinde communia et generalia."

Ibid [fol. 84va, ll. 6-9, 18-19, 28-32]: "Debet etiam confessio nostra esse nuda, ut penitens et contritus mundet se interius, confitendo spiritualia peccata exterius

many of these sermons is a concern, common to many sermons of this time, over pentitents lapsing into sin once the Lenten season is over.

The second sub-group preached by E2, or perhaps by a third Dominican, is made up of sermons 53, 90 and 77, preached on 2 March 1281, 15 March 1282, and 28 March 1283 respectively. If these summaries are studied in Appendix 11, their similarity to the sermons already noted is apparent. In sermon 53 there is the threefold division of penance being prompt, upright and prudent;[88] while the practical advice about making confession is similar to that in sermons 50 and 78.[89] The images for Lent are slightly different. In sermon 50, Lent is the desert which is reached only after a three-day journey whose spiritual meaning is contrition, confession and satisfaction; while in sermon 77 the experience of pilgrimage, with an overtone of crusade, is Lent's image.[90] In sermon 53, the development of the divisions of penance is taken from strong women of the Old Testament: contrition being the unknown woman who killed Abimelech; confession being Judith, who slew Holofernes; satisfaction is Jael, who despatched Sisera with a nail. These three illustrate the allegorical interpretation of Scripture drawn partly from the stories, partly from

---

pandendo carnalia....[line 18] sic etiam confessio integra, scilicet sine divisione, sine diminutione....[line 28] debet etiam esse nuda, ut nude ex omni parte manifestans, sublato omni velamine defensionis et excusationis."

[88] Sermon 53 [fol. 55va, ll. 26-27]: "Sic ergo penitentia nostra debet esse festina, recta et discreta."

[89] Sermon 53 [fol. 55vb line 42–fol. 56a, line 3]: "Non solummodo penitendum est modo eo, quod tempus iubet, ecclesia precipit, consuetudo fidelium hoc habet, // vel quia presbiteri parati sedent in ecclesia, sed solum ea intentione ut Deo placeas et animam salves."

Sermon 77 [fol. 93b, ll. 27-32]: "Omnes vero illi qui propter consuetudinem ecclesie, vel vanam laudem hominum, vel alia quacumque de causa quam propter Dei laudem et peccatorum remissionem confessi sunt, crucem Domini non ferunt, set magis diaboli."

[90] Sermon 77 [fol. 93a, ll. 11-18, 39–fol. 93b, line 5]: "Sed multi vestrum, Deo dante, in hac quadragesima crucem penitentie assumpserunt, proponentes ire in celestem Ierusalem, et ibidem sine fine cum Domino remanere. Et isti vere peregrini sunt singulis enim diebus post assumptam penitentie crucem unam dietam versus illam terram beatam fecerunt....Crux ista vera penitentia est. Isti cruce signati sunt quotquot, cum lacrimis, dolore, et suspiriis, peccata sua precogitarunt, post modum ea integre nude et plane confessi sunt nunquam, per Dei gratiam, recidivando, demum consilio ecclesie Deo satisfacere parati fuerint; beati sunt omnes ill qui isto modo crucem penitentie assumpserunt."

etymology.[91] In the context of Abbess Anora's death some time before 10 June in the same year as the sermon was preached this sermon, which delineates strong women doing the hard thing, could have been chosen deliberately by the preacher to strengthen his hearers. In sermon 90 penitence and penance are treated in a meditative approach that is also compassionate. In this it is very like sermon 136. The context is Christ's suffering and death, undergone out of love in order to call forth love.[92] It is through this healing love, which was not content to effect a minimum redemption, that we are forgiven our sins.[93] The aim of the preacher here is to arouse in his audience sympathy with, and sorrow for, the suffering of Christ, and so to educate the heart.[94]

[91] Sermon 53 [fol. 56b, ll. 7-11, 17-21, 23-32]: "Quedam mulier, expugnata ab Abimoles, submisit lapidem et confregit cerebrum eius. Hec mulier compunctio est que lapide contritionis occidit diabolum....[line 17] Judith, filia Merari, id est meroris, id est confessionis ex amaritudine cordis, procedens occidit Holofernem, id est diabolum, gladio lingue sue, id est confessionis verbo....[line 23] Jael, uxor Abel Cinei, que interpretatur expectans vel ascendens, et figurat proficientem per satisfactionem, que est opere pregnans et plenam reconciliationem expectat, occidit Sisarum clavo, id est opere satisfactionis, que coniungit penitentem Deo quasi ad osculum, licet enim remittatur offensa in contritione, et revocatur peccator in confessione, non tamen plene reconciliatur nisi in satisfactione quando per osculum, id est, unione spiritus coniungitur."

[92] Sermon 90 [fol. 101a, ll. 30-40; fol. 101b ll. 1-11]: "Ecclesia in alia parte quadragesime que precessit, usa est multis exemplis ad animandum eos, qui non erant in penitentia, ad aggrediendum penitentiam et ad consolandum et confirmandum eos qui iam aggressi sunt penitentiam ad portandum eam. Nunc quasi in fine quadragesime, exemplo efficacissimo utitur, scilicet, Christi passione, reducens eis ad memoriam Dominicam passionem et eius sanguinem....Scitis enim quod ignis elicitur a petra ex percussione ferri, et similiter ignis amoris Dei, ex recordatione clavorum hispidorum pedum et manuum Christi etiam a corde humano, quamvis lapideo, elicitur, et nutritur ignis iste, primo spinis corone Christi, deinde ligno crucis et lancea, malleis et flagellis, et sic comburatur ignis amoris et diligamus Christum quoniam ipse prior dilexit nos [1 John 4:10]. Amor enim melius quam amore recompensari non potest."

[93] Sermon 90 [fol. 101b, ll. 15-19, 21-26]: "Cum igitur totum genus humanum a commestione pomi vetiti infirmitatem nimiam contraxisset, Christus, Filius Deo caro [sic] et frater noster, sanam carnem assumpsit de virgine....quam fecit minui in habundatia proprio sanguine, et non alieno, cum tamen minima eius gutta ad redemptionem humani generis sufficeret, ut dicit Bernardus. Fuit etiam in illa minutione satis calidus per internam affectionem."

[94] Ibid, fol. 101vb], ll. 25-35]: "Qui vero tempore precedente ad lacrimas et contritionem non est fractus, saltem modo cum Christi sanguinem et passionem tota die audierit in ecclesia recitari, ad lacrimas et contritionem moveatur, quia per propri-

Preacher E2 is not significantly different in his choice of sermons from our manuscript, from preacher E1. He probably chose sermon 53 because of its feminine illustrations. It does not seem that any of the sermons preached at Elstow could fall into any category of *ad status* sermons, *ad moniales*, though they could well be *ad mulieres*. The nine sermons so far discussed were ordinary sermons for ordinary people, but selected from the book in an attempt to preach relevant sermons to the Elstow nuns. It is also probable that the Dominicans who preached at Elstow in these years found little difference between the nuns in the cloister and the pious women who came to their new preaching churches in the towns.

The bias of most of these sermons is the sacrament of penance. The same vocabulary is used in Gregory the Great as in the thirteenth century and as in recent times. In fact Gregory is often quoted. But the meanings of the words used are not necessarily the same in Gregory as in the Elstow sermons. In fact there is greater continuity between the thirteenth and the twentieth centuries in the vocabulary and meaning of the sacrament of penance, than there is between the eighth and the thirteenth centuries. The difference is the emergence of a radical change in sacramental practice, from having been a very harsh infrequent one in the time of Gregory, to a more merciful and frequent practice with more emphasis on the formation of individual conscience, especially after 1215.[95] The new approach, in fact, began to require a far more nuanced attitude to human sinfulness

---

um sanguinem introivit in sancta [Heb. 9:12]. Hiis diebus seras celestis amenitatis omnibus nobis patentes reliquit, festinemus, per penitentiam et bona opera, ingredi in illam requiem ubi melior est dies una etc, ubi Christus nos expectat etc."

[95] This is not the place for a history of the sacrament of penance, but it is worth noting that the sacrament has seen at least three significant changes in direction in its history. The first is linked with the emergence of the penitential practices of the Irish church which, hard though they were in actuality, did allow for the human experience of repeated sin. The second is the change associated with the Fourth Lateran Council of 1215, which required the practice of sacramental confession at least once a year. This led not only to a more sophisticated casuistry, but to important developments in the idea of personal conscience, and to the growth of moral and pastoral theology. The third is the change associated with the Second Vatican Council, which saw the practice of personal confession in a wider context, to allow for the individual contribution to corporate sin. Helen Forshaw, "The Pastoral Ministry of the Priest Confessor in the Early Middle Ages, 600-1100" (London Ph.D. thesis, 1976); Alexander Murray, "Confession as a historical source in the thirteenth century," in *The Writing of History in the Middle Ages: Essays Presented to Richard William Southern*, ed. R.H.C. Davis and J.M. Wallace-Hadrill (Oxford: Clarendon Press, 1981) 275-322.

and is the cause of the fast and full development of pastoral and moral theology, much of which was fostered by Dominicans like Raymund of Penaforte and William Peraldus. What had not changed was the teaching about the virtue of penitence. As the vocabulary for the virtue and for the sacrament is identical, it was possible to use what Gregory wrote about the virtue and apply it fruitfully to an understanding of the sacrament. In fact it was possible to use most patristic sources in this way. The difference between the thirteenth and the twentieth centuries' use of these sources within the same subject is that most thirteenth-century theologians were historically uncritical of the semantic change, and assumed that in their talk of the virtue of penance the Fathers were in fact writing about the sacrament of penance. An awareness of interpreting language in terms of its original meaning is one that has been fostered by critical biblical studies and transferred to other fields of theological and catechetical perception, and this is seen particularly in the growth of historical theology.

iv. The Time-Dated Sermons

The remaining time-dated sermons do not differ significantly from the sermons known to have been preached at Elstow from 1275 to 1283. They share with the Elstow sermons a slight bias towards women. Certainly they could have been preached there. Instead of treating each sermon as a whole, points of interest only will be selected.

Sermon 64, preached on the second Sunday of Lent, 14 March 1283, is very like the sermons on penance already seen. There is the image of the three-day journey into the desert standing for contrition, confession and satisfaction; sin is seen as a disease; and the practical instructions about confession are similar to those already noted, with the addition of advice about a suitable confessor.[96] The general tenor of the sermon is emphasis on God's love and mercy; for example, confession is one of the best gifts brought to us by the best man of all, Jesus.[97] This gift is not exercising on us revenge for sin, as sometimes seems under the Old Law,

---

[96] Sermon 64 [fol. 70va, ll. 29-36]: "Item, ut sacerdotem discretum eligat. Item, propria seipsum non alterum accusans, quia si alterum accusas, non eris criminis corrector sed proditor."

[97] Sermon 64 [fol. 70a, line 38–fol. 70b, line 2]: "Cum enim Dominus, ante adventum suum, multa bona per nuncios suos mundo mandaverit, ipse tamen quedam in propria persona attulit, ut est dilectio inimicorum de pace habenda et servanda, et confessio homini singulariter facta. Optima enim est, quia optimus eum // mundo adduxit; optimi enim est optima adducere."

but is full of the goodness of God.⁹⁸ The image for the suffering, grief, and compunction that can mark contrition is the pain of childbirth. In this way the loss of a living soul is made more actual to us.⁹⁹

Sermon 207 was preached on 4 July 1277, the sixth Sunday after Trinity. It focusses beautifully on the mercy of God. The antitheme takes the example of a journey-pilgrimage,¹⁰⁰ and the anxiety travellers have for a safe, well-directed journey. This is the image for the human journey through life to heaven. The best guide on this journey is the Word of God. The slight ambiguity between word as Scripture and Word as Jesus Christ makes this introduction telling. As in sermon 77, a contrast is made between the swift justice of the Old Testament, and the compassion and tenderness of God in Christ.¹⁰¹ But in his exegesis of the parable of the prodigal son, the preacher puts all the emphasis on the forgiving Father, refusing to make a dichotomy between the Father and the Son.¹⁰²

---

⁹⁸ Sermon 64 [fol. 70b, ll. 15-17, 18-21]: "Nunc, in tempore gratie, quia homini plenam voluntatem habenti confitendi remittit Deus peccatum...ibi dicit Cassiodorus: 'magna pietas Dei, qui ad solam promissionem peccata dimittit votum enim pro operatione iudicatur.'"

⁹⁹ Sermon 64 [fol. 70a, ll. 13-15, 26-33]: "Talis debet esse dolor contriti sicut parturientis que non potest esse sine dolore....Pena amarissima est inter omnes penas parturire et dolor gravissimus unigenitum perdere, et certe in infinitum plus dolore deberet; unusquisque de morte anime proprie quam de morte corporis alterius. Cum tanto dolore gemitu et planctu confiteri debemus peccata nostra."

¹⁰⁰ Sermon 207 [fol. 170vb, ll. 1-24]: "Itinerantes et peregrini, precipue cum elongati fuerint a propria patria, singulis diebus in mane Domini diligenter exorant ut ducatum eis prebeat congruum. Iter faciat securum, et ad salutem sed sua voluntate opera eorum dirigat et disponat. Set omnes nos hic congregati itinerantes sumus, quia cotidie per unam dietam ad mortem tendimus peregrini, quia elongati a terra nostra paradiso vel celo in hoc exilio commoramur. Secundum Apostolum quam diu sumus in hoc seculo peregrinamur a Domino, et sicut itinerantes, viam sibi incognitam diligenter querunt et addiscunt, sic nos utinam ad celum tendentes, viam discamus, sed nichil in mundo nobis tam bene viam illam instruit sicut Scriptura Sancta et doctrina Verbi Dei."

¹⁰¹ Sermon 207 [fol. 171a, ll. 12-17]: "Set ista iustitia Deitatis mitigata est per misericordiam humanitatis, postquam enim Deus carnem nostram induit et homo devenit, et in forma humana sedet ad dexteram maiestatis in excelso, ire et vindicte obliviscitur."

¹⁰² Sermon 207 [fol. 171vb, ll. 29-42]: "Exemplum ad hoc operum de filio prodigo et patre, Luc 15, qui cum substantiam suam luxuriose vivendo cum meretricibus vivendo consumpsisset, reversus ad patrem, penitentia ductus, dixit: 'Pater, peccavi in celum etc,' et recipiens pater in amplexus fecit proferri stolam primam, dedit

The last division of this sermon is devoted to salvation and, given human freedom, its corollary, damnation. It is always difficult for a preacher to describe heaven. This one, however, expresses it as above all friendship with the Blessed Trinity, then loving friendship with Our Lady and all the saints. We are totally surrounded by joy, like fish by the sea.[103] In its feeling, if not totally in its imagery, this passage is lyrical. But it is in the contrasting section on eternal punishment[104] that the preacher reaches the heights of passion. His greatest invective, however, is reserved not for the murderers, nor the unbelievers, nor the adulterers, the perjurers etc., but for those who defrauded over payment of tithes, "the false tithers"! Here, the language is stirring. Moreover, the preacher gives himself instructions for further expanding these descriptions and condemnations.[105] This particular sermon was originally included in the

anulum in manu, vitulum saginatum occidit, epulas adhibuit, convivium fecit, dicens: 'epulari et gaudere qui hic filius meus etc.'"

[103] Sermon 207 [fol. 171va, ll. 4-40]: "Salus illa et gaudium tam ineffabile est, quod penitus supereminet sensui et cogitationi humane. Nam quis potest cogitare gaudium quod de seipso unusquisque habebit, cum fuerit socius et amicus Altissimi, cum viderit Patrem et Filium et Spiritum Sanctum unum in substantia et trinum in persona, cum viderit spem nostram et refugium, Virginem Gloriosam ibi, tantum honoratam, apostolos, martires, confessores, angelos, et alios sanctos? Nullus, sine dubio, quia in presenti nullus illud umquam [sic] expertus est; quid si illud idem gaudium amico tuo karissimo, duobus vel tribus vel etiam centum Deus daret, quos non minus te ipso diligeres, quantum creditis excresceret tuum gaudium; certe non potest cogitari; quilibet enim ibi alium diliget sicut seipsum et de alieno gaudio tamquam de proprio congaudebit; gaudium illud tam magnum est ut omnes capiat in se, omnibus supereminet, superfluit et superhabundat omnes circumdabit omnibus, ex omni parte; erit sicut enim pisces maris undique circa se habent mare; sic Sancti Dei illam suavitatem gaudii magnificam circa se undique habebunt, et sine fine possidebunt, quibus dicet misericordia Divine pietatis 'Venite benedicti' etc. [Matt. 25:34]."

[104] Sermon 207 [fol. 171va, line 41–fol. 171vb, line 16]: "Sed quid faciet tunc Dei Iustitia de reprobis, adulteris, homicidis, periuris, falsis decimatoribus, // et excommunicatis,...[line 10] si enim esset ibi statutus terminus aliquod solatium esset, sed quamdiu Deus durat, hoc erit semper, et sancti eius cum eo glorianter ardebunt, et peribunt et erunt dampnati in fine et sine fine.

[105] Sermon 207 [fol. 171vb, ll. 16-37]: "Sed inter omnes dampnatos falsi decimatores profundius dampnabuntur, quia iustum est ut qui plus maledicantur profundius dampnentur, et isti maledicti sunt a Deo, et omnibus Sanctis, ab Ecclesia, et hominibus sanctis, apostolis, cardinalibus, archiepiscopis, episcopis, monachis, sacerdotibus, non semel in anno sed pluries, in conciliis, synodis, capitulis, et aliis congregationibus maledicti sunt dormiendo, vigilando, stando,

Liber Proprius by the compiler. One can see why he chose it, for its treatment of the love and mercy of God is moving. The original composer of this sermon, however, was less likely to be a friar than a secular priest. One wonders whether he really thought false tithing was the worst possible sin his people could commit, or whether his oratory reflects feelings about the tithe offerings he received. If this sermon had been preached to the nuns at Elstow, the rhetoric on being cheated of tithes could be a comment on their problems with their churches.[106]

Sermon 231 was preached on the feast of the Assumption, 1279. The dating is annotated in the two styles, solar and lunar, while the writing has a definite likeness to the hand of preacher E1. Again it must be emphasised that it is not certain whether this sermon was preached at Elstow, but it would have been highly appropriate for the nuns there. In this sermon celebrating Mary's ascension to heaven, the preacher describes three Old Testament figures of Our Lady: Bathsheba, Esther and Eve. Bathsheba as the mother of the reigning king, Solomon, was the all-important woman at court. Mary, as the Mother of the Son of God, is so close to him that she can express her thoughts to him. If, when she was on earth, Mary, mistress of the world, was protecting it by her goodness and her good works, how much more effective must her intercession for us be now that she is enthroned beside her Son![107] The story of Esther is taken not only as an image of Mary's concern for the Church, but also for the love and respect Christ has for his mother. Allegorized, this has all the elements of

---

sedendo, etc. *finge* maledicti sunt hyeme, estate, autumpno, quadragesima, omnique anni tempore; *adde plura huius.* Dicatur (Gen. 4:1-16) de fumo sacrificiorum Abel et Chaym, uno ascendente et alio descendente in signum quod boni decimatores ad celum ibunt, falsi vero in inferni supplicium etc,. *finge plura.*" (The italicized words are preacher's notes for further amplification.)

[106] See pp. 136-138 above.

[107] Sermon 231 [fol. 200va, ll. 10-20; fol. 200vb, ll. 2-15]: "Legitur in figura Regum III quod, veniente Bersabe, surexit Rex in occursum eius, adoravitque eam et sedit super trhonum [sic] suum; positus est thronus matris eius a dextris eius, et sedit super thronum, scilicet unde secreta consilia sibi imposita penes filium liberius valet intimare et expedire....[200vb, l. 2] 'Maria' lingua syra 'Domina' interpretatur mundi; si ergo ista Domina Mundi cum adhuc in terra esset conversata, que multum distat a celo, bonis suis operibus et precibus dulcissimis mundum salvaverit, quanto magis nunc cum iuxta tronum Filii sui collocatur supra omnes, Sanctos Christo propinquius residens et honorabilius mundo potest subvenire et Filium interpellare magna fiducia unicuique sibi ministranti et veneranti."

a dramatic confrontation of good and evil.[108] A third traditional counter image from the Old Testament is that of Eve. Very neatly, the preacher takes the statement about Esther being much loved by the people and applies it to Mary. He then says that all women should greatly love Our Lady for, while in the past women have been despised and belittled because of Eve, now all women share in the respect and honour given to Mary and the former allegations cannot be made.[109] Again, this sermon focusses on the mercy of the New Testament; for the fullness of God's mercy could be seen only in the humanity of Christ, which came to him through Mary.[110] As in the Fathers, the greatness of Mary is firmly placed in her Motherhood of God. So the preacher encourages due honour being paid to Our Lady; for example, Saturday devotions—still traditional, lighting candles, praying to her in need.[111] The modern listener would, perhaps correctly, question the implication in the earlier part of the sermon that Mary was placating Christ on behalf of humanity. On the other hand, that element does reflect some of the medieval style of devotion to

[108] Ibid. [fol. 200vb, ll. 19-20, 18-30, 32-38; fol. 210a, ll. 5-11]: "Quod salvavit mundum legitur in figura Hester....per Assueram intellige Christum benignum, qui vere benignus....per Hester absconditam intellige Virginem istam Beatam que, in salutatione angelica, non in foro, non in teatro, non in tumultu, non in congregatione, sed clausa in thalamo orationibus insistendo....per Aman ita dominantem intellige dyabolum, principem quondam mundi, in populum Dei et Virginis conspirantem, et pendere volentem, sed precibus huius regine confusum et convictum."

[109] Ibid. [fol. 201a, ll. 16-34]: "Legitur in Hester multum diligenda est ab omnibus, que salutis nostre causa fuit, et maxime de mulieribus quarum obprobrium abstulit; multo enim amplius quondam despectatores ferunt et viliores quam nunc sunt, et sepius inferebatur eis a multis quod mulier peccavit per lignum, mulier seduxit virum, mulier dampnavit genus humanum, scilicet Eva; sed iam cessant omnia ista, quia quod Eva deliquit ista correxit, que Eva destruxit ista restauravit, quos illa dampnavit ista salvavit; hanc quibus pro salute sua, iugiter imploret iugiter deprecetur."

[110] Ibid. [fol. 201b, ll. 1-13]: "Ista victricem manum Domini in Veteri Testamento misericordissimam prebuit in Novo, ut qui peccata vindicando alios percussit et afflixit se post modum pro peccatis aliorum percuti et affligi permisit et qui antea, peccatores pro peccatis morte affecit, et condempnavit eterne morti, nobis per Mariam factus est tam benignus et mansuetus quod postea seipsum morti turpissime condempnari permisit. Ista attraxit nobis a celis Christum Filium Dei."

[111] Ibid. [fol. 201b, ll. 23-31]: "Hanc speciali laude et prerogativa commenda, vel salutacione per ipsam transeundo, vel saltem semel in ebdomada, missam eius cum devotione audiendo, vel candelam aut cereum diebus sabbatorum in honore eius accedendo, vel ad missam eius oblationem faciendo vel consimile aliud."

Our Lady, which in its turn reflects an inadequate perception of the place of the Holy Spirit within the Trinity and in the life of the Church.

It is notable that these three time-dated sermons are not significantly different from the sermons certainly known to have been preached at Elstow. Were they preached there, they would have confirmed the encouragement being given by the Dominicans to the nuns, by their stressing the love and mercy of God, and by their manifest respect for women as women.

D. THE TIME-AND-PLACE-DATED SERMONS AS ONE GROUP

The first thing that is striking is that, of the thirteen sermons, ten are closely related to the virtue and sacrament of penance. Of the remaining three, one, sermon 136, is devoted to the Passion of Christ—celebrated after Easter; sermon 153 to prayer, and sermon 231 to Our Lady. All the sermons are related to the liturgical year, and the themes, with the exception of sermon 231, are taken from the epistle or gospel readings of the day. With so many of the sermons treating penance and, as we have already seen, having virtually identical content, it is yet a fact that the sermons differ. Either their use of Scripture authorities gives a flavour, as in sermons 78 and 53 with their emphasis on women in Scripture; or the *exempla* add a different dimension. The real cause of the differentiation, however, is the application of distinctions or divisions to the themes. The sermons preached, mostly at Elstow, are witness to the flexibility that the new "scholastic" method of making sermons gave to regular preaching. It must be remembered that, although the preaching to this particular audience occurred in the last quarter of the thirteenth century, many of the sermons in this compilation were made before 1250, at a time when the new method was still fresh. Furthermore, the sermons are far simpler than the theory of the *artes praedicandi* indicates. This may reflect, however, the popular rather than the scholarly nature of this group of sermons. It can also illustrate one of the main principles of sermon theory that initiative in the actual preaching of the sermon must be left to the preacher.

In so far as the actual "division" of the sermon themes is concerned, it should be noted that not all the sermons actually have the divisions defined in the opening of the sermon. This may have been the decision of the person who made the *reportatio* which has eventually appeared in this manuscript, and could have happened at the initial recording of the sermon as heard. Further modification could have occurred in the copying of the sermon into a sermon or model collection which, as we know from above, happened with some of the sermons of Peter of Rheims. A further potential for modification occurred when the sermon was copied into the source book. Yet again, our compiler could have modified what was copied into MS Laud Misc. 511. The only hard evidence we have is the actual existing manuscript. In several cases with the dated sermons, divisions are outlined but not all are amplified. Within the sermons themselves there is some variety in both the length and the manner of the amplification. Some are developed by comment on Scripture content, some by allegory; for example, the story of Hester in sermon 231. Some are developed by etymology; for example, Jerusalem as *visio pacis* in sermon 77. Some are amplified by extended *exempla*, of which more later. These differences emphasise that a too literal application of the theory of the *artes praedicandi* does less than justice to actual sermons.

The analysis of the "authorities" used in these sermons is of interest in this context. As far as possible all have been noted. although a few Scripture ones are still not identified. The gaps, however, are not numerous enough to invalidate the general picture. In the thirteen sermons there are 158 quotations from the Old Testament: thirty-four from the historical books; twenty-seven from the Psalms; forty-five from the Wisdom literature; and fifty-two from the prophets. From the New Testament there are 135 quotations: eighty-four from the Gospels of which thirty-five are from Matthew alone; thirty-six from the Pauline Epistles, and one from Hebrews; ten from the other epistles; and five from the Apocalypse. In all 294 located authorities are from the Scriptures. From the Fathers there are nineteen authorities: two from Augustine; three from Gregory; and eleven from Bernard; while Cassiodorus, Isidore and Jerome are credited with one each. It should be observed that, sometimes when it is possible to identify the actual patristic source, the wrong Father has been credited in the sermon. Such inaccuracy probably results from inaccessibility to the texts of the Fathers, except what was available in florilegia. There are no references to the Gloss, except for two in sermon 136. As for etymologies, nine are found in seven sermons.[112] The interesting group of authorities for

---

[112] Etymologies used in the time-dated sermons:

Sermon 52 [fol. 56b, ll. 23-26]: "Jael uxor Abel Cinei que interpretatur expectans vel ascendens et figurat proficientem per satisfactionem, que est opere pregnans, et plenam reconciliationem expectat."

Sermon 72 [fol. 84b, ll. 27-28]: "per Josue qui et Jesus dictus est per quem salvator interpretatur."

Sermon 77 [fol. 93a, ll. 31-34]: "In hoc quod dicit Jerusalem que visio pacis interpretatur denontat ibi pacem esse firmam."

Sermon 100 [fol. 107vb, ll. 10-11]: "In Jerusalem que interpretatur visio pacis."

these dated sermons is liturgical. Most are drawn from the Divine Office: antiphons, hymns, and versicles with responses. Sermon 231, for the Assumption, the theme of which is an antiphon from the Office, has several examples. Sermon 77 has two references, one to the liturgical season, the other to an Office hymn. Sermon 136 has a quotation from the *Officium* of the Mass for the day, and sermon 230 has reference to the gospel pericope of the preceding day's feast. A list of these liturgical authorities is found in Appendix 8, "The Liturgical Context of the Manuscript." It has not been possible to identify any literary or academic authorities in the dated sermons. In fact it is unlikely that there are any. So the authorities of these sermons, preached mainly at Elstow, are heavily Scriptural. This fits well with what is known of the general pattern of popular preaching by the friars.

Attention should be drawn in this group of sermons to their underlying "English" character. Sermon 78, an adaptation of a sermon by Hugh of St. Cher, has a story about a Cistercian lay-brother of Roche Abbey in Yorkshire. Doubtless, someone substituted an English for a non-English example. Many stories are told about the king of England. Two of the sermons have Latin versions of English idiom. Sermon 100, like some of the Advent sermons discussed below, has the story of the house being prepared for a guest "against his coming," *contra ipsius adventum.*[113] This use of *contra* is not Latin usage. Similar is the command of the king in another story in the same sermon; the Latin text reflects English idiom, not Latin usage.[114] Such illustrations reinforce the conclusion reached above about the English provenance of this sermon collection.

The question of the actual language used by the preachers at Elstow arises here. We have already seen that the nuns were not particularly well-educated.[115] Certainly nuns in thirteenth-century England did not have the contact with university education available to their Benedictine brethren. It is unlikely that the Latin sermons of MS Laud Misc. 511 used at Elstow were delivered in Latin. Depending on the vernacular language most

---

Sermon 78 [fol. 94a, line 3]: "Pascha quod transitus interpretatur."

Sermon 78 [fol. 94vb, ll. 19-21]: "Holofernes interpretatur infirmans vitulum saginatum hic est diabolus."

Sermon 153 [fol. 141va, line 9]: "Jesus enim salvator interpretatur."

Sermon 231 [fol. 200vb, ll. 2-3]: "Quia Maria lingua syra Domina interpretatur mundi."

[113] See n. 81.

[114] See n. 72.

[115] See pages 29-30 and 139-141 above.

familiar to the preachers, the nuns would have heard the sermons either in Anglo-Norman or English. The bias is probably towards English, as the linguistic usages noted above indicate.

These time-dated sermons are rich in *exempla*. While a full discussion of their function is found later, an excursus into the lighter side of sermon content would not go amiss here.[116]

In the fifty or so items listed as *exempla*, often by marginal annotation, there are a number of categories. There are metaphors, mainly commonplace; for example, the "division" of sin,[117] and the Scriptural one "that mortal sin is spiritual leprosy."[118] Some are illustrations from nature like the bee-sting[119] and/or the storm.[120] Some are observations from human actions, like imagining the curiosity of the crowds flocking to Bedford to see St. Peter,[121] or the behaviour of boys at school,[122] or going to school,[123] or men at sea in calm and storm.[124] Two reflect the domestic scene, such as preparing for a visitor,[125] or the tracelessness of water compared with milk, honey or oil.[126] Six of the *exempla* seem to be stories known to the general collections, such as St. Nicholas fasting as an infant and the king marrying his daughter to the Emperor.[127]1 The stag is a parti-

---

[116] See Chapter 6, section B.

[117] Sermon 64 [fol. 69vb, ll. 41-42]: "Nec mirum; peccati enim dividit nos et Deum."

[118] Ibid. [fol. 70b, ll. 27-29]: "Qui in peccato mortali est leprosam spiritualem."

[119] Sermon 90 [fol. 101b, ll. 8-29]: "Sicut apis in vulnere aculeum suum relinquit."

[120] See n. 46.

[121] See n. 82.

[122] Sermon 100 [fol. 107vb, ll. 1-4]: "Magister enim, docens puerum, dulciter blanditur et affatur, sed cum ludis et trussis intenderit et nesciat attendere, flagellat eum virgis asperimis [sic]."

[123] See n. 71.

[124] Sermon 100 [fol. 107a, l. 41–fol. 107b, l. 4]: "Mare enim alioquin est pacificum et quietum, et homines in eo navigantes et securi ludunt iocantur et frivola lo // cuntur; et post pauca insurgit tempestas; tunc clamant, tunc vovent, vota sed statim, cum pedem ad terram posuerint, ad pristinam stultitiam redeunt."

[125] See n. 81.

[126] Sermon 72 [fol. 84va, ll. 24-28]: "Sicut aquam quoniam in effusione olei mellis olei aut lactis de vase, remanet aliud de substantia vel colore vel sapore, sed in effusione aque nullum horum remanet vestigium."

[127] See Appendix 7, "The *Exempla*" for identification.
Sermon 50 [fol. 54b, line 41]: "*Exemplum* de Juda Machabeo."
Sermon 53 [fol. 55va, ll. 30-33]: "Hii etiam sunt sancti imitatores Nicholai qui

cularly popular one, being found in most bestiaries.[128] The most interesting, however, are those featuring *Rex Anglie* or *Rex Francie*, or customs of kings and princes. This group will be discussed in more detail.

Five dated sermons[129] contain references to the king and court life. Sermon 53 has an *exemplum* concerning the custom of making war in spring.[130] The same sermon has a story about losing the realm of France to a powerful enemy, and how the best grounds for resistance should be chosen.[131] This would have topicality for Elstow during the reign of Edward I. In sermon 64 the practice of the king of England sending writs is referred to in an imagined cure for leprosy.[132] Sermon 100 contains the extended comparison about earthly kings, their panoply and their end, compared with the kingship of Christ.[133] The same sermon describes an imaginary visit of the king of England to a house, and the ensuing preparations.[134] Sermon 136 has a parable of a king showing great mercy to

---

adhuc incunis iacens servabat ieiunia."

Sermon 53 [fol. 56a, ll. 4-5]: "*Exemplum* de Karolo et Sancto Egidio."

Sermon 72 [fol. 84va, ll. 32-33] "Sicut rex quidam potentissimus dans filiam suam in coniugium imperatori." Cf Sermon 78 [fol. 94vb, ll. 35-41].

Sermon 230 [fol. 199vb, ll. 15-19]: "Exemplum de Frederico impiissimo, comite sancti Egidii [Raymond of Toulouse?], Rege Johanne et huiusmodi etiam iudeos et paganos castigat Ecclesia."

Sermon 231 [fol. 201va, ll. 26-30] "Consideret prius Teophilum, quoniam cartam fecerat dyabolo, et homagium et adhuc cartam ei restituit, et in celum introduxit."

[128] See n. 51.

[129] Sermons 53, 64, 100, 136, 230.

[130] Sermon 53 [fol. 55b, ll. 27-29]: "Terrarum principes et reges regnorum hiis diebus, scilicet Martii, solent ad bella procedere et inimicos debellare."

[131] Sermon 53 [fol. 56a, ll. 8-16]: "Si enim regnum Francie pro delicto amississes, et haberes inimicum potentissimum et prudentissimum et fortissimum, qui te regnum deforciaret et necessitate haberes pugnare cum eo, nonne, si unus locus esset aptior pugne quam reliquus, et una armatura melior quam altera et securior, et posses eligere, nonne eligeres locum aptiorem et armaturam meliorem et securiorem?"

[132] Sermon 64 [fol. 69va, ll. 39-43]: "Si enim Rex Anglie mitteret tibi cartam ad curandum te de leprosa libenter audires, et intelligeres tum propter sanitatem recuperandam tum propter regis auctoritatem."

[133] See n. 72.

[134] See n. 81.

a fugitive.[135] In sermon 230 is a reference to the king of England crowning his son. (This could be Henry II.) The last story in the group is perhaps the most interesting,[136] with its references to the Justiciar, the assize, and the plea *coram rege*. Whether the king was well-loved or not, or had full control of his kingdom or not, he was still the symbol of earthly power and, in the thirteenth century, the embodiment of the reality of earthly power. The king of England was the source of justice in the land and, through his judges, law on the whole prevailed. There must have been very few places in thirteenth-century England which did not have some real experience of the king, either because their sheriff still had to take the taxes of the shire to the exchequer yearly; or because the king was seen as he progressed through the country in peace-time, eating his supplies from various manors; or because he was known to be meeting his magnates. In less peaceful times he was at war, either with his barons, or the Welsh or the Scots, or in France fending off the ambitions of the French king. For the nuns at Elstow, the power of the king could bear hard, if he took their land-holdings to himself in an interregnum between abbesses. They had contact with the court at that time through their proctors, while some of the nuns undoubtedly had active court connections. *Rex Anglie* was a known figure, and allusion to him in any sermon was bound to rouse or revive interest in the audience.

The final group of *exempla* are those relating to a characteristic phenomenon of the thirteenth century, the crusade. "Taking the cross" was an action which cut across all social barriers, and had a meaning for all. In the strictly religious sense, calling a crusade was the responsibility of the Pope. In the twelfth century, with St. Bernard as its most influential preacher, a crusade was predominantly a religious activity. It was also a very powerful political phenomenon, gathering together as it did desire for land, martial activities and possibility of loot; and as such it became increasingly impossible for the Church to control in any religious sense. As the thirteenth century progressed, the call to take the cross still drew

---

[135] Sermon 136 [fol. 127vb, ll. 25-29]: "Si enim rex aliquis, pro suo ribaldo fugitivo maximas subiret penas, ut ipsum doceret viam revertendi ad se, ut cum eo regnaret, quomodo non insaniret nisi attenderet redire ad dominum?"

[136] Sermon 230 [fol. 199a, line 37–fol. 199b, line 8]: "Si enim peteres terram coram Rege, et frater tuus factus est Iusticiarius et iussu Regis teneret placitum, acciperet // assisam et iudicio dirimeret, nonne multum sperares lucrandi terram petitam, immo etiam si minimum ius haberes in re, quia crederes fratrem tuum tibi favorabilem esse quam alteri parti, maxime si pars adversa inimicus esset Regis et fratris tui?"

forth a strong religious response. but the nature of a crusade modified, and its motivation as well as its operation became less clear. While the Pope called for a crusade for the Holy Land, following two councils at Lyons, the one in 1245, the other in 1274, a crusade had also been called for other parts of Christendom, and looked very much like territorial intervention for other than religious motives. Moreover, in the preaching of a crusade, for which the friars were mobilised, money had to be collected for its implementation. Naturally, if the Pope wanted money from the faithful, the king expected his cut. This considerably modified the development and practice of crusading.

As far as England was concerned, the influence of several princes was not without effect. In 1236 Richard of Cornwall, brother of Henry III, went on crusade, returning successfully after 1240. The rival French king, in the person of Louis IX, answered the call to crusade after 1245. His going made the crusade very fashionable, though his capture in 1250 did affect the complexion of the activity. Henry III took the cross in 1250, undertook in 1252 to leave in 1256, and in 1254 had his vow commuted by the Pope to helping the Church in Sicily. The Lord Edward went on crusade in 1268, returning only in 1274, having been reigning king since 1272. Edward's second attempt—he took the cross again in 1287—never came to fruition. Eventually the money collected for the crusade was shared between Pope and king for other ploys. Undoubtedly, while a crusade was a religious ideal for winning back the Holy Land for Christendom, its actuality was an exercise partaking of elements of pilgrimage, adventure, land hunger, social advancement, vandalism, political intrigue, terrorization, military campaign. For the preacher, the following of Christ as enjoined in the gospel (Luke 14:27) was provided with a well-known if ambiguous image in the crusade. The dated sermons have at least three references to crusading activity, and they reflect some of the above elements. Sermon 77 has an *exemplum* about those who wonder what the Holy Land is like.[137] Sermon 100 has interesting comments about true and false palmers,[138] and sermon 207 refers to travellers and pilgrims praying for safety in travel.[139]

---

[137] Sermon 77 [fol. 93a, ll. 2-10]: "Si aliquis vestrum hic esset crucis caractere insignitus, qui proponeret in Terram Sanctam accedere et ibidem manere, multum congratularetur si audiret bona de terra illa, et magnum solatium esset illi audire bonos rumores sicut habundanciam cibariorum, summam pacem, concordem, dilectionem, nullius boni defectum, et huiusmodi."

[138] See n. 76.

[139] See n. 100.

Undoubtedly, the use of *exempla* added a powerful human touch to the preaching of sermons, not only by way of application of gospel truth to everyday life and so being parabolic in function, but also by being renewers of the interest and attention of the audience. Maybe also, through the desire for entertainment by stories, the *exempla* used by the friars in their preaching helped to attract the large crowds of laity who in the thirteenth century flocked to hear the friars preach. In so far as the nuns of Elstow are concerned, the *exempla* throw little light on their actual community life. This is only to be expected as the *exempla* related here come from pre-existing sermons, the choice of which for preaching to the Elstow community was based on their liturgical occasion and their catechetical content rather than on the relevance or entertainment value of their *exempla*.

E. SOME CATECHETICAL ELEMENTS IN THE DATED SERMONS

The methodology of preaching as catechesis is culturally conditioned. The more preaching is rooted in the current culture, the more effective is the actual teaching of the sermon. Unlike the content of theology, which as a speculative discipline is exploring Christian doctrine both in its development and in its frontiers, the content of catechesis is both a constant as found in the Creeds and a continuum. So while the method of catechesis is constantly changing, the content of catechesis remains constant. The same message is handed on. Summed up in the Creeds, this tradition of handing on the message, or catechesis, centres on the mystery of God, belief in Jesus Christ as God made man, and his message of forgiveness. The only other theological question asked of these particular sermons is what images of God, of Christ, of sin and of human destiny are portrayed therein?

Where the sermons talk about God it is as Name. This is the use in six sermons.[140] But images are used to give more meaning to the Name. In sermon 153 on prayer, the image behind the use of the name "God" is that of Father. This is to be expected in view of the sermon theme, "Whatsoever you ask of the Father in my name...he will give it to you" (John 16:23). Sermon 230 also uses a phrase reminiscent of Ephesians, "God and Father."[141] In sermon 207 the attribute of God that is most dwelt on is

---

[140] Sermons 64, 72, 77, 78, 90, 100.
[141] See n. 68.

mercy. As we have seen, this runs throughout the sermon.[142] Sermon 230 briefly touches on the same theme in describing the tenderness of God.[143] In sermons 64, 207 and 231,[144] a contrast is made between the justice of God in the Old Law and the hand of God's mercy in the New Dispensation. There is only one reference to the Blessed Trinity, couched in the terms of the Athanasian creed.[145] Despite the reference to the good Spirit which makes the path of penance straight,[146] this is only an allusion to the Holy Spirit by assimilation, as in the comparison of Wisdom with the Word of God, rather than a direct statement. Such reticence as these sermons display about defining God seems orthodox.

In the dated sermons, far more images are used for Christ. Many of these spring directly from the gospels as, for example, Christ as judge.[147] But Christ is a judge who suffered for the guilty, and a judge who is our

---

[142] Sermon 207 [fol. 171a, ll. 1-7, 12-14]: "Attende; quis est qui expectat, quoniam Deus cuius magnitudinis secundum ps [144:3] non est finis. Et quam quoniam peccatorem, vita indignum, miserum vermiculum de terra plasmatum et queretur ad miserendum, non ad puniendum...set ista iustitia Deitatis mitigata est per misericordiam humanitatis.

Ibid [fol. 171b, ll. 8-14]: "Magna enim misericordia Dei circa genus humanum; tam misericors est quod sua bona et beneficia tam inimicis quam amicis; tam sibi per bona opera ministrantibus, quam se per peccatum impugnantibus prestat."

See n. 101.

[143] Sermon 230 [fol. 199b, ll. 27-37]: "Sicut dicit Augustinus: 'Nemo de Dei pietate diffidat quia maior est Dei misericordia quam nostra miseria, et si quis ad eum toto corde clamaverit, exaudiet illum, quia misericors est; tardius enim videtur ei veniam peccatori dare quam ipsi peccatori accipere.' Sic enim festinat absolvere reum a tormento conscientie sue quasi plus cruciet ipsum compassio miseri quam ipsum miserum compassio sui."

[144] See n. 98, 101, 110.

[145] See n. 103.

[146] Sermon 52 [fol. 55va, ll. 17-20]: "...quod penitentia nostra debet esse recta, tamquam a spiritu bono, et bona intentione facta ps [142:10] 'Spiritus tuus bonus deducet me in terram rectam.'"

[147] Sermon 136 [fol. 127vb, ll. 7-21]: "Quis enim unquam audivit quod iudex pro reis sponte pateretur? Hoc enim fecit Christus et beneficium huius gratie semper attendendum est; unde ecc 3: 'Gratiam fideiussoris ne obliviscaris in finem,' dedit enim pro te animam suam; fideiussor noster aput Patrem Christus est, sed Adam prevaricatus est transgressum, et mandata Dei in paradiso; unde oportuit eum satisfacere aut perire, sed ille, qui neminem vult perire 'sed omnes salvos fieri, et ad agnitioni sui nominis venire,' factus est homo, et hominis fideiussor aput Patrem, et posuit pro eo animam suam."

brother and therefore puts family interests before those of the accuser.[148] Christ as our brother is also used in sermon 90.[149] Christ as the life of the soul,[150] Christ as light,[151] Christ as Master,[152] Christ as true Temple,[153] Christ as seeking a home in us,[154] are all images within the gospel and Church tradition. Often these images are further described in terms of the customs of the times; for example, Christ being described as judge at an assize;[155] and, as noted above, a judge who gave precedence to "family." Other scriptural comparisons are used: David is Christ,[156] the fatted calf in the parable of the prodigal son represents Christ,[157] Christ as healer,[158] Christ as Saviour.[159] Christ is also declared to be "the best of men,"[160] "the Saint of saints,"[161] "our tender Lord."[162] Some images belong more specifically to the thirteenth century. The image of Christ as king, always

---

[148] See n. 136.

[149] See n. 68, 93.

[150] See n. 83.

[151] See n. 45.

[152] Sermon 64 [fol. 70a, line 36]: "...Dominus optimus magister."

[153] Sermon 78 [fol. 94b, line 42–fol. 94vb, line 1]: "Nomine templi passum Christi corpus in cruce intellige de quo ipse dicit Judeis: // 'Solvite templum hoc et in tribus diebus...'"

[154] Sermon 90 [fol. 101a, ll. 18-25]: "Et tamen ita ingrati sumus eiusdem pro omnibus beneficiis suis quod cum pulsat ad hostium cordis nostri vocando nos per gratiam suam ad penitentiam non aperimus ei. Immo quod peius est ipsum sepe admissum expellimus ab hospicio suo per peccatum quia non habitabit in corpore subdito peccatis."

Sermon 100 [fol. 107vb, ll. 17-21]: "Sic oportet nos contra adventum excelsi regis mundare domum conscientie nostre a fedis peccatis, et ornare eam omni honestate et scientate quia ipse dicit in apo 3 (Apoc. 3:20): 'Ecce sto ad ostium et pulso.'"

[155] See n. 136.

[156] Sermon 52 [fol. 55vb, line 10]: "Dixit David scilicet Christo ad Echay...."

[157] Sermon 78 [fol. 94vb, ll. 23-25]: "Vitulus saginatus est Christus sola caritate incarnatus et passus."

[158] See n. 93.

[159] See n. 61.

[160] See n. 97.

[161] Sermon 72 [fol. 83vb, ll. 9-10]: "...Dominus noster Jesus Christus sanctus sanctorum."

[162] Sermon 153 [fol. 141a, ll. 2-35] "Dominus noster, pius Jesus, magnam audaciam orandi magnamque fiduciam impetrandi singulis in hoc confert evangelio fidelibus dicens...."

somewhat ambiguous in the gospel narratives, is given importance in several sermons.[163] In sermon 100 the parallel between Christ and earthly kings is drawn out in the antitheme.[164] In sermon 230, Christ is described as king crowned in heaven making Peter his doorkeeper.[165] In sermon 231 Christ's kingship is compared to that of Ahasuerus.[166] In a number of sermons, as seen in the preceding section, the *exempla* which speak of *Rex Anglie* in some incident, real or imagined, are by implication referring to Christ the king. The images of Christ as the fortress,[167] or as the quarry in the hunt,[168] belong more completely to medieval culture than most of the other images used. It is significant, as coinciding with the tradition of the Church, that far more images are used for the Second Person of the Blessed Trinity as God made man, than for the Father or the Holy Spirit.

Next, there is the matter of imagery for sin. In twelve out of thirteen sermons, 136 being the exception, there are about thirty-three references. Thirteen of the images are drawn from Scripture: eight compare sin with sickness, or a wound or leprosy; others are darkness, blindness and dumbness. The ass and the colt of the Palm Sunday procession into Jerusalem are allegorized as the old and the young sinner.[169] Other images used

---

[163] J. Leclercq, *L'Idée de la Royauté du Christ au Moyen Age* (Paris, 1959).

[164] See n. 72.

[165] Sermon 230 [fol. 199a, ll. 14-21]: "...Sic Dominus noster Jesus Christus iam coronatus in celis, volens ut omnibus patefieret introitus in regnum celorum, constituit pauperes et peccatores ianitores regni sui dando claves Petro et eius successoribus."

[166] See n. 108.

[167] Sermon 90 [fol. 101va, ll. 16-41]: "Tertio, ut castrum fortissimum de se, ipso tempore guerre, ad se fugientibus prepararet...ps 'Turris fortissima nomen Domini' ...ad munitionem enim loci ita quod sit inexpugnabilis quinque sunt necessaria; oportet enim, ut sit bene et profunde fossatus; item, aqua viva intus et foris, maxime munitus trabibus magnis et spinis hirsutis, muris fortissimis circumdatus, supra rupem altam fundatus, et quod cibis et potibus et aliis necessariis sit instauratus; sic locus iste refugii qui est Christus clavis et lancea profunde fuit fossatus, 'unus militum....' [line 35] item, fuit aqua et sanguine vallatus.... [line 40] item, hirsutus fuit spinea corona, lancea quattuor angulis crucis...."

[168] Sermon 136 [fol. 127a, ll. 5-10]: "Canibus enim venaticis sequentibus vestigia fere sauciate, frequenter venator acclamat, ne forte insequi desistant, aut tepescant; fera nostra fortiter sauciata est Christus..."

[169] Sin as sickness, wound, leprosy: Sermon 50 [fol. 54b, ll. 8-14, 36-40], Sermon 53 [fol. 55vb, ll. 23-33], Sermon 64 [fol. 69va, line 37–fol. 69vb, line 3; fol. 70b, ll. 25-40], Sermon 90 [fol. 101b, line 12–fol. 101va, line 16], Sermon 230 [fol. 199va, ll. 15-

once only are drawn from human experience:[170] sin is a division between God and man; is like a war; is poison, is stupdity; the sinner's life
is under threat like being under the sword of Damocles, like having a frail
body easily shattered like glass. Mortal sin is mentioned several times.[171]
Three of the references are didactic: mortal sin as separating us from God
and—unpurged—leading to hell,[172] and a distinction betweeen original
sin and actual sin.[173] The listing of sins occurs three times only in the
sermons:[174] one showing the sins of the tongue that impede prayer; one
elaborating the list in the Apocalypse; and the third listing in general sins
of the senses. Only two sins are singled out for gravity, and that once
only, namely pride and despair.[175] The conclusion is that the context of
the treatment of sin is pastoral, aiming at stimulating contrition, encourag-
ing honest examination of conscience, rather than giving information
about specific sins. On the whole, the message of the sermons is that the

---

36].
    Sin as darkness: Sermon 64 [fol. 69vb, ll. 14-17].
    Sin as blindness: Sermon 72 [fol. 83vb, ll. 25-26].
    Sin as dumbness: Sermon 72 [fol. 84a, ll. 13-27].
    Sin like the ass: Sermon 100 [fol. 107a, line 27 seq].
[170] Sin as division; Sermon 64 [fol. 69vb, ll. 41-42].
    Sin like war: Sermon 64 [fol. 70va, ll. 1-1].
    Sin like stupidity: Sermon 50 [fol. 54b, line 4 seq].
    Sinful situation is like a hanging sword: Sermon 77 [fol. 93b, line 39 seq].
    Sinful situation is like glass: Sermon 77 [fol. 93va, ll. 11-19].
[171] Images for mortal sin:
Mouth of devil: Sermon 64 [fol. 70b, ll. 40-41].
Demoniac: Sermon 72 [fol. 83vb, ll. 27-29].
Mansion in hell: Sermon 77 [fol. 93va, ll. 38-39].
Gate of hell: Sermon 77 [fol. 93va, ll. 26, 31].
[172] Mortal sin separates us from God: Sermon 72 [fol. 84b, ll. 1-2].
Mortal sin, unpurged, leads to hell: Sermon 78 [fol. 94b, ll.24-26].
[173] Sermon 64 [fol. 69vb, ll. 21-25] "Sicut anima dupliciter polluitur per originale
peccatum et actuale, sic dupliciter mundatur, purgatur sive sanctificatur, ab originali enim purgatur per baptismum, ab actuali per penitentiam."
[174] Sins impeding prayer: Sermon 153 [fol. 141vb, line 35 seq].
    Sin in list from Apocalypse: Sermon 207 [fol. 171va, line 41–fol. 171vb line 5]:
"incredibilis, homicidis, adulteris, periuriis, execratis."
    Sins of five senses: Sermon 231 [fol. 200vb, line 38 seq].
[175] Sin is impediment to prayer: Sermon 153 [fol. 141va, ll. 21-23].
    Sin of pride: Ibid. [fol. 141vb, line 23 seq].
    Sin of despair: Sermon 230 [fol. 199a, ll. 23-32].

evil of sin is to be recognised, so that the hearers of sermons should be sensitive to the need for penance and practise it.

Because of a common assumption that the sermons of the medieval centuries were full of hell and devils, it is of interest to single out this topic for examination in the dated sermons. As one of the four last things, hell has serious significance. In the thirteen sermons there are about twenty-nine references to hell and its denizens: eight to the devil;[176] eight to the place, Hell;[177] eight quotations from Scripture about the devil, or the casting out of demons.[178] Of these Scripture references five are figures or parallels; for example, Pharaoh, Sehon, Holofernes, Maccedah, Haman are all Old Testament persons or places the names of which are interpreted as the devil.[179] It is clear that the frequency of reference to hell and the devil is low in the dated sermons and, moreover, descriptions are few. A certain realism, but not cynicism, concerning the human capacity for evil is found in these sermons. Other imagery for man's last end, namely death, judgement and heaven, is sparse. For death there is the death of Christ only. For judgement and heaven there is the rhetoric and drama of sermon 207, which, as we have seen, describes heaven as a place of friendship with the Blessed Trinity and all the saints, a place where joy is like the water surrounding the fish of the sea.

[176] References to the devil in the time-dated sermons: Sermon 50 [fol. 53vb, ll. 26-35; fol. 54a, line 12 seq], Sermon 64 [fol. 70a, ll. 3-4], Sermon 72 [fol. 84a, line 2], Sermon 77 [fol. 93va, line 21], Sermon 100 [fol. 107b, ll. 15-16; fol. 107va, ll. 5-6], Sermon 230 [fol. 199b, ll. 18-22].

[177] References to hell in the time-dated sermons: Sermon 77 [fol. 93b, line 43; fol. 93va, ll. 28-29; fol 93va, ll. 37-38], Sermon 78 [fol. 94b, ll. 21-22; ll. 25-32 (story of the lay-brother of Roche Abbey)], Sermon 136 [fol. 127a, line 15 seq], Sermon 207 [fol. 171a, ll. 24-26; fol. 171vb, ll. 5-16], Sermon 231 [fol. 201b, ll. 1-13].

[178] References to casting out demons: Sermon 64 [fol. 70va, ll. 40-42].

References to Mary Magdalene from whom 7 demons were cast out; one to the casting out of a legion, 6666, of demons: Sermon 72 [fol. 83vb, ll. 30-34].

Prayer casts demons out: Sermon 153 [fol. 141b, ll. 32-36].

[179] Old Testament figures for the devil: Sermon 53 [fol. 56a, ll. 24-25]: "scilicet penitentie persecutus est pharao cum suis, id est diabolus." Sermon 53 [fol. 56a, ll. 38-40]: "Seon interpretatur callidus vel temptacio, et figurat diabolum qui callidus est." Sermon 53 [fol. 56b, ll. 18-19] "...occidit Holofernem, id est diabolum." Sermon 72 [fol. 4b, ll. 33-36]: "...Maceda quoque exustio interpretatur et percutit in ore gladii, id est, in gladio oris." Sermon 231 [fol. 201a, ll. 5-8]: "...per Aman ita dominantem, intellige dyabolum, principem quondam mundi."

F. CONCLUSION

We began this chapter with a question about the importance of the audience. From the foregoing discussion it can be seen that the Dominican preachers at Elstow took care to select appropriate sermons for the nuns, although it seems clear that none of the sermons were officially *ad moniales*. It is unlikely that the sermons from our manuscript were the only ones preached to the community during these years. Nevertheless, we are certain about the preaching of ten sermons, one of them twice. It is some indication of the state of the community that the Dominican preacher-confessors thought that the same kind of sermons as those preached to laity, and perhaps some specifically to women, were of practical use to the nuns at Elstow. It confirms the impression that the nuns were pious, not particularly learned but, despite the trouble caused by Anora de Baskervil and Agatha Giffard, well-meaning women. Their confessors encouraged them, preaching a God of mercy and compassion; emphasising the need for dealing honestly, speedily and resolutely with sinfulness; fostering devotion to the humanity of Christ, especially through contemplation of the Passion; teaching about prayer; and placing Our Lady and other women from the Scriptures before them as models. These sermons are part of a long tradition of catechesis. The cultural dress of the sermons, particularly in the *exempla*, throw no significant light on the audience at Elstow, although they witness in general to many aspects of thirteenth-century life.

With regard to the question with which we began this chapter, namely, "Does the audience matter?" we are left with two, perhaps contradictory, conclusions. If an audience can be identified, then the use of sermons in particular can be addressed. In the context of sermon theory, the appropriateness of the preacher's choice of sermon for his hearers can be assessed. In the case of Elstow the sermons from our manuscript were happily chosen; and it is clear that to the Dominicans preaching there, the answer to the question, "Does the audience matter?" is undoubtedly positive. In so far as the study of medieval sermons in general is concerned, their content can be studied and analysed and the results prove honest and complete, despite the omission of any consideration of audience, in which case the audience does not matter.

6

Sermon Aids in the Handbook

While sermons constitute the major portion of MS Laud Misc. 511, they are not the only items. One of the problems in listing the contents of the manuscript was to sort out the nature of the short bits. Initially I called most of these pieces "distinctions," but closer study showed that many of them fitted neither the late twelfth-century style of listing different biblical meanings or contexts of one word or phrase nor the later thirteenth-century pattern of sermon distinctions. Reflection on the problem of the transmission of sermons, on the elusive place of the sermon reporter with the resultant *reportationes* in this process, and on the variety of material a thirteenth-century preacher collected, led to a different analysis of the contents of the manuscript. As a result, I reclassified many of my initially-defined distinctions as sermons.

Of the remaining material, some were catenas of quotations from the Fathers, which I thought of as a *mini-Patrologia*. It is still not clear, however, whether the compiler (of manuscript or of its source book) excerpted the Fathers for himself, or whether these selections were from existing *florilegia*, and hence second-hand anthologies. The catenas were liturgically related through their subject. A few distinctions were identified, but there were other items less easy to categorise. One group was the marginal annotations which proved to be summaries of the sermons on the page. At this stage more of the excellent technical organisation of the manuscript became clear, particularly the identification of *exempla* and of patristic authorities in the text by marginal notes. Finally the few remaining unidentified items could only be generally classified as sermon material.

Having looked in detail at the separate categories of items within the manuscript and then put them together in manuscript context, it became very clear that MS Laud Misc. 511 was not just a sermon collection from a variety of sources arranged in liturgical order, it possessed as well a highly organised set of sermon aids. This chapter examines the various forms taken of these sermon aids—marginal summaries, distinctions, *exempla*, florilegia and miscellaneous sermon material.

A. Sermon Summaries or Distinctions in the Marginalia

The catalogue of the manuscript (Appendix 1) shows the incidence of marginalia, especially those which are sermon summaries or distinctions. Of the 180 items in this category, all but one are related to the texts of sermons and *reportationes* in the main columns of the manuscript.

Before discussing the technicalities and content of these sermon summaries or distinctions, it is necessary to examine the meaning of the term "distinction." It is a general-purpose word in much thirteenth-century literature, particularly that connected with the Schools. In the late twelfth and early thirteenth centuries it seems to have had two main meanings: on the one hand a schematic description or analysis of content, and on the other a description of method. Either way it denotes much the same thing.

In the context of sermon studies biblical distinctions illustrate a content connotation of "distinctions." Many scholars have contributed to the current understanding of biblical distinctions. The studies of Beryl Smalley and Andre Wilmart[1] identified some of the early collections of biblical distinctions and drew attention to their exegetical function in aiding the understanding of the different meanings of Scripture, better known perhaps as "the four senses of Scripture,"[2] namely the literal, allegorical, tropological and anagogical meanings. In practice, as Peter Tibber has shown,[3] there were two main meanings of Scripture, the literal and the symbolic; the latter subsuming an allegorical and moral approach to the text; the former increasing in importance as Christian scholars learnt more from their Jewish contemporaries. Richard and Mary Rouse[4] and Louis Bataillon[5] have contributed much in recent years to further understanding about the composition and use of biblical distinctions. Moreover, the latter in his studies of the distinction collections attributed to Maurice de Provins

---

[1] Smalley, *Bible*, 246-249; Andre Wilmart, "Un Répertoire d'exégèse composé en Angleterre vers le début du xiiie siècle," *Memorial Lagrange* (Paris: Libraire Lecoffre, 1940), 307-346.

[2] M.D. Chenu OP, *La Théologie au douzième siècle* (Paris, 1957) 191-209; Henri de Lubac, *Exégèse médiévale, les quatre sens de l'Écriture* (Paris, 1959-1964).

[3] Peter H. Tibber, "The Origins of the Scholastic Sermon c1100—c 1210," unpublished thesis deposited in Bodley MS D Phil c 5001 1983, pp. 65-114.

[4] Rouse, "Biblical Distinctions," 27-37; Rouse, *'Manipulus Florum'*, 69-87; R.H. and M.A. Rouse, "Biblical Distinctiones, the Thematic Sermon and Peter of Capua," paper given at the MSS Symposium, Oxford July 1982.

[5] L.J. Bataillon OP, "Les Instruments de travail des prédicateurs au xiiie siècle," *Culture et travail intellectuel dans l'occident médiéval* (Paris, 1978) 200-205; idem, "Intermediaires entre les traites de morale pratiques et les sermons: les distinctions bibliques alphabetiques," in *Les genres littéraires dans les sources théologiques et philosophiques médiévales: Définition, critique et exploitation* (Louvain la Neuve, 1982) 213-226; idem, "L'Agir humain d'àpres les distinctions bibliques du xiiie siècle," *L'Homme et son univers au moyen âge* (Louvain la Neuve, 1986), 776-790.

and Nicholas Biard has illustrated the contributions of distinction collections to the composition of sermons.

The second connotation of "distinctions" is description of a method.[6] In the new learning of the Paris schools and the emerging universities of the late twelfth and early thirteenth centuries, the making of distinctions became a significant technique or method in academic work as an analysis showing how the subject would be treated. This was soon commonplace in the study of Arts and Law as well as of Scripture and Theology. The distinctions can be descriptive or analytical, or summary/precis, or a mixture. And they do not have to be linked with Scripture. Sermon 163, which is found in Appendix 9, "Selected Texts," is a good example of this methodology.

A brief look at Grosseteste's *Templum Dei*[7] demonstrates a double use of "distinction," both as method and as analysis of content. Grosseteste wrote this book during his episcopate, probably for parish priests as a summary of elementary instruction in the Christian faith. Each section of prose is followed by summaries in distinction form. For example, the first pages of the treatise are summarised as follows:

Templum Dei[8]
    ⌐corporale est corpus hominis cuius partes sunt
        ├fundamentum scilicet venter renes etc.—temperantia
        ├parietes scilicet latera dorsum pectus—fortitudo ⟶ sunt ornamenta
        └tectum scilicet caput in suis sensibus—prudentia
    └spirituale est anima hominis cuius partes sunt
        ├fundamentum scilicet vis cognoscitiva—fides
        ├parietes vis potentialis—spes ⟶ sunt ornamenta
        └tectum vis activa* affectiva**—caritas

Such is the content and style of the whole text. So in Grosseteste's treatise the method of distinction-making is used to provide a summary of content.

In MS Laud Misc. 511 both biblical distinctions and summaries in distinction form are found. The former are represented by two examples

---

[6] Wenzel, *Verses in Sermons*, 75-76; Tibber, "Scholastic Sermons," 86-87.

[7] S. Harrison Thomson, *The Writings of Robert Grosseteste* (Cambridge: CUP, 1940) 138-140, notes at least 66 surviving MSS of *Templum Domini*: 13 in Oxford, 12 in London, 12 in Cambridge. I have examined 6 in London and 3 in Oxford and have chosen London, British Library MS Harley 3244 fol.138-145 and Oxford, Bodleian Library MS Bodley 631 fol.183v-196v as the source of my text. Both are 13th-century, written in clear bookhands. See Robert Grosseteste, *Templum Dei*, edd. Joseph Goering and F.A.C. Mantello (Toronto: PIMS, 1984).

[8] MS Harley 3244 fol. 138v reads *activa*. MS Bodl. 631 fol. 183v reads *affectiva*. Goering and Mantello read *affectiva* (p. 30).

only: a set of distinctions on *Pax*, and a set on *Humilitas est*. The text of the latter is found in Appendix 9, "Selected Texts." The numerous marginal distinctions[9] are summaries of the whole or successive parts of a sermon; whether the sermon be full, summary, or *reportatio*. This close link between the actual sermon text and the marginal distinctions is well illustrated in the version of Sermon 13 in Appendix 9, "Selected Texts." The pattern of distinctions is reproduced as nearly as possible as in the manuscript itself.

Now to turn to the actual distinctions in MS Laud Misc. 511. They are most numerous in the first quarter of the manuscript. As seen in a previous chapter, there are several annotating hands. Up to folio 33v the marginalia hand is clearly Hand A. From folio 34v to 38v brown ink is used for the marginalia. From folio 39a to 46a, the hand is the same, but the ink colour different. Whether the marginalia hand is Hand A is less certain.

The distinctions for Sermon 118 are made in annotating Hand F, which uses the axe-shaped paraph mark. In sermons 128, 162, 180a, the marginalia are written in Hand B. In sermons 220 and 225 it is not possible to be specific about the identity of the hand. Up to and including folio 38v, the sermon summaries are rubricated. The majority of the summaries are written in the bottom margin which, in the practice of the Schools, is narrowly ruled for the addition of notes, references or extra text. Following dictionary usage and the practice recommended by Richard and Mary Rouse, I am taking the word *lemma* to indicate the introductory sentence or clause or phrase or word which is the "subject" of the distinction /summary. 154 distinctions are single, that is, they consist of the *lemma* and one set of distinctions. Eighteen have two sets of distinctions; six have three sets and one has four sets, making 180 in all. Appendix 1, "A Catalogue of MS Laud Misc. 511," gives a list of the *lemmas* of the marginal distinctions/sermon summaries.

It is necessary to examine some of these distinctions to discern their style and function. The examples of the second and much larger group illustrate some of the stylistic forms advocated by many writers of the *artes predicandi*,[10] such as assonance; internal and end-of-line rhymes; gramma-

---

[9] MS Laud Misc. 511, the distinction on *Pax*, no 199 in the catalogue (Appendix 1); on *Humilitas est*, no. 109 in the catalogue. Marginal distinctions in the manuscript are found on folios 5 to 46, and thereafter sporadically on folios 52va, 53va, 55va, 73vb, 74a, 101a+b. All the marginal distinctions have straight lines drawn from the initial *lemma* to each part of the distinction. If there are second and third sets, lines are drawn in the same way. The capital letters as written by the distinction-maker have been retained.

[10] H. Caplan, "'Henry of Hesse' on the Art of Preaching," in Caplan, *Of Eloquence*, 40-78; Thomas Waleys OP, *De Modo Componendi Sermones*, in Th. M. Charland, *Artes*

tical parallels either of tense, word-function or endings; and contrasts of meanings that medieval preachers were advised to use to add colour to their sermons. Richard of Thetford, one of the earliest writers of an *ars predicandi*, advises the use of "dilation," which

> consisted in choosing words of the same grammatical form but different prefixes etc. eg. he says if the theme is *querite eius pacem semper*, it can be developed by adding *"queritur"* in *baptismo*, *"requiritur"* in *penitencia* and so on for as many variations of the root-word as can be found.[11]

Thomas Waleys calls this practice "colours of sounds."[12] He comments on the value of making lists of parallel words, phrases, and internal rhymes, not only as a personal preaching aid but also as a stimulus to fresh insights in preaching.[13] Certainly some of the distinctions in the manuscript seem to function in the manner Waleys was to advise some fifty or sixty years later. The following five distinctions illustrate rhythmic endings, internal assonances, and contrasts of sounds and meanings:

Praedicandi: Contribution à l'histoire de la rhétorique au moyen-âge (Paris, Ottawa, 1936), 325-403, at 327ff.; St. Augustine, *De Doctrina Christiana*, L. IV, section ii-vi.

[11] Jennifer Sweet, "English Preaching," 36.

[12] Waleys, *De Modo*, 372-373. "Quantum ad sonum vocis, moderno tempore, observatur quidam color rhythmicus in fine membrorum divisionis, ut scilicet dictiones finales illarum in sono consimili terminentur. Et quidam non sunt contenti quod talis color appareat tantum in ultimis dictionibus, sed etiam in penultimis, et adhuc etiam in aliis, quando scilicet membra divisionum sunt aliquantulum longa et habent multas dictiones,...//...Quid autem valeant isti colores rhythmici, non video, nisi quod delectent aures audientium; et si fiant in excessum, sicut excedunt aliqui totum sermonem replentes de bilis et trilis, et osus et bosus; tunc constat quod [non] delectant auditorem bene dispositum, scilicet volentem aedificari et spiritualiter refici;...Impediunt autem fructum sermonis, quia, dum aures exteriores nimis occupantur in suavitate vocis, aures interiores ipsius cordis minus hauriunt de virtute rei et sententiae sicut et qui multum delectatur in cantu minus attendit ad rem quae canitur."

[13] Waleys, *De Modo*, 374-375."Ego mihi recollegi de verbis, quando se sponte offerebant memoriae, multas summas verborum quae simili modo terminantur, et in scriptus redegi, ut in divisionibus praedictis possem ea habere praedicta in promptu. Et sensi quod valde mihi profuit talis recollectio, non solum ad habendum prompte verba, sed etiam frequenter ad habendum sententiam divisionis quae, priusquam verba inspicerem, mihi non occurrebat. Occurrebatque mihi quandoque sententia ad verba primi membri divisionis mihi accepta, et non secundi membri divisionis aut tertii....//...Et hoc feci, ut faciliter invenire possem colorem rhythmicum quem volebam."

1. Sermon 34, fol. 35a
   Elemosina
   - Peccatum necat
   - Deo placet
   - Bona temporalia multiplicat
   - Diabolum impugnat
   - Petita a Deo impetrat
   - Ad finem bonum perducit
   - Morienti societatem prebet
   - In infernum ire non permittit
   - In iudicio liberat

2. Sermon 36, fol. 37vb
   Vocat nos Deus
   - a labore ad requiem
   - a mutabilitate ad immutabilitatem
   - a servitute ad libertatem
   - a paupertate ad thesaurum multiplicem
   - a fame ad saturitatem
   - a vilitate ad honorem
   - ab amaritudine ad dulcedinem
   - a merore ad iocunditatem
   - a miseria et bello ad concordiam ⟨et pacem⟩[14]

3. Sermon 67, fol. 73vb
   Agenda est penitentia
   - quia Deo desiderabilis
   - quia anime est utilis
   - quia Dei regnum instaurat
   - quia regnum diaboli conterit

4. Sermon 118, fol. 116vb
   Recidivans
   - Deum contra se provocat
   - demones letificat
   - animam suam vilificat
   - animam suam deturpat
   - angelos gaudio privat
   - resurrectionis Dominice derogat
   - ⟨ceteris creaturis peccator⟩ contrarius existit[15]

[14] Words in brackets added from body of text.

[15] Parchment damaged; phrase in brackets reconstituted from sermon text.

5. Sermon 225, fol. 194a
   Reddere rationem debemus de
         ├─pacto quod infregimus
         ├─precepto quod contempsimus
         └─commisso quod male tractavimus

Each of these distinctions has matching sounds of word-endings and parallel constructions, while some have a common pattern of rhythm, even a beat measure. In the thirteenth century, the process of learning depended mainly on the ears. In the lecture room the master was the only one to have a book, which he expounded to his listening students. For modern students, who have ready access to many books, the eyes are far more important than the ears. These different ways of learning require different ways of memorising. Such verbal harmonies as the above distinctions possess could be as useful a mnemonic to the preacher and his hearers as it would be to the master and his students.

The next distinction is an example of one with three parts. This is to illustrate the complex nature of a few of the distinctions in the manuscript. It is interesting to see how comprehensive is the possible development of the initial comparison of charity with fire. It also illustrates that the development travelled one-third of a path each time. In fact, the very content of the distinction shows how other developmental routes are present in it. There are twelve other distinctions in this Sermon 31, which together give an excellent summary of the whole sermon.

Sermon 31, fol. 31v
   Caritas est velud ignis
        ├─quia tendit sursum
        ├─quia in aliquid agit
        └─quia exardescit et crescit meditando de
               ├─Dei beneficiis que nobis contulit
               ├─debitis que dimisit. Condonavit enim nobis omnia delicta
                       ├─que multa sunt
                       ├─pondere gravia
                       └─effectum sordida
               └─bonis que promisit

The first five distinctions recorded above were selected from various parts of the manuscript to illustrate the fact that marginal summary distinctions were not limited to its first quarter. Nevertheless, this first part is characterised by numerous marginal distinctions. Most of them are written in the narrow lines ruled in the bottom margins of each folio beneath the writing block. These summary distinctions prove to be closely related, either through analysis or description, to the prose text in the neighbouring columns. Sometimes they are linked with arabic numerals written in

the side margins. Up to folio 38v, which is mostly in Hand A, the marginal
distinctions are rubricated. So they not only belong to the original text, but
were planned to be so. It is more probable that they were not found in the
original source books, otherwise marginal distinctions would have been
copied into the remaining three-quarters of the manuscript from the source
books. It could be that an attempt to continue the practice of making distinction summaries in the margins is reflected in the slightly differing annotating hands of folios 34v-46a. To compose marginal distinctions as summaries requires skill in making a precis. The marginal distinctions vary in
their quality as summaries. The next group of eight distinctions is chosen
to illustrate different ways of summarising content.

1. Sermon 1, fol. 5b
    Dies dicitur Christus quia
        ├─Rubuit in mane
        ├─Splenduit in meridie
        └─Palluit in passione

2. Sermon 5, fol. 7b
    Christus homo fieri voluit
        ├─ut homo eum videre posset
        ├─ut haberet quod offerret pro hominis salutis
        ├─ut homo hominem liberaret
        ├─ut diabolus ab homine vinceretur
        ├─ut diabolus gaudium hominis videret
        ├─ut homo Dei cerneret erga cum caritatem
        └─ut homo peccare non auderet

3. Sermon 8, fol. 10b
    Detractores
        ├─bona diminuunt
        ├─mala exaggerant
        ├─dubia pervertunt
        └─famam tollunt

4. Sermon 15, fol. 17va
    Ad regem spectant[16]
        ├─subditos protegere
        ├─contra unumquemque defendere
        ├─pacem reformare
        ├─pacis perturbatores corrigere
        ├─ius suum cuilibet tribuere
        └─hostes destruere et expugnare

[16] This is similar to the coronation oath that the kings of England swore. See
Chapter 8.

5. Sermon 22, fol. 21vb

Christus uno die[17]
- A Magis est adoratus
- A Johanne est baptizatus
- Aquam in vinum in nuptiis mutavit

6. Sermon 24, fol. 22b

Penitentia debet esse
- spontanea
- propria
- viva
- pura
- placida
- discreta

7. Sermon 32, fol. 34r

Dolet ecclesia ex presentia tristabilium
- In pauperum afflictione
- In peccatorum inundacione
- In adversariorum multiplicacione
  - saracenorum
  - corasminorum
  - tartarorum
  - hereticorum
  - falsorum Christianorum

8. Sermon 36, fol. 37b[18]

○ ———
- pro mane est pueritia
- hora tertia, adolescentia
- hora nona, senectus
- hora undecim, decrepitus

In these examples there is a marked absence of biblical distinctions: though the one quoted from sermon 36 (fol. 37b) is an allegorical interpretation of the parable of the labourers in the vineyard (Matt. 20:1-16); while that taken from sermon 22 (fol. 21vb) is a conflation of the mysteries of the life of Christ celebrated liturgically on the feast of the Epiphany. The distinctions from sermon 1 (fol. 5b) and sermon 36 (fol. 37b) are metaphor and allegory; while the one taken from sermon 5 (fol. 7vb) is a doctrinal summary of reasons for the incarnation. Those quoted from sermon 8 (fol. 10b) and from sermon 24 (fol. 22b) are moral exhortation. That from ser-

---

[17] This is similar to the Magnificat antiphon for the feast of the Epiphany.

[18] This distinction has no *lemma*, only a large red spot. To add clarity a *lemma*, *Reddet Deus mercedem laborum*, is taken from the sermon.

mon 15 (fol. 17va) is a neat summary of the king's duties deriving from the coronation oath. The three-stage distinction from sermon 32 (fol. 34r) gives a desolate picture of the Church, but an interesting nomination of the groups seen as enemies.

To gain a further insight into the function of the distinction as a sermon summary, it is useful to examine the distinctions together with the full transcript of sermon 13 in Appendix 9, "Selected Texts," and also the distinctions of sermon 18 (fol. 18a-20va) which are transcribed below. In the first place, the marginal distinctions of both sermons give the preacher a brief summary of most of the sermon's content. Secondly, the order of the summary distinctions gives a clearer picture of the organisation of the sermon, while the verbal patterns and rhymes aid—as we have seen—the preacher's memory. Lastly, such summary distinctions made it possible for a preacher to deliver a new sermon from the written structure before him in the manuscript. For the user of a collection of sermons, margin distinctions could reduce preparation time and permit a more flexible use of the material than reading or declaiming a sermon written out in full.

Distinction 1, fol. 19a
    Est convivium
            ├demonum
            ├potatorum
            ├bonorum
            └beatorum

Distinction 2, fol. 19vb
    Fercula in convivio diaboli
            ├longa scessio (sic)
            ├bolismus, id est, appetitus
            ├prepropera comestio
            ├superflua laucio
            ├studiosa ciborum preparatio
            ├crapula in cibo
            ├ebrietas in potu
            ├prodigalitas in divitibus
            ├tenacitas in pauperibus
            ├de bonis collatis ingratitudo
            └in nugis nimia dissolutio

Distinction 3, fol. 19vb
    Consideranda sunt in comedendo
            ├fames
            ├labor
            └complexio

Distinction 4, fol. 19vb
    Consideranda sunt in bibenda
        ├─sitis
        ├─vis potus
        └─ciborum qualitas

Distinction 5, fol. 20a-20b
    Convivium
        ├─linguarum
        ├─cordium—fercula huius convivii
        │   ├─Oratio
        │   ├─Confessio
        │   ├─Praedicatio
        │   ├─Sacra lectio
        │   ├─Catholica disputatio
        │   ├─Gratiarum actio
        │   ├─Honorabilis abstinentia
        │   └─Fortitudo sancta in
        │   ├─consiliis
        │   ├─predicationibus
        │   └─iudiciis
        └─bonorum operum

Distinction 6, fol. 20b
    per picem intelliguntur
        ├─Superbia
        ├─Invidia
        ├─Ira
        ├─Accidia
        └─Cupiditas terrena

The small compass that such distinctions use on a page, as well as the clarity that the diagrammatic pattern gives, shows the value of this technique of summarising sermons to the preacher. Perhaps too it was the ability to write down distinctions while another was preaching that enabled hearers to make *reportationes*. In scholastic exercises, such an ability would be helpful to the young preacher who had to continue at collation the sermon begun that morning by the master. In his inimitable manner, Thomas Waleys has comments on the making of divisions.[19] The practice

[19] Waleys, *De Modo*, 370-371. "Verum est tamen quod talis modus est facilis praedicatori ipsi, et potest faciliter in infinitum procedere, donec thema suum oblivioni tradiderit, si hoc sibi expediens videatur. V.g. potest enim primo thema suum dividere duobus aut tribus aut quattuor modis, vel pluribus si vult et postmodum auctoritates quibus membra divisionum confirmatur iterum dividere et iterum subdividere sicut prius thema fecerat, et iterum membra illius subdivisionis auctoritatibus

exemplified in MS Laud Misc. 511 would fall into the category of distinc-
tion- or division-making that he approved.

If the distinctions used as illustration in the preceding pages are
looked at in conjunction with the list of *lemmas* some interesting trends
emerge. There is a predominance of distinctions concerning God, Jesus
Christ, charity, sin, penitence. It is equally interesting to note, contrary to
a common expectation of medieval religious teaching, the small number
of distinctions relating to the devil and hell.

It is difficult to find a point of comparison for the sermon distinctions
written in MS Laud Misc. 511. I have had opportunity only to look at distinctions on *Navis* by Nicholas Biard;[20] on *Navicula* by Maurice of Provins;[21] and at a sermon by William of Mailly on the text, *Domine, salva
nos, perimus* (Matt. 8:25).[22] These three preachers were probably mendicants, but evidence of their specific membership of an Order is weak. The
sermon collections of William of Mailly and Nicholas Biard are mentioned
in the first Paris list of prices of *exemplaria* before 1275.[23] As preachers,
they were active in the second half of the thirteenth century. Their work
is either contemporary with, or just later than, the composition of some of
the sermons in MS Laud Misc. 511. There is only one sermon in the manuscript that treats at some length of *navis*, namely, sermon 30. So the following comments are in the nature of a microcosmic approach.

Nicholas uses three distinctions: *Navis dicitur crux Christi; Navis est
penitentia*; and *Navis dicitur homo*. Each distinction is expanded by reference

---

confirmare et illas auctoritates iterum subdividere sicut priores auctoritates divise-
rat, et eodem modo facere de illis sicut de prioribus, et sic in infinitum procedere.
Sed, cum infinitas reprobetur, tam a natura quam ab arte, et dicta superflua milti-
plicatio nec aedificet nec utilitatem aliquam afferat audientibus, immo quamdam
confusionem et obscuritatem intellectioni ingerat, melius est ad certum numerum
divisiones et subdivisiones reducere. Sufficit autem ut fiat divisio thematis, sive illa
sit tantum simplex divisio ejus, sive sit duplicata vel triplicata modo superius expla-
nato; at quod fiat subdivisio auctoritatum confirmantium membra divisionis thematis; quae quidem subdivisio auctoritatum non sit duplicata vel triplicata, sicut for-
san erat divisio thematis, sed una tantum simplex. Et sic vidi ab optimis praedicato-
ribus observari."

[20] Nicholaus de Biard, *Distinctiones*, in Paris, BN MS lat. 16489, fol. 169vb-173rb.

[21] Maurice de Provins, *Distinctiones*, in Paris, BN MS lat. 3271, fol. 157va-158ra.

[22] Guiaullme de Mailly, Sermon for the Fourth Sunday after Epiphany in
Venezia, MS La Fava 39, fol. 27r-29v.

[23] Denifle and Chatelain, *Chartularium*, 2: 648-650. The printer of the volume put
these entries of documents at the end of the book, so that they are out of chronological order. The first Paris list pre-dates 1275.

to authorities, especially Scripture. The interpretations fit with different senses of Scripture.

Maurice of Provins gives a similar treatment, but more in note form than Nicholas. Each element in the distinction is illustrated, sometimes by Scripture. His main distinctions are taken from the prose text. There are no patterns as in our manuscript.

> Nota quod triplex est navicula. Est enim navicula ecclesie, navicula anime, navicula penitencie. Ecclesia dicitur navis ratione continentie, eminentie et sustinentie. Item anima dicitur navis ratione triplici sicut et ecclesia, ratione materie, forme, et finalis cause. Item penitentia dicitur navis...et hoc triplici ratione, facture, portature, et gubernatoris.

Each of the elements in each distinction has been followed with suitable Scripture references. In the last distinction, however, *gubernatoris* is developed further than *facture* or *portature*, as follows:

> Item ratione gubernatoris. Et nota quod ad hoc bene gubernetur navicula. Necesse est quod naute habeant remos, velum, et anchoram et hastorium.

Then there is a brief development of each of these elements, and the passage ends with the comment:

> Et nota quod exeunti de navicula hac occurrit diabolus ad temptandum.

William of Mailly's sermon is more like Sermon 30 than the other two sets of distinctions. William describes the ship of holiness and penitence in which men take refuge, giving four reasons for their boarding the ship:

> ad naviculam sanctitatis sive penitencie confugiunt...Notandum igitur quod propter quattuor solent homines navem ascendere
> Primum ad diluvium evadendum...
> Secundo ascendunt homines navem ad transfretandum...
> Tercio ascenditur navis ad mercandum...
> Quarto ascendunt navem ad piscandum...

In the second part of the sermon William shows seven ways in which the ship is salvation in the storm:

> Notandum quod, sicut ad salvationem navis in tempestate alius navem exhonerat, alius exhaurit, alius rupturas obstruit, alius anchoram iacet, alius velum deponit, alius gubernaculum sumit, alius navigando aquas superat...
> Primo, igitur paupertas navem exhonerat, nam divicie mergunt.
> Secundo, humilitas navem anime exhaurit aquas peccati...
> Tercio, timor rupturas obstruit...

Quarto, spes anchoram iacet...
Quinto, paciencia sive benignitas velum deponit et ventus iniurie sibi
illate viam habet...
Sexto, prudencia sive sapiencia gubernaculum sumit...
Septimo, iustitia undas superat...

Each section of the sermon is developed in the usual way with commentary and Scriptural authorities.

Sermon 30 in MS Laud Misc. 511, fol. 25vb-29va, comes from the source book, *Niger Minor*, and was composed for the Fourth Sunday after Epiphany, like William of Mailly's. The theme, however, was Matthew 8:23, "Ascendente Jesu in naviculam, secuti sunt eum discipuli eius." The annotator has summarised the sermon in seven distinctions of which the *lemmata* are noted here: *Terra est triplex; Duplex est navis una; In cupiditate; Caritas dicitur navis propter; Pericula maris; Periclitati sunt;* and *Divitie sunt*. Of these seven distinctions, unlike the ones of William and Maurice above, which are solely on the word *navicula*, only three are related to *navis*:

1. Distinction 2, fol. 26a
   Duplex est navis, una
   ⎰qui vehit ad celum
   ⎱qui vehit ad infernum

2. Distinction 4, fol. 26va
   Caritas dicitur navis propter
   ⎰famis subventionem
   ⎨equitudinem
   ⎩expeditionem

3. Distinction 5, fol. 29a
   Pericula maris
   ⎰Cirtes, Avaritie est
   ⎪Sirene
   ⎨Serenina[24] duplex Superbia
   ⎪Cilla, Luxurie ⟨est⟩
   ⎩Caribdis, Gula est

In comparison with the biblical distinctions of Maurice and William it seems clear that our distinction maker, Scribe A, is not interested in working out numerous useful parallels of meanings of "navis" with appropriate authorities from Scripture; that is, composing biblical distinctions. Rather, he is providing only a simple summary of a sermon. The biblical

---

[24] *Serenina*: This should be replaced with "Acroceraunia," a promontory in Epirus dangerous to mariners. This distinction shows some knowledge of Greek myths.

distinctions of Maurice and William, however, illustrate the utility and versatility of the distinction as method, and the value of specific distinction collections: namely, that the same image can be given such variety in application that the freshness and impact of the image is maintained. At its best, the use of distinctions could foster spontaneity in the preacher and eager listening in the sermon hearers so that the message could be heard, reflected on, prayed about and acted out, as if for the first time.

Nevertheless, the making of distinctions could become as mechanical as any other device in rhetoric: it could lapse into commonplaces which would bore the listeners. Perhaps the danger of this would be greatest with well-known distinctions; for example, on "contritio," "confessio" and "satisfactio." In MS Laud Misc. 511 there are five distinctions clearly linked with this commonplace.

Distinction 1, Sermon 7, fol. 9v
    mundemur per
        ├contritionem
        ├confessionem
        └satisfactionem

Distinction 2, Sermon 12, fol. 13va
    Dies adventus docet nos
        ├per veram contritionem Christum querere
        ├per veram confessionem invenire
        └per bona opera ipsum sequi ad eterna

Distinction 3, Sermon 27, fol. 24b
    Triplex peccamus
        ├corde
        ├ore
        └opere
               └sic triplex satisfaciamus
                    ├cordis contritione
                    ├oris confessione
                    └operis satisfactione

Distinction 4, Sermon 67, fol. 74va
    Mundari contingit tripliciter in
        ├contritione
        ├confessione
        └satisfactione

Distinction 5, Sermon 50, fol. 54r
    Tres diete penitentia
        ├contritio triplex quod
            ├diabolo consensit
            ├peccatum perpetravit

        └nunquam ulterius recidivabit
    ─confessio sit in festina quia
        ├ibi incipiendum est ps. precinit Domino in confessione
        ├plus valet ieiunium unius diei sub vera confessione quam mille
                                           annorum in peccato
        ├tunc manus abluunt quando cibum sumpserunt et non ante
        ├ferrum extrahunt ante vulnus sanatum est
        └in cibum Domini fel apponunt
    └satisfactio

Two of the five quoted above are standard in division and content,
the first one and the fourth. These could be the tired commonplace distinction. The remaining three are good examples of a creative distinction, as
each throws a different light on the understanding of the sacrament of
penance: one linking it to the discovery and following of Christ; one to
actions of the heart, of speech and of deed; one to the penitential aspect
of the sacrament. It is useful to compare these three with the nuanced and
well-nigh contemporary teaching on contrition, confession and satisfaction
in the sacrament of penance by St. Thomas Aquinas in chapter 72 of Book
4 of his *Summa contra Gentiles*, "On the Necessity of Penance and Its
Parts.[25] In the teaching of Thomas and in the distinctions noted above,
the involvement of the penitent through conversion of heart is fostered.
Like any other kind of sermon aid, distinctions are only as good, creative
and relevant as their preacher-authors and preacher-users.

It is difficult to assess with exactitude the value of the marginal
distinctions in our manuscript. The above commentary has dealt with only
twenty-eight of the 180 in the manuscript, and has illustrated some of the
variety, simplicity and complexity of their style and content. But most of
the 180 appear regularly only in the first quarter of the manuscript. For
this portion they provide as it were a useful table of contents. Nothing in
the codicology of the manuscript indicates why marginal distinctions were
not made through the whole book, or at least through the first fifteen
gatherings. The process of analysis is time-consuming, however, and perhaps only the first part was so treated before the book was bound. It is
also possible that scribe B did not have the same interest and skill in making distinctions as scribe A, who wrote most of the folios 5-50 which are
supplied with marginal distinction summaries. What is certain is that the

---

[25] Saint Thomas Aquinas, *Summa contra Gentiles*, Book 4: *Salvation*, trans. Charles
J. O'Neill (Notre Dame/London: Univ. of Notre Dame Press, 1975) 277-282; see also
St. Thomas Aquinas, *Theological Texts*, selected and edited by Thomas Gilbey,
(Oxford: OUP, 1955), 378-382.

marginal distinctions as found in the manuscript contribute not only to its usefulness as a sermon collection, but also to its function as a preacher's handbook.

B. THE *EXEMPLA* IN MS LAUD MISCELLANEOUS 511

The *exempla* to be found in our manuscript throw further light upon the thoughts and intentions of the compiler of the handbook. Collections of *exempla* have fascinated students of sermons for over a century. Lecoy de la Marche, Crane and Hervieux have edited *exempla* collections by Etienne de Bourbon OP, Jacques de Vitry and Odo of Cheriton.[26] Scholars like Little and Welther continued the pattern with editions of several popular but anonymous collections, and Beryl Smalley showed the link between the lecture in the Schools and *exempla* collections in her article on Langton's *exempla*, most of which found their way into Odo of Cheriton's collection.[27] Two manuscripts initially used as codicological comparisons with MS Laud Misc. 511, namely MS Harley 3244, a library version of a Dominican preacher's handbook, and MS Roy 7 D i, a Cambridge Dominican's portable book of *exempla*, seem to be largely based on Odo of Cheriton's work. It is not surprising that an English collection should be preferred by, and perhaps be more accessible to, English compilers.[28] All these works have helped to provide a context in which to place the *exempla* noted in the manuscript.

There are over 450 *exempla* in our manuscript. Appendix 7, "The *Exempla*," lists as many as I have been able to locate and, in many cases, to identify. Of the 450, at least 355 are indicated as such by the scribes and annotators, mainly by side marginal notation (sometimes hidden in the

---

[26] A. Lecoy de la Marche, *Anecdotes historiques legendes et applogues tirés du receuil inédit d'Etienne de Bourbon, dominicain du xiiie siècle* (Paris, 1877); T.F. Crane, *The Exempla or Illustrative Stories from the Sermones Vulgares of Jacques de Vitry* (London, 1890); L. Hervieux, *Les Fabulistes depuis le siècle d'Auguste jusqu'à la fin du moyen age*, vol 4. *Etudes de Cheriton et ses derivés (Les Fabulae et Parabolae de Odo de Cheriton)* (Paris, 1896).

[27] A.G. Little, *Liber Exemplorum ad Usum Praedicantium* (Aberdeen, 1908); J.Th. Welter, *Le Speculum Laicorum, édition d'une collection d'exempla composée en Angleterre a la fin du xiiie siècle* (Paris, 1914); idem, *La Tabula Exemplorum secundum ordinem alphabeti: recueil d'exempla compilé en France a la fin du xiiie siècle* (Paris/Toulouse, 1926); Beryl Smalley, "'Exempla' in the Commentaries of Stephen Langton," *Bulletin of the John Rylands Library* 17, no 1, January 1933.

[28] Ward and Herbert, *Catalogue of Romances*, 3: 457-458, 477-478.

binding or even partially trimmed off) ex^m. A few *exempla* are identified by drawings of fingers, faces, or by the writing of titles or comments. At least another forty are found to be repetitions of *exempla* already marked; some as well-known literary references, some as stories about the king and Court, some similar to items already indicated as *exempla*, and some as *exempla* identified in the standard collections. About another fifty have been included because the material parallels items already marginally marked as *exempla*. The most difficult decision has concerned the comparisons, either metaphor or simile. The criterion I have applied is the difference between illustrative images and theological images. The latter are more closely related to Scripture. On the whole, I have omitted the latter and retained the former. It must be emphasised that, in the manuscript, items which are neither story nor anecdote are identified as *exempla* by the compiler. Clearly, the compiler had a broader concept of what an *exemplum* is than did the contemporary compilers of the standard collections.

The practical decision of what to include or omit raises the real question, what is an *exemplum*?[29] In the thirteenth century, Odo of Cheriton pointed the way in distinguishing between *fabulae* and *parabolas*. For the use of the latter all Christian preachers have a venerable *exemplar*. Thus it is that the theological content of an *exemplum* cannot be ignored as, "just an *exemplum*." Holcot's "pictures" seem to be grappling with just such a problem. A further element in the attempt at defining an *exemplum* is the temptation to regard it as a literary genre like "the ballad," or "the novel." It seems to me that the word "*exemplum*" is really the medieval preacher's word, a common noun, for any illustrative material, sacred or secular, poetic or comic, fact or fiction. The analogical use of illustrative material is the teacher's or preacher's method of explanation, using the known to discover, to illuminate, but not to identify with, the unknown. The more apt the illustrative material, the better will be the quality of understanding engendered. Used in this way, the *exemplum* is important as the possible

---

[29] L.J. Bataillon, "Les 'Exempla' dans les sermons universitaires" (unpublished paper from the author) has a valuable discussion on this question. See also Claude Bremond, Jacques Le Goff and Jean Claude Schmitt, *L"Exemplum"* (Turnhout: Brepols, 1982); also L.J. Bataillon OP, "'Similitudines' et 'exempla' dans les sermons du xiiie siècle" in *The Bible in the Medieval World: Essays in Memory of Beryl Smalley*, edd. Katharine Walsh and Diana Wood, SCH Subsidia 4 (Oxford: Basil Blackwell, 1985) 191-205; idem, "Les Images dans les sermons du xiiie siècle," *Freiburger zeitschrift für Philosophie und Theologie* (Sonder Abdruck Aus BD 37, 1990) Heft 3, 327-395; Jacques Berlioz and M.A. Polo de Beaulieu, *Les Exempla médiévaux* (Garae Hesiode, 1993).

catalyst of understanding. This function of the *exemplum* as method under-
lies my choice of extra, non-indicated *exempla* in the manuscript. But the
exemplum is Janus-like. The more effective it is as an aid to spiritual understanding, the greater is its value in illustrating the earthy, ordinary, human
life in which the spiritual is rooted. Hence historians have used the *exemplum*, whose primary use by the preacher was for spiritual instruction, as
historical evidence. So the following description of the *exempla* found in
our manuscript has a two-fold focus: what these stories and illustrations
can tell us of matters of interest, knowledge or practice in mid-thirteenth
century England; and how the *exempla* are effective or otherwise as a resource to practising preachers of the time.

The *exempla* in the manuscript can be placed in five groups: actual
stories whether fact, fiction, myth, fable, legend; pious anecdotes or comparisons about Christ, the saints, the devil; *de natura rerum*—illustrations
taken from animals, birds, inanimate things, science; stories and comparisons from daily life: household, family, sickness, health, foibles, occupations, pilgrimages, travels, hospitality; illustrations from the life of the
king, cort, war, government, processes of justice. Parenthetical references
in the text are to the entries in the catalogue of *exempla* found in Appendix
7; thus: (*Serm.* 13 [3]) refers to the third *exemplum* identified in Sermon 13.

In the first group the stories about Alexander, Antiochus, Constantine, Julian, Charlemagne were likely to be found in the literary works of
the time, or through the collections of stories like Jacques de Vitry's or
Odo of Cheriton's. The Lives of the Saints contained stories like those of
Nicholas and Theophilus. Nor should the function of the Second Nocturn
of Matins as a source of stories of the saints be forgotten. Stories of Circe,
Scylla and Charybdis came from classical poetry, and possibly seamen's
tales. Of more interest to the historian are the stories which record a real
event like the execution of the Mariscoes (*Serm.* 13 [9]), or like the Paris
Master (*Serm.* 46 [5]) with his change of mind about pluralism. The story
of the *conversus* of Roche, with its English verse, seems more like the pious
anecdotes which abound in the *Vitae Fratrum*, *Liber Exemplorum* and the
Cambridge Dominican's collection. On the other hand, the tantalising
references to a duel at Stamford (*Serm.* 232 [2]), and the theft of forty
marks from King Philip's exchequer (*Serm.* 226 [3]), seem to indicate real
and well-known events. It is not clear whether the mention of John Mauntel at the end of Sermon 232 (*Serm.* 232 [3]) is a reference to the famous
clerk who was a civil servant of Henry III,[30] but it is a possibility. In

---

[30] F.M. Powicke, *The Thirteenth Century*, 2nd ed. (Oxford: Clarendon Press, 1962),
references to John Maunsel: 113n, 116, 145n, 154, 162-164, 170-171, 175, 178, 278, 339,
590-591. See also Emden, *BRUO*, 2: 1217-1218.

most of the sermons, these *exempla* were only named, leaving the development—either as illustrations of a point already made, or as the base for moralising—to the preacher's initiative. The stories most detailed, the Paris Master and the Mariscoes, were more illustration than moralisation.

The pious *exempla* include a number about Christ. One compares the poor to the feet of Christ (*Serm.* 29 [8]), a sentiment likely to appeal to the early friars who still observed the practice of walking on their journeys. Two compare Christ to a master (*Serm.* 38, 39 [1]). One refers directly to the Schools (*Serm.* 57 [7]), comparing Christ to the master writing in the ink of his blood on the parchment of his body. Christ is also linked with the image of the ship (*Serm.* 206 [2]) and the wrestler (*Serm.* 89 [2] and 99 [3]). One *exemplum* is about Saint Peter (*Serm.* 72 [1]), describing an imaginary visit to Bedford by the apostle. Herein the preacher chides his hearers for being readier to come and see Peter than to accept the real presence of Christ. *Exempla* about the devil are few, about six only. One describes the devil in the traditional imagery of lion and serpent (*Serm.* 57 [12]). Another (*Serm.* 74 [1]) refers to the fall of the devil and his sons. Images of the devil and his effects are found in (*Serm.* 7 [1], 13 [6, 7]), while (*Serm.* 46 [8]) is the "horrible story" about the man whose call on the devil was unexpectedly answered.

Many *exempla* fall into the category, *de natura rerum*. Some are devoted to animals, real and mythical: the ass (*Serm.* 100 [3]) with its weak foreparts; the cat (*Serm.* 118 [3]) that longs for fish but does not like getting its paws wet; the dog (*Serm.* 229 [2], 130 [3]) as occupant of the butcher's shop, as barking at passers-by, as following at its master's heel (*Serm.* 32 [1]); pigs which can reduce a garden to a wallow (*Serm.* 229 [3]); the loss of a horse (*Serm.* 164 [1]); the timidity and gregariousness of sheep (*Serm.* 69 [2]). Such *exempla* of ordinary village and town life show a continuity in human experience which makes good preaching material. Other animal and bird stories: the elephant as battle animal (*Serm.* 95 [2]), the peculiarity of the hare's eyesight (*Serm.* 46 [1, 4]), the salamander (*Serm.* 8 [3]), the stag which sheds its coat etc. after drinking (*Serm.* 12 [2], 78 [3]), the pelican feeding its young with its blood (*Serm.* 64 [3] and 95 [11]), the peacock with its weak feet (*Serm.* 46 [7]), the bee-sting (*Serm.* 90 [3]), the fly (*Serm.* 47 [1]), and the bird laying three eggs but hatching only two (*Serm.* 29 [1]) reflect the knowledge available in the bestiaries. To the preacher all these *exempla* were fruitful sources of interest and information, valuable for moralisation. The *exemplum* which notes that all animals however rapacious love their own kind (*Serm.* 29 [2]), which is more than can be said of humans, is a good example of the use to which this kind of *exemplum* could be put.

The sub-category of non-living things has a significant number of *exempla*. Several draw on the imagery of light, heat, cold etc. One (*Serm.* 82 [6]) uses the contrast of heat and cold to speculate about the glorified body; several (*Serm.* 17 [1], 82 [6], 205 [2], 208 [3], 209 [4]), from four different sermons, use the image of the sun and its atoms. Other matters of scientific interest are found. The lyrical description of spring (*Serm.* 118 [1]), and the exciting description of a storm (*Serm.* 78 [1]), also reflect accuracy of observation. Similarly exact are the *exempla* on coal (*Serm.* 114 [2]) and asbestos (*Serm.* 209 [4]). The action of fire in its small beginnings (*Serm.* 72 [3], 90 [1]), its baleful destructive effects (*Serm.* 7 [2], 31, 66 [4], 209 [2, 3]), and its utility in metal-working (*Serm.* 67 [4], 101 [3], 223 [1, 2]) is the subject of numerous *exempla*. The rapid destruction that fire could cause among wooden and thatched buildings is perhaps best illustrated by the *exemplum* (*Serm.* 210 [3]) which advises against burning your enemy's house down if he is your neighbour: the danger to your own home was too great! The twofold nature of fire as destructive and purifying made it a valuable image to the preacher. Scientific theorising provides three *exempla*: two (*Serm.* 90 [4], 221 [4]) refer to the theory that goat's blood could split hard rock; and one *exemplum* (*Serm.* 74 [5]) describes the effect of the moon crashing to earth. It is significant that so many *exempla* in the manuscript reflect an interest in accurate knowledge about the properties of things.

The most numerous set of *exempla* in our sermon collection, however, is that relating to daily life. In some ways these are the most interesting, because of the light they throw on the manner of life and customs of the times. A few refer to relationships among family and friends (*Serm.* 14 [3], 37 [4], 160, 205 [1]); and to values such as the unity of mankind (*Serm.* 29 [5]). Another sub-group comprises *exempla* dealing with health: gratitude for good health (*Serm.* 37 [5]), the weakness and frailty of the human body (*Serm.* 77 [2], 114 [3]), and some physical handicaps like deafness (*Serm.* 221 [1, 3]), or dumbness (*Serm.* 74 [3]). References to medical treatment are few: the importance of the blood for healing (*Serm.* 90 [2]), the effectiveness of eye-lotion (*Serm.* 17 [2, 3]) and the instinctiveness of sleep (*Serm.* 114 [1]) illustrate the fact that real remedies for sickness were limited in the thirteenth century. Four *exempla* deal with the loss of an eye (*Serm.* 37 [6]), of a finger in preference to the head (*Serm.* 147), of foot or hand (*Serm.* 13 [10]) or arm (*Serm.* 95 [9]). The last two in this group refer to death (*Serm.* 74 [4], 145 [7]). The latter is a graphic description of a death-bed, with a distraught wife and wailing servants. A further sub-group relates to food and feasting: one (*Serm.* 13 [1]) refers to the feast of Christmas as being celebrated by people of all conditions and attitudes; in

another (*Serm.* 221 [2]) the preacher comments that his listeners prefer
their breakfast to his words! Two *exempla* describe cooking: the roasting
of a bird (*Serm.* 203 [3]), and how the cook turns the herring with a wet
hand and so avoids being burnt (*Serm.* 203 [4]). A miscellaneous sub-group
describes a number of practical points: columns supporting a building
(*Serm.* 184 [2]); gifts of a ring (*Serm.* 47 [4]) or necklace (*Serm.* 138 [1], 227
[3]); that good cloth is kept carefully (*Serm.* 204 [2]); that it is easier to
shave wet than dry (*Serm.* 203 [5]); a nauseating recipe for household soap
(*Serm.* 67 [2]); and a practice for reminding oneself of something by writing it down or binding a finger (*Serm.* 130 [5]). The use of such *exempla*
made everyday things the stuff of preaching.

Another small group uses human wickedness and folly as *exempla*:
greed (*Serm.* 30 [3], 69 [4]); robbers are frightened off the job by noise
(*Serm.* 152 [2]); a thief flees to a monastery for sanctuary (*Serm.* 69 [6]);
shameful behaviour (*Serm.* 142 [3]). Foolish behaviour of various kinds is
castigated: washing of hands after a meal not before (*Serm.* 50 [1]); attempting to cure a wound without removing the weapon (*Serm.* 50 [3]); the
vices of luxury (lust) and anger (*Serm.* 18 [1]); compromising happiness
(*Serm.* 35 [3]); doing something beyond one's physical strength (*Serm.* 61
[1]); cultivating barren instead of fertile land (*Serm.* 209 [1]); weeding after
harvest (*Serm.* 50 [2]); giving hospitality to your murderer (*Serm.* 73 [2]).
This last type of *exemplum* has a style often used in these stories which
begins "If you were to..." followed by an imaginary action, and a moral
judgement on the value of that action.

A further number of *exempla* I have grouped around the topic of employment. One (*Serm.* 145 [3]) refers to hard work as being easier for those
who are used to it; another to the carpenter (*Serm.* 138 [3]); still another
to the importance of the sower's occupation compared with many others
(*Serm.* 39 [4]), and of a full barn to the farmer (*Serm.* 40 [1]). A smaller
group within the category of employment relates to masters and scholars:
Latin is to be used only with those who understand it (*Serm.* 30 [6]) (a useful comment on the language of preaching); scholars do not always go
willingly to school, but when they learn they are happy despite the hard-
ships of study (*Serm.* 230 [6]); while the master first uses persuasion to
interest his pupils and then blows if they do not respond (*Serm.* 100 [9]).
Then there are three *exempla* about students' attitudes: there is no point in
learning the subtleties of geometry before knowing the meaning of the
terms (*Serm.* 30 [7]); bad scholars are those who mark only the "less desir-
able" parts of Scripture and not the good parts, and who have only criticism for the sermons they hear (*Serm.* 146 [1]); some students pay no attention, whatever method the master uses (*Serm.* 184 [1]). Another three

exempla stress the importance of preachers using as Christ did ordinary illustrations and parables from daily life rather than complex examples from geometry, astronomy etc (*Serm.* 38, 39 [1], 69 [1]). There are a few *exempla* which are themselves "illustrations of scholastic method" (*Serm.* 1 [1, 2, 3]), being philosophical rather than imaginative.[31] The last sample of this group is from Simon of Hinton's sermon (*Serm.* 66 [1]).

The last portion of the sub-group, employment, comprises *exempla* about important trades. One refers to the experienced merchant (*Serm.* 37 [2]), another to the desire of merchants to trade profitably (*Serm.* 57 [11]), others to activity in the market-place (*Serm.* 37 [1]) and the buyer (*Serm.* 200c [2]). A further set is about ships and sailors. One (*Serm.* 30 [18]) refers to the vessel, while three relate to the captain's function and skill (*Serm.* 30 [5, 10], 206 [2]), and another to the crew (*Serm.* 30 [13]). Yet others take up the perils and advantages of travel by sea: how to cross the sea (*Serm.* 213); the ship as the fastest form of travel (*Serm.* 30 [11]); the difficulties and perils of sailing—rocks, storms, seasickness (*Serm.* 57 [3], 224 [3, 5]); the ship lost at sea (*Serm.* 30 [2]); the ship saved after the storm by the concerted efforts of all on board (*Serm.* 224 [4]); the sea and its dangers, its bitterness (*Serm.* 30 [1], 100 [4], 224 [2]); seeing the harbour from deck, and all the people on the shore (*Serm.* 30 [12]). Certainly in our manuscript the number of references to ships and the sea is one of the highest on any single topic. This possibly owes its importance to the first apostles, especially Peter, being fishermen; and to imagery in the early Church in which the fish denoted Christ. That England was a seafaring nation, and that all contact with the Continent at that time was perforce by boat, would have made this imagery specially appealing to English hearers.

A further group of *exempla* refers to other modes of travel and their implications. Several are concerned with the actual road of the traveller: that he needs to hold to the road (*Serm.* 57 [6]); that a little light is very welcome when the way is dark and muddy (*Serm.* 64 [2]); that the high road is safer from robbers and violence, and easier too (*Serm.* 145 [6]). Alternatively, the untrodden path is harder (*Serm.* 145 [1]), so it is more prudent to go by the middle way (*Serm.* 57 [8]). Travelling abroad whether forced or free, is the subject of several *exempla*: the difficulties of exile (*Serm.* 21 [1]); the problems of not knowing foreign languages, especially French (*Serm.* 200a [1]); the daily prayer of pilgrims and travellers for a

---

[31] MS Laud Misc. 511, fol. 5b, l. 26: quod dicuntur propinqui qui fratres appropinquavit. Ibid., l.31: *exemplum*, quod dicuntur aliqui esse prope illorum quibus conferunt bona. Ibid., l. 34: *exemplum* de eo qui dicitur esse prope alium, qui omnia que facit alius.

safe journey and a happy return (*Serm.* 207 [1]). Another *exemplum* refers to false palmers who have never even crossed the Mediterranean (*Serm.* 100 [6]); yet another describes the desire to go to the Holy Land (*Serm.* 77 [1], 100 [7]). The last *exemplum* about travel noted here is an interesting one about pilgrims crossing the Alps, using special metal nails on their boots and in their hands so as not to slip, and to keep their grip on the path more secure (*Serm.* 145 [2]).

Linked with travel is the inn or hostelry or house at which the traveller hopes to lodge. Several *exempla* emphasise the need for cleanliness in the guest room (*Serm.* 12 [3], 13 [5], 14 [4], 15 [1]); another emphasises the welcome of a large fire (*Serm.* 203 [2]). One of the pleasures of the inn is its drink, and the sign of a good brew is the circular wreath (*Serm.* 204 [1]). A related *exemplum* (*Serm.* 30 [9]) comments that the regular drinker of wine has a better-educated palate than the occasional drinker!

To end this section on daily life there are a number of *exempla* about the poor in society. The poor who are hungry often have to beg, clamouring loudly outside the lord's hall, putting up with blows, having to stand in a line if they are to have a hope of help (*Serm.* 25 [1], 152 [8], 200b [2], 200c [1], 221 [5], 69 [3]). The practice of poor people making their children cry to attract alms is described (*Serm.* 203 [1]), as is also the noise that children and beggars make to draw attention to themselves (*Serm.* 152 [6]).

While no complete picture of mid-thirteenth century life is given in these *exempla*—for example, there is nothing about the relationships of men and women either in or out of marriage—some aspects of daily life are well pictured. It is interesting to notice the emphasis on town experience and travel, rather than on country pursuits and occupations. This would reflect the mendicant pattern of life and work, with the strong emphasis on the task of preaching frequently to the people of the fast-growing towns. It is equally interesting to note that the *exempla* described in the previous paragraphs provide valuable illustrative material for the preacher, both in their own right and as a potential for development by moralisation or or by an allegorical or spiritual interpretation.

The last group of *exempla* that I have defined relates to the life of the ruling classes rather than to the ruled. Of this group over forty are concerned with the king and the royal family.[32] Twelve of these are about

---

[32] *Exempla* concerned with royalty: (*Serm.* 8 [1], 11 [1, 4], 15 [2], 29 [6], 33 [1, 3], 46 [4], 72 [4], 82 [1, 4], 93, 132 [3], 141 [1, 2], 142 [4], 152 [4], 162, 214, 220); with the king's son: (*Serm.* 13 [8, 9], 33 [5], 40 [2], 96, 145 [4]).

Rex Anglie.[33] Several of these will be discussed in the comment on the specific sermons studied. Most of the stories seem to be imaginary, stressing the magnanimity and condescension of the king to someone beneath him, as in *Serm.* 21 [2], 25 [2], 26 [3], 33 [2], and 174a. Two *exempla* point out that the king's wife is, by virtue of the relationship, Lady of England (*Serm.* 82 [1, 2]). Two *exempla* (*Serm.* 82 [3], 142 [4]), however, are about the dishonouring of the queen and of the king's daughter. Is Eleanor de Montfort the subject of this last *exemplum*? In the stories are allusions to palaces, servants, ministers, castles, wealth and grandeur. Many *exempla* are about the king's family, particularly his son (*Serm.* 13 [8, 9], 33 [5], 96, 145 [4]). In one of this group (*Serm.* 33 [5]), the Lord Edward is named. Is it significant in historical terms that four of these stories are about attempts to kill the prince, or are these just preacher's stories with the obvious parallel of the death of the Son of the King of Heaven? It is interesting that only four *exempla* refer to *Rex Francie* (*Serm.* 53 [4], 54 [1], 95 [3], 100 [1]) and these in a context of hostility rather than of friendship. Three (*Serm.* 8 [1], 15 [2], 132 [3]) describe the duties of the king, two of them in words reminiscent of the coronation oath, while the third emphasises the duty of the king to stamp out evil customs. A further *exemplum* (*Serm.* 93) alludes to the king's writ containing orders to be obeyed by his representatives in different regions. Several *exempla* are related to war and campaigning. Two (*Serm.* 89 [1], 198 [1]) give contrasting aspects of the declaration of war; the first concerning the military preparation of collecting gold, hiring knights and foot soldiers, assembling the host; the second the weeping and wailing among civilians at the prospect of war. Two more *exempla* (*Serm.* 51 [2, 3]) illustrate the episodic nature of war at this time, starting mostly in spring, *in diebus Martii*; one (*Serm.* 89 [3]) emphasises the function of the standard bearer. Of the last two *exempla* in this set, one (*Serm.* 162) describes the return of the victorious king, made more worthy if he has freed those captured in war; the other (*Serm.* 123 [1]) describes the victor despatching his beadles to towns and villages, proclaiming the peace. One *exemplum* (*Serm.* 29 [4]) is the story of the man who is the friend of the king, of whom no-one dares to be an enemy. A further five (*Serm.* 82 [4], 136 [3], 141 [2], 184 [3], 198 [4]) emphasise the mercy and forgiveness of the king. The last two *exempla* in the group (*Serm.* 32 [3], 205 [4]) note that death respects not kings: they can be on the throne yesterday, on their sick-bed today, and in the tomb tomorrow. It is interesting to note that four *exempla* in the sermon of Richard Fishacre, Sermon 82, are

[33] *Exempla* concerned with Rex Anglie: (*Serm.* 14 [1, 2], 21 [2], 25 [2], 26 [3], 33 [2], 64 [1], 100 [1, 10], 133 [3], 174a, 230 [1]).

about the king and/or the queen. Several Dominican friars were personally linked with the Plantagenets in the thirteenth century as confessors, and often as diplomatic agents, while John of Darlington was a member of Henry III's council.[34]

There are two remaining sub-groups in this royal section: life among nobles and knights; the law and judgement. In the first two *exempla* (*Serm.* 37 [3], 200a [2]), the courtesy and generosity of nobles are described; three (*Serm.* 130 [1]), relate the pride of the knight in his wounds, whether gained in battle (*Serm.* 130 [2]) or in the tourney (*Serm.* 130 [6]); one (*Serm.* 136 [1]) refers to hunting while two others (*Serm.* 26 [2], 95 [4]) describe the festive part of life particularly at court. Two (*Serm.* 211 [2] and 130 [4]) describe service to a magnate, and also dereliction of feudal duty. The second (*Serm.* 130 [4]) is a repetition of the *exemplum* in *Serm.* 174a, except that the subject of the latter is the king and of the former a magnate. For other aspects of life in a palace or great castle, there are only three *exempla*: one (*Serm.* 200b [1]) is about the almoner giving alms, but only to those standing in line; while two (*Serm.* 152 [4], 200c [3]) refer briefly to the organisation of manors, hundreds and honours. The last *exemplum* in this subgroup (*Serm.* 74 [2]) declares that, like a vase, a great man can fall from a height. Some of the elements of conflict and disloyalty in these stories could reflect the troubled times of Henry III.

The final sub-group relates to a variety of matters concerning law: three *exempla* (*Serm.* 32 [2], 54 [4], 134) refer to the heirs seeking or losing their inheritance, and to the will governing inheritance; another (*Serm.* 15 [3]) to a charter which confirms possession. The rest of these legal *exempla* relate in one way or another to law court procedure, judgement, or punishment. Three (*Serm.* 226 [1], 230 [2], 234) describe either royal justice or a law court of significance. Eight (*Serm.* 27 [3, 4], 35 [2], 36 [2], 37 [7], 54 [3], 119 [1], 147) relate to the death penalty and going to execution or to reprieve and commutation of the sentence. The last *exemplum* in this group (*Serm.* 226 [1]) concerns final judgement before God, not human judgement. *Exempla* concerning kingship, power, or law were particularly fruitful for the preacher.

The *exempla* in our manuscript illustrate how the preachers drew on the experience of their times, both the realities of ordinary daily life and the less ordinary realities symbolised by the life of king and court. Many people would have seen the king as he moved around the country eating up the produce of his manors; and some would have had recourse to royal justice during the same progress. So the preacher found ample illustrative

[34] Hinnebusch, *Early English Friars*, chapters 22 and 23.

material for describing the life and work of Christ, especially in his incarnation and acts of redemption; and for showing the mercy and condescension of God in the daily life of mid-thirteenth century England illustrated by these *exempla*. But it is also significant that, taken as a group, the *exempla* in the manuscript display real divergences from those in the collections of Jacques de Vitry, Etienne de Bourbon and Odo of Cheriton. In the first place the compiler by his annotating of *exempla* displays a broader concept than the standard collections, for he includes comparisons, metaphors, images and scripture events, as well as anecdotes and stories. Secondly, there are differences of emphasis, demonstrated by the compiler's choice of content. Compared with the three collections noted, the Laud manuscript has few *exempla* on the devil and demons; few on marriage, women, clerical concubinage and allied themes; neither are there many on usury, nor from the *Vitae Patrum*. It must be concluded that our manuscript was a very useful resource to a preacher as a handbook providing many identified and original *exempla* which would complement, but not replace, the *exempla* available in the well-known and oft-used standard collections.

C. MS Laud Misc. 511 as a Miscellaneous Sermon Aid

i. Distinctions and Sermon Material

The use of marginalia for sermon summaries/distinctions in MS Laud Misc. 511 and the annotation of the manuscript as an *exempla* collection have been discussed. There remains, mostly in the body of the text but in a few cases in the bottom margin, material organised under the *Temporale* of the liturgical calendar which is neither sermons, portions of sermons, nor summaries thereof. It is, however, material of use to a preacher who wished to compose a fresh sermon, or modify an existing one with extra authorities and or distinctions. I have taken the size and style of writing as a guide in sorting out the few cases of marginalia in this category of sermon material. If the hand has been more or less the same kind of book hand, albeit smaller, as in the the body of the text, I have included it in sermon material.

In making a list of this sermon material, I have divided it into three groups: distinctions; sermon material; and quotations from the Fathers, a mini-florilegia. None of the elements of this sermon material seems to have any internal relationship with the others. The unity of the material is an external one, directed by the liturgical order of the *Temporale*.

The section on distinctions arises from the nature of the material. Two sections, 149 and 150, are actually marginally annotated *dist'* while items 109 and 129 in the Appendix 1, "A Catalogue of MS Laud Misc. 511," have been identified already as biblical distinctions. In dealing with our manuscript it seemed necessary to try and sort out what the compiler was doing, and to be wary of imposing more order than existed. The sticking point was whether a sermon copied into the manuscript in whole or in part was a sermon or a distinction. It seemed best to allow a favoured Dominican adjective, *perutilis*, to be the criterion.[35] "Usefulness," especially for preaching, is the standard applied to much Dominican study, composition and writing in the thirteenth century. So where the piece in the manuscript seemed to be a sermon, whether complete or incomplete, no matter how incomplete the portion, and regardless of its literary form, it was listed as a sermon. Similarly, pieces in the small hand of the marginal material which were completions of sermons, the contents of which overran the writing block, were retained as sermons.[36] The remaining pieces were neither sermon, nor biblical distinction, nor sermon summary, but pieces of material useful towards making a sermon that were written up in distinction style.[37] The material falls into three groups. The first group, including two biblical distinctions, are in distinction style; the three items of the second group are themes with the divisions outlined; the third group consists of material similar in content to that found in *Summas of Virtues and Vices* written up in distinction style.

[35] *Utilis/Perutilis*: see Humbert of Romans, *De Vita Regulari*, 2: 390-392; 2: 258, n. 2; also chapter titles 1: 143—"De remediis contra elationem de bonis propriis et de utilitate humilitatis in praedicatore"; 2: 28—"De utilitate studii in nostro ordine."

[36] MS Laud Misc. 511, Sermon 38, fol. 39b-40b; Sermon 99, fol. 105b-106va; Sermon 123, fol. 120vb-121vb; Sermon 165, fol. 149b-149vb.

[37] Distinctions:
Group 1:
  for Holy Week—109
  for Easter on peace—128, 129
  for Fifth Sunday of Easter—149, 150
  for Third Sunday after Trinity on humility—179, 180a
Group 2. Themes with divisions:
  First Sunday after Nativity—20
  Fourth Sunday of Lent—85, 87
Group 3. Sermon material in distinction style:
  for Third Sunday after Trinity on humility and obedience—180b, 181
  for Fourth Sunday after Trinity on mercy and almsgiving—190, 191, 192, 194, 196
  for Fifth Sunday after Easter and Fifth Sunday after Trinity on tears—155, 203

The remaining pieces[38] are "gobbets" in no particular style, extracts large and small, which relate to a specific Sunday or time of the *Temporale*, and which could be of use to a preacher looking either for authorities, or for expansion of a topic, or for extra sermon material. This group I call "named sermon material." It has not been possible to identify the sources except for a small sub-group of vernacular phrases. One gobbet, under the liturgical heading of Palm Sunday, describes the suffering of Our Lady as linked with that of her Son when the sword of sorrow pierced her, and then continues:

> *Anglice* Maiden stod at welle and wep,
> Weila wei late comet ye lith of dai.

This is one of six fragments of Middle English in the manuscript.[39] Siegfried Wenzel has made a thorough study of verses in sermons,[40] and has shown the popularity of verse-making in the later middle ages. It was considered "a proper medium for teaching and study," for it "not only helps our memory but also expresses things succinctly and gives us pleasure."[41] Mendicant preachers, the Franciscans more often than the Dominicans, used verses when preaching to congregations of lay people;[42] and presumably, even if they were preaching to more learned audiences, they would not translate the English into Latin. The present parallel is the vernacular hymn. In arousing compassion for the sufferings of Christ, verse would be more powerful in effect. It is significant that five out of the six pieces of Middle English in this manuscript relate to Christ's passion and death. Another piece is the opening line of a well-known thirteenth-century poem on Christ's sufferings.[43] Although our manuscript is not a good example in general of the use of verses in sermons, the compiler thought them worth including in his collection of sermon material.

---

[38] Sermon Material for Palm Sunday and Holy Week on the passion of Christ—106a, 106c, 106g, 106h, 113a, 113b, 113c; for Fifth Sunday after Easter—149b, 149c; for Fourth Sunday after Trinity on mercy—189, 196; for Fifth Sunday after Trinity on prayer—200a, 200b, 200c.

[39] See Appendix 1: *Serm.* **78, 82, 95, 96, 106a, 130,** and **134.**

[40] Wenzel, *Verses in Sermons*, Chapter 2.

[41] Ibid., 61, 67-68.

[42] Ibid., 93; see also H.G. Pfander, *The Popular Sermon of the Medieval Friars in England* (New York, 1937) 20-43.

[43] See Rosemary Woolf, *The English Religious Lyric in the Middle Ages* (Oxford, 1968), 33-34: "Wan Ics on rode se Iesu mi leman."

ii. Florilegia

On the principle that a bird in the hand was worth two in the bush, the compiler of our manuscript culled from the gardens of the Fathers and the hedges of commonplace a small bouquet or gathering of spiritual and devotional items. These were inserted in the order of the *Temporale* according to the main thrust of the liturgical celebration as the compiler saw it. Thus an element of personal choice, probably the only one, is clearly to be seen in this aspect of the manuscript's contents.

The contents of the mini-florilegia and their liturgical positions are noted below.[44] The Fathers drawn on, with the number of authorities cited from each, include Ambrose (3), Anselm (1), Augustine (36), Bede (3), Bernard (17), Cassiodorus (2), John Chrysostom (3), Eusebius (1), Gregory the Great (34), Jerome (3), Leo (1), Peter of Ravenna (5), Rabanus Maurus (1), and a *Summa* (2). Of the above Fathers, the majority are well-known. It is difficult, however, to know which Eusebius is meant, as there were several in the early Church. There is a slight problem with Peter of Ravenna. He is called such in the *Patrologia Latina* of Migne, though the better-known theologian of that name belongs to the sixteenth century. The numerical balance of authorities that the above list displays, together with the preponderance of Western Fathers, is characteristic of the sermon collection as a whole. St. Augustine and St. Gregory from the earlier centuries and St. Bernard from the recent Church, are the most widely quoted, while a few standard authorities are also included. It is important to note, however, that a thirteenth-century ascription of an authority to a particular Father is not necessarily accurate, especially in the case of anything ascribed to Chrysostom. During the thirteenth century an interest in the Greek Fathers increased, notably through the activities of St. Thomas Aquinas. In England an interest in the Greek language was characteristic of Robert Grosseteste when he was bishop of Lincoln.[45] Neither of these interests is represented in the manuscript. Nevertheless, the presence of the *florilegium* is significant, and the search for its possible sources important.

The study by Richard and Mary Rouse of a very popular medieval *florilegium*, the *Manipulus Florum*, has not only shown its sources, structure

---

[44] Florilegia for Palm Sunday for Holy Week on the passion of Christ: 106b, 106d, 106e, 106f, 107; for Third Sunday after Trinity on humility: 175, 176, 177, 178; for Fourth Sunday after Trinity on mercy and almsgiving: 187, 188; for Fifth Sunday after Trinity on prayer: 199a, 199b, 201, 202.

[45] D.A. Callus OP, "The Contribution to the Study of the Fathers made by the Thirteenth-Century Oxford Schools" *JEH* 5 (1954) 141.

and use, but has set the book in the context of sermon aids and *florilegia* as a whole.[46] Their researches have drawn attention to the new thirteenth-century application of alphabetization,[47] to the organisation of information and its speedy retrieval. Before this methodology was realised, medieval writers had great difficulty in finding information when its organisation depended on memory and/or rational order. The sheer number of works from the Fathers of the Church and their successors, of which Migne's *Patrologia Latina* is a mute but incomplete witness, illustrates the related problem of trying to index themes. In this context of numerous patristic sources, how could limited medieval resources of expensive parchment and comparatively slow scribes ever permit the copying of the whole works of the Fathers? The classical practice of making *florilegia* was continued gratefully by medieval scholars and students. C.H. Talbot quotes Seneca's commendation of the practice:

> He says that the plethora of books has a numbing effect on the mind and that it is better to restrict oneself to what one can usefully absorb than to peruse superficially everything that is available; and he adds that he himself was accustomed to cull from books certain passages which he could think over during the day and from which he could draw profit.[48]

Following some of the references in the works of Philippe Delhaye[49] and of Richard and Mary Rouse, I examined a number of manuscripts and printed books,[50] including what I could find of Kilwardby's *Tabulae super Originalia Patrum*. In none of these was a possible source of the patristic contents of MS Laud Misc. 511 identified. But in the course of the search it became clearer that the *mini-florilegia* in our manuscript

---

[46] Rouse, 'Manipulus Florum'.

[47] Rouse, "Biblical Distinctions," 27-37.

[48] C.H. Talbot, *Florilegium Morale Oxoniense* (Louvain/Lille, 1956), 2: 6-8; M.C. Murray SND, *Rebirth and Afterlife* (Oxford, 1981) 135 n. 46, which shows that the compilation of *florilegia* was in existence by 649, and actively fostered by the Lateran Council and the sixth Ecumenical Council of 787; see also Callus, "Contribution," 139-148.

[49] Philippe Delhaye, *Florilegium Morale Oxoniense*, pars 1 (Louvain/Lille, 1955).

[50] Oxford, Lincoln College MS Lat. 98E; printed book: Oxford, Bodleian Auct 6Q.4.40; Robert Kilwardby, *Tabulae Super Originali Patrum*: Oxford, Bodleian MS Laud Misc. 128; *Liber Deflorationum seu Excerptorum ex Diversis Patribus*, Oxford, Bodleian P.8.12.Th.; *Glossa Ordinaria* (Antwerp, 1617); *Speculum Religiosorum* and *Speculum Ecclesie*, ed. Helen Forshaw SHCJ, in *Auctores Brittanici Medii Aevi* (London: British Academy, 1973).

were derived from other *florilegia* rather than directly from the Fathers. The attempt to identify in the actual works of the Fathers the passages cited in the manuscript was a long task. Even with resources such as the Indexes of the *Patrologia Latina*, of the *Concordance of Augustine*,[51] and the advice of skilled scholars, the results were meagre. They are recorded in Appendix 1.

It is worth noting that one of the quotations from John Chrysostom is from the medieval writer now called Pseudo-Chrysostom, and that a few references were wrongly ascribed in our manuscript.[52] There is the further problem in the use of the Fathers either in an "original" text or in a *florilegia* of how far textual equivalence could be achieved. That problem is partly the impossibility of knowing the accuracy of the source books of our manuscript; partly the element of scribal error in transmission of medieval texts; and partly the improvement of modern texts through both linguistic discoveries and literary criticism, which has modified some original patristic texts in relation to their medieval versions. Lastly, there is one difference between the generality of medieval *florilegia* and MS Laud Misc. 511 in that the former included non-Christian sources as well as Fathers, while in the manuscript the *mini-florilegia* are patristic only.

As well as the specific small collection of *florilegia* in MS Laud Misc. 511 other references to the Fathers in the manuscript can be identified by the marginal annotation of patristic authorities quoted in the adjoining column of text. The Fathers most commonly noted are Augustine, Bernard and Gregory. Some further access to patristic authorities was provided, not only for the compiler, but for other users of the manuscript. In this manner the general utility and comprehensiveness of the manuscript as a preacher's handbook are enhanced.

iii. The Religious Content of the Sermon Material

While, as has been noted, the contents of the sermon material have no intrinsic unity, they do have a firm purpose related specifically to five occasions in the Church year: Holy Week and Easter; the Fifth Sunday after Easter; and the Third, Fourth, and Fifth Sundays after Trinity.

---

[51] D. Lenfant OP, *Concordantiae Augustinianae*, 2 vols. (1656-65); photo-reprint (Brussels, 1965). Appendix 1 lists those sources which have been identified.

[52] Many years ago a research student informed me that some of the authorities ascribed to John Chrysostom in MS Laud Misc. 511 belonged to Pseudo-Chrysostom: see the notes on religious authorities to Sermon 187 in Appendix 1, "A Catalogue of MS Laud Misc. 511."

The emphasis of the sermon material under Palm Sunday and in Holy Week is on the passion of Christ and its effects. There is realisation of the harshness of his sufferings;[53] emphasis on Christ choosing to die, not in his bed but on the cross, as a sign of love.[54] As a result, not only is our sin forgiven, but we can have great confidence in God.[55] The content is balanced between knowledge of and feeling for the depth of Christ's suffering, together with an acknowledgment of human guilt. The other material under this liturgical heading is the set of distinctions on humility.[56] Again in this text, the practicalities of the Christian life of prayer, gratitude to God, growth in goodness, courtesy and fidelity are emphasised. The distinction on *Pax* under the liturgical heading of Easter exalts the value of peace as an effect of the resurrection:[57] peace adorns the religious life, is a mark of God's children, strengthens unity, leads out from vice, and is a symbol of God. These samples give the flavour of the content.

The sermon material under the Fifth Sunday after Easter relates to the text from St. James' Epistle, *Vir duplex est* (James 1:8). Items 149a,b,c, 150 and 151 come under this general grouping. Number 150 is entitled in the margin *distinctio*. All are concerned in one way or another with the suitable behaviour of a preacher. Items 150 and 151 relate in broad outline to aspects of dress and behaviour suitable to a preacher though nowhere is the word *frater* or *predicator* used, rather *iactator*. There is no link with the intructions of Humbert of Romans on the religious life, or on preaching in these pieces, though I found a slight similarity in two instances:

---

[53] MS Laud Misc. 511, fol. 110vb, ll. 30-35: Consueverunt homines nobiles in festis eorum sedere in imo sed tamen habere aliquos curiales qui cum eis pranderet et de meliore in celario, sed Christus, econtra, quia cum iniquis deputatus est, scilicet, duobus latronibus et de peiore in celario.

Ibid., Sermon 106g, fol. 110vb, ll. 24-28: *Glosa* Non solum occidere sed crucifigere volunt, ut, manibus et pedibus ad lignum confixis, producta morte necaretur, ne dolor cito finiretur, et ut in cruce diu videretur.

[54] Sermon 113c [fol. 112vb, ll. 42-43]: Christus non in strato suo (sed in cruce) mori voluit ut, quod ultimum fuit pudoris, signum esset supprimi amoris.

[55] Sermon 113a [fol. 112vb, ll. 34-37]: Scio quod non est iniquitas sicut iniquitas mea, sed econtra non est dolor sicut dolor eius, qui me redemit; si supra modum peccavi, non despero quia supra modum doluit, in quo respiro.

Sermon 113b [fol. 112vb, ll. 39-40]: Si exasperatur Deus immensitate sceleris mei, mitigatur, procul dubio, satisfactione Filii sui.

[56] See Appendix 9, "Selected Texts" (fol. 111vb, ll. 1-32).

[57] Sermon 129 [fol. 123va, ll. 1-32]: Pax...Religionem decorat...in filios Dei adoptat...unitatem vult et firmat...ymaginem Dei representat...a vitio educit....

150's *Iactator graviter egrotat* has a little link with Humbert's *De merito prae-dicatoris*;[58] and 151's *Ad vestem vilitatem* has a small affinity with Humbert's *Commentary on the Rule of St. Augustine*, chapter 112, *De vestitu*.[59] While these items in MS Laud Misc. 511 do not constitute an *ars predicandi*, they do contain admonitory material about suitable behaviour and, more significantly, about the inner integrity a preacher requires. The week after the Fifth Sunday after Easter contains the Rogation days, while a fortnight later occur the Ember days, traditional days for conferring various stages of ordination to priesthood. The liturgical link, however, is not strong enough to draw any conclusions about a specific connection of this material with the education of priests and preachers.

    The other three liturgical times in which the compiler places material other than sermons are the Third, Fourth and Fifth Sundays after Trinity. For these he selects—based on the pericopes—the themes of humility, mercy with almsgiving, prayer and tears. It is at this place in the manuscript that the *mini-florilegia* are found. It is useful to examine how Werner of St. Blaize and Simon of Hinton treat the above topics. In his *Deflorationes*, Werner deals with humility in his treatment of the Fall, and of penance and envy.[60] Under mercy he has a long discussion on mercy and truth.[61] On prayer he has very little. In his *Summa Juniorum*,[62] Simon of Hinton concentrates largely on the sacraments of penance and eucharist —the latter in terms of devotion to the real presence; on a commentary on the creed and the *pater noster*, and on virtues and vices. I did not find any similarity between the treatment in Simon's treatise and the material included by the compiler in MS Laud Misc. 511. It was noticeable, however, that both of them emphasised the positive elements of forgiveness and the practice of virtue.

    On the theme of mercy there are six portions, four of them (190, 191, 192, and 196) comment on the mercy of God to us as sinners. These pieces show that God is loving, kind, not vengeful, reluctant to condemn, constantly offering opportunities for forgiveness, showing mercy and patience

---

[58] Humbert of Romans, *De Vita Regulari*, 2: 404-406.

[59] Humbert of Romans, *De Vita Regulari*, 1: 356-367.

[60] PL 157: 1035-1036.

[61] PL 157: 1039-1041.

[62] Simon of Hinton, *Summa Juniorum* in Oxford, Bodleian MS Laud Misc. 379; P.A. Walz OP, "The 'Excepciones' from the 'Summa' of Simon of Hinton," *Angelicum* 13 (1936) 283-368; A. Dondaine OP, "La Somme de Simon de Hinton," *RTAM* 9 (1937) 5-22, 204-218; V. Burch, "The 'Excepciones' from Simon of Hinton's Summa," *MEH* 3 (1948) 69-80.

to the reprobate, delaying in applying punishment.[63] In one piece the spiritual and corporal works of mercy are described: for the spiritual works, Tobit is the source; for the corporal works, the judgement parable of Matthew 25.[64] None of these analyses match with any discussion of mercy in the *Summae Virtutum* that I have been able to see. They do share, however, a similar approach. It is most likely that this identifies one of the great commonplaces of the spiritual life, for these balancing tables of virtues, sins, gifts of the Holy Spirit, beatitudes, petitions of the Our Father, are frequently found in the *Summae*, but few of them are absolutely identical. In Richard Fishacre's *Commentary on the Sentences*, Book 3, a similar table is found.

In the manuscript the only corporal work of mercy that is treated is almsgiving in item 189.[65] Almsgiving was closely associated with the third of the necessary elements for the full reception of the sacrament of

[63] For example:

Sermon 190 [fol. 161b, ll. 35-46]: Multa fuit misericordia Dei erga nos, que, cum ex nobis nichil eramus, ad esse perduxit quod esse in infinitum a nichil esse distat item, quia a malo esse in bonum esse elevavit; item, multa fuit in remittendo (Isaiah)...item, multa est in dando (Isaiah)...item, multa est secundum essentiam (Ecc'o).

Sermon 196 [fol. 162a, ll. 27-42]: Tres sunt miserationes Dei circa [?] electos: prima quod invitos ad se venire compellit cum flagellis cum beneficiis...Item Christus multociens contemptus contemptores suos dulciter suscipit...tertia, quod eis facile omnia remittit.

Sermon 196 [fol. 162b, ll. 9-35]: Tres sunt miserationes Dei circa [?] reprobos quantum [?] penitentia est, quia cum sint eius inimici, eos non privat omni bono. Hic satis inconsueta sunt hominibus....Diu ad penitentiam patienter expectat, cum tamen peccata eorum vix sunt portabilia...Tertio, quod citam condignum dampnat.

[64] Sermon 190 [fol. 161b, ll. 27-30]: Septem elemosine sunt spirituales et septem corporales que ennarrantur mt 25 et septem spirituales, Tobit.

Sermon 191 [fol. 161va, ll. 1-23]: Septem sunt misericordie Domini; prima est conservare a peccato....Secunda est ultionis misericors expectatio....Tertia ad penitentiam conversio....Quarta est peccatorum remissio....Quinta est continendi et melius vivendi virtutis prestatio....Sexta est gratia vitam eternam promittendi....Septa est spes eam optinendi.

[65] Sermon 189 [fol. 161b, ll. 8-12]: Nulla plus valet peccatorum curatio quam eleemosynam largitio, quia frustra pro peccatis suis rogaturus manus suas ad Domini extenderit, qui has pro posse ad [pauperem] Domini non extendit.

Sermon 189 [fol. 161b, ll. 21-27]: Non ut sufficiat elemosyna ad emundationem culpe, sed ut sit principalius motivum ad remissionem peccati vel pene, sed ex Dei misericordia unius cuius vulneris est propria medicina a sacerdote adhibenda ut contraria contrariis curentur.

penance: contrition, confession, satisfaction. Almsgiving had the advantage of not identifying too specifically the sins for which some reparation was being made—an advantage in a small community. In all these pieces related to mercy, however, the emphasis is on the overwhelming kindness and love of God. All these passages could be of use to a preacher searching for material for preaching, particularly preaching on the sacrament of penance.

Under the Fifth Sunday after Trinity a large supplementary section on prayer is included. The extracts from the Fathers, including passages about *lectio* seem to be chosen for preaching to religious, as lay-people in the thirteenth century had little skill in liturgical reading apart perhaps from that needed for the Little Office of Our Lady. Another section from the Fathers, item 201, has the *pater noster* as its subject. From the directives of Synods in the Church in England in the thirteenth century, teaching on the Our Father was part of every parish priest's duty, and one that preaching friars would also fulfil. The three items 200a, b, and c, are teaching on prayer. The first piece underlines the importance of the prayer of adoration: "so does God give himself to the man who praises him with a pure heart."[66] The second piece stresses the importance of communal prayer, and disparages the one who absents himself from the Divine Office.[67] The third piece not only repeats the last point, but also encourages perseverance in prayer.[68] The image of the poor man for one who prays is significant in the mendicant context of Dominican life. The short selection on prayer contains something of use to all groups in the Church at that time.

The other section of material on prayer is found in item 203 on tears.[69] This also has a marginal note referring back to item 155 on *lacrime*.

---

[66] Sermon 200a [fol. 165a, ll. 18-19]: Sic Deus donat seipsum illi qui eum laudat puro corde.

[67] Sermon 200b [fol. 165b, ll. 5-9]: Ita laudes multorum in communitate acceptabiles a Deo reputantur non bene censum solvit; econtra, qui privatim horas dicit et[?] a communitate se separat.

[68] Sermon 200c [fol. 165b, ll. 17, 22-25]: Efficaciter impetrat pauper...sic qui vult Domini delicate orationibus pascere et si possit eum pluribus, pascere, privatis debet, tamen conferre communes que fuit cum cantu.

[69] Sermon 203 [fol. 166b, ll. 13 seq.]: ⟨Lacrime⟩ (from margin) Deum cogent....Ad misericordiam Deum provocant....Deum hospitari faciunt....Coram presenti Dei preveniunt...mundant quia humide a peccatore immunditias.

Lacrime
┌conservant a putredine quia salto
├dissolvant quia calide
└illuminant quia clare

me. For many centuries in the Church the "gift of tears" was highly valued. It is better recognised in Thomas a Kempis's "compunction," the gift of experiencing sorrow for one's sins. Teaching on contrition has always emphasised that it is less a matter of feeling than of will. Compunction is more than feeling. In the Dominican tradition it was a virtue closely associated with St. Dominic himself. By comparison with the Franciscans, Dominicans have very little of story or writing about their founder. This makes the book, *On the Nine Ways of Prayer of St. Dominic,*[70] all the more noteworthy. Its anonymous author wrote it before 1260. It is very probable that he drew on the evidence taken before the official canonisation of St. Dominic in 1234.[71] In his introduction to the English edition, Simon Tugwell quotes one of Dominic's contemporaries, the Abbot of St. Paul's, Narbonne:

> I never saw anyone pray so much, nor anyone who wept so much....He used to pray so loudly that he could be heard everywhere.[72]

In the treatise itself, the author describes Dominic's prayer when he is dealing with the fourth way of prayer:

> But also, at times, he spoke in his heart and his voice was not heard at all, and he would remain on his knees, his mind caught up in wonder, and this sometimes lasted a long time. Sometimes when he was praying like this, his gaze seemed to have penetrated into the spiritual heavens, and he would suddenly be radiant with joy, wiping away the abundant tears running down his face."[73]

If this is a tradition written within forty years of Dominic's death, it is not surprising that allusion to this way of praying should be found in the manuscript. It seems likely that the origin of this material on prayer is the Dominican tradition which prizes highly the Fathers of the Church and the Fathers of the Desert. The content in the manuscript probably

---

[70] Ed. I. Taurisano OP, *Analecta OP* 15 (1922), 93 seq.

[71] *MOPH* 16, "Acta Canonizatione St. Dominici." See also Augusta T. Drane, *The History of St. Dominic* (London and New York: Longmans, 1891), xi, xii and chapter 19 about the Acts of Bologna, "consisting of the depositions of nine of the brethren who were most familiar with the Saint during his life, and whose evidence was taken at the time of the Process of Bologna," that is, prior to the canonization of St. Dominic.

[72] Trans. and ed. Simon Tugwell OP as *The Nine Ways of Prayer of St. Dominic* (Dublin, 1978) 6.

[73] Ibid., 26.

arose from usage within the community. The inclusion, however, of teaching on the Our Father and of sermons on prayer, of which item 163 in Appendix 9, "Selected Texts," is a good example, indicates that teaching on prayer was an essential part of popular preaching too.

It is useful to reflect on the extra sermon material in our manuscript as a whole. It has not been possible to trace the sources of every item and so establish a wider context for the material. Nevertheless the contents themselves indicate something about the compiler of the manuscript. He evidently thought that the spiritual life was important for members of his Dominican community, for lay-people and presumably for clergy. While some of his extra material, from both patristic and other sources, is related to the sacrament of penance, it is not fanciful to see all the things he added, and the liturgical context in which he added them, as part of his preaching approach. He could have added extra sections about sin, about hell and judgement, about the devil and the tricks of demons, but he did not. Rather his aim was the positive spiritual formation of his listeners: the model is Christ in his suffering; this means prayer, compunction, alms-giving and the virtues of humility, obedience and mercy. In this he is part of the new emphasis in the Church of the thirteenth century on devotion to the humanity of Christ, and on the living out of the apostolic life. Through the work of the friars, these developments were not left as the prerogatives of clerics and religious, but were opened to all members of the Church. Is the compiler of MS Laud Misc. 511 speaking only for himself in this, or can he be considered a representative English Dominican of the mid-thirteenth century?

D. CONCLUSION

Thus MS Laud Misc. 511 is not simply a sermon collection in portable form. Analysis of its contents shows that it contains not only sermons in various patterns: long, short, summary, distinction style, popular and clerical. It also offers a preacher, through marginal annotations, a collection of *exempla* and a collection of patristic authorities. Moreover, organised in a liturgical context, a small *florilegia* is included as well as extra material for preaching on specialised topics. The manuscript proves in fact to be a comprehensive preacher's handbook.

7

Paschal Preaching

In this chapter two sets of Eastertide preaching from our manuscript will be examined: the sermons for Easter Sunday briefly, the sermons for the Second Sunday after Easter more extensively. The sermons for Easter Sunday contain matters of codicological and catechetical interest, while the sermons for the Second Sunday after Easter are significant for their catechetical context and content.

For Easter Sunday the compiler has chosen nine sermons, drawn from five different source books.[1] Moreover, apart from sermons 121, 117, and 119, the themes of which are taken from the epistle for the Easter Vigil, the epistle for Easter Sunday and the responsory *Haec dies*, the themes are not related, as normally, to the pericopes of the feast but to texts about the resurrection of Christ.

In contrast, for the second Sunday after Easter, known in the Dominican calendar and in our manuscript too, as the First Sunday after the Octave of Easter, the compiler has chosen eleven sermons—the last one out of liturgical order—nine of which are preached on the epistle of the day, one on the gospel pericope, and one on a related theme from the first letter of St. Peter.[2] Of the nine preached on the epistle pericope, seven have the same theme: *Christus passus est pro nobis, relinquens exemplum ut sequamini vestigia eius* [1 Pet. 2:21].

Apart from the fourteen sermons for the First Sunday of Lent, many

---

[1] See Appendix 1, "A Catalogue of MS Laud Misc. 511," 114-122: 114 *Parvus Rubeus* Theme, Numquid qui dormit non adiiciet ut resurgat; 115 *Rubeus Minor* Theme, Si consurrexistis cum Christo; 116 *Rubeus Minor* Theme, Christus resurgens ex mortuis; 117 *Rubeus Minor*, Petrus de Remis OP Theme, Pascha nostrum; 118 *Confessionum Augustini* Theme, Transi hospes et orna mensam; 119 *Quaternus Oxoniensis* Theme, Haec est dies quam fecit Dominus; 120 *Proprius* Theme, Christus resurgens ex mortuis; 121 *Proprius* Theme, Si consurrexistis cum Christo; 122 *Niger Minor* Theme, Qui comederit de sanctificatis etc.

[2] See Appendix 1, "A Catalogue of MS Laud Misc. 511," 131-140, 147: 131 *Minimus* 1 Pet. 2:25; 132 *Parvus Rubeus* 1 Pet. 3:18; 133 *Parvus Rubeus* 1 Pet. 2:21; 134 *Parvus Rubeus* 1 Pet. 2:21; 135 *Parvus Rubeus* 1 Pet. 2:21; 136 *Niger Maior* 1 Pet. 2:21 preached at Elstow; 137 *Rubeus Minor* 1 Pet. 2:21; 138 *Proprius* 1 Pet. 2:21; 139 *Confessionum Augustini* John 10:11; 140 *Parvus Rubeus* 1 Pet. 2:21; 147 *Niger Minor* 1 Pet. 2:23.

of which are on the theme *Ductus est Jesus* [Matt. 4:1], the eleven sermons for the Second Sunday after Easter are the most numerous group for one liturgical occasion in our manuscript. This in itself suggested an investigation, and the choice was confirmed when the results of a search through Schneyer's *Repertorium* for other sermons on the same theme emerged. The search in volumes one to six yielded a harvest of about twenty-two sermons.[3] Of the twenty-two, one is anonymous, seven are by named Dominicans, five by anonymous Dominicans, five by a named Franciscan and four by secular masters, of which two are by John of Abbeville. MS Laud Misc. 511 is the only manuscript catalogued in Schneyer's *Repertorium* to have such a large number of sermons on this one theme. Moreover, in the twenty-two other sermons, twelve are of Dominican provenance.[4] These facts further support the initial decision to study the sermons for the Second Sunday after Easter to ascertain whether anything of significance, particularly of a catechetical nature, emerged.

To provide a comparison, five other sermons on the theme *Christus passus est*, were selected. The sermon of Hugh of Hartlepool OFM, which he preached at Greyfriars, Oxford, on Good Friday 1291, is a superb exam-

---

[3] Some sermons on the theme *Christus passus est*, 1 Pet. 2:21, in Schneyer, *Repertorium*, vols. 1-6: Pseudo-Eckhart (2: 30) nos 144, 145; Guy d'Evreux OP (2: 322) no. 33, (2: 335) no. 217; Hugh of St. Cher OP (2: 767) no. 153, (2: 773) no. 238; John de Castello OFM (3: 388) nos. 180, 181, 182, (3: 407) no. 433, (3: 415) no. 547; John of Abbeville (3: 515) nos 82, 83; Nicholas Gorran OP (4: 262) no. 114; Petrus de Remis OP (4: 727) no. 43; Radulphus Ardens (5: 5) no. 56; Stephen Langton (5: 469) no. 37; Thomas Aquinas OP (5: 587) no. 99; subprior OP (6: 45) no. 151; Paris master (6: 85) no. 51; OP (6: 550) no. 47; OP anon (6: 590) no. 84.

Sermons I have located in MSS on the theme *Christus passus est*: Cambridge, Trinity B.15.21 fol. 98a-99vb John of Abbeville; Kues MS 21 fol. 172a-172b Pseudo-Eckhart; London, BL MS Harley 755 fol. 216vb-217b Hugh of St. Cher OP; MS Harley 4951 fol. 63a-63b John of Abbeville; London, Lambeth Palace MS 71 fol. 208a-b Stephen Langton (MS notes this); MS 127 fol. 36b-36vb John of Abbeville; Oxford, Bodleian MS Bodl 25 p 186-189 OP anon; MS Bodl 50 fol. 38v Nicholas Gorran OP; MS Bodl 157 fol. 25va-vb Hugh of St. Cher OP; MS Bodl 406 fol. 22-22v Petrus de Remis OP; MS Greaves 53 fol. 205va-vb John de Castello OFM; MS Laud Misc. 172 fol. 17vb-18a anon (German); MS Laud Misc. 320 fol. 118v-119 anon; MS Laud Misc. 323 fol. 135v, and 135v-136 both by Petrus de Remis OP; MS Laud Misc. 376 fol. 63v Thomas Waleys OP; Paris, BN lat. 15005 fol. 120vb-121vb sub prior OP; lat. 15966 fol. 46b-47vb Guy d'Evreux OP; Migne PL vol 155, col. 1870-1872 Homilia LVI Radulphi Ardentis.

[4] The commentary of Hugh of St. Cher on 1 Pet. had no link with these sermons.

ple of a *sermo ad scolares*.[5] None of the others match it. The four other
examples, all assigned to the second Sunday after Easter, are by thirteenth-
century preachers more or less contemporary with the compiler. They are
one by Aldobrandinus de Cavalcantibus OP, prior provincial in the Italian
province of Tuscia in the 1260s—a contemporary of Thomas Aquinas when
he was in Italy; two by William Peraldus, a famous Dominican preacher
in southern France in the mid-thirteenth century; and a sermon wrongly
ascribed to St. Thomas Aquinas, but composed by an anonymous Italian
Dominican before 1274.[6]

Apart from the first section, when the authorities used in the two sets
of sermons will be considered together, the enquiries about the two
groups will proceed separately but, it is hoped, will lead to common conclusions.

A. THE AUTHORITIES IN THE PASCHALTIDE SERMONS

As in the other groups of sermons the authorities fall into two main
groups: those from Scripture, and those from the Fathers, Doctors and
other sources. Similar to the other sermons, the most numerous authorities
come from the Scriptures. The following table indicates their disposition.
Within the Old Testament at least 86 for Easter Sunday (ES), 97 for the
Second Sunday after Easter (S2) and 45 for the comparative group (C) are
noted. For the Easter Sunday set the Psalms are the largest number; in the
other two groups authorities from Isaiah, the Psalms, Job and Jeremiah are
the origin of more than half the Old Testament authorities. References to
the New Testament number at least 84 for the Easter Sunday group, 101
for the Second Sunday after Easter group and 46 in the comparative sermons. For the Easter Sunday set just 49 are from the Gospels and 35 from
the Epistles, eleven of which are from I Corinthians. In the Second Sunday
set the majority of authorities, unusually, are from the Epistles. Given the

[5] Little and Pelster, Appendix I, pp. 192-204: Sermon of Hugh of Hartlepool
OFM, preached at Greyfriars Oxford on Good Friday 1291, edited from Worcester
Cathedral MS Q 46 fol. 159v-162r.

[6] Aldobrandinus de Cavalcantibus, Wroclaw, Biblioteka Uniwersyteka MS I.Q.
427, fol. 135v-137r. Peraldus, Sermon 1, p. 67 col. 2–p. 68 col. 2 and Sermon 2, p. 68
col. 2–p. 69 col. 1; printed in William of Auvergne, *Opera Omnia* (Orléans: Francis-
cum Hotot 1674). (Père L.J. Bataillon informed me that these sermons, ascribed to
William of Auvergne, are really by Peraldus.) Pseudo-Thomas de Aquino (an unknown Italian Dominican, xiii s.), ed. Vives, in Thomas Aquinas, *Opera Omnia*
(Paris, 1886) 29: 234.

TABLE 1. SCRIPTURAL AUTHORITIES IN THE PASCHALTIDE SERMONS

Old Testament

	ES	S2	C		ES	S2	C
Genesis	5	3	2	Canticales	3	3	3
Exodus	7	1	2	Wisdom	2	7	0
Leviticus	1	0	1	Ecclesiasticus	5	2	2
Numbers	4	0	1	Isaias	6	22	4
Deuteronomy	1	4	0	Jeremias	3	8	5
Josue	1	0	0	Lamentations	2	8	2
Judges	0	1	0	Ezechiel	0	2	0
Ruth	0	1	0	Osee	1	2	0
1 Kings	1	0	0	Joel	0	1	0
2 Kings	2	1	1	Amos	0	1	0
3 Kings	1	0	0	Micheas	0	0	1
1 Paralipomenon	0	0	1	Habacuc	0	1	0
Tobias	0	1	1	Zacharias	0	2	0
Job	2	6	1	Malachias	2	0	0
Psalms	29	18	13	1 Machabees	0	1	0
Proverbs	4	0	5				
Ecclesiastes	4	1	0	Totals	86	97	45

New Testament

	ES	S2	C		ES	S2	C
Matthew	12	16	4	1 Thessalonians	1	1	0
Mark	0	2	0	1 Timothy	0	2	0
Luke	13	9	7	2 Timothy	0	3	0
John	24	15	9	Titus	0	0	1
Acts	0	1	0	Hebrews	3	4	3
Romans	4	4	6	James	2	3	0
1 Corinthians	11	5	4	1 Peter	6	9	3
2 Corinthians	1	3	2	2 Peter	0	3	1
Galations	1	4	0	1 John	2	3	0
Ephesians	0	1	0	Apocalypse	2	9	1
Philippians	1	3	2				
Colossians	1	1	3	Totals	84	101	46

ES = Sermons for Easter Sunday
S2 = Sermons for Easter II
C = Comparative Sermons

fact that the comparative group of sermons is barely half the total of sermons from our manuscript, several differences in choice of authorities
emerge: the greater use of Matthew's Gospel and of Peter's Epistles in the
Laud sermons, while in the comparative group there is a greater use of
Luke's Gospel, Romans and I Corinthians. In all three groups of sermons
the references to John's Gospel outnumber Matthew—this emphasises the
significance of John's Gospel for Paschaltide. In the manuscript sermons
for the Second Sunday after Easter the authorities from the Apocalypse are
proportionately greater than in the comparative group. The balance in the
authorities is quite different from the pattern shown either in the Elstow
or in the Advent sermons.[7]

In the Easter Sunday sermons there are five references each to Augustine and Gregory, two to Jerome, one to Rabanus Maurus, two to Anselm,
six to Bernard and six also to John Damascene. In the manuscript sermons
for the Second Sunday after Easter there is one authority only from the
Fathers, and six authorities from St. Bernard. In the five comparative
sermons eighteen references to the Fathers and six to St. Bernard are
found in three sermons: two authorities from Bernard in that by Aldobrandinus; two references to Bernard and one to Gregory in the first sermon
of Peraldus; but nineteen authorities in Hugh of Hartlepool's university
sermon—fifteen from Augustine, two from Bernard, one from Chrysostom
and one from Gregory. The proportion of authorities taken from the
Fathers is significantly different in Hugh of Hartlepool's sermon compared
with any others of the Paschaltide sermons, except perhaps sermon 114.

Only two references to the *Gloss* are found in the Easter sermons:
one in sermon 117 by Petrus de Remis, looking at the meaning of Pasch
in Greek, Hebrew and Latin; the other in the sermon of Aldobrandinus,
a comment on Philippians 2:8 that death on the Cross is more ignominious
than any other.[8] Etymologies show a similar paucity: none in the Easter
Sunday sermons—four only for the other group: two giving the interpretation of "Christ" as meaning "anointed"; one giving the meaning of "mare"
as "bitter"; and one interpreting the name "Sydon" as "hunters."[9] Literary

---

[7] See Chapter 5 and Chapter 8.

[8] Sermon 117 [fol. 115vb, ll. 5-6]: Glosa: pasch in grece, phase in hebraice, transitus latine.
    Wroclaw MS I.Q.427, fol. 136va: phi ii mortem autem crucis, glosa que erat ig-
nominiscior inter alias.

[9] Worc. Cath. MS Q 46, fol. 161r found in Little and Pelster, 198: Secundum Papi-
as Christus nomen grecum est, et est idem quod unctus. Wroclaw MS I.Q.427, fol.
136b: Christus enim unctus interpretatur.

references are equally few: two quotations from Seneca, one in sermon 131, the other in the sermon of Hugh of Hartlepool. In the second sermon of Peraldus there is a reference to the *Ethicus*. In the antitheme of his Good Friday sermon Hugh embarks on a sophisticated linguistic analysis based on grammatical usage with regard to transitive and intransitive verbs as an image for Christ.[10]

Liturgical authorities are slightly more numerous. In the Easter Sunday sermons there are eight liturgical references. In sermon 114 three hymns are quoted, two for Passiontide—the Matins hymn, *Pange lingua gloriosi prelium*, verse 3;[11] the Vesper hymn, *Vexilla regis*, verse 2;[12] and an Advent hymn, *Intende qui regis Israel*, verse 3.[13] In sermon 119 the Paschaltide Matins hymn, *Aurora lucis rutilat*, verse 4 is quoted.[14] In the same sermon there is a comment about the greatness of Easter among the three feasts of Christmas, Easter and Ascension.[15] Finally, references to the

---

Sermon 137 [fol. 128a, ll. 16-18]: Erubesce Sydon ac mare per mare amaritudo Passionis Christi interpretatur.

Ibid. [ll. 21-25]: Sydon autem venationem interpretatur et significat voluptuosam qui gaudia venatur forinseca et tales confundi possunt considerata Passione Christi.

[10] Sermon 131 [fol. 125a, ll. 25-26]: Error enim, ut dicit Seneca, est declinatio anime a veritate. Worc. Cath. MS Q 46, fol. 161v, found in Little and Pelster, 202: Et hoc dicit Seneca quod exitus vite eminentis est cadere fortuna alta, quoniam cum splendit tunc frangitur.

Peraldus, Sermon 2, p. 68 col 2: Ethicus Ex vitiis leviter quidquid patiare ferendum est. Quae venit indigne poena dolenda fuit.

Worc. Cath. MS Q 46, fol. 159v, found in Little and Pelster, 193: Sermo iste ultimus potest dupliciter exponi ex hoc quod genitivus 'Christi' potest construi transitive vel intransitive.

[11] Sermon 114 [fol. 113b, ll. 34-37], *Pange lingua gloriosi prelium*, verse 3: Hoc opus nostrae salutis / Ordo depoposcerat / Multiformis proditoris / Ars ut artem falleret / Ut medelam ferret inde / Hostem unde leserat.

[12] Sermon 114 [fol. 113b, ll. 37-38], *Vexilla regis*, verse 2: impleta sunt que concinit / David fideli carmine / Dicens: in nationibus / Regnavit a ligno Deus.

[13] Sermon 114 [fol. 114b, ll. 13-14], from an Advent hymn, *Intende qui regis Israel*, verse 3: "non virili semine sed divino spiramine."

[14] Sermon 119 [fol. 118a, ll. 38-40], *Aurora lucis rutilat*, verse 4: solutis doloribus inferni et ruptis vinculis eius inferni.

[15] Sermon 119 [fol. 118b, ll. 18-22]: Cum autem sint tria festa principalia: Natale, Pascha, et Ascensio, istud pre ceteris excellentissimum est, cum sit festum Dei, hominum, et angelorum, et omnium creaturarum.

words of eucharistic consecration are made in sermons 114 and 121.[16]

In the sermons of the second Sunday after Easter and the comparative group there are four liturgical authorities: one in sermon 136, quoting the Introit of the Mass for the day;[17] one at the conclusion of sermon 138, referring to St. John the Baptist and his awe of Christ at the baptism of the Lord, through quoting the third antiphon of the Vespers of the Octave of the Epiphany.[18] The second sermon of Peraldus lists three other Sundays of which the epistle touches on the mysteries of the sufferings of Christ.[19] Fourthly, the conclusion of Hugh of Hartlepool's sermon paraphrases the Good Friday 'Reproaches'.[20] For men whose lives were partially structured by the daily celebration of the Divine Office, liturgical allusions became second nature.

Equally sparse in both groups of sermons from our manuscript are usages found in the Elstow and Advent sermons. For example, there is only one quotation in English, a proverb in the antitheme of sermon 134

---

[16] Sermon 114 [fol. 114va, ll. 14-16]: Unde in cena dixit 'hoc est corpus meum quod pro vobis datur...infra hic est calix etc quod pro vobis fundetur'.

Sermon 121 [fol. 120b, line 1]: verbum 'hoc est corpus meum' etc.

[17] Sermon 136 [fol. 127vb, ll. 21-22]: In principio Misse canit Ecclesia hodie: 'Misericordia Domini plena est terra.' (Office of Sunday Pasch II or I post oct' Pasche: "Misericordia Domini plena est terra, alleluia; verbo Domini caeli firmati sunt. Alleluia.")

[18] Sermon 138 [fol. 129vb, ll. 17-18]: Item, Baptista contremuit et non audet tangere sanctum Christi verticem.

Compare: Antiphon 3, Lauds and Vespers, Octave of Epiphany: Baptista contremuit, et non audet tangere sanctum Dei verticem, sed clamat cum tremore: Sanctifica me, Salvator. (F. Proctor and C. Wordsworth, ed., *Breviarum ad usum insignis ecclesiae Sarum*, 3 vols. [Cambridge, 1882-1886], 1: ccclvii—ccclviii; *Breviarum Sacri Ordinis Praedicatorum*, 2 vols. [Mechlin, 1865-1893], 1: 177-178.)

[19] Peraldus, Sermon 2, p. 68 col 2: De Passione etiam Dominica invenies in sermonibus illius Epistolae 'Quicumque baptizati sumus' (Trinity 6) Et in illo sermone 'Tradidi vobis in primis' etc. (Trinity 9) Et in illa Epistola 'Hoc sentite in vobis' (Palm Sunday).

[20] Worc. Cath. MS Q 46, fol. 162r, found in Little and Pelster, 204: Quid dicet homo quando Christus dicet sibi: Popule meus, ego dedi tibi vitam; tu autem quantum in te est me occidisti quando in peccatum cecidisti. Ego dedi tibi escam et potum, tu potasti me aceto. Coronam spineam pro te portavi; tu contra me coronam auream vel rosam. Ego dilexi te, tu me despexisti. Ego nudus pependi pro te; tu autem delicate vestibus insurgis contra me. Sanguinem cordis mei dedi pro redemptione tui, et tu extraxisti a me amorem cordis tui. Ei enim debemus totum amorem nostrum rependere et omnes ad invicem diligere.

for the Second Sunday after Easter.[21] Only one reference to 'natural history' is made, namely some commonplace observations about sheep in sermon 131.[22] None of the comparative sermons have any vernacular usage
or information from the Bestiaries, except that of Hugh of Hartlepool.
Hugh has a veritable zoo of references: to turtledove, sparrow, pigeon,
sheep, ox, goat, later to the beetle and the pig and later still to the donkey.[23] He also draws on the science of the day for several images and
comparisons.[24]

With regard to *exempla*, the number in both manuscript groups of
sermons is small, about fourteen in each group.[25] There is only one *exemplum* worth recording, namely, an evocative description of spring as an
image for resurrection. This is found in full in sermon 118;[26] and an
active copyist, at an appropriate point in sermon 119, refers to this "being
found in the above sermon just before the middle."[27] The printed
sermons of Peraldus and pseudo-Aquinas do not really yield any, neither
does the sermon of Aldobrandinus. Hugh of Hartlepool's has at least
sixteen. His use of them is not only an attention reviver for his hearers,

---

[21] Sermon 134 [fol. 126b, line 8]: Wo is ute bisteken he is inne forgeten. Probably
from R. Morris, ed., "The Proverbs of Alfred," in *An Old English Miscellany*, E.E.T.S.
49 (London, 1872), 134, ll. 554-6. See Appendix 1, "A Catalogue of MS Laud Misc.
511."

[22] Sermon 131 [fol. 125a, ll. 15-16, 19: ovis enim animal simplex est....ovis est animal mansuetus....

[23] Worc. Cath. MS Q 46, fol. 160r, in Little and Pelster, 195: In turture invenitur...
agilitas circulationis.

 Ibid., fol. 160v and p. 197: Scarebeus bene scit...aromatico.

 Ibid., fol. 161r and p. 200: Sic est de istis sicud narratur de quodam rustico
quod faceret asinum.

[24] Worc. Cath. MS Q 46, fol. 160v, in Little and Pelster, 197: sicud ad oculum
requiritur illuminatio...sed sicud causatur eclipsis naturalis.

 Ibid., fol. 160v and p. 198: Noscis enim quod imago relucens in speculo. Lux
enim solaris delectat.

[25] See Appendix 7, "The Exempla": Easter Sunday 114 [1]-**120** [5]; second Sunday
after Easter **132** [1]-**138** [3], **147**.

[26] Sermon 118 [fol. 116vb, line 39–fol. 117a, line 4]: Post pascha enim germinat
terra herbam virentem, arbores frondent et florent; aves nidificant; ova ponunt et
excubant, tam animalia dormita quam indormita, pulos renovant et fecundant,
tempus fulget, dies elongatur, noctes decrescunt, et sic omnes creature quasi
renovantur et reviviscunt quasi Resurrectioni Dominice applaudentes.

[27] Sermon 119 [fol. 118va, ll. 11-12]: quere supra sermone proximo ante medium.

but also amusing and apt.[28] Of course, Hugh's is a full university sermon, not a portion thereof. Also he is Franciscan. Certainly the *exempla* are recorded more fully in Hugh's sermon than in many of the Dominican sermons in our manuscript, where often the title only of the story is given.

Of the sixteen sermons in the total group, Hugh of Hartlepool's is the only identified "university" sermon. It is, even allowing for the shortening of a sermon because it comes from a *reportatio* instead of from the original composer, considerably longer and fuller than any of the fifteen other sermons on the theme *Christus passus est*. Moreover, it quotes significantly more authorities other than Scripture. Despite lack of any specific ascriptions, it seems unlikely that any of the other sermons in this Second Sunday after Easter group are "university" sermons. As for the nine sermons for Easter Sunday, they are varied in length and content. It is possible that sermons 114 and 118 were intended originally for clerics or for the brethren. But in default of any clear indications, it is preferable not to categorize the the audience for the remaining fifteen sermons in the groups.

B. THE SERMONS FOR EASTER SUNDAY: A CODICOLOGICAL SIGNIFICANCE

The nature of our manuscript as a compilation the greater part of which has only one editor is well illustrated by these nine sermons for Easter Sunday, which are selected from six different source books. The technical patterns and probable appearance of these source books have been discussed above.[29] Here, in conjunction with the fact that one of these paschal sermons, number 117, has been identified as composed by Petrus de Remis OP, the two questions of the nature of MS Laud Misc. 511 as a sermon collection on the one hand and, on the other, the process of the transmission of sermons by writing—as exemplified by our manuscript—can be fruitfully raised.

Schneyer's *Repertorium* offers a good picture of the variations in

---

[28] Worc. Cath. MS Q 46, fol. 161r, in Little and Pelster, 200: miles strenuus...et quidam similes hystrionibus.

Ibid., fol. 161r and pp. 201-2: cuidam sacerdoti qui vovebat adire Romam.

Ibid., fol. 161v and p. 202: sicud venatores..sicud de pueris quando primum equitant.

Ibid., fol. 161v and pp. 202-3: Sic de Christo sicud de magistro et pueris quando primo ponuntur ad literaturam.

Ibid., fol. 161v and p. 203: Unde Christus fecit sicud auceps qui situat se.

[29] See Chapter 3.

medieval sermon collections: some can be beautifully ordered according
to the *Temporale, Sanctorale,* Common of Saints; other collections follow the
pattern of the life of Christ; others yet again are higgledy-piggledy. Some,
like those of Peraldus or Hugh of St. Cher, are "model" collections. In this
context the term "model" does not mean model as an ideal, but rather
model in the sense of something to copy. A model collection is a written
collection of sermons for common use by other preachers. Some of the
sermons, possibly many of those of Peraldus, like those of Humbert of
Romans, were written from their very inception for the use of others. It is
unlikely that that kind of composed, written, model collection was actually
preached initially by the composer. Other sermons, starting as oral and
aural occasions, could be circulated in writing either in a full copy or in
reportatio form. These could become part of a collection gathered by an individual preacher for his own use. Such a collection by its use and function can become a model collection; but unless it is copied and circulated
as a collection, it does not become a standard collection. MS Laud Misc.
511 is an example of this middle position. It is a "one-off" model collection
derived from at least thirteen other collections of sermons which, by virtue
of being gathered into such a book, became available for common use as
models. The preaching at Elstow is an example of our manuscript being
used as a model collection.

But at this point we must turn to a further codicological fact about
our manuscript illustrated by part of sermon 120, the whole of sermon 121
and 122 for Easter Sunday, together with sermons 138 and 140 for the
Second Sunday after Easter and sermon 141 for the third Sunday. These
are the two replacement *bifolia* written by the much-corrected scribe C.[30]
The originals written by scribe B were rejected, but bound at the front of
the manuscript. As already noted above, the parchment of the rejected
bifolia is poor in quality, while the format and neatness of the layout and
hand are less careful than the rest of scribe B's work. The existence of the
rejected bifolia does raise a question about whether a rought draft of
gatherings i-xv was produced. The technical problems of copying over two
hundred sermons in correct liturgical order, with very few out of place,
from at least thirteen source books, must have been formidable and would
have required meticulous organisation, so that the production of a draft
before a best copy would not have been unreasonable. But if there was a
rough draft, where are the other rejected 178 pages? It is a puzzle without

[30] MS Laud Misc. 511, folios 1-4v, the reject bifolia, replaced in the body of the
manuscript by bifolia one, folios 119, 119v, 130, 130v and bifolia 2, folios 120, 120v,
129, 129v.

a present answer. It does, however, identify clearly the two-stage production of our manuscript.

The second codicological question is, how did the identified sermon 117 reach MS Laud Misc. 511? Its composer, Petrus de Remis OP, was a Frenchman whose duties in the Order kept him focussed on France from 1224 to 1233 and again from 1245 to 1247. It is unlikely that he himself brought his manuscript to England. Rather, we know from its other contents that *Liber Rubeus Minor* was not an exemplar of Peter's sermons, so that 117 is one sermon from one collection. The diagram represents the sources of the known sermons present in our manuscript. The sermons of Simon Hinton OP, H. de Mordon and Richard Fishacre, of whose sermon two versions at least have been identified, were already in England. The sermons of Peraldus OP, Hugo de St. Caro, Johannes Halgrinus de Abbeville and Petrus de Remis were all composed in France. It is unlikely that the original version of these sermons crossed the Channel. Moreover, the sermons of Peraldus, Hugh and Peter belong initially to model collections for which there would be at least one exemplar. An early copy of a complete exemplar could have been brought to England. Alternatively, a sermon or sermons could come in a personal sermon collection similar to *Liber Proprius* in the haversack of any friar travelling from France to England. Whatever the mode of transportation, there are at least two stages, possibly three, between the composing of the original sermon and its appearance in one of five of the thirteen source books. As illustrated by sermon 117, these could be: stage one, Peter's composition; stage two, the placing of that sermon in the model collection exemplar; stage three, the copy of that exemplar brought to England; stage four, the sermon copied into *Liber Rubeus Minor*; stage five, sermon 117 copied into the compiler's part of the manuscript, perhaps in draft, perhaps in final copy; stage six, the binding of the compiler's larger portion with the smaller portion of gatherings xvi, xvii and at least one other. It is clear that logically there is a minimum of five stages between the initial composition of sermon 117 and its appearance in MS Laud Misc. 511. Moreover, these stages have historical and geographical variants, and different scribes or copyists would be involved.

If it is reasonable to posit these stages, with their accompanying hazards, of the transmission of the actual identified sermons, we can extend a similar supposition of staged process to the rest of the contents of our manuscript. Furthermore, we can note how distant are these sermons from any occasion of oral delivery. Lastly, we can see how the palaeographical information in our manuscript itself throws valuable light on its written contents.

TABLE 2. DIAGRAMMATICAL REPRESENTATION OF SOURCES OF SOME OF THE SERMONS IN MS LAUD MISC. 511

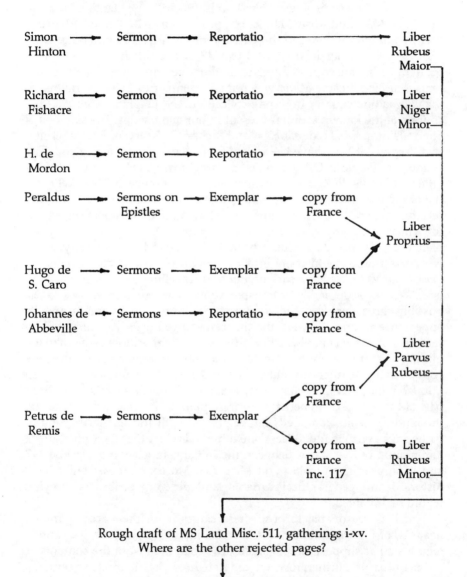

Rough draft of MS Laud Misc. 511, gatherings i-xv.
Where are the other rejected pages?

Binding together in the existing manuscript of gatherings i-xv
and gatherings xvi-xvii, plus at least one more,
together with the rejected pages 120, 121, 122, 138, 140 and 141.

C. THE CATECHETICAL CONTENT OF NINE SERMONS FOR EASTER SUNDAY

Clearly, the compiler was interested in having a variety of sermons for Easter Sunday, as he did for the feast of the Ascension. These emphases are in strong contrast to the paucity of sermons for the important feast of Christmas. The nine sermons for Easter Sunday[31] have several significant topics in common, some of which would be well accepted today, for example, the passion and death of Christ, the Resurrection itself, the eucharist, and confession (this in one sermon only). At least one topic would not find much sympathy from a congregation today, namely the preachers' preoccupation with those known as *recidivantes* or *recidivandi*, who lapse into sin at Eastertide, having repented during Lent.

Four sermons comment, some at considerable length, on Christ's sufferings and death.[32] Sermon 114 gives a wealth of detail concerning the date of creation, 18 March—although April is also mentioned—and not only the synchronicity of the fall of man with Christ's death on Calvary, but also the parallels between the tree of knowledge of good and evil and the tree of the cross.[33] The other sermons share common comments on Christ's humility, his terrible sufferings, his painful death, and the poverty expressed through it, the love he showed by the extent of his sufferings.[34] Many of these sermons emphasise the ingratitude of those who fall back into sin after their Easter communion.[35] So listeners are urged to imitate Christ in his humility, patience and poverty. This emphasis on the suffering humanity of Christ is, as we have already seen and will see

---

[31] English summaries of these sermons are found in Appendix 9, "Selected Texts."

[32] Sermons 114, 118, 120, 122.

[33] Sermon 114 [fol. 113a, ll. 16-28]: Factus est enim mundus octavadecima die Martii scilicet ubi 'C' est tertia littera Dominicalis et illa fuit Dominica....hec omnia si consideras patent quod homo lapsus est mense lunationis Aprilis sexta feria post plenilunium. Et hec etiam concurrerunt in Passione Domini quando homo reparatus est, per hoc quod homo vicit diabolum.

Ibid. [fol. 113b, ll. 24-27]: Sicut hominem vicit et occidit in Paradiso per delectationem in ligno asssumptam, sic ab homine victus est in medio mundi, non per delectationem sed per penam in ligno passam.

[34] Sermon 118 [fol. 117b, ll. 38-41]: Iterum secundum ferculum fuit perfecta Christi caritas suos scilicet docendo et etiam traditorem suum manu propria cibando hic fuit summa Christo caritas.

Sermon 120 [fol. 119b, ll. 24-28]: Christus destruxit peccatum in nobis mortuus est in cruce ut cum eo peccatum crucifigeretur et corporaliter passus ut nos spiritualiter pati et in peccatis mori doceret.

[35] Sermons 118, 119, 120, 121.

again, characteristic of thirteenth-century devotion, especially in the mendicant tradition.

As one would expect for sermons for Easter Sunday itself, resurrection is prominent, but it is less emphasised than Christ's sufferings and death. Two sermons, 115 and 121, contain a threefold tropological interpretation of the resurrection: Samuel by witchcraft, standing for sinfulness; Lazarus who rose from death, but had to die again, standing for those who lapse into paschaltide sin after Lenten repentance; Christ, the real and total resurrection, standing for commitment to living a life of repentance and good works.[36] In sermon 114 the attitude of Our Lady as a constant believer in Christ's resurrection is contrasted with the doubting attitudes of the apostles.[37] This seems to be a nuanced way of emphasising the resurrection as a mystery of faith. Sermon 119 shows that of the three feasts, Christmas, Resurrection and Ascension, the greatest is Easter —a feast of God, of the angels, of humankind and of all creation.[38] "The season is bright, the days longer, the nights shorter, and thus all creatures are renewed and revivified, as though applauding the resurrection of the Lord."[39] Sermon 120 is the most thorough in its treatment of resurrection: Christ rose physically, we rise to repentance and virtue; Christ will not die again, neither must we die by falling back into sin; the risen Christ is present with us to the end of time, but his resurrection continues Christ's gift of his body and blood in the eucharist.[40]

---

[36] Sermon 115 [fol. 115b, line 33-115va, line 3]: quia triplex est resurrectio, aliter enim surrexit Samuel, aliter Lazarus, aliter Christus. Samuel enim non in veritate sed in apparentia ut videbatur Sauli, cum quo resurgat yprocite simulatores, qui in veritate mortui sunt, videntur tamen vivere. Lazarus surrexit in veritate set iterum moriturus, cum quo resurgent qui a peccato resurgant per penitentiam sed iterum incident in peccatum. Christus autem vere surrexit, iterum non moriturus, cum quo resurgent qui ita dimittunt peccata / ut amplius ea non committant; ideo dicit cum Christi excludens alios resurrectiones.

[37] See also Sermon 121 [fol. 120, ll. 6-16] for the same distinction.

Sermon 114 [fol. 114b, ll. 8-10, 21-26]: Si desideratis, potest esse vox Gloriose Virginis. Ipsa enim de eius divina potentia non dubitavit, et ideo nec de eius resurrectione quam predixerat....Si autem hec interrogatio exprimat affectum dubitantis, potest esse vox Apostolorum et discipulorum Christi qui non senserunt de ipso nisi sicut de homine, et ideo videntes eum mori de eius divinitate dubitaverunt, et ideo de eius resurrectione.

[38] See n. 15.

[39] See n. 26.

[40] Sermon 120 [fol. 119b, ll. 32-37]: Sed Christus iam non moriturus, ut et nos in peccato nunquam recideremus; hic dulcissime Dominus pro nobis mortuus nobis-

It is in fact the eucharistic dimension which is most striking in all these sermons. Sermon 114, using authorities from John Damascene, has a whole division devoted to it.[41] Sermons 117 and 121 mention it briefly. Sermons 118, 119 and 120 significantly comment on the eucharist,[42] while summary sermon 122 is totally eucharistic. The emphasis is less on the celebration of Mass, although the consecration is mentioned several times, than on the reception of Christ in holy communion and particularly the Easter communion. In view of the infrequent reception of holy communion by most people in the thirteenth century, the Easter communion would be given a very strong focus.

At least four of these sermons treat of the Easter communion in the context of those who come back to Christ during Lent by their sincere repentance and confession, but when Easter is celebrated or over, lapse back into their old ways of sin. They are recidivists.[43] So they share the body and blood of the Lord unworthily and merit punishment. One sermon only, 116, itself incomplete, talks exclusively about punishment.[44] Sermon 118 describes the table of the devil and of sin.[45] Sermon 119 talks of the ingratitude and wickedness of the sinner who sinks back into "idleness, sporting licentiousness, gluttony, luxurious living and other sins."[46]

---

cum tamen semper presens est....corpusque suum et sanguinem concedit fidelibus.

[41] Sermon 114 [fol. 114vb, line 19–fol. 115a, line 29].

[42] Sermon 119 [fol. 118b, ll. 1-5]: Hodie quod est excellentissimum corpus suum et sanguinem in singulis ecclesiis, singulis fidelibus partitur manibus sacerdotum et distribuit.

[43] Sermon 118 [fol. 116vb, ll. 8-11]: Karissimi, talis hospes qui ita inconstans est et post pascha recidivat Deum contra se provocat.

Sermon 119 [fol. 118va, ll. 4-8, 15-16]: Unde valde ingratus est Christo et multum derogat Dominice Resurrectione, qui a bona vita iam in Quadragesima incepta recedit, et in peccatum recidivat.

Sermon 120 [fol. 119a, ll. 6-11] Istam mortem incurrunt omnes balneantes se in peccatis et in deliciis et precipue qui postquam translati sunt de morte ad vitam per concordiam Deo factam in penitentia in Pascha recidivant.

[44] Sermon 116 [fol. 115va, line 20–fol. 115vb, line 2].

[45] Sermon 118 [fol. 117vb, ll. 9-16]: Multa ferculorum multiplicatio; ventris in gluvies retributio in divites, tenacitas in pauperes, nimia garrulitas fatuorum, cantuum multiplicitas simplicium absentium, detractio, murmur, et litigatio nocivorum ultra modum super corporum destructionem, clamosa disputatio quandoque sanguinis effusio....

[46] Sermon 119 [fol. 118va, ll. 38-42]: et cum ipsum sacramentaliter receperit tunc otiis, ludis lasciviis, tunc gule, luxurie et ceteris peccatis immergunt.

Sermon 120 refers briefly but luridly to the punishment of hell,[47] but sermon 121 shows how confession can rescue sinners from the clutch of Satan and the possibility of hell and restore them to God.[48] On balance, however, sin and hell are given less attention than the other three areas: Christ's suffering and death, his resurrection and the eucharist.

The last element of content to be commented on is that of types and images. Sermon 117 by Petrus de Remis is the most significant here, as he expresses the suffering and death of Christ in the Scripture types of the paschal lamb, the bronze serpent, and the gift of manna in the Old Testament as a type of Christ.[49] The idea of the "exodus" itself, the journey out of Egypt through the desert, is the image of the human journey—collectively and individually—to God.[50] No other sermon so clearly uses these commonplace types. Sermons 114 and 115 link the first with the second Adam;[51] while sermon 118, quoted by 119, uses the image of spring —referred to above—as an image of resurrection.[52] Sermon 119 also uses the image of the Sun of Justice, with its implicit English pun, as an image of resurrection.[53] Sermon 122 has images for the eucharist in the "bread

---

[47] Sermon 120 [fol. 119b, ll. 9, 14-18]: In ista morte pessima eternaliter cremabuntur....autem eius nullus est finis; hanc penam habebunt precipui gulosi et luxuriosi contra ardorem luxurie preparatur cum ignis sulphurus in inferno qui nunquam extinguetur.

[48] Sermon 121 [fol. 119vb, ll. 15-18]: dicatur nostro de homine eunte ad confessionem a diabolo ducto, sic omnia peccata, ut videtis, tegit confessio, occultat a diabolo, restituit penitentem Deo.

[49] Sermon 117 [fol. 115vb, ll. 23-25]: sicut illi fuit eius agnus in viaticum, sanguis in defensionem contra angelum exterminatorem. Ibid. [line 39]: Isti haec manna in cibum.... Ibid. [ll. 43-44]: scripture serpens....

[50] Sermon 117 [fol. 115vb, ll. 26-29]: Sic in ista pascha habemus carnem Christi in viaticum, sanguinem gratia, scilicet protectionem, crux vel Passio in ductorem.

[51] Cf. Sermon 114 [fol. 113a, line 41–fol. 113b, line 26, especially line 41–line 1]: et sicut dicit Augustinus super Genesam ad litteram 'sic operatur Deus ab initio in operibus creationis ad prefigurandum ordinem sue / future operationis in operibus recreationis'.

Sermon 115 [fol. 115b, ll. 22-26]: Sic mors antecessit? mortem corporis in Ada et causa eius existit infra oportet quod resurrectio anime precedat resurrectionem corporis si ad gloriam resurgere volumus.

[52] See n. 26.

[53] Sermon 119 [fol. 118b, ll. 9-17]: Sic Christus qui in Mal 4 vocatur 'sol iustitie'; nascens mundo fecit diem, scilicet gratie, quia ante illam nox fuit peccatorum, et fuit quasi una dies a Nativitate usque ad eius Passionem. Tunc enim sol occidens, et ad tempus absconditur in sepulcro, sed hodie, post occasum, resurgens fecit

of angels" and the "new tree of life."[54]

After this brief account we are in a position to analyse the main catechetical content of these sermons. Firstly, there is the emphasis on the saving mysteries of Christ's passion, death and resurrection. A few of these have overtones of the Anselmian theory of redemption, especially the talk of freedom and the firm defeat of Satan, with no mention of Satan's rights.

Secondly, there is a strong emphasis on the eucharist. The focus is more on the annual reception of holy communion and the concomitant expectations of Christian living, than on an understanding of the eucharist as sacrifice. The interpretation of the mystery of the resurrection in all four gospels sees the death and suffering of Christ as a a journey, the "return," of Christ from this world to the Father. At the same time, the meaning and understanding of the Resurrection in the gospels for the Christian community *in via* is seen as sharing in the eucharist. In other words, the significant catechetical content of these nine thirteenth-century sermons for Easter Sunday is identical with the teaching of the gospel and with continuous tradition in the Church.

Thirdly, there is one large omission compared with other times in the Church; namely, the lack of any preaching on baptism. This is the first of the sacraments—baptism, penance, eucharist—ecclesially related to the Easter celebration. In all nine sermons for Easter Sunday there is one reference only to baptism, in an authority from Augustine quoted in sermon 118.[55] Its context is not baptism itself, but post-baptismal sin.

Fourthly, there is the emphasis on the *recidivandi*. It seems that this reflects the early pastoral dilemma of the friars in coping with the experience of human sinfulness. The tradition of the old penitentials which placed absolution only after the performance of penance had gradually declined. The newer tradition empowered by the Fourth Lateran Council put what had been the order of the virtue of penitence into the order of the sacrament, namely, contrition, confession, absolution, satisfaction or penance. There was clearly a pastoral problem in dealing with post-baptismal sin. In these early years, after radical changes developing in the

---

diem istum gloriosum.

[54] Sermon 122 [fol. 120va, ll. 15-17] quoting Wisdom: panem de celo prestitisti eius.

Ibid. [ll. 25-26]: per esum hoc panis tamquam de ligno vite subsequentur vita.

[55] Sermon 118 [fol. 116vb, ll. 20-25]: Augustinus: 'Anime que Christi sponsa est accepta in Baptismo gratiam Spiritus scilicet vel in vera penitentia post peccatum longe clarior lucidior est radiis solis. Deformatio vero per peccatum, nigrior deformior que est quibuslibet visibilibus.'

practice of the sacrament of penance in the twelfth century were confirmed conciliarly in 1215, the moral teaching about mortal sin and the
repetition of sin was much less nuanced than it later became, after longer
times of pastoral practice and experience. Only once, and this in the context of receiving holy communion, is the forgiveness of venial sin by the
reception of communion noted.[56] Yet it was in the direction of emphasising the love and mercy of God, rather than with a sin-punishing God, that
mendicant preaching was developing in the thirteenth century; and hence
there was a more realistic, as well as a more Christocentric, moral theology
of the experience and actuality of human sin.

    We can conclude that in catechetical terms these sermons were fulfill-
ing a twofold need of instruction in the mysteries of faith as well as education of the consciences of the hearers about the demands of the Christian life. The priorities in preaching for Easter Sunday that these sermons
contain differ little from those of the creeds.

D. BACKGROUND TO THE SERMONS FOR THE SECOND SUNDAY AFTER EASTER

In none of the sermons under discussion is soteriology as such being
preached in detail, but there is no doubt that the doctrine of redemption
is the essential background or context of these sermons. Wherever they
describe the passion and death of Christ, together with some elements of
its meaning and application in the Christian life, soteriology comes imper-
ceptibly to the forefront. It is not valid to discuss the meaning of these sermons totally in twentieth-century soteriological categories, hence the need
for some historical excursus into theories in the doctrine of redemption. In
this kind of study Newman provides a reliable guide.[57] The history of
doctrine as an organised study is comparatively recent, and reflects a number of different theological stances. Perhaps the establishment of a common approach in biblical studies by scholars of most Christian groups has
stimulated a similar development among historians of Theology. Moreover, as historical method has become more rigorous, this development has
influenced the history of Theology, which is also being seen as part of the
history of ideas.

    The more objective historical studies of soteriology such as those by

---

[56] Sermon 122 [fol. 120va, ll. 30-32]: Septa: quia hic datur ad remedium peccatorum venialium que cotidie committuntur.

[57] J.H. Newman, *Development of Christian Doctrine* (1878 edition; London 1903).

Aulen and Turner[58] have shown the need to ascertain what the Fathers said about the Scriptural teaching on redemption, and not to judge the content of that teaching solely by current valuations which can be influenced by cultural as well as theological factors.

There are several elements which help to provide the context of a history of soteriology. First, there is the fact of redemption and faith in it as part of the Christian consciousness from the very beginning. That is to say there is a context of soteriology for the doctrines of the Trinity and the incarnation; for the work or activity of Christ cannot be described or analysed apart from enquiry, within the limits of human language, into who Christ was. Trinitarian and Christological discussions, often burgeoning into controversies, occupied the early Church for the first five centuries. A series of Church councils formulated dogmatic definitions about God, the Trinity, the person and nature of Christ, the function of the Mother of God.[59] On the whole these definitions set the parameters for doctrinal orthodoxy. It is significant perhaps that, despite considerable patristic, magisterial and tridentine discussions of soteriology, no dogmatic definitions have ever been made which present one coherent doctrine of redemption.

[58] Some studies in historical order: J. Tixeront, *L'Histoire du dogmes* (Lyons, 1904), trans. as *History of Dogmas* (London, 1930); J. Rivière, *Le Dogme de la rédemption* (Paris, 1905), trans. (London, 1909); J. de Ghellinck, *Le Mouvement théologique du xiiie siècle* (1st ed. Paris, 1914; 2nd ed. Bruges, 1948); L.W. Grensted, *A Short History of the Doctrine of Atonement* (Manchester, 1920); C. Lattey, ed., *The Atonement* (Cambridge, 1928); G. Aulen, *Christus Victor*, trans. A.G. Hebert (London, 1931); J. Rivière, *Le Dogme de la rédemption au début du moyen âge* (Paris, 1934); H.E.W. Turner, *The Patristic Doctrine of Redemption* (London, 1952); M.D. Chenu, *La Théologie comme science au xiii siècle* (Paris, 1943), trans. A.H.H. Green-Armytage as *Is Theology a Science?* (London: Hawthorn Books, 1959); idem, *La Théologie au douzième siècle* (Paris, 1957), trans. by J. Taylor and L.K. Little as *Nature, Man and Society in the Twelfth Century* (Chicago, 1968); Y. Congar, *La Tradition et les traditions* (Paris, 1960, 1963), trans. M. Naseby and T. Rainborough as *Tradition and Traditions,* (London: Burns and Oates, 1966); Paul Tillich ed. C.A. Braaten, *A History of Christian Thought* (London 1968); J. Daniélou, A.H. Couratin, John Kent, *The Pelican Guide to Modern Theology*, vol. 2, (London, 1971); J. Pelikan, *Historical Theology: Continuity and Change in Christian Doctrine* (London and New York, 1971); J. Daniélou, *A History of Early Christian Doctrine*, vol. 3, (London, 1977); J. Pelikan, *The Growth of Medieval Theology* (Chicago and London: Univ. of Chicago Press 1978); vol. 3 in *The Christian Tradition—a History of the Development of Doctrine.*

[59] Council of Nicaea, 325; First Council of Constantinople, 381; Council of Ephesus, 431; Council of Chalcedon, 451.

Secondly, in discussing the history of soteriology, the place and function of tradition cannot be ignored. In the nineteenth century significant advances in the historical study of their tradition were made by Protestant scholars. This confessional differentiation has paradoxically shown the importance of tradition in the history of Christian doctrine. In an illuminating essay, Congar describes tradition in the early Fathers as a process of transmitting or handing on the "rule of faith" of the apostles.[60]

This has relevance for the history of doctrine and for the history of catechetics. Turner emphasised the importance of *lex orandi* for *lex credendi*.[61] The relationship between living, praying and believing is a constant tension in the life of the Church. Sometimes liturgical prayer and belief and practice are in good harmony; sometimes the liturgy in its content, prayer and rubrics preserves—like fossils found in a rock—traces of earlier practices.[62] A further element is popular devotion, which often incarnates, sometimes to the dismay of theologians and purists, not only some of the mixture of beliefs of the Christian people but a mixture of their religious feelings too. While much of what is accepted in soteriology comes from direct teaching of Scripture, the Fathers and the Church, such teaching has to be situated in the wider context of prayer and the Christian life. For the redemption is part of that "mystery of faith" which finds its most complete sacramental practice in the eucharist. Ultimately, while not contrary to reason, the actions of God transcend human reason.

There is a third factor in the context of soteriology, namely the use of analogies. It is commonplace that human understanding progresses largely by analogy. The gospels abound in the analogies of the parables which, in some cases, are transformed into allegories. In the Church the traditional practice of exegesis for many centuries was bound up with

---

[60] Congar, *Tradition*, 27—29. "The rule of religious practice and truth is not the authority of the ministers as such, but rather that which they guard and transmit.... The rule of faith, that is to say, the apostolic and Christian teaching, is not the whole of tradition. It is its principal part, but other things are also 'transmitted': rules of discipline or of behaviour, usages especially in worship or liturgy, examples or ways of doing things."

[61] Turner, *Redemption*, 13, 17, 23, 43, 48, 107.

[62] Examples of this are found in the use of Roman clothing as liturgical garments and in the description of the worshipping group in the first Roman canon as standing round the altar, "circumstantes." For many centuries now, the standing has been replaced by kneeling. The "angel Christology," dating from the first century where Christ is often identified as the "angel" of Isaiah, is found in the fourth-century Roman canon. It remains today as a further example of "fossilization."

variants on the literal, anagogical, moral and eschatalogical levels of the meaning of Scripture.[63] From the earliest evangelical and apostolic times typology was an important mode of understanding, especially for Christ and his work. Images come from both Testaments.[64] It seems, however, that some of the problems of soteriology come from putting too much logical and intellectual content with some of these images. This is well exemplified in much of the discussion of the notion of "ransom" and "the devil's rights." Where allegories are linked with doctrinal expression, safety seems to lie in numbers, in the use of multiple images. This is clearly seen in Matthew's gospel where, after the allegorical interpretation of the parable of the sower is given, a number of parables on seed and growing follow.[65] The counterbalance of images not only adds depth and variety to the meaning, but also indicates the limitations of words in expressing religious truth. The variations in popularity and acceptance of some theories of redemption are linked with the popularity and acceptance of the images. For example, some modern writers have dismissed the theory of the devil's rights as crude and unfitting.[66]

[63] H. de Lubac, *Exégèse médiévale*, 2 vols. (Paris, 1959-1964); O. Lottin, *Psychologie et morale au xiie et xiiie siècles*, 6 vols. (Louvain, 1942-1960).

[64] These types of Christ's work of salvation were incorporated at a very early time into the Christian tradition. Listed more or less in the Vulgate scriptural order they are: Adam; the Tree of Knowledge of Good and Evil; the death of Abel; the birth of Seth; the Deluge and the Ark; the birth, and particularly the sacrifice, of Isaac; Jacob; Joseph sold by the brothers he later saved; Moses the prophet; the paschal lamb; the passage of the Red Sea; the cloud by day and fire by night; the bronze serpent; Joshua; saviours from the time of the judges; David the King; the prophets, especially Elijah, Jonah, Daniel in the lions' den; the servant in Isaiah (sometimes called the fifth gospel of the passion); the dry bones in Ezekiel; the destruction and restoration of Jerusalem and the temple; the stone that is rejected; Susanna; Esther, the Remnant of Israel; the three boys in the furnace. See Congar, *Tradition*, 70: "A certain number of biblical references quoted by the Fathers...constitute an intermediate area between an exegetical tradition properly speaking...and an exclusively oral tradition....This could be called typological tradition...a history which, while fully historical, is equally divine, the history of salvation; a history which is made by men and the Holy Spirit together."

[65] Matt. 13:1-23, 24-30, 31-32.

[66] Aulen, *Christus Victor*, 63-64: "It should be evident that the historical study of dogmas is wasting its time in pure superficiality if it does not endeavour to penetrate to that which lies below the outward dress, and look for the religious values which lie concealed underneath....The religious motive lying behind the mythological language is plainly the desire to assert the guilt of mankind, and the judgement

The problem of language which is here identified is ultimately a philosophical one. In so far, however, as nineteen centuries of belief, prayer, practice, dispute and discussion go, a certain credal language has evolved. Despite the intrinsic limitations of any language for talking about God and the work of God, it is necessary to use it.

The foundation of the teaching of the Church on redemption lies in the Scriptures and in the writings of the Fathers of the Church. But before any of the accepted Fathers formulated theories about redemption, the Church had reached a traditional consensus about types of Christ and his work of salvation.[67] This resulted from the apostolic exegesis of the Old Testament building on the gospel,[68] where the salvation history of the Old Testament, being fulfilled in Christ, was continued and applied in his body the Church. It led naturally to an exegesis of Scripture which established first a textual reading, leading to a Christological reading and then to an ecclesial reading.

As the Fathers of the Church reflected and disputed, and tried to articulate in human language what the Church believed and worshipped, Christian doctrine began to be formulated. How did they try to describe the work of Christ the Redeemer? In terms of 1 Peter 2, Christ was seen as the exemplar, the teacher—pedagogue—of how to live. In the prologue to John's gospel Christ is the Word who enlightens, the Illuminator. Another emphasis showed the function of the Word, the Word which is God audible as well as God visible, while the Alexandrian Fathers emphasised the Word as knowledge, the *gnosis* particular to Christians. This primitive soteriology was seen as a living up to the demand of a better life that Christ required of his followers in a world made better through the cross.

In the context of increasing disputes about the nature of God and who Christ was, a second soteriological approach emerged, that of Christ the Victor, who freely chooses to conquer evil in his death, and who, as the New Man, gives new life to the human race. The dualism implicit in this view[69] indicates a radical but not absolute opposition between good and evil. The evil is a rebellion against God from within his own creation, which Christ Victor conquered and in so doing redeemed humankind.

A third soteriological theory is Christ as "ransom," a metaphor which led to a long-running discussion about the "rights of Satan." The question of God's justice—in the legal sense—is also raised, for it accepts the real

---

of God on human sin."

[67] Daniélou, *History*, 298-306; Congar, *Tradition*, 71-82.

[68] Luke 24:25-32.

[69] Aulen, *Christus Victor*, 20-21.

destruction that sin brings, and sees redemption as a real action; and so the question about how the devil is defeated involves justice.[70] In this theory Christology was developing: Christ the Word as the second Adam, the new man who re-creates humankind, gives all people a second chance of life, in whose victory is redemption for humankind. The theory also enabled Our Lady to be brought in as the second Eve.

A fourth variant of soteriological theory sees Christ as Giver of divine life and immortality. This theory to some extent incorporates the Pauline teaching about humanity being "in Christ," through the free gift, the grace, of God. Through Christ's saving actions humanity is adopted by grace into what Christ had by nature, sonship of God. Thus humankind is restored to God's original creation. The balance of the human and divine elements in Christ's redemptive work raises questions about Christology, while the sorting out of the function of the Father, the Son and the Holy Spirit in the same redemptive work asks questions about the Trinity.

The soteriological theory which sees Christ as Victim is a fifth. On the whole this theory was stronger among the western Fathers, but not exclusive to them. The advantage of this theory is that it makes much more room for the human elements of Christ's suffering and death. The Christ-victim theory draws heavily on the typology of Isaiah, chapter 53, concerning the suffering servant who gave his life for many, and on the typology of sacrifice, both of the Old Testament and of the epistle to the Hebrews. It makes the shedding of Christ's blood which, in the Christ-victor theory is paid in a fashion to the devil, a sacrifice of adoration to the Father. Satisfaction for sin also becomes part of the Christ-victim theory. At the same time a fresh perception of the moral imperative of the Christian life was emerging.

On the whole it is true to say that while these five soteriological theories can be distinguished, they cannot necessarily be separated. There was no single formulation of doctrine about redemption in patristic times, nor has there ever been. As far as the eastern Church is concerned, elements of the five emphases make up their traditional soteriology, with a correspondingly different sacramental celebration, stressing the transcendence and mystery of God. John Damascene, the last of the Greek Fathers, adds nothing significant to what he received from the classical times of the eastern Fathers. In the western Church, where discontinuity of cultural

---

[70] Turner, *Redemption*, 61: "The devil, for all his startling success at the expense of humanity is a revolted subject, and not an independent being dividing the sovereignty of the world with God by nature and of right."

setting was more marked than continuity,[71] medieval theologians—led by Anselm—raised on the trinitarian and christological definitions of the Fathers a soteriological theory which related more closely, although not exclusively, to the Christ-victim theory.

The writings of St. Anselm of Bec represent a turning-point in the theological speculation of the early middle ages.[72] St. Bernard of Clairvaux has been called "the last of the Fathers,"[73] and undoubtedly his spiritual influence was profound. In soteriology, however, he relied on the now traditional teachings, but with a greater emphasis on the sufferings of Christ as an expression of love.[74] Bernard's prayers to the suffering Christ struck a chord in many Christian hearts of the time, and have had

---

[71] The real survival of the Fathers was in the eastern Church. Origen was largely lost through being condemned for heresy. and the Syrian tradition was lost to the whole Church by the spread of Islam. As knowledge of Greek was lost so the Greek Fathers became closed books to the West, unless anything of them existed in Latin translation. The western Church was confined mainly to the Latin Fathers, the greatest of whom was Augustine. As the pattern of classical education broke down, so the coherent intellectual context of these patristic works disappeared, though the monasteries did a great work in conserving many patristic texts. The thought of Augustine was largely mediated to the medieval Church by Gregory the Great; and much of Tertullian's influence came into it with the formulation of canon law, a process which was strong in the twelfth century. Early medieval theology was modified by its new limitations in culture, geography and communications. One of the greatest effects of all these changes was the slow loss of the linguistic culture implicit in the writings of the Fathers, so that medieval reading of the Fathers occurred within medieval thought patterns that were critically unaware of the patristic usage of language. The work of the Celtic and Benedictine monasteries in preserving some continuity in the face of so much discontinuity was crucial to theological development in the later middle ages.

[72] Brief bibliography of Anselm: R.W. Southern, *Saint Anselm: a Portait in a Landscape* (Cambridge: CUP, 1990); idem, *St. Anselm and His Biographer* (Cambridge, 1963); idem, ed. *The Life of St. Anselm by Eadmer* (London, 1962); G.R. Evans, *Anselm and Talking about God* (Oxford: Clarendon Press, 1978); idem, *Anselm and a New Generation* (Oxford: Clarendon Press, 1980); idem, *Anselm* (London: Geoffrey Chapman, 1989); J. McIntyre, *St. Anselm and his Critics: a Reinterpretation of the Cur Deus Homo* (Edinburgh and London: Oliver and Boyd, 1954); Benedicta Ward, *The Prayers and Meditations of St. Anselm* (London: Penguin, 1973).

[73] Pius XII, Encyclical letter "Doctor Mellifluus," Pentecost 1953, commemorating the 800th anniversary of St. Bernard's death; quoting Mabillon in "Praefatio Generalis," n. 23 to *Bernardi Opera*, Migne PL 182: 26.

[74] Cf. Sermon XI, "On the Mode and Fruits of Redemption," trans. from St. Bernard, *Sermons on the Canticle of Canticles* (Dublin, 1920) 1: 90-99.

a lasting effect on devotion in the Church. Nevertheless, despite Bernard's significance, Anselm is greater theologically. While he holds a bridging position between the theology of the early middle ages and that of the twelfth to thirteenth centuries in western Europe, he cannot be called either the last of the early theologians or the first of the scholastics. Anselm is unique.

In soteriology Anselm, in the spirit of "faith seeking understanding," applies grammatical, logical, and philosophical analysis directly to credal statements. His *Cur Deus Homo*,[75] once his assumptions are accepted, develops a very clear but complex set of arguments postulating a theory of redemption which relates most closely to the Christ-victim theory of the Fathers. In the form of a dialogue with Boso, one of his students and a fellow monk, Anselm disposes rapier-like of earlier theories, especially that of the devil's "rights," and bases the redemption on the making of satisfaction to God in justice for the dishonour done by human sin, both original and actual. To make satisfaction properly on behalf of humanity, the redeemer had to be human; to make adequate satisfaction to God, the redeemer had to be God. Within the Trinity, the person appropriate in terms of their interrelationship to be redeemer was the Son. Hence the incarnation. As soteriology, however, *Cur Deus Homo* needs to be balanced with his *Meditation on Human Redemption*. It is paradoxical that one who sums up in himself the breadth of culture implicit in the monastic tradition should yet be a forerunner of a scholastic method which distinguished firmly, and sometimes narrowly, between Philosophy and Scripture and Theology. It is also interesting to note the influence of Anselm's soteriology on twelfth-and-thirteenth-century theologians. None of them accepts without reserve Anselm's philosophical approach to soteriology.

B.P. McGuire[76] has patiently tracked down the use of Anselm's *Cur Deus Homo* by theologians of the twelfth and thirteenth centuries. Among the Victorines, Richard of St. Victor exhibits no real influence of Anselm. His emphasis, unlike Anselm's, is on the human response in love to the redemptive work of Christ. Hugh of St. Victor "consciously adopted and adapted some of Anselm's language and concepts,"[77] but ultimately pre-

---

[75] *Cur Deus Homo and The Fool by Gaunilon*, 2nd ed. (La Salle, 1962); see also Grensted, *History*, 120-157; Evans, *Talking About God*, especially chapters 7-8; Evans, *New Generation*, 150-192.

[76] B.P. McGuire, "The History of St. Anselm's Theology of Redemption in the Twelfth and Thirteenth Centuries," unpublished D.Phil thesis, (Oxford, 1970), Bodleian Library MS D Phil d 4990.

[77] Ibid., 79-80, 130-132.

ferred the Augustinian tradition of the school of Laon. In the thirteenth century, however, Anselm's *Cur Deus Homo* becomes influential through the schools of Paris and the adoption of his terms by William of Auxerre.[78] Of greater significance, however, is the extensive use of Anselm's soteriology by Alexander of Hales in his *Glossa in IV Libros Sententiarum*, and by Robert Grosseteste in his *Questiones*.[79] Through these two masters, Anselm's thinking on redemption becomes part of the teaching in the Franciscan schools. It is important to note, however, that Anselm's theories are neither taken uncritically nor in their totality.

Of great significance for soteriology from the mid-twelfth century is the *Sentences* of Peter Lombard. As a theologian, Peter is not particularly original. But the methodology of breaking credal statements into chapters, and discussing them with added "gobbets" from the Fathers as supporting authorities, set a new pattern of theological commentary which took its place beside the traditional method of commenting on the Bible, *sacra pagina*.[80] The distinctions used in the *Sentences* were probably added by Alexander of Hales. Peter Lombard uses none of Anselm's soteriology or his vocabulary in distinctions 18 to 22 of his *Sentences*, in the part on soteriology. Rather he draws very fully on Augustine, Ambrose, Hilary and Gregory, including a section on the devil's "rights."[81] It seems that most of these patristic authorities come from the *Gloss*, not directly from the Fathers. As the *Sentences* became a standard textbook for part of the course in Theology, Anselm's soteriology was effectively bypassed in the schools, unless and until it was brought in by individual masters in their own commentaries, as exemplified by Alexander of Hales. But the ubiquity and popularity of Anselm's *Meditations and Prayers* equally effectively bypassed the schools. Through the *Meditation on Human Redemption* many of Anselm's conclusions about soteriology became doctrinal commonplaces by the thirteenth century.

As McGuire has shown, the English Franciscans, following Robert Grosseteste and Alexander of Hales, incorporated much of Anselm's soteriology. No comment, however, was made by McGuire about the English Dominicans. Richard Fishacre, the first Oxford-educated Dominican to become a master of theology at Oxford, wrote a long commentary on Peter

---

[78] Ibid., 205-213.

[79] Ibid., 215-226, 254-263.

[80] Smalley, *Bible*, ch 2.

[81] Peter Lombard, *Sententiae in IV Libris Distinctae*, [ed. I. Brady], 3rd ed., 3 vols. (Grottaferrata, 1971-1981), 2: 111-140 (Liber 3) and relevant footnotes.

Lombard's *Sentences*.[82] It exists today in manuscript only.[83] Having made a close study of the marginal summaries of Book 3, distinctions 18–22, and a cursory reading of a densely and minutely written text lacking indicative markings such as coloured initials or underlinings, I conclude that Fishacre does not use Anselm. Certainly he does not quote him among his authorities. The latter are drawn, like the Lombard's, very frequently from Augustine, sometimes from Ambrose, Bede, and the Master of the *Histories*, and in one place from John Damascene. In one summary Fishacre uses the *affectus aspectus* distinction that is a commonplace with Grosseteste and others, when he describes the deliverance—*liberatione* from evil being *per accensionem affectis caritate* and *per illuminationem aspectus fide*.[84] Despite their regular contact with Grosseteste, together with the considerable friendship he had with Robert Bacon and John of St. Giles, the Dominicans were less theologically dependent on Grosseteste than the Franciscans.[85] There are too few extant theological texts from Oxford Blackfriars at this time to allow of any conclusions. The elementary theological treatise, the *Summa Juniorum*,[86] by Simon of Hinton, which expounds the Apostles' Creed, gives only a simple commentary on the death of Christ, referring to the Psalms, Isidore and John Damascene.[87] It must be emphasised, however, that apart from Anselm's own work, soteriology was not studied systematically in separation from the overall theological commentaries at this time. I have not looked at anything of Hugh of St. Cher's except his commentary on the epistles of St. Peter. This showed nothing germane to the topic of soteriology. Thomas Aquinas, however,

---

[82] Robert Bacon, who was a Paris master of theology, was the first master of the Oxford Dominican school. Richard Fishacre was probably one of his first pupils to incept in theology.

[83] For this section I have used Oxford, Oriel College MS 43, fol. 283v-292vb and London, BL MS Royal 10 B vii, fol. 222v-228v. The publication of Fishacre's *Commentary on the Sentences* will be undertaken by the Bavarian Academy of Sciences between 1995 and 2005. The international editorial team is led by R.J. Long.

[84] London BL, MS Royal 10 B vii, fol. 227; Oxford Oriel College MS 43, fol. 289v; see also D.A. Callus OP, *Robert Grosseteste, Scholar and Bishop* (Oxford, 1955), 21.

[85] Smalley, *Bible*, 279-280. In his letter criticising the new methods of teaching theology at Oxford, Grosseteste had Fishacre's ways in mind.

[86] Oxford, Bodleian Library MS Laud Misc. 379, fol. 106a-152b: manuscript of the *Summa Juniorum* of Simon of Hinton. P.A. Walz, "The 'Exceptiones' from the 'Summa' of Simon of Hinton," *Angelicum* 13 (1936), 283-368. There is no expressed soteriology in either of these texts.

[87] MS Laud Misc. 379 fol. 108va-109a; Walz, 296-297.

had his own originality. While he made some reference to Anselm,[88] he
showed a greater concern for drawing on as many Greek Fathers as he
could.

By the end of the thirteenth century, however, Anselm's concepts of
"satisfaction" and "honour" had become part of western soteriological vocabulary. Moreover, it is significant that no theologian took seriously any
longer the theory of the devil's "rights." Anselm had effectively disposed
of them. But even more significant is that no other twelfth- or thirteenth-
century theologian had tried to answer the question, *Cur Deus Homo*, nor
had any theologian attempted a single coherent answer as did Anselm. As
McIntyre has shown and Southern's study confirms,[89] Anselm, using his
training in grammar about the precision of the meaning of words; his
Benedictine formation in *meditatio* based on the *lectio divina*, his long reading of Augustine in original sources not in florilegia, deliberately eschewing Scripture and with no known philosopher to inspire him, had pains-
takingly thought his way through this question *Cur Deus Homo*? In other
words, *Cur Deus Homo* is itself an exercise in the limitations of theological
language. When Boso argues in Book 2 that Christ was not free since he
was fulfilling the Father's will already determined, and so his actions
could neither be deemed meritorious nor as making supererogatory satisfaction, Anselm can only answer that the freedom of Christ comes from
his divine subject, and that as man he finds freedom in his absolute obedience to the Father's will. This in itself is not a philosophical statement, and
the question stands. So for all his philosophy, Anselm was not attempting
as it were "to tie God down" but was maintaining God's freedom of action.
It is no wonder that Anselm's question, *Cur Deus Homo*, has fascinated so
many philosophers and theologians since. The use of Anselm's terminology: satisfaction, honour, justice, gave a further impetus to the popularity
of emphasis on the Christ-Victim theory. It is significant that "honour" was
an important social concept of those times, and hence could catch the ima-
gination of contemporaries.

It is important to emphasise the continuing influence of the patristic
teaching in medieval theology. There were the existing florilegia.[90] There
were snippets of the Fathers to be found in the *Gloss* and in the Lombard's *Sentences*. There was the regular reading of extracts from the Fathers

---

[88] Grensted, *History*, 150-153.

[89] McIntyre, *St. Anselm*, chapter 4, 152-160; see also Southern, *Anselm...Portrait*.

[90] M.C. Murray, *Rebirth and Afterlife* (Oxford, 1981), 135 n. 46. The practice of
excerpting from the Fathers to make florilegia is an early one and marked already
by the Lateran Council of 649.

in the daily Divine Office. In the later thirteenth century there was the active interest of Kilwardby in providing annotations to the works of St. Augustine. There was the active interest at the same time in the learning of Greek, and in the obtaining of Greek authors and the Greek Fathers. There is also the implication of the *Registrum Anglie*,[91] an incomplete catalogue made by the Franciscans of works of the Fathers existing in monastic libraries in England and Wales, and available to Franciscans as a thirteenth-century "inter-library loan." According to MS Tanner 165, at least thirty of the early Fathers are represented in monastic libraries. Augustine heads the list with over 300 works available; but Jerome is listed with 114, Ambrose with 92, John Chrysostom with 40, Origen with 32, Eusebius and Cassiodorus with 12 each, Basil with 8, Athanasius with 19, Gregory Nazianzus with 16, Cyprian with 32, and Didymus with 3. In other words, many works of the Fathers were available; probably many of them were read. We have seen that practice in Anselm. So, despite the many hazards in the transmission of the Fathers and even more in the transmission of patristic understanding, their living influence on the theological studies of the twelfth and thirteenth centuries cannot be discounted.

Though not as important as the written and spoken word in formal study, but perhaps of greater influence in popular devotion, is the pictorial representation of religious events and truths. Between many of the icons of the eastern Church[92] and the illuminations in western church manuscripts, particularly of the twelfth and early thirteenth centuries there are many parallels. Gospel picture-books, sometimes found at the beginning of psalters,[93] contain a pictorial life of Christ. The representations of the main events, the annunciation, the birth of Jesus, the visit of the Magi, the baptism, the crucifixion, the resurrection, and the coming of the Holy Spirit are remarkably close in content, colour, and often in the position and gesture of the main figures, to icons of the eastern Church. It seems

---

[91] Paper read to Oxford Medieval Society in May 1982; now published with an introduction and notes by R.H. and M.A. Rouse, the Latin text established by R.A.B. Mynors, *Registrum Anglie de Libris Doctorum et Auctorem Veterum*, Corpus of British Medieval Library Catalogues (London: British Library/British Academy 1991).

[92] Murray, 140 n.3.

[93] London, BL MS Arundel 157, MS Royal 1 D x, and MS Royal 2 A xxii. Note also William de Brailles' illustrations in Cambridge, MS Fitzwilliam 330; Psalter: Oxford, New College MS 322; illustrated Bible: Bodleian Library, MS lat bibl. E7; and Book of Hours: London, BL MS Add 49999. See also Sydney C. Cockerell, *The Work of W. de Brailles* (Cambridge: Roxburghe Club, 1930), 192.

that up to the mid-thirteenth century at least, the western Church shared
with the eastern Church the same artistic tradition.

In England, through the depredations of later centuries, medieval
stained glass is rare, and what remains is often of a later date than the
thirteenth century. Nevertheless, bearing in mind that glass was often related to a catalogue and so similar patterns were widespread, and that it
was a "conservative" rather than an "adventurous" artistic style, it is of
significance that medieval stained glass not only pictured the life of Christ,
but also parallel selections of Old Testament typology. Some of the win-
dows in Canterbury and York cathedrals survive to show this, while the
Gloucestershire church in Fairford shows the use of stained glass in a
parish context. The link between religious pictures in manuscripts, stained
glass, wall-paintings, and popular devotion is probably a commonplace.
It is interesting that the glass contains the oldest form of typology, together with an emphasis on the human sufferings of Christ and the punishment of the Last Judgement. These images should not be denied a significance in the perception of soteriology in the thirteenth century.

E. The Sermons for the Second Sunday after Easter: Catechetical Content

Having looked briefly at the development of soteriology in the western
Church to the thirteenth century, it is now possible to see how the sermons for the Second Sunday after Easter in our manuscript, together with
the five comparative sermons, fit into the context of the doctrine of redemption as understood at the time. In the course of prolonged study of
fifteen of the sermons, I have been increasingly impressed by their content. As it has not been possible to give the same quality of attention to
the sermon of Hugh of Hartlepool, I have only included references to it
occasionally.[94]

In trying to make a catechetical assessment of the sermons, the nature of our manuscript as a compilation is of first importance, for it represents a deliberate selection from many sources. Moreover, the liturgical

---

[94] It is interesting to note that, despite the Anselmian bias in soteriology of the
Oxford Franciscan school, Hugh shows little of it in his sermon beyond what had
become commonplace. He rests firmly on Augustine's approach, but with little
emphasis on the "devil's rights." He draws significantly on the typology of the Old
Testament sacrifices. His concern for the need to imitate Christ is no different from
the other fourteen sermons. His exposition and style, however, are more sophisticated and complex than those of any others in the group.

positioning of the sermons is significant. As we see from Hugh of Hartlepool's sermon on the theme *Christus passus est*, it was preached on Good
Friday. Seven of the sermons in the manuscript and four of the comparative group were preached on the first Sunday after the Easter octave. In
the eleven sermons he chooses to include, the compiler has selected only
two on the Good Shepherd, the subject of the gospel of that Sunday; the
remaining nine sermons are on the sufferings of Christ as suggested by
the epistle. This choice shows a change from the very early typology of
the good shepherd as an image of the Redeemer to the Christ-victim
image of the crucified one. This balance in Easter sermons seems strange
to those of us accustomed to celebrating Christ's resurrection victory for
forty days, having contemplated his life and sufferings in the previous
forty days. That this balance was not peculiar to the compiler is shown by
the fact that the comparative group, two from France and two from Italy—
the latter two definitely Dominican—agree liturgically with it. It could be
that at this time the octave of Easter was considered sufficient celebration
of the feast.

Sermons 136, 138, that of Aldobrandinus and the first sermon of Peraldus all have a statement to the effect that, Easter having been celebrated,
it is necessary not to forget the sufferings of Christ. Sermon 136 opens,
"Recently, in the season of the Lord's passion we heard much about his
sufferings. Now, having broken off for the paschal season, there is once
again a solemn commemoration of his passion." Sermon 138 has the same
idea: "lest for greatness of joy we forget the death of Christ."[95] Peraldus
concurs[96] and, like Aldobrandinus, develops the thought at length with
the encouragement not to lapse from the renewed holiness of Easter.[97]

---

[95] Sermon 136 [fol. 127a, ll. 1-5]: Nuper tempore Passionis Dominice multa audivimus de eius Passione nunc interiectis Paschalibus solempniis iterum memoratur
eius Passio.

Sermon 138 [fol. 129a, ll. 11-16]: Item, ne obliviscamur mortis Christi, beneficia
interpositione Paschalium gaudiorum et ad exultationem et gaudium nimium dis-
solvamur cum extrema gaudii luctus occupet dicit nobis Ecclesia, 'Christus passus
est' etc.

[96] Peraldus, Sermon 1, p. 67 col. 2: Specialiter autem memoranda est Paschali
tempore. Unde Dominus post resurrectionem spiritualiter apparens discipulis suis
loca vulnerum suorum ostendit.

[97] Aldobrandinus [Wroclaw MS I.Q.427, fol. 135vb-136a]: Quia consueverunt nimis leta/dissolvere ideo ecclesia post gaudium resurrectionis rememorat nobis supplicium passionis et hoc propter quattuor causis...Prima est ne tanti beneficii obliviscamur sicut pueri post festa obliviscuntur eorum que scripta sunt in tabulis...Se-
cunda est recidivare vereamur...Tercia est ut ad eius amorem ferventius accenda-

The danger of "recidivism" which we have already seen strongly in our texts for Easter Sunday was a topic thirteenth-century preachers often took, and seems to be the main pastoral reason for preaching on Christ's passion. In two sermons, 132 and 138, this danger is implied[98] but not described at any length.

In the eleven sermons from our manuscript studied as a group, the soteriological emphases are as follows: the status or nature of the Christ who suffers; our redemption; his sufferings; his motivation for suffering; the application of all this through the sacraments—this latter, however, while mentioned is not greatly developed; and our imitation of the suffering Christ.

Several sermons take the etymology of Christ, "the anointed one," as a starting point, and describe him in terms of his anointing either as priest[99] and/or as king but not as prophet. His divine nature as God and his relationship as Son are emphasised in four of the sermons.[100] This

---

mur...Quarta est ut eum imitemur.

[98] Sermon 132 [fol. 125b, ll. 16-19]: Inde Augustinus quantum delinquunt contra ipsum qui peccata faciunt nec volunt dimittere et penitere pro peccatis propriis tollendis.

Sermon 138 [fol. 129vb, ll. 6-13]: Omnes nos, in hac quadragesima preterita, Christum secundum modum nostrum per penitentiam sequebamur, et die Pasce admisimus corporaliter sumendo; si enim animas nostras et corpora munda servavimus ante eius assumptionem, multo mundius ea servari oportet post incorporationem.

See also n. 43: Easter Sunday preaching on recidivism.

[99] Sermon 134 [fol. 126b, ll. 9-13]: Quattuor hic tanguntur pacientis dignitas Christus, id est unctus, pre particibus suis ad regiam dignitatem 'in cuius femore scriptum est Rex regum et Dominus dominantium'; ad pontificalem dignitatem.

Aldobrandinus [MS I.Q.427, fol. 136vb]: Verum triplicem unctionem Christus enim unctus interpretatur...aliquid ad fortiorem conflictum sicut pugiles...aliqui ad altiorem gradum sicut reges et sacerdotes...

Hugh of Hartlepool [Little and Pelster, 196]: et ibidem dicit quod solum inungi debent reges et sacerdotes in signum dignitatis. Christus autem non solum unctus est unctione materiali set spirituali, sicud igitur spiritualia excellunt temporalia in dignitate, sic dignitas Christo alios excellit.

[100] Sermon 135 [fol. 126va, ll. 36-38]: Quippe ille qui fuit Deus immutabilis secundum divinitatem, secundum hominem subiit mortem que est penarum ultima et finis.

Sermon 135 [fol. 127b, ll. 2-3]: Quid enim mirabilius quam quod Deus et Dei Filius patiatur.

Sermon 139 [fol. 128va, ll. 1-2, 9-10]: Dominus Deus noster...misit ergo Filium

in turn is linked in three sermons to kingship, especially the title, King of Kings (Apoc. 19:16).[101] The image of king is the subject of three *exempla* in these sermons.[102] In relation to the remarks in the preceding sentences, it is interesting to note how Grosseteste in his *Templum Dei* links Christ's kingship to his resurrection. This in turn reflects an emphasis similar to that of the Greek Fathers. In one sermon Christ is described as the judge who saves those on trial.[103] All this imagery is emphasising the nature and dignity of the Christ who suffered. It also has links with the thought of Anselm, for whom the nature of Christ as God was fundamental to his whole theory. Only one reference to Christ as priest has a sacrificial element, which is perhaps punning on the twofold meaning of *hostia* as sacred host in the Mass, and as the victim of sacrifice.[104]

Several of the themes common to the soteriology of the Fathers are found, albeit briefly, in many of the sermons. There is one reference only to the price being paid for our redemption but, the preacher goes on, the devil was not able to retain it.[105] This is the only reference to that aspect

ut quereret in agro isto ovem. Cf. Hugh of Hartlepool in Little and Pelster, 196-9.

Sermon 147 [fol. 137b, ll. 31-32]: ...spiritus virtutis, id est Christus, qui est Dei virtus.

[101] Sermon 132 [fol. 125b, ll. 14-16]: Ex quo ergo qui est 'Rex regum' etc., cuius gloria non potest augmentari vel minui, mortuus est pro peccatis nostris tollendis.

[102] Sermon 132 [fol. 125b, ll. 19-24]: Item si Rex multum laborasset et expendisset pro consuetudine mala tollenda, et postea prohiberet sub pena vite et rerum, ut nullus eam faceret, quid faceret postea de faciente [end of text in MS].

Sermon 133 [fol. 125vb, ll. 36-41]: Sed quid fieret de homine, pro quo Rex Anglie poneret tertiam partem regni sui in vadimonio ut redimeret aliquem, et redemptus, statim adiret Regem Francie et totis viribus Regem Anglie persequeretur?

Sermon 136 [fol. 127vb, ll. 25-30]: Si enim rex aliquis pro suo ribaldo fugitivo maximas subiret penas, ut ipsum doceret viam revertendi ad se, ut cum eo regnaret, quomodo non insaniret nisi attenderet redire ad dominum et sic intrare in regnum celorum?

MS Bodl. 631, fol. 184v]: De Christo qui est Deus et homo, Rex et Sacerdos, Rex in quantum Deus, sacerdos in quantum homo. Homo quidem in Nativitate, Sacerdos in Passione, Rex in Resurrectione, Deus in Ascensione.

[103] Sermon 136 [fol. 127vb, ll. 7-10]: Quis enim unquam audivit quod iudex pro reis sponte pateretur? Hoc enim fecit Christus, et beneficium huius gratie semper attendendum est.

[104] Sermon 133 [fol. 125va, ll. 2-4]: Item pro penis tollendis I Pe 3 mortuus ut nos offeret Deo sicut sacerdos hostiam. Cf. Hugh of Hartlepool, Little and Pelster, 195.

[105] Sermon 139 [fol. 128va, ll. 25-27, 29-30]: Sed vide quod precium pro ove optulit, scilicet, animam suam dilectam....Sed diabolus precium istud retinere non potuit.

of the Christ-victor theory, and perhaps reflects the success of Anselm in destroying in soteriology the concept of the devil's "rights." The idea of God's honour requiring satisfaction, another echo of Anselm, is found in the second sermon of Peraldus (and also very briefly in Hugh of Hartlepool) where Peraldus moves up the social scale until the infinite honour of God is reached.[106] The idea of satisfaction is found in three sermons, two of which actually use the term.[107] According to sermon 136, only Christ is able to make satisfaction for the sin of Adam—another strand of Anselm's argument—and he has done so of his own accord, laying down his life. Love not justice, is the implication here. Aldobrandinus has a more technical attitude to satisfaction as making up for our sins. In sermon 138, however, while satisfaction is implicit, the idea of Christ recapitulating human experience by taking on our infirmities is equally strong. In fact, several of the sermons emphasise, as Anselm did, that Christ "freely" suffered;[108] and one, sermon 139, implies Christ's free ac-

---

[106] Peraldus, Sermon 2, p. 68 col. 2: Primum est personae patientis sublimitas; major est contumelia quae infertur militi, quam quae rustico, et si inferatur comiti, tunc etiam major erit; si regi, tunc longe major; si in infinitum majori, tunc in infinitum major, ut videtur. Cf. Hugh of Hartlepool, in Little and Pelster, 204.

[107] Sermon 136 [fol. 127vb, ll. 12-20]: Fideiussor noster aput Patrem Christus est, sed Adam prevaricatus est transgressum et mandata Dei in Paradiso. Unde oportuit eum satisfacere aut perire, sed ille qui neminem vult perire, sed omnes salvos fieri et ad agnitionem sui nominis venire, factus est homo et hominis fideiussor aput Patrem et posuit pro eo animam suam.

Sermon 138 [fol. 129b, ll. 6-16]: Nec mirum quoniam ipse passus est ut nos ab omni infirmitate curaret. Est infirmitas quedam a qua nullus potest curari nisi sanguine hominis prius de illa infirmitate curati; sed Christus recepit omnes infirmitates in se preter ignorantiam et peccatum qui iam sanatus est, et reliquid nobis sanguinem suum ad nos curandum.

Aldobrandinus [MS I.Q.427, fol. 136va-vb]: Et ponit triplicem effectum passio-/nis ipsius in nobis. Unus est satisfactio peccatorum, unde, qui peccata nostra pertulit id est penam pro peccatis.

[108] Sermon 135 [fol. 126vb, ll. 22-24]: Cum ipse nichil horum meruerit sed pro nostra utilitate hec omnia sponte assumpsit. See also n. 101.

Sermon 139 [fol. 128vb, ll. 2-10]: Sed attende quod habuit quod homo non habuit, et ideo dare potuit et dedit quod homo dare non potuit; habuit enim vitam ⟨im⟩mortalem, id est non mori possibilem. Dico secundum quod homo peccatum enim non habuit, et ideo mortem que est pena peccati vitare potuit, sicut primus Adam. Vita enim hominis necessario est mortalis. Cf. Hugh of Hartlepool, in Little and Pelster, 196.

Pseudo-Aquinas, 234: Circa secundum, notandum quod eius patientia ostenditur in tribus. Primo quia passioni se sponte obtulit...

ceptance of his passion and death, for he went to death without needing to die. The implication of two *exempla* in sermon 132 should not be missed: that Christ's passion and death freed humankind from sin as from prison and slavery.[109] Seeing redemption in terms of liberation reflects the language of Lombard's *Sentences* and Fishacre's *Commentary* thereon; but it also, in so far as the freedom of Christ in going to death is concerned, reflects some of the theory of Anselm. Probably by the mid-thirteenth century Anselm's terminology is commonplace.

So in some of the ideas about redemption that come through these sermons, influences of the Fathers can be discerned: Christ as the man who takes on human life in order to save and sanctify it, the recapitulation theme; and Christ laying down his life freely—something that many of the Fathers were anxious to safeguard. Some of the images and types of Christ as Redeemer are found in some of these sermons: Christ as the Lamb of God, as the Good Shepherd giving his life for the sheep; as linked with Adam; as the Tree of Life; as healing with blood; as being foreshadowed by the sacrifices of the Old Law; as the new Moses.[110] In this context of typology it is important to note the constant use, in a traditional manner, of texts and images from the last song of the suffering servant (Isa. 53).

The main emphasis in most of these sermons, however, is on the sufferings and cruel death of Christ.[111] The preachers tend to use more

---

[109] Sermon 132 [fol. 125b, ll. 7-9]: Si aliquis deberet proici in fetidum carcerem et alius eum liberaret, bonum magnum ei faceret.

Sermon 132 [fol. 125b line 11]: Item, si quis liberaret alium a gravi servitute etc.

[110] Lamb of God and Good Shepherd: Sermon 139 [fol. 128va, ll. 9-12]: Misit ergo Filium ut quereret in agro isto ovem, et ne a principe cognosceretur tamquam heres, agnum induit eum, secundum quod rogavit Isaia line 32 Vere bonus pastor vere bonus.

Adam: n. 107, n. 108.

Tree of Life: Peraldus, Sermon 1, p. 68 col. 1: Notandum quod Christus Lignum Vitae est.

Healing Blood: n. 107.

Sacrifices of Old Law: Hugh of Hartlepool, in Little and Pelster, 195.

Christ, the new Moses: Hugh of Hartlepool, in Little and Pelster, 196.

Sermon 135 [fol. 126va, ll. 28-30]: Talis in Passione factus est ut pre livore plagarum et vulnerum et operimento sputorum, leproso similis factus est.

[111] Sermon 134 [fol. 126b, ll. 19-25]: Passionis ineffabilitas ibi passus tanta gravia vilia et turpia passus est quod nescivit exprimere. Ideo posuit sine determinatione. Nam quantumcumque posuisset minus quam fuit in re posuisset. Ideo Jero: 'Dolor meus super dolorem'.

analysis of the ways in which Christ suffered, especially through humility, poverty, abasement, shame, ingratitude, disfigurement and punishment,[112] without giving too many actual descriptions, unless they are couched in scriptural allusion, especially to the Psalms and to Isaiah. Sometimes the sufferings of Christ are portrayed graphically and with much sensitivity, to stir the hearts of the listeners through compassion.[113] More often than not on such occasions, however, the preacher is using St. Bernard,[114] and once St. Augustine.[115] As befits sermons selected by a friar, two of them, 135 and 137, refer to the great poverty of Christ in his passion:[116] he had no garment, no sustenance, no lodging,

[112] See Appendix 11, "Summaries of Selected Sermons," for the descriptive content of the sermons, especially numbers 133-139, 147, Aldobrandinus and Peraldus, Sermon 2, pp. 68-69.

[113] Sermon 136 [fol. 127b, ll. 35-40]: Sibi mirabile et magis miserabile quod non ab omnibus attenditur. Quam creditis penam intulit Passio Christi presentialiter inflicta, que tam habundantem expressit sanguinem cum premeditaretur? Christus de sua Passione factus est sudor eius sicut gutte sanguinis decurrentis in terram.

[114] Sermon 136 [fol. 127a, ll. 30-35]: Bernardus 'O bone Jesu omnes te volunt assequi sed pauci sequi, "Non sic impii, non sic" [Psalm 114] Det nobis Deus, sic clamare et exhortari ad Christum nunc sequendum, ut tunc ipsum assequi possimus.'

Sermon 136, [fol. 127b, ll. 26-33]: Omnibus enim insensibilibus insensibilior est homo qui Christum passum non attendit nec admiratur. Unde Bernardus: 'Si non attendis, timeas quod sis mortuus aut plusquam mortuus. Si Christus parva passus fuisset, non esset mirum si homines non attenderent sed nunc ex quo nullus umquam tantum sustinuit.'

Sermon 137 [fol. 128a, ll. 30-31]: Bernardus 'O bone Jesu tu maiorem habuisti qui animam pro inimicis posuisti.' This is quoted also in Sermon 138 [fol. 129a, ll. 38-40].

Sermon 138 [fol. 129b, ll. 32-40]: Bernardus 'Respice in faciem Christi tui' [PS 83:10] et videbis eum dorso flagellatum, capite vepribus compunctum, confossis pedibus, manibus perforatis, volue et revolue illud Dominicum corpus a latere in latus a summo usque deorsum, et circumquaque invenies dolorem quia cruorem. Idem Bernardus: Lignum defuit capiti, terra pedi, indumentum corpori, potus ori, amicus consolationi.

Aldobrandinus [MS I.Q.427, fol. 136a]: Bernardus: 'super omnia reddit te michi amabile bone Jesu, calicem quem bibisti opus nostre redemptionis.'

[115] Sermon 138 [fol. 129b line 40–129va line 4]: Augustinus: Gaudet pectus nudatum, rubet latus perforatum lancea, / languent decora lumina, pallent ora regia, protera rigent, brachia tensa arent, viscera pendent, crura marmorea. Hugh of Hartlepool uses Augustine extensively.

[116] Sermon 135 [fol. 126va, ll. 5-12]: Christus in Passione incessit per viam summe paupertatis; cum enim eius essent omnia que erant patris...tantum depauperatus

not even a foothold on the earth. Sermon 136 has an effective use of the imagery of the cross, both to arouse devotion and to encourage good living.[117] Several of the sermons, following the *Gloss*, stress the ignominy of Christ in actually suffering crucifixion.[118] Despite the opportunity for pious rhetoric offered by these sermons, their style is not explicit in emotional appeal, but restrained—understated, even.

In so far as the sermons give any reasons for Christ's undergoing such suffering in his passion and death, the emphasis falls mostly on his love and mercy towards weak, sinful humankind. Of the two motives, love is most frequently appealed to.[119] This is an echo of Augustine's ap-

---

est in Passione ut non haberet vestimentum...nec victum...nec hospitium quia extra portam passus est.

Sermon 137 [fol. 128b, ll. 11-16]: Christus enim passus est magnam paupertatem non habuit domum...maiorem, quia quo tegeretur non habuit, scilicet vestimentum...maximam quia non habuit pedem super terram.

[117] Sermon 136 [fol. 127va, line 39–fol. 127vb, line 5]: Nisi homo sit prophanatus habebit crucifixum semper in memoria / in templis dedicatis et Deo consecratis sunt cruces intus et extra in parietibus, et vos certe estis templa Deo consecrata. Unde in parietibus habere debetis templa, scilicet penitentie, vel cruces cruciatus, in recordationem Passionis Dominice.

[118] Sermon 135 [fol. 126va, ll. 20-23]: Ideo nobilissimus deputatus est cum personis vilissimis, scilicet latronibus, et in dampnationem mortis, scilicet vilissime.

Sermon 137 [fol. 128b, ll. 23-24]: ...maximam quando non tantum suspenditur sed inter latrones quasi esset unus eorum.

Aldobrandinus [MS I.Q.427, fol. 136va]: 'mortem autem crucis' glosa que erat ignominiosior inter alias.

[119] Sermon 134 [fol. 126b, ll. 36-37]: Compassionis modus ibi ut sequamini vestigia eius sed pes spiritualis est amor.

Sermon 137 [fol. 128a, ll. 26-27]: notatur caritatis eius insinuatio per hoc quod dicit passus pro nobis.

Sermon 138 [fol. 129a, ll. 37-38]: quotes John 14, "maiorem caritatem."

Sermon 139 [fol. 128va, line 39–128vb, line 5]: Sed dices quid magna pro me dedit quod pro ipso dare non possim; vitam mortalem pro me dedit / et vitam meam temporalem pro ipso dare non possum. Sed attende quod habuit quod homo non habuit, et ideo dare potuit, et dedit, quod homo dare non potuit.

Peraldus, *Sermones*, 1: 68. Si enim sentis te aliquo labore in servitio Christi gravatum, recurre ad memoriam Dominicae Passionis, ibi enim accenditur homo ad amorem Dei. Amor enim nescit esse otiosus, operatur enim magna, si est; si autem operari renuit, amor non est.

Pseudo-Aquinas, 234: Tertio, ineffabilis ipsius caritas...ostenditur caritatem eius magna fuisse in tribus. Primo, quia peccata nostra ipse abstulit....Secundo, in modo oblationis, quia in corpore suo poenas peccatorum nostrorum ipse pertulit....Tertio,

proach to the reasons for the redemption, with the corollary of the human response of love. The other main motive for God's redeeming work in Christ is seen as mercy.[120] Hugh of Hartlepool balances these two motives most acutely. Given the largely Dominican context of these sermons, it is of interest to note that in a "moralising" sermon preached on Passion Sunday, Robert Kilwardby declared that "the devil and every kind of wickedness are less than the mercy of God."[121]

Five of the sermons deal with the application of Christ's redemption to the members of the Church through the sacraments. Although there is a brief reference to baptism, it is not, in Kilwardby's sermon, linked with the Resurrection of Christ.[122] Effectively, two sacraments, holy eucharist

---

quia tam crudelem mortem pro peccatis nostris auferendis sustinuit. Cf. Hugh of Hartlepool, in Little and Pelster, 201.

[120] Sermon 133 [fol. 125vb, ll. 12-22]: Vestigia eius secutus est pes meus, que sunt misericordia et veritas [line 18] Mare cuius aque; attracte in nubes, dulces sunt et de facili moventur; significat peccatores mobiles et ad penitentiam habiles, super quos ponit Deus pedum dexterum, id est misericordiam.

Sermon 136 [fol. 127vb, ll. 20-23]: Pro hac inestimabili gratia, in principio Misse canit Ecclesia hodie 'Misericordia Domini plena est terra.' Igitur gratiam fideiussoris tui ne obliviscaris in finem.

Sermon 147 [fol. 137va, ll. 3-7]: Tre iii 21: 'Misericordie Domini multe sunt quod non sumus consumpte.' Si ergo te tam gravia delinquentem in Deum totiens te frequens misericordia sustinuit.

Hugh of Hartlepool, in Little and Pelster, 201: Ante istam Passionem discordia erat inter misericordiam et iusticiam.

[121] Robert de Kilwardby, "Sermo in Dominica in Passione" (Cambridge, Trin. Coll. MS 373, ff. 212v-215v), ed. P. Osmund Lewry OP, AFP (1982); fol. 214r, ll. 271-272: Diabolus enim et omnis nequicia minor est quam Dei misericordia.

[122] Sermon 138 [fol. 129a, ll. 23-33]: Si enim amicus vester recederet a te peregrinationis causa vel alia huiusmodi, et daret tibi anulum vel monile vel aliquod huiusmodi, semper, cum videres illud, benediceres datorem. Sed, Christus, secundum Bernardum, amicus est dulcis, consiliarius prudens, defensor fortis. Ipse enim dedit nobis carnem in cibum, sanguinem in potum, se ipsum totum in mortem et dampnationem, pro vita nostra restauranda. Nonne ingrati sumus nisi de ipso habeamus memoriam?

Sermon 139 [fol. 128vb, ll. 26-27, 43-44]: Jesus pastor bonus oves redemit sed modo videamus qualiter paverit....Tactum refecit in palpatione vulnerum, gustum esurientem satiavit, bonis dicens 'Accipite et commedite, hoc est corpus meum.' O vere pastor bonus, alii enim se pascunt de ovibus, tu econtrario, pavisti oves de te.

Peraldus, Sermon 1, p. 67 col. 2: Notandum Passionem Christi memorandam esse fidelibus omni tempore. Hoc enim Dominus docuit discipulos suos, quando in brevi erat recessurus ab eis, ut magis memoriae eorum infigeretur. Luc: 'Hoc

and penance, are treated. Sermons 138, 139 and Peraldus 1 link the remembrance of the passion and death of Christ with its sacramental celebration in the eucharist. The eucharist is a gift to be used, food to be eaten and drunk with a good conscience. Given the sparse participation in the Mass through communion in these centuries, it is interesting to note the emphasis on communion in these sermons. It could reflect the fact that most people's communion was an annual event, mainly at Easter. Given the customary focus of most mendicant sermons, it could have been expected that the sacrament of penance would have featured more strongly in our texts. In fact, sermon 131 relates to penance by implication, for it describes the state of the sinner and his repentance in terms of a straying sheep returning to the shepherd. The language of return is similar to the advice given in other sermons about confession.[123] Sermon 140 is a standard exhortation to follow the Lord's steps through the sacrament of penance: in purity of heart as regards contrition, in truth of confession, in vigorously undertaking satisfaction.[124] It is similar to many sermons in our manuscript.

None of these sermons leave preaching about the redemption of Christ just at the levels of catechetical knowledge or of feeling compassion. They are practical about moral applications. The sermons on the theme *Christus passus est* have an inbuilt third division, *ut sequamini vestigia eius*. Hence the following or imitation of Christ is preached. The listeners are reminded that the servant is not greater than the master,[125] so the

facite in meam comemorationem'; I Cor: 'Quotiescumque manducabitis panem hunc et calicem bibetis, mortem Domini annunciabitis, donec veniat.'

Peraldus, Sermon 1, p. 68 col. 1: Hoc fit quotidie, quando in sanguine suo, qui est in specie vini in altari, lavat Ecclesiam, quae ad ornatum et honorem Christi facit, propter quod stola vel vestis ejus dicitur. Qui sanguinem Domini in calice haberet, multum diligenter eum custodiret, et valde reus esset si eum projiceret. Sic valde reus est, qui pulchritudinem sanguine Christi comparatam, per negligentiam amittit.

[123] Sermon 131 [fol. 125a, ll. 38-41]: Qualiter sit convertendi et cui qualiter tripliciter: velociter...universaliter...perseveranter.

[124] Sermon 140 [fol. 129vb, ll. 22-23, 32-33, 37-38]: In cordis puritate quod spectat ad contritionem....In verbi veritate quod pertinet ad confessionem....In operis strenuitate quod spectat ad satisfactionem.

[125] Sermon 135 [fol. 126vb, ll. 17-22]: Si ille Dominus noster et magister per has vias incesserit, ut daret nobis exemplum, quanto magis nos servi sic incedemus, presertim cum deceat servum sequi dominum, et cum non sit servus maior domino suo.

Sermon 147 [fol. 137va, ll. 37-40]: Si Deus sustinuerit contumeliam falsam, et

way of the cross becomes part of daily life. The passage from sermon 138 could well be a guide to the moral virtues and the corporal and spiritual works of mercy. The particular virtues, both in Christ and recommended as part of the following of Christ, are penance, patience and above all love.[126] While sin and its effects are not ignored, the positive importance

---

non est servus maior Domino suo, debet servus saltem sustinere contumeliam in verbis.

[126] Sermon 138 [fol. 129b, ll. 24-27]: Per crucem enim penitentie sequendus est Christus, et sicut Christus in omnibus membris passus est corporaliter, sic et nos oportet spiritualiter.

Sermon 138 [fol. 129va, ll. 7-31]: Respiciamus in faciem Christi nostri et crucifigamus caput nostrum oculos ne videant vanitates, aures ne audiant detractiones, scurrilia, vaniloquia et cetera huiusmodi, os ne aperiatur ad vaniloquia, mendacia, falsa iuramenta et huiusmodi. Item, crucifigamus manus nostras abstinendo eas ab illicitis tactibus et immundis, a pravis operibus et iniquis, ab omni opere diebus Dominicis et Festivis; exercendo eas in pauperum elemosinas, in curando corporaliter et spiritualiter infirmos, et in reddendo unicuique quod suum est. Item, crucifigamus pedes nostros abstinendo eos a viis iniquis, gressibus pravis, exercendo eos in viis Ecclesie peregrinationis et huiusmodi. Item, crucifigamus linguam nostram compessendo eam a pravis loquelis, scurilibus, detractionibus, mendaciis, falsis iurationibus et huiusmodi. Item, crucifigamus corda nostra, abstinendo ea a pravis cogitationibus et iniquis voluntatibus, et memorialiter in mente retinere Crucem et Passionem Jesu Christi.

Sermon 147 [fol. 137b, ll. 21-25, 32-36]: Si ergo Christus et sui tam gravia sustinuerunt ut docerent nos patientiam, nonne tantos labores frustramus et adnichilamus si manemus impatientes?...Item, alia ratione simus patientes, lex equitatis est ut sicut tecum fit, sic conservo tuo facias, sed considera quam patienter tecum actum est cum peccasti.

Sermon 147 [fol. 137vb, ll. 1-5, 9-10]: Igitur et tu vera patienter sustine sed non poterit tibi dici contumelia nisi vera. Si enim peccasti, sepius vel semel, mortaliter factus es omnium reus....Igitur quantamcumque contumeliam patienter debes sustinere.

Peraldus, Sermon 2, p. 68 col. 2–p. 69 col. 1: Et notandum quod tripliciter solet aliquis aliquid sequi....Primo modo sequuntur Christi incipientes qui cavent ab inimicitiis proximi, et instant operibus / misericordiae....Secundo modo sequuntur eum proficientes, quos jam incipit delectare odor exempli Christi et odor praemii aeterni....Tertio modo sequuntur Christum perfecti, qui desiderant mori pro Christo sicut pro eis Christus mortuus est, qui a carcere corporis cupiunt liberari.

Pseudo-Aquinas, 234: Ista sunt tria vestigia in quibus debemus illum sequi. Primo in innocentiae puritate....Secundo in patientiae firmitate....Tertio in caritate.

Sermon 138 [fol. 128vb, ll. 17-25]: Considerate, igitur, fratres karissimi, vitam Christi precium nostrum, et nemo se contempnat vel proximum. Nullus nostrum sic vilescat in tantum, ut se servum peccati pro modica delectatione faciat 'empti

of mercy and love are preached, so that the effectiveness of Christ's loving redemption is answered by love.

When one looks at the inevitable compression of the soteriology of the selected sermons, it is clear that some subjects that could have been expected are either not there, or present in such small measure that they are clearly of little significance in this context. While sin is mentioned, it is not given a central position. References to Hell and the devil are surprisingly sparse.[127] There is also no etymology of Jesus as Saviour: it could be that the interchangeability of the terms "redeeming" and "saving" in modern soteriology did not exist then. Anselm is present, not as a specific theologian of the doctrine of redemption, but in those elements of his teaching which by the thirteenth century were accepted as commonplace insights into soteriology—in themselves a most powerful theological contribution. In three-quarters of our manuscript, however, there are only four references in all to Anselm which have any link with *Cur Deus Homo*.[128]

---

enim estis precio magno'. Nullus proximum condempnet dives pauperem, sanctus nocentem, justus iniustum, cum utriusque equale sit precium.

[127] Sermon 136 [fol. 127a, ll. 15-18]: Unde plus dolebunt reprobi de ipsius amissione in extremo examine quam de tormentis Gehenne. Cf. Sermon of Richard Fishacre OP, fol. 99b.

Sermon 136 [fol. 127vb, ll. 39-40]: Sic qui Christum iterum peccando crucifigunt et eius sanguinem fundunt maledicti sunt, et cum reprobis ibunt in supplicium eternum.

Sermon 139 [fol. 128va, ll. 5-7]: Princeps autem mundi huius ovem errantem in agro suo inclusit.

See n. 105.

Sermon 140 [fol. 129vb, ll. 26-30]: Qui in baptismo adesistis Christo et postea ipso contempto adesistis diabolo et sequitur ibi modus purificandi, miseri estote, lugete et plorate; risus vester convertatur in lucem et gaudium.

See n. 126.

Peraldus, Sermon 1, p. 68 col. 1: Recurrat ad memoriam Dominicae Passionis. Hanc enim multum timet diabolus.

Pseudo-Aquinas, 234: Mors Christi. Primo, quia nos liberavit a malo culpe.

[128] References to Anselm's work in MS Laud Misc. 511:

Sermon 47 [fol. 52a, ll. 9-11]: Dulcis est amor pro quo tam dulces sunt iniurie que et ipsam mortem dulcem facit.

Sermon 46 [fol. 48b, ll. 20-28]: Beatus Anselmus cum dixit: O misera sors hominis cum hoc perdidit...remansit quod per se non nisi miserum est.

Sermon 114 [fol. 115a, ll. 37-40]: In Meditationibus quod tollerabilius fetet putridus canis coram hominibus quam anima peccatrix coram Deo.

Sermon 187 [fol. 160b, ll. 31-38]: O Misericordia Dei, de qua opulenti dulcedine ...illos meritis repugnantibus.

All the sermons, the two French, the two Italian, the university sermon, together with the eleven from our manuscript, have shown a consensus in preaching on soteriology. There is no strong didactic or information content as such. Nor are specific soteriological theories discernible. The general framework is credal, while the focus is very much the passion and death of Christ. Devotion to Christ is fostered in this context. Such a devotion points up the real humanity of Christ, and prevents this belief from being swamped by belief in his divinity. The moral formation fostered by the sermons encourages virtues like compassion, courage, charity and patience, and tries to educate consciences without resorting to fear and guilt based on fear as motivation for right action. The presence of the Scriptures and the Fathers is pervasive. These sermons reflect not so much a specific soteriology as the function of tradition in the teaching, preaching and praying Church.

F. CONCLUSION

On the whole, the paschal preaching in our manuscript represents genuine pastoral teaching and pastoral care. The inclusion in our manuscript of all the sermons for the Second Sunday after Easter clearly reflects the choice of its compiler. The preoccupation with the passion and death of Christ in Eastertide is less surprising when one considers the content of the Divine Office and the readings thereof, together with the use of the Acts of the Apostles in the epistles of paschaltide. The balance in the thirteenth century and in the present is different, but the perception of the unity of the saving mysteries of the passion, death and resurrection of Christ is the same. There is a further significant aspect of this preaching, namely, that its thrust is firmly catechetical, concerned with handing on the message of Christ, but the catechesis is guided by the theological learning, understanding and insights of the preacher. It would seem that in the mind of the preachers there is no confusion between the function of the theologian and the function of the catechist; neither is there any expectation that these functions are identical.

8

Advent Sermons on Liturgical Themes

In 215 of the 234 pieces, mostly sermons, in MS Laud Misc. 511, the theme of the sermon, or the link for the sermon material, is the epistle or gospel reading of the day. This accords with the venerable tradition of Christian preaching which has given us collections of seasonal homilies from Leo the Great, Gregory the Great and others of the Fathers. Of the remaining nineteen sermons, eleven have themes drawn from the Divine Office, four from the Sanctoral cycle, and seven from the Temporal cycle. Of these seven, six belong to Advent. The source book provision of these sermons is equally interesting; for one, No. 8, is from an unnamed source, and one, No. 5, is from *Liber Niger Maior*, but four, Nos 12, 13, 14, and 15, come from the compiler's *Liber Proprius*. Such a deliberate inclusion in MS Laud Misc. 511 of this group of sermons preached directly on a liturgical theme seemed worth examining.

The six Advent sermons are liturgically indicated as for the First, Second and Third Sundays,[1] but Sermon 15 has two parts. The first and longer part relates to the Third Sunday of Advent, and the second shorter part is meant for the Fourth Sunday.[2] These sermons, in common with those in the first few gatherings of the manuscript, possess margin distinctions which are summaries of the section of the sermon beside them. In the study of these six sermons, the margin distinctions were helpful. A glance at the text of Sermon 13 will demonstrate this. Before looking at the specific content of these sermons it is necessary to examine some evidence about the language of sermons and in particular, the dating of MS Laud Misc. 511, and in general, the process of the transmission of sermons, that these Advent sermons provide.

---

[1] English summaries of the 6 sermons are found in Appendix 11, "Summaries of Selected Sermons," while in Appendix 9, "Selected Texts," a transcription of sermon 13 is found. The marginal summaries have been discussed in Chapter 6.

[2] Sermon 15 [fol. 17b, ll. 26-27 margin note]: Post hoc sermo super Dominica Quarta Adventum.

A. Some Specific Characteristics of These Advent Sermons

Some of the linguistic peculiarities of this group of sermons further strengthen the belief that the manuscript was produced in England. Four of them contain idiomatic English usage translated into Latin. In each case it is the same phrase, namely the use of the word "against" (*contra*), meaning "preparation for" instead of the standard meaning of "opposition to."[3] Such a cultural usage is not confined to England. Some thirteenth-century French sermons not only contain French phrases translated into Latin, but also express a mode of French which can be identified regionally.[4] Modern linguistic philosophers like Vygotsky have shown how the use of language reflects thinking patterns. It is very probable that the cultural thought behind these four Advent sermons is English. This confirms the likelihood of the English provenance of MS Laud Misc. 511.

There is a small textual link of Sermon 13 with Sermon 14. An examination of the edited text shows that a passage in both sermons is identical,[5] and that the portion in Sermon 14 is the more accurate. A similar repetition of a small part of a sermon has occurred in two sermons for Easter Sunday. The reason for this repetition is not known, except that it was recognised as appropriate and not reprehensible for a preacher to use another's sermon without acknowledgment. So taking an attractive part of another sermon into one's own was acceptable practice.

Sermon 13, the transcription of which is found in Appendix 9, "Selected Texts," is interesting in its catechetical content, which will be considered later; in its *exempla*; and in the unique fact that it is the only sermon in the manuscript to possess an internal date, to wit, 1251.[6] Initially, the written evidence of a date seemed conclusive for the date of the composition of the sermon. But it is not quite so simple. It is useful first to look in detail at the long *exemplum* about *rex anglie* and the abuse of royal hospitality committed by William de Marisco, one of the two "seductores

---

[3] Sermon 8 [fol. 9vb, ll. 38-40]: Ecce veniet rex ut et ipsi mundi sint contra suum adventum et parati ipsum recipere.... This usage is found in Sermon 12 [fol. 14vb ll. 4-5], Sermon 13 [fol. 15a, ll. 5-6, 8-10}, Sermon 15 [fol. 17b, ll. 38-39], and also in a sermon preached at Elstow, Sermon 100 [fol. 107vb, ll. 14-17].

[4] L.J. Bataillon, "Classifying Medieval Sermons," *Leeds Studies in English* NS 11 (1980) 19-35.

[5] Sermon 13 [fol. 15a, line 29–fol. 15b, line 11]; Sermon 14 [fol. 16va, line 33–fol. 16vb, line 12].

[6] Sermon 13 [fol. 15a, ll. 22-23]: Et intellige quod sicut olim mccli venit Dominus in carne.

regis" named in Sermon 13.[7]

F. M. Powicke has reconstructed the saga of the Marisco family, scions of which were the Willelmus and Johannes of the *exemplum*, and the executions of whom were the end of one turbulent chapter in the family fortunes.[8] The trouble had started with the murder of an Irish clerk, Henry Clement, when he was on a mission to the king's court in 1235. William de Marisco was the chief suspect. For the next seven years he led a fugitive, sometimes lucrative, life as a pirate from his base on the family property of Lundy Island off the north Devon coast. From this life of outlawry William de Marisco was also the chief suspect behind an attempt, graphically chronicled by Matthew Paris,[9] on the life of Henry III and his Queen in 1238. After a long search, William was captured in 1242, imprisoned in the Tower, and tried with some sixteen others. The condemned men were executed according to the custom, but before his death William was shriven by the well-known Dominican, John of St. Giles.

Some of these dramatic events are partially recorded in the long *exemplum* in Sermon 13. As sermons are an ephemeral genre it is probable that, if real life stories were being used as *exempla*, contemporary events would be chosen. If this is so, it is more likely that the orginal version of Sermon 13 was composed around 1242, not in 1251. The source book of sermon 13 is the *Liber Proprius*. Its composer could have been the compiler himself; or it could have been a *reportatio* of a sermon heard by the compiler; or it could have been found in another written source and copied into the *Liber Proprius* by the compiler. The real significance of using the date, 1251, is not about the date as such of the sermon, but as a record of one use of the sermon in Advent as a teaching point to emphasise that Christ was coming this Christmas of 1251. Then why was the sermon date not updated when the *Liber Proprius* was used as a source book for the manuscript, when this was made between 1256 and 1275? Scribe Hand A was copying, not editing or updating, an existing text. The date, 1251, has significance in the *Liber Proprius*, but not necessarily in MS Laud Misc. 511. In other words, in sermons internal dates can no more be taken at face value than external dates. They have to be balanced with any other evi-

---

[7] Sermon 13 [fol. 15va, ll. 20-21].

[8] F.M. Powicke, *King Henry III and the Lord Edward* (Oxford, 1941), vol. 2, Appendix B, 740-759; idem, *Ways of Medieval Life and Thought* (London, 1949), 38-68; see also *Royal and Other Historical Letters Illustrative of the Reign of Henry III*, ed. W.W. Shirley, Rolls Series 27 (London, 1866) Letter ccccxxv, 2: 15-16.

[9] Matthew Paris, *Chronica Majora*, ed. H.R. Luard, Rolls Series 57 (London, 1876), 3: 497-498.

dence that is available. This is further exemplified by Sermon 14, which contains an *exemplum* about *rex anglie*,[10] who is not only king of England, but also of Ireland, Wales and Gascony. In this *exemplum* the English king's claim to Normandy, the foundation of the Anglo-Norman monarchy, is not mentioned. By the Treaty of Paris (1259), Henry III agreed with Louis IX to abrogate this title. Perhaps this *exemplum* is an indication of an actual date of composition. One cannot form a definite conclusion about the dating of our manuscript on one piece of evidence. Nevertheless, these two illustrations of possible dates within sermons show with what circumspection dates within sermons need to be treated.

Two other sermons in the group of six are also noted. When the liturgical content of Sermons 8 and 15 is examined, anomalies emerge which are best answered by positing an earlier composition before 1256, in that part of England where the York use was paramount. In an earlier chapter, a hypothetical reconstruction of the stages by which the identified sermons, all composed before 1250, reached the compilation MS Laud Misc. 511 has been presented. Among this group of six Advent sermons, selected only by liturgical function of their themes, three are older than the Laud manuscript. This fact draws attention to the process of transmission of sermons in the thirteenth century.

B. The Authorities in the Advent Sermons

The authorities used in these six sermons are of interest. They contain at least 147 references to Scripture: seventy-seven from the Old Testament and seventy from the New. Of these quotations only two are repeated (Baruch 2:14 in Sermons 13 and 14 and Isaiah 45:8 in Sermons 12 and 15). The Psalms, the only prayer-book in the Bible and the staple prayer of the Divine Office, account for thirty-four Old Testament authorities. There are fourteen from Isaiah. Between them these two books provide almost two-thirds of the Old Testament references. The use of Isaiah would be charac-

---

[10] Sermon 14 [fol. 16a, ll. 30-38]: Specialiter tamen Rex hominum nuncupatur, et hoc tribus de causis: quia nostram naturam assumpsit, quia nos redemit, quia intimo cordis amore pre cunctis creaturis nos dilexit. Quia nostram naturam assumpsit: quia *Rex anglie* cum sit et Hybernie, Wallie, Gasconie, et aliarum terrarum Rex et Dominus, solummodo *Rex anglie* nuncupatur et hoc quia ab Anglicis traxit originem et in Anglia natus. Sic Christus....

Professor Lawrence has drawn my attention to the fact that the King of England included "Dux Normanniae" in his titles until the Treaty of Paris (1259) when it was dropped.

teristic of Advent. The remaining third include twelve references to the Wisdom books, and six single references to other prophets.[11] Of the seventy New Testament quotations, forty-two are from the gospels (twenty of those taken from Matthew), and twenty-four from the epistles (twenty from St. Paul).[12] Authorities from the Fathers and Masters number five only: two from St. Augustine, one each from Origen, Chrysostom and St. Bernard.[13]

There is one etymology, but there are neither references to the *Gloss* nor to any secular literature. These sermons contain over thirty *exempla*: natural history, images from daily life, from known stories, an interesting set of *exempla* about *rex anglie*, and a long reference to the story of the stag.[14]

Apart from the Scriptures, the greatest single source of authorities in these six sermons is the liturgy, which supplies seventeen references used at least thirty-six times—fourteen from the Divine Office, and three from the epistle or gospel of the Sunday. While Sermon 5 has only one liturgical reference, its theme, and Sermon 14 only two, the other sermons possess a greater number.[15] Compared with the studies of other groups of sermons in the manuscript, these Advent sermons have a higher proportion of authorities from the liturgy than either the sermons preached at Elstow, or those available for preaching on Easter Sunday and on the Second Sunday after Easter.

[11] Old Testament authorities: Psalms 34; Isaiah 14; Wisdom 7; Genesis 4; Proverbs 3; 1 Kings 3; Baruch 3; Exodus 2; and 1 each from Job, Ecclesiastes, Ecclesiasticus, Jeremiah, Sophoniah, Zachariah, Malachiah.

[12] New Testament authorities: Matthew 20; John 12; Luke 8; Romans 6; Philippians 4; 1 Corinthians 4; Apocalypse 3; Galatians 3; 1 John 3; Mark 2; Titus 2; and 1 each from Acts, Colossians, 1 Peter.

[13] Augustine: fol. 7vb, line 23 seq, and fol. 15a, ll. 2-4. Origen: fol. 14b, ll. 7-13. Chrysostom (probably pseudo-Chrysostom) on Matt. 10:16: fol. 16vb, ll. 27-32. Bernard: fol. 17vb, ll. 20-22.

[14] A full list of *exempla* is found in Appendix 7, "The *Exempla*," and discussed in Chapter 6. Here the references to *rex anglie* only are given: fol. 16a, ll. 34-38; fol. 15va, ll. 6-27; fol. 16b, ll. 7-23. The story of the stag is in Sermon 12 [fol. 14b, ll. 22-35]: De cervo, nota exemplum: Cervus, cum venit ad loca spinosa et lutosa, transilit.... Cervus deserit valles et ascendit montes.... Item, cervus senescens, devorat serpentem, et tunc nimio ardore currit ad fontem, post cuius potum deponit veterem pellem et cornua, et reiuvenescit. This *exemplum* is thoroughly discussed by J. Sweet in her thesis.

[15] Most of these sources are found in Appendix 8, "The Liturgical Context of the Manuscript," Table 5.

The discussion of the content of these six Advent sermons will look in varying depth at three points only: the liturgical links of these sermons, the teaching about Advent found in them, the possible audience of their actual preaching.

C. The Liturgical Links of the Six Advent Sermons

The initial realisation that the themes of the six Advent sermons were not in the respective epistles or gospels led to a search. Nothing in Schneyer, either the *Wegweiser* or the *Repertorium*, gave a clue. From having sung Sunday Vespers for many years, however, I knew that the theme of Sermons 13 and 14 came from the Advent Office. In turn that led to examination of other Offices in the Breviary and the discovery of the other four sermon themes in the invitatory of Matins for the Advent Sundays and for the Advent ferias. Initially this scrutiny was done for the Dominican, Sarum and York uses. Several years later I made a systematic comparison of the Dominican and Paris uses from manuscript with the Franciscan, Sarum and York uses from the printed editions. Some of the results of these investigations are recorded in the introduction to Table 6 in Appendix 8, "The Liturgical Context of the Manuscript."

It can be seen from the tables that in every case Sermons 5, 12, 13 and 14 fit into the general Advent pattern, and in particular to the Dominican use. Given the similarity of the first two weeks of the Advent liturgy, this is not surprising. It is worth noting, however, that none of the liturgical authorities of these sermons fits with the Franciscan use. In the quotations from the Advent Invitatories, where the differences of the five uses are most marked, these four sermons follow the Dominican, not the Sarum, use. Sermons 8 and 15 differ from the other four. Their sermon themes do not belong to the Dominican pattern. Within each sermon was a short passage indicating the order of Advent celebrations as seen by the preachers. Sermon 8 for the Second Sunday of Advent has the statement: "A week ago the Gospel, 'Behold your King comes,' was read; next week the Church will sing 'Rex noster adveniet'; and today the first words are 'Surgite vigilemus quia venit Rex'."[16] In Sermon 15 for the Third Sunday of Advent, the preacher's comment runs: "Secunda Dominica legebatur,

---

[16] Sermon 8 [fol. 9vb, ll. 27-33]: Specialiter tamen rex hominum nuncupatur sicut hodie; in unam septimana; Prima Dominica Adventus legebatur in Evangelio, "ecce Rex tuus venit," et hodie, in octam dies canet Ecclesia, "Rex noster adveniet" etc., et hodie, in primo verbo cantus nostri dicitur, "Surgite, vigilemus quia venit Rex."

'Surgite vigilemus quia venit rex scilicet noster', hodie canit ecclesia sicut audistis 'Rex noster adveniet'."[17] The liturgical order which matches these two preachers' descriptions is the York use. But sermon 15 also quotes an antiphon which is identical with the Magnificat antiphon in the Dominican use for the First Vespers of the Second Sunday of Advent, "Veni, Domine, visitare in pace."[18] This same antiphon is also found in the Paris use, but its liturgical place there is unclear. The neatest theory to fit these differences is to posit the making of these two sermons in the northern province of the Church in England before 1256. Such a theory is consistent with the compilatory nature of MS Laud Misc. 511, which has the strong probability of having been made in Oxford. The Oxford priory, as the first and major *studium* of the province, would draw students from the whole country, north as well as south of the Trent.

This group of Advent sermons has drawn attention to the fact that a minority of sermons made in the thirteenth century have their themes taken from the liturgy. Such a link is not at variance with the general practice of preaching sermons on the Mass pericopes of the day, for the liturgy of the Breviary is but the setting for the celebration of the Mass. Moreover, such examples indicate the value of examining the liturgical background of sermons. The detailed discussion in Appendix 8, "The Liturgical Context of the Manuscript," is a contribution to this study.

There is another significance to this particular group of sermons. Leclercq[19] pointed out that the invitatory for the First Sunday of Advent —which is related to the gospel in the Dominican, Paris, Sarum and York uses—was an important theme in medieval times for preaching on the kingship of Christ. Four of the sermons in this group have this preaching.

But the theme of the kingship of Christ draws attention to the identification of the start of the liturgical year. That Advent is the beginning of the Church year is not a foregone conclusion. It took many centuries to establish it, for the problem about a cyclical celebration is how the end is reached and the beginning begun.[20] The gospel pericopes of the Roman

[17] Sermon 15 [fol. 17a, ll. 36-39].

[18] Sermon 15 [fol. 17b, ll. 18-19].

[19] J. Leclercq, *L'Idée de la Royauté du Christ au Moyen Age* (Paris, 1959), 111.

[20] The earliest liturgical celebrations which became the focus of the liturgical year were the Passion, Death, Resurrection and Ascension of Christ, lasting from Holy Week to Pentecost. On the model of Christ's forty days in the desert (together with several Old Testament examples), 40 days—not counting Sundays—of preparation for the Paschal mysteries were inserted. So Lent came into being. Later, 50, 60 and 70 days before Easter became the Septuagesima cycle of three

Temporal use followed the author order of the synoptic gospels, Matthew Mark and Luke, and within each gospel followed the content order now identified by chapter and verse. There is one further problem about following gospel order, in that each gospel has two main sections: the passion narratives and the ministry narratives. The accounts of the passion, death and resurrection of Christ, which most exegetes acknowledge were the earliest written elements of the gospels, were made first. The first written gospel, that known as Mark, was significant in establishing the literary genre of "gospel." In this the passion, death and resurrection narratives are preceded by groups of events, miracles,teaching and parables associated with the ministry of Christ in Galilee, Perea and Judea. The end of this ministry part of the gospel is the eschatalogical accounts and the parables about the kingdom of heaven. Because the passion and resurrection narratives are used as pericopes only in Holy Week and Eastertide, the eschatalogical accounts and parables about the kingdom are the virtual end of the gospel. On a parallel with the paschal cycle, the feast of the Nativity of Christ was preceded eventually by a preparation time. The thematic link between the end of one liturgical year and the start of the next emerged as the kingship of Christ. Only after the second Vatican Council was this finally acknowledged, when the feast of the Kingship of Christ was removed from the sanctoral cycle and placed at the end of the temporal cycle. It is interesting to note that many of the catechetical insights of the twentieth-century celebration are found in four of the six Advent sermons which are the subject of the present study.

Sundays preceding Lent. The date of the Paschal celebration was dictated by the movable Jewish feast of Passover. The second focus for the liturgical year emerged later as the celebration of the Incarnation, which was fixed to canonise the pagan Roman feast of December 25th, Saturnalia. With one fixed and one movable focus the liturgical year was bound to have problems in how the two main cycles related. Initially the Sundays after Pentecost were grouped together around saints' feasts. By the end of the 8th century, as D.A. Wilmart showed in "Le *Comes* de Murbach," *Revue Bénédictine*, 30 (1913), 35-53, the series of Sundays after Trinity with their Epistles and Gospel pericopes were established in the Roman rite. Thus the *Temporale* was clarified. Up to the 10th/11th centuries there was still confusion about the point in the annual cycle when the liturgical year ended and began. In some traditions the Vigil of the Nativity was the start: this is the day accepted by some of the earliest liturgical sources viz. Wurzburg M.p.th.f. 62 (mid 7th cent.), *Murbach Epistles and Gospels* (end 8th cent.), *Liber Comitis* of Corbie (10th cent.) and the Anglo Saxon *Capitulare Evangelium* (pre 1066). In others the feast of the Annunciation, 25th March, was the start. By the second half of the 11th century the liturgical year was starting with Advent. Christian liturgy is not a structure but a growth.

D. The Catechetical Content of the Six Advent Sermons

It is now appropriate to turn to the doctrine of Advent as found in these six sermons. Despite the two passages in Sermons 13 and 14 of repetition[21] and the common use of *exempla*, these Advent sermons are different from each other. Any unity they have results from a common catechetical approach to Advent, which is seen as a time of preparation for, and expectation of, the coming of Christ. The season is compared with the time of the prophets and patriarchs, who in the Old Testament were awaiting the Messiah.[22] The coming of Christ, however, is not seen as one thing but as threefold: a coming in history, a coming in the present, and a coming at the end of time. This cosmic aspect of Christ is expressed in terms of kingship, but the kingship itself is not interpreted as a simple parallel with human kingship. There is careful distinction between Christ's universal lordship as creator, and his kingship as man of humanity. The kingship of Christ has a clear objective: the conquest of the devil and of sin. The conflict is described sometimes in terms of fighting the devil, who wounded our first parents, sometimes in terms of redemption, sometimes in terms of personal repentance through the sacrament of penance, sometimes in terms of judgement at the end of time. It is worth noting that, apart from one slight reference,[23] there is no mention of that saint popular in the middle ages, John the Baptist, in any of these sermons. The obvious parallel of making him the herald of the king is not used.

It is helpful to compare the content of these sermons from MS Laud Misc. 511 with the study of the Kingship of Christ in Leclercq's monograph. None of the political or social matters mentioned by Leclercq seem to emerge in these Advent sermons. There is no discussion whatever of poverty,[24] a topic often used by Franciscans in their presentation of Christ as king. Neither is there any overt political or theological discussion about kingship in the manner of Grosseteste's theories.[25] Neither is there

---

[21] See n. 5.

[22] Sermon 12 [fol. 14va, ll. 30-32]: Antiqui patres contra adventum se preparabant Christi, ut digni essent redemptione futura.

Sermon 15 [fol. 17b, ll. 1-4]: Et representat tempus istud adventus totum tempus illud quod fuit ante Christi nativitatem, in quo Sancti Patres Patriarche et Prophete multipliciter adventum Christi in carnem desiderabant.

[23] Sermon 12 [fol. 14b, ll. 21-22]: De hac via clamavit Precursor: "Parate viam Domini, rectas facite semitas eius" [Matt. 3:3].

[24] Leclercq, *L'Idée*, 37-39, 133-143.

[25] Leclercq, *L'Idée*, 35-37, 49-51.

any ideological support for the growth of the temporal power of the papacy on monarchical lines.[26] Unlike the thirteenth-century French sermons referred to by Leclercq, these six sermons have no discussion of human kingship in itself apart from a listing of the king's duties,[27] and the implicit theory in the *exempla* about *rex anglie*, his attitude to law and his attitude to his subjects.

There is, however, a similarity in spirit between the listed duties of a king in some of the sermons, and the coronation promises or oath that the king of England made at his coronation.[28] From about the eighth century the rituals surrounding king-making were sacralised under the influence of the Church. The Anglo-Saxon bishops were initiators herein, adopting some elements from the rite in use for imperial coronations and some from the rite of coronation of a pope. Some of these rituals also borrowed from the sacrament of orders. In these centuries the link between king and Church reflected the social and "political" structures of the times. That they should work together for the common good was axiomatic. It is not so surprising then to note the links made in these sermons. The greatest consonance I have found between Leclercq's study of political and social aspects of the kingship of Christ, and the six Advent sermons of the Laud manuscript, is in his edition of and comment on a sermon preached by St. Thomas Aquinas in Paris, probably on the First Sunday of Advent in 1270.[29] Most of the topics mentioned as general to these six

---

[26] Up to the time of Innocent III the title the Pope used was *vicarius Petri*. The title used later was *vicarius Christi*. There is also the growing claim of the papacy to the right to exercise the kingship of Christ. Opposition to such theories was strong by the end of the 13th century, especially from Giles of Rome.

[27] Sermon 8 [fol. 10a, ll. 2-5]: Quia sicut vos scitis quod ad regem pertinet suos protegere et defendere, perturbatores pacis evellere, inimicos destruere, ius suum unicuique tribuere.

Sermon 15 [fol. 17va, ll. 16-20]: Vos scitis quoniam ad regem pertinet suos subditos protegere, et contra unumquemque defendere, pacem reformare, et pacis perturbatores corrigere, ius suum unicuique tribuere, hostes destruere et expugnare.

[28] The Coronation Promise or Oath (London, BL, MS Cotton Claudius A III, fol. 19r-19v): In Christi nomine promitto hec tria populo Christiano et michi subdito; in primis me precepturum et opem pro viribus impensurum ut Ecclesia Dei et omnis populus Christianus veram pacem / nostro arbitrio in omni tempore servet; aliud ut rapacitates et omnes iniquitates omnibus gradibus interdicam; tercium ut in omnibus iudiciis, equitatem et misericordiam precipiam ut michi et vobis indulgeat suam misericordiam clemens et misericors Deus. See also J. Wickham Legg, *Three Coronation Orders*, Henry Bradshaw Society 19 (London, 1900).

[29] Leclercq, *L'Idée*, 80, 83-107.

sermons are used by Thomas in his sermon, while those elements of social and political interest described by Leclercq are not dealt with at all. This lack of involvement in a contemporary political interpretation of the kingship of Christ, in both the sermon of Thomas Aquinas and the six Laudian sermons, could indicate a nice appreciation of the theological limitations of the topic as well as the fact that Thomas was one of the few thirteenth-century scholars to have some appreciation of politics in Aristotle's sense of the word. It certainly does not indicate unfamiliarity with royal matters. Dominicans in England were in constant touch with the court. It could reflect some of the active difficulties of the English monarchy during the reign of Henry III, especially after 1256.

It is time to turn to some of the doctrinal themes, with detailed reference to the sermons. The kingship of Christ is clearly distinguished from other types of kingship,[30] resting on his Lordship of the universe[31] as creator.[32] All this is called his "kingship in general."[33] In the

---

[30] Sermon 5 [fol. 7va, ll. 17-19]: Sunt enim quinque reges, qui suis militibus diversa prebent stipendia, hii sunt reges: Rex terre, caro, mundus, diabolus, Rex in celo.

[31] Sermon 14 [fol. 15vb, ll. 30-36; fol. 16a, ll. 1 and 13]: Dominus iste est Dominus noster Jesus Christus de quo dicit ps [99:3]: "Scitote quia Dominus ipse est Deus utique Deus et Dominus omnium universorum quia conditor et creaturarum creator." Ipse enim fecit mundum ex nichilo et omnia produxit in esse. Propter hoc ubique dominatur et optinet principatum.... / Iste Dominus magnus est et magne potestatis.... Iste Dominus sapientissimus est.

[32] Sermon 15 [fol. 17a, ll. 15-27]: Rex iste Rex regum est per quem regnant omnes reges cuius imperio omnes reges subiciuntur et parent in cuius nomine [Phil. ii 10]: "flectitur omne genu celestium, terrestrium et infernorum" qui etiam regnorum omnium et terrarum Rex et Princeps nuncupatur et non tantum hoc immo contentorum inter celum et terram, maris, solis, venti, fluminum luneque stellarum, qui omnium dominatur eo quod omnia de nichilo condidit et creavit. Iste est Rex qui omnes reges iudicaturus est, comites, barones et imperatores, et duces quotquot fuerunt sunt et erunt.

Sermon 12 [fol. 13va, ll. 7-15]: O quam mundum, quam sanctum, quam splendidum, oportet esse habitaculum, quod Rex regum, Dominum mundi, Creatorem celi et terre, suscipere debet. Quam felix hospes apud quem talis ac tantus Dominus dignatur pernoctare. Quam gloriosum habitaculum ubi ille, in quo omnes quiescunt, requiescit.

[33] Sermon 8 [fol. 9vb, ll. 24-28]: Rex iste Rex regum est qui reges et imperatores iudicaturus est secundum opera illorum, qui quamvis omnium rerum creaturarum factor, gubernator et Rex generaliter dicatur, specialiter tamen Rex hominum nuncupatur.

eastern Church Christ in this function is called Pantocrator. The images of the Pantocrator—Christ full face, seated, right hand raised in blessing, left hand holding the book of the gospels—is also a common image in many late twelfth and early thirteenth-century gospel picture-books in manuscript.[34] In three dimensions one of the most beautiful images of the Pantocrator is "le beau Dieu," the statue of Christ made about 1239 and found on the front of the cathdedral at Amiens.[35] It seems clear that when these six sermons are referring to the "general kingship" of Christ, this is the context of thought and image.

In most of the sermons, however, the particular kingship of Christ is described, namely Christ as the king of humanity, of men. This is so because he became a man, assuming our human nature to redeem us from sin. He did this out of a particular love for humankind.[36] One preacher uses the distinction of *rex anglie* as specially king of England as describing Christ's kingship of humanity, and *rex anglie* as king of all his lands including Wales and Gascony—as describing Christ's kingship in general.[37]

---

[34] London, BL, MS Roy 1 D x, fol. 8v; MS Arundel 157, fol.12v; Oxford, Bodleian Library, MS Rawl. G 185, fol. 20; MS Lat. Bibl. E 7, fol. 194; Cambridge, Fitzwilliam Museum, MS 330, leaf 5. The last two MSS are decorated by William de Brailles.

[35] Marcel Aubert, *High Gothic Art* (London, 1964) 64, 67.

[36] Sermon 8 [fol. 10a, ll. 6-29]: Propter hoc, Rex hominum, Christus, de celis ad terras descendit ut diabolum mundo dominantem, ab ipso mundi principem vocatum, pacis scilicet perturbatorem, ius hominum occupantem et viribus detinentem, destrueret et enervaret. Ipse enim adveniens per angelum suum pacem suam statim clamare fecit: "Gloria in excelsis Deo" etc., suos fideles cotidie contra diabolum protegit et defendit, hereditatem nostram perditam, hoste devicto, plene restituit libertati. Dicitur etiam Rex hominum quia pro homine et de homine natus, in terris conversatus, ut verbo et exemplo viam regni demonstraret, et quia tandem pro homine turpissime morti condempnatus. Item, dicitur Rex hominum quia nos de nichilo creavit, vivificavit, ad ymaginem et similitudinem suam formavit [Gen. i 26], et quia omnia quecumque sunt, propter hominem subiugavit et servituti hominum deputavit. Dicitur tamen specialiter Rex hominum propter tria: quia nostram naturam assumpsit, quia nos redemit, quia nos intimo cordis amore pre cunctis creaturis dilexit. Querantur alia exempla ad hec tria. Tot et tanta fecit pro hominis dileccione ut hominis amorem ad se attraheret.

[37] Sermon 14 [fol. 16a, ll. 30-38]: Specialiter tamen Rex hominum nuncupatur, et hoc tribus de causis: quia nostram naturam assumpsit, quia nos redemit, quia intimo cordis amore pre cunctis creaturis nos dilexit. Quia nostram naturam assumpsit: quia *Rex anglie* cum sit et Hybernie, Wallie, Gasconie, et aliarum terrarum Rex et Dominus, solummodo *Rex anglie* nuncupatur et hoc quia ab Anglicis traxit originem et in Anglia natus. Sic Christus....

The same sermon also uses the image of the favourite son as revealing God's special relationship with man.[38] The kingship of Christ as king of humanity is given in fact a more subtle treatment than at first seems: there is the awareness that Christ's kingship is not self-contained but is held under the Father. This is well conveyed in a long *exemplum* about the King of England's son, the young Lord Edward.[39] Another sermon has a long section on Christ, the redemeer-king, drawing on the powerful patristic interpretation of Christ, the good samaritan, going to the succour of the fallen human race.[40] These differences in emphasis between Christ as creator-king and Christ as the king of humanity are clearly made by St.

[38] Sermon 14 [fol. 16va, ll. 8-14]: Qui enim plures habet filios, si unum excellenter diligat, pre aliis diligat, applaudit ei citius, et vultum hillariorem pre ceteris ostendit, dicens, "Hic est puer meus, hic est filius meus," et tamen omnes sunt filii eius. Sic Dominus cum sit Pater et Creator omnium hominum, pre ceteris vocat Filium dicens per ps : "Dominus dixit ad me, Filius meus es tu."

[39] Sermon 13 [fol. 15va, ll. 6-27]. See edited sermon in Appendix 9, "Selected Texts." This *exemplum* tells the story about William and John de Marisco.

[40] Sermon 14 [fol. 16b, ll. 7-24 and line 27–fol. 16v, line 7]: Si enim *rex anglie* duos comites nobiliores sui propter eorum delicta maxima, seditionem magnam a regno exularet, si postea pietate et misericordia motus unum illorum per nuncium suum ad pacem revocaret, signum magni amoris esset. Sed quid, si Rex ipse a regali sede descenderet, personaliter eum quereret per multa terrarum spatia, pedibus ambulando, et tandem in longinqua regione inveniret eum, miserum et omnibus bonis destructum, et ipsum sibi reconciliaret et ad pristinum statum revocaret, certe signum maioris dileccionis esset, et cum alium per se vel per alium nullo modo quereret, signum esset quod de ipso vim non constitueret. Sic Rex regum, angelum et hominem, tocius regni sui, nobiliores, barones, propter peccata eorum a regno deiecit; demum pietate ductus hominem, per prophetas scilicet, multipliciter quesivit, postmodum sicut legitur in sap [xviii 14–15]...et in Johanne [xvi 28]: "Exivi a Patre et veni in mundum," et ad quid? Certe, "querere et salvum facere quod perierat" [Matt. xviii 11]. Demum per triginta annos et amplius, circuiendo terram et provincias sicut legitur in Marco [ix 35]...tandem invenit hominem qui descenderat ad Ierusalem in Iericho, iacentem extra viam rectam, scilicet veritatis, spoliatum omnibus bonis, moribus et virtutibus, vulneratumque peccatis multipliciter, inciderat enim in latrones, scilicet demones. Et quid? Curam illius egit donec sanaretur et ad statum primum reduxit in omnemque gloriam sublimavit. Angelum vero nunquam per se nec per alium quesivit, hominem quesivit, invenit et care redemit.... Propter quod maior est / ei cura de homine quam de angelo et propter hoc Dominus et Rex dicitur et hominum non angelorum et altarum creaturarum et quia maior est ei cura de homine quam de angelo.... Item, quia intimo cordis amore hominem preter cunctis creaturis dilexit.

Thomas,[41] who preaches that Christ is our king because we are made in his image, because he bears us a special affection, because he has a particular care of humankind, and because he shares our human nature. These are in fact the same distinctions which are made in the six Advent sermons. The one sermon which does not follow the above pattern is Sermon 12. Taking the distinction that Christ is the king of kings, lord of the world, and maker of heaven and earth, the preacher looks at the individual's need to prepare by penance for the coming of Christ in the context of corporate human sin. Humankind is blind, deaf, lame and dumb before Christ's coming.[42] He, the redeemer-king, brings healing; and the sinner, like the stag in the famous *exemplum*,[43] is rejuvenated. Sermon 12, in fact, makes explicit what remains implicit in the other five sermons, namely the Advent call to repentance.

A second theological theme is the coming of Christ. In no sermon is this seen as a mere historical event in time. Sermon 5 is a good example of the threefold distinction on Christ's coming.[44] In his first coming in history, he came humbly to redeem humankind; his second coming, which is hidden, is to justify sinners; while his third coming, in full publicity, will be as judge. Sermon 8 describes the joy of Christ coming in grace to his waiting people.[45] Sermon 13 makes the point that 1251 years ago Christ came to us in time, and will come to us in grace in the approaching feast.[46] In his sermon, Thomas Aquinas describes Christ's coming as four-

[41] Leclercq, *L'Idée*, 95-100.

[42] Sermon 12 [fol. 13vb]:

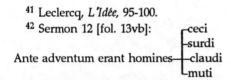

Ante adventum erant homines — ceci / surdi / claudi / muti

[43] See note 14, where the story of the stag is told: how it leaps over dirt and brambles, up hill and down dale, until it consumes the serpent, and being poisoned, seeks the fountain and is rejuvenated.

[44] Sermon 5 [fol. 7va, ll. 36-42]: Huius Regis tres sunt adventus: in primo venit hominem redimere, in secundo venit peccatores iustificare, in tertio iudicaturus.... In primo venit iudicandus, in secundo venit iustificaturus, in tertio veniet iudicaturus. In primo venit humilis, in secundo occultus, in tertius veniet manifestus.

[45] Sermon 8 [fol. 9vb, ll. 31-34]: "Surgite,vigilemus, quia venit Rex"; cotidie de adventu istius regis clamat Ecclesia propter gaudium adventus eius, per gratiam in die natalis, et representat tempus istud adventus, scilicet totum tempus illud ante legem in quo Sancti Patres adventum Christi in carne tantum desiderabant.

[46] Sermon 13 [fol. 15a, ll. 22-28]. See Appendix 9, "Selected Texts."

fold.[47] These manifold descriptions of the coming of Christ have been a standard way for many centuries of trying to express some of the meaning of the incarnation. Sermon 5 gives a comprehensive set of reasons for Christ becoming man[48] which fills out the threefold distinction (Sermon 8) of Christ assuming our nature to redeem us and give us love.[49]

In most of the sermons, the coming of Christ as a man, as king of men, is seen as conquest of sin. In this context, the image of Christ as king making war on the devil is potent. Two of the sermons recognise the duties of kingship[50] as including the establishment of peace, the destruction of enemies and the calming of troublemakers. Christ came to break the power of Satan over this world[51] and to free humankind as the sinful progeny of Adam and Eve, from the effect of sin.[52] In his sermon, Thomas

---

[47] Leclercq, L'Idée, 85: "Scire debetis quod quadruplex legitur Christi adventus. Primus est quo venit in carnem. Secundus eius adventus est quo venit in mentem. Tertius Christus adventus est quo venit in morte justorum. Sed quartus Christi adventus est quo venit ad iudicandum." Note that Thomas takes a more personal, even moral, stance compared with the sermons in MS Laud Misc. 511.

[48] Sermon 5 [fol. 7vb, ll. 3-15]: ...ut hominem redimeret diverse sunt cause.Prima est hic quia nisi divinitas in humanitate lucem suam temperaret, homo eum videre non posset, unde dicit [Eod. xxxiii 20]: "Non videbit me homo et vivet." Secundo, ut haberet quid offerret pro salute hominum. Tertia est quia homo sese et genus humanum perdidit decens erat ut homo eum liberaret. Quarta est ut diabolus qui hominem vicit vinceretur ab homine. Quinta, ut diabolus videret gaudium hominis apud Dominum suum quando passus est propter eum. Sexta, ut homo videret amorem quem Dominus suus exhibuit ei. Septima, ut homo non auderet peccare in forma in qua vidit Dominum suum.

[49] See note 36.

[50] See note 27.

[51] Sermon 8 [fol. 10a, ll. 6-15]: Christus de celis ad terras descendit ut diabolum mundo dominantem, ab ipso mundi principem vocatum, pacis scilicet perturbatorem, ius hominum occupantem, et viribus detinentem, destrueret et enervaret. Ipse enim adveniens per angelum suum pacem suum statim clamare fecit: "Gloria in excelsis Deo" etc....suos fideles cotidie contra diabolum protegit et defendit, hereditatem nostram perditam, hoste devicto, plene restituit libertati.

Sermon 15 [fol. 17va, ll. 21-32]: Propter hoc Rex regum, Christus, videns humanum genus suum plasma principi diabolo fore subiectum, item, diabolum illis insidiantem et multipliciter illos impugnantem, guerram hostilem in terra sua propria sibi et suis movere quam sibi fraude et sedicione adquisierat menciendo primis parentibus nostris, item, vidit humanum genus hereditate sua et iure defraudari; a celis ad terras descendit "in similitudinem hominum factus" est "et habitu inventus ut homo" [Phil. ii] suos subditos homines a demonibus obscessos liberavit.

[52] Sermon 13 [fol. 15b, line 25–fol. 15va, line 4]. See Appendix 9, "Selected Texts."

Aquinas gives little attention to the devil,[53] but devotes the greater part of his sermon to describing the life of grace given to humankind in and through Christ.[54]

Finally a personal response to the coming of Christ is preached in all six sermons. It is going to confession,[55] or eschewing sin[56]—this shows the application of the image of the stag—or practising neighbourly charity,[57] or preparing the soul by being cleansed from sin and being decorated with virtue.[58] In this way the coming of Christ is celebrated. As

[53] Leclercq, *L'Idée*, 90, 94.

[54] Leclercq, *L'Idée*, 100-103, 106.

[55] Sermon 12 [fol. 13va, bottom margin]:

Dies adventus docet nos—
- per veram contritionem Christum querere
- per veram confessionem invenire
- per bona opera ipsum sequi ad eterna

[56] Sermon 12 [fol. 14b, ll. 35-40]: Similiter, tu occide diabolum per contritionem, curre ad fontem Christum vel Ecclesiam et depone veterem hominem, scilicet superbiam, iram, invidiam, luxuriam, cupiditatem, et cetera mala per veram confessionem.

[57] Sermon 8 [fol. 10b, ll. 2-17]: Qui enim diligit Deum, diligit proximum, diligit inimicum, diligit etiam omnem creaturam. Qui enim odit aliquod, vel invidet, vel detrahit, non diligit Deum.... [line 8] Signum est quod pauci diligunt Deum quia pauci diligunt proximum, immo multi persecuntur detrahendo, quorum quidam in tantum replentur diabolo quod statim, aversa facie, ad eis [sic], corrodunt aliis et detrahunt, bona diminuunt, mala exaggerant, dubia pervertunt, famam tollunt. Tales commedunt carnes crudas et certe nisi habuerint potum compunctionis morientur. Tales persequitur Christus et persequetur in tremendo iudicio.

Sermon 5 [fol. 8a, ll. 13-15]: Adoremus Regem celi confessione, ieiuniis, vigiliis; adoremus veniendo ad ecclesiam, pauperes pascendo, vestiendo.... (This is one of the few occasions in the sermons of Laud Misc. 511 where explicit advice is given about *satisfactione*. In the time-dated sermons this particular point was rarely amplified.)

[58] Sermon 12 [fol. 14va, line 40–fol. 14vb, line 8]: Nonne domos vestras eggregie ornaretis / si ad vos venturus esset Imperator temporalis? Ornate ergo virtutibus animas vestras et corda ut Regem angelorum digne recipiatis. Cogita de magno festo futuro. Non est vetula tam paupercula quin contra illud festum domum purgabit, cineres asportabit, caput et vestimenta lavabit, vestes conservet et reparabit, maiori sollicitudine in omni pro posse providebit.

Sermon 13 [fol. 15a, line 35–fol. 15b, line 9]; see Appendix 9, "Selected Texts."

Sermon 14 [fol. 16va, line 38–fol. 16vb, line 10]: Qui ergo vult Christum in suo adventu hospitare, necesse est primo eicere a templo Dei omnia grossa vilia et fetentia: demum area [sic] purgare lacrimis semper irrigantibus coinquinata lavare. Ultimo, / templum Christi ramis virtutum et floribus bonorum operum decorare,

already noted, Sermon 12 is specific about actual confession. All the sermons, however, preach at some length on the evil of sin, but above all on the need for repentance so as to have the necessary purity of heart for Christ to enter with love into the soul. In this aspect there is much similarity with the sermons preached at Elstow. In a very practical way, then, these six Advent sermons focus the minds and hearts of the listeners on the mysteries of God's greatness, power, love and mercy; and show them made flesh in Christ, who offers forgiveness of sin and a share in the divine life and love.

It is useful to put these six sermons in the context of the remaining thirteen sermons for Advent available in MS Laud Misc. 511. The other sermons are preached on themes chosen traditionally from the Mass pericopes. In content they refer to Advent as a time of Christ's coming; they treat of sin, grace, good and evil works, judgement, the sacrament of penance, in much the same manner as the six sermons discussed. If, however, the compiler had not chosen to include the six sermons noted; that is, those with themes from the Divine Office, no Advent preaching on the kingship of Christ would have been available in MS Laud Misc. 511.

E. TO WHOM WERE THESE SERMONS PREACHED?

There is one last point to be discussed about this group of sermons; namely for what audience were they intended? As we have already seen, this is a current problem for students of sermons. There is no explicit inscription in any of these sermons. Four of them, Sermons 8, 12, 13, and 15, imply considerable familiarity with much of the Divine Office; while Sermons 8 and 15 assume that the hearers have recently sung the antiphons concerned.[59] If active participation in the Divine Office is assumed by the preacher, then sermons 8 and 15 could have been composed *ad clerum* or *ad religiosum*. Also, in the antitheme of Sermon 15, the preacher declares "you do not often have sermons preached to you."[60] Either his

---

ut nichil sub vel supra in angulis vel cavernis lateat, quod oculum Christi venientis offendat, sicut faciunt in magnis villis qui hospites recipiunt. Primo, domos suas sordibus mundant et purgant circumquaque, utensilia lavant et oculis transeuntium lucentia reddunt et cum talis honestas videtur a transeuntibus, in domo descendunt et ibi nocte commorantur. Sic Christus nobiscum cohabitabit si munditiam cordis sui templi nostri respexerit.

[59] Sermon 8 [fol. 9vb, ll. 28-33] and Sermon 15 [fol. 17a, ll. 36-39].

[60] Sermon 15 [fol. 17a, ll. 2-3]: Raro predicatur vobis verbum Domini et quanto rarius annunciatur....

audience were non-churchgoers, or were not served by a regular preacher, or they were oftener in the pulpit than on the benches. The reference to *confratres* in the same sermon strengthens the impression that the original sermon was composed for the brethren.[61] Sermon 8 too in its emphases— love of one's neighbour in the context of daily life and condemnation of backbiting—has an authentic note of community life.[62] It is possible that these two sermons came from a Dominican priory in the northern pro- vince of York. On the other hand, bearing in mind episcopal legislation in England in the thirteenth century, it is important not to assume that lay people could not appreciate preaching closely related to the Divine Office; or that sermons other than exhortations to receive the sacrament of pen- ance were never preached to the laity. Sermon 13 would have been of interest to any audience, with its topical references to king and court and its memories of past scandals. But further, it is to be remembered that the way the sermons were used and re-used makes it impossible to identify an audience, unless the information is given in the annotation. Moreover, that first audience is the only one of any significance, because the thirteenth- century practice of preaching encouraged multiple use of any given sermon.

The range of enquiry engendered by the study of these six sermons preached on liturgical themes suggests that it is worth examining in some detail these kinds of sermon as contrasted with the more numerous sermons preached directly on the pericopes of the epistle and gospel.

---

[61] Sermon 15 [fol. 17vb, ll. 23-25]: Quia multi confratrum nostrorum, qui dies suos hic compleverunt, hereditatem celestem adepti sunt.

[62] Sermon 8 [fol. 10b, ll. 26-28]: Avertere enim deberent quod auris aperta est ante et clausa retro, in signum quod nos non debemus audire detractatoria que retro dicuntur.

Afterword

Dr Daniel Callus's assessment of MS Laud Misc. 511 as a significant Dominican manuscript has been borne out by the foregoing studies. The manuscript was carefully and consciously designed as a preacher's handbook with sermons, *exempla*, distinctions, *florilegia* on some topics, and sermon material. All are easily identifiable, partly by liturgical order, partly by annotation and numbering of columns and lines, and partly by the colourful flourishing of the introductory initial of each piece. If the earlier dating I have suggested for this manuscript is acceptable, together with its highly probable Oxford origin, then we have in MS Laud Misc. 511 not only one of the earliest known English sermon collections in the new preaching practice of the twelfth to thirteenth century, but also useful evidence to contribute to our growing knowledge of the "book-trade" in mid-thirteenth century England.

As a sermon collection MS Laud Misc. 511 seems to indicate that the practical implementation of the information and advice contained in the *Artes Praedicandi* about making sermons could be much simpler than the actual theory. Of greater significance, however, is the fact that this manuscript contains identified sermons from the earliest generations of Preachers after Saint Dominic. It is witness then, not only to the effective fulfilment of Dominic's ideas in France by known Dominicans, but to similar activity of mainly anonymous Dominicans in England in the second quarter of the thirteenth century, for the compiler drew on at least thirteen existing sermon collections for his own new handbook. The preaching of sermons from this manuscript at Elstow Abbey in the last quarter of the thirteenth century confirms the continuing usefulness of the compiler's work.

From the aspect of sermon content, the manuscript has proved equally significant. The need to have linguistic, literary, social and political studies of medieval sermons cannot be disputed. Such contribute to the history of ideas. But it is equally helpful to make catechetical and liturgical studies of medieval sermons. These might well provide a more realistic context for the social and literary analysis.

It is interesting to note a continuity from the methodology of the medieval sermon into catechetical patterns of the eighteenth, nineteenth and early twentieth centuries; and to note the central position—rarely acknowledged—of St Augustine's *De Doctrina Christiana* in the theory and practice of catechetics. If some of the doctrinal contents of the sermons in MS Laud Misc. 511 seem surprisingly topical in the twentieth century, then such continuity witnesses to the perennial problem for preachers and cate-chists alike of effectively communicating the gospel to the current genera-tion. But equally, discontinuities and unfamiliar emphases in the sermon contents of the manuscript witness to the cultural, social and historical embeddedness of preaching and catechetics. Both these facets of the ser-mons in our manuscript draw attention to a deeper need: namely how to discern the universal message of the gospel, and distinguish that from its linguistic, cultural and historical expressions. Such a conclusion underlines the need to make historical studies of doctrine and of pastoral practice.

Appendix 1

A Catalogue of MS Laud Misc. 511

This appendix provides a comprehensive catalogue of the sermons or sermon material contained in MS Laud Misc. 511. Each item follows manuscript order and is numbered sequentially in **bold**; where necessary, subdivisions of an item are assigned a letter. In a few cases, items which have been separated by the scribes have been conflated; alternatively, some items not clearly divided by the scribes have been numbered separately. Only a small number, however, are so treated.

Each entry in the catalogue consists of a concise analytic description, organized under several headings separated by the marker: folios; source-book; theme; incipit; thema; explicit; lemmata; marginalia; religious authorities cited; other authorities; vernacular phrases; notes; and a liturgical reference. Here is a typical entry:

> **12** *Folios* 13va– 14vb ☐ *Runnning title* Dominica iia adventus ☐ *Source book* Proprius ☐ *Theme* Rex noster adveniet quem Johannes predicavit agnum esse venturum ☐ *Incipit* Dies isti adventus Domini representant Dominum nobis venturum, appropinquare per gratiam de die in diem et in magno festo futuro ☐ *Thema* Ante adventum Domini, fratres, tantis tenebris genus humanum involutum est ☐ *Explicit* Non sis ergo pigrior munditie anime tue et saluti providere quam corpori etc. ☐ *Lemmata* [7]: Mundum debet esse habitaculum Christi; Dies adventus docet nos; Ante adventum erant homines; Adam primus parens transgrediendo fuit; Ante adventum Christi fuit genus humanum; Cervus; Sic peccator ☐ *Marginalia* scribal ann.; distinc. ☐ *Notes* Theme is Invitatory for Matins Advent II in Dominican, Paris and Sarum uses; Advent III in York use. ☐ *Schneyer* T2

A brief explanation of the rubrics may be useful here. The compass of the sermon or sermon material in the manuscript is supplied under *Folios*. Most of the sermons or sermon material in the manuscript are identified scribally by liturgical function and source-book: first, in minute black headings in the top or bottom margins of the page, given as the *Running title* in the catalogue; second, by a red title or rubric in the column at the start of the sermon / sermon material, or, in a few cases, in the side margin. As the original folios were trimmed in the binding process some of these cues are missing. As far as possible, all cues are included in the catalogue.

The specific sermon collection used will be found under *Source book*. An index to the source-books used, as well as the total number of citations to specific source-books, throughout the manuscript can be found in Appendix 6.

For each sermon or piece of sermon material the *Incipit* and *Explicit* are provided. Where the sermon has an antitheme, the *incipit* of the theme is also given under the heading *Thema*. This information should help readers in identifying individual sermons, as copiers of sermons often omitted the original antitheme starting at the main section of the sermon which is indicated by the restatement of the theme. The relevant Scriptural reference is provided in parentheses for all pieces. Theme, incipit, and thema are listed in alphabetical order in Appendix 5.

Some fifty-four sermons have short summaries or distinctions written in the margin (mostly the bottom margin). The first section or *lemma* of these distinctions is recorded in the catalogue after the *explicit* of the sermon / sermon material to which it belongs under the rubric **Lemmata**. The number of sets of distinctions under the heading is indicated by a numeral in parentheses after the *lemma*; the total number is indicated in square brackets immediately after the heading. The majority of these distinctions, being rubricated, belong to the original making of the manuscript.

Many of the entries also contain additional material, in the form of marginal annotations or interlinear comments, which seem to have been made by the users of the manuscript rather than by its scribes. These are gathered under the heading *Marginalia*, and are subdivided into three groups: (i) *annotations*: original *scribal* annotations (because rubricated), and *unidentified* annotations (written by other than the identified scribes); (ii) *distinctions*: marginal distinctiones attached to the sermons or sermon material; and (iii) *enumeration*: arabic numerals in the side margins indicating the members of distinctions within the sermon text.

The rhetorical and argumentative resources of the *ars praedicandi* are revealed in the wide-ranging quotation and citation from patristic, religious, and secular sources that is characteristic of the sermons in this manuscript. These are grouped in the catalogue under **Religious authorities** and **Other authorities** and are cited from the conventional editions in the *Patrologia graeca* (PG) and *Patrologia latina* (PL). It is important to remember that quotations preserved in the sermons do not always correspond to these latterly established texts, the result no doubt of errors to which a much copied text is inevitably prone. Inexact verbal concordance between the manuscript and the modern texts is signalled by cf. A few items contain **Vernacular phrases**. Six are signalled by 'dicitur anglice,' one by 'sed dicitur Gallice.'

The sermons in MS Laud Misc. 511 also contain over four hundred and fifty *exempla*: these are not included here, but are listed separately in manuscript order in Appendix 7.

Matters relating to date and provenance, liturgical or codicological information have been recorded in the *Notes* section after each item. Finally, the liturgical code from the Sigeltabellen included in each volume of the *Repertorium* edited by J.B. Schneyer is provided under the heading **Schneyer**. Readers should also consult the concordance between this catalogue and Schneyer's description of MS Laud Misc. 511 in the *Repertorium* found in Appendix 4.

1 *Folios* 5a–5b □ *Runnning title* Dominica ia adventus, sermo primus □ *Source book* Minimus □ *Theme* Nox precessit dies autem appropinquavit (Rom 13:12) □ *Incipit* Duo tangit in hiis verbis Apostoli, videlicet, noctis abscessum et diei adventum □ *Explicit* tribulationem sustinentibus Ps. cum ipso sum in tribulatione □ *Lemmata* [4]: Mundus dicitur nox quia (2); Mundus declinat animum a veritate duplici; Dies dicitur Christus quia; Appropinquavit nobis Christus (2) □ *Marginalia* scribal ann.; distinc. □ *Schneyer* T1

2 *Folios* 5va □ *Runnning title* Dominica prima adventus □ *Source book* none □ *Theme* Abiciamus opera tenebrarum et induamur arma lucis (Rom 13:12) □ *Incipit* Duo sunt necessaria ad vitam: declinare a malo et facere bonum □ *Explicit* quod patet ex eorum descensu; sunt etiam mala quod patet ex eorum effectu □ *Lemmata* [1]: Peccata dicuntur opera tenebrarum quia (4) □ *Marginalia* scribal ann.; distinc. □ *Schneyer* T1

3 *Folios* 5vb–6a □ *Runnning title* Dominica ia adventus □ *Source book* Tabulatus □ *Theme* Ro xiii Dies autem appropinquavit (Rom 13:12) □ *Incipit* Nativitas bene dicitur dies, primo quia quid est dies nisi presentia solis □ *Explicit* luculus precedens ortum solis et ideo tunc desierunt stelle apparere □ *Lemmata* [1]: Nativitas dicitur dies quia (2) □ *Marginalia* scribal ann.; distinc. □ *Other authorities* 5vb.5–8: cf. Aristotle, *De generatione et corruptione* 2.10 (336a32) and 2.10 (336b17–18); 5vb15–19: cf. Abū Ma'shar, *Introductorium in astronomiam*. □ *Schneyer* T1

4 *Folios* 6a–7va □ *Runnning title* Dominica ia adventus. □ *Source book* Niger Minor □ *Theme* Abiciamus opera tenebrarum et induamur arma lucis. (Rom 13:12) □ *Incipit* Verba sunt beati Apostoli ad Ro xiii, fratres mei, socii et amici karissimi, oremus in principio sermonis nostri Deum misericordiam. □ *Thema* Verba ista beati Apostoli ad Ro xiii duas in se continent exhortaciones. □ *Explicit* ad nos per Virginem gloriosam preparatam in nobis inveniet mansionem. □ *Lemmata* [3]: Opera mala dicuntur opera tenebrarum; Opera tenebrarum; Opera lucis dicuntur bona opera. □ *Marginalia* scribal ann.; distinc. □ *Schneyer* T1

5 *Folios* 7va–8a □ *Runnning title* Dominica ia adventus vel secunda □ *Source book* Niger Maior □ *Theme* Regem venturum Dominum, venite adoremus □ *Incipit* Quia adventum ingressi sumus proposuimus nobis aliquid de adventu regis dicere □ *Explicit* Ipse, inquam, vocat te ad mensam suam in celis. Quod nobis prestare dignatur □ *Lemmata* [3]: Quinque sunt reges; Tres sunt adventus; Christus homo fieri voluit ut □ *Marginalia* scribal ann.; distinc.; enumeration □ *Notes* Theme is taken from the Invitatory for Advent weekday. Matins in the Dominican, Paris, Sarum and York Breviaries. This sermon could be Schneyer category T1 or T2. □ *Schneyer* T1

6 *Folios* 8a–8vb □ *Runnning title* Dominica ia adventus □ *Source book* Proprius □ *Theme* Abiciamus opera tenebrarum et induamur arma lucis (Rom

13:12) □ *Incipit* In principio sermonis nostri oret unusquisque Deum ut ipse Deus, largitor gratiarum dives □ *Thema* Duo dicenda sunt. Que sint opera tenebrarum et quare abicienda sint □ *Explicit* immo in gaudio hic viam consummabit, et post ad gaudium transibit angelorum quod nobis etc. □ *Lemmata* [2]: Peccata dicuntur opera tenebrarum quia.; Abicienda sunt opera tenebrarum quia. □ *Marginalia* scribal ann.; distinc. □ *Schneyer* T1

7 *Folios* 9a–9vb □ *Runnning title* Dominica ia adventus □ *Source book* Proprius □ *Theme* Hora est iam nos de sompno surgere (Rom 13:11) □ *Incipit* Verba sunt Apostoli in epistola hodierna in quibus monet fideles excitari a sompno peccati □ *Explicit* dies isti preparatorii sunt quibus nos omnes preparat Dominus et mundos facit contra tanti regis adventum □ *Lemmata* [4]: Peccatum sompno comparatur quia; Surgendum est a peccato quia; Occurramus Deo (2); Mundemur per □ *Marginalia* unidentified ann.; distinc. □ *Schneyer* T1

8 *Folios* 9vb–10b □ *Runnning title* Dominica iia adventus □ *Source book* none □ *Theme* Surgite vigilemus quia venit rex □ *Incipit* Brevi diei brevis debetur sermo, sermo divinus magna diligentia est audiendus □ *Thema* Duo sunt querenda; quis sit ille rex, et quare dicatur rex noster, et quare venerit □ *Explicit* Narratio de divite mortuo et heremita stante ad portam vidente demones transire etc. □ *Lemmata* [2]: Christus Rex hominum specialiter dicitur quia; Detractores □ *Marginalia* scribal ann.; distinc. □ *Notes* Theme is taken from liturgy, Invitatory of Advent II, York, and Advent III, Dominican, Breviaries. □ *Schneyer* T2

9 *Folios* 10va–11b □ *Runnning title* Dominica iia adventus □ *Source book* Proprius □ *Theme* Tunc videbunt filium hominis venientem in nube cum potestate <magna> et maiestate (Lc 21:27) □ *Incipit* Mater Ecclesia temporibus istis adventus, multum recitat nobis adventum Christi □ *Thema* Duplicem adventum hiis diebus rememorat nobis □ *Explicit* id est incommunicabilia veritatis et sapientie ut si non licere etc., et alibi Augustinus ibi vacabimus etc. [end of *De Civitate Dei*] □ *Lemmata* [3]: Adventus (2); Christus veniens mundo invenit (2); Remunerabit Deus (2) □ *Marginalia* scribal ann.; distinc. □ *Schneyer* T2

10 *Folios* 11b–12b □ *Runnning title* Dominica iia adventus □ *Source book* Proprius □ *Theme* Quecumque scripta sunt ad nostram doctrinam scripta sunt (Rom 15:4) □ *Incipit* Filius sapiens letificat patrem suum □ *Thema* Omnes doctrina scripture ad hoc tendit ut vitetur malum ut fiat bonum □ *Explicit* (Jac 3: 7) linguam autem nullus unquam hominum domare potuit □ *Lemmata* [5]: Peccatum scriptum est; Pedes nos instruunt; Manus nos instruunt; Os instruit nos; Lingua instruit nos □ *Marginalia* scribal ann.; distinc.; enumeration □ *Notes* The theme and incipit of this sermon are found in Schneyer, *Repertorium* 2: 544, no. 134, a sermon of Guilelmus Peraldus OP. □ *Schneyer* T2

11 *Folios* 12va–13b □ *Runnning title* Dominica iia adventus □ *Source book* Proprius □ *Theme* Virtutes celorum movebuntur (Lc 21:26) □ *Incipit* Reges

terrenos venientes ad civitates et castra precedent buccinatores ... cum tubis magnum sonitum et tumultum emittentes □ *Thema* In evangelio precedentis dominice egit ecclesia de humili Christi adventu in carnem quia sedens super asinam □ *Explicit* Anselmus in *Meditatione* ... foris mundus ardens latere erit impossibile apparere intollerabile etc. □ *Lemmata* [4]: Adventus Christi triplex (3); Adventus; Districtum erit iudicium in; Horribile erit iudicium quia □ *Marginalia* scribal ann.; distinc. □ *Schneyer* T2

12 *Folios* 13va-14vb □ *Runnning title* Dominica iia adventus □ *Source book* Proprius □ *Theme* Rex noster adveniet quem Johannes predicavit agnum esse venturum □ *Incipit* Dies isti adventus Domini representant Dominum nobis venturum, appropinquare per gratiam de die in diem et in magno festo futuro □ *Thema* Ante adventum Domini, fratres, tantis tenebris genus humanum involutum est □ *Explicit* Non sis ergo pigrior munditie anime tue et saluti providere quam corpori etc. □ *Lemmata* [7]: Mundum debet esse habitaculum Christi; Dies adventus docet nos; Ante adventum erant homines; Adam primus parens transgrediendo fuit; Ante adventum Christi fuit genus humanum; Cervus; Sic peccator □ *Marginalia* scribal ann.; distinc. □ *Notes* Theme is Invitatory for Matins Advent II in Dominican, Paris and Sarum uses; Advent III in York use. □ *Schneyer* T2

13 *Folios* 14vb-15vb □ *Runnning title* Dominica iiia adventus □ *Source book* Proprius □ *Theme* Veniet Dominus et non tardabit □ *Incipit* Duo dicenda sunt hic, primo de adventu Domini et hoc est *veniet Dominus.* Secundo quid tardat eius adventum et hoc est *et non tardabit* □ *Explicit* teste Salamone dicente: Memorare novissima tua et in eternum non peccabis. Dicatur narratio de nobili rege Grecie etc. □ *Lemmata* [3]: Verus sol Christe; De hospes Christi debet; Abiciendum est peccatum □ *Marginalia* scribal ann.; distinc.; enumeration □ *Notes* Theme is the First Antiphon for Lauds and Vespers Advent III, Dominican, Paris, Sarum and York uses □ *Schneyer* T3

14 *Folios* 15vb-16vb □ *Runnning title* Dominica iiia adventus □ *Source book* Proprius □ *Theme* Veniet Dominus et non tardabit □ *Incipit* Sancta mater nostra Ecclesia intendit hodie, in verbo proposito, corda filiorum suorum □ *Explicit* in sua eterna claritate. Quam oculus non vidit et auris non audivit et in cor hominis non ascendit etc. □ *Lemmata* [2]: Christus dicitur rex hominum; Abiciendum est peccatum quia □ *Marginalia* scribal ann.; distinc.; enumeration □ *Notes* See note for sermon 13. □ *Schneyer* T3

15 *Folios* 17a-18a □ *Runnning title* Dominica iiia adventus □ *Source book* Proprius □ *Theme* Rex noster adveniet quem Johannes predicavit agnum esse venturum □ *Incipit* Raro predicatur vobis verbum Domini, et quanto rarius annunciatur, tanto diligencius audiri debet □ *Thema* In presenti verbo tria possunt considerari, videlicet quis sit iste rex et quare dicatur rex noster □ *Explicit* et non patietur animam quibuscumque peccatis depressam, ne in tenebras dicatur de heremita et de divite mortuo etc. □ *Lemmata* [2]: Tria

dicuntur (Rex); Ad regem spectant □ *Marginalia* unidentified ann.; distinc. □
Notes See note on sermon 12. For the *explicit,* cf. Sermon 8. Fol. 17b side
margin, pencil drawing of a flower. □ *Schneyer* T3

16 *Folios* 18a-18va □ *Running title* Dominica iiia adventus □ *Source book*
Parvus ... □ *Theme* Qui me iudicat Dominus est (1 Cor 4:4) □ *Incipit* Duo
tanguntur, cui iudicare conveniat in hoc quod dicitur Dominus, et quis
iudicari debeat □ *Explicit* In quibus omnibus manifestum est filium Dei ceteros
omnes excellere □ *Lemmata* [5]: Tria dicunt esse in iudice; Deus est (2); Deus
potens est quia omnia facit aliquando; Due sunt partes iustitie; Opus bonum
dividetur in opus □ *Marginalia* scribal ann.; distinc. □ *Schneyer* T3

17 *Folios* 18va-19a □ *Running title* Dominica iiia adventus □ *Source book*
Parvus Niger □ *Theme* Ceci vident etc. (Mt 11:4-5) □ *Incipit* Duo sunt hic
attendenda et duo dicenda, primo de cecitate humana □ *Explicit* super idem
Ps. Juxta est Dominus etc. Deus quidem altus est et vicinatur humili non se
erigenti □ *Lemmata* [2]: Excecant hominem spirituali; Videre debemus □
Marginalia scribal ann.; distinc. □ *Schneyer* T3

18 *Folios* 19a-20va □ *Running title* Dominica iiiia adventus □ *Source
book* Niger Minor □ *Theme* Faciet Dominus exercituum omnibus populis hoc
convivium in monte pinguium medullatorum vindemie defecate (Is 25:6) □
Incipit Ista verba leguntur in ysaya xxv et possunt exponi tripliciter, scilicet,
de convivio secularium in natali, de convivio bonorum in vita presenti, vel de
convivio bonorum in celesti patria □ *Explicit* ait anima calida quasi ignis
ardens non extinguetur donec aliquid glutiat □ *Lemmata* [6]: Est convivium;
Fercula in convivio diaboli; Consideranda sunt in commedendo; Consideranda
sunt in bibendo; Convivium (3); Per picem intelliguntur □ *Marginalia* scribal
ann.; distinc. □ *Notes* Isaiah is read throughout Advent in the Office; this part
is used in Lesson 2, Matins of Week II, feria 4. □ *Schneyer* T4

19 *Folios* 20va-20vb □ *Running title* Dominica iiiia adventus □ *Source
book* Liber Virginis Gloriose □ *Theme* Gaudete in Domino semper iterum dico
gaudete (Phil 4:4) □ *Incipit* In hiis verbis monet Apostolus fideles ad
gaudendum, et hoc est *gaudete* □ *Explicit* In Domino ergo Deo gaudendum,
quia si hoc gaudium nostrum, nemo tollet a nobis. Ad quod gaudium etc. □
Lemmata [2]: Gaudendum est in Domino; Deo placere non possunt □
Marginalia scribal ann.; distinc. □ *Schneyer* T4

20 *Folios* 21, margin □ *Running title* none □ *Source book* Minimus □
Theme Puer natus est nobis (Is 9:6) □ *Marginalia* none □ *Notes* The entire text
reads: Tria dicuntur: Veneranda filii nativitas ibi NATUS; / nascentia qualitas
ibi PUER; / nascendi utilitas ibi NOBIS. □ *Schneyer* T7

21 *Folios* 21a-21va □ *Running title* Dominica ia natale / infra natale □
Source book Proprius □ *Theme* Annuntio vobis gaudium magnum quod erit
omni populo quia natus est vobis salvator mundi etc. (Lc 2:10-11) □ *Incipit*

Verbum Domini summa diligencia et devotione ad omnibus audiri debet □ *Thema* Verba ista leguntur in evangelio quod legitur in Christi nativitate et sunt verba angelica et in hiis quattuor possunt considerari □ *Explicit* propter hoc enim venit in terris sicut ipse dicit, "non sum missus nisi ad oves que perierunt domus Israel,"et in Johanne, "ego sum pastor bonus" Bonus pastor etc. □ *Lemmata* [3]: Verbum Domini; Christus natus; Natus est Christus ut □ *Marginalia* scribal ann.; distinc. □ *Schneyer* T7

22 *Folios* 21vb □ *Runnning title* Dominica infra natale □ *Source book* Proprius □ *Theme* Invenerunt puerum cum Maria matre eius (Mt 2:11) □ *Incipit* Salvator hominum a sinu procedens Patris in uterum matris □ *Explicit* Reges isti, more Persarum, offerunt munera aurum, thus et mirram; auro regem, thure Deum, mirra mortalem significantes □ *Lemmata* [1]: Christus uno die □ *Marginalia* scribal ann.; distinc. □ *Notes* Margin note: quare sermonem istum alibi valde plene □ *Schneyer* T7

23 *Folios* 22a–22b □ *Runnning title* Dominica infra oct' epiphanie □ *Source book* Parvus Rubeus □ *Theme* Optulerunt ei munera aurum, thus et mirram (Mt 2:11) □ *Incipit* Sicut Deo huius seculi de quo I Cor Deus huius seculi excecavit mentes infidelium offeruntur a suis tria dona □ *Explicit* Si secundum carnem vixeritis, moriemini, si autem spiritu facta carnis mortificaveritis, vivetis □ *Lemmata* [3]: Offeruntur diabolo; Offeruntur Deo; Humiliandum est □ *Marginalia* scribal ann.; distinc. □ *Schneyer* T11

24 *Folios* 22b–22va □ *Runnning title* Dominica ia post epiphanie □ *Source book* Parvus Rubeus □ *Theme* Obsecro vos ut exhibeatis corpora vestra etc. (Rom 12:1) □ *Incipit* Hic innuit Apostolus vii que necessaria sunt vere penitenti, scilicet, ut penitentia sit spontanea □ *Explicit* Qui indiscrete penitet, animal cecum offert, quod prohibetur □ *Lemmata* [1]: Penitentia debet esse □ *Marginalia* scribal ann.; distinc. □ *Schneyer* T11

25 *Folios* 22va–23b □ *Runnning title* Dominica iia post epiph' □ *Source book* Proprius □ *Theme* Implete ydrias aqua et impleverunt etc. (Jo 2:7) □ *Incipit* Scitis quod pauper stans ad ianuam divitis, longe ab aula vehementer clamans, non auditur □ *Thema* Dicatur narratio evangelii si libeat. In verbis premissis tria possunt considerari □ *Explicit* omni bonitate et salute, quod fit per contritionem, confessionem et satisfactionem etc. □ *Lemmata* [5]: Tria dicuntur (implete hydrias); Coronabatur quidam (2); Ministri sunt; Corda humana sunt; Infernus triplex □ *Marginalia* scribal ann.; distinc. □ *Notes* The liturgical reference is written in red and black, compare with 26. □ *Schneyer* T12

26 *Folios* 23b–23vb □ *Runnning title* Dominica iia oct'epiph'/Dominica ia post epiph' □ *Source book* Proprius □ *Theme* Implete ydrias aqua etc. (Jo 2:7) □ *Incipit* Legitur in Libro Antiquorum de populo Israelitico in captivitatem ducto □ *Thema* Dicatur narratio evangelii. In verbo presenti tria queri possunt □ *Explicit* miser ribaldus divitiis honeratus, per latam viam credit intrare celum.

Non. □ *Lemmata* [1]: Nuptie Christe magne erunt propter □ *Marginalia* scribal ann.; distinc. □ *Notes* Marginal note: Antithema. The variants in the liturgical placing reflect the differences between the Sarum and Paris/Dominican uses for this Sunday. □ *Schneyer* T12

27 *Folios* 24a–24va □ *Running title* Dominica iiia post epiph' □ *Source book* Proprius □ *Theme* Cum descendisset Jesus de monte etc. (Mt 8:1) □ *Incipit* Narretur evangelium mistice. Dominus descendens de monte, quando de celo in mundum descendens, carnem humanam assumpsit □ *Explicit* quia nichil potest nocere homini nisi per peccatum. Unde solum fugiat illud, et non sunt timendi ceteri □ *Lemmata* [2]: Triplex peccamus (3); Peccatum vitandum est □ *Marginalia* scribal ann.; distinc.; enumeration □ *Schneyer* T13

28 *Folios* 24va–24vb □ *Running title* Dominica iiia post epiph' □ *Source book* Niger Minor □ *Theme* Cum descendisset Jesus de monte (Mt 8:1) □ *Incipit* Dupliciter possunt hec verba exponi, uno modo de ipso descendente de sublimitate maiestatis, ad quem montem non presumunt turbe, id est, pauperes et humiles □ *Explicit* ascendentes in montem inebriati vino sacre scripture, filios ex concupiscentia carnis et propria voluntate generant □ *Marginalia* none □ *Schneyer* T13

29 *Folios* 24vb–25vb □ *Running title* Dominica a post epiph' □ *Source book* Proprius □ *Theme* Diliges proximum tuum sicut teipsum (Rom 13:9) □ *Incipit* Scriptum est a sapientia. In initio cuiuslibet operis Deum invoca □ *Thema* Ista verba sunt Apostoli scripta in epistola hodierna sumpta de evangelio Matthei xxii ubi legitur istud idem □ *Explicit* Qui diligit proximum legem implevit, et hoc dupliciter sicut patet alibi etc. □ *Lemmata* [3]: Diligendus est proximus; Triplex est amor ad; Proximus malus amandus est propter □ *Marginalia* scribal ann.; distinc.; enumeration □ *Notes* "Foreword" on fol. 24vb line 19 Nota bene totum sermonem subsequentem. □ *Schneyer* T14

30 *Folios* 25vb–29va □ *Running title* Dominica a post epiph' □ *Source book* Niger Minor □ *Theme* Ascendente Jesu in naviculam secuti sunt eum discipuli eius (Mt 8:23) □ *Incipit* Qui navigant mare dupplici indigent suffragio, scilicet, navis et stelle □ *Thema* Hic tria dicenda sunt, primo de navicula, secundo de ascensu in ipsam, tertio de transfretacione per ipsam □ *Explicit* ut cum gubernatore perveniamus ad portam salutis eterne, amen □ *Lemmata* [7]: Terra est triplex; Duplex est navis una; In cupiditate; Caritas dicitur navis propter; Pericula maris (2); Periclitati sunt; Divitie sunt □ *Marginalia* scribal ann.; distinc. □ *Other authorities* 27a.41–27b.1: cf. Aristotle, *Meteorologica* 2.3 (359a1–4); 28b.20–22: cf. Aristotle, *Meteorologica* 2.3 (359a7–9). □ *Schneyer* T14

31 *Folios* 29vb–32a □ *Running title* Dominica v post epiphaniam □ *Source book* Niger Maior □ *Theme* Ad colo 3. Super omnia autem hec caritatem habete quod est vinculum perfectionis (Col 3:14) □ *Incipit* Caritas autem, ut dicunt Augustinus et Gregorius, amor est. Amor autem in amantis voluntate,

tria solet efficere □ *Thema* Duo principaliter tanguntur in hiis verbis □ *Explicit* unde Jac ubi zelus et contentio ibi inconstancia et omne opus pravum □ *Lemmata* [13]: Amans amati; Solent homines; Amor est triplex; Dividitur bonum in; Temporalia nocent; Tria requiruntur in habendo divitias ut; Carnalis affectio consistit circa; Inducere dicunt ad penitentiam; Caritas super omnia haberi debeat quia est (2); Caritas est velud ignis (3); Provocant ad amorem Christi beneficium; Ignis deficit per; Contraria caritati sunt □ *Marginalia* scribal ann.; distinc. □ *Other authorities* 30a.23–24: cf. al-Ghazzālī, *Maqāsid al-falāsifah* 2.5.3 (ed. J.T. Muckle, *Algazel's Metaphysics* [Toronto, 1933]); 31vb.20–22: cf. Aristotle, *De generatione et corruptione* 2.4–5 (some similiarity but not congruence with suggested source); 31vb.36–37: cf. Aristotle, *Topica* 2.2 (109b36–37). □ *Schneyer* T15

32 *Folios* 32a–34b □ *Runnning title* Dominica in septuagesima □ *Source book* Niger Maior □ *Theme* Circumdederunt me gemitus mortis (Ps 17:5) □ *Incipit* Recordata est Jerusalem dierum afflictionibus sue prevaricationis □ *Explicit* In adversariorum multiplicatione ut Saracenorum, Tartarorum, Corasminorum, cismaticorum, hereticorum, et falsorum Christianorum etc □ *Lemmata* [6]: Circumdederunt hic notatur; Recordata est hodie Ecclesia (2); Dolores mortis (2); Ecclesia est (3); Consolantur filii matrem Ecclesiam (2); Dolet Ecclesia ex presentia tristabilium (2) □ *Marginalia* scribal ann.; distinc. □ *Other authorities* 32va.4–5: Pseudo-Seneca, *De remediis fortuitorum* 10.4 (ed. F.G.H.C. Haase [Leipzig, 1895], 2: 451). □ *Schneyer* T16

33 *Folios* 34b–35b □ *Runnning title* Dominica in lxxa □ *Source book* Proprius □ *Theme* Memor esto unde excideris et age penitentiam (Apoc 2:5) □ *Incipit* Dominus loquens per Jeremiam prophetam 26b omnibus curam animarum habentibus dicit noli subtrahere verbum □ *Thema* A nativitate Domini usque modo solet tempus expendi scilicet in gaudio seculari □ *Explicit* si renuisses et parvipenderes nonne ammes esses ita est Christus; Rex regum vocat te, mater Ecclesia vocat te, etc. □ *Lemmata* [3]: Invitat nos Ecclesia (2); Cecidisti a; De penis malorum □ *Marginalia* scribal ann.; distinc. □ *Schneyer* T16

34 *Folios* 35va–35vb □ *Runnning title* Dominica in septuagesima □ *Source book* Proprius □ *Theme* none □ *Incipit* Mater nostra Ecclesia, semper de salute filiorum sollicita, recolit nobis in officio hodierno peccatum primi parentis nostri, propter quod eiectus fuerat de paradyso amenitatis ad mundum □ *Explicit* Item cogita quis petat, et quid et ad quid et quod tu necesse habens petere □ *Lemmata* [1]: Elemosina □ *Marginalia* scribal ann.; distinc. □ *Notes* Marginal note: *hodierno* is a correction from *divino*. The Responsories of Matins for Septuagesima Sunday tell the story of the Fall; they also make the *historia dominicalis*. □ *Schneyer* T16

35 *Folios* 36a–37a □ *Runnning title* Dominica in septuagesima □ *Source book* Proprius □ *Theme* Nescitis quoniam hii qui in stadio currunt omnes quidem currunt etc. (1 Cor 9:24) □ *Incipit* Vita cuiuslibet hominis peregrinatio,

secundum sanctum, ad mortem est □ *Thema* Apostolus in epistola hodierna omnes in mundo videntes comparat currentibus □ *Explicit* carnis desideria minuat et restringat ut velocius currat. Dominus Jesus Christus etc. □ *Lemmata* [2]: Triplex est cursus; Oportet currentem esse expeditum □ *Marginalia* scribal ann.; distinc. □ *Schneyer* T16

36 *Folios* 37a–38a □ *Runnning title* Dominica in septuagesima □ *Source book* Proprius □ *Theme* Simile est regnum celorum homini patrifamilias etc. (Mt 20:1) □ *Incipit* Dominus predicaturus in mundum, sermones suos leves fecit et omnibus intelligibiles, ne possit ei aliquis in die iudicii respondere □ *Explicit* Item perpetua est ys li letitia sempiterna erit eis Idem xiii Gaudium et exultatio etc. □ *Lemmata* [7]: (De laborantibus in vinea); (Reddet Deus mercedem laborum); Peccatores stant in ; Penitendum est; Otiositas; Vocat nos Deus a; Merces est □ *Marginalia* scribal ann.; distinc. □ *Notes* In the MS the first two lemmas are indicated by dots. □ *Schneyer* T16

37 *Folios* 38a–39b □ *Runnning title* Dominica xviii post trin' □ *Source book* Proprius □ *Theme* Diliges Dominum Deum tuum ex toto corde tuo etc. (Mt 22: 37) □ *Incipit* Quando mercatores sunt in nundinis, si Deus signaret eis, per angelum suum vel seipsum vel aliquem qui de celo venisset quas merces emere deberent, fatui essent si eas emere pigritarent □ *Explicit* Ipse enim voluit fieri de terra nostra et nasci in mundo isto ut amabilior nobis esset □ *Lemmata* [4]: Dilectio ab omnibus habenda est quia (2); Dedit Deus homini; Diligendus est Deus quia; Celum sancti comparabant alii (2) □ *Marginalia* scribal ann.; distinc.; enumeration □ *Notes* This sermon is one of two out of liturgical order fol.5–180. □ *Schneyer* T59

38 *Folios* 39a–40b □ *Runnning title* Dominica in sexagesima □ *Source book* Proprius □ *Theme* Semen est verbum Dei (Lc 8:11) □ *Incipit* Narretur evangelium etc. Unicus Dominus et magister omnium, seminaturus mundum sterilem verbo doctrine sue, elegit sibi doctrinam simplicem et facillimam predicationem per parabolas et exempla vulgaria et omnibus manifesta □ *Thema* In hiis verbis quattuor sunt attendenda quare verbum comparatur semini □ *Explicit* Unde legitur Beatam Ceciliam dixisse Domino, Domine Jesu Christe, seminator casti consilii, suscipe seminum fructus quos in Cecilia seminasti □ *Lemmata* [5]: Doctrina Christi per; Ut de (parabola); (Parum dixit) de; Quattuor attende (semen est verbum Dei); Verbum Dei comparatur semine quia □ *Marginalia* scribal ann.; distinc.; enumeration □ *Notes* The *explicit* quotes the Antiphon of the second Nocturn of Matins for the feast of St. Cecilia: "Domine Jesu Christe seminator casti consilii, suscipe seminum fructus, quos in Caecilia seminasti" (see BL MS Add. 23935, fol. 358va; OP Breviary 2: 729; Sarum Breviary 3: 1082; York 2: 708; for clarity lemmata are completed from the MS). □ *Schneyer* T17

39 *Folios* 40va–42a □ *Runnning title* Dominica in sexagesima □ *Source book* Niger Minor □ *Theme* Semen est verbum Dei (Lc 8:11) □ *Incipit* Karissimi, unicus Dominus noster et magister omnium qui ait, "Vos vocatis me magister et Domine bene dicitis, sum etenim"; per parabolas et exempla non per astronomica non mechanica qualia moderni appetunt, set vulgaria et omnibus manifesta et capabilia veritatis et vite, viam edocit □ *Thema* Tria sunt hic dicenda scilicet cum verbum Dei dupliciter dicatur scilicet substantiale et vocale qualiter utrumque potest dici semen □ *Explicit* et qui seminat in Spiritu, de Spiritu metet vitam eternam □ *Marginalia* marginal headings □ *Other authorities* 40vb.23- 28: cf. Plato, *Timaeus* 29e, trans. Calcidius (ed. J.H. Waszink, *Plato Latinus*, vol. 4 [1962; London, 1975]); 41vb.5- 7: Horace, *Epistulae* 1.6.1- 2. □ *Schneyer* T17

40 *Folios* 42b- 43a □ *Running title* Dominica in sexagesima □ *Source book* Niger Minor □ *Theme* Semen est verbum Dei (Lc 8:11) □ *Incipit* In hiis verbis innuuntur duo, scilicet, que debentur verbo Dei ex parte auditorum, et ex parte predicatoris; ex parte predicatoris debet esse humilitas sine arrogantia, ex parte audientium debet esse fides et obedientia □ *Thema* In hiis verbis tria considerare debemus quare scilicet, verbum Dei comparetur semini □ *Explicit* Hec enim est causa quare tam diu sedent □ *Lemmata* [1]: Terra cordis nostri debet □ *Marginalia* unidentified ann.; distinc.; enumeration □ *Schneyer* T17

41 *Folios* 43a- 44b □ *Running title* Dominica in sexagesima □ *Source book* Niger Minor □ *Theme* Exiit qui seminat seminare semen suum (Lc 8:5) □ *Incipit* Ut legitur in Prov 13 Sermo purus firmabitur a Deo; sermo purus est cum terrenitate non est permixtus □ *Thema* Ut dicit beatus Augustinus super Genesem ad litteram, ipsa Domini narracio proverbium fuit □ *Explicit* cruciabit sed pavorem non fugabit; ab hiis penis nos defendat qui sine fine vivit etc. □ *Lemmata* [11]: Sermo; Quicquid est aut est; Sermo Dei est; Loquetur Dominus in evangelio; Tres sunt status in Ecclesia; Quid sit (parabola); Diligendus est Deus quia; Exitus Christi; Pars mundi; De semine verbo Dei colligitur messis eterna; Demones dicunt aves quia □ *Marginalia* unidentified ann.; distinc. □ *Schneyer* T17

42 *Folios* 44b- 44va □ *Running title* Dominica in quinquagesima □ *Source book* Rubeus Minor □ *Theme* Cecus sedebat iuxta viam (Lc 18:35) □ *Incipit* De duobus agitur in hoc evangelio, scilicet, de Christi passione et ceci illuminatione, in quibus ostenditur Christi humanitas et divinitas □ *Explicit* dulcissimus ad serviendum, potentissimus et largissimus ad remunerandum □ *Lemmata* [4]: Quattuor notantur (in quibus ostenditur Christi humanitas); Angustia Christi ostenditur in; Quare fit mentio de Passione Christi ante quam quadragesimam; Miseria peccatoris □ *Marginalia* unidentified ann.; distinc. □ *Schneyer* T18

43 *Folios* 44va- 45a □ *Running title* Dominica in quinquagesima □ *Source book* Proprius □ *Theme* Cecus sedebat iuxta viam mendicans (Lc 18:35) □ *Incipit* Per istum cecum intellige quemlibet peccatorem, qui foris viam sedet, non in via veritatis □ *Explicit* qui pro tam modico dant animam diabolo, corpus ribaldo, cui non darent sotulares suos □ *Lemmata* [2]: In luxurie sunt; Peccatum luxurie □ *Marginalia* unidentified ann.; distinc. □ *Schneyer* T18

44 *Folios* 45a–45va □ *Runnning title* Dominica in quinquagesima □ *Source book* Proprius □ *Theme* Jesu fili David miserere mei (Lc 18:38) □ *Incipit* Narretur evangelium et exponatur cecus iste tripliciter miser comprobatur, tum quia cecus, tum quia mendicus, tum quia extra viam positus □ *Explicit* Glosa: celestia me extendo propter hoc cedet in partem que a sinistris est □ *Lemmata* [6]: Cecus iste miser fuit tum quia; Temporalia dantur, Creature Dei facte sunt in; Hec omnia (liber vite); Multi sequuntur, Sequi Jesum est □ *Marginalia* unidentified ann.; distinc. □ *Notes* Two of the lemmas belong to Sermon 45: viz. *Multi sequuntur* and *Sequi Jesus est.* An indexing symbol of the pattern linked with Grosseteste is found in the margin of this sermon. □ *Schneyer* T18

45 *Folios* 45vb–46a □ *Runnning title* Dominica in la □ *Source book* Rubeus Maior □ *Theme* Confestim vidit (Lc 18:43) □ *Incipit* Tria possunt hic notari, scilicet, subdita gratie illustratio, Jesu imitatio, et intentionis rectificatio □ *Explicit* Jo 8 b Qui sequitur me non ambulat in tenebris etc., ad quod nos ducat etc. □ *Lemmata* [6]: Tria hic notatur (confestim vidit); Concurrunt ad imitationem Jesum; Necessaria sunt ad sequendum Jesum; Sequendus est Jesus; Multi sequuntur, Sequi Jesum est □ *Marginalia* unidentified ann.; distinc. □ *Notes* The text of this sermon is the same as Sermon 48. □ *Schneyer* T18

46 *Folios* 46a–49va □ *Runnning title* Dominica in la □ *Source book* Niger Minor □ *Theme* Jesu fili David miserere mei (Lc 18:38) □ *Incipit* Adducite michi psaltem in II regum 3 legitur quod Heliseus □ *Thema* Hec fuit petitio ceci corporalis per quam sicut tangit Glosa intelligitur cecus spiritualis □ *Explicit* cum adolescentulis in odorem hoc unguenti curratis, sic currite ut comprehendatis etc. □ *Lemmata* [3]: Aperiendum est os ad; Miseria ceci triplex quia; Jesus dicitur filius □ *Marginalia* unidentified ann.; distinc.; marginal headings □ *Other authorities* 46b.7–8: cf. Boethius, *De consolatione philosophiae* 1.1; 47b.18–23: Averroes, *Compendia librorum Aristotelis qui Parva naturalia vocantur* (ed. A.L. Shields and H. Blumberg [Cambridge, MA, 1949], p. 6.63–65); 47va. 21–23: ibid 70.44–45; 47va.29–34: Aristotle, *Ethica Nichomachea* 2.9 (1109b.9–11); 49a.13–23: Petrus Comestor, *Historia scholastica,* Liber Exodi 27 (PL 198: 1155); 49a.24–32: ibid, Liber Esther 4 (PL 198: 1496cd–1497a). □ *Schneyer* T18

47 *Folios* 49va–52b □ *Runnning title* Dominica in quinquagesima □ *Source book* Rubeus Maior □ *Theme* Si caritatem non habuero nichil sum (1 Cor 13:12) □ *Incipit* Tria ut frequencius solent attendere sermocinantes, scilicet materie delectabilitatem, et eiusdem securitatem, et audientium utilitatem □ *Thema* Sicut ex serie littere patet quod intendit hic Apostolus specialiter commendare caritatem □ *Explicit* videbis quante dilectionis signum fuerit inter tot mala delicias reputare cum filiis hominum habitare □ *Marginalia* unidentified ann. □ *Other authorities* 49vb.37–39: cf. Aquinas, *In 1Sent.* 35.1.2.2; 49vb.40–50a.2: Johannes Blund, *Tractatus de anima* 23 (ed. D.A. Callus and R.W. Hunt [London, 1970], pp. 87–88, §323). □ *Notes* In the middle of this sermon, there is a change of scribal hand. □ *Schneyer* T18

48 *Folios* 52va–52vb □ *Runnning title* Dominica in quinquagesima □ *Source book* Rubeus maior □ *Theme* Confestim vidit (Lc 18:43) □ *Incipit* Tria possunt hic notari scilicet: subdita gratie illustratio / Jesu imitatio / intentionis rectificatio □ *Explicit* Qui sequitur me non ambulat in tenebris etc., set habebit lumen vite etc. □ *Lemmata* [1]: Moderni sequuntur □ *Marginalia* unidentified ann.; distinc. □ *Notes* This text is the same as that of Sermon 45. □ *Schneyer* T18

49 *Folios* 53a–53va □ *Runnning title* Dominica ia quadragesima □ *Source book* Proprius □ *Theme* Ductus est Jesus in desertum etc. (Mt 4:1) □ *Incipit* Legitur in libro antiquorum quod populus Israel postquam introivit in terram promissionis, peccavit contra Domini voluntatem ydolotrando et sacrificando diis alienis □ *Thema* Legitur in evangelio hodierna de quodam spirituali bello inter Christum et diabolum □ *Explicit* Jonatas enim addictus fuit morti, eo quod ante bellum finitum, parum de melle in summitate virge gustasset. Redeamus ad primum □ *Marginalia* Ann. □ *Schneyer* T19

50 *Folios* 53va–54b □ *Runnning title* none □ *Source book* none □ *Theme* Ductus est Jesus etc. (Mt 4:1) □ *Incipit* Sciendum quod duplex est desertum, culpe et penitentie □ *Explicit* bona opera narrando, tacendo peccata, exemplum de Juda Machabeorum etc. □ *Lemmata* [2]: In deserto; Tres diete in penitentia (2) □ *Marginalia* scribal ann.; distinc.; enumeration □ *Notes* Margin Note: predicatur sermo iste aput Eln' prima dominica quadragesime anno domini m.cc.lxx.viii. □ *Schneyer* T19

51 *Folios* 54va–55a □ *Runnning title* none □ *Source book* Proprius □ *Theme* Ecce nunc tempus acceptabile ecce nunc dies salutis (2 Cor 6:2) □ *Incipit* Legitur in evangelio hodierno quod non in solo pane vivit homo sed in omni verbo quod procedit de ore Dei □ *Thema* Solent principes et reges regnorum quando pugnaturi sunt cum inimicis, premonere populum □ *Explicit* hodie canit Ecclesia, sicut aqua extinguet ignem, ita elemosyna extinguet peccatum □ *Marginalia* scribal ann.; distinc.; enumeration □ *Notes* Explicit quotes sixth responsory for first Sunday of Lent: MS Add. 23935, fol. 276a; OP Breviary 2: 239 □ *Schneyer* T19

52 *Folios* 54v, bottom margin □ *Runnning title* Antithema aliud □ *Source book* none □ *Incipit* Non in solo pane vivit homo. Homo conficitur ex corpore et anima □ *Explicit* adversus carnem et sanguinem sed adversus principes et potestates etc. □ *Marginalia* none □ *Notes* Probably this text is an alternative antitheme for Sermon 51 □ *Schneyer* none

53 *Folios* 55b–56b □ *Runnning title* none □ *Source book* Proprius □ *Theme* Ductus est Jesus in desertum etc. (Mt 4:1) □ *Incipit* Quando aliqui frequentius et sepius audiunt verbum Dei, nec per illud proficiunt □ *Thema* Cum tempus istud quadragesimali tempus spiritualis pugne denotetur □ *Explicit* Unde potest dicere illud Cant 1, osculetur me osculo oris sui; exemplum huius est ii Reg 14 de Absalome, patri suo David reconciliato □ *Lemmata* [3]: Penitentia debet esse (2); Quidam penitent; De tribus dietis □ *Marginalia* unidentified ann.; distinc. □ *Notes* Marginal note reads: "predicatur aput Elnest' anno circuli lunaris ix." □ *Schneyer* T19

54 *Folios* 56va- 57a □ *Runnning title* none □ *Source book* Rubeus Maior □ *Theme* Quasi tristes semper autem gaudentes (2 Cor 6:10) □ *Incipit* Duo dicuntur, tristitia apparens et gaudium perseverans □ *Explicit* set in sap, Cum nobis disciplinam das, inimicos nostros multipliciter flagellas, scilicet, demones, ergo etc. □ *Marginalia* none □ *Schneyer* T19

55 *Folios* 57b- 59a □ *Runnning title* none □ *Source book* Niger Maior □ *Theme* Ductus est Jesus in desertum ut temptaretur a diabolo mt 4 et deut 4 (Mt 4:1) □ *Incipit* Non in solo pane vivit homo sed in omni verbo qui procedit ex ore Dei. Sicut enim panis corporalis est refectio corporis, sic panis spiritualis est verbum Dei □ *Thema* Quamvis omni tempore pugnandum sit contra hostes spirituales, id est mundum carnem et demonum et contra eorum opera, id est peccata □ *Explicit* licet enim remittatur offensa in contritione, et revocetur in confessione, non tamen plene reconciliatur peccator nisi in satisfactione. Exemplum huius 3 Reg 14 de Absalome patri suo David reconciliato. □ *Marginalia* Ann. □ *Schneyer* T19

56 *Folios* 59b- 60vb □ *Runnning title* none □ *Source book* Niger Maior □ *Theme* Ductus est Jesus in desertum a Spiritu (Mt 4:1) □ *Incipit* Hic verba scripta sunt Mt 4 in quibus tanguntur tria que predicatoribus sunt necessaria, scilicet eminentia vite, sapientie sive scientia doctrine, et collatio gratie □ *Thema* Circa hec verba ad presens videamus tria, primo cum multiplex sit desertum, quod sit illud desertum quo Jesus ducitur □ *Explicit* duo pertinent ad esse penitentie, et duo ad bene esse; ad esse pertinent munditia et abstinentia, ad bene esse caritas et humilitas. □ *Marginalia* scribal ann.; marginal headings; enumeration □ *Other authorities* 59vb.41- 42: cf. Aristotle, *Metaphysica* 1.1 (980a21); 59vb.42- 43: cf. Cicero, *De senectute* 19.68; 60a.1- 2: Aristotle, *Ethica Nichomachea*, trans. Grosseteste, 1.1 (94a3). □ *Notes* The protheme / antitheme section is very long, and has been given separate flourishing and rubrication by the scribe. □ *Schneyer* T19

57 *Folios* 61a- 64vb □ *Runnning title* none □ *Source book* quaterna Oxon' □ *Theme* Ductus est Jesus in desertum a Spiritu (Mt 4:1) □ *Incipit* Sicut magister noster Christus a Spiritu Sancto ductus, desertum intravit, sicut habetur ex verbis propositis. Ita qui volunt esse ipsius discipuli verbi sui auditores fructuosi □ *Thema* Cum omnis Christi actio nostra sit instructio ista Christi actio quia ducatur Spiritus Sancti exiit in desertum spiritualis est instructio penitentium et possunt in isto facto Jesu notari tria ad penitentes pertinentia □ *Explicit* per transeuntes cum filiis Israel hereditabunt terram promissionis, terram lacte et melle manantem. Ad quam nos perducat etc. □ *Marginalia* scribal ann.; marginal headings; enumeration □ *Schneyer* T19

58 *Folios* 65a- 66b □ *Runnning title* none □ *Source book* Parvus Rubeus □ *Theme* Hortamur vos ne in vacuum gratiam Dei accipiatis (2 Cor 6:1) □ *Incipit* Videndum est que sit hec gratia de qua hic loquitur Apostolus □ *Explicit* Et ideo illi qui sunt elemosinarii audituri sunt in die iudicii, Venite benedicti Patris mei, percipite regnum etc. □ *Marginalia* unidentified ann.; marginal headings □ *Schneyer* T19

59 *Folios* 66b- 66va □ *Runnning title* none □ *Source book* Parvus Rubeus □ *Theme* Ductus est Jesus etc. (Mt 4:1) □ *Incipit* Nota quod desertum dicitur multipliciter dicitur enim desertum status peccatoris, status penitentis, status triumphantis. □ *Explicit* in corde contritio recogitare et ad unitatem reducere; quod cum fecerimus, apparet nobis quasi ignis omnia consumens et delens □ *Marginalia* none □ *Schneyer* T19

60 *Folios* 66va- 67b □ *Runnning title* none □ *Source book* Parvus Rubeus □ *Theme* Ecce nunc tempus acceptabile (2 Cor 6:2) □ *Incipit* Tempus scilicet gratie, vel tempus quadragesimale ad medendum scilicet et ad negotiandum □ *Explicit* sed priores reficiunt et medentur. De hoc foro apo 4 facit □ *Marginalia* none □ *Notes* Petrus de Remis OP, †1247: see Schneyer, *Repertorium* 4: 726, no. 27 □ *Schneyer* T19

61 *Folios* 67b- 67vb □ *Runnning title* none □ *Source book* Parvus Rubeus □ *Theme* Ecce nunc tempus acceptabile (2 Cor 6:2) □ *Incipit* Reis ad reconciliandum, peccatoribus ad satisfaciendum □ *Explicit* melius est esse duos simul quam unum; habent enim emolumentum societatis sed Ve soli etc., hoc erit in inferno □ *Marginalia* none □ *Schneyer* T19

62 *Folios* 67vb- 68vb □ *Runnning title* none □ *Source book* Parvus Rubeus □ *Theme* Ecce nunc dies salutis (2 Cor 6:2) □ *Incipit* Sicut autem duplex est malum vel morbus, culpa et pena, sic duplex est salus □ *Explicit* si sic agis dico tibi quia securus es, scilicet de patria ad quam nos perducat etc. □ *Marginalia* none □ *Schneyer* T19

63 *Folios* 68vb- 69a □ *Runnning title* none □ *Source book* Rubeus Minor □ *Theme* Ductus est Jesus in desertum (Mt 4:1) □ *Incipit* Antithema. Vox Domini conucientis desertum etc. Desertum populus peccator, vel mundus, in quo vox Domini □ *Thema* Mistice illud desertum est mundus vel populus peccator □ *Explicit* exterius ypocrisi et tunc assumit 7 spiritus nequiores se et ingressi habitant ibi et post eum solitudo deserti □ *Marginalia* enumeration □ *Schneyer* T19

64 *Folios* 69va- 70vb □ *Runnning title* Dominica iia quadragesima □ *Source book* Proprius □ *Theme* Hec est voluntas Dei sanctificatio vestra (I Thess 4:3) □ *Incipit* Cum mundus iste lacrimarum vallis denominetur, et tempus presentis vite deploratio culpe □ *Thema* Sicut anima dupliciter polluitur per originale peccatum et actuale □ *Explicit* discoperui Esau, revelavi abscondita eius, et celari non poterit. Esau significat quemlibet peccatorum □ *Marginalia* unidenti-

fied ann.; enumeration □ *Notes* Margin Note: predicatur sermo anno lun' xi
□ *Schneyer* T20

65 *Folios* 70vb–72b □ *Runnning title* Dominica iia quadragesima □ *Source book* Proprius □ *Theme* Hec est voluntas Dei sanctificatio vestra (1 Thess 4:3) □ *Incipit* Salamone in proverbiis, audiens sapiens sapientior erit, stultus enim quantumcumque audierit, non erit eo sapientior □ *Thema* In verbo isto ostendit nobis Apostolus primo quid sit voluntas Dei quoniam sanctificare sive mundare □ *Explicit* Introduxit me rex in cubiculo suo; cubiculum est locus quietis et requiei, ad quam nos perducat etc. □ *Marginalia* unidentified ann. □ *Schneyer* T20

66 *Folios* 72va–73va □ *Runnning title* Fratris S. de Henton □ *Source book* Niger Minor □ *Theme* Hec est voluntas Dei sanctificatio vestra (1 Thess 4:3) □ *Incipit* In primo aspectu duo occurrunt consideranda, que sit Dei voluntas, et quare sit facienda □ *Explicit* Item requiritur presentia agentis in eo in quod agitur non solum in superficie sed etiam in profundo □ *Marginalia* unidentified ann. □ *Notes* Simon de Hinton OP: See Schneyer, *Repertorium* 9: 61, no. 67. □ *Schneyer* T20

67 *Folios* 73vb–74vb □ *Runnning title* Dominica iia quadragesima □ *Source book* Rubeus Maior □ *Theme* Hec est voluntas Dei sanctificatio vestra (1 Thess 4:3) □ *Incipit* Sicut dupliciter polluitur anima, sic duplex est purgatio, mundatio sive sanctificatio □ *Explicit* et qui ante delicata, modo grossa comedat, donec voluptatem extraxerit □ *Lemmata* [4]: Agenda est penitentia quia; Qui penitet seipsum sacrificat; Deus procurat penitentiam fieri per (3); Mundari contigit tripliciter in □ *Marginalia* unidentified ann.; distinc. □ *Schneyer* T20

68 *Folios* 75a–75va □ *Runnning title* Dominica iia quadragesima □ *Source book* Rubeus Maior □ *Theme* Ecce mulier Cananea etc. (Mt 15:21) □ *Incipit* Tria hic precipue designantur videlicet, vite veteris mutatio, perfecta seculi abrenuntiatio, et devota Jesu invocatio □ *Explicit* per hoc, quod subdit fili David, et ideo merito, dicit ei Jesus, mulier, magna est fides tua □ *Marginalia* none □ *Schneyer* T20

69 *Folios* 75b–80a □ *Runnning title* none □ *Source book* Niger Maior □ *Theme* Egressus inde Jesus etc. (Mt 15:21) □ *Incipit* Ad perfectum magistrum pertinet ut sit doctor in verbo, ductor in exemplo □ *Thema* In hiis enim verbis ad litteram signatur egressus a regione nativitatis secundum humanitatem, id est, a Judea in regionem gentium et signat egressum a regione nativitatis sue secundum Deitatem, in regionem nostram; id est, a sinu Patris in mundum □ *Explicit* ecce tranquillitas, et sequitur felicitas, que consistit in duobus, in gaudio et gloria, Ps: exaltabunt Sancti in gloria etc. Ad quam gloriam etc. □ *Marginalia* unidentified ann. □ *Other authorities* 76a.10–14: cf. Aristotle, *De generatione et corruptione* 1.7 (323b–324a). □ *Schneyer* T20

70 *Folios* 80b–81vb □ *Runnning title* Dominica iiia in quadragesima □ *Source book* Proprius □ *Theme* Cum eiecisset Jesus demonium (Lc 11:14) □ *Incipit* Scitis quod homo perficitur ex corpore et anima. Anima autem multo nobilior est quam corpus, quia in eternum duratura □ *Thema* Narrat evangelista de Christo quod cum operaretur salutes hominum et sanabat infirmitates □ *Explicit* multi enim tot et tanta in terrenis expendunt edificiis, et peractis omnibus, moriuntur, et de medietate expensarum possent sibi pallatium construxisse in celum, duraturum in vitam eternam. □ *Marginalia* unidentified ann.; enumeration □ *Schneyer* T21

71 *Folios* 82a–83va □ *Runnning title* Dominica 3 in quadragesima □ *Source book* Proprius □ *Theme* Cum eiecisset Jesus demonium etc. (Lc 11:14) □ *Incipit* Si ita esset quod Dominus noster Jesus Christus nunc, sicut olim, ambularet in terris et fecisset denunciare quod quicumque ad eum accederet verbum eius audituri haberent eius benedictionem, non credo multos esse presentes □ *Thema* Dominus per terram ambulando multas et diversas languentibus potentia sua in simul cum misericordia contulit sanitates □ *Explicit* Item, quod minimum est si frangatur circulus, vel etiam virgula unde ligatur circulus, adhuc potest esse causa effusionis totius vini □ *Marginalia* unidentified ann. □ *Schneyer* T21

72 *Folios* 83vb–84va □ *Runnning title* Dominica 3a in quadragesima □ *Source book* Proprius □ *Theme* Cum eiecisset Jesus demonium etc. (Lc 11:14) □ *Incipit* In fine huius evangelii legitur Beati qui audiunt verbum Dei et custodiunt illud. Si beatus Petrus Apostolus nunc, sicut olim, in terris ambularet, et denunciasset in ecclesiis circumquaque quod quicumque aput Bedeford' ad verbum suum audiendum accederet, benedictionem suam reciperet, multi sunt qui diligenter accurrerent et libenter eum audirent. Sed Dominus noster Jesus Christus □ *Thema* Legitur in evangelio quod Dominus eiecit demonium a quodam qui mutus fuerat □ *Explicit* qui dicit conversus de Rupe laborabat in extremis etc. Ideo in Prov, Qui abscondit scelera sua non dirigetur etc. □ *Marginalia* none □ *Notes* Margin Note: predicatur aput Elnest' anno circuli lun' vi □ *Schneyer* T21

73 *Folios* 84vb–86a □ *Runnning title* Dominica 3a in quadragesima □ *Source book* Proprius □ *Theme* Estote imitatores Dei sicut filii karissimi (Eph 5:1) □ *Incipit* Mater nostra Ecclesia de salute Christianorum valde sollicita, qui filii eius sunt sacri baptismatis regeneratione □ *Explicit* et oculorum concupiscentia evacuetur, per orationem Deo serviatur, et ipse qui superbivit humilietur □ *Marginalia* unidentified ann. □ *Schneyer* T21

74 *Folios* 86b–90b □ *Runnning title* Dominica 3a in quadragesima □ *Source book* Parvus Niger □ *Theme* Cum eiecisset Jesus demonium locutus est mutus (Lc 11:14) □ *Incipit* Duo hic videnda: de eiectione et concomitantibus eam. Circa primum tria; quid eicitur, quis eicit, et quam utilis eiectio illi a quo

fit □ *Explicit* ad misericordiam provocare facta sua confiteri sicut patet in Judit
et fere per totum Vetus Testamentum.Ideo Prov 9, qui abscondit scelera sua
non dirigetur etc. □ *Marginalia* enumeration □ *Schneyer* T21

75 *Folios* 90va - 91va □ *Running title* none □ *Source book* Rubeus Maior
□ *Theme* Erat Jesus eiiciens demonium etc. (Lc 11:14) □ *Incipit* Duo dicuntur:
cur diabolus reddit peccatorem mutum et quare □ *Explicit* Quamvis enim
misericors sit, tamen iustus est Dominus. Unde quidem in peccatores respicit
ira illius. Gregorius: ad iustitiam Dei pertinet ut nunquam careant supplicio,
qui nunquam voluerunt carere peccato □ *Marginalia* unidentified ann. □
Schneyer T21

76 *Folios* 91vb- 92vb □ *Running title* Dominica 3a in quadragesima □
Source book Rubeus Maior □ *Theme* Cum eiecisset Jesus demonium locutus est
mutus (Lc 11:14) □ *Incipit* Hic notatur ordo iustificationis impii; primo enim,
accepta gratia, conteritur peccator, et tunc eicitur demonium □ *Explicit* Vera
sine mundatio, secundum illud ys ecc 4 pro anima tua non confundaris dicere
verum; est enim confusio adducens peccatum etc □ *Marginalia* unidentified
ann. □ *Schneyer* T21

77a *Folios* 93a- 93vb □ *Running title* Dominica in media quad' □ *Source
book* Proprius □ *Theme* Illa que sursum est Jerusalem libere est mater nostra
(Gal 4:26) □ *Incipit* Si aliquis vestrum hic esset, crucis caractere insignitus, qui
proponeret in Terram Sanctam □ *Explicit* et tamen vellet metere eternam
benedictionem, non avertens illud Apostoli, quecumque seminaverit homo hac
et metet et Prover 21 Quecumque in iuventute tua nec congregasti quomodo
invenies in senectute tua □ *Marginalia* enumeration □ *Notes* Margin Note
predicatur sermo iste apud Eln' anno lun' xi □ *Schneyer* T22

77b *Folios* 93vb □ *Running title* Antithema sermonis predicte □ *Source
book* none □ *Theme* Illa que sursum est etc. (Gal 4:126) □ *Incipit* Karissimi,
doctrina sacri libri in principio operum nostrorum □ *Explicit* summe nichil
potestis facere □ *Marginalia* none □ *Notes* 77a and 77b are possibly part of a
sermon by Guilelmus Peraldus OP: see Schneyer, *Repertorium* 2: 552, no. 260
□ *Schneyer* none

78 *Folios* 94a- 94vb □ *Running title* Dominica in media quad' □ *Source
book* Proprius □ *Theme* Erat proximum pascha dies festus Judeorum (Jo 6:4) □
Incipit Legitur in evangelio hodierno quod imminente Pascha, quod transitus
interpretatur, venit ad Jesum multitudo magna quasi quinque milia hominum
□ *Explicit* sicut rex quidam potentissimus dans filiam suam Imperatori etc.,
sicut alibi propter hoc, Job 31, Si abscondit quasi homo peccatum meum etc.,
et in Prov 28 qui abscondit scelera sua etc. □ *Marginalia* unidentified ann.;
enumeration □ *Vernacular phrases* "yus ssal I brenne al so hot fo alle mine
sinnes yat no man ne Wot" (fol. 94b 30- 32) □ This phrase is followed by the
Latin direction *et narretur totum*. It is part of a story, *exemplum*, about a
lay- brother of the Cistercian Abbey of Roche in Yorkshire. The preacher

makes a Latin note to tell the complete story. □ *Notes* Marginal note reads: "Iste sermo predicatur aput Elnest' a° do^i m.cc.lxx.quinto." Hugonis de S. Caro OP: see Schneyer, *Repertorium* 2: 760, no. 39 □ *Schneyer* T22

79 *Folios* 95a–95va □ *Runnning title* Dominica in media quad' □ *Source book* Rubeus Maior □ *Theme* Nunc vadimus ad domum Dei habentes panem ac vinum, in meos et ancille usus (Jud 19:18–19) □ *Incipit* In hiis verbis tangitur et loquitur quicquid hodie geritur in Ecclesia Dei, et sunt tria □ *Explicit* qui loquitur victorias co ad confessionem, ad quam domum nos perducat etc. □ *Marginalia* none □ *Schneyer* T22

80 *Folios* 95va–96a □ *Runnning title* Dominica in media quad' □ *Source book* Rubeus Maior □ *Theme* Letare sterilis que non paris (Gal 4:27) □ *Incipit* Iste textus Apostoli sumptus est de ys 54 ubi dicitur: Lauda sterilis etc. □ *Explicit* de hac discordia ro 7: video aliam legem in membris meis repugnantem legi mentis mee □ *Marginalia* none □ *Schneyer* T22

81 *Folios* 96b–96va □ *Runnning title* Dominica in media quad' □ *Source book* Rubeus Maior □ *Theme* Illa que sursum est Jerusalem libera est (Gal 4:26) □ *Incipit* Cum sit tempus penitentie et propter hoc fletus et doloris, invitat tamen mater Ecclesia filios suos multipliciter ad letitiam spiritualem in principio Misse, et hoc propter plura □ *Explicit* quem voluit Abraham mactare Domino, sed ariete occiso, rediit cum eodem □ *Marginalia* enumeration □ *Schneyer* T22

82 *Folios* 96va–99va □ *Runnning title* Sermo fratris R. de Fisac^r □ *Source book* Rubeus Maior □ *Theme* Non enim heres erit filius ancille cum filio libere (Gal 4:30) □ *Incipit* Hic quinque consideremus: que sit ancilla, que libera, quis filius ancille, quis libere, quare non sit heres cum eo □ *Explicit* propter hoc, frigus vel calor in celo non est passibilis. Apoc 7: non esurient nec sitient amplius, et non cadet super illos sol neque ullus estus □ *Marginalia* none □ *Vernacular phrases* "Sed dicitur Gallice. Ki a mauveis sert. tot son service pert" (fol. 97b 32–33) □ There is no indication in the manuscript of the language in which this sermon was preached: Latin, English or French. In the version found in MS Ipswich 6, this proverb is given in Latin. Cf. J. Morawski, *Les proverbes français anterieurs au XVe siècle* (Paris, 1925): "Qui mauves sert son loier pert" (no. 1987); "Son loier pert qui mauves sert" (no. 2271). □ *Notes* Richardus de Fishacre OP: see Schneyer, *Repertorium* 5: 149, no. 25; see also Ipswich MS 6, fol. 76r. □ *Schneyer* T22

83 *Folios* 99va–99vb, bottom margin □ *Runnning title* Dominica in media quad' □ *Source book* Rubeus Minor □ *Theme* Eice ancillam et filium eius (Gal 4:30) □ *Incipit* Filii Agar sunt peccatores que interpretatur festum suscitans □ *Explicit* Ideo ge 16, e regione umbre mortis, figet tabernacula □ *Marginalia* none □ *Notes* Petrus de Remis OP, †1247: see Schneyer, *Repertorium* 4: 727, no. 33. Numbers 83–88 are fitted into three columns and the bottom margins of both folios, and in half the right margin of folio 100. It seems that the scribe underestimated the space. □ *Schneyer* T22

84 *Folios* 99va–100a □ *Runnning title* in media quadragesima □ *Source book* Rubeus Maior □ *Theme* Letare sterilis etc. (Gal 4:27) □ *Incipit* Hiis notatur tria, videlicet / Status culpe recordatio / Penitentis exultatio / et bonorum operum exultatio (sic) □ *Explicit* et bonis operibus celestis hereditas exhibetur ps: dedisti hereditatem timentibus nomen tuum □ *Marginalia* none □ *Schneyer* T22

85 *Folios* 100a (9 lines) □ *Runnning title* Dominica in media quad' □ *Source book* Minimus? □ *Theme* Letare sterilis etc. (Gal 4:27) □ *Incipit* Nota hic Beate Virginis commendatio et eius ad gaudium invitatio □ *Explicit* habebit fructum etc. co ad tertium □ *Marginalia* none □ *Schneyer* T22

86 *Folios* 100b (9 lines) □ *Runnning title* In media quadragesima □ *Source book* Minimus □ *Theme* Sequebatur eum multitudo magna (Jo 6:2) □ *Incipit* Tria sunt quare ipsum sequi conveniat □ *Explicit* per amicitiam copulati Christus magister et nos eius discipuli □ *Marginalia* none □ *Schneyer* T22

87 *Folios* 100b (4 lines) □ *Runnning title* in media quadragesima □ *Source book* Minimus □ *Theme* Abraham duos filios habuit (Gal 4:22) □ *Marginalia* none □ *Notes* The entire text reads: "debemus esse Abraham per efficaciam credendi / propter modum vivendi / propter vim gignendi." □ *Schneyer* T22

88 *Folios* 100b and bottom margin □ *Runnning title* none □ *Source book* Confessiones Augustini □ *Theme* Eice ancillam et filium eius (Gal 4:30) □ *Incipit* Videamus hic tria, scilicet, qui sint eiciendi et ubi sint eiciendi et quo proiciendi □ *Explicit* tria consideremus, scilicet, matris turpitudinem, a tanta dulcedine eiectionem, in tanta miseria proiectionem □ *Marginalia* none □ *Schneyer* T22

89 *Folios* 100va–100vb □ *Runnning title* Dominica in passione Domini □ *Source book* Proprius □ *Theme* Vexilla regis prodeunt □ *Incipit* Scitis quoniam reges et principes terrarum qui et iusti et misericordes et liberales existunt □ *Explicit* cum ad bella processerint, generaliter omnes et singulos (last words lost in the binding) □ *Marginalia* none □ *Notes* Theme is the opening of the Vesper Hymn for Passion Sunday: MS Add. 23935, fol. 27a, 372b; OP Breviary 1: 360; Sarum Breviary 1: dccxiii (see p. 373 below). □ *Schneyer* T23

90 *Folios* 101a–101vb □ *Runnning title* Dominica in passione Domini □ *Source book* Proprius □ *Theme* Christus per proprium sanguinem semel introivit in sancta (Hebr 9:12) □ *Incipit* In hiis verbis excellens Christi caritas humano generi commendatur, qui ovem perditam nec auro nec argento, non angelo vel alia creatura, sed sanguine proprio voluit comparare □ *Thema* Ecclesia in alia parte quadragesimale que precessit □ *Explicit* per penitentiam et bona opera ingredi in aliam requiem ubi melior est dies una etc., ubi Christus nos expectat etc. □ *Lemmata* [1]: Ecclesia vocat nos (2) □ *Marginalia* unidentified ann.; distinc. □ *Notes* Margin Note: predicatur aput Eln' anno lun' x □ *Schneyer* T23

91 *Folios* 101vb and bottom margin □ *Runnning title* none □ *Source book* Rubeus Minor □ *Theme* Christus assistens pontifex (Hebr 9:11) □ *Incipit* Templum dedicando primum uterum virginis □ *Explicit* Sed multi vado transeunt aquam fluminis, id est, voluptatis carnalis quia lata est via etc. Ubi etiam inferiora discooperiunt quidam navigio quidam equis □ *Marginalia* none □ *Schneyer* T23

92 *Folios* 102a (24 lines) □ *Runnning title* none □ *Source book* Rubeus Maior □ *Theme* Christus per proprium sanguinem etc. (Hebr 9:12) □ *Incipit* Tria notantur, passio Christi, efficacia eius, et effectus □ *Explicit* quia ex ipso vita procedit et quia peccatum invadit voluntatem □ *Marginalia* none □ *Schneyer* T23

93 *Folios* 102a- 102vb □ *Runnning title* none □ *Source book* Rubeus Maior □ *Theme* Si quis sermonem meum servaverit etc. (Jo 8:51) □ *Incipit* Duo tanguntur, scilicet, meritum cum dicit *si quis sermonem meum servaverit* □ *Explicit* debetur vita eterna et hac ratione effectus triplicis et ideo bene dicit Petrus Domino Jo 6 Verba vite eterne habes □ *Marginalia* enumeration □ *Schneyer* T23

94 *Folios* 103a- 103b □ *Runnning title* Dominica in passione Domini □ *Source book* Parvus Rubeus Minor □ *Theme* Christus per Spiritum Sanctum semetipsum obtulit Deo immaculatum (Hebr 9:14) □ *Incipit* Hiis verbis excellens Christi caritas et quid nobis agendum sit declaretur □ *Explicit* ex caritate et timore casto, non ex timore servili, de quo ro 8; non accepistis iterum spiritum servitutis ex timore sed accepistis etc. □ *Marginalia* enumeration □ *Schneyer* T23

95 *Folios* 103b- 104b □ *Runnning title* none □ *Source book* Rubeus Minor □ *Theme* Christus per proprium sanguinem etc. (Hebr 9:12) □ *Incipit* Ut se nos amare ostenderet. Dicitur quod per minimum foramen cognoscitur amicus; igitur per ampliora et plura melius et efficacius □ *Explicit* frater noster devenit et postea sanguinem suum fudit, quia dicitur anglice: "sib blod same rennit." □ *Marginalia* enumeration □ *Vernacular phrases* "quia dicitur anglice sib blod same rennit" (fol. 104b53) □ This phrase seems to be a proverb-, "kindred blood runs together." In the context of the sermon the preacher is referring to the love which Christ, "our brother," has for us. Cf. B.J. and H.W. Whiting, *Proverbs, Sentences and Proverbial Phrases* (Cambridge, MA and London, 1968): "Blood draws to blood" (B359); "Like to Like" (L270); "Sib is dearest to each" (S293). □ *Schneyer* T23

96 *Folios* 104va- 104vb □ *Runnning title* none □ *Source book* Parvus Rubeus □ *Theme* Christus per proprium sanguinem introivit in sancta (Hebr 9:12) □ *Incipit* Triplex notatur, effectus fusionis sanguinis Christi, quia per ipsum janua celi reseratur, homo a peccato mundatur □ *Explicit* Si quis interfecisset filium regis et cum cultello extracto et manibus sanguinolens ministraret coram rege numquid placeret ei servitium □ *Marginalia* enumeration □ *Vernacular phrases* "ye Vieie is al grene lef in to yi bur" (104va. 42- 104vb.1) □ The context of this phrase is Lam 1:4 which refers to the de-

struction of Sion. Ivy is a traditional symbol for Our Lady. The sermon is
about Christ shedding his blood through his sufferings; cf. Luke 23:27–31. See
R.H. Robbins and John Cutler, *Supplement to the Index of Middle English Verse*
(Lexington, 1965): "Ivy is both far & gren" (1651.5). □ *Schneyer* T23

97 *Folios* 104vb (21 lines) □ *Running title* none □ *Source book* Parvus
Rubeus □ *Theme* Introivit in sancta (Hebr 9:12) □ *Incipit* Hic duo possunt
notari, scilicet, humana redemptio, et janue apertio □ *Explicit* et in pace et in
bello ea premia vincentibus tribuent □ *Marginalia* none □ *Schneyer* T23

98 *Folios* 105a (30 lines) □ *Running title* none □ *Source book* Parvus
Rubeus 181 □ *Theme* Christus assistens pontifex etc. (Hebr 9:11) □ *Incipit*
Dominica ista appropriatur Dominica in Passione Domini □ *Explicit* que et
amigdalas proferat, que sunt cibus infirmorum □ *Marginalia* none □ *Notes* The
text and first few words of this sermon are found in a sermon by Johannes
Halgrinus de Abbatisvilla, noted by Schneyer, *Repertorium* 3: 514, no. 67. The
explicits and most of the text, however, are not the same. □ *Schneyer* T23

99 *Folios* 105b–106va □ *Running title* Dominica in passione Domini □
Source book Niger Minor □ *Theme* Recordare paupertatis mee et transgressionis
absinthii et fellis (Lam 3:19) □ *Incipit* Verba sunt Domini per Jeremiam. Sicut
bonus pastor curam habet de gregibus suis, sic Christus de suis subditis □
Thema Huius auctoritatis est sensus memorare passionis mee que consistit in
tribus: in penalitate, paupertate, vilitate □ *Explicit* ut ad illam beatitudinem
perveniamus de qua dicitur; Beati qui audiunt verbum Dei et custodiunt illud
□ *Marginalia* unidentified ann. □ *Notes* The Thema is indicated by a decorated
initial. □ *Schneyer* T23

100 *Folios* 106vb–107vb □ *Running title* Dominica palmarum □ *Source
book* Confessiones Augustini □ *Theme* Noli timere filia Syon; ecce rex tuus etc.
(Jo 12:15) □ *Incipit* Tria sunt hic notanda: quis sit iste rex et quare vocetur rex
et qualis sit eius adventus □ *Explicit* Nec in celo locus dignior regali solio quo
mariam Marie filius sublimavit. Ad quod solium nos perducat etc. □ *Marginalia* none □ *Notes* The marginal note reads: predicatur sermo anno lun' v
aput Eln' usque ibi "Cantandum est." Similiter anno lun' xi. These separate
annotations indicate that this sermon was preached twice at Elstow; the
second time only part of the text available was used by the preacher. □
Schneyer T24

101 *Folios* 108a–108vb □ *Running title* none □ *Source book* Rubeus Maior
□ *Theme* Ecce rex tuus venit tibi mansuetus (Mt 21:5) □ *Incipit* Videndum quis
venit, quoniam rex ad quid innuitur quod ad utilitatem nostram □ *Explicit* De
tertio, mansuetus venit ut nos, exemplo eius, tales essemus secundum quod dicit Mt ii Discite a me quia mitis sum et humilis corde, et hoc est contra tiran-
nos maledictos et inimiciarum observatores □ *Marginalia* none □ *Schneyer* T24

102 *Folios* 108vb- 109vb □ *Runnning title* none □ *Source book* Rubeus Maior □ *Theme* Hoc sentite in vobis etc. (Phil 2:5) □ *Incipit* 3a notantur videlicet: sentiendi exortatio; / obiecti sensus demonstratio; / ei ipsius assimulatio; □ *Explicit* Hec vulnera debemus in nobis sentire iuxta illud; Gal 6, stigmata Christi Jesu in corpore meo porto; can 4, pone me ut signaculum super cor tuum □ *Marginalia* none □ *Schneyer* T24

103 *Folios* 109va- 109vb □ *Runnning title* none □ *Source book* Rubeus Maior 57 □ *Theme* Hoc sentite in vobis etc. phil (Phil 2:5) □ *Incipit* Non dicit quantum, quia eius dolor super omnem dolorem et incomparabilis fuit □ *Explicit* et addit, torrentes iniqui conturbaverunt me propter multitudinem peccatorum □ *Marginalia* none □ *Schneyer* T24

104 *Folios* 109va- 110b □ *Runnning title* In ramis palmarum □ *Source book* Rubeus Minor □ *Theme* Vox Domini preparantis cervos (Ps 28:9) □ *Incipit* 3a sunt in Dominica Palmarum; primum est pueri Hebreorum, secundo turba cervis assimulatur, arbores densiores spoliantur □ *Explicit* Item venenosa mortificant Col: Mortificate membra vestra que sunt super terram □ *Marginalia* none □ *Notes* The text of this and Sermon 124 are the same. □ *Schneyer* T24

105 *Folios* 110b- 110va □ *Runnning title* none □ *Source book* Rubeus Minor □ *Theme* Hoc sentite etc. (Phil 2:5) □ *Incipit* Dilectionis insinuationem Bernardus, verius est anima ubi amat quam ubi animat □ *Explicit* Iterum facta est hereditas mea quasi leena □ *Marginalia* none □ *Notes* The Theme is written in the margin. □ *Schneyer* T24

106a *Folios* 110va (7 lines) □ *Source book* Rubeus Minor □ *Incipit* Gloriose Virginis imitationem □ *Explicit* *Anglice*: Maiden stod at Welle and Wep Weila Wei / Late comet ye lith of dai □ *Marginalia* none □ *Vernacular phrases* "Anglice. Maiden stod at welle and wep weilawei. late comet ye lith of dai" (fol. 110va 28- 30) □ This phrase is found in a section which is sermon material rather than a sermon. It is part of a commentary on a text from Lamentations *O vos omnes qui transitis per viam* ... which is commonly applied in the liturgy to Our Lady. No source can be found. □ *Notes* Items 106a- 106h are pieces of sermon material. □ *Schneyer* none

106b *Folios* 110va (5 lines) □ *Source book* Rubeus Minor □ *Incipit* Recompensationem in Mt 24; Esurivi etc.; sitivi etc □ *Explicit* sustinet nostram quasi suam (sic) □ *Marginalia* none □ *Schneyer* none

106c *Folios* 110va (3 lines) □ *Runnning title* none □ *Source book* Rubeus Minor □ *Theme* Tuitionis in certitudinem I Reg; cum esset David in Geth non addidit ultra Saul prosequi eum; Geth interpretatur torcular vel opprimens □ *Marginalia* none □ *Notes* This is the whole text. □ *Schneyer* none

106d *Folios* 110va- 110vb (7 lines) □ *Runnning title* none □ *Source book* Rubeus Minor □ *Incipit* Divisiones....certitudinem. Bernardus □ *Explicit* Vita nostra Christus est, unde, si eo non compatimur, mortui sumus □ *Marginalia* none □ *Schneyer* none

106e *Folios* 110vb (9 lines) □ *Runnning title* none □ *Source book* Rubeus Minor □ *Incipit* Effectu. Bernardus horum dulcis memoria lacrimas allicit □ *Explicit* Bernardus: Ingratitudo est ventus urens siccans venas pietatis □ *Marginalia* none □ *Schneyer* none

106f *Folios* 110vb (9 lines) □ *Source book* Rubeus Minor □ *Incipit* Peccatorum odium; Ambrosius: Ve tibi amaritudo peccatorum meorum □ *Explicit* quod extrema gaudii luctus occupat sicut sonitus spinarum □ *Marginalia* none □ *Schneyer* none

106g *Folios* 110vb (6 lines) □ *Runnning title* none □ *Source book* Rubeus Minor □ *Incipit* Attendite et videte si est dolor etc. Productio. Glosa □ *Explicit* ne dolor cito finietur, et ut in cruce diu videretur □ *Marginalia* none □ *Schneyer* none

106h *Folios* 110vb (7 lines) □ *Runnning title* none □ *Source book* Rubeus Minor □ *Incipit* Turpissima; Sap: morte turpissima condemnemus eum □ *Explicit* et de peiore in celario Ps: in siti mea potaverunt etc. □ *Marginalia* none □ *Schneyer* none

107 *Folios* 110vb–111a □ *Runnning title* none □ *Source book* Rubeus Minor □ *Incipit* A discipulo procurata quid vultis michi dare etc. □ *Explicit* propter persone reverentiam, quia creatorem omnium rerum qui secundum Apostolum complet omnia verbo, virtus tua □ *Marginalia* none □ *Schneyer* none

108 *Folios* 111a–111va □ *Runnning title* none □ *Source book* Rubeus Minor 208 □ *Theme* Hoc sentite in vobis etc. (Phil 2:5) □ *Incipit* Hoc sentite sensu, scilicet, experientie quod in Christo Jesu, sensu, scilicet, cognitionis et tanguntur hic tria □ *Explicit* nullus affectus ardentior quam quod est pro nobis unicus ne remaneret unus □ *Marginalia* enumeration □ *Notes* Petrus de Remis OP: see Schneyer, *Repertorium* 4: 727, no. 37. □ *Schneyer* T24

109 *Folios* 111vb (32 lines) □ *Runnning title* none □ *Source book* Rubeus Minor □ *Incipit* Orationis sublevatio 23 similar statements are complement to the subject □ *Explicit* quia in immo est, recipit humiditatem et calorem □ *Marginalia* none □ *Notes* The title "Humilitas est" is found at fol. 111vb, col. 410 (top). This piece consists of distinctions on humility □ *Schneyer* none

110 *Folios* 111vb–112b □ *Runnning title* none □ *Source book* Rubeus Minor □ *Theme* Cum appropinquasset etc. (Mt 21:1) □ *Incipit* Videamus tria: quare palma portatur, quare passio processionem sequatur, et quare Christus pateretur □ *Explicit* scientes quoniam extrema gaudii luctus occupat □ *Marginalia* unidentified ann.; enumeration □ *Schneyer* T24

111 *Folios* 112b (9 lines) □ *Runnning title* none □ *Source book* Rubeus Minor □ *Theme* Ascendam in palmam (Cant 7:8) □ *Incipit* Palma precipue

Christus quia mascula □ *Explicit* sed querat paganus divitias, qui sine Deo vivit □ *Marginalia* unidentified ann. □ *Schneyer* T24

112 *Folios* 112b- 112vb □ *Runnning title* none □ *Source book* Rubeus Minor □ *Theme* Clamans voce magna emisit spiritum (Mt 27:50) □ *Incipit* Nota quod Matheus dicit "emisit spiritum,"Johannes "tradidit," Lucas et Marcus, "exspiravit □ *Explicit* Item a clericis in corona, id est, honoris ambitione. Vestium superfluitate crucifigitur etiam generaliter ab omnibus He 9 rursum crucifigentes Filium Dei □ *Marginalia* none □ *Schneyer* T24

113a *Folios* 112b (4 lines) □ *Source book* Rubeus Minor? □ *Incipit* Scio quod non est iniquitas sicut iniquitas mea □ *Explicit* quia supra modum doluit in quo respiro □ *Marginalia* none □ *Schneyer* none

113b *Folios* 112vb (2 lines) □ *Source book* Rubeus Minor? □ *Marginalia* none □ *Notes* The entire text reads: "Si exasperatur Deus immanitate sceleris mei mitigatur procul dubio satisfactione filii sui. □ *Schneyer* none

113c *Folios* 112vb (5 lines) □ *Source book* Rubeus Minor? □ *Incipit* Christus non in strato suo sed in cruce □ *Explicit* et infernus reperiretur in summo celi cardine □ *Marginalia* none □ *Schneyer* none

114 *Folios* 113a- 115b □ *Runnning title* In die pasche □ *Source book* Parvus Rubeus □ *Theme* Numquid qui dormit non adiciet ut resurgat (Ps 40:9) □ *Incipit* In hiis verbis primo, mors Christi certa supponitur ibi *qui dormit*, secundo, de eius resurrectione queritur ibi *numquid non adjiciet ut resurgat* □ *Explicit* tamquam ad quiescendum Jesum Christum reclinat. Honoremus eum omni puritate anime et corporis □ *Marginalia* unidentified ann. □ *Schneyer* T28

115 *Folios* 115b- 115va □ *Runnning title* none □ *Source book* Rubeus Minor 1.76 □ *Theme* Si consurrexistis cum Christo etc. (Col 3:1) □ *Incipit* Homo existens ex duabus naturis dupplicem habet mortem, scilicet, corporis et anime, et sic dupplicem habet resurrectionem □ *Explicit* Ad ea querenda sive Christum nos monent quattuor, anime natura, corporis statura, Christi exaltatio, nostra professio □ *Marginalia* none □ *Schneyer* T28

116 *Folios* 115va- 115vb □ *Runnning title* none □ *Source book* Rubeus Minor 1.73.1 □ *Theme* Christus resurgens ex mortuis etc. (Rom 6:9) □ *Incipit* Est mors nature cui neque divites neque pauperes resistunt □ *Explicit* tunc erit miseris mors sine morte quando in corpore et anima cruciabuntur □ *Marginalia* none □ *Schneyer* T28

117 *Folios* 115vb- 116a □ *Runnning title* none □ *Source book* Rubeus Minor 1.77.1 □ *Theme* Pascha nostrum etc. (1 Cor 5:7) □ *Incipit* Glosa: paschin grece pati latine. Triplex pascha celebraverunt filii Israel, primum in exitu de Egipto □ *Explicit* caritas adimplebitur quando Deus erit perfecte (sic) omnia in omnibus et hoc est vita eterna □ *Marginalia* none □ *Notes* Petrus de Remis OP †1247: see Schneyer, *Repertorium* 4: 727, no. 39. □ *Schneyer* T28

118 *Folios* 116a-117vb □ *Runnning title* none □ *Source book* Confessiones Augustini □ *Theme* Transi hospes orna mensam (Eccli 29:33) □ *Incipit* In hiis verbis quattuor, quattuor consideranda sunt, scilicet, quis hospes, et quis eius transitus, que mensa, et quis eius ornatus □ *Explicit* Ad quam mensam nos perducat etc. □ *Lemmata* [1]: Recidivans □ *Marginalia* unidentified ann.; enumeration □ *Schneyer* T28

119 *Folios* 118a-118vb □ *Runnning title* none □ *Source book* quaterna Oxon' □ *Theme* Hec est dies quam fecit Dominus etc. (Ps 117:24) □ *Incipit* Si nos omnes, hic congregati, adiudicati essemus morti pro nostris iniquitatibus, et cum duceremur versus suspendium, compararet aliquis innocens □ *Thema* Propheta per Spiritum Sanctum altitudinem huius diei expavescens longe ante Christi nativitatem dixit *hec est dies* etc. □ *Explicit* non dicit, qui ferre debetis, quasi ante receptionem, sed qui fertis scilicet postquamque incorporastis □ *Marginalia* none □ *Schneyer* T28

120 *Folios* 118vb-119b □ *Runnning title* none □ *Source book* Proprius □ *Theme* Christus resurgens ex mortuis etc. (Rom 6:9) □ *Incipit* Hic est Christus qui pridie passus, hodie resurrexit, nunquam post hoc moriturus. Sciendum est etiam quod triplex est mors: nature, culpe, Gehenne □ *Explicit* quia magis expediret eis se ipsos suspendere dicatur etiam quid credendum etc. □ *Marginalia* none □ *Notes* The replacement bifolia occur halfway through this sermon. □ *Schneyer* T28

121 *Folios* 119va-120b □ *Runnning title* in pasche □ *Source book* Proprius □ *Theme* Si consurrexistis cum Christo que sursum sunt querit (Col 3:1) □ *Incipit* Verbum Domini a fidelibus audiendum est et intelligendum saltem propter mercedem □ *Thema* Quicumque cum Christo resurgere desiderat modum resurrectionis Christi tenere oportet □ *Explicit* Mundamini ergo qui ferre vultis vasa Domini et scitis mundi cum pueris David; positum est enim corpus Jesu in monumento novo etc. □ *Marginalia* unidentified ann. □ *Schneyer* T28

122 *Folios* 120b-120vb □ *Runnning title* none □ *Source book* Niger Minor □ *Theme* Qui comederit de sanctificatis per ignorantiam addet quintam partem cum eo qui comedit (Lev 22:14) □ *Incipit* Hic misterium corporis et sanguinis Christi designatur de hoc sanctificato per ignorantiam commedit, qui virtutem dignitatem atque circumstantiam sacramenti penitus ignorat □ *Explicit* Juste enim punitur in corpore suo qui peccat in corpus Christi □ *Marginalia* unidentified ann.; enumeration □ *Schneyer* none

123 *Folios* 120vb-121vb □ *Runnning title* In octavas pasche □ *Source book* Proprius □ *Theme* Stetit Jesus in medio <discipulorum suorum> et dixit: pax vobis etc. (Jo 20:19) □ *Incipit* Sic est de Christo sicut de aliquo rege terreno, qui postquam pugnaverit et dimiserit inimicos facit pacem suam □ *Thema* Scriptum est in psalmo: ad vesperum demorabitur fletus et ad matutinum letitia. Scitis quod sole tendentes ad occasum vincti et incarcerati tristiores efficiuntur □

Explicit Item pax temporalis est arra pacis eterne ys ultimo, erit sabbatum ex sabbatho, id est, requies ex requie et Jer 29: querite pacem civitatis ad quam migrare vos fecit Dominus etc. □ *Marginalia* enumeration □ *Schneyer* T29

124 *Folios* 122a □ *Runnning title* none □ *Source book* none □ *Theme* Vox Domini preparantis cervos etc. (Ps 28:9) □ *Incipit* Tria sunt in Dominica Palmarum □ *Explicit* et can 2: In foraminibus petre etc. Item libro 8 cui □ *Marginalia* none □ *Notes* Title at head of sermon notes reads: "Ista scribitur supra." This sermon is the same text as Sermon 105. □ *Schneyer* T24

125 *Folios* 122b–122va □ *Runnning title* Dominica ia post pascha / oct' pasc' □ *Source book* Parvus Rubeus □ *Theme* Quis est qui vincit mundum etc. (1 Jo 5:5) □ *Incipit* Qui credit Jesum esse Filium Dei, credit Deum Patrem ei dedisse sapientiam □ *Explicit* Nota quod fides est fundamentum, et diabolus minator huius fundamenti □ *Marginalia* none □ *Schneyer* T29

126 *Folios* 122va–122vb □ *Runnning title* Feria ii post pascha □ *Source book* Rubeus Minor □ *Theme* Mane nobiscum Domine (Lc 24:29) □ *Incipit* Nota quod non solum Dominus est rogandus ut maneat sed compellendus □ *Explicit* Sed rogare debemus in prosperitate sicut in adversitate ys 21: si queritis querite etc. □ *Marginalia* none □ *Schneyer* T28/2

127 *Folios* 122vb–123b □ *Runnning title* In octavas pasche □ *Source book* Rubeus Minor □ *Theme* Gavisi sunt discipuli viso Domino (Jo 20:20) □ *Incipit* Ps ad vesperum Passionis demorabitur fletus, et ad matutinam scilicet, resurrectionis, letitia □ *Explicit* ad maiorem confusionem monstraret Za 12; aspicient ad me apo 1, Za 13 que sunt etc. □ *Marginalia* none □ *Notes* Petrus de Remis OP †1247: see Schneyer, *Repertorium* 4: 727, no. 42. □ *Schneyer* T29

128 *Folios* 123b □ *Runnning title* none □ *Source book* Rubeus Minor □ *Theme* Pax vobis (Jo 20:21) □ *Incipit* Non treuga quod cito transit. Istam accipiunt qui proponunt recidivare post pascha □ *Explicit* et hoc iudicat securitatem quod alii famem □ *Lemmata* [1]: Sanum reddunt hominem □ *Marginalia* scribal ann.; distinc. □ *Schneyer* T29

129 *Folios* 123va □ *Runnning title* none □ *Source book* Rubeus Maior □ *Incipit* Recipit donum □ *Explicit* Utinam abscidantur qui nos conturbant □ *Marginalia* none □ *Notes* This is a set of distinctions on "pax." *Pax* is found in the margin with the drawn lines linking it to the distinctions written in the adjoining column. □ *Schneyer* T29

130 *Folios* 123vb–124vb □ *Runnning title* In octavas pasche □ *Source book* Rubeus Minor □ *Theme* Ostendit eis manus et latus (Jo 20:20) □ *Incipit* Possunt tria dici, primo, quare Christus resurgens a mortuis, cicatrices in suo corpore reservavit. Secundo, quare eos non solum ad videndum sed ad tangendum invitavit ibi □ *Explicit* vita eterna nobis ergo merito conferetur quod nobis annuat Dominus etc. □ *Marginalia* unidentified ann.; enumeration □ *Vernacular phrases* "anglice. Wan Ics on rode se Iesu mi leman, ..." (fol. 124va.22–24).

This poem refers to the suffering of Christ, particularly from his wounds gained in the battle with the devil. □ Cf. Carleton Brown, *English Lyrics of the XIII Century* (Oxford, 1932), pp. 61- 64: "Wose seye on rode ihesus is lef- mon" (no. 34); "Wenne hic soe on rode idon ihesus mi leman" (no. 35); "Vyen i o þe rode se Faste nailed to þe tre, Iesu mi lefman" (no. 36); "Quanne I zenke onne þe rode" (no. 37) See also Rosemary Woolf, *The English Religious Lyric in the Middle Ages* (Oxford, 1968): "No Latin original for this is known, though it has various manuscript ascriptions: in St. John's 15, for instance, it is described as *verba Sancti Augustini et Sancti Bernardi*. There is, however, nothing in the verse to suggest that it is a paraphrase of one of the great Latin commonplaces" (pp. 33- 34). □ *Other authorities* 124a.25- 28: Seneca, *Epistola ad Lucillium* 1.4.2; 124va.29- 34: Petrus Comestor, *Historia Scholastica*, Evangelia 192 (PL 198: 1640b- c). □ *Schneyer* T29

131 *Folios* 125a □ *Running title* Dominica 3a post pascha [later hand] □ *Source book* Minimus □ *Theme* Eratis enim sicut oves errantes sed nunc conversi estis ad pastorem et episcopum animarum vestrarum (1 Petr 2:25) □ *Incipit* In hiis verbis notantur status duplicis hominis status, scilicet, peccatoris, status hominis penitentis □ *Explicit* Universaliter Joel, convertimini ad me in toto corde vestro perseveranter; Apostolus qui perseveraverit □ *Marginalia* none □ *Schneyer* T30

132 *Folios* 125b □ *Running title* none □ *Source book* Parvus Rubeus □ *Theme* Christus semel pro peccatis nostris mortuus est (1 Petr 3:18) □ *Incipit* Hic notantur patientis dignitas ibi Christus, pene acerbitas *mortuus* □ *Explicit* quid faceret postea de faciente □ *Marginalia* none □ *Schneyer* T30

133 *Folios* 125b- 126a □ *Running title* none □ *Source book* Parvus Rubeus □ *Theme* Christus passus est pro nobis relinquens exemplum (1 Petr 2:21) □ *Incipit* Nota quod Christus mortuus est pro iniustis Pe 4 □ *Explicit* Sap x Justum deduxit Dominus per vias rectas. Vie recte sunt tribulationes ac item introducendus ut supra □ *Marginalia* none □ *Notes* Petrus de Remis OP †1247: see Schneyer, *Repertorium* 4: 727, no. 43. □ *Schneyer* T30

134 *Folios* 126b □ *Running title* none □ *Source book* Parvus Rubeus □ *Theme* Christus passus est etc. (1 Petr 2:21) □ *Incipit* Solent heredes petere, post mortem patris, quid ei testamento reliquerit □ *Thema* Quattuor hic tanguntur, patientia, dignitas □ *Explicit* quod non potest ea invenire quid dicit Job 23, Vestigia eius secutus est pes meus □ *Marginalia* none □ *Vernacular phrases* "dicitur anglice. Wo is ute bisteken he is inne forgeten" (fol. 126b.7- 8) □ This phrase is found at the end of the antitheme in the sermon above on the sufferings of Christ. The preacher is emphasising the use of reminders. Cf. *The Proverbs of Alfred*, ed. R. Morris in *An Old English Miscellany*, Early English Texts Society 49 (London, 1872): "Foe he þat is ute biloken, he is inne sone forgeten" (p. 134.554- 556). Morris dated the original text about 1250; the manuscript has since disappeared from the British Library. □ *Schneyer* T30

135 *Folios* 126va–126vb □ *Runnning title* none □ *Source book* Parvus Rubeus □ *Theme* Christus passus est pro nobis relinquens exemplum etc. (1 Petr 2:21) □ *Incipit* Tria hic tanguntur, Christi passio ibi, *Christus passus;* nostra imitatio ibi, *ut sequamini vestigia eius* □ *Explicit* ad regnum pervenire valemus quia Ac 14, per multas tribulationes oportet nos intrare in regnum celorum □ *Marginalia* none □ *Schneyer* T30

136 *Folios* 127a–127vb □ *Runnning title* none □ *Source book* Niger Maior □ *Theme* Christus passus est pro nobis etc. (1 Petr 2:21) □ *Incipit* Nuper tempore passionis, Dominice multa audivimus de eius passionis; nunc interiectis paschalibus solempnis □ *Thema* Tria hic notanda sunt, quod Christus passus est, quod pro nobis, quod nobis in exemplum □ *Explicit* sic qui Christum iterum peccando crucifigunt, et eius sanguinem fundunt, maledicti sunt et cum reprobis ibunt in supplicium eternum □ *Marginalia* unidentified ann. □ *Notes* Margin Note: Dominica secunda post pascha anno circuli lun' vi predicatur apud Eln'. □ *Schneyer* T30

137 *Folios* 128a–128b □ *Runnning title* none □ *Source book* Rubeus Maior □ *Theme* Christus passus est etc. (1 Petr 2:21) □ *Incipit* Hic tria notantur, videlicet, passionis Christi rememoratio, caritatis Christi insinuatio, et vite nostre informatio □ *Explicit* quando non tantum suspenditur sed inter latrones, quasi esset unus eorum; econtra superbi Mt: amant primos recubitus □ *Marginalia* unidentified ann. □ *Schneyer* T30

138 *Folios* 128b; 129a–129vb □ *Runnning title* none □ *Source book* Proprius □ *Theme* Christus passus est etc. (1 Petr 2:21) □ *Incipit* Scriptum est in Ps. Verbo Domini celi firmati sunt □ *Thema* Verba sunt Beati Petri et innuunt nobis duo □ *Explicit* Item mulier que sanguinis fluxum patiebatur tremens tetigit fimbriam vestimenti Christi □ *Marginalia* none □ *Notes* This sermon is in the latter part of the replacement bifolia □ *Schneyer* T30

139 *Folios* 128va–128vb □ *Runnning title* Dominica 3a post pascha □ *Source book* de libro Augustini □ *Theme* Ego sum pastor bonus (Jo 10:11) □ *Incipit* Dominus Deus, noster Christus, centum oves habuit sed una de agro Domini sui □ *Explicit* sic oves reficit in presenti, deinde in futuro reficiet de hiis que nec oculus vidit etc. □ *Marginalia* none □ *Schneyer* T30

140 *Folios* 129vb □ *Runnning title* none □ *Source book* Parvus Rubeus □ *Theme* Sequamini vestigia eius (1 Petr 2:21) □ *Incipit* In cordis puritate quod spectat ad contritionem □ *Explicit* resistimus imminentibus iam temptationibus et peccatis □ *Marginalia* none □ *Schneyer* T30

141 *Folios* 130a–130vb □ *Runnning title* Dominica 4 post pascha □ *Source book* Parvus Rubeus □ *Theme* Obsecro vos tanquam advenas et peregrinos etc. (1 Petr 2:11) □ *Incipit* Tria sunt hic notanda, scilicet, quid monetur abstinere, scilicet, a carnalibus desideriis □ *Explicit* te solam desiderant, optabunt qui te veementer oderunt, apo 9; desiderabunt mori, et fugiet mora ab eis □ *Marginalia* none □ *Schneyer* T31

142 *Folios* 131a–132vb □ *Running title* none □ *Source book* Proprius □ *Theme* Obsecro vos tanquam advenas et peregrinos etc. (1 Petr 2:11) □ *Incipit* Cibus mentis, secundum Gregorium, est verbum Dei □ *Thema* Beatus Petrus custos et prelatus totius Ecclesie in epistola hodierna subditos suos quibus de iure imperare potuit □ *Explicit* Job 40; Neemoth in locis humentibus habitat; loci humentis sunt gulosi et luxuriosi □ *Marginalia* enumeration □ *Schneyer* T31

143 *Folios* 132a □ *Running title* Dominica 4 post pascha □ *Source book* Parvus Rubeus □ *Theme* Vado ad eum qui me misit (Jo 16:5) □ *Incipit* In hiis verbis possunt notari duo, scilicet, vite nostre transitus, et quo transire debeamus □ *Explicit* utique ad illum Patrem, a quo omnis paternitas in celo et in terra eph 3 □ *Marginalia* none □ *Schneyer* T32

144 *Folios* 132b–132vb □ *Running title* none □ *Source book* Proprius fol. 6 □ *Theme* Vado ad eum qui me misit (Jo 16:5) □ *Incipit* In epistola hodierna legitur, sit omnis homo velox ad audiendum, scilicet, verbum Dei □ *Thema* Quasi dicat sicut misit me Pater a summo celo ad terras carnem ab homine assumpturum et pro homine moriturum □ *Explicit* diligamus ergo Deum ex toto corde etc. Et dicatur aliqua narratio de dilectione proximi □ *Marginalia* enumeration □ *Schneyer* T32

145 *Folios* 133a–134vb □ *Running title* none □ *Source book* Proprius fol. 1 or 7 [?MS] □ *Theme* Vado ad eum qui me misit me (Jo 16:5) □ *Incipit* Christus, Dei filius, qui ab initio, sicut dicit Apostolus, dilexit nos, cum transiret de hoc mundo ad Patrem, in finem etiam dilexit nos. □ *Explicit* Eia ergo advocata nostra illos tuos misericordes oculos ad nos converte, et Jesum benedictum fructum ventris tui, nobis post hoc exilium ostende. □ *Marginalia* none □ *Notes* The explicit is the latter part of the "Salve Regina," the Marian antiphon used at the end of Compline during the year. □ *Schneyer* T32

146 *Folios* 135a–137a □ *Running title* none □ *Source book* Parvus Niger .67 □ *Theme* Vado ad eum qui me misit (Jo 16:5) □ *Incipit* Tria sunt genera auditorum, quidam sermonem Dei audire contempnunt □ *Thema* In hiis verbis duo possunt notari Christi, labor in via et eius bravium in patria □ *Explicit* Recogitate eum, qui talem sustinuit a peccatoribus adversus semetipsum contradictionem, ut ne fatigemini animis vestris deficientes et hec de via □ *Marginalia* unidentified ann. □ *Schneyer* T32

147 *Folios* 137a–137vb □ *Running title* Dominica ii post pascha □ *Source book* Niger Minor □ *Theme* Cum malediceretur non maledicebat etc. (1 Petr 2: 23) □ *Incipit* Duppliciter experitur patientia, verbis scilicet et verberibus □ *Explicit* ergo quecumque contumelia tibi dicatur vera est, igitur quantamcumque contumeliam patienter debes sustinere □ *Marginalia* unidentified ann. □

Notes Up to fol.180 this is the second sermon only to be out of liturgical order. □ *Schneyer* T30

148 *Folios* 137vb- 138a □ *Runnning title* none □ *Source book* Parvus Rubeus 1.38.20. black; 38.20.red □ *Theme* Estote factores verbi et non auditores tantum (Jac 1:22) □ *Incipit* Ut supplicium gravius vitemus Luc 2: ille servus qui cognovit voluntatem Domini et non fecit □ *Explicit* administrantur vobis introitus in regnum eternum et ideo Joh' 2: qui facit voluntatem Dei manet in eternum sicut Deus manet in eternum □ *Marginalia* none □ *Notes* This sermon is very similar to Sermon 156. □ *Schneyer* T33

149a *Folios* 138a- 138b □ *Runnning title* none □ *Source book* none □ *Theme* Vir duplex est (Jac 1:8) □ *Incipit* Vas beneficiis vacuum, exemplum de doleo quod sonat vacuum □ *Explicit* qui promisit homini immortalitatem, Deo assimilationem, et maiorem scientiam, sed persolvit penitus contraria □ *Marginalia* none □ *Notes* All of 149a- c and 150 are introduced by a large flourished initial; 149a- c seem to be sermon material rather than sermons. □ *Schneyer* T33

149b *Folios* 138b (8 lines) □ *Source book* none □ *Incipit* Ignis sine calore; quippe sunt ignis depictus a longe, apparet calidus □ *Explicit* Iste est rectus ordo, quia ab interiore caritate debent procedere verba □ *Marginalia* none □ *Schneyer* none

149c *Folios* 138b (8 lines) □ *Source book* none □ *Incipit* Fons sine humore fons enim est per apparentiam, sed caret aqua □ *Explicit* Dilectio sine emulatione □ *Marginalia* none □ *Schneyer* none

150 *Folios* 138b- 138va □ *Source book* none □ *Incipit* Iactator graviter egrotat, quippe bona opera sunt cibus spiritualis anime □ *Explicit* mal 1: dixistis, ecce de labore et exsufflastis illud □ *Marginalia* none □ *Notes* In the side margin is the annotation: "Distinctio." □ *Schneyer* none

151 *Folios* 138va.35- 138vb.41 □ *Running title* none □ *Source book* none □ *Theme* none □ *Incipit* Ad vestium vilitatem, Augustinus, non affectitis vestibus placere sed moribus □ *Explicit* Econtraria etiam esse deberet; Ps edent pauperes et saturabuntur □ *Marginalia* none □ *Schneyer* none

152 *Folios* 139a- 141a □ *Running title* none □ *Source book* Confessiones Augustini □ *Theme* Petite et accipietis ut gaudium vestrum sit plenum (Jo 16:24) □ *Incipit* In hiis verbis tria tanguntur, primo monet ut petamus, secundo docet quid petere debeamus, tertio permittit ut petendi fiduciam habeamus □ *Explicit* sed potius ictus, sic nec religiosus absentans se a communitate, exemplum parva pira parva oboli veteres nummi per se non recipiatur in emptione, et tamen inter alios multos bene admittuntur □ *Marginalia* unidentified ann. □ *Schneyer* T33

153 *Folios* 141a- 142b □ *Runnning title* none □ *Source book* Proprius □ *Theme* Si quid petieritis Patrem in nomine meo etc. (Jo 16:23) □ *Incipit* Sermo

noster hodiernus erit de oratione; ad hanc nos admonet lectio evangelica □
Thema Dominus noster pius Jesus magnam audaciam orandi magnamque
fiduciam impetrandi singulis in hoc confert evangelio fidelibus □ *Explicit* Illa
enim ostendit Filio pectus et ubera; Filius ostendit Patre latus et vulnera; non
potest oratio esse repulsa ubi tot caritatis occurrunt insignia □ *Marginalia*
unidentified ann. □ *Notes* Margin Note: Iste sermo predicatur aput Elnest'
Dominica proxima ante Ascensionem a.do^i m.cc.lxxv □ *Schneyer* T33

   154 *Folios* 142a–142vb □ *Runnning title* none □ *Source book* Proprius □
Theme Petite et accipietis ut gaudium vestrum sit plenum (Jo 16:24) □ *Incipit*
Evangelium hodiernum multum nobis commendat orationem, spem promittens
petentibus petita recipere □ *Thema* In hiis verbis primo monet nos Dominus
ad petendum ibi *petite*; secundo quid petere debeamus ibi *ut gaudium vestrum
sit plenum*; tertio impetrandi fiduciam confert ibi *accipietis* □ *Explicit* Qui ergo
videre Deum sicut est desiderat, in ipsa figat oculos, in ipsa cohabitet, in ipsa
quiescat, ut cum ipsa sine fine requiescat □ *Marginalia* unidentified ann. □
Notes This sermon possesses very extensive interlinear comment in a later
hand. □ *Schneyer* T33

   155 *Folios* 142v, bottom margin note □ *Source book* none □ *Incipit* O
lacrima cum oratione humili □ *Explicit* ordinabiliter tibi, sociabiliter proximo,
humiliter Deo. □ *Marginalia* none □ *Notes* Nota infra 6.20 (ie. 203, fol. 166b);
this piece is probably sermon material. □ *Schneyer* none

   156 *Folios* 143a–143b □ *Runnning title* none □ *Source book* Rubeus Maior
□ *Theme* Estote factores verbi et non auditores tantum (Jac 1:22) □ *Incipit* Ut
supplicium gravius vitemus quia Luce 2 ille servus qui cognovit □ *Explicit* et
ideo Jo 2; qui facit voluntatem Dei manet in eternum, quoniam Deus manet
in eternum □ *Marginalia* none □ *Notes* This text is similar to Sermon 148. □
Schneyer T33

   157 *Folios* 143b–144a □ *Runnning title* none □ *Source book* Rubeus Maior
□ *Theme* In hoc vocati estis ut hereditate possideatis benedictionem (1 Petr 3:9)
□ *Incipit* In hiis verbis duo notantur, unum quod spectat ad gratiam, ibi in *hoc
vocati estis*, aliud quod spectat ad gloriam *ut hereditate* etc. □ *Explicit* ad istam
benedictionem vocati sumus sed quis inveniet eam? Ille qui queret eam ut
rorem, scilicet, mane; unde qui mane vigilant ad me invenient me □
Marginalia none □ *Schneyer* none

   158 *Folios* 144b (32 lines) □ *Runnning title* In die ascensionis □ *Source
book* Rubeus Maior □ *Theme* Ascendo ad Patrem meum et Patrem vestrum etc.
(Jo 20:17) □ *Incipit* Duo sunt que precipue impellunt tristitiam ab aliquo divi
ab eo separatur □ *Explicit* Ascendens in altum captivam duxit captivitatem □
Marginalia none □ *Schneyer* T36

   159 *Folios* 144b–144va (15 lines) □ *Runnning title* In die ascensionis
Domini □ *Source book* Rubeus Maior □ *Theme* Ascende ad me in montem et

esto ibi ex 24 (Ex 24:12) □ *Incipit* Hic notatur ascensus in eminentia vite □ *Explicit* perseverans scilicet in bonis □ *Marginalia* none □ *Schneyer* T36

160 *Folios* 144va-145a □ *Running title* none □ *Source book* Parvus Rubeus □ *Theme* Levabo ad celum manum meam etc. (Deut 32:40) □ *Incipit* Christus dicitur manus propter magnum laborem et modicam sumptuositatem □ *Explicit* penitens vero semper speret de venia ad protegendum ys 49, sub umbra manus sue protexit me □ *Marginalia* unidentified ann. □ *Schneyer* T36

161 *Folios* 145a-145b □ *Running title* none □ *Source book* Rubeus Maior □ *Theme* Ascendet iter pandens ante eos mich 2 (Mich 2:13) □ *Incipit* Ascendet pandens quia via ignota fuit; ideo quidam volentes ascendere ceciderunt ut Lucifer, Adam, filii Sem □ *Explicit* Ps. Iniquitates mee supergresse sunt caput meum □ *Marginalia* none □ *Notes* In the MS the Scripture reference precedes the Theme. □ *Schneyer* T36

162 *Folios* 145b-148a □ *Running title* none □ *Source book* Parvus Rubeus □ *Theme* Hic Jesus qui assumptus est a vobis in celum, sic veniet etc. ac.1 (Act 1:11) □ *Incipit* Duo hic tanguntur, quorum primum nos erigit in spem, secundum deprimit nos per timorem □ *Explicit* qui oderunt te induentur confusione, et Ps. operientur sicut diploide confusione sua; et ys in finem; erunt usque ad satietatem visionis omni carni □ *Marginalia* scribal ann. □ *Notes* In the Bottom Margin of fol.148a is a note: *Antithema quando voluis* in distinction form, starting *Scriptura.* □ *Schneyer* T36

163 *Folios* 148b □ *Running title* Dominica ia post ascensionem □ *Source book* Rubeus Maior □ *Theme* Vigilate in orationibus, pe 4 (1 Petr 4:7) □ *Incipit* Hoc enim faciendum est multis rationibus, scilicet, ut Christum et sanctos eius imitemur □ *Explicit* Luc 18, oportet semper orare et non deficere □ *Lemmata* [2]: Orandum est ut; Orandum est □ *Marginalia* distinc. □ *Schneyer* T37

164 *Folios* 148va-149a □ *Running title* none □ *Source book* Proprius □ *Theme* Ante omnia <fratres> mutuam caritatem habentes (1 Petr 4:8) □ *Incipit* Sermo noster hodiernus erit de amore. Amor enim in amantis voluntate tria solet efficere etc., ut supra in sermone, "super omnia habetis etc." □ *Thema* In hiis verbis monet nos beatus Petrus ad duo: ad habendum ante omnia caritatem; et habendi ponit rationem ibi quia caritas operit multitudinem peccatorum □ *Explicit* Caritas ergo toto cordis desiderio amplectanda est, quia caritas / locumplectat / mortuum vivificat / in celum introducit □ *Marginalia* none □ *Notes* See Sermon 31. The distinction ends the *explicit.* □ *Schneyer* T37

165 *Folios* 149b-149vb □ *Running title* none □ *Source book* Proprius □ *Theme* Estote prudentes et vigilate in orationibus (1 Petr 4:7) □ *Incipit* In principio sermonis nostri invocemus salvatoris suffragium □ *Thema* Legitur quod tempore isto medio inter ascensionem et pentecosten □ *Explicit* quare tam necligentes sunt et tepidi Ecclesiam adire, orationem proferre, Deum invocare, cum dulcis sit labor et parum durans per que celestia comparantur,

mirum est □ *Marginalia* unidentified ann. □ *Notes* Guilelmus Peraldus OP: see Schneyer, *Repertorium* 2: 547, no. 183. □ *Schneyer* T37

166 *Folios* 150a □ *Runnning title* Sermo fratris H de Mordon in die pent' □ *Source book* none □ *Theme* Repleti sunt omnes Spiritu Sancto (Act 2:4) □ *Incipit* Quando festum alicuius magnatis debet commendari, oportet ut tria concurrant; quod multi sint vocati, quod habundanter exhibiti, quod de bono procurati □ *Explicit* Omne datum optimum et omne donum perfectum etc. □ *Marginalia* none □ *Notes* Liturgical day: in die pent', Whit Sunday. □ *Schneyer* T39

167 *Folios* 150a–150va □ *Runnning title* In die pentecosten □ *Source book* Proprius □ *Theme* Spiritus Domini replevit orbem terrarum (Sap 1:7) □ *Incipit* Invocemus Spiritum Sanctum in principio sermonis nostri, ut descendat super nos et inflammet dono scientie sue □ *Thema* Spiritus iste Spiritus Sanctus est qui hodierna die a throno procedens Apostolorum pectora invisibilia penetrabit □ *Explicit* Ignis iste neminem accendit iracundum, nec invidia repletum: exemplum de illo nobili cuius cor noluit comburi nisi prius extracto veneno etc. □ *Marginalia* unidentified ann. □ *Notes* The Thema is related to the Third Responsory for Matins of Pentecost: BL MS Add. 23935, fol. 298vb; OP Breviary 1: 352; Sarum Breviary 1: mvi (see p. 381 below). □ *Schneyer* T39

168 *Folios* 150vb–151b □ *Runnning title* none □ *Source book* Confessiones Augustini □ *Theme* Apparuerunt illis dispertite lingue etc. (Act 2:3) □ *Incipit* Adveniens hodie, Spiritus Sanctus in Apostolos Domini linguis igneis apparuit suum nobis demonstravit effectum □ *Explicit* Ignis lucidus est sic de eloquium Domini unde Luc 3; nemo accendit lucernam et ponit sub modio etc. □ *Marginalia* unidentified ann. □ *Schneyer* T39

169 *Folios* 151va–151vb □ *Runnning title* Dominica de trinitate □ *Source book* Parvus Rubeus / Rubeus Minor □ *Theme* Tres sunt quoniam testimonium dant in celo (1 Jo 5:7) □ *Incipit* Primo videndum qui sunt illi tres testes, secundo ubi ferant testimonium, tertio quando est quibus □ *Explicit* separatum est enim convivium eorum ab aliis etc. Similiter nec luxuriosi etc. □ *Marginalia* none □ *Notes* The rubrics for source book conflict: the black writing indicates *Parvus Rubeus*; while the red writing indicates *Rubeus Minor*. □ *Schneyer* T40

170 *Folios* 152a–152b □ *Runnning title* Dominica ia post trin' □ *Source book* Proprius □ *Theme* Fili recordare quia recepisti bona etc. (Lc 16:25) □ *Incipit* Scitis quoniam cera ab igne calefacta liquescit, ab igne vero elongata durescit; set cor hominis et mulieris est sicut cera □ *Thema* Narretur transcurrendo vis evangelii horribile multum est quod legitur in evangelio hodierno □ *Explicit* Ad hanc perfectam indesinantemque jocunditatem habendam, precipue cum detestatione peccati, valet mortis memoria sicut dicit sap: memorare novissima tua etc. □ *Marginalia* none □ *Schneyer* T42

171 *Folios* 152va–152vb □ *Runnning title* Dominica iia post trin' □ *Source book* Proprius □ *Theme* Homo quidam fecit cenam magnam (Lc 14:16) □ *Incipit*

Narretur evangelium et fiat oratio; homo iste Dominus noster est Jesus Christus □ *Thema* Immensa Christi potestas ibi *fecit cenam magnam*; et excellens Christi liberalitas ibi *vocavit multos* □ *Explicit* Item, propter que et quot, convivium magnum erit, quere in sermone: *Implete ydrias* □ *Marginalia* none □ *Notes* Hugonis de S. Caro OP: see Schneyer, *Repertorium* 2: 762, no. 62. The sermons with the theme, "Implete hydrias" are 25, 26. □ *Schneyer* T43

172 *Folios* 153a □ *Runnning title* none □ *Source book* Minimus □ *Theme* Homo quidam fecit cenam magnam (Lc 14:16) □ *Incipit* Tria tanguntur in hiis verbis perfecta, Christi humilitas *homo quidam*; eius operative potestas, *fecit cenam magnam*; excellens eius liberalitas, *vocavit multos* □ *Explicit* Ideo nec mirum si admirans dixit Petrus; Domine tu michi lavas pedes □ *Marginalia* none □ *Schneyer* T43

173 *Folios* 153b- 153vb □ *Runnning title* none □ *Source book* Minimus □ *Theme* Multi sunt vocati etc. (Mt 22:14) □ *Incipit* Duo in hiis verbis tanguntur scilicet, vocatio multorum et electio paucorum: circa primum tria; primo si vocantur multi, secundo ad quid sint vocati; tertio de modo vocandi □ *Explicit* quare debet habere propositum de non committendo quere alibi □ *Marginalia* unidentified ann. □ *Notes* The phrase "quere alibi" is rubricated. □ *Schneyer* T43

174a *Folios* 154a- 154vb □ *Runnning title* Dominica 3a post trin' □ *Source book* Proprius □ *Theme* Humiliamini sub potenti manu Dei etc. (1 Petr 5:6) □ *Incipit* Tria dicit hic Apostolus quod humiliandum sit, ibi humiliamini et cui humiliandum □ *Explicit* III Reg 2, sedit rex super tronum suum, positusque est tronus matris ad dexteram eius, et sedit super tronum suum etc. □ *Marginalia* none □ *Schneyer* T44

174b *Folios* 154, bottom margin □ *Runnning title* none □ *Source book* none □ *Theme* Humiliamini etc. (1 Petr 5:6) □ *Incipit* Verba sunt beati Petri et tanguntur hic tria remedia tribus viciis principalibus respondentia □ *Explicit* sed quia sine Deo nichil possumus. Rogemus etc. □ *Notes* The margin note indicates that this is an Antitheme, possibly of 174a. □ *Schneyer* T44

175 *Folios* 154vb □ *Marginalia* none □ *Religious authorities* 154vb.34- 38: cf. Gregory, *Moralia in Iob* 24.11.27 (PL 76: 301C); 154vb.39- 43: Gregory, *Moralia in Iob* 15.17.21 (PL 75: 1092B) □ *Notes* Three quotations (one of which has not been identified) from Gregory, *Moralia in Iob*: (a) l[iber]'mor[alium] 6: Legem daturus ... caliginem erroris obscuraret; (b) l' 24: Hostis noster ... necligit expugnare; (c) l' 15: Luet que fecit ... vivet in pena. □ *Schneyer* T44

176 *Folios* 155a.1- 21 □ *Source book* none □ *Marginalia* none □ *Religious authorities* 155a.6- 9: cf. Augustine, *De trinitate* 4.proem (PL 42: 885, 887); 155a.10- 11: Pseudo- Augustine, *De diligendo Deo* 8 (PL 40: 854) □ *Notes* Quotations on humility (seven in all, five of which are not identified) from Augustine. □ *Schneyer* T44

177 *Folios* 155a.22–41 □ *Source book* none □ *Religious authorities* 155a.22–24: Gregory, *Homiliae in Evangelia* 1.7.4 (PL 76: 1103A); 155a.25–26: Gregory, *Moralia in Iob* 19.21.34 (PL 76: 119C); 155a.27–28: cf. Gregory, *Moralia in Iob* 22.7.16–17 (PL 76: 222–223) □ *Marginalia* none □ *Notes* Quotations on humility (seven in all, four of which are not identified) from Gregory. □ *Schneyer* T44

178 *Folios* 155b □ *Source book* none □ *Marginalia* none □ *Religious authorities* 155b.1–2: Bernard, *Sermones in Cantica* 16.10 (PL 183: 853AB); 155b.3–5: Bernard, *Super 'Missus est angelus' homiliae* 4.9 (PL 183: 84C) □ *Notes* Quotations on humility (ten in all, eight of which are not identified) from Bernard. □ *Schneyer* T44

179 *Folios* 155va □ *Runnning title* none □ *Source book* none □ *Incipit* Humilitas est utilis / ut faciliter intretur ad regnum / ut evadatur demonis aspectus / ut evadatur diaboli laqueus □ *Explicit* evadet laqueos diaboli □ *Marginalia* none □ *Notes* This item is a distinction on humility. □ *Schneyer* T44

180a *Folios* 155va–155vb □ *Source book* none □ *Incipit* Ex propria estimatione quia qui □ *Explicit* illam administret sicut boni dispensatores etc. □ *Lemmata* [1]: Humilitas perpenditur ei □ *Marginalia* marginal heading: Qui se humiliat exaltabitur □ *Notes* This piece is a set of Distinctions on Humility. □ *Schneyer* T44

180b *Folios* 155vb: 24–41 □ *Runnning title* none □ *Source book* none □ *Incipit* Tum propter retributionis modum □ *Explicit* Alioquin erit illud Ps. ascendunt ad celos etc. □ *Marginalia* none □ *Notes* The title, *Humili debetur exaltatio,* is found in mid-column at the start of the text. □ *Schneyer* T44

181 *Folios* 155v: 43–46 □ *Source book* none □ *Incipit* Obediendum est non solum exterius sed interius □ *Explicit* interiora eius plena sunt <dolo> ... . □ *Marginalia* none □ *Notes* This is a piece on obedience. The end of this brief text is lost in the binding. □ *Schneyer* T44

182 *Folios* 156a–157a □ *Runnning title* none □ *Source book* Niger Maior □ *Theme* Humiliamini sub potenti manu Dei etc. (1 Petr 5:6) □ *Incipit* Quattuor sunt cause humilitatis paupertas, vilitatis conditio impotentia merendi □ *Explicit* quod si Pater est abbas et omnes fideles eius monachi, omnes sumus a servitute liberati □ *Marginalia* de manu H' □ *Schneyer* T44

183 *Folios* 157b–157b: 41–44 □ *Runnning title* none □ *Source book* Parvus Rubeus 1.64 □ *Theme* Humiliamini sub potenti manu Dei etc. (1 Petr 5:6) □ *Incipit* Tria dicuntur quod humiliandum est, propter quam utilitatem humiliandum propter se, et propter alias virtutes quod patet auctoritate et ratione □ *Explicit* presbitero humilia animam tuam quantum ad interiorem et magnato etc., quantum ad exteriorem □ *Marginalia* none □ *Schneyer* T44

184 *Folios* 157va-158a □ *Runnning title* none □ *Source book* Parvus Rubeus 2 ii □ *Theme* Humiliamini sub potenti manu Dei etc. (1 Petr 5:6) □ *Incipit* Tria dicuntur quod humiliandum sit, et cui, et propter quid, ut dicitur supra, de humilitate que superbie opponitur dicendum □ *Explicit* et hoc ut nos instrueret et formaret docendo humilitatem □ *Marginalia* unidentified ann. □ *Schneyer* T44

185 *Folios* 158b-159b □ *Runnning title* Dominica 4a post trin' □ *Source book* Proprius □ *Theme* Estote misericordes etc. (Lc 6:36) □ *Incipit* In evangelio hodierno invitat Dominus omnes fideles ad misericordiam, et hoc ad similitudinem Dei Patris □ *Explicit* veniens Christus ad iudicium ante de misericordia disputat quam iudicet de reatu □ *Marginalia* enumeration □ *Notes* This sermon has marginal drawings of at least nine devil faces. □ *Schneyer* T45

186 *Folios* 159va-159vb □ *Runnning title* none □ *Source book* Parvus Rubeus 231.4 □ *Theme* Estote misericordes etc. (Lc 6:36) □ *Incipit* Augustinus: O anima insignita Dei ymagine, decorata eius similitudine, dotata fide, redempta sanguine, particeps beatitudinis, capax bonitatis □ *Explicit* et egrediamur ad regem Israel, forsitan salvabit animas nostras □ *Marginalia* none □ *Schneyer* T45

187 *Folios* 160a-160va.27 □ *Runnning title* none □ *Source book* Parvus Rubeus 229.1 □ *Theme* Estote misericordes etc. (Lc 6:36) □ *Incipit* Ecc° miserere anime tue □ *Explicit* ut revertamur munera promittit □ *Marginalia* none □ *Religious authorities* (a catena of patristic and theological quotations) 160a.11-13: cf. Augustine, *Enarrationes in Psalmos* 36.8 (PL 36: 388); 160a.13-21: Augustine, *Epistulae* 127.5 (PL 33: 486); 160a.27-36: cf. Augustine, *Enarrationes in Psalmos* 38.12 (PL 36: 422-424); 160a.43-160b.6: Bernard, *Sermones in sanctis: in purificatione B. Mariae* 1.2 (PL 183: 366D); 160b.6-9: Augustine, *De civitate Dei* 9.5 (PL 41: 261); 160b.10-11: Ambrose, *Expositio Evangeli secundum Lucam* 3.9-14 (PL 15: 1662D); 160b.12-18, "*Glosa chrysostom super idem*": cf. pseudo-Chyrsostom, *Eruditi commentarii evangelium Matthaei incerto auctore* 26.10.40 (PG 56: 770); 160b.25-29: Augustine, *De civitate Dei* 9.5 (PL 41: 260-261); 160b.31-38: Anselm, *Proslogion* 9, *Opera omnia*, ed. F.S. Schmitt [6 vols., Edinburgh, 193-1961], 1: 107.22-25); 160b.40-42: cf. Peter of Ravenna, *Sermones* 8 (PL 52: 211A); 160b.42-46: Peter of Ravenna, *Sermones* 42 (PL 52: 318C); 160va.1-3: Peter of Ravenna, *Sermones* 3 (PL 52: 193A); 160va.4-5: cf. Peter of Ravenna, *Sermones* 2 (PL 52: 188B); 160va.5-9: Gregory, *Moralia in Iob* 20.36.25 (PL 76: 180B); 160va.12-23: probably from Cassiodorus, *Expositio psalmorum*, not from the letters. □ *Notes* Unidentified religious authorities: Augustine (1); Bernard (2); Glosa Chrysostom (1); Gregory (1); Peter of Ravenna (1). □ *Schneyer* T45

188 *Folios* 160va.28-161b.6 □ *Runnning title* none □ *Source book* Parvus Rubeus 8.1 □ *Incipit* Augustinus: Qui elemosyna dat tedio interpellantis □ *Explicit* panis esurientem est quod tu detines nudorum vestimentum, quod tu recludis etc. □ *Marginalia* none □ *Religious authorities* (a catena of patristic and theological quotations) 160va.28–30: Augustine, *Enarrationes in Psalmos* 42.8 (PL 36: 482); 160va.31–32: cf. Augustine, *Sermones* 123.5 (PL 38: 686); 160vb.8–9: not Augustine but Leo the Great, *Sermo in II Quadragesima*, (see Ermenelgido Lio, "Finalmente rintracciata la fonte del famoso testo patristico 'Pasce fame morientem ...,'" *Antonianum* 27 [1952], 349–366, esp. 356); 160vb.10–13: cf. Gregory, *Homiliae in Evangelia* 2.37.5 (PL 76: 1277 AB); 160vb.14–15: Gregory, *Homiliae in Evangelium* 2.37.5 (PL 76: 1277B); 160vb.19–22: Gregory, *Regula pastoralis* 3.21.22 (PL 77: 87B); 160vb.23–27: Gregory, *Moralia in Iob* 12.51.57 (PL 75: 1013A); 160vb.28–31: Augustine, *Sermones* 82.3.5 (PL 38: 508); 161a.1–4: Gregory, *Moralia in Iob* 12.51.57 (PL 75: 1013B); 161a.5–8: Gregory, *Moralia in Iob* 12.51.57 (PL 75: 1013B); 161a.28–31: cf. Ambrose, *De Nabuthe Jezraelitica* 12.53 (PL 14: 783B); 161a.32–34: not Bede, but cf. Rabanus Maurus *Commentaria in Matthaeum* 4, in Mt 12:13 (PL 107: 923A); 161a.38–39 not Bede, but cf. Peter Lombard, *Collectanea in epistolas S. Pauli*, in Ep. 1 ad Tim. (PL 192: 348D); 161b.2–6: not Ambrose but Basil, *Homiliae quas transtulit Rufinus* 3 (PG 31: 1752BC). □ *Notes* Unidentified religious authorities: Augustine (9); Bede (2); Gregory (4); Jerome (1); Leo Papa (1); Rabanus Maurus (1). □ *Schneyer* T45

   189 *Folios* 161b: 7–27 □ *Running title* none □ *Source book* Parvus Rubeus 26.25 □ *Incipit* Glosa super idem Mt xii: extende manum tuam,nulla plus valet (cf Mt 12:13) □ *Explicit* ut contraria contrariis curentur □ *Marginalia* none □ *Schneyer* T45

   190 *Folios* 161b: 27–46 □ *Source book* Parvus Rubeus 27.1 □ *Incipit* Septem elemosyne sunt spirituales et septem corporales □ *Explicit* et misericordia ipsius cum ipso est □ *Marginalia* none □ *Schneyer* T45

   191 *Folios* 161va: 1–25 □ *Running title* none □ *Source book* Parvus Rubeus 27.15 □ *Incipit* Prima est conservare a peccato □ *Explicit* ad Thim: reposita est michi corona □ *Marginalia* none □ *Notes* In the left margin, beside the start of the text, are found the words: "Septem sunt misericordie Domini." □ *Schneyer* T45

   192 *Folios* 161va: 26–45 □ *Running title* none □ *Source book* Parvus Rubeus 28.10 □ *Incipit* Misericordia est amor relevandi a miseria □ *Explicit* quam homo miseretur carni sue □ *Marginalia* none □ *Schneyer* T45

   193 *Folios* 161vb.1–31 □ *Running title* none □ *Source book* Parvus Rubeus 33.1 □ *Incipit* Disciplina non est servanda sine misericordia nec econtrario □ *Explicit* nec rigor sit rigidus nec mansuetudo dissoluta □ *Marginalia* marginal headings □ *Notes* "Gregorius in Moralium" is found in the right margin beside the start of the text. □ *Schneyer* T45

   194 *Folios* 161vb–162a □ *Running title* none □ *Source book* Parvus Rubeus 2.35.1 □ *Incipit* Dicitur in Ps: Benigna est misericordia tua, ad differentiam triplicis crudelis misericordie □ *Explicit* peccatoribus (sic) statim ultiones adhibere magni beneficii est iudicium □ *Marginalia* none □ *Schneyer* T45

195 *Folios* 161vb bottom margin □ *Source book* none □ *Marginalia* none □ *Notes* Entire text reads: De triplici miseria peccatoris / Supra in sermone "Cecus sedebat" /Item ibidem de misericordia Dei (cf 42 and 43). □ *Schneyer* T45

196 *Folios* 162a- 162b □ *Source book* Confessiones Augustini fol.ult. □ *Incipit* Tres sunt miserationes Dei circa electos, prima quod invicos ad se venire compellit □ *Explicit* Ps: non secundum peccata nostra fecit nobis etc. □ *Marginalia* none □ *Schneyer* T45

197 *Folios* 162va □ *Running title* Dominica 5a post trin' □ *Source book* Parvus Rubeus □ *Theme* Per totam noctem laborantes etc. (Lc 5:5) □ *Incipit* Tria possunt hic notari de vita cuiuslibet peccatoris, videlicet quod sit tenebrosa, laboriosa, infructuosa □ *Explicit* heres bonitatis, particeps rationis, quid tibi cum carne □ *Marginalia* enumeration □ *Schneyer* T46

198 *Folios* 162vb- 163vb □ *Running title* none □ *Source book* Proprius fol.59 □ *Theme* Omnes unanimes in ratione estote (1 Petr 3:8) □ *Incipit* Officium Ecclesie hodiernum multum et sepe tangit de oratione, □ *Thema* Glosa super illud Psalmi aput me oratio Deo vite mee dicit iustitia hominis in hac vita est ieiunium, oratio, et eleemosyna □ *Explicit* et alia mala verba sentit in Ose et sic de aliis portis □ *Marginalia* enumeration □ *Notes* Guilelmus Peraldus OP: see Schneyer, *Repertorium* 2: 548, no 196; and 443, no. 279. □ *Schneyer* T46

199a *Folios* 164a- 164va.16 □ *Source book* Parvus Rubeus □ *Incipit* Magna est excellentia pure orationis □ *Explicit* aput secretissimas aures Dei valenciores voces sunt vite quam verba □ *Marginalia* none □ *Religious authorities* 164a.1- 4: not Augustine but Peter Lombard, *Commentaria in Psalmos* 87.2 (PL 191: 811D); 164a.5- 6: Augustine, *In Iohannis Evangelium tractatus* 9.2.13 (PL 35: 1464); 164a.7- 10: not Augustine but Isidore, *Sententiae* 3.8.1 (PL 83: 679AB); 164a.11- 12: cf. Augustine, *Enarrationes in Psalmos* 37.14 (PL 36: 404); 164a.15- 19: Augustine, *Epistulae* 3.10.20 (PL 33: 502); 164a.20- 25 cf. Augustine, *Enarrationes in Psalmos* 87.14 (PL 37: 1118); 164a.26- 29: William Peraldus *Summa virtutum* 3.5.7.3; 164a.34- 35: not Gregory, but Hugh of St. Victor, *Exposito super Regulam S. Augustini* 3 (PL 176: 892B); 164a.36- 38: Gregory, *Moralia in Iob* 22.17.43 (PL 76: 238C; see below, 166a.37- 42); 164a.39- 41: Gregory, *Moralia in Iob* 33.22.43 (PL 76: 701B); 164a 42- 164b 4: Gregory, *Moralia in Iob* 9.16.23 (PL 75: 872C); 164b.5- 9: Gregory, *Moralia in Iob* 35.11.21 (PL 76: 761AB); 164b.10- 11: Gregory, *Moralia in Iob* 33.22.43 (PL 76: 701A); 164b.12- 14: Gregory, *Dialogi* 3.15 (PL 77: 256C) □ *Notes* General heading at this point in the MS is: "De Oratione," *nota multa bona de parvo libro rubeo.* This piece is a catena of quotations from the Fathers on prayer: the unidentified religious authorities are from Augustine (1), Gregory (1), and *Summa* (1). □ *Schneyer* T46

199b *Folios* 164va.17-164vb.20 □ *Source book* Parvus Rubeus □ *Incipit* Lectionem frequenter interrumpat oratio □ *Explicit* effugat angelus, aggaudet, tenet, stans cor que ligatur □ *Marginalia* none □ *Notes* A catena of quotations on prayer from the Fathers: Bede, Cassiodorus, Augustine, Origen, etc. □ *Schneyer* T46

200a *Folios* 164vb.21-165a.32 □ *Source book* Parvus Rubeus □ *Incipit* Oratio animam letificat □ *Explicit* et homo exacuit faciem amici sui □ *Marginalia* none □ *Notes* Preaching material on prayer. □ *Schneyer* T46

200b *Folios* 165a.33-165b.15 □ *Source book* Parvus Rubeus □ *Incipit* Ad suscipiendum gratiam Dei se humilitat □ *Explicit* Multi viri misericordia, virum autem fidelem quis inveniret □ *Marginalia* none □ *Notes* Preaching material on prayer. □ *Schneyer* T46

200c *Folios* 165b.16-35 □ *Source book* Parvus Rubeus □ *Incipit* Oratio efficaciter impetrat □ *Explicit* Deus in amorem animarum nostrarum □ *Marginalia* none □ *Notes* Preaching material on prayer. □ *Schneyer* T46

201 *Folios* 165b.37-165vb.6 □ *Source book* Parvus Rubeus □ *Incipit* Petrus Ravenensis: Christus breviter orare docet □ *Explicit* patrem nolite vocare vobis super terram □ *Marginalia* none □ *Notes* A catena of quotations from the Fathers on the *Pater Noster.* □ *Schneyer* T46

202 *Folios* 165vb.7-166b.11 □ *Runnning title* none □ *Source book* Parvus Rubeus □ *Theme* Ps. Benedictus Deus qui non amovit orationem etc. (Ps 65:20) □ *Incipit* Magnum aliquid reputat continuam orationem □ *Explicit* de quo amarior amaritudo nunquam emanat oratio □ *Marginalia* none □ *Religious authorities* 165vb.14-16: Augustine, *De nuptiis et concupiscentia* 1.33.38 (PL 44: 435); 165vb.16-19: Gregory, *Moralia in Iob* 10.15.29 (PL 75: 937A); 165vb.20-28: cf. Cassiodorus, *Expositio in psalmorum* 13.5-6 (CCL 97: 130.163-6); 165vb.29-32: Jerome, *Epistolae* 22.37 (PL 22: 421); 166a.6-9: cf. Gregory, *Moralia in Iob* 1.34.47 (PL 75: 548C); 166a.10-15: Augustine, *De doctrina christiana*, prol. 5 (PL 34: 17); 166a.24-26: Gregory, *Moralia in Iob* 15.47.53 (PL 75: 1108A); 166a.30-34: Augustine, *Enarrationes in Psalmos* 65.24 (PL 36: 801); 166a.37-39: cf. Gregory, *Moralia in Iob* 22.17.43 (PL 76: 238C) □ *Notes* A catena of quotations from the Fathers. Religious authorities not identified: Bernard (2); Jerome (1). □ *Schneyer* T46

203 *Folios* 166b.12-166va.34 □ *Runnning title* none □ *Source book* Parvus Rubeus □ *Incipit* Lacrime Deum cognat □ *Explicit* Ecc° 12 pungens oculum de lacrimis □ *Marginalia* none □ *Notes* *Lacrime* is found as a title in the right margin. Marginal note: fol. 166va (see 155): Nota supra auctoritatem de lacrimis 5.29, O lacrima etc. This is a piece in Distinction style. □ *Schneyer* T46

204 *Folios* 166vb-167vb □ *Runnning title* Dominica 6a post trin' □ *Source book* Proprius □ *Theme* Quicumque baptizati in Christo Jesu etc. (Rom 6:3) □ *Incipit* Legitur in Deut quod Deus loquens ad Moysen dixit: Ligabis verba mea quasi signum in manu tua □ *Thema* In Christo Jesu baptizatus est qui in iustificatione eius scilicet in nomine Sancte Trinitatis baptizatus est □ *Explicit* unde minus misericordes sunt parentes qui nolunt filios suos cito ab hiis ardoribus liberare □ *Marginalia* enumeration □ *Schneyer* T47

205 *Folios* 168a–168vb □ *Runnning title* Dominica 7a post trin' □ *Source book* Proprius □ *Theme* Stipendia peccati mors (Rom 6:23) □ *Incipit* Audiendum est verbum Dei ab omnibus, propter promissionem factam a Domino auditoribus, quibus loquitur □ *Thema* Et notandum quod cum triplex sit mors: carnalis, spiritualis et infernalis □ *Explicit* quoniam stipendia bonorum operum sunt vita eterna ad quam nos perducat etc. □ *Marginalia* none □ *Schneyer* T48

206 *Folios* 169a–170va □ *Runnning title* Dominica 7a post trin' □ *Source book* Proprius □ *Theme* Stipendia peccati mors (Rom 6:23) □ *Incipit* Predicanti verbum Dei tria sunt necessaria, eminentia vite, sapientia sive scientia doctrina, collatio gratie □ *Thema* Verba sunt Apostoli in epistola hodierna sciendum est quod peccatum primi hominis occasio fuit mortis □ *Explicit* Iterum memoria districti iudicii valde motiva est. Jero' sive commedo etc. □ *Marginalia* unidentified ann. □ *Schneyer* T48

207 *Folios* 170vb–171vb □ *Runnning title* Dominica via post trin' □ *Source book* Proprius □ *Theme* Misereor super turbam etc. (Mc 8:2) □ *Incipit* Itinerantes et peregrini precipue cum elongati fuerint a propria patria, singulis diebus in mane, Deum diligenter exorant □ *Thema* Dominum Salvatorem in terris ambulantem et viam celestem instruentem secuta est turba multa usque in solitudinem □ *Explicit* ad celum ibunt, falsi vero in inferni supplicium etc. *finge plura* □ *Marginalia* none □ *Notes* Marginal note reads: Dominica hoc antithema a.d. m.cc.lxx.vii. The theme is taken from the Gospel of the 7th Sunday after Trinity. This contradicts the liturgical reference in the MS. □ *Schneyer* T48

208 *Folios* 172a–173b □ *Runnning title* Dominica viiia post trin' □ *Source book* Proprius □ *Theme* Omnis arbor que non facit fructum bonum (Mt 7:19) □ *Incipit* Quattuor in verbo proposito possunt considerari, primo iudicantis equitas ibi, *omnis arbor* □ *Explicit* unde si decimam non dederis tu ad decimam non voceris etc. □ *Marginalia* none □ *Schneyer* T49

209 *Folios* 173va–175va □ *Runnning title* Dominica 8a post trin' □ *Source book* Parvus Rubeus □ *Theme* Omnis arbor que non facit fructum bonum (Mt 7:19) □ *Incipit* Arbor iste est quilibet electus, can 2, sicut malus inter ligna silvarum □ *Explicit* et erit terra eius in picem ardentem, nocte et die non extinguetur in sempiternis □ *Marginalia* enumeration □ *Schneyer* T49

210 *Folios* 175vb–177vb □ *Runnning title* Dominica ixa post trin' □ *Source book* Proprius □ *Theme* Non simus concupiscentes malorum etc. (1 Cor 10:6) □ *Incipit* Apostolus in epistola hodierna monet nos mala non concupiscere de quibus per nos moniti esse deberemus □ *Explicit* in decimis primitiis et oblationibus vos maledicti estis ecce pena □ *Marginalia* unidentified ann.;

enumeration □ *Notes* There are nine blank lines before the next sermon. □ *Schneyer* T50

211 *Folios* 177vb–178b □ *Runnning title* none □ *Source book* Parvus Rubeus Minor □ *Theme* Neque fornicemur sicut quidam ex eis fornicati sunt (1 Cor 10:8) □ *Incipit* Quare non sit fornicandum multiplex potest assignari ratio □ *Explicit* que enim participatio iustitie cum iniquitate etc. □ *Marginalia* none □ *Schneyer* T50

212 *Folios* 178va–180va □ *Runnning title* none □ *Source book* Niger Minor □ *Theme* Qui se existimat stare videat ne cadat (1 Cor 10:12) □ *Incipit* Rogemus cum Apostolo ut Deus aperiat nobis hostium sermonis sui, quod duplex est: hostium enim per quod exit sermo predicatoris est os; hostium per quod intrat aures sunt audientium, quorum utrumque Deus nobis aperiat ita ut me proponere, et vos saluberrime audire, concedat □ *Thema* Sciendum est quod spiritualiter quidam iacent quidam sedent quidam stant □ *Explicit* Det igitur Deus nobis sic stare, constare, instare, obstare, et substare, ut cum regnare possimus, astare; de qua Ps. astitit regina etc. □ *Marginalia* marginal headings □ *Other authorities* 180b.3–8: cf. Aristotle, *Ethica Nichomachea* 9.9 (1169b33). □ *Schneyer* T50

213 *Folios* 180vb □ *Runnning title* Dominica xa post pent'; post trin' □ *Source book* Proprius 38 □ *Theme* Videns Jesus civitatem Jerusalem flevit super eam (Lc 19:41) □ *Incipit* Si nos omnes hic congregati de necessitate mare transiremus, et venientes ad portum, inveniremus navem fortem et levem □ *Explicit* ut det mihi aliud dicere de evangelio et vos audire etc. □ *Marginalia* none □ *Notes* This is an antitheme only; and is similar to the first part of 217, also numbered 38. The second liturgical reference, *post trin'*, is correct. □ *Schneyer* T51

NOTE *From this point in the manuscript, there is a change of hand (Scribe D). No more source-books are named, although some numbers are added in a later hand; other codicological evidence indicates that the remainder of the manuscript has a different provision.*

214 *Folios* 181a–181va □ *Runnning title* none □ *Theme* Videns Jesus etc (Lc 19:41) □ *Incipit* Per Jerusalem, que interpretatur "visio pacis," intelligit anima fidelis que Christum iugiter videre debet per gratiam et bona opera □ *Explicit* Bernardus: quia felices sunt ille lacrime quas sanctissima manus salvatoris absterget □ *Marginalia* none □ *Schneyer* T51

215 *Folios* 181vb–181va □ *Runnning title* Eadem dominicam quam prius □ *Source book* none □ *Theme* Videns Jesus civitatem flevit super eam (Lc 19:41) □ *Incipit* Cum Dominus destructionem defleverit futuram, et nos in facto suo hoc idem docuerit, quid dicendum est de illis qui non solum inimicos non diligunt immo amicos odio habent □ *Explicit* manuum tuarum quam retribuens est Dominus et septies tantum reddet □ *Marginalia* none □ *Schneyer* T51

216 *Folios* 182a-183va □ *Runnning title* Dominica iiia post trin' □ *Source book* none □ *Theme* Humiliamini sub potenti manu Dei etc. (1 Petr 5:6) □ *Incipit* Legitur in ecc° fons sapientie verbum Domini in excelsis. Diligentes ergo sapientiam, verbum Domini diligenter audiant cum magno desiderio □ *Thema* Tria dicit quod humiliandum sit ibi *humiliamini* et cui quia *sub potenti manu Dei* et quare □ *Explicit* ut medicina respondeat vulneri et precium obligationi □ *Marginalia* none □ *Schneyer* T44

217 *Folios* 183va-184b □ *Runnning title* Dominica x post trin' □ *Source book* none □ *Theme* Videns Jesus civitatem Jerusalem flevit super eam et dixit etc (Lc 19:41) □ *Incipit* Si nos omnes hic congregati de necessitate mare transiremus, et venientes ad portum, inveniremus <navem> fortem et levem □ *Thema* Dicatur narratio evangelii ad litteram et etiam mistice □ *Explicit* a sinistris infinita demonia fugere erit impossibile, manere intolerabile □ *Marginalia* none □ *Notes* This sermon is a repetition of part of Sermon 213. □ *Schneyer* T51

218 *Folios* 184b-184va □ *Runnning title* Dominica xxiv post trin' □ *Source book* none □ *Theme* Reddite ergo que sunt Cesaris Cesari etc. (Mt 22:21) □ *Incipit* Videndum est quis sit iste Cesar, que sint sua ei reddenda. Per istum Cesarem intellige dyabolum propter multa □ *Explicit* fugat pacem non sustinet dileccionem □ *Marginalia* none □ *Notes* From the Gospel, this Sunday should be xxiii post trin'. □ *Schneyer* T64

219 *Folios* 184va-186b □ *Runnning title* Dominica xi post trin' □ *Source book* none □ *Theme* Duo homines ascenderunt etc. (Lc 18:13) □ *Incipit* Narretur hystoria evangelii et fiat oratio. Cum Christus, sponsus Ecclesie que est mater omnium fidelium, suos electos sibi coniunxerit tanquam membra corpori et corpus capiti per fidem et operationem bonam □ *Explicit* Item eiusdem id est: ecce ego ad te mons pestifer □ *Marginalia* none □ *Other authorities* 185a.4-8 (versus): Claudianus, *De IV Consolata Honorii* 305 (see H. Walther, *Proverbia sententiaeque latinitatis medii aevi*, 6 vols. [Göttingen, 1963-1967], 2: 12465). □ *Schneyer* T52

220 *Folios* 186b-187a □ *Runnning title* Dominica xi post trin' □ *Source book* none □ *Theme* Publicanus a longe stans nolebat etc. (Lc 18:13) □ *Incipit* Narretur evangelium et fiat oratio. In hiis verbis notantur quinque que necessaria sunt omni penitenti, primo timor □ *Explicit* Quod si non credit ymaginibus mortuis crede saltem visis. Nonne vides puniri? □ *Lemmata* [1]: Peccator timere potest (2) □ *Marginalia* unidentified ann.; distinc. □ *Schneyer* T52

221 *Folios* 187a-189a □ *Runnning title* Dominica xii post trin' □ *Source book* none □ *Theme* Adducent ei surdum et mutum etc. (Mc 7:32) □ *Incipit* In initio Misse hodierne diei canit Ecclesia: "Deus in adiutorium meum intende," et non tantum in Missa canit istud, immo consuetudine habet appropriata. Ad omnes Horas diei cotidie Deum invocate (sic) "in adiutorium" □ *Thema* Legitur in evangelio hodierno quod Dominus exiens de una provincia ad aliam provinciam adduxerunt ei quidam cecum et mutum □ *Explicit* Dicatur narratio de clerico suaviter nutritio intrante religionem etc. □ *Marginalia* none □ *Notes* The Office of the Mass is quoted in the *incipit*. For Trinity xii it runs: "Deus in adiutorium meum intende: Domine ad adiuvandum me festine, confundantur et revereantur inimici mei qui querunt animam meam." □ *Schneyer* T53

222 *Folios* 189a- 189vb □ *Runnning title* Dominica xviii post trin' □ *Source book* none □ *Theme* Diliges Dominum Deum tuum ex toto corde tuo et ex toto anima tua etc. (Mt 22:37) □ *Incipit* Nulli tedeat verbum Dei audire, homo enim etc. □ *Thema* Duo dicenda sunt quare Christus diligendus est et qualiter □ *Explicit* scilicet per vitam suam laboriosam scitis enim quod inter omnes actus corporales etc. □ *Marginalia* none □ *Notes* Note sermons 70, 71 and 72 in the above list. □ *Schneyer* T59

223 *Folios* 189vb- 191vb □ *Runnning title* Dominica 19 post trin' □ *Source book* none □ *Theme* Renovamini spiritu mentis vestre etc. (Eph 4:23- 24) □ *Incipit* Verba sunt ad Eph Apostoli 4, in quibus hortatur nos spiritualiter in mente secundum animam scilicet renovari □ *Explicit* que fit in glorificationem corporum quando impletur, idem apo 21: ecce nova facio omnia □ *Marginalia* none □ *Schneyer* T60

224 *Folios* 191va- 192vb □ *Runnning title* Dominica nona decima post trin' □ *Source book* none □ *Theme* Ascendens Jesus in naviculam etc. (Mt 9:1) □ *Incipit* Antiphona de Officio huius diei "Salus populi ego sum dicit Dominus" etc. □ *Thema* Naute mare transeuntes in tenebris noctis maxime beneficio lucis stellarum nimium indigent □ *Explicit* transfretabimur in navem cum Domino in civitatem suam celestem, quod nobis prestare etc.. □ *Marginalia* enumeration □ *Notes* The Officium of the Mass for Trinity 19 runs: "Salus populi ego sum, dicit Dominus: de quacunque tribulatione clamaverint ad me, exaudiam eos: et ero illorum, Dominus in perpetuum. □ *Schneyer* T60

225 *Folios* 192vb- 194vb □ *Runnning title* Dominica xxiii post trin' □ *Source book* none □ *Theme* Redde rationem villicationis tue etc. (Lc 16:2) □ *Incipit* Narra evangelium et fiat oratio. Notandum quod Deus, Pater misericordiarum, in evangelio comparatur homini secundum sex modos □ *Explicit* quia qui abscondit scelera sua non dirigetur, qui autem confessus fuerit et reliquerit ea, misericordiam consequetur etc □ *Lemmata* [1]: Reddere rationem debemus de □ *Marginalia* distinc.; enumeration □ *Notes* The theme is from the Gospel of Trinity xi. The Concordance for *Reddite* (Mt 22: 21) may have suggested this text for Trinity xxiii. □ *Schneyer* none

226 *Folios* 194vb- 196b □ *Runnning title* Dominica xxii post trin' □ *Source book* none □ *Theme* Omne debitum dimisi tibi quoniam rogasti me (Mt 18:32) □ *Incipit* Dominus in evangelium hodierno narrat quidam exemplum in signum venturi iudicii magni □ *Explicit* Narretur de Comite Blesensi et de

monacho suo, item de heremita et divite mortuo, item quodam de S.Nichalao testamentum □ *Marginalia* enumeration □ *Schneyer* T63

227 *Folios* 196b–197va □ *Runnning title* In exaltatione Sancte Crucis □ *Source book* none □ *Theme* Exaltabo ad populos meos signum meum etc. (Is 49: 22) □ *Incipit* Hec prophetia in festo hodierno impleta est ubi duo notantur, venerande crucis exaltatio □ *Explicit* Narretur de Judeo qui divertit in templum Apollinis □ *Marginalia* none □ *Schneyer* S66

228 *Folios* 197va–197vb □ *Runnning title* Dominica xxiv post trin' □ *Source book* none □ *Theme* Reddite que sunt Cesaris Cesari etc. (Mt 22:21) □ *Incipit* Dicatur narratio evangelii, inprimis invocemus Dominum Jesum Christum □ *Thema* Cesar dicitur dyabolum duplici ratione. Dicitur enim Cesar quia cesus erat de utero matris sui □ *Explicit* non habitabit in medio domus mee qui facit superbiam □ *Marginalia* none □ *Notes* Compare this liturgical reference with 218. □ *Schneyer* T64

229 *Folios* 197vb–198vb □ *Runnning title* De quocumque confessore □ *Source book* none □ *Theme* Homo quidam peregre proficiscens etc. (Mt 25:14) □ *Incipit* Dicatur antithema supra positum, narratio evangelii, dicatur et exponatur sic: homo iste Dominus est Jesus Christus qui propter hominum salutem homo factus, qui ad celos ascendens a mundo isto □ *Explicit* propter hoc inhibet Dominus hoc dicens: nolite iudicare et non iudicabimini □ *Marginalia* none □ *Notes* Possibly Hugonis de S. Caro OP: see Schneyer, *Repertorium* 2: 785, no. 418. □ *Schneyer* C7

230 *Folios* 198vb–200a □ *Runnning title* Dominica proxima post Nativitas Joh' Baptiste □ *Source book* none □ *Theme* Quodcumque solveris super terram etc. (Mt 16:19) □ *Incipit* Dominus noster Jesus Christus, rex et conditor omnium creaturarum, sine principio Deus in fine seculorum, pro salute hominis factus est homo □ *Thema* Istud non tantum Petro dicitur immo omnibus in apostolatum Petro succedentibus □ *Explicit* qui enim perseveraverit in finem hic salvus erit □ *Marginalia* unidentified ann. □ *Notes* The liturgical reference has an addition in a different hand: *vel de Sancto Petro.* Margin Note: Iste sermo predicatur aput Elnest' a° do^i m.cc.lxx.quinto. □ *Schneyer* S46

231 *Folios* 200a–201va □ *Runnning title* Dominica in oct' assumptionis (BVM) □ *Source book* none □ *Theme* Que est ista que ascendit quasi aurora consurgens etc. (Cant 6:9) □ *Incipit* Sermo noster, Deo dante, erit de Virgine Gloriosa, cuius hodie ad celum assumpcio in omni memoratur Ecclesia □ *Thema* Verba ista sunt Salamonis scripta in Cantico et sunt tria querenda □ *Explicit* Consideret prius Teophilum, qui cartam fecerat dyabolo et homagium et adhuc cartam ei restituit et in celum introduxit □ *Marginalia* none □ *Notes* The Theme comes from the Benedictus Antiphon for the day. Note reads "predicatur iste sermo in assumptione beate virgine circuli lun' vii a° dn^i m.cc.lxxix." □ *Schneyer* S59

232 *Folios* 202va–203a □ *Runnning title* In Assumptione Beate Virgine □ *Source book* none □ *Theme* Exaltata est Sancta Dei Genitrix □ *Incipit* Legitur in prov 1 in persona Gloriose Virginis: qui me audierit absque timore quiescit etc. □ *Thema* Queri potest quibus de causis in tantum sit exaltata et potest dici quod pluribus □ *Explicit* Item narretur de duello Stanfordensi Johannis Mauntel et alicuius miseri cantantis semper "Ave Maria" □ *Marginalia* none □ *Notes* The Theme is from Antiphon 1 of the First Nocturn of Matins. □ *Schneyer* S59

233 *Folios* 203a–204va □ *Runnning title* De Assumptione □ *Source book* none □ *Theme* Que est ista que ascendit sicut aurora consurgens pulchra ut luna electa ut sol terribilis ut castrorum acies ordinata (Cant 6:9) □ *Incipit* Virgo Maria de qua presens fiet sermocinatio dicitur inventrix gratie □ *Thema* Cum aurora sit finis noctis et origo diei profecto aurora designatur Virgo Maria □ *Explicit* portas aperuit paradysi; pete audacter quod vis et impetrabis □ *Marginalia* unidentified ann. □ *Notes* The Theme comes from the Benedictus Antiphon for the day. □ *Schneyer* S59

234 *Folios* 204va–204vb □ *Runnning title* In nativitate Beate Virginis □ *Source book* none □ *Theme* Cum jocunditate nativitatem Beate Marie celebremus ut ipsa intercedat. □ *Incipit* Qui mare navigant etc., ut alibi fiat oratio *Cum jocunditate* etc. □ *Thema* Si quis vestrum haberet aliquam arduam causam coram iudice iustissimo discuciendam □ *Explicit* cum igitur talis ac tanta sit et tantum possit impetrare, immo quantum mens … . □ *Marginalia* unidentified ann. □ *Notes* The Theme is from Antiphon 5 of Lauds for the feast. □ *Schneyer* S65

NOTE *Sermon 234 is incomplete, for the manuscript ends at this point; at least one gathering is missing.*

Appendix 2

The Rejected Folios

The rejected folios in MS Laud Misc. 511 are 119–20, 129–30, recto and verso in both cases (columns designate the numbers at the top of each folio). The scribe who copied these sermons, now bound into the manuscript at the correct place, treated his two bifolia as a small gathering. He copied the extra material from col. 2vb (having already copied the antitheme in the correct place) onto the *fifth* page of his small gathering (fol. 129a). Realizing his error, he cancelled the 6 lines copied at the top of fol. 129a (the marks are like a Union Jack) and continued copying Sermon 138.

[i] *Folios* 1- 1b (columns 439, 440) □ *Incipit* Homo mortuus □ *Explicit* seipsos suspendere dicitur est quid credendi etc □ *Notes* This is the last part of Sermon 120, written on fol. 119 "Christus resurgens."

[ii] *Folio* 1, bottom margin □ *Incipit* Dominica proxima post festum □ *Explicit* ad Annunciationem Beate Marie (d)uodecim denarios pro mercede □ *Notes* This is a form of contract, probably a rough draft, printed in the Bodleian Library's *Quarto Catalogue,* rev. R.W. Hunt (Oxford, 1973), Addenda, 567.

[iii] *Folios* 1va- 2a (columns 441, 442, 443) □ *Incipit* Si consurrexistis □ *Explicit* in monumento novo etc □ *Notes* This is Sermon 121, written on fol. 119va- 120b: "Si consurrexistis cum Christo."

[iv] *Folios* 2b- 2va (columns 444, 445.) □ *Incipit* Qui commederit de □ *Explicit* qui peccat in corpus Christi □ *Source Book* Niger Minor □ *Notes* This is Sermon 122, written on fol. 120b- 120va: "Qui comederit de sanctificatis."

[v] *Folio* 2vb (column 446) □ *Source Book* Proprius □ *Title* in oct' pasche □ *Incipit* Stetit et □ *Explicit* sum fine letitia □ *Notes* This is the first part of Sermon 123, fol. 120vb. The bottom margin contains the antitheme of the Sermon (*incipit* Sic est de Christo; *explicit* clamat, Pax vobis).

[vi] *Folios* 3a- 3vb.21 (columns 479, 480, 481, 482) □ *Incipit* Et producit in medium Dominicam Passionem □ *Explicit* tetigit fimbriam vestimenti Christi *Notes* This is Sermon 138, written on fol. 129a- 129vb: "Christus passus est."

[vii] *Folio* 3vb.23 (column 482) □ *Incipit* Sequamini vestigia eius, in cordis □ *Explicit* iam temptationibus et peccatis □ *Notes* This is Sermon 140, written on fol. 129vb (19 lines).

[viii] *Folios* 4a- 4vb (columns 483, 484, 485, 486.) □ *Incipit* Obsecro vos tamquam □ *Explicit* mori et fugiet mors ab eis □ *Notes* This is Sermon 141, written on fol. 130a- 130vb.

[ix] *Folio* 4v, bottom margin □ *Title* Octa philosophi de Alexandro Magno □ *Incipit* Alexander ex aure fecit □ *Explicit* not clear □ *Notes* This is an annotation not connected with the sermon above.

Appendix 3

The "Missing" Sermons

There are several references in MS Laud Misc. 511 to the sources of other relevant sermons not already catalogued. This list of the 'missing' sermons, mostly described in the manuscript by the phrase: *Deficiunt hic ... sermones*, includes references to at least 28 sermons from 8 of the source books already recorded. Column/line and folio references are scribal.

Folios 9v bottom margin □ *Running title* Sun I Advent □ *Source Book* Rubeus Maior: *Sermons missing* 2 □ *Source Book* Rubeus Minor: Sermons missing 1

Folios 14v bottom margin □ *Running title* Sun II Advent □ *Source book* Rubeus Maior: *Sermons missing* 2 □ *Source book* Rubeus Minor □ *Sermons missing* 1

Folios 18a bottom margin □ *Running title* Sun III Advent □ *Source book* De Beate Virgine, scilicet 40.24 *Nolite* ante tempus iudicare (1 Cor 4:5): *Sermons missing* 1

Folios 21va bottom margin □ *Running title* Sun IV Advent □ *Source book* none: *Sermons missing* "plures"

Folios 38a top margin *Running title* Septuagesima □ *Source book* none: *Sermons missing* 8 □

Folios 49v bottom margin □ *Running title* Sexagesima □ *Source book* Parvus Tabulatus in fine *Libenter* etc. (2 Cor 1:19): *Sermons missing* 1

Folios 52vb bottom margin □ *Running title* Quinquagesima □ *Source book* Rubeus Maior 36.84 □ *Sermons missing* 2

Folios 69v bottom margin □ *Running title* Sun I Lent □ *Source book* Niger Minor *agite penitentiam*: *Sermons missing* 1 □ *Source book* In libro Confessiones Augustini: *Sermons missing* 1

Folios 100 bottom margin □ *Running title* Sun IV Lent □ *Source book* Rubeus Minor 24.18 (red) and 28.18 (black): *Sermons missing* 1 □ *Source book* Minimus: *Sermons missing* 1

Folios 152 bottom margin □ *Running title* Sun I post Trin' □ *Source book* Rubeus Maior: *Sermons missing* 1

Folios 153 bottom margin □ *Running title* Sun II post Trin' □ *Source book* Proprius, fol. 9: *Sermons missing* 1

Folios 157v bottom margin □ *Running title* Sun III post Trin' □ *Source book* none: *Sermons missing* 2/3

Folios 180v bottom margin □ *Running title* Sun IX post Trin' □ *Source book* De Beate Virgine: *Sermons missing* 1

Appendix 4

Concordance: Schneyer–O'Carroll

This list concords the Catalogue of MS Laud Misc. 511 in Appendix 1 and the description of the manuscript found in Schneyer, *Repertorium* (abbreviated *Rep*, below) 9: 58–69. The Notes identify the sermons and their printed and/or manuscript sources. * indicates sermon or part thereof, identified since volume 9 of Schneyer's *Repertorium* was published.

Catalogue	Schneyer	Notes
1	1	
2	2	
3	3	
4	4	
5	5	
6	6	
7	7	
8	8	
9	9	
10	10	Guilelmus Peraldus OP (*Rep.* 2: 544, no. 134)
11	11	
12	12	
13	13	
14	14	
15	15	
16	16	
17	17	
18	18	
19	19	
20		omitted from Schneyer, sermon distinction
21	20	
22	21	
23	22	
24	23	
25	24	
26	25	
27	26	
28	27	
29	28	
30	29	
31	30	
32	31	
33	32	
34	33	

35	34	
36	35	
37	36	
38	37	
39	38	
40	39	
41	40	
42	41	
43	42	
44	43	
45	44	
46	45	
47	⌈ 46	is the antitheme
	⌊ 47	is the full sermon exposition
48	48	
49	49	
50	50	
51	51	
52		an alternative antitheme; omitted by Schneyer
53	52	
54	53	
55	54	
56	⌈ 55	is the antitheme
56	⌊ 56	is the full sermon exposition
57	⌈ 57	is the antitheme
58	⌊ 58	is the full sermon exposition
58	59	
59	60	
60	61	Petrus de Remis OP (*Rep.* 4: 726, no. 27)
61	62	
62	63	
63	64	
64	65	
65	66	
66	67	Simon of Hinton OP (*Rep.* 5: 459–60, no. 1)
67	68	Schneyer puts this as *collatio* of 67; it is not.
68	69	
69	70	
70	71	
71	72	
72	73	
73	74	
74	75	

75	76	
76	77	
*77 b+a	78	probably part of a sermon by Guilelmus Peraldus OP (*Rep.* 2: 552, no. 260)
*78	79	Hugonis de S. Caro OP (*Rep.* 2: 760, no. 39)
79	80	
80	81	
81	82	
82	83	Richard Fishacre OP (*Rep.* 5: 149, no. 25)
83	84	Petrus de Remis OP (*Rep.* 4, 727, no. 23)
84		omitted by Schneyer: *Letare sterilis* from *Liber rubeus maior*
85	85	
86	86	
87	87	
88	88	
89	89	
90	90	
91	91	
92	92	
93	93	
94	94	
95	95	
96	96	
97	97	
98	98	Johannis Halgrinus de Abbatisvilla (*Rep.* 3: 514, no. 67); this is not by Peraldus
99	⌈ 99	is the antitheme
	⌊ 100	is the full sermon exposition
100	101	
101	102	
102	103	
103	104	
104	105	
105	106	
106 a–h		omitted by Schneyer; sermon material
107		omitted by Schneyer; possibly *florilegia*
*108	107	Petrus de Remis OP: (*Rep.* 4: 727, no. 37)
109		omitted by Schneyer; distinction on humility
110	108	
111	109	
112	110	
113 a–c		omitted by Schneyer; sermon material

114	111	
115	112	
116	113	
117	114	Petrus de Remis OP (*Rep.* 4: 727, no. 39)
118	115	
119	116	
120	117	
121	118	
122	119	
123	120	
124	121	
125	122	
126		omitted by Schneyer, *Mane nobiscum Domine* from *Liber rubeus minor*
*127	123	Petrus de Remis OP (*Rep.* 4: 727, no. 42)
128	124	
129		omitted by Schneyer, *Pax vobis*, distinctions
130	125	
131	126	
132		omitted by Schneyer, *Christus semel pro peccatis* from *Liber parvus rubeus*
*133	127	Petrus de Remis OP (*Rep.* 4: 727, no. 43)
134	128	
135	129	
136	130	
137	131	
138	132	
139	133	
140	134	
141	135	
142	136	
143	137	
144	138	
145	139	
146	140	
147	141	
148	142	
149a–c		omitted by Schneyer, distinctions
150		omitted by Schneyer, distinctions
151		omitted by Schneyer, sermon material
152	143	
153	144	
154	145	

155		omitted by Schneyer; sermon material
156	146	
157	147	
158	148	
159	149	
160	150	
161	151	
162	152	
163	153	
164	154	
*165	155	Guilelmus Peraldus OP (*Rep.* 2: 547, no. 183)
166	156	H. de Mordon
167	157	
168	158	
169	159	
170	160	
*171	161	Hugonis de S. Caro OP (*Rep.* 2: 762, no. 62)
172	162	
173	163	
174a	⌈ 164	is the sermon exposition
174b	⌊ 165	is the antitheme
175–181		omitted by Schneyer: *florilegia,* sermon material
182	166	
183	167	
184	168	
185	169	
186	170	
187	171	*florilegia*
188–196		omitted by Schneyer: *florilegia,* sermon material
197	172	
*198	173	Guilelmus Peraldus OP (*Rep.* 2: 548, no. 196; also 2: 553, no. 279)
199a–203		omitted by Schneyer: *florilegia,* sermon material
204	174	
205	175	
206	176	
207	177	
208	178	
209	179	
210	180	
211	181	
212	182	
213	183	
214	184	

215	185	
216	186	
217	187	
218		omitted by Schneyer: *Reddite ergo que sunt cesaris* (no book)
219	188	
220	189	
221	190	
222	191	
223	192	
224	193	
225	194	
226	195	
227	196	
228	197	
*229	198	possibly Hugonis de S. Caro OP (*Rep.* 2: 785, no. 418); no MS available to check
230	199	
231	200	
232	201	
233	202	
234	203	

Appendix 5

Sermon Theme, Incipit, and Thema

This appendix is an alphabetical list of the theme, incipit, and thema of all the sermons or sermon material found in MS Laud Misc. 511, here referred to by the common abbreviation *Serm.*, followed by a numeral bold corresponding to the numbers in the Catalogue of the manuscript found in Appendix 1. Biblical references are provided in parentheses.

THEME

Abiciamus opera tenebrarum et induamur arma lucis (Rom 13: 12) □ *Serm.* 2–6
Abraham duos filios habuit (Gal 4: 22) □ *Serm.* 87
Adducent ei surdum et mutum etc. (Mc 7: 32) □ *Serm.* 221
Annuntio vobis gaudium magnum quod erit omni (Lc 2: 10–11) □ *Serm.* 21
Ante omnia <fratres> mutuam caritatem habentes (1 Petr 4: 8) □ *Serm.* 164
Apparuerunt illis dispertite lingue etc. (Act 2: 3) □ *Serm.* 168
Ascendam in palmam (Cant 7: 8) □ *Serm.* 111
Ascende ad me in montem et esto ibi ex 24 (Ex 24: 12) □ *Serm.* 159
Ascendens Jesus in naviculam etc. (Mt 9: 1) □ *Serm.* 224
Ascendente Jesu in naviculam secuti sunt eum discipuli (Mt 8: 23) □ *Serm.* 30
Ascendet iter pandens ante eos mich 2 (Mich 2: 13) □ *Serm.* 161
Ascendo ad Patrem meum et Patrem vestrum etc. (Jo 20: 17) □ *Serm.* 158
Benedictus Deus qui non amovit orationem etc (Ps 65: 20) □ *Serm.* 202
Ceci vident etc. (Mt 11: 4–5) □ *Serm.* 17
Cecus sedebat iuxta viam mendicans (Lc 18: 35) □ *Serm.* 42, 43
Christus assistens pontifex (Hebr 9: 11) □ *Serm.* 91
Christus assistens pontifex etc. (Hebr 9: 11) □ *Serm.* 98
Christus passus est pro nobis etc. (1 Petr 2: 21) □ *Serm.* 133–138
Christus per Spiritum Sanctum semetipsum obtulit Deo (Hebr 9: 14) □ *Serm.* 94
Christus per proprium sanguinem etc. (Hebr 9: 12) □ *Serm.* 90, 92, 95, 96
Christus resurgens ex mortuis etc. (Rom 6: 9) □ *Serm.* 116, 120
Christus semel pro peccatis nostris mortuus est (1 Petr 3: 18) □ *Serm.* 132
Circumdederunt me gemitus mortis (Ps 17: 5) □ *Serm.* 32
Clamans voce magna emisit spiritum (Mt 27: 50) □ *Serm.* 112
Confestim vidit (Lc 18: 43) □ *Serm.* 45, 48
Cum appropinquasset etc. (Mt 21: 1) □ *Serm.* 110
Cum descendisset Jesus de monte (Mt 8: 1) □ *Serm.* 27, 28
Cum eiecisset Jesus demonium locutus est etc. (Lc 11: 14) □ *Serm.* 70–72, 74, 76
Cum jocunditate nativitatem Beate Marie celebremus ut ipsa □ *Serm.* 234
Cum malediceretur non maledicebat etc (1 Petr 2 23) □ *Serm.* 147
Dies autem appropinquavit (Rom 13: 12) □ *Serm.* 3
Diliges Dominum Deum tuum ex toto corde tuo etc. □ *Serm.* 37, 222

Diliges proximum tuum sicut teipsum (Rom 13: 9) □ *Serm.* 29
Ductus est Jesus in desertum etc. (Mt 4: 1) □ *Serm.* 49, 50, 53, 55, 56, 57, 59, 63
Duo homines ascenderunt etc. (Lc 18: 13) □ *Serm.* 219
Ecce mulier Cananea etc. (Mt 15: 21) □ *Serm.* 68
Ecce nunc tempus acceptabile (2 Cor 6: 2) □ *Serm.* 51, 60–62
Ecce rex tuus venit tibi mansuetus (Mt 21: 5) □ *Serm.* 101
Ego sum pastor bonus (Jo 10: 11) □ *Serm.* 139
Egressus inde Jesus etc. (Mt 15: 21) □ *Serm.* 69
Eice ancillam et filium eius (Gal 4: 30) □ *Serm.* 83, 88
Erat Jesus eiiciens demonium etc. (Lc 11: 14) □ *Serm.* 75
Erat proximum pascha dies festus Judeorum (Jo 6: 4) □ *Serm.* 78
Eratis enim sicut oves errantes sed nunc conversi estis (1 Petr 2: 25 □ *Serm.* 131)
Estote factores verbi et non auditores tantum (Jac 1: 22) □ *Serm.* 148, 156
Estote imitatores Dei sicut filii karissimi (Eph 5: 1) □ *Serm.* 73
Estote misericordes etc. (Lc 6: 36) □ *Serm.* 185–187
Estote prudentes et vigilate in orationibus (1 Petr 4: 7) □ *Serm.* 165
Exaltabo ad populos meos signum meum etc. (Is 49: 22) □ *Serm.* 227
Exaltata est Sancta Dei Genitrix) □ *Serm.* 232
Exiit qui seminat seminare semen suum (Lc 8: 5) □ *Serm.* 41
Faciet Dominus exercituum omnibus populis hoc convivium (Is 25: 6) □ *Serm.* 18
Fili recordare quia recepisti bona etc. (Lc 16: 25) □ *Serm.* 170
Gaudete in Domino semper iterum dico gaudete (Phil 4: 4) □ *Serm.* 19
Gavisi sunt discipuli viso Domino (Jo 20: 20) □ *Serm.* 127
Hec est dies quam fecit Dominus etc. (Ps 117: 24) □ *Serm.* 119
Hec est voluntas Dei sanctificatio vestra (1 Thess 4: 3) □ *Serm.* 64–67
Hic Jesus qui assumptus est a vobis in celum, sic veniet (Act 1: 11) □ *Serm.* 162
Hoc sentite in vobis etc. (Phil 2: 5) □ *Serm.* 102, 103, 105, 108
Homo quidam fecit cenam magnam (Lc 14: 16) □ *Serm.* 171, 172
Homo quidam peregre proficiscens etc. (Mt 25: 14) □ *Serm.* 229
Hora est iam nos de sompno surgere (Rom 13: 11) □ *Serm.* 7
Hortamur vos ne in vacuum gratiam Dei accipiatis (2 Cor 6: 1) □ *Serm.* 58
Humiliamini sub potenti manu Dei (1 Petr 5: 6) □ *Serm.* 174a–b, 182–184, 216
Illa que sursum est Jerusalem libere est (Gal 4: 26) □ *Serm.* 77a–b, 81
Implete ydrias aqua et impleverunt etc. (Jo 2: 7) □ *Serm.* 25, 26
In hoc vocati estis ut hereditate possideatis (1 Petr 3: 9) □ *Serm.* 157
Introivit in sancta (Hebr 9: 12) □ *Serm.* 97; see 90–92, 95, 96
Invenerunt puerum cum Maria matre eius (Mt 2: 11) □ *Serm.* 22
Jesu fili David miserere mei (Lc 18: 38) □ *Serm.* 44, 46
Letare sterilis etc. (Gal 4: 27) □ *Serm.* 80, 84, 85
Levabo ad celum manum meam etc. (Deut 32: 40) □ *Serm.* 160
Mane nobiscum Domine (Lc 24: 29) □ *Serm.* 126
Memor esto unde excideris et age penitentiam (Apoc 2: 5) □ *Serm.* 33

Misereor super turbam etc. (Mc 8: 2) □ *Serm.* 207
Multi sunt vocati etc. (Mt 22: 14) □ *Serm.* 173
Neque fornicemur sicut quidam ex eis fornicati sunt (1 Cor 10: 8) □ *Serm.* 211
Nescitis quoniam hii qui in stadio currunt omnes quidem (1 Cor 9: 24) □ *Serm.* 35
Noli timere filia Syon; ecce rex tuus etc. (Jo 12: 15) □ *Serm.* 100
Non enim heres erit filius ancille cum filio libere (Gal 4: 30) □ *Serm.* 82
Non simus concupiscentes malorum etc. (1 Cor 10: 6) □ *Serm.* 210
Nox precessit dies autem appropinquavit (Rom 13: 12) □ *Serm.* 1; see 2, 4, 6
Numquid qui dormit non adiciet ut resurgat (Ps 40: 9) □ *Serm.* 114
Nunc vadimus ad domum Dei habentes panem (Jud 19: 18-19) □ *Serm.* 79
Obsecro vos tanquam advenas et peregrinos etc. (1 Petr 2: 11) □ *Serm.* 141, 142
Obsecro vos ut exhibeatis corpora vestra etc. (Rom 12: 1) □ *Serm.* 24
Omne debitum dimisi tibi quoniam rogasti me (Mt 18: 32) □ *Serm.* 226
Omnes unanimes in ratione estote (1 Petr 3: 8) □ *Serm.* 198
Omnis arbor que non facit fructum bonum (Mt 7: 19) □ *Serm.* 208, 209
Optulerunt ei munera aurum, thus et mirram (Mt 2: 11) □ *Serm.* 23
Ostendit eis manus et latus (Jo 20: 20) □ *Serm.* 130
Pascha nostrum etc. (1 Cor 5: 7) □ *Serm.* 117
Pax vobis (Jo 20: 21) □ *Serm.* 128
Per totam noctem laborantes etc. (Lc 5: 5) □ *Serm.* 197
Petite et accipietis ut gaudium vestrum sit plenum (Jo 16: 24) □ *Serm.* 152, 154
Publicanus a longe stans nolebat etc. (Lc 18: 13) □ *Serm.* 220
Puer natus est nobis (Is 9: 6) □ *Serm.* 20
Quasi tristes semper autem gaudentes (2 Cor 6: 10) □ *Serm.* 54
Que est ista que ascendit quasi aurora consurgens (Cant 6: 9) □ *Serm.* 231, 233
Quecumque scripta sunt ad nostram doctrinam scripta sunt (Rom 15: 4) □
    Serm. 10
Qui comederit de sanctificatis per ignorantiam addet (Lev 22: 14) □ *Serm.* 122
Qui me iudicat Dominus est (1 Cor 4: 4) □ *Serm.* 16
Qui se existimat stare videat ne cadat (1 Cor 10: 12) □ *Serm.* 212
Quicumque baptizati in Christo Jesu etc. (Rom 6: 3) □ *Serm.* 204
Quis est qui vincit mundum etc. (1 Jo 5: 5) □ *Serm.* 125
Quodcumque solveris super terram etc. (Mt 16: 19) □ *Serm.* 230
Recordare paupertatis mee et transgressionis absinthii (Lam 3: 19) □ *Serm.* 99
Redde rationem villicationis tue etc. (Lc 16: 2) □ *Serm.* 225
Reddite ergo que sunt Cesaris Cesari etc. (Mt 22: 21) □ *Serm.* 218, 228
Regem venturum Dominum, venite adoremus (Advent Invitatory) □ *Serm.* 5
Renovamini spiritu mentis vestre etc. (Eph 4: 23-24) □ *Serm.* 223
Repleti sunt omnes Spiritu Sancto (Act 2: 4) □ *Serm.* 166
Rex noster adveniet quem Johannes predicavit (Advent invitatory) □ *Serm.* 12, 15
Semen est verbum Dei (Lc 8: 11) □ *Serm.* 38-40
Sequamini vestigia eius (1 Petr 2: 21) □ *Serm.* 140; *see also Serm.* 133-138
Sequebatur eum multitudo magna (Jo 6: 2) □ *Serm.* 86

Si caritatem non habuero nichil sum (1 Cor 13: 2) □ *Serm.* 47
Si consurrexistis cum Christo que sursum sunt (Col 3: 1) □ *Serm.* 115, 121
Si quid petieritis Patrem in nomine meo etc. (Jo 16: 23) □ *Serm.* 153
Si quis sermonem meum servaverit etc. (Jo 8: 51) □ *Serm.* 93
Simile est regnum celorum homini patrifamilias etc. (Mt 20: 1) □ *Serm.* 36
Spiritus Domini replevit orbem terrarum (Sap 1: 7) □ *Serm.* 167
Stetit Jesus in medio <discipulorum suorum> et dixit: (Jo 20: 19 □ *Serm.* 123)
Stipendia peccati mors (Rom 6: 23) □ *Serm.* 205-206
Super omnia hec caritatem habete quod est vinculum (Col 3: 14) □ *Serm.* 31
Surgite vigilemus quia venit rex (Invitatory, Advent II York) □ *Serm.* 8
Transi hospes orna mensam (Eccli 29: 33) □ *Serm.* 118
Tres sunt quoniam testimonium dant in celo (1 Jo 5: 7) □ *Serm.* 169
Tunc videbunt filium hominis venientem in nube cum (Lc 21: 27) □ *Serm.* 9
Vado ad eum qui me misit (Jo 16: 5) □ *Serm.* 143-146
Veniet Dominus et non tardabit (Advent Invitatory) □ *Serm.* 13, 14
Vexilla regis prodeunt (Hymn) (Advent Invitatory) □ *Serm.* 89
Videns Jesus civitatem Jerusalem flevit (Lc 19: 41) □ *Serm.* 213, 214, 215, 217
Vigilate in orationibus, pe 4 (1 Petr 4: 7) □ *Serm.* 163
Vir duplex est (Jac 1: 8) □ *Serm.* 149a
Virtutes celorum movebuntur (Lc 21: 26) □ *Serm.* 11
Vox Domini preparantis cervos (Ps 28: 9) □ *Serm.* 104, 124

INCIPIT
A discipulo procurata quid vultis michi dare etc. □ *Serm.* 107
Ad perfectum magistrum pertinet ut sit doctor in verbo □ *Serm.* 69
Ad suscipiendum gratiam Dei se humilitat □ *Serm.* 200b
Ad vestium vilitatem, Augustinus, non affectitis vestibus □ *Serm.* 151
Adducite michi psaltem in II regum 3 legitur quod Heliseus □ *Serm.* 46
Adveniens hodie, Spiritus Sanctus in Apostolos Domini □ *Serm.* 168
Antiphona de Officio huius diei "Salus populi ego sum ... □ *Serm.* 224
Antithema. Vox Domini conucientis desertum etc. Desertum □ *Serm.* 63
Apostolus in epistola hodierna monet nos mala non concup' □ *Serm.* 210
Arbor iste est quilibet electus, can 2, sicut malus inter □ *Serm.* 209
Ascendet pandens quia via ignota fuit; ideo quidam volent' □ *Serm.* 161
Attendite et videte si est dolor etc. Productio. Glosa □ *Serm.* 106g
Audiendum est verbum Dei ab omnibus, propter promissionem □ *Serm.* 205
Augustinus: O anima insignita Dei ymagine, decorata eius □ *Serm.* 186
Augustinus: Qui elemosyna dat tedio interpellantis □ *Serm.* 188
Brevi diei brevis debetur sermo, sermo divinus magna □ *Serm.* 8
Caritas autem, ut dicunt Augustinus et Gregorius, amor est. □ *Serm.* 31
Christus dicitur manus propter magnum laborem et modicam □ *Serm.* 160
Christus non in strato suo sed in cruce □ *Serm.* 113c
Christus Dei filius qui ab initio sicut dicit Apostolus □ *Serm.* 145

Cibus mentis, secundum Gregorium, est verbum Dei □ *Serm.* 142

Cum Dominus destructionem defleverit futuram, et nos in □ *Serm.* 215

Cum mundus iste lacrimarum vallis denominetur, et tempus □ *Serm.* 64

Cum sit tempus penitentie et propter hoc fletus et dolor' □ *Serm.* 81

De duobus agitur in hoc evangelio, scilicet de Christi □ *Serm.* 42

De triplici miseria peccatoris □ *Serm.* 195

Debemus esse Abraham per efficaciam credendi □ *Serm.* 87

Dicatur antithema supra positum, narratio evangelii □ *Serm.* 229

Dicatur narratio evangelii, in primis invocemus Dominum □ *Serm.* 228

Dicitur in Ps: Benigna est misericordia tua, ad differentiam □ *Serm.* 194

Dies isti adventus Domini representant Dominum nobis □ *Serm.* 12

Dilectionis insinuationem Bernardus, verius est anima □ *Serm.* 105

Disciplina non est servanda sine misericordia nec □ *Serm.* 193

Distinctions on Humility □ *Serm.* 109

Divisiones ... certitudinem. Bernardus □ *Serm.* 106d

Dominica ista appropriatur Dominica in Passione Domini □ *Serm.* 98

Dominus Deus, noster Christus, centum oves habuit sed una □ *Serm.* 139

Dominus in evangelium hodierno narrat quidam exemplum in □ *Serm.* 226

Dominus loquens per Jeremiam prophetam 26b omnibus curam □ *Serm.* 33

Dominus noster Jesus Christus, rex et conditor omnium □ *Serm.* 230

Dominus predicaturus in mundum sermones suos leves fecit □ *Serm.* 36

Duo dicenda sunt hic, primo de adventu Domini et hoc est □ *Serm.* 13

Duo dicuntur, tristitia apparens et gaudium perseverans □ *Serm.* 54

Duo dicuntur: cur diabolus reddit peccatorem mutum et quare □ *Serm.* 75

Duo hic tanguntur, quorum primum nos erigit in spem □ *Serm.* 162

Duo hic videnda: de eiectione et concomitantibus eam □ *Serm.* 74

Duo in hiis verbis tanguntur scilicet, vocatio multorum et □ *Serm.* 173

Duo sunt hic attendenda et duo dicenda, primo de cecitate □ *Serm.* 17

Duo sunt necessaria ad vitam: declinare a malo et facere □ *Serm.* 2

Duo sunt que precipue impellunt tristitiam ab aliquo divi □ *Serm.* 158

Duo tangit in hiis verbis Apostoli, videlicet, noctis □ *Serm.* 1

Duo tanguntur, cui iudicare conveniat in hoc quod dicitur □ *Serm.* 16

Duo tanguntur, scilicet, meritum cum dicit si quis sermonem □ *Serm.* 93

Dupliciter possunt hec verba exponi, uno modo de ipso □ *Serm.* 28

Duppliciter experitur patientia, verbis scilicet et verber' □ *Serm.* 147

Effectu. Bernardus horum dulcis memoria lacrimas allicit □ *Serm.* 106e

Est mors nature cui neque divites neque pauperes resistunt □ *Serm.* 116

Evangelium hodiernum multum nobis commendat orationem □ *Serm.* 154

Ex propria estimatione quia qui □ *Serm.* 180a

Filii Agar sunt peccatores que interpretatur festum □ *Serm.* 83

Filius sapiens letificat patrem suum □ *Serm.* 10

Fons sine humore fons enim est per apparentiam, sed caret □ *Serm.* 149c

Gloriose Virginis imitationem □ *Serm.* 106a

Glosa super idem Mt xii: extende manum tuam, nulla plus □ *Serm.* 189
Glosa: paschin grece, pati latine.Triplex pascha celebrav' □ *Serm.* 117
Hec prophetia in festo hodierno impleta est ubi duo notan' □ *Serm.* 227
Hic duo possunt notari, scilicet, humana redemptio, et □ *Serm.* 97
Hic est Christus qui pridie passus, hodie resurrexit □ *Serm.* 120
Hic innuit Apostolus vii que necessaria sunt vere penitenti □ *Serm.* 24
Hic misterium corporis et sanguinis Christi designatur de □ *Serm.* 122
Hic notantur patientis dignitas ibi Christus, pene acerbitas □ *Serm.* 132
Hic notatur ascensus in eminentia vite □ *Serm.* 159
Hic notatur ordo iustificationis impii; primo enim, accepta □ *Serm.* 76
Hic quinque consideremus: que sit ancilla, que libera, quis □ *Serm.* 82
Hic tria notantur, videlicet, passionis Christi rememoratio □ *Serm.* 137
Hic verba scripta sunt Mt 4 in quibus tanguntur tria que □ *Serm.* 56
Hiis notatur tria, videlicet Status culpe recordatio □ *Serm.* 84
Hiis verbis excellens Christi caritas et quid nobis agendum □ *Serm.* 94
Hoc enim faciendum est multis rationibus, scilicet, ut Xtm □ *Serm.* 163
Hoc sentite sensu, scilicet, experientie quod in Christo Jesu □ *Serm.* 108
Homo existens ex duabus naturis dupplicem habet mortem □ *Serm.* 115
Humilitas est utilis □ *Serm.* 179
Iactator graviter egrotat, quippe bona opera sunt cibus □ *Serm.* 150
Ignis sine calore; quippe sunt ignis depictus a longe □ *Serm.* 149b
In cordis puritate quod spectat ad contritionem □ *Serm.* 140
In epistola hodierna legitur, sit omnis homo velox ad audi' □ *Serm.* 144
In evangelio hodierno invitat Dominus omnes fideles ad □ *Serm.* 185
In fine huius evangelii legitur Beati qui audiunt verbum □ *Serm.* 72
In hiis verbis duo notantur; unum quod spectat ad gratiam □ *Serm.* 157
In hiis verbis excellens Christi caritas humano generi □ *Serm.* 90
In hiis verbis innuuntur duo, scilicet, que debentur verbo □ *Serm.* 40
In hiis verbis monet Apostolus fideles ad gaudendum □ *Serm.* 19
In hiis verbis notantur status duplicis hominis status □ *Serm.* 131
In hiis verbis possunt notari duo, scilicet, vite nostre □ *Serm.* 143
In hiis verbis primo, mors Christi certa supponitur ibi qui □ *Serm.* 114
In hiis verbis quattuor consideranda sunt, scilicet, quis □ *Serm.* 118
In hiis verbis tangitur et loquitur quicquid hodie geritur □ *Serm.* 79
In hiis verbis tria tanguntur, primo monet ut petamus □ *Serm.* 152
In initio Misse hodierne diei canit Ecclesia: "Deus in adj. □ *Serm.* 221
In primo aspectu duo occurrunt consideranda, que sit Dei □ *Serm.* 66
In principio sermonis nostri invocemus salvatoris suffrag' □ *Serm.* 165
In principio sermonis nostri oret unusquisque Deum ut □ *Serm.* 6
Invocemus Spiritum Sanctum in principio sermonis nostri □ *Serm.* 167
Ista verba leguntur in ysaya 25 et possunt exponi triplici □ *Serm.* 18
Iste textus Apostoli sumptus est de ys 54 ubi dicitur, Lauda □ *Serm.* 80
Itinerantes et peregrini precipue cum elongati fuerint a □ *Serm.* 207

Karissimi, unicus Dominus noster et magister omnium qui ait □ *Serm.* 39
Karissimi, doctrina sacri libri in principio operum nostrorum □ *Serm.* 77b
Lacrime Deum cognat □ *Serm.* 203
Lectionem frequenter interrumpat oratio □ *Serm.* 199b
Legitur in Deut quod Deus loquens ad Moysen dixit: Ligabis □ *Serm.* 204
Legitur in Libro Antiquorum de populo Israelitico in capt' □ *Serm.* 26
Legitur in ecc° fons sapientie verbum Domini in excelsis □ *Serm.* 216
Legitur in evangelio hodierno quod imminente Pascha, quod □ *Serm.* 78
Legitur in evangelio hodierno quod non in solo pane vivit □ *Serm.* 51
Legitur in libro antiquorum quod populus Israel postquam □ *Serm.* 49
Legitur in prov 1 in persona Gloriose Virginis: qui me aud' □ *Serm.* 232
Magna est excellentia pure orationis □ *Serm.* 199a
Magnum aliquid reputat continuam orationem □ *Serm.* 202
Mater Ecclesia temporibus istis adventus, multum recitat □ *Serm.* 9
Mater nostra Ecclesia de salute Christianorum valde solli' □ *Serm.* 73
Mater nostra Ecclesia, semper de salute filiorum sollicita □ *Serm.* 34
[Ecco] Miserere anime tue □ *Serm.* 187
Misericordia est amor relevandi a miseria □ *Serm.* 192
Narra evangelium et fiat oratio. Notandum quod Deus, Pater □ *Serm.* 225
Narretur evangelium et exponatur cecus iste tripliciter □ *Serm.* 44
Narretur evangelium et fiat oratio. In hiis verbis notantur □ *Serm.* 220
Narretur evangelium et fiat oratio; homo iste Dominus noster □ *Serm.* 171
Narretur evangelium mistice. Dominus descendens de monte □ *Serm.* 27
Narretur evangelium etc. Unicus Dominus et magister omnium □ *Serm.* 38
Narretur hystoria evangelii et fiat oratio. Cum Christus □ *Serm.* 219
Nativitas bene dicitur dies, primo quia quid est dies nisi □ *Serm.* 3
Non dicit quantum, quia eius dolor super omnem dolorem et □ *Serm.* 103
Non in solo pane vivit homo sed in omni verbo qui procedit □ *Serm.* 55
Non in solo pane vivit homo. Homo conficitur ex corpore et □ *Serm.* 52
Non treuga quod cito transit. Istam accipiunt qui proponunt □ *Serm.* 128
Nota hic Beate Virginis commendatio et eius ad gaudium □ *Serm.* 85
Nota quod Christus mortuus est pro iniustis Pe 4 □ *Serm.* 133
Nota quod Matheus dicit emisit spiritum, Johannes tradidit □ *Serm.* 112
Nota quod desertum dicitur multipliciter dicitur enim □ *Serm.* 59
Nota quod non solum Dominus est rogandus ut maneat sed comp' □ *Serm.* 126
Nulli tedeat verbum Dei audire, homo enim etc □ *Serm.* 222
Nuper tempore passionis, Dominice multa audivimus de eius □ *Serm.* 136
O lacrima cum oratione humili □ *Serm.* 155
Obediendum est non solum exterius sed interius □ *Serm.* 181
Officium Ecclesie hodiernum multum et sepe tangit de oratio' □ *Serm.* 198
Oratio animam letificat □ *Serm.* 200a
Oratio efficaciter impetrat □ *Serm.* 200c
Palma precipue Christus quia mascula □ *Serm.* 111

Peccatorum odium; Ambrosius: Ve tibi amaritudo peccatorum □ *Serm.* 106f
Per Jerusalem, que interpretatur visio pacis, intelligit □ *Serm.* 214
Per istum cecum intellige quemlibet peccatorem, qui foris □ *Serm.* 43
Petrus Ravenensis: Christus breviter orare docet □ *Serm.* 201
Possunt tria dici, primo, quare Christus resurgens a mortuis □ *Serm.* 130
Predicanti verbum Dei tria sunt necessaria, eminentia vite □ *Serm.* 206
Prima est conservare a peccato □ *Serm.* 191
Primo videndum qui sunt illi tres testes, secundo ubi □ *Serm.* 169
Ps ad vesperum Passionis demorabitur fletus, et ad matutinam □ *Serm.* 127
Quando aliqui frequentius et sepius audiunt verbum Dei □ *Serm.* 53
Quando festum alicuius magnatis debet commendari, oportet □ *Serm.* 166
Quando mercatores sunt in nundinis, si Deus signaret eis □ *Serm.* 37
Quare non sit fornicandum multiplex potest assignari ratio □ *Serm.* 211
Quattuor in verbo proposito possunt considerari, primo □ *Serm.* 208
Quattuor sunt cause humilitatis paupertas, vilitatis □ *Serm.* 182
Qui credit Jesum esse Filium Dei, credit Deum Patrem ei □ *Serm.* 125
Qui mare navigant etc. ut alibi fiat oratio "Cum jocunditate" □ *Serm.* 234
Qui navigant mare dupplici indigent suffragio, scilicet □ *Serm.* 30
Quia adventum ingressi sumus proposuimus nobis aliquid de □ *Serm.* 5
Raro predicatur vobis verbum Domini, et quanto rarius annun' □ *Serm.* 15
Recipit donum □ *Serm.* 129
Recompensationem in Mt 24; Esurivi etc.; sitivi etc □ *Serm.* 106b
Recordata est Jerusalem dierum afflictionibus sue prevar' □ *Serm.* 32
Reges terrenos venientes ad civitates et castra precedent □ *Serm.* 11
Reis ad reconciliandum, peccatoribus ad satisfaciendum □ *Serm.* 61
Rogemus cum Apostolo ut Deus aperiat nobis hostium sermonis □ *Serm.* 212
Salamone in proverbiis, audiens sapiens sapientior erit □ *Serm.* 65
Salvator hominum a sinu procedens Patris in uterum matris □ *Serm.* 22
Sancta mater nostra Ecclesia intendit hodie, in verbo □ *Serm.* 14
Sciendum quod duplex est desertum, culpe et penitentie □ *Serm.* 50
Scio quod non est iniquitas sicut iniquitas mea □ *Serm.* 113a
Scitis quod homo perficitur ex corpore et anima. Anima aut' □ *Serm.* 70
Scitis quod pauper stans ad ianuam divitis, longe ab aula □ *Serm.* 25
Scitis quoniam cera ab igne calefacta liquescit, ab igne □ *Serm.* 170
Scitis quoniam reges et principes terrarum qui et iusti □ *Serm.* 89
Scriptum est a sapientia.In initio cuiuslibet operis Deum □ *Serm.* 29
Scriptum est in Ps. Verbo Domini celi firmati sunt □ *Serm.* 138
Septem elemosyne sunt spirituales et septem corporales □ *Serm.* 190
Sermo noster hodiernus erit de amore. Amor enim in amantis □ *Serm.* 164
Sermo noster hodiernus erit de oratione; ad hanc nos admonet □ *Serm.* 153
Sermo noster, Deo dante, erit de Virgine Gloriosa, cuius □ *Serm.* 231
Si aliquis vestrum hic esset, crucis caractere insignitus □ *Serm.* 77a
Si exasperatur Deus immanitate □ *Serm.* 113b

Si ita esset quod Dominus noster Jesus Christus nunc, sicut □ *Serm.* **71**
Si nos omnes hic congregati de necessitate mare transiremus □ *Serm.* **213**
Si nos omnes hic congregati de necessitate mare transiremus □ *Serm.* **217**
Si nos omnes, hic congregati, adiudicati essemus morti pro □ *Serm.* **119**
Sic est de Christo sicut de aliquo rege terreno, qui post' □ *Serm.* **123**
Sicut Deo huius seculi de quo I Cor iiii Deus huius seculi □ *Serm.* **23**
Sicut autem duplex est malum vel morbus, culpa et pena □ *Serm.* **62**
Sicut dupliciter polluitur anima, sic duplex est purgatio □ *Serm.* **67**
Sicut magister noster Christus a Spiritu Sancto ductus □ *Serm.* **57**
Solent heredes petere, post mortem patris, quid ei testamento □ *Serm.* **134**
Templum dedicando primum uterum virginis □ *Serm.* **91**
Tempus scilicet gratie, vel tempus quadragesimale ad medend' □ *Serm.* **60**
Tres sunt miserationes Dei circa electos, prima quod invicos □ *Serm.* **196**
Tria dicit hic Apostolus quod humiliandum sit, ibi humiliam' □ *Serm.* **174a**
Tria dicuntur Veneranda filii nativitas ibi *natus*; □ *Serm.* **20**
Tria dicuntur quod humiliandum est, propter quam utilitatem □ *Serm.* **183**
Tria dicuntur quod humiliandum sit, et cui, et propter quid □ *Serm.* **184**
Tria hic precipue designantur videlicet, vite veteris mutat' □ *Serm.* **68**
Tria hic tanguntur, Christi passio ibi, Christus passus; □ *Serm.* **135**
Tria notantur viz; sentiendi exortatio; □ *Serm.* **102**
Tria notantur, passio Christi, efficacia eius, et effectus □ *Serm.* **92**
Tria possunt hic notari de vita cuiuslibet peccatoris, viz □ *Serm.* **197**
Tria possunt hic notari, scilicet, subdita gratie illustratio □ *Serm.* **45**
Tria possunt hic notari scilicet: □ *Serm.* **48**
Tria sunt genera auditorum, quidam sermonem Dei audire conte' □ *Serm.* **146**
Tria sunt hic notanda, scilicet, quid monetur abstinere □ *Serm.* **141**
Tria sunt hic notanda; quis sit iste rex et quare vocetur □ *Serm.* **100**
Tria sunt in Dominica Palmarum □ *Serm.* **124**
Tria sunt in Dominica Palmarum primum est pueri Hebreorum □ *Serm.* **104**
Tria sunt quare ipsum sequi conveniat □ *Serm.* **86**
Tria tanguntur in hiis verbis perfecta, Christi humilitas □ *Serm.* **172**
Tria ut frequencius solent attendere sermocinantes, scilicet □ *Serm.* **47**
Triplex notatur, effectus fusionis sanguinis Christi, quia □ *Serm.* **96**
Tuitionis in certitudinem I Reg; cum esset David in Geth non □ *Serm.* **106c**
Tum propter retributionis modum □ *Serm.* **180b**
Turpissima; Sap: morte turpissima condemnemus eum □ *Serm.* **106h**
Ut legitur in Prov 13 Sermo purus firmabitur a Deo; sermo □ *Serm.* **41**
Ut se nos amare ostenderet. Dicitur quod per minimum foramen □ *Serm.* **95**
Ut supplicium gravius vitemus Luc 2: ille servus qui cognovit □ *Serm.* **148**
Ut supplicium gravius vitemus quia Luce 2 ille servus qui □ *Serm.* **156**
Vas beneficiis vacuum, exemplum de doleo quod sonat vacuum □ *Serm.* **149a**
Verba sunt Apostoli in epistola hodierna in quibus monet fi' □ *Serm.* **7**
Verba sunt Domini, per Jeremiam. Sicut bonus pastor curam □ *Serm.* **99**

Verba sunt ad Eph Apostoli 4, in quibus hortatur nos spirit' □ *Serm.* 223
Verba sunt beati Apostoli ad Ro xiii, fratres mei, socii et am' □ *Serm.* 4
Verba sunt beati Petri et tanguntur hic tria remedia tribus □ *Serm.* 174b
Verbum Domini a fidelibus audiendum est et intelligendum □ *Serm.* 121
Verbum Domini summa diligencia et devotione ad omnibus audi' □ *Serm.* 21
Videamus hic tria, scilicet, qui sint eiciendi et ubi sint □ *Serm.* 88
Videamus tria: quare palma portatur, quare passio processionem □ *Serm.* 110
Videndum est que sit hec gratia de qua hic loquitur Apostol' □ *Serm.* 58
Videndum est quis sit iste Cesar, que sint sua ei reddenda. □ *Serm.* 218
Videndum quis venit, quoniam rex ad quid innuitur quod ad ut □ *Serm.* 101
Virgo Maria de qua presens fiet sermocinatio dicitur inven' □ *Serm.* 233
Vita cuiuslibet hominis peregrinatio, secundum sanctum, ad □ *Serm.* 35

THEMA

A nativitate Domini usque modo solet tempus expendi scil' □ *Serm.* 33
Ante adventum Domini, fratres, tantis tenebris genus humanum □ *Serm.* 12
Apostolus in epistola hodierna omnes in mundo videntes com' □ *Serm.* 35
Beatus Petrus custos et prelatus totius Ecclesie in epist' □ *Serm.* 142
Cesar dicitur dyabolum duplici ratione. Dicitur enim Cesar □ *Serm.* 228
Circa hec verba ad presens videamus tria, primo cum multip' □ *Serm.* 56
Cum aurora sit finis noctis et origo diei profecto aurora □ *Serm.* 233
Cum omnis Christi actio nostra sit instructio ista Christi □ *Serm.* 57
Cum tempus istud quadragesimali tempus spiritualis pugne □ *Serm.* 53
Dicatur narratio evangelii ad litteram et etiam mistice □ *Serm.* 217
Dicatur narratio evangelii si libeat. In verbis premissis □ *Serm.* 25
Dicatur narratio evangelii. In verbo presenti tria queri □ *Serm.* 26
Dominum Salvatorem in terris ambulantem et viam celestem □ *Serm.* 207
Dominus noster pius Jesus magnam audaciam orandi magnamque □ *Serm.* 153
Dominus per terram ambulando multas et diversas languentibus □ *Serm.* 71
Duo dicenda sunt quare Christus diligendus est et qualiter □ *Serm.* 222
Duo dicenda sunt. Que sint opera tenebrarum et quare abic' □ *Serm.* 6
Duo principaliter tanguntur in hiis verbis □ *Serm.* 31
Duo sunt querenda; quis sit ille rex, et quare dicatur rex □ *Serm.* 8
Duplicem adventum hiis diebus rememorat nobis □ *Serm.* 9
Ecclesia in alia parte quadragesimale que precessit □ *Serm.* 90
Et notandum quod cum triplex sit mors: carnalis, spiritualis □ *Serm.* 205
Glosa super illud Psalmi aput me oratio Deo vite mee dicit □ *Serm.* 198
Hec fuit petitio ceci corporalis per quam sicut tangit □ *Serm.* 46
Hic tria dicenda sunt, primo de navicula, secundo de ascensu □ *Serm.* 30
Huius auctoritatis est sensus Memorare passionis mee que □ *Serm.* 99
Immensa Christi potestas ibi fecit cenam magnam; et excellens □ *Serm.* 171
In Christo Jesu baptizatus est qui in iustificatione eius □ *Serm.* 204
In evangelio precedentis dominice egit? ecclesia de humili □ *Serm.* 11

In hiis enim verbis ad litteram signatur egressus a regione □ *Serm.* 69
In hiis verbis duo possunt notari Christi, labor in via et □ *Serm.* 146
In hiis verbis monet nos beatus Petrus ad duo: ad habendum □ *Serm.* 164
In hiis verbis primo monet nos Dominus ad petendum ibi pet' □ *Serm.* 154
In hiis verbis quattuor sunt attendenda quare verbum compar' □ *Serm.* 38
In hiis verbis tria considerare debemus quare scilicet, □ *Serm.* 40
In presenti verbo tria possunt considerari, videlicet quis □ *Serm.* 15
In verbo isto ostendit nobis Apostolus primo Quid sit volunt □ *Serm.* 65
Ista verba sunt Apostoli scripta in epistola hodierna □ *Serm.* 29
Istud non tantum Petro dicitur immo omnibus in apostolatum □ *Serm.* 230
Legitur in evangelio hodierna de quodam spirituali bello □ *Serm.* 49
Legitur in evangelio hodierno quod Dominus exiens de una □ *Serm.* 221
Legitur in evangelio quod Dominus eiecit demonium a quodam □ *Serm.* 72
Legitur quod tempore isto medio inter ascensionem et pent' □ *Serm.* 165
Mistice illud desertum est mundus vel populus peccator □ *Serm.* 63
Narrat evangelista de Christo quod cum operaretur salutes □ *Serm.* 70
Narretur transcurrendo vis evangelii horribile multum est □ *Serm.* 170
Naute mare transeuntes in tenebris noctis maxime beneficio □ *Serm.* 224
Omnes doctrina scripture ad hoc tendit ut vitetur malum ut □ *Serm.* 10
Propheta per Spiritum Sanctum altitudinem huius diei expav' □ *Serm.* 119
Quamvis omni tempore pugnandum sit contra hostes spirituales □ *Serm.* 55
Quasi dicat sicut misit me Pater a summo celo ad terras □ *Serm.* 144
Quattuor hic tanguntur, patientia, dignitas □ *Serm.* 134
Queri potest quibus de causis in tantum sit exaltata et □ *Serm.* 232
Quicumque cum Christo resurgere desiderat modum resurrecti' □ *Serm.* 121
Sciendum est quod spiritualiter quidam iacent quidam sedent □ *Serm.* 212
Scriptum est in psalmo: ad vesperam demorabitur fletus et ad □ *Serm.* 123
Si quis vestrum haberet aliquam arduam causam coram iudice □ *Serm.* 234
Sicut anima dupliciter polluitur per originale peccatum et □ *Serm.* 64
Sicut ex serie littere patet quod intendit hic Apostolus □ *Serm.* 47
Solent principes et reges regnorum quando pugnaturi sunt □ *Serm.* 51
Spiritus iste Spiritus Sanctus est qui hodierna die a thro' □ *Serm.* 167
Tria dicit quod humiliandum sit ibi humiliamini et cui quia □ *Serm.* 216
Tria hic notanda sunt, quod Christus passus est, quod pro □ *Serm.* 136
Tria sunt hic dicenda scilicet cum verbum Dei dupliciter □ *Serm.* 39
Ut dicit beatus Augustinus super Genesem ad litteram, ipsa □ *Serm.* 41
Verba ista beati Apostoli ad Ro xiii duas in se continent □ *Serm.* 4
Verba ista leguntur in evangelio quod legitur in Christi □ *Serm.* 21
Verba ista sunt Salamonis scripta in Cantico et sunt tria □ *Serm.* 231
Verba sunt Apostoli in epistola hodierna sciendum est quod □ *Serm.* 206
Verba sunt Beati Petri et innuunt nobis duo □ *Serm.* 138

Appendix 6

The Source-Books

Confessiones Augustini: 88, 100, 118, 139, 152, 168, 196 □ TOTAL 7

Liber Minimus: 1, 20, 85, 86, 87, 131, 172, 173 □ TOTAL 8

Liber Niger Maior: 5, 31, 32, 55, 56, 69, 136, 182 [de manu H'] □ TOTAL 8

Liber Niger Minor: 4, 18, 28, 30, 39, 40, 41, 46, 66 [Simon of Hinton OP], 100, 122, 147, 212 □ TOTAL 13

Liber Proprius: 6, 7, 9, 10 [William Peraldus OP], 11, 12, 13, 14, 15, 21, 25, 26, 27, 29, 34, 35, 36, 37 [not in liturgical place], 38, 43, 44, 49, 51, 53, 64, 65, 70, 71, 72, 73, 77 [William Peraldus OP], 78 [Hugh of St Cher OP], 89, 90, 120, 121, 123, 138, 142, 144, 145, 153, 154, 155, 164, 165 [William Peraldus OP], 167, 170, 171 [Hugh of S. Cher OP], 174, 185, 198 [William Peraldus OP], 204, 205, 206, 207, 208, 210, 213 □ TOTAL 61

Liber Rubeus Maior: 45 same as 48, 47, 48 [same as 45], 54, 67, 68, 75, 76, 79, 80, 81, 82 [Richard Fishacre OP], 84, 92, 93, 101, 102, 103, 129 [sermon material], 137, 156 [see *Parvus Liber Rubeus*: 148], 157, 158, 159, 161, 163 □ TOTAL 26

Liber Rubeus Minor: 42, 63, 83 [Peter of Rheims OP], 91, 95, 104 [same as 124, no book], 105, 106–107 [sermon material], 108 [Peter of Rheims OP], 109 [sermon material], 110, 111, 112, 113 [sermon material], 115, 116, 117 [Peter of Rheims], 126, 127 [Peter of Rheims OP], 128 [sermon material], 130 □ TOTAL 22

Liber Tabulatus: 3 □ TOTAL 1

Liber Virginis Gloriose: 19 □ TOTAL 1

Quaternus Oxoniensis: 57, 119 □ TOTAL 2

Parvus Liber Niger: 17, 74, 146 □ TOTAL 3

Parvus Liber Rubeus: 23, 24, 58, 59, 60 [Peter of Rheims OP], 61, 62, 96, 97, 98 [John of Abbeville], 114, 125, 132, 133 [Peter of Rheims OP], 134, 135, 140, 141, 143, 148 [same as 156: see *Liber Rubeus Maior*], 160, 162, 169, 183, 184, 186, 187–193 [sermon material], 194, 197, 199–203 [sermon material], 209 □ TOTAL 41

Parvus Liber Rubeus Minor: 94, 211 □ TOTAL 2

No book cited: 2 [margin cropped], 8, 16 [*Parvo Libro co*], 50, 52 [extra anti-theme: see *Liber Proprius*], 124 [same as 104: see *Liber Rubeus Minor*], 149, 150, 151, 166 [fr H. de Mordon], 175, 176, 177, 178, 179, 180, 181, 195, □ TOTAL 18

The table below shows that the compiler made specific citations (often with folio, line, or column) to many sermons from the 8 Source Books. References to 5 of them are not numerous enough to reveal any significant patterns except for their use of arabic numerals. In references to the 3 others (*Liber Proprius, Rubeus Minor, Parvus Liber Rubeus*), however, distinct patterns emerge. The manuscript incorporates the source book sermons in liturgical order. When citations to them are re-ordered numerically a different pattern emerges. This pattern is not liturgical but probably chronological.

Source-Book	Manuscript Order	Source-Book order
Confessiones Augustini	118 (T28).17.	118 (T28).17.
	196 (T45) ult' fol.'	196 (T45) ult' fol.',
Liber Niger Maior	5 (T 1) li' ii	
Liber Niger Minor	212 (T50).1.02	
Liber Rubeus Maior	103 (T24) 57	103 (T24) 57
	137 (T30) 57.35	137 (T30) 57.35,
Parvus Liber Niger	46 (T32) 67	
Liber Proprius	144 (T32) fol. 6	145 (T32) fol. Vn (bl)
		fol. 7 (red)
	145 (T32) fol. Vn (bl)	144 (T32) fol. 6
	7 (red)	
	198 (T46) fol.59	213 (T51) 38
	204 (T47) 67	198 (T46) fol. 59
	210 (T50) 1.Vi **	204 (T47) 67
	213 (T51) 38	
Liber Rubeus Minor	108 (T24) 208	116 (T28).1.73.1
	115 (T28).1.76	115 (T28).1.76
	116 (T28).1.73.1	117 (T28).1.77.1
	117 (T28).1.77.1	108 (T24) 208,
Parvus Liber Rubeus	98 (T23) 181	188 (T45) 8.1
	148 (T33) 138.24	192 (T45) 24.10
	183 (T44) 165	189 (T45) 26.27
	184 (T44) 2.ii**	190 (T45) 27.1
	186 (T45) 231.4	191 (T45) 27.15
	187 (T45) 229.1	193 (T45) 33.1
	188 (T45) 8.1	148 (T33) 138.24
	189 (T45) 26.27	183 (T44) 165
	190 (T45) 27.1	98 (T23) 181
	191 (T45) 27.15	187 (T45) 229.1
	192 (T45) 24.10	186 (T45) 231.4
	193 (T45) 33.1	194 (T45) 235.1
	194 (T45) 235.1	

Note □ A double asterisk (**) above indicates difficulty in interpreting the medieval number. Most of the dots in the numbers are found in the middle of the space, not at the bottom of the line. A 1 or 2 followed by such a dot, often indicates a numerical hundred.

Appendix 7

The *Exempla*

This compendium of the *exempla* in MS Laud Misc. 511 is organized in manuscript order. The sermon number in **bold** (corresponding to those of the Catalogue of the Manuscript in Appendix 1), is followed by each *exemplum*, together with the appropriate folio reference (page number with column a or b, and line number preceded by a period). Where there is more than one *exemplum*, each is numbered sequentially in square brackets: thus, *Serm.* **78** [3] indicates the third *exemplum* in Sermon 78.

Most exempla are indicated in the margin by ex^m; where they are not, other marginalia may be used, in isolation or together with ex^m (they are indicated below by a + sign). These additional marginalia include: *narratio*, which may appear in full or abbreviated in the manuscript (given here as *narr*); *face*, *finger*, and *title*. Any Latin phrase quoted is from a scribe or annotator. About 77 out of some 463 *exempla* are not designated in the margin of the text by the annotation exm, or by title, narr., or pattern such as face or finger. Nevertheless some of these unidentified *exempla* have parallels among those identified. A list is given here: *Serm.* 12 [4], 13 [9], 26 [1], 27 [1], 29 [2, 3], 30 [3, 4, 12, 15, 16], 32 [2, 3], 37 [3], 39 [3], 46 [6], 47 [1], 50 [1, 2, 3], 53 [1, 2, 3], 57 [6], 66 [4], 69 [1, 5], 72 [3, 4], 77 [1, 2], 78 [4], 82 [1, 2], 89 [3], 90 [3], 100 [3, 6], 114 [2, 3, 4], 118 [2, 3], 123 [1], 134 [1], 145 [1, 2, 4, 5, 8], 146 [1, 2], 153, 162, 170 [1], 204 [1, 2], 205 [3], 207 [1, 2], 218, 221 [4], 224 [3, 4], 226 [2, 4] 227 [2], 228, 130 [4, 6] 231, 232 [2, 3, 4] 233 [3, 4] 234.

A brief synopsis of the *exemplum* follows this codicological information (a lack of title indicates that the meaning of the *exemplum* is unclear; a brief description is provided where possible). SOURCES and analogues for an *exemplum* are placed in parentheses, cited according to the list of manuscript and printed sources below. Where relevant, cross-references are provided.

REFERENCES
Manuscripts
London: British Library, MS Harley 3244: catalogued in *Catalogue of Romances* (see below) 3: 457– 463

London: British Library, MS Royal 7 D i: catalogued in *Catalogue of Romances* (see below) 3: 477– 503

Printed Collections of Exempla and Indexes
An Alphabet of Tales: An English 15th-Century Translation of the 'Alphabetum narrationum,' ed. M.M. Banks, Early English Texts Society 126– 127 (London, 1904– 1905)

Catalogue of Romances in the Department of Manuscripts in the British Museum, ed. H.L.D. Ward and J.A. Herbert, 3 vols. (London, 1883– 1910) [cited as CatRom with vol. number]

Etienne de Bourbon, *Tractatus de diversis materiis praedicabilibus*, ed. A. Lecoy de la Marche in *Anecdotes historiques, légendes et apologues tirés du recueil inédit d'Etienne de Bourbon, Dominicain du XIIIe siècle* (Paris, 1877)

Gesta Romanorum: cited from the *Catalogue of Romances* (see above)

Jacques de Vitry, *The Exempla or Illustrative Stories from the 'Sermones Vulgares' of Jacques de Vitry*, ed T.F. Crane, (London, 1890) [See also *CatRom* 3: 1-30]

Liber Exemplorum ad usum praedicantium, ed. A.G. Little (Aberdeen, 1908)

Odo of Cheriton: various fables in manuscript; cited from the *Catalogue of Romances*: see *CatRom* 3: 31-77

Odo of Cheriton, *Fabulis addita collectio tertia*; *Fabulae*; and *Parabolae*: all cited from *Les Fabulistes Latins depuis le siècle d'Auguste jusqu'à la fin du moyen age*, ed. Léopold Hervieux, vol. 4 (Paris, 1896)

Le 'Speculum Laicorum': *Edition d'une collection d'exempla, composée en Angleterre à la fin du XIIIe siècle*, ed. J. Th. Welter (Paris, 1914). See also *CatRom* 3: 370-405, which describes the version found in MS Additional 11284.

La 'Tabula Exemplorum' secundum ordinam alphabeti: Receuil d'"exempla" compilé en France à la fin du XIIIe siècle (Paris-Toulouse, 1926) [exempla from this collection do not seem to appear in MS Laud Misc. 511]

Frederick C. Tubach, *Index Exemplorum: A Handbook of Medieval Religious Tales* (Helsinki, 1969) [cited by the abbreviation Tubach and number]

S.L. Forte, OP, "A Cambridge Dominican Collector of *Exempla* in the Thirteenth Century [some from British Library, MS Royal 7 D i] *AFP* 28 (1958), 115-148 [exempla from this collection do not seem to appear in MS Laud Misc. 511]

THE EXEMPLA IN MS LAUD MISC. 511

Sermon 1 [1] fol. 5b.26: Verbal analysis □ [2] fol. 5b.31: Verbal analysis □ [3] fol. 5b.33: Verbal analysis

Sermon 6 [1] fol. 8b.35: Fear and horror of perils of darkness in unknown area □ [2] fol. 8va.6: Fear □ [3] fol. 8va.17, *narr.*: Story of King Antiochus at death (Peter Comestor?) □ [4] fol. 8vb.26: Rough road to the Holy Land

Sermon 7 [1] fol. 9a.34: Sleeping near a thief; cf. *Serm.* 13 [6], *Serm.* 57 [12] □ [2] fol. 9b.21: Extinguishing fire □ [3] fol. 9b.26: Fire □ [4] fol. 9b.37: Rescuing animals from mud (SOURCES Odo of Cheriton, *Sermones* 2.62 [*CatRom* 3: 75, no. 178; unique to BL, MS Arundel 231]) □ [5] fol. 9va.8: A woman's horror at giving birth to a toad or serpent (SOURCES Odo of Cheriton, *Sermones* 2.42 [*CatRom* 3: 68, no. 97; unique to MS Arundel 231]) □ [6] fol. 9vb.1: Prepare for feast with clean clothes and cloths □ [7] fol. 9vb.3: Clean the house to welcome friends; cf. *Serm.* 12 [4], *Serm.* 67 [3]

Sermon 8 [1] fol. 10a.3: The King's duties; cf. *Serm.* 15 [2] □ [2] fol. 10a.33: Stupid behaviour □ [3] fol. 10b.29, title: The salamander (SOURCES BL, MS Harley 3244, fol. 80b; Odo of Cheriton, *Parabolae* 97 [ed. Hervieux, p. 302], *Collection tertia* 3.3 [p. 406]; *Gesta Romanorum* [*CatRom* 3: 163, no. 105]; Tubach 4156]) □ [4] fol. 10b.40: Hermit and dead rich man (SOURCES BL, MS Harley 3244, fol. 75vb-76a [cf. *CatRom* 3: 459, no. 30]; Odo of Cheriton, *Parabolae* 4 [ed. Hervieux, pp. 266-267]); cf. *Serm.* 15 [4], *Serm.* 226 [5]

Sermon 9 fol. 10vb.21: God's servants suffer now, will be rewarded hereafter

Sermon 11 [1] fol. 12va.1: Fanfare for King's entry to Town □ [2] fol. 12vb.20: Christ's Second Coming □ [3] fol. 12vb.23: A wounded part afflicts whole body □ [4] fol. 12vb.38: City rising against King; cf. *Serm.* 214

Sermon 12 [1] fol. 14b.13: Ark returned from Philistines □ [2] fol. 14b.23, *ex^m bonum*, title: The stag (SOURCES BL, MS Harley 3244, fol. 41v; Tubach 4270; Odo of Cheriton, *Collection tertia* 16 [ed. Hervieux, p. 412]; Robert Holcot, *Convertimini* [see *CatRom* 3: 139, no. 34]; Jacques de Vitry, *Sermones* 71 [*Exem.* 274, ed. Crane; cf. *CatRom* 3: 23, no. 195]); cf. *Serm.* 78 [3], *Serm.* 104 □ [3] fol. 14va.40: Preparing a guest room; cf. *Serm.* 13 [5], *Serm.* 14 [4], *Serm.* 100 [10], *Serm.* 119 [2] □ [4] fol. 14vb.4: Cleaning house, furnishings and clothes in preparation for feast; cf. *Serm.* 7 [7], *Serm.* 67 [3]

Sermon 13 [1] fol. 14vb.27: Christmas a feast for all □ [2] fol. 15a.22: It is 1251 years since the Lord came as man □ [3] fol. 15a.30: Mildew of sin □ [4] fol. 15a. 35: Temple of soul cleansed for Christ's coming (this *ex^m* is repeated at fol. 16va.38) □ [5] fol. 15b.3: Clean-up of Inn; cf. *Serm.* 12 [3], *Serm.* 14 [4], *Serm.* 100 [10], *Serm.* 119 [2] □ [6] fol. 15b.25, finger: Snake in bed (SOURCES Odo of Cheriton, *Fabulae* 59 [ed. Hervieux, p. 231], *Parabolae* 53 [pp. 285–286]); cf. *Serm.* 7 [1], *Serm.* 36 [1], *Serm.* 57 [12] □ [7] fol. 15b.35: No hospitality to a murderer □ [8] fol. 15va.6: King's son □ [9] fol. 15va.20: The execution of William and John de Marisco, 1243 (SOURCES see Chapter 8) □ [10] fol. 15va.35: Amputated foot or hand □ [11] fol. 15vb.9, *narr.*: King of Greece (SOURCES Odo of Cheriton, *Parabolae* 75 [ed. Hervieux, pp. 194–195]; Tubach [two columns of references]); cf. *Serm.* 206 [4]

Sermon 14 [1] fol. 16a.35, footnote bottom margin: King of England, Ireland, Wales and Gascony □ [2] fol. 16b.7: King of England □ [3] fol. 16va.8: Favourite son □ [4] fol. 16vb.3: Clean-up of Inn; cf. *Serm.* 12 [3], *Serm.* 13 [5], *Serm.* 100 [10], *Serm.* 119 [2] □ [5] fol. 16vb.20: Son of God equal and similar to the Father

Sermon 15 [1] fol. 17b.30: Visit to a home from a Lord □ [2] fol. 17va.16, title: King's duties; cf. *Serm.* 8 [1] □ [3] fol. 17vb.22, face: Charter-giving (seisin) □ [4] fol. 18a.30, *narr.*: Hermit and dead rich man (SOURCES MS Harley 3244, fol. 75vb–76a; Odo of Cheriton, *Parabolae* 4 [ed. Hervieux, pp. 266–267]) □ Cf. *Serm.* 8 [4], *Serm.* 226 [5]

Sermon 17 [1] fol. 18vb.40: Sun's rays and their atoms; cf. *Serm.* 82 [6], *Serm.* 205 [2], *Serm.* 208 [3], *Serm.* 209 [4] □ [2] fol. 19a.4 and 10: Eye lotion

Sermon 18 [1] fol. 19b.2 and 13: Stupid behaviour □ [2] fol. 19vb.15: Fish takes little bites to avoid hook

Sermon 21 [1] fol. 21b.38, face: Englishman exiled and in trouble □ [2] fol. 21va.6, face: King of England □ [3] fol. 21va.21, face: Sons of powerful men abuse peasant girls □ [4] fol. 21va.22, footnote: Countryman's garment (SOURCES Jacques de Vitry, *Sermones* 73 [*Exem* 288, ed. Crane; cf. *CatRom* 3: 25, no. 210])

Sermon 25 [1] fol. 22va.15: Beggar □ [2] fol. 22vb.25: King of England

Sermon 26 [1] fol. 23b.29: Wedding at Cana was Apostle John's □ [2] fol. 23va.16: Well- prepared feast □ [3] fol. 23vb.24: King of England

Sermon 27 [1] fol. 24a.4: Mountains above plains and valleys □ [2] fol. 24b.25, title: Naaman and Constantine cured of leprosy (2 Reg 5) (SOURCES 'Siluestri Confessoris, ' *Alphabetum narrationum* 713, in *An Alphabet of Tales: An English 15th-Century Translation of the 'Alphabetum narrationum, '* ed. M.M. Banks, Early English Texts Society 126- 127 [London, 1905], p. 478; the preamble to the Donation of Constantine also refers to this cure) □ [3] fol. 24va.19: Wishing only son hanged □ [4] fol. 24va, bottom margin, footnote: One's own hanging

Sermon 29 [1] fol. 25a.27, *narratio bona*: Bird lays three eggs, can hatch only two □ [2] fol. 25a.36: Animals care for own kind (SOURCES Tubach 254) □ [3] fol. 25b.9: Elements agree with each other □ [4] fol. 25b.16: The crab and the oyster (SOURCES Tubach 1310; *CatRom* 3: 377, no. 66) □ [5] fol. 25b.20: Unity of the human race □ [6] fol. 25b.42: King's friends not to be offended □ [7] fol. 25va.24: Brotherly love □ [8] fol. 25va.41: The poor are the feet of Christ (SOURCES Tubach 990) □ [9] fol. 25vb.5: Pyx (SOURCES *Speculum laicorum* 265 [pp. 52- 53])

Sermon 30 [1] fol. 25vb.32: Aids to sailing; cf. *Serm.* 224 [1] □ [2] fol. 26b.5: Ship foundered; cf. *Serm.* 57 [3] □ [3] fol. 26b.34: Greedy man's fear □ [4] fol. 26va.21: Millstone sinks immediately □ [5] fol. 27a.2: Ship's captain; cf. [10] below, *Serm.* 206 [2] □ [6] fol. 27va.2: Speak Latin only to those who under-stand it □ [7] fol. 27va.5: Scholar needs to know terms before theorems □ [8] fol. 27va.11: Nut and shell (SOURCES *Speculum laicorum* [*CatRom* 3: 377, no. 60]); cf. *Serm.* 230 [5] □ [9] fol. 27va.13: Wine- taster □ [10] fol. 27va.33: Ship's captain; cf. [5] above, *Serm.* 206 [2] □ [11] fol. 27vb.7: Ship as fast transport; cf. *Serm.* 57 [3] □ [12] fol. 28b.2: Seeing quay from deck □ [13] fol. 28b.41: Sailors' skill □ [14] fol. 28vb.30, title: Scylla and Charybdis □ [15] fol. 29a.5: Charybdis □ [16] fol. 29a.12: Sirens (SOURCES Tubach 4495) □ [17] fol. 29b.1, title: Circe □ [18] fol. 29b.12: Ship; cf. *Serm.* 57 [3]

Sermon 31 fol. 31b.11: Fire expels coal's blackness

Sermon 32 [1] fol. 32va.1, later ann.: Dog with master □ [2] fol. 32va.9: Heirs' dispute; cf. *Serm.* 134 □ [3] fol. 32va.24: Human glory passes

Sermon 33 [1] fol. 34va.26: King and opulent building □ [2] fol. 34vb.17: King of England □ [3] fol. 35a.9: King and noble □ [4] fol. 35b.12: Tears □ [5] fol. 35b.20: The Lord Edward

Sermon 35 [1] fol. 36a.32: Runner □ [2] fol. 36b.4: Condemned man and flowers; cf. *Serm.* 36 [2], *Serm.* 170 [2] □ [3] fol. 36b.27: Foolish behaviour □ [4] fol. 36va.2: Running for a prize □ [5] fol. 36vb.7: Running for one prize only □ [6] fol. 36vb.25: Wife of prisoner works to free him

Sermon 36 [1] fol. 37b.29: Scorpion in house; cf. *Serm.* 13 [6] □ [2] fol. 37b.34: Condemned man going to death; cf. *Serm.* 35 [2], *Serm.* 170 [2] □ [3] fol. 37va.2: Gardener

Sermon 37 [1] fol. 38a.25: Trading in market □ [2] fol. 38b.32: Skilled merchant □ [3] fol. 38va.2: Noble □ [4] fol. 39a.23: Son's love for father □ [5] fol. 39a.29: Blessing of having a body □ [6] fol. 39a.35: Loss of eye; cf. *Serm.* 13 [10] □ [7] fol. 39b.3: Reprieved from execution; cf. *Serm.* 54 [3], *Serm.* 119 [1], *Serm.* 147

Sermon 38 fol. 39b.28: Christ preached parables and stories not astronomy or geometry; cf. *Serm.* 39 [1], *Serm.* 57 [7], *Serm.* 69 [1], *Serm.* 198 [2]

Sermon 39 [1] fol. 40va.2, face: Christ as good teacher (magister); cf. *Serm.* 38, 57 [7], 69 [1], 119, 174, 198 [2], 201, 366 □ [2] fol. 41a.21: Mistaking mirror- like reflections for reality □ [3] fol. 41va.4: Elements □ [4] fol. 41vb.34: Importance of sowing

Sermon 40 [1] fol. 42b.15: Farmer and full barn □ [2] fol. 42vb.22: Killing King's son

Sermon 42 [1] fol. 44va.4: Prodigal Son (Luc 15:11- 52) □ [2] fol. 44va.27: Nebuchadnezzar and Sedechias (4 Reg 25:1- 7) □ [3] fol. 44vb.3, *narr.*: Stench of luxury

Sermon 46 [1] fol. 45va.23: Hare sees sideways (SOURCES Tubach 2436; Nicholas of Bozon, *Contes moralisés* [*CatRom* 3: 105, no. 46]); cf. [4] below □ [2] fol. 45vb.25: Hounds follow scent of quarry; cf. *Serm.* 95 [3], *Serm.* 136 [1] □ [3] fol. 46b.7, *narr.*: Demons repulsed by harp (Boethius?) □ [4] fol. 46vb.15: Hare sees sideways; cf. [1] above □ [5] fol. 46vb.36, *narr.*: A Master of Paris (Peter the Chanter?) (SOURCES See J.W. Baldwin, *Masters, Princes and Merchants* [Princeton, 1970], 1: 117- 120, 2: 79- 81; see also Thomas de Cantimpré, *Bonum universale de apibus* 1.19 [about Chancellor Philippe de Greve], ed. Georges Colvener [1627]) □ [6] fol. 48a.29: The swallow □ [7] fol. 48b.5, title: The peacock (SOURCES Odo of Cheriton, *Fabulae* 66 [ed. Hervieux, p. 238]; *Speculum laicorum* 389.i [p. 76]; *Vitae patrum*, in PL 73: 881, 911]); cf. *Serm.* 206 [3] □ [8] fol. 49b.11; *horribilis narratio*: The man who called on Satan (SOURCES cf. Gregory, *Dialogues* 3.20, cited in Jacques de Vitry, *Sermones* 74 [*Exem.* 295, ed. Crane; cf. *CatRom* 3: 26, no. 218])

Sermon 47 [1] fol. 49vb.16: A living fly worth more than dead gold □ [2] fol. 50b.9: The leading man in the kingdom □ [3] fol. 50b.23, finger + face: Merchants seek merchandise □ [4] fol. 51a.27: A ring; cf. *Serm.* 138 [1], *Serm.* 227 [3] □ [5] fol. 51a.41, very faint: Death- bed repentance

Sermon **49** [1] fol. 53a.20: World like a prison □ [2] fol. 53a.42: Do not let yourself be beaten up □ [3] fol. 53b.34: Soldiers' provisions in war □ [4] fol. 53b.39, story in margin: The King or prince helps his wounded followers

Sermon **50** [1] fol. 54a.40 and 54b.5, 7: Stupid behaviour □ [2] fol. 54b.41, *ex^m* in text: Judas Macabeus (SOURCES cf. BL, MS Harley 3244, fol. 72b)

Sermon **51** [1] fol. 54va.4: Humans need food □ [2] fol. 54va.21: Going to war, cf. [3] below, *Serm.* **53** [1], *Serm.* **198** [1] □ [3] fol. 54vb.29: Going to war in March: Alexander and Charlemagne (SOURCES Tubach 945); cf. [2] above, *Serm.* **53** [1], *Serm.* **198** [1]

Sermon **53** [1] fol. 55b.27: Going to war, cf. *Serm.* **51** [2, 3], *Serm.* **198** [1] □ [2] fol. 55va.31: S. Nicholas (SOURCES see *Acta Sanctorum* for numerous sources); cf. *Serm.* **226** [6] □ [3] fol. 56a.4, face: Charles and St. Giles (SOURCES Tubach 951) □ [4] fol. 56a.8: King chooses best battle- ground □ [5] fol. 56a.28: Saul in David's hands (1 Reg 24)

Sermon **54** [1] fol. 56va.5: King of France □ [2] fol. 56va.24: Consecration of a church. Liturgical practice of anointing of the crosses on walls of Church during ceremony of consecration. □ [3] fol. 56va.40: Reprieved from execution; cf. *Serm.* **37** [7], *Serm.* **119** [1], *Serm.* **147** □ [4] fol. 56vb.1: Loss of inheritance □ [5] fol. 56vb.33: Cure poisoning by its opposite

Sermon **55** [1] fol. 58vb.24: Success in fighting enemy □ [2] fol. 58vb.34: Israelites crossing Red Sea (Exodus 14); cf. *Serm.* **65** [2] □ [3] fol. 59a.42: Absalom and David (2 Reg 13- 19)

Sermon **56** [1] fol. 60b.16: Cup of suffering (Gregory, Homilies?) □ [2] fol. 60va.40: Grave illnesses

Sermon **57** [1] fol. 61b.33: The Lord's teaching on prayer (Mt 6:6) □ [2] fol. 61b.40: Preaching: exterior and interior ears □ [3] fol. 62a.16: Ship; cf. *Serm.* **30** [2, 11, 18] □ [4] fol. 62a.32, *ex^m bonum*: Taming an animal □ [5] fol. 62b.33: Christ on the Cross Mt 27:42 □ [6] fol. 62va.34: Keeping to the road □ [7] fol. 63a.2, title: Christ the Master, cf. *Serm.* **38**, *Serm.* **39** [1], *Serm.* **69** [1], *Serm.* **198** [2] □ [8] fol. 63b.25: Way of salvation □ [9] fol. 64a.1: Bitter- sweet □ [10] fol. 64a.23: Gravity and levity □ [11] fol. 64b.16: Businessmen □ [12] fol. 64vb.19; 2 faces: Snake, lion, thief in bed; cf. *Serm.* **7** [1], *Serm.* **13** [6]

Sermon **58** fol. 65va.6: Whole body benefits from food

Sermon **61** [1] fol. 67va.1: Stupid behaviour □ [2] fol. 67va.8, face: St. Arsennius

Sermon **62** [1] fol. 68b.37: Hot water freezing quickly □ [2] fol. 68b.40, *ex^m* in text: Iron burning before tow

Sermon **64** [1] fol. 69va.39: King of England □ [2] fol. 69vb.10: Dark night □ [3] fol. 70a.18: pelican (SOURCES Tubach 3657, 3658; Odo of Cheriton, *Fabulae* 57

[ed. Hervieux, p. 229], *Parabolae* 10 [p. 269], *Collection tertia* 1 [p. 405]); cf. *Serm.* 95 [11] □ [4] fol. 70va.24: Pure water □ [5] fol. 70va.38: Enemy

Sermon 65 [1] fol. 71vb.11: Purity of sun, moon, stars □ [2] fol. 71vb.38: Israelites crossing Red Sea (Ex 14); cf. *Serm.* 55 [2]

Sermon 66 [1] fol. 72vb.23: Verbal analysis □ [2] fol. 73a.19: *Diaphonum* – transparency (light versus opacity) □ [3] fol. 73b.18: God, like an artist, makes an image □ [4] fol. 73b.42: Statue disfigured by fire

Sermon 67 [1] fol. 74b.39: Working hard to please a master □ [2] fol. 74va.36: Soap-making like contrition □ [3] fol. 74vb.7: Maid cleans house; cf. *Serm.* 7 [7], *Serm.* 12 [4] □ [4] fol. 74vb.16, title: Goldsmith □ [5] fol. 74vb.20: Cleaning a silver vessel

Sermon 69 [1] fol. 75vb.29: Christ good teacher; cf. *Serm.* 38, *Serm.* 39 [1], *Serm.* 57 [7], *Serm.* 198 [2] □ [2] fol. 76a.14, *ex^m* in text: Sheep crossing bridge □ [3] fol. 76va.33: Rich man and beggar □ [4] fol. 77a.13, face: Greedy one like a wolf □ [5] fol. 77b.1: Greedy one like a crane □ [6] fol. 79a.26, face: Thief flees to monastery for sanctuary

Sermon 70 [1] fol. 80va.29, *ex^m* in text: Dog, horse □ [2] fol. 80vb.34: Excessive hate □ [3] fol. 81b.8: Enemies of man

Sermon 71 [1] fol. 82a.1: Christ on earth now □ [2] fol. 83va.21: Full wine- cask

Sermon 72 [1] fol. 83vb.3: St. Peter in Bedford □ [2] fol. 84a.18: Injury / sickness must be described to be cured □ [3] fol. 84va.3: Fire □ [4] fol. 84va.23: Properties of water, oil, milk, honey □ [5] fol. 84va.32: King gives daughter as wife of Emperor (SOURCES cf. *Gesta Romanorum* 1; Holcot, *Moralitates* [*CatRom* 3: 110- 111, no. 33]); cf. *Serm.* 78 [4] □ [6] fol. 84va.36, face: Popular saying: lay brother of Roche Abbey; cf. *Serm.* 78 [2]

Sermon 73 [1] fol. 85va.16: All rivers flow seaward □ [2] fol. 86a.10: Stupid behaviour

Sermon 74 [1] fol. 86va.16: Fall of devil and sons □ [2] fol. 86vb.17: Fall of vase from height (SOURCES Odo of Cheriton, *Parabolae* 39 [ed. Hervieux, p. 280]) □ [3] fol. 87vb.26: Dumbness □ [4] fol. 88va.11: Walking into death □ [5] fol. 88va.29: Moon crashing to earth

Sermon 75 fol. 90va.21: Egress from castle

Sermon 76 [1] fol. 92a.16: Eating a morsel □ [2] fol. 92a.40: Shame

Sermon 77 [1] fol. 93a.2: The Holy Land □ [2] fol. 93va.15: A stone can kill a human

Sermon 78 [1] fol. 94a.31: Storm □ [2] fol. 94b.27: The lay- brother of Roche Abbey; cf. *Serm.* 72 [6] □ [3] fol. 94va.14, title: The stag; cf. *Serm.* 12 [2], *Serm.* 104 □ [4] fol. 94vb.39: King gives daughter to Emperor; cf. *Serm.* 72 [5]

Sermon 79 [1] fol. 95a.42: Water drowns many □ [2] fol. 95b.2, *ex^m* in text: Tears delete writing (SOURCES Odo of Chariton, *Fabulae* [*CatRom* 3: 55, no. 105]; cf. *Speculum laicorum* 531 [cf. *CatRom* 3: 380, no. 123]; cf. Caesarius of Heisterbach, *Dialogus miraculorum* [*CatRom* 3: 351, no. 15]; Jacques de Vitry, *Sermones* 74 [*Exem.* 301, ed. Crane; cf. *CatRom* 3: 13, no. 88]; also cf. Tubach 1202)

Sermon 82 [1] fol. 96va.35: King and Queen □ [2] fol. 96vb.43: Queen of England □ [3] fol. 97a.7: Queen dishonoured (SOURCES *Vie des anciens Pères* [*CatRom* 3: 344, no. 26]) □ [4] fol. 97vb.4: King's servant □ [5] fol. 98vb.38: Fire, weeping and tears □ [6] fol. 99va.30: Sun's rays, its atoms; cf. *Serm.* 17 [1], *Serm.* 205 [2], *Serm.* 208 [3], *Serm.* 209 [4]

Sermon 89 [1] fol. 100va.1: Declaration of war □ [2] fol. 100va.21: The wrestler; cf. *Serm.* 99 [3] □ [3] fol. 100vb.31: The standard bearer

Sermon 90 [1] fol. 101b.1: Striking a spark □ [2] fol. 101b.13: Blood heals □ [3] fol. 101b.28: Bee- sting □ [4] fol. 101vb.16: Adamant and goat's blood; cf. *Serm.* 221 [4]

Sermon 93 fol. 102va.23: The king's friend

Sermon 95 [1] fol. 103va.4: Ox □ [2] fol. 103va.17: Elephant (SOURCES cf. BL, MS Harley 3244, fol. 39, 76va) □ [3] fol. 103va.23: Hunted animal; cf. *Serm.* 46 [2], *Serm.* 136 [1] □ [4] fol. 103va.29: Feast □ [5] fol. 103va.39: Not washing battle-stained tunics □ [6] fol. 103vb.5: Not talking about family □ [7] fol. 103vb.15: Healthy blood needed for healing □ [8] fol. 103vb.25: Properties of rosewater □ [9] fol. 103vb.29: Arm amputated to heal body □ [10] fol. 103vb.42: A weak person becomes weaker □ [11] fol. 104a.10: Pelican; cf. *Serm.* 64 [3] □ [12] fol. 104b.42: Covenant in blood □ [13] fol. 104b.47: Damping flame with blood

Sermon 96 fol. 104vb.19: King's son murdered

Sermon 99 [1] fol. 105b.2: Good shepherd □ [2] fol. 105b.10: Rich man's indifference to beggar □ [3] fol. 105b.19: Wrestler; cf. *Serm.* 89 [2]

Sermon 100 [1] fol. 106vb.4, title: King of England, King of France □ [2] fol. 106vb.27: Disobeying the king □ [3] fol. 107a.20: The ass' weak foreparts, strong hindparts (SOURCES *Speculum laicorum* 182 [p. 405]; the same is said of 'Ursus,' Bartholomew Anglicus, *De proprietatibus rerum*; Tubach 396) □ [4] fol. 107a.40: The sea □ [5] fol. 107b.19: Following advice □ [6] fol. 107b.41: The palm □ [7] fol. 107va.6: Going on crusade □ [8] fol. 107va.16: The mocking of Christ □ [9] fol. 107va.42: The schoolmaster □ [10] fol. 107vb.14: King of England; cf. *Serm.* 12 [3], *Serm.* 13 [5], *Serm.* 14 [4], *Serm.* 119 [2]

Sermon 101 [1] fol. 108a.14: Senses and members of body like city streets meeting at centre □ [2] fol. 108a.20: Business matters stay secret □ [3] fol. 108b.28: Fire purifies and softens metal □ [4] fol. 108va.40: Master sets slave free; cf. *Serm.* 132 [2]

Sermon **104** fol. 109vb.36: Detailed comparison of the stag; cf. *Serm.* **12** [2], *Serm.* **78** [3]

Sermon **105** fol. 110b.35: Mother's tears

Sermon **114** [1] fol. 113va.9: Sleep is instinctive □ [2] fol. 115a.7: Coal □ [3] fol. 115a.13: Physical effects of heat and cold □ [4] fol. 115a.32: Respect for Sacred Host

Sermon **118** [1] fol. 116vb.38; 118va.11, finger: Spring and Easter □ [2] fol. 117b.1: Vulture □ [3] fol. 117b.12: Cat (SOURCES Tubach 890)

Sermon **119** [1] fol. 118a.2: Reprieved from execution; cf. *Serm.* **37** [7], *Serm.* **54** [3], *Serm.* **147** □ [2] fol. 118va.29: Preparing for visitors; cf. *Serm.* **12** [3], *Serm.* **13** [5], *Serm.* **14** [4], *Serm.* **100** [10]

Sermon **120** [1] fol. 119a.11: Runaway robber recaptured □ [2] fol. 119a.30: Redeemed from Saracens □ [3] fol. 119a.34: Merchant at fair □ [4] fol. 119b.10: Damned soul is restless □ [5] fol. 119vb.29: King forgives a traitor

Sermon **123** [1] fol. 120vb.6: Peace-making after war □ [2] fol. 120vb.14: Sunset and prisoners' sadness

Sermon **130** [1] fol. 123vb.10: Pride in wounds □ [2] fol. 123vb.26: Two knights on battlefield □ [3] fol. 124a.19: Barking dogs and passers by □ [4] fol. 124a.34: Dereliction of military duty □ [5] fol. 124b.5: Aids to memory □ [6] fol. 124va.9: Knights wounded in tournament

Sermon **132** [1] fol. 125b.7: Prisoner freed □ [2] fol. 125b.11: Freed from slavery; cf. *Serm.* **101** [4] □ [3] fol. 125b.19: King tries to destroy bad customs

Sermon **133** [1] fol. 125va.16: Mill, ceaseless in movement, yet static □ [2] fol. 125vb.30: Man's imprisonment by corruption □ [3] fol. 125vb.36: King of England

Sermon **134** fol. 126b.1: Heirs seeking the will; cf. *Serm.* **32** [2]

Sermon **136** [1] fol. 127a.6: Huntsman and dogs in the chase; cf. *Serm.* **46** [2], *Serm.* **95** [3] □ [2] fol. 127va.35: Respect for crucifix and cross □ [3] fol. 127vb.30: King and fugitive

Sermon **138** [1] fol. 129a.23: Gift of ring or necklace; cf. *Serm.* **47** [4], *Serm.* **227** [3] □ [2] fol. 129b.8: Incurable weakness □ [3] fol. 129va.37: Carpenter

Sermon **141** [1] fol. 130b.13: King and portrait □ [2] fol. 130b.29: King's servant □ [3] fol. 130va.32: Clean feet dirtied by walking in mud □ [4] fol. 130vb.5: Depriving a weak person of food

Sermon **142** [1] fol. 131a.3: Banquet for noble and rich □ [2] fol. 131b.1: Travellers avoid bad food □ [3] fol. 131va.28: Shameful behaviour, fornication □ [4] fol. 131va.42: King of England's daughter; cf. *Serm.* **72** [5], *Serm.* **78** [4]

Sermon **144** fol. 132vb.5: Felony

Sermon **145** [1] fol. 133a.30: Unused path is hard going (SOURCES Tubach 4113) □ [2] fol. 133b.2: Pilgrims use nails on hands and feet to cross the Alps □ [3] fol. 133va.8: Hard work easier for one used to it □ [4] fol. 133va.10: King's son, living hard □ [5] fol. 133vb.25: Saints Andrew and Peter, and the Martyrs □ [6] fol. 134a.7: Highway or royal way (SOURCES Tubach 4111) □ [7] fol. 134a.17: Deathbed worries □ [8] fol. 134va.44: Julian the Apostate (SOURCES BL, MS Harley 3244, fol. 77a–77b; Tubach 2881; Odo of Cheriton, *Parabolae* 16 [ed. Hervieux, p. 271]; *Miracles of the Virgin Mary* [CatRom 2: 602–603, no. 4]) □ [9] fol. 134vb.2: Theophilus (SOURCES Tubach 3572; *Speculum laicorum* 370 [p. 74]; Anonymous collection of tales [CatRom 2: 595–596, no. 156]; *Liber exemplorum ad usum praedicantium* 47, ed. A.G. Little [Aberdeen, 1908], pp. 29–30, with notes on p. 134 [where he claims this is Peraldus' version]); cf. *Serm.* **231**

Sermon **146** [1] fol. 135a.17: Bad scholars □ [2] fol. 135a.35: Ill-treated horses

Sermon **147** fol. 137va.15: Reprieved from death, sentence commuted; cf. *Serm.* **37** [7], *Serm.* **54** [3], *Serm.* **119** [1]

Sermon **149a** fol. 138a.44: Contradiction of thought with word

Sermon **150** fol. 138b.27: Good works are spiritual food

Sermon **152** [1] fol. 140vb.12: Moses (Exodus) □ [2] fol. 140vb.19, *ex^m* in text: Robbers frightened off □ [3] fol. 140vb.30, *ex^m* in text: Contrasting behaviours □ [4] fol. 140vb.41, *ex^m* in text: King's writ □ [5] fol. 141a.1, *ex^m* in text: Two servants □ [6] fol. 141a.5, *ex^m* in text: Noisy children and beggars heard □ [7] fol. 141a.8, *ex^m* in text: Manor customs □ [8] fol. 141a.12, *ex^m* in text: Poor have to queue for alms; cf. *Serm.* **200b** [1], *Serm.* **200c** [1], *Serm.* **221** [5] □ [9] fol. 141a.15, *ex^m* in text: A quantity of small herrings or coins is valuable; cf. *Serm.* **200b** [3]

Sermon **153** fol. 141b.41: A little old lady at prayer

Sermon **160** fol. 144vb.25: Mother, child, and fruit

Sermon **162** fol. 145b.41: Victorious king returns with freed prisoners

Sermon **164** [1] fol. 148vb.2, *ex^m* in text: Horse, stolen or lost □ [2] fol. 149a.26, *narr.*: Noble and poison

Sermon **167** [1] fol. 150b.26, *narr.*: Merchants □ [2] fol. 150va.43, *narr.*: Noble

Sermon **170** [1] fol. 152a.1: Wax liquefies in heat □ [2] fol. 152b.6: Condemned man gazes at meadow; cf. *Serm.* **35** [2], *Serm.* **36** [2]

Sermon **174a** fol. 154a.15: King of England and servant

Sermon **180a** fol. 155va.27: Formation of a baby

Sermon 184 [1] fol. 157va.5: Learner inattentive to teachers □ [2] fol. 157va.19: Column as support □ [3] fol. 158a.8: The king as servant

Sermon 193 fol. 161vb.25: Holy Spirit compared to dove

Sermon 198 [1] fol. 163a.11: Preparation for war; cf. *Serm.* 51 [2] and [3], *Serm.* 53 [1] □ [2] fol. 163a.28: Christ the Master (Teacher); cf. *Serm.* 38, *Serm.* 39 [1], *Serm.* 57 [7], *Serm.* 69 [1] □ [3] fol. 163b.42, face: Use of thurible □ [4] fol. 163va.4: Offending the King

Sermon 200a [1] fol. 164vb.38: Learning French language and customs □ [2] fol. 165a.15: Noble gives hunting bird

Sermon 200b [1] fol. 165a.34: Almoner only distributes alms to those who queue; cf. *Serm.* 152 [8], *Serm.* 200c [1], *Serm.* 221 [5] □ [2] fol. 165a.42, face: Beggar □ [3] fol. 165b.1: Many small things are valuable; cf. *Serm.* 152 [9]

Sermon 200c [1] fol. 165b.17: Beggar out of queue receives only blows; cf. *Serm.* 152 [8], *Serm.* 200b [1], *Serm.* 221 [5] □ [2] fol. 165b.19: Buying fine bread □ [3] fol. 165b.26: Tenants have to follow shire or hundred

Sermon 201 fol. 165va.19: Like father, like son

Sermon 203 [1] fol. 166b.18: Beggars make children cry to attract alms □ [2] fol. 166b.26: Generosity of host □ [3] fol. 166b.41, *ex^m* in text: Roasting a bird □ [4] fol. 166va.20, *ex^m* in text: How cook avoids burning the hand □ [5] fol. 166va.26, *ex^m* in text: It is less painful to shave a wet surface

Sermon 204 [1] fol. 166vb.7: The wreath as sign of good ale (SOURCES cf. Richard Fishacre *In 4Sent.* d. 3 BL, MS Roy 10.B.vii, fol. 272rb; Città del Vaticano, Biblioteca Apostolica Vaticana, MS Vat. Ottob. lat 294, fol. 275ra: "Sicut circulus expositus est signum vini in cellario, et expositio circuli, scilicet usus quidam eius, est signum expositionis vini ad venditionem, similiter et aqua est signum ut circulus et tinctio ut usus circuli, scilicet expositio eius.") □ [2] fol. 167a.20: Good cloth is kept carefully □ [3] fol. 167b.6: The true Cross (SOURCES Tubach 1339 [St. Helena; cf. Petrus Comestor or *Acta Sanctorum*]) □ [4] fol. 167vb.15: Baptism is like a purifying bath

Sermon 205 [1] fol. 168va.11: Murder of a loved brother □ [2] fol. 168va.24: Christ on the cross surrounded by demons like atoms; cf. *Serm.* 17 [1], *Serm.* 82 [6], *Serm.* 208 [3], *Serm.* 209 [4] □ [3] fol. 168vb.16: Antiochus and destruction of Temple (1 Mac 1:23-25) □ [4] fol. 168vb.29, *narr.*: Death respects not kings – King of Greece

Sermon 206 [1] fol. 169va.14: Father of family □ [2] fol. 170a.23: Captain's station is at stern of ship; cf. *Serm.* 30 [5, 10] □ [3] fol. 170b.25: Peacock: superb tail, weak feet □ Cf. *Serm.* 46 [7] □ [4] fol. 170va.35, *narr.*: King of Greece's long face (SOURCES cf. Jacques de Vitry, *Sermones* 19 [*Exem.* 8 and 42, ed. Crane [cf.

CatRom 3: 26–27, no. 2]; also cf. *Speculum laicorum* [*CatRom* 3: 391, no. 303]; *Gesta Romanorum* 143; as well as Tubach 4994]) □ Cf. *Serm.* 13 [11]

Sermon 207 [1] fol. 170vb.1: Travellers and pilgrims pray daily for safe return □ [2] fol. 172a.35: Trees in fertile and infertile ground

Sermon 208 [1] fol. 172va.14: In time, chipping–away destroys □ [2] fol. 172va.29: Imprisonment □ [3] fol. 172va.40: Sun and atoms; cf. *Serm.* 17 [1], *Serm.* 82 [6], *Serm.* 205 [2], *Serm.* 209 [4] □ [4] fol. 172vb.25: Pruning in a garden □ [5] fol. 173b.15, *narr.*: Knight and rector

Sermon 209 [1] fol. 174b.34: Stupid behaviour □ [2] fol. 175b.42, *ex*^{m} in text: Coal burns to crumbling embers □ [3] fol. 175va.13, *ex*^{m} in text: Fire discolours white wood □ [4] fol. 175va.16: Asbestos; cf. *Serm.* 17 [1], *Serm.* 82 [6], *Serm.* 205 [2], *Serm.* 208 [3] □ [5] fol. 175va.20: Lamps prepared for vigils

Sermon 210 [1] fol. 176vb.16: Stupid behaviour □ [2] fol. 177a.6: You cannot wound your enemy if he is standing next to your parents □ [3] fol. 177a.12: Don't burn your enemy's house if he's your neighbour!

Sermon 211 [1] fol. 177vb.37: Humiliation of Christ □ [2] fol. 178a.33: Not welcoming your Lord to stay □ [3] fol. 178b.20: Offending your Lord

Sermon 213 fol. 180vb.2; 183va.20 [textual repetition]: Crossing the sea

Sermon 214 fol. 181a.35: City rising against the king; cf. *Serm.* 11 [4], *Serm.* 217 [2]

Sermon 216 fol. 182b.25: Service to a magnate

Sermon 217 [1] fol. 183vb.14: Sailing □ [2] fol. 184a.37: City rising against the king 'supra est hoc exemplum'; cf. *Serm.* 214

Sermon 218 fol. 184b.17: Julius Caesar's birth; cf. *Serm.* 228

Sermon 220 fol. 186va.26: King's judgement

Sermon 221 [1] fol. 187va.32: Deafness; cf. [3] below □ [2] fol. 187vb.12: Congregation prefers breakfast to a sermon □ [3] fol. 187vb.33: Stone–deafness; cf. [1] above □ [4] fol. 188a.24: Hard stone broken by goat's blood; cf. *Serm.* 90 [4] □ [5] fol. 188vb.19: Beggar out of queue is given blows not alms; cf. *Serm.* 152 [8], *Serm.* 200b [1], *Serm.* 200c [1] □ [6] fol. 188vb.29, *ex*^{m} in text: Tenants of hundred or shire

Sermon 222 fol. 189vb.29: ?

Sermon 223 [1] fol. 190va.24: Purifying metal through fire □ [2] fol. 190vb.2: Effects of fire on gold and rust

Sermon 224 [1] fol. 191va.38: Sailors steer by stars; cf. *Serm.* 30 [1] □ [2] fol. 192b.19: Nothing taken from sea without bitterness □ [3] fol. 192b.27: Careful navigation □ [4] fol. 192b.38: At sea, all co–operate in danger □ [5] fol. 192va.24: Seasickness

Sermon 226 [1] fol. 195a.26, face: Lawcourt compared with Doomsday ☐ [2] fol. 195b.19: Doomsday equal for rich and poor ☐ [3] fol. 195vb.24: King Philip and the thief who stole 40 marks ☐ [4] fol. 196b.24: Count of Blois and the monk (SOURCES cf. Odo of Cheriton, *Fabulae* 51 [ed. Hervieux, pp. 222–223]) ☐ [5] fol. 196b.26: Hermit and dead rich man; cf. *Serm.* 8 [4], *Serm.* 15 [4] ☐ [6] fol. 196b.27: St. Nicholas (SOURCES *Speculum laicorum* 238 [p. 49]; Etienne de Bourbon, 'De accusatoribus et testibus, ' *Tractatus de diversis materiis praedicabilibus* 2.43, ed. A. Lecoy de la Marche in *Anecdotes historiques, légendes et apologues tirés du recueil inédit d'Etienne de Bourbon, Dominicain du XIIIe siècle* [Paris, 1877], pp. 51–52]); cf. *Serm.* 53 [2]

Sermon 227 [1] fol. 196va.5: Cross as penalty ☐ [2] fol. 196vb.13: St. Andrew and his cross ☐ [3] fol. 196vb.28, *ex^m* in text: Gift of ring or necklace; cf. *Serm.* 47 [4], *Serm.* 138 [1] ☐ [4] fol. 197va.14, *ex^m* in text: Jew in Temple of Apollo (SOURCES *Speculum laicorum* 142 [p. 33]; Gregory, *Dialogues* 3.7.3, 8 [PL 77: 229, 231; ed. Adalbert de Vogüé, 3 vols. [Paris, 1978–1980], 2: 281, 283, 285])

Sermon 228 fol. 197va.32: Caesar's name; cf. *Serm.* 218

Sermon 229 [1] fol. 198b.36: Lion and wolf love own kind (SOURCES Tubach 254) ☐ [2] fol. 198va.2: Dog in butcher's shop ☐ [3] fol. 198va.8: face: Pigs roll in flower garden

Sermon 230 [1] fol. 199a.9: King of England ☐ [2] fol. 199a.37: Appearing before your brother who is Justiciar ☐ [3] fol. 199vb.15, *ex^m* in text: Frederick, Count St. Giles, King John ☐ [4] fol. 199vb.19: Keeper of castle's keys ☐ [5] fol. 199vb. 34; 200a.5: To obtain nut, crack shell; cf. *Serm.* 30 [8] ☐ [6] fol. 200a.9: Unwillingly to school

Sermon 231 fol. 201va.27: Theophilus; cf. *Serm.* 145 [9]

Sermon 232 [1] fol. 203a.28, *narr.*: The sacristan and his lady (SOURCES Tubach 3370; Jacques de Vitry, *Sermones* 72 [*Exem.* 282, ed. Crane; *CatRom* 3: 24, no. 204]; Etienne de Bourbon, 'De tribulacionis utilitate, ' *Tractatus* 5.519, ed. de la Marche [see *Serm.* 226 [6] above], pp. 448–449]) ☐ [2] fol. 203a.33: The duel at Stamford ☐ [3] fol. 203a.35: John Mauntel(?), the king's clerk (SOURCES cf. A.B. Emden, 'Mansel, John, ' in *A Biographical Register of the University of Oxford*, 3 vols. [Oxford, 1957–1959], 2: 1217–1218]) ☐ [4] fol. 203a.35: Those who call on Mary with *Ave Maria* (SOURCES *Miracles of the Virgin Mary* [*CatRom* 2: 612])

Sermon 233 [1] fol. 203va.40: *narr.*: The virgin saved from temptation through praying *Ave Maria* (SOURCES Tubach 3098) ☐ [2] fol. 203vb.3: Dawn and new day ☐ [3] fol. 204b.1, *narr.*: Canon helped by Our Lady (SOURCES Tubach 3450) ☐ [4] fol. 204va.1: Mary, Lady of Heaven

Sermon 234 fol. 204va.13: Having a good advocate in court

Appendix 8

The Liturgical Context of the Manuscript

This appendix explores the liturgical context of the sermon themes in MS Laud Misc. 511. It aims to provide a brief overview of thirteenth-century liturgy and, in particular, its development among the Dominicans and Franciscans; it also seeks to show the relevance of other regional variants from the Roman rite common throughout western Europe in the Middle Ages by studying elements from the liturgy in its Paris, Sarum, and York uses.

I

The liturgy of the Church as celebrated in the Mass, the sacraments and the Divine Office was an enduring element in the life of the Church and of the preacher, but it also has a life in history. The Roman rite that was the common one used in much of western Europe, but local variants or uses were found in different regions. Initially the friars, both Dominicans and Franciscans, used the liturgy appropriate in their locality. With the growth of the orders, however, this led to considerable confusion of practice. Both orders were faced with the problem of arranging the liturgy so that it served both the unity and needs of a mobile, international group of preachers as well as the needs of the people to whom they preached.

From its beginning, the Order of Preachers had no doubt about its corporate obligation to celebrate the liturgy, both the conventual Mass and the Divine Office. The canonical influence on the Order is discernible here. After the establishment of provinces by St. Dominic, and with the rapid growth of membership of the order in its first two decades, problems regarding worship came to the fore. The main problem was that increasing diversity of liturgical practice was endangering unity. In 1244 the chapter at Bologna decreed that the diffinitors should bring the rubrics and the notation of liturgical books for the night and day Offices, Gradual, and Missal to the next chapter, so that the various books could be brought into harmony. The chapter of 1245, held in Paris, established the Commission of the Four Friars - one each from the provinces of France, England, Lombardy and Germany - to work at Angers on the revision of the liturgy. At the same time, Humbert of Romans, erstwhile provincial of the Roman province, then provincial of France, was commissioned to revise the lectionary.[1]

Despite acceptance of these revisions, and despite the quality of the work, the chapter of 1250 demonstrated considerable unease in the Order about the new liturgy. Bonniwell suggests that the four brethren considerably modified the Paris liturgical practice which had become increasingly established within the Order in the first two decades, but acceptance of their changes was not

---

1. See P. Gleeson OP, "Dominican Liturgical Manuscripts from Before 1254," *AFP* 42 (1972) 86 seq., and W.R. Bonniwell OP, *A History of the Dominican Liturgy 1215–1945* (New York, 1945), pp. 75–81.

widespread. Whatever the reason for the difficulties, it is significant that in 1254 Humbert of Romans, the newly elected master-general, was commissioned by the general chapter to put the Divine Office in order and to correct the liturgical books: his authority to do so was to be recognised as final. By 1256 Humbert had completed his task, and together with the chapter had made practical arrangements for the copying and circulation of the text. To ensure uniformity, all copying of the mastertexts was to be done at S. Jacques, the Paris priory and *studium generale*, and a tax was levied on the whole Order to pay for the work. The main copy of this work survives in Santa Sabina, MS XIV L.1, while the Master General's copy, a portable record of the revision known as the *Portiforium*, is now in London, BL MS Add 23935. Papal confirmation on 7 July 1267 finally assured the revision of success. The comparatively few changes made in the Dominican liturgy after 1267 testify to the integrity, quality and - ultimately - acceptability, of Humbert's revision, probably because it had considerable continuity with previous practice.[2]

The Franciscans' liturgical problem was essentially different. They had not just to sort out how they were to celebrate Mass and Divine Office, but whether they were bound to the Office or not. This was a different process marked by suffering and conflict at each stage. The liturgical outcome, however, was remarkably similar to that of the Dominicans.[3]

While the Dominicans had a clear canonical background to their foundation, the Franciscans in their foundation were essentially an order of laymen. But the thirteenth-century Church had no category for religious who were not *monachi* or *canonici*, except the *conversi* of the Cistercian Order, and the function of the *conversi* was clearly defined in economic terms within the structure of the monastery. There was no easy place for lay people as active members of the apostolate in the Church of time.[4] This was part of the

2. Bonniwell, *History*, pp. 82, 84, 191–192, 213–214. See also F.M. Guerrini, *Ordinarium juxta ritum sacri ordinis fratrum praedicatorum* (Rome, 1921); *Litterae Encyclicae MOPH* 5, 42; *De Vita Regulari* 2, 503; Humbert of Romans: *De Vita Regulari*, ed. J.J. Berthier, 2 vols. (Rome, 1889), 2: 503: "Rogo autem ut detis operam ad correctionem illius secundum illa, ut uniformitas Officii diu desiderata in Ordine inveniatur ubique ... .Ut autem scire possitis utrum habeatis officium, noveritis XIV esse volumina in quibus multipliciter continentur, videlicet: Ordinarium, Antiphonarium, Lectionarium, Psalterium, Collectarium, Martyrologium, Libellum processionale, Graduale, Missale majoris altaris, Evangelistarium ejusdem, Epistolarium ejusdem, Missale pro minoribus altaribus, Pulpitorium et Breviarium portatile" (cited Bonniwell, *History*, p. 84).

3. What follows relies heavily on the work of S.J.P. van Dijk, especially his *Sources of the Roman Liturgy: The 'Ordo Missalis' of Haymo of Faverham* (Leiden, 1963); he has done much to sort out the intricacies of papal and Franciscan liturgies in the thirteenth century.

4. Cf. Innocent III and the 'Humiliati': see Brenda Bolton, "Innocent III's Treatment of the 'Humiliati,'" *SCH* 8 (1984) 73–82, for an attempt to recognise laity.

dilemma of the early Franciscans. Francis himself eventually accepted the diaconate and took on the obligation of the Divine Office, but he took it at a personal level, and was unable or unwilling to give his brethren any help in understanding the corporate and institutional implications of the introduction of clerical status into his Order. Thus the Franciscans had no canonical tradition on which to draw, something that gave them freedom to choose and to adapt. It was perhaps incidental that Francis chose to give his brethren the order of Divine Office used by the canons of his home town, Assisi. The canons of Assisi used the books of the papal chapel. In such unplanned manner did the significant Franciscan influence on the Roman liturgy begin.

It was natural that the Franciscans, relatively untutored in liturgical practice, should seek papal advice and follow papal patterns in their adaptation of the usage of the papal chapel. Van Dijk brings out very clearly the distinction between the practice of the Roman Church and that of the papal court or Roman Curia. The latter was undoubtedly Roman in inspiration, but already modified by the liturgical changes made by Innocent III in the Divine Office, and by Honorius III in the Mass. As van Dijk has shown, the interaction in liturgy between the papal chapel and the Franciscan Order was not some highly organised blueprint to be followed unwaveringly, but rather a process of mutual aid. Both were interested in modifying the monastic flavour of the liturgy and the Mass; the Franciscans had the same need for uniformity as the Dominicans - more pressing, in fact, because of the division in the Order about the Divine Office, and more practical because the members of the Order, lacking a tradition, needed clear instructions for liturgical practice.

The person who answered this need was Haymo of Faversham. After many years of service, both as regent master, and as provincial of the Franciscans in England, Haymo was elected minister general in 1240.[5] Despite only four years in office, he carried through with papal permission and support a major liturgical reform which showed his genius for clarification and simplification. He gave to the Order two completed works: the *Indutus Planeta* presented to the chapter at Bologna in 1243, and the *Ordo Missalis*. The *Indutus Planeta* is an order of Mass which includes instructions not only about words but also about actions. It is the first such manual of its kind, and, as it met an ecclesiastical need that existed long before the Franciscans, its use and influence spread rapidly throughout the Church. It is in fact the origin of the simple Low Mass which has become increasingly common practice in the Roman Church since the thirteenth century. The *Ordo Missalis* provided a clear pattern containing all the parts necessary for the celebration of Mass in the temporal and sanctoral cycles. At the time of his death in 1244, Haymo was working on the *Ordinationes* or instructions about the celebration of the Divine Office. He left it in the form of unrevised notes. All three works, including the

5. S.J.P. van Dijk and J.H. Walker, *The Origins of the Modern Roman Liturgy* (London, 1960), chapter 10.

unfinished *Ordinationes*, were promulgated authoritatively in the Franciscan Order by Haymo's successor, John of Parma after 1247 (the promulgation of the *Ordinationes* in the form left by Haymo caused much confusion, because their unrevised state was not recognised). The full story of the Franciscan revision is magisterially recorded in the work of Stephen van Dijk.[6]

It is significant that during the thirteenth century the liturgical uses of both Dominicans and Franciscans were accepted by groups and geographical areas outside their immediate sphere of influence. In fulfilling the requirements of their Orders, they both moved away from a monastic-dominated liturgy towards a liturgy more easily understood by the laity.[7] In the event, the cooperation in liturgical change between the papacy and the Franciscan Order was the more influential. The Franciscans accepted the modified papal liturgy, reshaped it to suit their requirements and promulgated it throughout the Order. So the practice of the Papal Chapel won a far wider public than it would ever have gained had it been imposed. Eventually a Dominican Pope, Pius V, was to give to the whole western Church, apart from a few clearly stated exceptions, the papal-court- Franciscan liturgy as the Tridentine reform.

II

Nearly 200 sermons in MS Laud Misc. 511 are in the liturgical order of the Temporale (i.e., the liturgy for the feast of Easter, Pentecost, Christmas, Epiphany and the Sundays of the year). Since sermons have traditionally been preached on themes taken from the two main readings of the Mass, the Epistle and Gospel, and, since this tradition firmly held both in the new scholastic sermon method delineated in the *artes praedicandi* and in the preaching revival of the friars, the liturgical analysis of the manuscript must correspondingly focus on the Mass pericopes or readings of the Temporale and their uses.

It was simpler to establish the order of the revised Franciscan use from the work of van Dijk. The revised Dominican pericpoes, however, had to be taken from manuscripts. The main list was extracted from Humbert of Romans' *Portiforium* in BL, MS Add. 23935 made in Paris 1255- 1263, in particular the *Epistolarium* (fols. 526- 545b) and the *Evangeliarium* (fols. 545v- 571vb). This list was checked against those found in BL, MS Add. 35085 and Add. 37487. A further comparison was made with a microfilm copy of Santa Sabina, MS XIV L.1,

---

6. See *The Franciscan Missal and Breviary: Sources of the Roman Liturgy*, ed. S.J.P. van Dijk, 2 vols. (Leiden, 1963); see also n. 5 above.

7. A good example of this is the Dominican emphasis on the office of Compline, followed by the solemn singing of the *Salve* and the solemn processsion in honour of Our Lady. This service proved popular with the townspeople who lived near the priories. It was a religious service they could appreciate, and was held at a time when they could attend. See Marguerite Aron, *St. Dominic's Successor: the Life of Bl.Jordan of Saxony, Master-General of the Dominican Order 1222–37* (London, 1955), pp. 69–70.

folios 9–11v. In this way a comparative table of the pericopes for the revised Dominican and Franciscan uses was established.[8]

To clarify this comparison further, the Dominican and Franciscan pericopes were compared with the Mass pericopes from the Paris, Sarum, and York missals. Of the five uses four are similar with a few variants, namely the Dominican, Paris, Sarum and York uses; the different one is the revised Franciscan use. The results of these investigations are recorded in Table 1 below.

Some valuable insights emerge from this comparative analysis of pericopes, and it may be useful to set forth some of them here. It is interesting, for example, to note that, with the exception of the Second Sunday of Lent[9] and some Gospels for the Palm Sunday procession, the liturgical readings are identical in all uses from Septuagesima to Pentecost. This reflects the fact that both the nucleus of the liturgy and the earliest liturgy developed by the Church celebrated the saving acts of Christ in the paschal mystery. The concept of the liturgical year – accepted readily in the twentieth century – was comparatively new in the thirteenth century. In fact there was much uncertainty about the timing of a new cycle, whether it was Christmas, or the present First Sunday of Advent, or even the feast of the Annunciation on 25 March. The time between the ending of the Christmas cycle and the start of Septuagesima was confused. It is worth noting that, while in the time after Epiphany the Dominican, Franciscan and Paris uses are the same at this stage, the two English uses are a week behind.

The season 'after Pentecost / after Trinity' was similarly uncertain, and at an earlier stage was related in blocks of Sundays to the sanctoral cycle. Moreover, it was not seen as a continuity. So it is not surprising that in the history of the pericopes of the Roman Mass temporal cycle, Pentecost to Christmas had a less definite structure. By the tenth century, however, the Roman temporal Mass readings seem to be clearly assigned. The difference in pericopes between Dominican and Franciscan lay not so much in Scripture content – the scriptural order of the epistles closely follows the order of the books in the Latin Vulgate – as in their liturgical *timing*. It is significant that the temporal Mass readings of the Dominican use reflect an older Roman tradition; while the those of the Franciscan use were to become a newer Roman tradition.

For a complete list of manuscript and printed sources, see p. 381 below.

For a complete list of manuscript and printed sources, see p. 381 below.

---

8. See Maura O'Carroll, "The Lectionary of the Proper of the Year in the Dominican and Franciscan Rites of the Thirteenth Century," *AFP* 49 (1979), 79–103.

9. Except the Second Sunday of Lent. In Morin's edition of Wurzburg, MS M.p.th. fol. 62, this Sunday is described, "Ebd II Die Dominico Vacat." This mid-seventh century MS contains the then current Roman practice. See "Comes and Capitulum Evangeliarum," ed. Dom G. Morin in "Les plus ancien 'Comes' ou Lectionnaire de l"Eglise Romaine,'" in *Revue Bénédictine* 27 (1910) 41–74; and "Liturgie et Basiliques de Rome au milieu du viie siècle," *Revue Bénédictine* 28 (1911) 298.

TABLE 1 *Mass Pericopes for the Temporal Cycle (Dominican-Franciscan Uses)*

This table compares Dominican (*OP*) and Franciscan (*OFM*) pericopes with the uses of Paris, Sarum, and York for Epistle (abbreviated *Ep*), Gospel (abbreviated *Ev*), and, where necessary, the Lesson (abbreviated *Le*). Where the liturgical name of a feast of the Temporale (which appears below in **bold**) is common to Dominican and Franciscan uses English is used; where they are different, the name reflects the Latin of the sources.

The sources of the Dominican pericopes are the Master General's copy of Humbert's liturgical revision found in BL, MS Add 23935 (cited by folio). Franciscan use is cited from *The Franciscan Missal and Breviary: Sources from the Roman Liturgy*, ed. S.J.P. van Dijk (abbreviated SRL, and cited by volume and page). The variant uses of Paris are cited from BL, MS Add. 38723 (cited as Paris, with folio numbers); those of Sarum from the printed version of *The Sarum Missal*, ed. J. Wickham Legg (cited by page); and those of York from W.G. Henderson's edition, *Missale ad usum insignis Ecclesiaem Eboracensis* (cited by volume and page number). It is difficult to determine Dominican, Sarum, or Paris uses from the common table; it is the Franciscan use that is unique. Variant usages (Dominican, Paris, Sarum, and York) are more helpful in liturgical identification and can be found below in items with the following codes from Schneyer: T11, T24, T35, T41, T64 to T66.

To provide an adequate representation of the texts within the limited compass available, common phrases and their variants are abbreviated: AADV for "amen, amen dico vobis"; CJDN/DJC/DNJC for variants of "Christus Jesus Dominus Noster," with adjustments of case where necessary; i s s for "in secula seculorum"; and SERC/SFERC for "simile est regnum celorum" or "simile factum est regnum celorum."

Sunday I Advent (Schneyer T1)
Ep *OP and OFM* Rom 13:11-14: Scientes quia hora est ... sed induimini DJC (MS fol. 526a-b; SRL 2: 207)
Ev *OP* Mt 21:1-9: Cum appropinquasset ... in nomine Domini (MS fol. 546a) *OFM* Lc 21:25-33: Erunt signa ... non transibunt (SRL 2: 207)

Sunday II Advent (Schneyer T2)
Ep *OP and OFM* Rom 15:4-13: Quecumque scripta sunt ... et virtute Spiritus Sancti (MS fol. 526b; SRL 2: 208)
Ev *OP* Lc 21:25-33: Erunt signa ... non transibunt (MS fol. 546a-b) □ *OFM* Mt 11:2-10: Cum audisset ... tuam ante te (SRL 2: 208)

Sunday III Advent (Schneyer T3)
Ep *OP* 1 Cor 4:1-5: Sic nos existimet ... a Deo (MS fol. 526b) □ *OFM* Phil 4:4-7: Gaudete ... in CJDN (SRL 2: 208)
Ev *OP* Mt 11:2-10: Cum audisset ... tuam ante te (MS fol. 546b) □ *OFM* Jo 1:19b-28: Miserunt Judaei ... baptizans (SRL 2: 208)

Sunday IV Advent (Schneyer T4)
Ep OP Phil 4:4-7: Gaudete ... in CJDN (MS fol. 526vb-7a) □ *OFM* Cor 4:1-5: Sic nos existimet ... a Domino (SRL 2: 210)
Ev OP Jo 1:19b-28: Miserunt Judaei ... baptizans (MS fol. 546va) □ *OFM* Lc 3:1-6: Anno quintodecimo ... Dei (SRL 2: 210)

Vigil of the Nativity (Schneyer T5)
Le OP and York Is 52:1-4: Propter Syon ... inhabitabunt (complacuit Domino in te) (MS fol. 527a; and p. 13) □ *OFM* none
Ep OP and OFM Rom 1:1-6: Paulus servus ... vocati J C D N (MS fol. 527a; SRL 2: 211)
Ev OP and OFM Mt 1:18-21: Cum esset desponsata ... a peccatis eorum (MS fol. 546va-b; SRL 2: 211)

Nativity: Midnight (Schneyer T6)
Le OP Is 9:2-7: Populus qui ... sempiternum (MS fol. 527a) □ *OFM* none
Ep OP and OFM Tit 2:11-15: Apparuit gratia ... hec loquare et exhortare (MS fol. 527a; SRL 2: 211)
Ev OP and OFM Lc 2:1-14: Exiit edictum a Cesare ... pax hominibus bone voluntatis (MS fol. 547b; SRL 2: 211)

Nativity: Dawn (Schneyer T6)
Le OP Is 61:1-62:12: Spiritus Domini ... redempti a Domino Deo nostro (MS fol. 527a-b) □ *OFM* none
Ep OP and OFM Tit 3:4-7: Apparuit benignitas ... spem vite eterne (MS fol. 527b; SRL 2: 211-2)
Ev OP and OFM Lc 2:15-20: Pastores loquebantur ... est ad illos (MS fol. 547b; SRL 2: 212)

Nativity: Day (Ad magnam Missam: Sarum, York) (Schneyer T6)
Le OP Is 52:6-10: Propter hoc sciet ... Dei nostri (MS fol. 527b) □ *OFM* none
Ep OP and OFM Heb 1:1-12: Multifarie multisque modis ... anni tui non deficient (MS fol. 527b-va; SRL 2: 212)
Ev OP and OFM Jo 1:1-14: In principio erat verbum ... gratie et veritatis (MS fol. 547b-va; SRL 2: 212)

Sunday in Octave of Nativity (Schneyer T7)
Ep OP and OFM Gal 4:1-7: Quanto tempore heres ... heres per Deum (MS fol. 527a; SRL 2: 214)
Ev OP and OFM Lc 2:33-40: Erant Joseph et Maria ... et gratia Dei erat in illo (MS fol. 547va; SRL 2: 214)

Octave of Nativity (Circumcision) (Schneyer T8)
Ep OP Mt Tit 3:4-7: Apparuit benignitas ... spem vite eterne (MS fol. 527va) □ *OFM* Tit 3:11-15: Apparuit gratia ... hec loquere et exhortare (SRL 2: 215)
Ev OP and OFM Lc 2:21: Postquam consummati sunt ... in utero conciperetur (MS fol. 547va; SRL 2: 215) □ *Paris, York, and Sarum* all correspond to OFM

Vigil of Epiphany (Schneyer T9)
Ep OP Tit 3:4–7: Apparuit benignitas ... spem vite eterne (MS fol. 527va) □
OFM Gal 4:1–7: Quanto tempore ... heres per Deum (SRL 2: 216)
Ev OP and OFM Mt 2:19–23: Defuncto Herode ... quoniam Nazarenus
vocabitur (MS fol. 547va; SRL 2: 216)

Epiphany (Schneyer T10)
Ep OP and OFM Is 60:1–6: Surge illuminare ... et laudem domino annuntian-
tes (MS fol. 527va; SRL 2: 216)
Ev OP and OFM Mt 2:1–12: Cum natus esset ... reversi sunt in regionem suam
(MS fol. 548b; SRL 2: 216)

Sunday in Octave of Epiphany (Schneyer T11)
Ep OP and OFM Rom 12:1–5: Obsecro vos per misericordiam ... alterius membra (MS fol. 527va; SRL 2: 217) □ *York* Rom 3:19–26: Scimus quoniam quae-
cunque lex ... qui est ex fide CJ (York 1: 33)
Ev OP and OFM Lc 2:42–52: Cum factus esset Jesus ... Deum et homines (MS
fol. 548b–va; SRL 2: 217) □ *York* Mt 3:13–17: Venit Jesus a Galilea ... complacuit (York 1: 34) □ *Sarum* Jo 1:29–34: Vidit Johannes Jhesum ... hic est filius Dei
(Sarum 39)

Octave of Epiphany (Schneyer T–)
Ep OP Is 25:1–8: Domine Deus meus ... in universa terra (MS fol. 527va–vb)
□ *OFM* Is 60:1–6: Surge illuminare ... et laudem domino annuntiantes (SRL 2: 217)
Ev OP Mt 3:13–17: Venit Jesus a Galylea ... complacui (MS fol. 548va) □ *OFM*
Jo 1:29–34: Vidit Johannes Jesum ... quia hic est filius Dei (SRL 2:17) □ *York*
Corresponds to OFM

Dom I post oct Epiph (*OP*) ¦ **Dom post Epiph** (*OFM*) (Schneyer T12)
Ep OP and OFM Rom 12:6–16: Habentes donationes ... humilibus consentien-
tes (MS fol. 527vb; SRL 2: 217) □ *Sarum and York* Schneyer T11
Ev OP and OFM Jo 2:1–11: Nuptie facte sunt ... et crediderunt in eum discipuli eius (MS fol. 548va; SRL 2: 217–8) □ *Sarum and York* Schneyer T11

Dom II post oct Epiph (*OP*) ¦ **Dom III post Epiph** (*OFM*) (Schneyer T13)
Ep OP and OFM Rom 12:16–21: Nolite esse prudentes ... sed vince in bono
malum (MS fol. 527vb; SRL 2: 218) □ *Sarum and York* Schneyer T12
Ev OP and OFM Mt 8:1–13: Cum descendisset Jesus ... puer in illa hora (MS
fol. 548va–vb; SRL 2: 218) □ *Sarum and York* Schneyer T12

Dom II post oct Epiph (*OP*) ¦ **Dom IV post Epiph** (*OFM*) (Schneyer T14)
Ep OP and OFM Rom 13:8–10: Nemini quicquam ... plenitudo legis est (MS
fol. 527vb–8a; SRL 2: 218) □ *Sarum and York* Schneyer T13
Ev OP and OFM Mt 8:23–27: Ascendente Jesus in naviculam ... obediunt ei
(MS fol. 548vb; SRL 2: 218) □ *Sarum and York* Schneyer T13

Dom IV post oct Epiph (*OP*) ¦ **Dom V post Epiph** (*OFM*) (Schneyer T15)
Ep OP Col 3:12–16: Induite vos sicut ... in cordibus vestris (MS fol. 528a) □

OFM Col 3:12- 17 Induite vos sicut ... agentes Deo et Patri (SRL 2: 218) □ *Paris*
OFM □ *Sarum and York* Schneyer T14
Ev OP and OFM Mt 13:24- 30: SFERC homini qui seminavit ... in horreum
meum (MS fol. 548vb; SRL 2: 218) □ *Sarum and York* Schneyer T14

Dom V post Epiph (*Sarum* and *York*) (Schneyer T15)
Ep Sarum and York Col 3:12- 17: Induite vos sicut ... Deo et Patri
Ev Sarum Mt 13:24- 30: SFERC homini qui seminavit ... in horreum meum □
York Lc 4:14- 22: Regressus est Jesus ... procedebant de ore ipsius

Septuagesima (Schneyer T16)
Ep OP and OFM 1 Cor 9:24- 10:4: Nescitis quod hii ... petra erat autem Christ
(MS fol. 528a1; SRL 2: 219)
Ev OP and OFM Mt 20:1- 16: SERC homini patri familias ... pauci vero electi
(MS fol. 548vb- 9a; SRL 2: 219)

Sexagesima (Schneyer T17)
Ep OP and OFM 2 Cor 11:19- 12:9: Libenter suffertis ... in me virtus Christi
(MS fol. 528a- b; SRL 2: 219)
Ev OP and OFM Lc 8:4- 15: Cum turba plurima ... afferunt in patientia (MS
fol. 549a; SRL 2: 219)

Quinquagesima (Schneyer T18)
Ep OP and OFM 1 Cor 13:1- 13: Si linguis hominum ... maior autem horum
est caritas (MS fol. 528b- va; SRL 2: 219)
Ev OP and OFM Lc 18:31- 43: Assumpsit Jesus duodecim ... dedit laudem Deo
(MS fol. 549a- b; SRL 2: 219)

Ash Wednesday Feria quarta in capite jeiunii (*OP*) ¦ **Feria quarta Cinerum**
(*OFM*) (Schneyer T18/4)
Ep OP and OFM Joel 2:12- 19: Convertimini ad me ... opprobrium in gentibus
(MS fol. 528va; SRL 2: 220)
Ev OP and OFM Mt 6:16- 21: Cum ieiunatis ... ibi est cor tuum (MS fol. 549b;
SRL 2: 221)

Dom I in Quadragesima (Lent I) (Schneyer T19)
Ep OP and OFM 2 Cor 6:1- 10: Hortamur vos ne in vacuum ... et omnia
possidentes (MS fol. 528vb- 9a; SRL 2: 222)
Ev OP and OFM Mt 4:1- 11: Ductus est Jesus ... et ministrabant ei (MS fol.
549va- vb; SRL 2: 222)

Dom II in Quadragesima (*OP*) ¦ **[Lent II]** (*OFM*) (Schneyer T20)
Ep OP and OFM 1 Thess 4:1- 7: Rogamus vos et obsecramus ... sed in
sanctificatione (MS fol. 530a; SRL 2: 225)
Ev OP Mt 15:21- 28: Egressus Jesus ... ex illa hora (MS fol. 550va) □ *OFM* Mt
17:1- 9: Assumpsit Jesus Petrum ... a mortuis resurgat (SRL 2: 225) □ *Paris*
Corresponds to OFM

Dom III in Quadragesima (*OP*) ¦ **[Lent III]** (*OFM*) (Schneyer T21)
Ep *OP and OFM* Eph 5:1-9: Estote imitatores Dei ... et iustitia et veritate (MS fol. 530vb-1a; SRL 2: 227)
Ev *OP and OFM* Lc 11:14-28: Erat Jesus eiciens demonium ... et custodiunt illud (MS fol. 551b; SRL 2: 227)

Dom IV in Quadragesima (*OP*) ¦ **[Lent IV]** (*OFM*) (Schneyer T22)
Ep *OP and OFM* Gal 4:22-31: Scriptum est quoniam Abraham ... Christus nos liberavit (MS fol. 532a-b; SRL 2: 229)
Ev *OP and OFM* Jo 6:1-14: Abiit Jesus trans mare ... est in mundum (MS fol. 552b; SRL 2: 229)

Dominica de Passione (*OP*) ¦ **[Lent V, Passion Sunday]** (*OFM*) (Schneyer T23)
Ep *OP and OFM* Heb 9:11-15: Christus assistens ... qui vocati sunt eterne hereditatis (MS fol. 533a; SRL 2: 232)
Ev *OP and OFM* Jo 8:46-59: DJ ... quis ex vobis arguet ... exivit de templo (MS fol. 553va; SRL 2: 232)

Dominica in ramis palmarum (*OP*) ¦ **In die Palmarum** (*OFM*) (Schneyer T24)
1 Blessing of Palms
Le *OFM* Exod 15:27-16:7: Venerunt filii Israel in Helium ... gloria ejus (SRL 2: 234) □ *Sarum and York* Correspond to OFM
Ev *OP and OFM* Mt 21:1-9: Cum appropinquasset Jesus Jerosolymam ... in nomine Domini (MS fol. 554b; SRL 2: 234) □ *Sarum and York* Jo 12:12-19: Turba multa ... mundus totus post eum abiit (Sarum 92; York 1: 84)
2 Mass
Ep *OP and OFM* Phil 2:5-11: Hoc sentite in vobis ... in gloria est Dei Patris (MS fol. 533vb; SRL 2: 236)
Ev *OP* Passio Mt 26:2-27:66: Scitis quia post biduum ... lapidem cum custodibus (MS fol. 554b-555vb) □ *OFM* Passio Mt 26:2-27:61: Scitis quia post biduum ... sedentes contra sepulchrum (SRL 2: 236)

Feria V, in cena Domini (Maundy Thursday) (Schneyer T25)
Ep *OP and OFM* 1 Cor 11:20-32: Convenientibus in unum ... ut non cum hoc mundo dampnemur (MS fol. 534a; SRL 2: 238)
Ev *OP and OFM* Jo 13:1-15: Ante diem festum pasche ... ita vos faciatis (MS fol. 558a; SRL 2: 238)
Variants The Dominican, Sarum and York Missals make provision for the reading of the Gospel of John 13:16 to 17:26

Feria VI, in parasceve (*OP*) ¦ **[Good Friday]** (*OFM*) (Schneyer T26)
Le *OP and OFM* Os 6:1-6: In tribulatione sua ... plus quam holocausta (MS fol. 534b; SRL 2: 240)
Le *OP and OFM* Ex 12:1-11: Mensis iste vobis ... id est transitus Domini (MS fol. 534b; SRL 2: 240)
Ev *OP and OFM* Jo 18:1-19:42: Egressus est Jesus ... quia iuxta erat monumentum posuerunt Jesum (MS fol. 559va-60b; SRL 2: 240)

In vigilia pascatis (*OP*) ¦ **[Holy Saturday]** (*OFM*) (Schneyer T27)
Ep OP and OFM Col 3:1–4: Si consurrexistis ... cum ipso in gloria (MS fol. 535a; SRL 2: 248)
Ev OP and OFM Mt 28:1–7: Vespere sabbati que ... ecce predixi vobis (MS fol. 561va; SRL 2: 248)

In die Sancto Pasche [EasterSunday] (*OP*) ¦ **Dominica Resurrectionis Domini** (*OFM*) (Schneyer T28)
Ep OP and OFM 1 Cor 5:7–8: Expurgate vetus fermentum ... sinceritatis et veritatis (MS fol. 535a–b; SRL 2: 251)
Ev OP and OFM Mc 16:1–7: Maria Magdalene ... sicut dixi vobis (MS fol. 561va; SRL 2: 251)

In octavis pasche (*OP*) ¦ **In octava Pasce** (*OFM*) (Schneyer T29)
Ep OP and OFM 1 Jo 5:4–10a: Omne quod natum ... testimonium Dei in se (MS fol. 535vb; SRL 2: 253)
Ev OP and OFM Jo 20:19–31: Cum esset sero die illo ... vitam habeatis in nomine eius (MS fol. 562b; SRL 2: 253)

Dom I post oct pasche Dom (*OP*) ¦ **II post pascha** (*OFM*) (Schneyer T30)
Ep OP and OFM 1 Petr 2:21–25: Christus passus est ... episcopum animarum vestrarum (MS fol. 535vb; SRL 2: 254)
Ev OP and OFM Jo 10:11–16: Ego sum pastor bonus ... unum ovile et unus pastor (MS fol. 562b–va; SRL 2: 254)

Dom II post oct pasche (*OP*) ¦ **Dom III post pascha** (*OFM*) (Schneyer T31)
Ep OP and OFM 1 Petr 2:11–19a: Obsecro vos tamquam advenas ... est enim gratia in CJ (MS fol. 535vb–6a; SRL 2: 254)
Ev OP and OFM Jo 16:16–22: Modicum et iam non videbitis ... nemo tollet a vobis(MS fol. 562va; SRL 2: 254)

Dom III post oct pasche (*OP*) ¦ **Dom IV post pascha** (*OFM*) (Schneyer T32)
Ep OP and OFM Jac 1:17–21: Omne datum optimum ... salvare animas vestras (MS fol. 536a; SRL 2: 254)
Ev OP and OFM Jo 16:5–14: Vado ad eum qui misit me ... et annuntiabit vobis (MS fol. 562va–b; SRL 2: 254)

Dom IV post oct pasche (*OP*) ¦ **Dom V post pascha** (*OFM*) (Schneyer T33)
Ep OP and OFM Jac 1:22–27: Estote factores verbi ... se custodire ab hoc seculo (MS fol. 536a; SRL 2: 254–255)
Ev OP and OFM Jo 16:23–31: AADV si quid petieritis ... a Deo existis (MS fol. 562va–b; SRL 2: 255)

In Rogationibus (*OP*) ¦ **In letaniis Maioribus** (*OFM*) (Schneyer T34)
Ep OP and OFM Jac 5:16–21: Confitemini alter utrum peccata ... multitudinem peccatorum (MS fol. 536a; SRL 2: 255)
Ev OP and OFM Lc 11:5–13: Quis vestrum habebit amicum ... spiritum bonum petentibus se (MS fol. 562vb; SRL 2: 255)

Vigil of Ascension (Schneyer T35)
Ep   OP and OFM Eph 4:7- 13: Unicuique nostrum data ... etatis plenitudinis
Christi (MS fol. 536a- b; SRL 2: 255) □ *Paris, Sarum, and York* Act 4:32- 35: Mul-
titudinis autem ... cuique opus erat (Paris fol. 97a- b; Sarum 154; York 1: 146)
Ev   OP and OFM Jo 17:1- 11a: Sublevatis Jesus oculis ... et ego ad te venio (MS
fol. 562vb; SRL 2: 255)

Ascension Day (Schneyer T36)
Ep   OP and OFM Act 1:1- 11: Primum quidem sermonem ... euntem in celum
(MS fol. 536b; SRL 2: 255)
Ev   OP and OFM Mc 16:14- 20: Recumbentibus undecim ... sequentibus signis
(MS fol. 562vb- 3a; SRL 2: 255)

Sunday in Octave of Ascension (Schneyer T37)
Ep   OP and OFM 1 Petr 4:7- 11: Estote prudentes et vigilate ... honorificetur
Deus per Jesum Christum (MS fol. 536b; SRL 2: 256)
Ev   OP and OFM Jo 15:26- 16:4: Cum venerit Paraclitus ... quia ego dixi vobis
(MS fol. 563a; SRL 2: 256)

Octave of Ascension
Ep   York Eph 4:7- 13: Unicuique nostrum data ... plenitudinis Christi (York 1:
150; Schneyer: none)
Ev   York Lc 24:49- 53: Ego mittam promissum Patris ... benedicentes Deum
(York 1: 150; Schneyer: none)

Vigil of Pentecost (Schneyer T38)
Ep   OP and OFM Act 19:1- 8: Factum est cum Apollo ... et suadens de regno
Dei (MS fol. 537a; SRL 2: 257)
Ev   OP and OFM Jo 14:15−21: Si diligitis me ... manifestabo ei me ipsum (MS
fol. 563a; SRL 2: 257)

Pentecost (Schneyer T39)
Ep   OP and OFM Act 2:1- 11: Cum complerentur dies ... magnalia Dei (MS fol.
537a; SRL 2: 258)
Ev   OP and OFM Jo 14:23- 31: Si quis diligit me ... Pater sic facio (MS fol.
563a- b; SRL 2: 258)

In festo Sancte Trinitatis (*OP*) ¦ **Dom I post Pent** (*OFM*) (Schneyer T40 ¦ T41)
Ep   OP 2 Cor 13:11- 13: Gaudete perfecte ... omnibus vobis amen (MS fol.
538a) □ *OFM* Jo 4:16b- 21: Deus caritas est ... diligat et fratrem suum (SRL 2:
261) □ *Paris* 2 Cor 13:13: Gratia DNJC et caritas Dei ... cum omnibus vobis
(Paris fol. 106b) □ *Sarum and York* Apoc 4:1- 10: Vidi ostium apertum ...
viventem in s s (Sarum 170; York 1: 213)
Ev   OP 6 Jo 3:1- 15: Erat homo ex phariseis ... habeat vitam eternam (MS fol.
563va- vb) □ *OFM* Lc 6:36- 42: Estote misericordes ... de oculo fratris tui (SRL
2: 261) □ *Paris* Jo 1:1- ?: In principio erat Verbum ... [no end-cue given] (Paris
fol. 106va) □ *Note* OFM missal in Haymo's revision has no Feast of the Trinity.

Dom I post festum SS Trinitatis (*OP*) ¦ **Dom II post Pent** (*OFM*) (Schneyer T42)
Ep OP 1 Jo 4:8- 21: Deus caritas est ... fratrem suum (MS fol. 538a) □ *OFM* 1
Jo 3:13- 18: Nolite mirari si odit ... sed opere et veritate (SRL 2: 261)
Ev OP Lc 16:19- 31: Homo quidam erat dives ... resurrexit credent (MS fol.
563vb- 4a) □ *OFM* Lc 14:16- 24: Homo quidam fecit cenam ... gustabit cenam
meam (SRL 2: 261) □ *Variants York* Dom I post octavas Pentecostes

Dom II post trin (*OP*) ¦ **Dom III post pent** (*OFM*) (Schneyer T43)
Ep OP 1 Jo 3:13- 18: Nolite mirari si odit ... sed opere et veritate (MS fol. 538b)
□ *OFM* 1 Petr 5:6- 11: Humiliamini sub potenti ... ipsi gloria in s s (SRL 2: 262)
Ev OP Lc 14:16- 24: Homo quidam fecit cenam ... gustabit cenam meam (MS
fol. 564a) □ *OFM* Lc 15:1- 10: Erant appropinquantes ... penitentiam agente
(SRL 2: 262)

Dom II post trin (*OP*) ¦ **Dom IV post pent** (*OFM*) (Schneyer T44)
Ep OP 1 Petr 5:6- 11: Humiliamini sub potenti ... ipsi gloria et imperium i s
s (MS fol. 538b) □ *OFM* Rom 8:18- 23: Existimo enim quod ... corporis nostri
(SRL 2: 262)
Ev OP Lc 15:1- 10: Erant appropinquantes ... penitentiam agente (MS fol.
564a) □ *OFM* Lc 5:1- 11: Cum turbe irruerent ... secuti sunt eum (SRL 2: 262)

Dom IV post trin (*OP*) ¦ **Dom V post pent** (*OFM*) (Schneyer T45)
Ep OP Rom 8:18- 23: Existimo quod non sunt ... corporis nostri in CJDN (MS
fol. 538b) □ *OFM* 1 Petr 3:8- 15a: Omnes unanimes in oratione ... in cordibus
vestris (SRL 2: 262)
Ev OP Lc 6:36- 42: Estote misericordes ... de oculo fratris tui (MS fol. 564a- b)
□ *OFM* Mt 5:20- 24: Nisi abundaverit ... offeres munus tuum (SRL 2: 262)

Dom V post trin (*OP*) ¦ **Dom VI post pent** (*OFM*) (Schneyer T46)
Ep 1 Petr 3:8- 15a: Omnes unanimes in oratione ... in cordibus vestris (MS fol.
538b- va) □ *OFM* Rom 6:3- 11: Quicumque baptizati sumus ... autem Deo in
CJDN (SRL 2: 263)
Ev OP Lc 5:1- 11: Cum turbe irruerent ... secuti sunt eum (MS fol. 564b) □
OFM Mc 8:1- 9: Cum turba multa esset ... et dimisit eos (SRL 2: 263)

Dom VI post trin (*OP*) ¦ **Dom VII post pent** (*OFM*) (Schneyer T47)
Ep OP Rom 6:3- 11: Quicumque baptizati sumus ... autem Deo in CJDN (MS
fol. 538va) □ *OFM* Rom 6:19- 23: Humanum dico propter ... Dei vita eterna in
CJDN (SRL 2: 263)
Ev Mt 5:20- 24: AADV nisi abundaverit ... munus tuum (MS fol. 564b) □ *OFM*
Mt 7:15- 21: Attendite a falsis ... in regnum celorum (SRL 2: 263)

Dom VII post trin (*OP*) ¦ **Dom VIII post pent** (*OFM*) (Schneyer T48)
Ep OP Rom 6:19- 23: Humanum dico ... Dei vita eterna in CJDN (MS fol.
538va) □ *OFM* Rom 8: 12- 17a: Debitores sumus non carni ... coheredes autem
Christi (SRL 2: 263)

Ev   OP Mc 8:1–9: Cum turba multa esset ... et dimisit eos (MS fol. 564b–va)
□ *OFM* Lc 16:1–9: Homo quidam erat dives ... eterna tabernacula (SRL 2: 263)

Dom VIII post trin (*OP*) ¦ **Dom IX post pent** (*OFM*) (Schneyer T49)
Ep   OP Rom 8:12–17a: Debitores sumus non ... coheredes autem Christi (MS
fol. 538va) □ *OFM* 1 Cor 10:6–13: Non simus concupiscentes. ..ut possitis
sustinere (SRL 2: 264)
Ev   OP Mt 7:15–21: Attendite a falsis ... in regnum celorum (MS fol. 564va) □
OFM Lc 19:41–47a: Cum appropinquaret Jesus ... cotidie in templo Dei (SRL
2: 264)

Dom IX post trin (*OP*) ¦ **Dom X post pent** (*OFM*) (Schneyer T50)
Ep   OP 1 Cor 10:6–13: Non simus concupiscentes ... ut possitis sustinere (MS
fol. 538va–vb) □ *OFM* 1Cor 12:2–11: Scitis quoniam cum gentes ... singulis
prout vult (SRL 2: 264)
Ev   OP Lc 16:1–9: Homo quidam erat dives ... in eterna tabernacula (MS fol.
564va) □ *OFM* Lc 18:9–14: Dixit Jesus ad quosdam qui in se confidebant ...
humiliat exaltabitur (SRL 2: 264)

Dom X post trin (*OP*) ¦ **Dom XI post pent** (*OFM*) (Schneyer T51)
Ep   OP 1 Cor 12:2–11: Scitis quoniam cum gentes ... singulis prout vult (MS
fol. 538vb) □ *OFM* 1 Cor 15:1–10a: Notum vobis facio ... in me vacua non fuit
(SRL 2: 264)
Ev   OP Lc 19:41–47a: Cum appropinquaret Jesus ... cotidie in templo (MS fol.
564va–vb) □ *OFM* Mc 7:31–37: Exiens Jesus de finibus ... et mutos loqui (SRL
2: 264)

Dom XI post trin (*OP*) ¦ **Dom XII post pent** (*OFM*) (Schneyer T52)
Ep   OP 1 Cor 15:1–10a: Notum vobis facio ... in me vacua non fuit (MS fol.
538vb) □ *OFM* 2 Cor 3:4–9: Fiduciam talem ... iustitie in gloria (SRL 2: 265)
Ev   OP Lc 18:9–14: Dixit Jesus ... confidebant ... humiliat exaltabitur (MS fol.
564vb) □ *OFM* Lc 10:23–37: Beati oculi qui vident ... et tu fac similiter (SRL 2:
265)

Dom XII post trin (*OP*) ¦ **Dom XIII post pent** (*OFM*) (Schneyer T53)
Ep   OP 2 Cor 3:4–9: Fiduciam talem habemus ... iustitie in gloria (MS fol.
538vb) □ *OFM* Gal 3:16–22: Abrahe dicte sunt ... daretur credentibus (SRL 2:
265)
Ev   OP Mc 7:31–37: Exiens Jesus de finibus ... et mutos loqui (MS fol. 564vb)
□ *OFM* Lc 17:11–19: Cum iret Jesus in Jerusalem ... te salvum fecit (SRL 2: 265)

Dom XIII post trin (*OP*) ¦ **Dom XIV post pent** (*OFM*) (Schneyer T54)
Ep   OP Gal 3:16–22: Abrahe dicte sunt ... daretur credentibus (MS fol.
538vb–9a) □ *OFM* Gal 5:16–24: Spiritu ambulate ... cum vitiis et concupiscentiis
(SRL 2: 265)
Ev   OP Lc 10:23–27: Beatis oculi qui vident ... tu fac similiter (MS fol.
564vb–5a) □ *OFM* Mt 6:24–33: Nemo potest duobus dominis ... adicientur
vobis (SRL 2: 265)

Dom XIV post trin Dom XV post pent (Schneyer T55)
Ep OP Gal 5:16–24: Spiritu ambulate et ... vitiis et concupiscentiis (MS fol. 539a) □ *OFM* Gal 5:25–6:10: Si Spiritu vivimus ... ad domesticos fidei (SRL 2: 266)
Ev OP Lc 17:11–19: Dum iret Jesus in ... te salvum fecit (MS fol. 565a) □ *OFM* Lc 7:11–16: Ibat Jesus in civitatem ... plebem suam (SRL 2: 266)

Dom XV post trin (*OP*) ¦ **Dom XVI post pent** (*OFM*) (Schneyer T56)
Ep OP Gal 5:25–6:10: Si Spiritu vivimus ... ad domesticos fidei (MS fol. 539a) □ *OFM* Eph 3:13–21: Obsecro vos ne deficiatis ... generationes s s amen (SRL 2: 266)
Ev OP Mt 6:24–33: Nemo potest duobus ... adicientur vobis (MS fol. 565a–b) □ *OFM* Lc 14:1–11: Cum intraret Jesus in domum ... se humiliat exaltabitur (SRL 2: 266)

Dom XVI post trin (*OP*) ¦ **Dom XVII post pent** (*OFM*) (Schneyer T57)
Ep OP Eph 3:13–21: Obsecro vos ne deficiatis ... generationes s s amen (MS fol. 539a–b) □ *OFM* Eph 4:1–6: Obsecro vos ego vinctus ... benedictus in s s amen (SRL 2: 266)
Ev OP Lc 7:11–16: Ibat Jesus in civitatem ... plebem suam (MS fol. 565b) □ *OFM* Mt 22:34–46: Accesserunt ... amplius interrogare (SRL 2: 267)

Dom XVII post trin (*OP*) ¦ **Dom XVIII post pent** (*OFM*) (Schneyer T58)
Ep OP Eph 4:1–6 : Obsecro vos ego vinctus.. benedictus s s amen (MS fol. 539b) □ *OFM* 1 Cor 1:4–8: Gratias ago Deo meo ... adventus DNJC (SRL 2: 268)
Ev OP Lc 19:1–11: Cum intraret Jesus in ... humiliat exaltabitur (MS fol. 565b) □ *OFM* Mt 9:1–8: Ascendens Jesus in naviculam ... talem hominibus (SRL 2: 268–269)

Dom XVIII post trin (*OP*) ¦ **Dom XIX post pent** (*OFM*) (Schneyer T59)
Ep OP 1 Cor 1:4–8: Gratias ago Deo meo ... in die adventus DNJC (MS fol. 540a) □ *OFM* Eph 4:23–28: Renovamini spiritu mentis ... necessitatem patienti (SRL 2: 269)
Ev OP Mt 22:34–46: Phariseis audientes ... amplius interrogare (MS fol. 565vb) □ *OFM* Mt 22:1–14: SFERC homini regi qui fecit nuptias ... vero electi (SRL 2: 269)

Dom XIX post trin (*OP*) ¦ **Dom XX post pent** (*OFM*) (Schneyer T60)
Ep OP Eph 4:23–28: Renovamini spiritu ... necessitatem patienti (MS fol. 540a) □ *OFM* Eph 5:15–21: Videte itaque quomodo caute ... in timore Christi (SRL 2: 269)
Ev OP Mt 9:1–8: Ascendens Jesus in ... talem hominibus (MS fol. 565vb–566a) □ *OFM* Jo 4:46–53: Erat quidam regulus ... et domus eius tota (SRL 2: 269)

Dom XX post trin (*OP*) ¦ **Dom XXI post pent** (*OFM*) (Schneyer T61)
Ep OP Eph 5:15–21: Videte quomodo caute ... in timore Christi (MS fol. 540a–b) □ *OFM* Eph 6:10–17: Confortamini in Domino ... quo est verbum Dei (SRL 2: 269)
Ev OP Mt 22:1–14: SFERC homini regi qui fecit nuptias ... vero electi (MS fol. 566a) □ *OFM* Mt 18:23–35: SFERC homini regi qui voluit rationem ... de cordibus vestris (SRL 2: 269)

Dom XXI post trin (*OP*) ¦ **Dom XXII post pent** (*OFM*) (Schneyer T62)
Ep *OP* Eph 6:10-17: Confortamini in Domino ... quod est verbum Dei (MS fol. 540b) □ *OFM* Phil 1:6-11: Confidimus in Domino Jesu ... in gloriam et laudem Dei (SRL 2: 270)
Ev *OP* Jo 4:46-53: Erat quidam regulus ... et domus eius tota (MS fol. 566a) □ *OFM* Mt 22:15-21: Abeuntes pharisei consilium ... que sunt Dei Deo (SRL 2: 270)

Dom XXII post trin (*OP*) ¦ **Dom XXIII post pent** (*OFM*) (Schneyer T63)
Ep *OP* Phil 1:6-11: Confidimus in Domino Jesu ... et laudem Dei (MS fol. 540b) □ *OFM* Phil 3:17-4:3: Imitatores mei estote ... in libro vite (SRL 2: 270)
Ev *OP* Mt 18:23-35: SFERC regi qui voluit rationum ... de cordibus vestris (MS fol. 566a-b) □ *OFM* Mt 9:18-26: Ecce princeps unus ... universam terram illam (SRL 2: 270)

Dom XXIII post trin (*OP*) ¦ **Dom XXIV post pent** (*OFM*) (Schneyer T64)
Ep *OP* Phil 3:17-4:3: Imitatores mei estote ... sunt in libro vite (MS fol. 540b) □ *OFM* Col 1:9-14: Non cessamus pro vobis ... et remissionem peccatorum (SRL 2: 270) □ *Sarum* Phil 3:17-21: Imitatores mei estote ... qua possit eciam subicere sibi omnia (Sarum 194)
Ev *OP* Mt 22:15-21: Abeuntes pharisei ... et que sunt Dei Deo (MS fol. 566b) □ *OFM* Mt 24:15-35: Cum videritis abominationem ... non preteribunt (SRL 2: 270)

Dom XXIV post trin (*OP*) (Schneyer T65)
Ep *OP* Col 1:9-11: Non cessamus pro vobis ... cum gaudio in CJDN (MS fol. 540b-va)
Ev *OP* Mt 19:18-26: Loquente Jesu ad turbas ecce princeps ... universam terram (MS fol. 566b-va) □ *Sarum* Mt 9:18-22: Loquente Jesu ad turbas ... mulier ex illa hora (Sarum 195)
Note There is no xxvth Sunday after Pentecost in the OFM missal

Dom XXV post trin (Schneyer T66)
Ep *OP* Jer 2:5-8: Ecce dies ... in terra sua (MS fol. 540va) □ *Paris* Heb 3:12-4:3 Videte ne forte sit ... qui credimus in DJC (Paris fol. 125va-125vb)
Ev *OP* Jo 6:5-14: Cum sublevasset ... est in mundum (MS fol. 566va) □ *Paris* Mc 10:29-34: AADV nemo est qui reliquerit domum ... et tertia die resurget (Paris fol. 125va-125vb). *Note* Paris Missal has Epistle and Gospel from **Dom XXVI post trin** as **Dom XXV post trin.**

III

Although the majority of sermons in MS Laud Misc. 511 were preached on themes taken from the pericopes of the Mass of the Temporale, a minority was preached on themes taken from other parts of the Mass of the Temporale, or from the Divine Office found in breviaries. Those changeable parts of the Mass in feasts, seasons, and Sundays of the Temporale, or in specific celebrations of saints' feast days (known as the Sanctorale) are called the Proper of the Mass. This is in direct contrast to those parts of the Mass which remain constant and are named the Ordinary of the Mass. The Proper of the Mass is found mainly in the opening antiphons and psalms, the responsory or gradual and alleluia verses between the pericopes, the offertory and Communion antiphons (with or without Psalms), the Preface to the Common and all the collects. Some illustrations of these usages can be found in Tables 2 and 4. Use of the breviary as a source of sermon themes is illustrated in Tables 3 and 5.

That both Mass texts and the Breviary provided the source for a minority of sermon themes in our manuscript prompted a closer analysis of the sources of those sermon authorities that proved to be of liturgical origin. This is exemplified by the liturgical authorities from the sermons preached at Elstow and from the six Advent sermons made on liturgical themes found in Tables 4 and 5.

TABLE 2 *Sermon Themes Derived from the Proper of the Mass in the Temporale*

This table has two parts: the first refers specifically to MS Laud Misc.511, showing sermon themes taken from parts of the *Temporale* other than epistles and gospels. Three come from the introductory Antiphon of the Mass known in the Dominican, Paris, Sarum and York uses as the *Officium,* and in the Franciscan and Tridentine uses as the *Introit.* The fourth theme comes from the special Easter Sunday and Octave Mass responsory. The second part of the table is derived from a comparative examination of the *Officium / Introit* for each Sunday of the *Temporale.* It records the small number of variants which are peculiar to each use.

Sermon 20
Theme Puer natus est nobis
Comparanda OP fol. 485va; Paris MS 38723 fol. 10b; Sarum 29; York 1: 18; OFM 2: 214)
Reference Schneyer T7: Sunday in Octave of Nativity
Source Office/Introit of Nativity, Day Mass; and of feast of the Circumcision

Sermon 32
Theme Circumdederunt me gemitus mortis
Comparanda OP fol. 486va; Paris MS 38723 fol. 17va; Sarum 45; York 1: 40; OFM 2: 218
Reference Schneyer T16: Septuagesima
Source Office/Introit of Septuagesima

Sermon 119
Theme Hec est dies quam fecit Dominus
Comparanda OP fol. 498vb; Paris MS 38723 fol. 85b; Sarum 136; York 1: 126; OFM 2: 251
Reference Schneyer T28: Easter Sunday
Source Responsory of the Mass

Sermon 167
Theme Spiritus Domini replevit orbem terrarum
Comparanda OP fol. 501a; Paris MS 38723 fol. 101va; Sarum 161; York 1: 152;
OFM 2: 258
Reference Schneyer T39: Pentecost
Source Office/Introit of Pentecost

*Variants in the Office/Introit of the Mass in the Dominican, Franciscan, Paris,
Sarum and York uses*

Fourth Sunday of Advent
Antiphon [1 and 2] Memento nostri Domine, in beneplacito populi tui; visita
nos in salutari tuo; ad videndum in bonitate electorum tuorum, in letitia gentis
tue; ut lauderis cum hereditate tua (OP fol. 485a; Paris MS 38723, fol. 7b–7va;
Sarum 24; York 1: 11) □ [3] Rorate celi et nubes pluant justum; aperiatur terra
... Salvatorem (OFM 2: 210)
Psalm [1] Confitemini Domino quoniam bonus; quoniam in seculum
misericordia eius (OP fol. 485a; Paris MS 38723, fol. 7b–7va; York 1: 11:) □ [2]
Peccavimus cum patribus nostris injuste egimus iniquitatem fecimus (Sarum
24) □ [3] Et justitia oriatur simul; ego Dominus creavi sum (OFM 2: 210)

Ascension
Antiphon Viri Galilei quid admiramini aspicientes in celum, alleluia, quem
admodum vidistis eum ascendentem in celum, ita veniet, alleluia alleluia,
alleluia (OP fol. 500va; Paris MS 38723, fol. 97vb; Sarum 155–156; OFM 2: 255;
York 1: 147)
Psalm [1] Cumque intuerentur ... dixerunt (OP fol. 500va) □ [2] Omnes gentes
plaudite manibus ... (Paris MS 38723, fol. 97vb) □ [3] Cumque intuerentur in
celum euntem illum; ecce duo viri astiterunt juxta illos in vestibus albis; qui
et dixerunt (Sarum 155–156; OFM 2: 255; York 1: 147)

Pentecost
Antiphon Spiritus Domini replevit orbem terrarum, alleluia; et hoc quod
continet omnia scientiam habet vocis, alleluia, alleluia, alleluia (OP fol. 501a;
Paris MS 38723, fol 101va; Sarum 161; York 1: 152; OFM 2: 258)
Psalm [1] Confirma hoc Deus quod operatus es in nobis a templo tuo quod est
in Jerusalem (OP fol. 501a) □ [2] Exsurgat Deus et dissipentur inimici eius; et
fugiant qui oderunt eum a facie eius (Paris MS 8723, fol 101va; Sarum 161;
York 1: 152) □ [3] Omnium est enim ... (OFM 2: 258)

TABLE 3 *Sermon Themes from the Breviary*

Tables 3 and 4 are strictly related to MS Laud Misc. 511. Table 3 identifies four sermons in the manuscript, in addition to the specific six Advent sermons, the themes of which are taken directly from the Divine Office. Three of the themes are from antiphons appropriate to the feasts; one of them from the hymn at Vespers. *Note* No Paris references are given for feasts of BVM as the MS used has no summer or autumn sections. Table 4 brings together ten specific liturgical authorities used in the thirteen sermons preached at Elstow, 1275 to 1283.

Sermon 89
Passion Sunday (Schneyer T23)
Theme Vexilla regis prodeunt
Comparanda OP fol. 372b; Paris 212vb; Sarum 1: dccxiii–iv; York 1: 343–4; OFM 2: 79
Source Opening phrase of the hymn for Vespers of Passion Sunday and Passiontide; used in OP, OFM, and Sarum Breviaries

Sermon 232
Assumption BVM (S59)
Theme Exaltata es sancta Dei Genitrix
Comparanda OP fol. 345a; Sarum 3: 686; York 2: 477; OFM 2: 155–156
Source Matins, antiphon 2: Dominican and Franciscan Breviaries: "Exaltata es sancta Dei Genitrix super choros angelorum ad celestia regna." In Franciscan, Sarum and York Breviaries this is a versicle and response: "V/ Exaltata es ... Genitrix R/ Super choros ... regna."

Sermons 231 and 233
Assumption BVM (S59)
Theme Que est ista ascendet quasi aurora consurgens pulcra ut luna electa ut sol, terribilis ut castrorum acies ordinata
Comparanda OP fol. 346a; Sarum 3: 699; York 2: 485; OFM 2: 156
Source Benedictus antiphon, Lauds of the Feast: "Quae est ista, quae ascendit sicut aurora consurgens: pulcra ut luna, electa ut sol, terribilis ut castrorum acies ordinata" Dominican, Sarum, York and Franciscan Breviaries.

Sermon 234
Nativity BVM (S65)
Theme Cum iocunditate nativitatem beate Marie celebremus ut ipsa intercedat
Comparanda OP fol. 350a; Sarum 3: 782; York 2: 542; OFM 2: 160
Source Antiphon 5, Lauds of the Feast: "Cum jocunditate Nativitatem sanctae Mariae celebremus, ut ipsa pro nobis intercedat ad Dominum Jesum Christum" Dominican, Sarum, York and Franciscan Breviaries.

TABLE 4 *Liturgical References in the Sermons Preached at Elstow, 1275–1283*

Sermon 77

fol. 93b.10–17: "quod tempus valde prope est quia die sabbati proximi ad vesperas incipiet Ecclesia Dominicam Passionem ab illa die usque ad Sabbatum Sanctum totum cantat Ecclesia et legit de sanguine Christi et eius cruce, penis, plagis, et passione ... ." □ *Notes* This describes the liturgical season of Passiontide, the last two weeks of Lent.

fol. 93b.22–23. "unde canit Ecclesia, 'Vexilla regis prodeunt.'" □ *Notes* This is the opening line of the Office Hymn for Passiontide (see Table 4).

Sermon 136

fol. 127vb.21–22: "In principio Misse canit Ecclesia hodie 'Misericordia Domini plena est terra ...'" □ *Notes* Officium/Introit for Sunday II after Easter: "Misericordia Domini est terra, alleluia, alleluia; verbo Domini celi firmati sunt, alleluia, alleluia" (OP fol. 499vb; Paris fol. 92va; Sarum 146; York 1: 140; OFM 2: 254).

Sermon 230

fol. 198vb.38: "sicut legitur in evangelio hodierno 'Quecumque solveritis': *Note* In 1275, "the Sunday nearest the feast of S. John the Baptist" – the title the annotator gave this sermon in the manuscript – was dated 30 June, the day after the feast of SS Peter and Paul of which this is the gospel pericope.

Sermon 231

fol. 200a.24–25: For sermon theme ("Que est ista ...") see Table 4.

fol. 200a.32–34: "Unde canit Ecclesia 'Mittet ad Virginem non quemvis angelum' ..." *Notes Mittet ad Virginem non quemvis angelum*: hymn to Our Lady for the feast of the Annunciation BVM, attributed to Peter Abelard (see *Hymni Latini Medii Aevi*, ed. F.J. Mone, 3 vols. [Freiburg, 1854] 2: 31, no. 343).

fol. 200b.35–37: "Hic est quod in festo isto canit Ecclesia: 'Ascendens Christus super celos preparavit sue castissime Matri immortalitatis locum'.." *Notes* Magnificat Antiphon of First Vespers of the Assumption BVM: "Ascendit Christus super caelos et praeparavit suae castissimae Matri immortalitatis locum; et haec est illa praeclara festivitas, omnium Sanctorum festivitatibus incomparabilis, in qua gloriosa et felix, mirantibus caelestis curiae ordinibus, ad aetherum pervenit thalamum, quo pia sui memorum immemor nequaquam exsistat" (OP fol. 344vb; Paris no MS; Sarum 3: 686–687; York 2: 477–78). The Franciscan Antiphon is "Virgo prudentissima, quo progredieris quasi aurora ... ut sol" (OFM 2: 156)

fol. 200b.39–fol. 200va.1: "De celestibus canit Ecclesia: 'Gaudent angeli et exultant archangeli' ... " *Notes* cf. Magnificat Antiphon of Christmas Day Vespers: "Hodie Christus natus est, hodie salvator apparuit, hodie in terra canunt angeli, letantur archangeli, hodie exultant iusti dicentes Gloria in excelsis. Alleluia" (OP fol. 261b; Paris fol. 118vb-119a; Sarum cxciv; York is different; OFM uncertain).

fol.200va.39-fol. 200vb.2: "Item tam preclara quia octo dies // attribuuntur celebrationi huius festivitatis ..." *Notes* This refers to the practice current until recent times of celebrating major feasts, including the Assumption of the BVM, with a solemn octave.

fol. 201b.22-31: "speciali laude et prerogativa commendatione vel salutatione per ipsam transeundo vel saltem semel in ebdomada Missam eius cum devotione audiendo vel candelam aut cereum diebus sabbatorum in honore eius accendendo vel ad Missam eius oblationem faciendo vel consimile aliquid ..." □ *Notes* This passage refers to liturgical and devotional Marian practices; some are still in use, especially the Saturday Mass of Our Lady.

IV

As mentioned above, MS Laud Misc. 511 contains six Advent sermons made on liturgical themes: Sermons 5 and 12 to 15. The themes of the six sermons are: "Regem venturum Dominum venite adoremus" (Sermon 5); "Surgite vigilemus quia venit rex" (Sermon 8); "Rex noster adveniet quem Johannes predicavit agnum esse venturum" (Sermons 12 and 15); and "Veniet Dominus et non tardabit" (Sermons 13 and 14). These themes are derived not from the Mass pericopes, but from the Divine Office. They contain seventeen different references to the liturgy, occurring at least thirty times. These are recorded below in Table 5, in many ways the most complicated table in this series.

When Table 5 is compared to Table 4, where ten liturgical authorities are used in thirteen sermons, the difference in number is too great to be explained by the choice of the preacher. It would be reasonable to conclude that in the six Advent sermons the liturgical content is important to the preachers who originally composed the sermons, to the compiler of MS Laud Misc. 511 who chose to put these six in his book, to the preachers who used the book subsequently, and finally to the listeners or audiences of these sermons.

The first three authorities in Table 5 are commonplace references to the Mass pericopes of the specific Sundays. The remainder come from a variety of sources: antiphons at Lauds, Prime, Terce; a Magnificat antiphon; versicles and responses; invitatories; parts of responsories. The cues of several of these contain the verb *venire*, expressing the petitionary Advent prayer, thus: Sermon 8 (fol 9vb.37-38): "Tota die clamat Ecclesia suis fidelibus veniet Dominus" (Adv II); Sermon 13 (fol. 15a.21-22): "Tota die clamat veniet veniet ut nos parati sumus" (Adv III); Sermon 15 (fol. 17va.1-3): "Nuntiat tibi adventum suum Ecclesia cotidie clamante veniet veniet Dominus" (Adv III).

I have made a comparison of the Dominican, Paris, Sarum and York breviaries for the Advent antiphons, versicles and responses and responsories. I have not examined the lessons of the three nocturns in Matins nor the hymns. Comparisons with the Franciscan breviary are incomplete: Haymo of

Faversham gives only short cues to all the components of a specific part of the Divine Office; some of these cues are common to different passages and hence are ambiguous. Where they can be determined with some certainty, specific references (to Dominican, Paris, Sarum, York and Franciscan sources) are given, with folio or page reference.

A close examination of these five uses in their Advent liturgy yields some useful observations (conclusions would necessitate a comparative examination of the five breviaries in the complete Temporale and the Sanctorale). There is no exact parallel between any of the five uses. Each follows its own pattern, although it depends on the same material; differences are thus more of placement than of content. The Benedictus and Magnificat antiphons for Advent follow two structures. In the first two weeks of Advent the Benedictus and Magnificat antiphons for the ferias are uniform in all five uses with two exceptions (for the first Vespers of the Second Sunday of Advent the Magnificat antiphon in the Dominican and Franciscan breviaries is the same, and different from the other three uses; in week two in the York use, the Magnificat antiphon for most ferias is a day behind the other four uses). In the second two weeks of Advent, there is far less uniformity among the five uses and it is not possible to describe the differences precisely. The 'O' Antiphons for the Magnificat ("O Sapientia, O Adonai, O Radix Jesse, O Clavis David, O Oriens, O Rex Gentium, O Emmanuel") for 16–23 December are the same in the five uses, but Sarum and Paris add two more alternatives: "O Virgo Virginum" and "O Thome Didime" (itself an alternative O Antiphon for the feast of St. Thomas Apostle, 21 December), while York adds only "O Virgo Virginum."

Another unexpected difference in the disposition of liturgical content is found in the responsories at Matins for the four Advent Sundays. Many of them had the same *response* but different *verse*. For example in the comparison between the Dominican and Paris breviaries for the Advent Sunday Matins, the following differences emerged: on Sunday I three were the same, six were different; on Sunday II four were the same, five were different; on Sunday III six were the same, three were different; on Sunday IV two were the same and seven were different. Sarum and York tended to be more similar to the Dominican breviary, but not consistently so. In fact there were more correlations between Dominican and Sarum, and between Paris and York. It is important not to attach too much significance to these differences; a comprehensive overview would require further detailed study.

Nevertheless, a few observations may be offered. First, a comparison of the five uses shows the clarity of the liturgical focus on the liturgical season in the Dominican and Franciscan uses in contrast with those of the Paris, Sarum and York breviaries. The latter are still tied with a variety of sanctoral commemorations in the different parts of the particular offices. Since preaching was the raison d'être of the Dominican Order, their early constitutions required that the Divine Office be celebrated "breviter et succinte." Their Advent breviary shows how successfully this requirement was observed. The Franciscan breviary is equally clear, and probably even more successful, as Haymo's reorganisation of the liturgy for the Franciscans reduced significantly the number of books needed. Second, all five uses essentially follow the Roman rite; the variants are insignificant compared to the similarities. When it is possible to identify differences, however, they can be used to indicate an initial liturgical source for some sermons. Finally, there is a need to question whether the Dominican and Paris uses are as close to each other as some have thought.

Here, then, are the liturgical authorities found in the six Advent sermons and their sources.

TABLE 5 *Liturgical Authorities in Six Sermons for Advent*

Hora est iam nos de sompno surgere abiciamus opera tenebrarum etc □ *Sermons* 12 and 13 (fols. 14va.35–37; 15a.14–15): Advent II and Advent III □ *Liturgical Source* Epistle Advent I Rom 13:11–14

Ob eius adventum monet Apostolus in Epistola hodierna gaudere fideles dicens: Gaudete in Domino semper etc. □ *Sermon* 15 (fol. 17vb.26–29): Advent IV □ *Liturgical Source* Epistle Advent IV Phil 4:4–7

Ecce rex tuus venit ... □ *Sermons* 8 and 15 (fols. 9vb.29; 17a.31–33): Advent II and Advent III □ *Liturgical Source* Gospel Advent I Mt 21:1–9.

Ecce venit rex occurramus obviam salvatori nostro □ *Sermons* 13 and 15 fols. 15a.19; 17b.23–24): Advent III □ *Liturgical Source* Invitatory Matins Advent I (OP 250va; Sarum 1: xvii; York 1: 8; Paris 80b)

Regem venturum Dominus venite adoremus □ *Sermons* 5, 8, and 15 (fols. 7va. 15–16; 9vb.32; 17a.39–17b.1): Advent I, Advent II, and Advent III □ *Liturgical Source* Invitatory Matins Advent Ferias (OP 252vb; Sarum 1: li; York 1: 19; Paris 85b; OFM 2: 20)

Emitte agnum Domine dominatorem terre □ *Sermons* 12 and 15 (fols. 13va.20–21; 17b.6–7): Advent II and Advent III □ *Liturgical Source* Versicle and Response before Lauds Advent Ferias (OP 251vb; Sarum 1: xxx; York 1: 20; Paris 83va-b)

Veni et libera nos Deus noster □ *Sermon* 15 (fol. 17b.17–18): Advent III □ *Liturgical Sources* Antiphon Prime Advent Ferias (OP 252b; Sarum 1: lvi); Antiphon Terce Advent Ferias (York 1: 23)

Veni Domine et noli tardare relaxa facinora plebis tue Israel □ *Sermon* 15 (fol. 17b.18) Advent III □ *Liturgical Sources* Antiphon Terce Advent Ferias (OP 252b; Paris is different); Antiphon None Advent Ferias (Sarum 1: lvi); Antiphon 3 Lauds Feria 6 Week III (Sarum 1: cxxv; York 1: 53); Antiphon 3 Lauds Feria 6 Week IV (OP 258va); Responsory Matins Advent III (OP 255a; Sarum 1: cvii; York 1:42; Paris 94b); Antiphon 4 Lauds Advent III (OP 255b; York 1: 43)

Veni ad liberandum nos Domine Deus virtutum □ *Sermon* 15 (fol. 17b.15–17): Advent III □ *Liturgical Source* Responsory Terce Advent Ferias (OP 252a; Sarum 1: xli; York 1:17; Paris 84vb; OFM 2: 20)

Rorate celi desuper □ *Sermons* 12 and 13 (fols. 13va.20–21; 17b.6): Advent II and Advent III □ *Liturgical Source* Versicle and Response Vespers Advent Ferias (OP 250va; Sarum 1: lvii; York 1: 18; Paris 80b; OFM 2: 27); Antiphon 1 Lauds Feria 4 Week III (Sarum 1: cxviii); Antiphon 1 Lauds Feria 3 Week IV (OP 258a; Paris 101b)

Rex noster adveniet Christus quem Johannes predicavit agnum esse venturum □ *Sermons* 8, 12, and 15 (fols. 9vb.30; 13va.1–2; 17a.1; 17a.38–39): Advent II and Advent III □ *Liturgical Sources* Invitatory Matins Adv II (OP 252vb; Sarum 1: lxxii; Paris 87va); Invitatory Matins Adv III (York 1:38); Responsory Matins Adv II (OP 253va; Sarum 1: lxxxix; York 1: 32; Paris 89vb)

Ecce Dominus veniet et omnes Sancti eius cum eo et erit in die illa lux magna □ *Sermons* 13 and 15 (fols. 15a.19–20; 17b.22–23): Advent II and III □ *Liturgical Source* Antiphon 3 Lauds Adv I (OP 251vb; Sarum 1: xxx; York 1:21; Paris 83vb; OFM 2: 19)

Veni Domine visitare nos in pace ut letemur coram te corde perfecto □ *Sermon* 15 (fol. 17b.18–19): Advent III □ *Liturgical Source* Magnificat Antiphon Ist Vespers Adv II (OP 252vb; OFM 2: 23) □ *Notes* Antiphon, liturgical function unclear (Paris 87b-va)

Ecce in nubibus celi Dominus veniet cum potestate magna alleluia □ *Sermon* 15 (fol. 17b.21–22; 17b.24–25): Advent III □ Antiphon 1 Lauds Adv II (OP 253va; Sarum 1: lxxxix; York 1:32; Paris 89vb; OFM 2: 23)

Surgite vigilemus venite adoremus quia nescitis horam quando veniet Dominus □ *Sermons* 8 and 15 (fols. 9vb.31; 17a.36–38): Advent II and III □ *Liturgical Sources* Invitatory Matins Adv II (York 1: 28); Invitatory Matins Adv III (OP 254b; Paris 92b)

Item Dominus prope est quasi totum quod canit Ecclesia de adventu Domini: Prope est iam Dominus venite adoremus □ *Sermon* 13 (fol. 15a.17–18): Advent III □ *Liturgical Sources* Responsory Matins Adv III (OP 254vb); Invitatory Matins Adv III Feria 4 (OP 255va; Sarum 1: cxiv; Paris none)

Veniet Dominus et non tardabit et illuminabit abscondita tenebrarum et manifestabit se ad omnes gentes □ *Sermons* 13, 14, and 15 (fols. 14vb.12; 15vb.12, 26–27; 17b.19–21): Advent III □ *Liturgical Source* Antiphon 1 Lauds Adv III (OP 255a; Sarum 1: cix; York 1:43; Paris 94va-b; OFM 2: 25)

Advent Invitatories

Adv I	Ecce venit rex occurramus obviam salvatori nostro (OP 250va; Sarum 1: xvii; York 1:8; Paris 80b; OFM not used)
Adv I	Regem venturum Dominus (OFM 2: 17)

Adv II	Rex noster adveniet Christus quem Johannes predicavit agnum esse venturum (OP 252vb; York 1:lxxxi-lxxxii; Paris 87va)
Adv II	Surgite vigilemus venite adoremus quia nescitis horam quando veniet Dominus (York 1: 28; OFM 2: 23)
Adv III	Surgite vigilemus venite adoremus quia nescitis horam quando veniet Dominus (OP 254b; Paris 92b)
Adv III	Ecce jam venit plenitudo temporis in quo misit Deus Filium suum natum de virgine factum sub lege (Sarum 1: c)
Adv III	Rex noster adveniet Christus quem Johannes; see above (York 1: 38)
Adv III	Domine prestolamur (OFM 2:24)
Adv IV	Ecce jam venit plenitudo temporis in quo; see above (OP 256va; Paris 104vb– 104va)
Adv IV	Prestolantes Redemptorem levate capita vestra quoniam prope est redemptio vestra (Sarum 1: cxxxiii)
Adv IV	Dicite filia syon ecce salvator tuus venit (York 1: 58)
Adv IV	Ecce veniet rex (OFM 2: 29)
Adv Feria	Regem venturum Dominus, venite adoremus (OP 252b; Sarum 1: li; York 1:19; Paris 85b; OFM 2: 20)
Adv III Feria	Prope est iam Dominus (OP 255va)

V

In our sermon collection a few sermons at the end of the manuscript constitute a small Sanctorale, that is feasts of saints that follow the pattern of the fixed calendar year, in contrast to feasts and seasons of the Temporale which, apart from Christmas and Epiphany, are related to the movable feast of Easter.

While sanctoral celebrations are specific to the saints, the specificity varies according to their significance in the Church local and/or universal. For a few saints the celebrations are wholly specific, but the majority are honoured by a few elements from a general collection of available collects, antiphons, pericopes, and psalms. This general provision is known as the Common of Saints. Within this general provision, different groupings or categories (such as Common of Doctors, Common of Martyrs - men, Common of Martyrs - women; Common of Virgins, Common of Confessors, etc) are found. In MS Laud Misc. 511 there is only one sermon from the Common of the sanctoral cycle, namely Sermon 229 for the Common Mass of One Confessor. A perusal of the comparisons in Table 6 shows that this sermon theme is not Franciscan. To declare categorically that it is Dominican, however, is not possible.

TABLE 6 *Liturgical Sources for the Theme of Sermon 229*

Table 6 shows the gospel pericopes of the Common Mass of One Confessor from the Dominican, Franciscan, Paris, Sarum and York uses to provide a context for the one sermon from MS Laud Misc. 511 with the theme "Homo quidam peregre proficiscens" (Mt 25:14). There is no provision for this pericope in the Franciscan Common Mass of One Confessor.

The Dominican Portiforium (MS Add 23935)
Sint lumbi vestri (Lc 12:35- 40): fol 570vb
Vigilate quia nescitis hora (Mt 24:42- 47): fol 571a
Homo quidam peregre proficiscens (Mt 25:14- 23): fol. 571a
Homo quidam nobilis (Lc 19:12- 28): fol. 571a- b
Nemo accendit lucernam (Lc 11:33- 36): fol. 571b

The Paris Missal (MS Add 38723)
Homo quidam peregre (Mt 25:14- 23): fol. 174a
Vigilate quia nescitis hora (Mt 24:42- 47): fol. 174a- b
Videte vigilate et orate MC 13:33- 37): fol. 174b
Nemo accendit lucernam (Lc 11:33- 36): fol. 174b
Sint lumbi vestri precincti (Lc 12:35- 40): fol. 174b- va

The Sarum Missal (*Sarum Missal*, ed. Wickham Legga, p. 374)
Vigilate quia nescitis qua hora (Mt 24:42- 47)
Homo quidam peregre (Mt 25:14- 23)
Homo quidam nobilis (Lc 19:12- 28)
Videte, vigilate et orate (Mc 13:33- 37)

The York Missal (*Missale ad usum insignis ...*, ed. Henderson, 2: 151)
Homo quidam peregre (Mt 25:14- 23):
Homo quidam nobilis (Lc 19:12- 28):
Misit Jesus duodecim (Mt 10: 5- 10):
Vos estis sal terre ... regnum celorum (Mt 5: 13- 19) [or two pericopes: (1) Vos estis ... ad hominem; (2) Vos estis lux mundi ... regnum celorum.
Nolite timere pusillus grex (Lc 12:32- 44)
Qui vos audit me audit (Lc 10:16- 20)
Vigilate quia nescitis hora (Mt 24:42- 47)
Videte vigilate et orate (Mc 13:33- 37)
Nemo accendit lucernam (Lc 11:33- 36)

The Franciscan Ordines (*Franciscan Missal and Breviary*, ed. van Dijk, 2: 315)
Vos estis sal terre (Mt 5: 13- 19)
Vigilate quia nescitis (Mt 24:42- 47)
Sint lumbi (Lc 12:35- 40)
Nemo accendit lucernam (Lc 11:33- 36)
Videte, vigilate et orate MC 13:33- 37)

Nolite timere pusillus grex (Lc 12:32-44)
Homo quidam nobilis (Lc 19:12-28)
Ecce nos reliquimus omnia (No ref. given.)

VI

Here is a list of manuscript and printed sources referred to in this appendix.

Manuscript Sources

Dominican *Portiforium*: London, BL (BM) MS Add 23935

Rome, Santa Sabina Archivium Generale Ordinis Praedicatorum: MS XIV L. 1. fol. 9-11v

Dominican *Graduale*: Oxford: Blackfriars MS 1

Paris Missal: London, BL (BM) MS Add 38723

Paris Breviary (Hiemalis): London BL (BM) MS Add 37399

BM MS Add 35085, fol. 676b-680vb [*Catalogue of Additions (1894-1899)*, 16: 145-146]: This MS is a *Vulgate Bible*, probably written in France in the mid-thirteenth century.

BM MS Add 37487, fol. 396a-397a [*Catalogue of Additions (1906-1910)*, 18: 51-52: This MS is a *Vulgate Bible* written in Italy in the thirteenth century. The table of epistles and gospels is added in a different but contemporary hand.

The following BM manuscripts were also consulted but not used significantly in the above tables, as they are all fifteenth-century manuscripts: MSS Harley 2927 (a Paris Breviary); Add 16416 (an OFM Missal); Harley 2897 (an OFM Breviary); Add 37519 (a Sarum Missal), Stowe 12 (a Sarum Breviary); and Add 17007 (a Dominican Missal).

Printed Sources

The Franciscan Missal and Breviary: Sources of the Roman Liturgy, ed. S.J.P. van Dijk, 2 vols. (Leiden, 1963).

Breviarium ad usum Sarum, Fasc. I, III, ed. F. Procter and C. Wordsworth (Cambridge, 1882-1886).

Graduale Sarisburiense, ed. W.H. Frere (London, 1894).

The Sarum Missal, ed. J. Wickham Legg (Oxford, 1916).

Breviarium ad usum insignis Ecclesiae Eboracensis, ed. W.G. Henderson, 2 vols., SS 71, 75 (Durham-London-Edinburgh, 1875).

Missale ad usum insignis Ecclesiae Eboracensis, ed. W.G. Henderson, 2 vols. SS 59, 60 (Durham-London-Edinburgh, 1874).

Missale Romanum (Antwerp, 1711).

Appendix 9

Selected Texts

Sermon 13: Third Sunday of Advent

De Libro Proprio, fol. 14vb–15va.

Veniet Dominus et non tardabit.

Duo dicenda sunt hic: primo, de adventu Domini et hoc est *veniet Dominus*; secundo, quid tardat eius adventum, et hoc est *et non tardabit*.

    Primum de primo. Sancta mater nostra Ecclesia hodie premunit filios
5   suos, scilicet omnes Christianos quotquot sunt, qui filii facti sunt Ecclesie
per veram fidem et sacre fontis Baptismatis regenerationem, de adventu
Domini nostri Jesu Christi qui erit ad hoc natale quando Dominus noster
pius Jesus pro salute humana de Virgine Gloriosa nasci dignabatur, ubi
salutis nostre initium emanavit. Tunc enim primo oriebatur sol iusticie in
10   mundo et fuit tota vita Christi quasi unica dies; occidit enim iste sol in
passione. Quod quidem festum omnis Ecclesia per orbem terrarum late diffusa colit et veneratur, et est festum omnium festorum. Quia tunc omnes
divites et pauperes, largi et tenues atque avari festa celebrant, vicinos convocant, convivia parant. De hoc festo magno, scilicet, adventu Christi pre-
15   munit hodie Ecclesia filios suos dicens *Veniet Dominus* etc. quasi dicat: 'vos
Christiani filii mei spiritualiter regenerati, tergite maculas, deflete culpas,
mundate culpas, quia rex regum, dominus dominantium, salvator omnium,
Emanuel, id est nobiscum Deus, *veniet*.' Et ne crederet aliquis quod posset
adhuc expectare et in sterquilinio peccati residere, statim adiungit et *non*
20   *tardabit*. Quasi dicat / *fol. 15a* / Ne tardetis converti ad Dominum, immo
statim, "lavamini et mundi estote." Quia sicut dicit Augustinus: "Qui penitenti hodie veniam spopondit peccanti diem crastinum non promisit."

10 mundo] luxit per predicat.... miraculorum.... et s... predicationem *add. in
marg.*   14 De hoc ... adventu *bis*

1   Antiphon 1, Lauds and Vespers, 3rd Sunday of Advent.
17   Apoc 19:16, cf. Responsory 1, Matins, 3rd Sunday of Advent.
18   Is 7:14.
20   Margin Distinction / Summary:
                                    Oritur in nativitate
            Verus sol Christus⎰Luxit miraculorum operatione
                                ⎱Occidit in Passione
21   Is 1:16.
21–22 *Augustinus: Enarratio in Psalmos* 101.10 (PL 37: 1301).

Dominus enim veniet et non tardabit et debet quilibet exemplo matris sue
Ecclesie contra Domini tanti adventum animam suam, templum scilicet
Domini, preparare, que propter fervens desiderium post sponsum suum   25
Christum se longe tempore elapso contra tantum adventum incepit preparare "Venite ascendamus ad montem Domini," etc. scilicet per contempla-
tionem celestium et desiderium eternorum, cogitando meditando de divi-
nis; sic enim intellexit Apostolus cum dixit: "nostra conversatio in celis
est," "Hora est iam nos de sompno surgere." Item, "abiciamus opera tene-   30
brarum" etc., "ut in die," scilicet adventus Domini, "honeste ambulemus."
Item, "Dominus prope est" quasi totum quod canit Ecclesia de adventu
Domini est, sicut *veniet Dominus et non tardabit*. "Ecce venit rex occurramus
obviam ei": "Ecce Dominus veniet et omnes sancti eius cum eo"; "Ecce ap-
parebit Dominus," tota die clamat 'Veniet, veniet' ut nos parati simus. Et   35
ex^m intellige quod sicut olim iam mccli venit Dominus in carne, Deus et homo
cum hominibus conversandus. Bar c iii: "In terra visus est" etc., sic in hoc
festo futuro per gratiam veniet non solum cum fidelibus sed in eorum animabus commansurus; et congrue potest tunc vocari Emanuel, id est, nobiscum Deus. Sed, pro certe, discant omnes quam sap: "malivolam animam   40
non introibit sapientia" Dei Patris eo quod tam suaviter deliciis celorum
nutritus est et tantis gaudiis assuetus quod animam peccato fetentem abor-
ret et cum rubigine vitiorum quiescere dedignatur. Mundum enim oportet
esse eius hospicium.

Qui ergo vult Christum in suo adventu hospitare, necesse est primo   45
eicere a templo Dei omnia immunda, grossa et vilia et fetencia, demum
aream purgare, lacrimis semper irrigantibus coinquinata lavare, ultimo

---

25 preparare] dicens filiis suis *add. in marg. post* celis est *et expunx.* dicens filiis   46
omnia – 56 *multa*: The text here is exactly the same as Sermon 14 *fol. 16va-b*, with
the following exceptions: l. 46 immunda *om. fol. 16*; l. 48 ramis et floribus] ramis
virtutum et floribus bonorum operum *fol. 16*: ll. 49–50 ostendat] offendat *fol. 16*;
l. 53 Christus nobiscum] Christum nobiscum cohabitabit *fol. 16*

27   Is 2:3.
29–30   Phil 3:20.
30–32   Rom 13:11–13.
32   Phil 4:5
33–34   Invitatory, Matins, 1st Sunday of Advent.
34   Antiphon 3, Lauds and Vespers, 1st Sunday of Advent.
34–35   Responsory 1, Matins, 3rd Sunday of Advent.
36ss.   ex^m: scribal insertions in the margins of the text.
36   This sermon seems to be the only one in the MS to contain a date.
37   Bar 3:38.
40–41   Sap 1:4.

templum Christi ramis et floribus decorare, ut nichil sub / *fol. 15b* / vel
supra in angulis vel cavernis lateat quod oculum Christi venientis osten-
50ex^m dat, sicut faciunt in magnis villis qui hospites recipiunt. Primo domos suas
a sordibus purgant et mundant circumquaque, utensilia lavant et oculis
transeuntium lutentia reddunt, et cum talis honestas videtur in domo a
transeuntibus descendunt et ibi commorantur nocte: sic Christus nobiscum
si mundiciam cordis templi sui respexerit. Quia ergo nichil est quod obsis-
55 tat Deo venienti nisi peccatum, abiciendum est peccatum a nobis propter
multa. Primo quia separat hominem a Deo, ys lix: "Iniquitates nostre divi-
serunt inter nos et Deum nostrum"; et non tantum hoc sed etiam coniungit diabolo. Postquam enim angelus apostata cecidit nunquam simul coha-
bitare potuerunt Deus et diabolus, immo quam cito anima existens in cari-
60 tate habens Christum per gratiam instigante diabolo et carnis delectatione
atque mera voluntate mortaliter peccaverit, recidit Christus, ingreditur diabolus et quot vicibus maculatur tot demonibus satiatur, teste evangelio de
Maria Magdalena: "De qua Dominus eiecit vii demonia," id est vii crimina-
libus peccatis purgavit eam; sic ergo patet quod predicitur.
65 Item quod peccator filius est diaboli et etiam diabolus et peior diabolo.
ex^m Heu, quam horrendum est diabolum incorporare. Credo quod quicumque
vestrum serpente cingeretur non audacter cubaret neque dormiret quousque liberaretur. Non. Nec, quod minus est, si sciretur serpens in stramine
alicuius, non ibi dormiret quousque deponeretur. Mirum ergo est quod ali-
70 quis scienter et prudenter dormit cum diabolo serpente infernali venenoso,
qui primos parentes nostros invidia sua intoxicavit, quam habuit quod
homo efficeretur heres illius regni quod ipse per superbiam suam perdidit
ex^m in eternum. Nonne amens esset qui illum secum cohabitandum gratis ad-
mitteret, qui patrem suum et matrem occidisset, et illummet totis viribus
75 nocte dieque ad perdendum quereret et investigaret? Immo talis est qui
diabolum per peccatum admittit in anima, qui Adam et Evam gustu / *fol.*

---

72 *post* homo *del.* scire   74 illummet] illuminet *MS*

48   Margin Distinction / Summary:

               eicere a templo Dei omnia immunda etc.
               per confessionem etc.
               aream mundare sub et subtus per precogitationem
hospes Christi debet — lacrimis irrigantibus maculas deflere
               ramis et floribus bonorum operum decorare
               item, locum quietis Christo mundissime conservare

56–57   Is 59:2.
63   Luc 8:2.
66   *quam horrendum*: In the MS a finger points to this phrase.

15va / pomi occideret et totam eorum postmodum progeniem spiritualiter occidere machinavit, non tantum in corpore sed etiam in anima eternalibus penis cruciare querit et satagit; merito ergo abiciendum est peccatum.

ex^m   Et vide quantam verecundiam peccator infert Domino quantum in ipso   80
est. Si enim haberes magnum palatium ad regem hospitandum et filius regis veniens hinc penes te hospitaret et premuniret te quod si inimicos eius reciperes nullam cum eis tecum moram faceret, et tu non obstante hac premunitione, postquam esset cenatus et in lecto causa quiescendi cubatus, inimicos eius capitales admitteres in hospitio, et ipse hac de causa media   85
nocte surgeret et hospitium reliqueret, et hac contumelia audita, Rex faceret te citare ad Banchium Londoniarem, nonne crederes furcis suspendi? Forte non! Immo melius crederes comburi, vel excoriari, vel equis tractari, sicut Willelmus et Johannes de Marisco, seductores Regis. Et ipse filius quasi rex est. Nonne omnes Anglie iuraverunt ei fidelitatem? Et quid si Rex   90
faceret istud attingere per Assisam et ita istud proponeret contra te, et sic convictus esses, et Rex consequenter diceret filio suo: 'Fili mi, iste iam super seditione vestra convictus est. Da Sententiam.' Sic est de abicientibus Filium Dei adveniente peccato et per consequens diabolo. Quando testis erit in iudicio contra te ipsum propria conscientia, iudicabit Filius Dei sicut   95
in Johanne: "Pater non iudicat quemquam; sed omne iudicium dedit Filio."

Item, abiciendum est peccatum quia privat omni ecclesiastico suffra-
ex^m gio. Qualiter fiat hoc? Videamus per exemplum. Si esset modo hic aliquis sententialiter truncatus pede vel manu et sic abiceretur manus vel pes a corpore, et postea reficeretur corpus deliciosis cibariis et potaretur vino   100
optimo vel pigmento, quid ista refectio manui vel pedi absciso proderetur? Nichil. Tota Ecclesia est quasi unicum corpus cuius caput Christus est, membra autem fideles: abscisus ergo per / *fol. 15vb* / mortale peccatum a corpore Ecclesie de dulci refectione Missarum, Matutinarum, et aliarum orationum, ubicumque et in quacumque religione nichil participat iste am-   105
plius quam membrum abscisum.

77   Margin Distinction / Summary
                              ⌐quia separat hominem a Deo etc.
Abiciendum est peccatum ⌐ quia peccator filius est diaboli diabolus et peior diabolo
                              ⌐quia privat hominem omni ecclesiastico suffragio prop-
                              ter incertitudinem hore mortis
87   *Londoniarem* is written thus in the MS.
89   For the story see first part of Chapter 8 on the Advent Liturgical Sermons.
96   Jo 5:22.
102–103 1 Cor 12 seq.
105   *Religione* is a term meaning religious life.

Item, propter incertitudinem hore mortis, Eze 7: "Veniet mors," etc; Eccles: "Vivens sciat quia morietur." Unde frequens memoria mortis aufert peccatum, teste Salomone dicente: "Memorare novissima tua et in Narr° eternum non peccabis." Dicatur narracio de nobili Rege Grecie, etc.

107   Ps 54:16.
108   Eccles 9:5.
109–110 Ecclus 7:40.
110   Narr°: scribal insertion in the margin of the text. *Fabulae and Parabolae of Odo of Cheriton*, ed. L. Hervieux (Paris, 1896) 75, 194–195, is a possible source; F.C. Tubach, *Index Exemplorum* (Helsinki, 1969) has two columns of references to stories about Alexander and other kings of Greece.

Sermon 66: by Simon of Hinton OP, for Second Sunday of Lent.

De Libro Nigro Minori, fratris S. de Henton, fol. 72va–73va

Hec est voluntas Dei sanctificatio vestra.

In primo aspectu duo occurrunt consideranda, que sit Dei voluntas et quare sit facienda. Primum est ibi: "sanctificatio vestra"; sanctificatio est sanctitatis factio. Sanctitas tamen, licet in Scriptura multipliciter accipitur, tamen 5 hic proprie pro munditia accipitur, unde in eadem Epistola: "Non enim vocavit nos Deus in immunditiam sed in sanctificationem." Propter hoc dicit: "ut abstineatis vos a fornicatione," ecce immunditia, "ut sciat unusquisque vas suum possidere," ecce perseverantia; quod enim possidetur ab aliquo manet ei. Ex hoc ergo duo sunt consideranda, munditia et perseverantia. 10 Consideremus ergo quid animam faciat immundam, secundo quomodo anima mundatur, tertio de perseverantia munditie.

De primo patet quod peccatum, auctoritate et ratione: Jere 2: "Si laveris te nitro" quod est genus salis multum abstersivum, "et multiplicaveris tibi herbam larith [*Vg* borith]," que est herba multum lavativa, "maculata es in 15 iniquitate tua coram me. Quomodo ergo dicis: non sum polluta. Vide vias tuas in convalle, scito quid feceris."

Ratione, sub quadam metafora, sic, anima sancta in Cantico orto comparatur, unde sponsus ait: "Ortus conclusus, soror mea sponsa, ortus conclusus," qui quidem vacuus non est sed consitus multi generis arboribus,

1   1 Thess 4:3.   12–16 Jere 2:22–23.
5–6   1 Thess 4:7.   18–21 Cant 4:12–13.
7–8   1 Thess 4:3–4.

unde sequitur: "emissiones tue paradisus malorum punicorum cum pomo- 20
rum fructibus," et in eodem sponsus dicit: "descendi in ortum meum ut
viderem poma convallium et inspicerem si floruisset vinea et germinasset
mala punica." Hee autem arbores virtutes sunt, quarum est ordo ut nulla
aliam excedat; fructus sunt bona opera. In hoc orto etiam florum suavitas
non deficit, qui sunt meditationes et affectiones ad modum florum, nunc 25
apparentes, inde transeuntes; unde de fructu et floribus, idem sponsus in
Can: "Dilectus meus descendit ad are<o>lam aromatis ut pascatur / *fol.
72vb* / in ortis," ecce fructus, "et lilia colligit," ecce flores. Sed certe, si talem ortum corporalem invaderet ignis, duo faceret, scilicet arborem cum
fructibus et floribus absumeret, et terram fedam relinqueret et horribilem 30
solitudinem. Quod autem est ignis naturaliter ad ortum corporalem, hoc
est peccatum ad ortum spiritualem, de quo peccato in Job: "Ignis est usque
ad consummationem devorans et eradicans omnia semina." Ideo per figu-
ram dicitur de exercitu diaboli qui mentem istam succendit, Joel: "Quasi
ortus voluptatis terra coram eo et post eum solitudo deserti" cuius tamen 35
ante parvum ponitur "ante faciem eius ignis vorans et post eum urens
flamma." Patet ergo quam feda, quam misera, et quam horribilis per peccatum efficiatur anima.

Item, quod peccatum immundam facit animam patere potest per locum
a minori sicut diabolus Mt 12 dicitur: "immundus spiritus," sed in ipso tria 40
contigit considerare, scilicet naturam, culpam et penam. Per naturam enim
immundus non est; sicut enim a summo bono non est nisi bonus, nec a
summo iusto nisi iustus sic nec a summo mundo et pulcro non potest esse
nisi mundus et pulcrus, etc. Cum ergo omnis creatura, unde natura est, sic
a Deo est qui est summe pulcher et summe mundus, cumque: "Deus lux 45
est, et tenebre in eo non sunt ille," non potest creatura, unde natura est,
esse nisi pulcra et munda; quod si hoc est verum de infima, quanto magis
de supprema et angelica. Unde et de diabolo pro statu illo quo fuit natura
eius sine peccato dicitur Eze 28: "Tu signaculum similitudinis plenus sapientia et perfect<us> decore fuisti in deliciis paradisi Dei." Item, nec pena 50
facit ipsum immundum quia tunc pre omnibus hominibus Christus immundus in hac vita fuisset, in persona cuius dicitur: "Dolor meus super
omnem dolorem," quod absit cum ipse sit Dei sapientia, in qua sapientia:

---

31 naturaliter *corr. ex* corporaliter *in marg.* | *post* ortum *del.* spi   34 mentem]
istem *MS*   43 sic nec ... pulcro *bis, correxit*

21–23	Cant 6:10.	40	Mt 12:43.
27	Cant 6:1.	45–46	Jo 1:5.
32–33	Job 31:12.	49–50	Ezech 28:12–13.
34–35	Joel 2:3.	52–53	Jere 8:18.

"nichil inquinatum incurrit." / *fol. 73a* / Restat ergo ut sola culpa sue immun-
55 ditie causa fuerit. Quod si angelum tam excellentis nature in celo existentem
et nulli inferiori nature unitum potuit culpa immundum facere, quanto
magis animam hac valle miserie captivatam et corpori coruptibili unitum;
unde Job: "Stelle non sunt munde in conspectu eius," id est Dei, scilicet
propter peccatum, "quanto magis homo putredo et filius hominis vermis?"
60 Item, per rationem potest patere quod peccatum immundam reddit
animam, quia, sicut ex diffinitione peccati que est aversio a bono incom-
mutabili ad bonum commutabile, in peccato sunt duo: aversio a luce <que
est Deus> et conversio ad hec inferiora. Scilicet unde avertit se a luce
cum sit tenebrosa; unde convertit se ad inferiora cum sit turbulenta, sicut
65 potest patere per exemplum. Diaphonum enim quod per naturam in medio
est inter luminosa et opaca verbi gratia aer, per absentiam luminosorum
fit tenebrosum, per immixtionem horum inferiorum ut vapor terrestrium
et aquarum fit turbulentum; sic et anima per naturam media inter Deum
et omnia corporalia, per hoc quod Deus est ipsi absens, licet numquam
70 Deo sit tenebrosa; per hoc autem quod hec inferiora per amorem non sibi
immiscet, verum etiam nunc fit turbulenta unde Boethius in *Libro Consola-*
tionis loquens de animabus dicit: "ubi oculi a summe veritatis luce ad hec
inferiora et tenebrosa deiecerint, mox inscitiae nube, caligant et perniciosis
turbantur affectibus."
75 Item, per rationem pulcritudinis que est sicut dicit Augustinus *De Civi-*
tate Dei liber 22: "Congruentia partium cum coloris suavitate," patet idem,
quia peccatum utramque partem pulcritudinis tollit, quod sic patet. Partes
anime preter vegetativam due sunt, scilicet sensibilis et rationalis, et rationalis duos habet, inferiorem et superiorem. Ordo autem naturalis istarum
80 partium, sicut patet per primum statum hominis, est ut superior secundum
nomen suum proponatur inferiori et non solum per naturam, verum etiam
per regimen, sic vir mulieri secundum Augustinum et inferior sen-/ *fol.*

56 unitum *corr. ex* initum *in marg.*   62–63 que est Deus *corr. ex* mutabili *in marg.*
63 inferiora] interiora MS   66 opaca] operata MS   73 inscitiae nube] inficit vile
MS   81 inferiori] superiori MS

54   Sap 7:25.
58–59   Job 25:5–6.
61–63   Cf. Thomas de Chobham, *Sermones* 3 l. 270; 4 l. 351 (CCCM 82A: 33–34, 49).
65ff.   The following two sentences share vocabulary and scientific ideas with
parts of the Sermon by Richard Fishacre in MS *Laud Misc. 511.*
72–74   Boethius: *De consolatione Philosophiae* 55, prosa 2.7 (PL 63: 837).
76   Augustinus: *De civitate Dei* 220.19.2 (PL 41: 781).
82   Augustinum: cf. *Quaestionum in heptateuchum libri septem* 1.153 (PL 34: 590).

73b /-sualitati, tamquam domina ancille secundum Apostolus ad Gal per peccatum autem fit istarum partium adversio ut subiciatur inferior pars rationis sensualitati, superior inferiori. Quorum primum concomitatur 85 abusio, quia secundum beatum Bernardum: "Dominam ancillari et ancillam dominari magna est abusio." Secundo, vero concomitatur inquietudo et confusio. De primo ecc 25: "Mulier si primatum habeat contraria erit viro suo"; de secundo in ecc dicitur de muliere: "Si non ambulaverit ad manum tuam, confundet te in conspectu inimicorum tuorum." 90

Item, aufert secundam partem pulcritudinis que est coloris suavitas; color quippe anime gratia est; quod ut melius pateat, attendamus sic fuisse de Deo in conditione anime, sicut de optimo artifice volente sui representativam ymaginem facere; talis quidem duo faceret; primum quod in natura congrua lineamenta figuraret et proportionaret, et hoc facto ymago 95 eius aliquo modo dici posset, quia ymago; sed ut complete representaret ipsum, ymaginem sic figuratam coloribus suis similibus sic supervestiret; quo facto completa esset. Sic Deus in natura anime que est incoruptibilis, qualis materia congruit ymagini eius cuius nulla potest esse corruptio, quo ad sui representationem, et quo ad divinitatis unitatem per unitatem essen- 100 tie, et quo ad Trinitatem personarum in trinitate positarum expressit. Unde quia natura etiam cum per peccatum anima fedatur, licet deturpata manet ymago sicut dicit Ps: "Verumtamen in ymagine pertransit homo, sed et frustra conturbatur." Sed volens Deus animam complete ipsum representare vestivit eam gratiis diversis, unde Ge 1 dicit Dominus: "Faciamus 105 hominem," scilicet interiorem scilicet animam, "ad ymaginem et similitudinem nostram"; Glosa: "Quo ad naturalia," ecce primum, "et similitudinem nostram quo ad gratuita," ecce secundum. Set yma-/ *fol.73va* /-ginem qualitercumque depictam, licet in materia incorruptibili sculptam, si in ignem proieceris et ipsam ignis invaserit et prevaluerit, nigrum et 110 horribilem aspectu reddit. Unde in tre 4 loquens de hominibus pro statu gratie, ait: "Candidiores Nazarei eius nive, nitidores lacte, rubicundiores

99 quo] co *MS*   108 quo] co *MS*   109 incorruptibili] incorruptibili (*sic*) *corr. ex* incorporali *MS*

83–85   Gal 4.
86–87   *Bernardum*: cf. *Sententiae* 88, series 3 (*Opera* 6,2: 134).
88–89   Ecclus 25:30.
89–90   Ecclus 25:35.
94ss   *ymaginem*: wherever "y" is found in the MS, it has a dot above it.
103–104 Ps 38:7.
105–107 Gen 1:26.
107–108 *Glosa*: gloss on Gen 1:26 (*Biblia sacra cum glossa ordinaria* 1: 30).
112–113 Tre 4:7.

ebori antiquo, saphiro pulcriores," et pro statu culpe subdit: "Denigrata est
super carbones facies eorum" etc. Hoc expavescens Jeremias, tre 2: "Filii
115   Syon incliti et amicti auro primo, quomodo reputati sunt in vasa testea,"
et parum ante: "Quomodo obscuratum est aurum, mutatus est color optimus." O quam misera et quam dolenda commutatio! Deus cum tanta diligentia et quasi cum deliberatione pre omnibus creaturis animam condidit
tam excellentem in natura, quia ad sui ymaginem, tam venustam in gratia,
120   quia ad similitudinem; et infelix homo tam crudelis sibi, tam ingratus Deo,
animam suam Deo similem ac in genere: "suo speciosior et supra omnem
stellarum dispositionem," consentiendo peccato facit peccato similem et
carbone nigriorem. Hoc expavescens Ecc 30 exclamat: "miserere anime tue
placens Deo, et contine, et congrega cor tuum in sanctitate"; miserere
125   anime tue, contra crudelitatem; placens Deo contra ingratitudinem.
        Sequitur secundum, scilicet videre quomodo mundetur, quod sic pate-
bit. Ad alterandum aliquid in contrariam dispositionem, necessario tria
requiruntur, scilicet agens habens actu vel virtute effectiva contrariam
dispositionem, ut, si de frigido fieri debeat calidum, exigitur habens actu
130   calorem, sicut est ignis, vel virtute effectiva, sicut sol: quod enim motus
calorem generat per accidens est et non in veritate motus. Item, requiritur
presentia agentis cum eo in quod agitur, non solum in superficie sed etiam
in profundo.

128 effectiva] infectiva MS

113–114 Tre 4:8.
114–115 Tre 4:2.
116–117 Tre 4:1.
121–122 Sap 7:29.
123–124 Ecclus 30:24.
125   This completes the first section of the sermon only.
133   The end of the sermon-text in MS Laud Misc. 511, but clearly not the end
         of this sermon.

109: Distinctions on Humility, Palm Sunday

De Libro Rubeo Minori, fol. 111vb

Humilitas est:

Oratio sublevatio: Ecc oratio humiliantis se nubes penetrabit;
Regie sedis adepcio: exemplum, de pueris;
Gratie susceptio: exemplum, de sedentibus ubi noti de curia sedent;

5   Dei honorificatio: exemplum, quanto materia operis incultior
                              tanto operarius nobilior,

Exenniorum receptio;
Virtutis augmentatio;
Laqueorum evasio;

10   Status certitudo: exemplum, de loco alto respicite;
Magni fructus ostensio: exemplum, fructus inclinat arborem;
                              respicite arbores etc.;

Virtutum conservacio;
Ascensionis manifestatio: exemplum, qui ascendit montem humiliat se;

15   Visus Domini attractio;
Curialitatis ostensio,   phi.2 b: "superiores invicem arbitrantes";
Fidelitatis exhibitio: ys: "Gloriam meam alteri";
Occultorum revelatio: exemplum, de descentibus in puteum;
Universitatis exhortatio: ps: "Humiliatus sum usquequaque";

20   Casus vitatio: ys: "Quomodo cecidisti, Lucifer" etc.;
Vite recordatio: exemplum, duo non possunt in unum saccum;
      ps: "Ecce, reges terre congregati sunt, convenerunt in unum";

Prostrati erectio;
Compassionis provocatio: leo enim parcit prostratis;

25   Hereditatis celestis adepcio: Bernardus: "O qualem oportet eum repperiri
                      qui debet succedere loco angeli repu<dia>ti";

Celestis edificii expeditio: Sanctus: "Vis magnam fabricam extruere celsitudinis
                      prius de radice cogita humilitatis";

Terre fructificatio   que in se sterilis est, sed quia
                      in imo est recipit humiditatem et calorem.

---

2   Ecclus 35:21.   19   Ps 118:107.
16   Phil 2:3.   20   Is 14:12.
17   Is 42:8, 48:11.   21   Is this a proverb?
18   *puteum*: Cf. Du Cange s.v.   22   Ps 47:5.

24   Cf. "Speculum animalium," cap. 1, l. 107, *Christiani Campililensis Opera poetica*
        (CCCM 19B: 296).
25   *Bernardus*: *Pro Dominica I Novembris, Sermo* 2.3 (PL 183: 384).
27   *Sanctus*: Augustine, *Sermo* 69.1.2 (PL 38: 441).

Sermon 136: Second Sunday after Easter

De Libro Nigro Maiori, fol. 127a–127vb.

Christus passus est pro nobis.

Nuper tempore passionis Dominice multa audivimus de eius passione,
nunc interiectis paschalibus solempniis iterum memoratur eius passio.
Canibus enim venaticis sequentibus vestigia fere sauciate frequenter vena-
5 tor acclamat ne forte insequi desistant aut tepescant. Fera nostra fortiter
sauciata est Christus, cuius vestigia sequi debemus, qui etiam "passus est
pro nobis *vobis relinquens exemplum ut sequamini vestigia eius.*" Hanc feram
oportet diligentissime sequi quoniam gravissimum dampnum est eam non
assequi, unde plus dolebunt reprobi de ipsius amissione in extremo exami-
10 ne quam de tormentis Gehenne: unde in apo 1: "Ecce venit in nubibus et
videbit eum omnis oculus et qui in eum pupugerunt. Et plangent se super
eum omnes tribus terre"; Glosa: id est omnes terreni et vitiis dediti quia
tunc erunt omnes reprobi interclusi quoniam de electis dicit Apostolus:
"Simul rapiemur obviam Christo in aera": et ibi dicit Glosa: "Non tantum
15 dolebunt de tormento quantum quod a tali separabuntur consortio." Qui
igitur tunc a tanto malo declinare volunt nunc studiosissime Christum se-
quantur quia aliter cum ipso esse non poterunt. Bernardus: "O bone Jesu
omnes te volunt assequi sed pauci sequi." "Non sic impii, non sic," det
nobis Deus sic clamare et exorare ad Christum nunc sequendum ut tunc
20 ipsum assequi possimus, et dicat quilibet "Pater noster."
   Christus passus est, etc. Tria hic notanda sunt: quod Christus passus est,
quod pro nobis; quod nobis in exemplum. Primum est diligenter attendendum; secundum, scilicet quod pro nobis passus, magis; tertium, maxime.
Quod Christus passus est / *fol. 127b* / multum attendendum quia multum
25 admirandum. Quid enim mirabilius quam quod Deus et Dei Filius patiatur?

---

11 oculos *corr. ex* populus   12 eum *super lineam*   17 poterunt] poterit *MS*   19
exorare] exortare *MS*

This sermon was preached at Elstow on 16 April 1279. "*Iste sermo predicatur
aput Elnstowe circuli lunaris vii.*"

1   1 Pet 2:21.
10–12   Apoc 1:7.
12–13   *Glosa*: gloss on Apoc 1:7 in *Biblia sacra cum glossa ordinaria ... et postilla
         Nicolai Lyrani* 6: 1461.
14   1 Thess 4:17.
14–15   *Glosa*: gloss on Apoc 1:7 (*Biblia sacra cum glossa ordinaria* 6: 1461).
17–18   *Bernardus*: cf. *Sermones de diversis* 62 (PL 183: 685–686).

·1· Angelici enim spiritus admirabantur: ys 53: "Quare rubeum est indumentum tuum, et vestimenta eius sicut calcantium in torculari." Indumentum anime corpus est.

·2· Item prophete admirabantur Jer 13: "Quare factus [*Vg* futurus] es velud vir vagus et [*Vg* ut] fortis qui non potest salvare." Dixerunt Judei: 30
"Alios salvos fecit seipsum non potest salvum facere. Si Filius Dei es, descende nunc de cruce et credemus." Sic dixerunt estimantes quod si Filius Dei esset pati non posset.

·3· Item, Petrus admirabatur quia cum Christus passionem suam discipulis prediceret admirans Petrus ait: "'Absit a te, Domine, non erit tibi hoc',   35
cui Christus respondit: 'Vade retro me Sathana'."

·4· Item, Christus admirans passionem suam dixit Patri cum pateretur: "Deus meus, ut quid me dereliquisti," mt 27.

·5· Item, universa creatura quasi admirabatur suam passionem cum pateretur: 40

·6·7·"Terra enim obstupuit et tremuit," celum obtenebratum est: "Petre scisse sunt."

·8· Item, mortui mirati sunt, "unde et monumenta aperta sunt." Omnibus enim insensibilibus insensibilior est homo qui Christum passum non attendit nec admiratur, unde Bernardus: "Si non attendis timeas, quod   45
sis mortuus aut plusquam mortuus." Si Christus parva passus fuisset, non esset mirum si homines non attenderent; sed nunc, ex quo nullus umquam tantum sustinuit, secundum illud, tre 1: "O vos omnes qui transitis per viam, attendite et videte" etc. Igitur, mirabile et magis miserabile quod non ab omnibus attenditur. Quam creditis penam intulit   50
passio Christi presentialiter inflicta que tam habundantem expressit sanguinem, cum premeditaretur Christus de sua passione, "factus est

52 premeditaretur *corr. in marg.*

The numbers in the left-hand margin indicate distinctions within the text. These numbers are scribal annotations.

26–27   Is 63:2.
29–30   Jer 14:9.
31–32   Mt 27:42.
35–36   Mt 16:22–23.
38   Mt 27:46.
41   Cf. Luc 23:44–45, i.e. Ps 75:9.
41–43   Mt 27:51–52.
45–46   *Bernardus*: cf. *Parabolae,* "De Aethiopissa," in *S. Bernardi Opera,* ed J. Leclerq and H. Rochais (Rome, 1972) 6,2: 293.
48–49   Tre 1:12.
52–53   Luc 22:44.

sudor eius sicut gutte sanguinis decurrentis in terram." / *fol. 127va* / Et
potest notari quod eius passio fuit amarissima, vilissima, iniuriosissima.
55   Amarissima, tre 3: "Replevit me amaritudinibus, inebriavit me absintho,"
et Jer 8: "Dolor meus super dolorem et in me cor meum merens." *Dolor,*
ecce amaritudo; super *dolorem,* ecce maior, *et in me cor meum merens,* ecce
quam maxima. Unde de eo dici potest: "Ecce in pace amaritudo mea amarissima." Item, fuit vilissima, Sap 2: "Morte turpissima condemnemus eum,"
60   et ys 53: "Vidimus eum et non erat aspectus, unde nec reputavimus eum,"
et hec omnia inter cognatos et notos, in die solempni, in loco eminenti.
Item, iniuriosissima quia solum pro beneficiis suis, iuxta illud: "Multa bona
operatus sum in vobis propter quod horum me vultis lapidari?" Jer: "Ego
erudivi eos et confortavi brachia eorum et in me cogitaverunt malitiam."
65   *Erudivit eos,* sed quomodo? "Nunquam sic locutus est homo sicut hic homo
loquitur." *Confortavit brachia,* sed quomodo? Sanando omnes male habentes.
Et ipsi cogitaverunt malitiam, quomodo? scilicet eum dolo tenerent et occi-
derent. Cum igitur Christi passio talis fuerit ac tanta, merito est attendenda
et recogitanda, He 22: "Recogitate eum qui talem sustinuit adversus seme-
70   tipsum contradictionem," et dicit talem, non qualem, sed tu potes dicere
amarissimam, vilissimam, iniuriosissimam. In omni ecclesia nisi forte sit per
aliquem sacrilegum prophanata, est ymago crucifixi reverenter collocata,
et dicit Apostolus: "Templum Dei sanctum quod estis vos." Sic nisi homo
sit prophanatus, habebit crucifixus semper in memoria. / *fol. 127vb* / In tem-
75   plis dedicatis et Deo consecratis sunt cruces intus et extra in parietibus; et
vos certe estis templa Deo consecrata, unde in parietibus habere debetis
cruces scilicet penitentie cruciatus: in recordationem passionis Dominice,
Gal 6: "Stigmata Christi Jesu in corpore meo porto."
Multum igitur attendendum est quod Christus passus est. Quis enim
80   unquam audivit quod Judex pro reis sponte pateretur? Hoc enim fecit
Christus, et beneficium huius gratie semper attendendum est, unde ecc 3:
"Gratiam fideiussoris ne obliviscaris in finem, dedit enim pro te animam
suam." Fideiussor noster aput Patrem Christus est. Sed Adam prevaricatus
est, transgressus est mandata Dei in Paradiso. Unde oportuit eum satis—

---

64 me *expunct. a rubricatore*   69 He *corr. ex* Eze   71 iniuriosissimam *corr. in*
marg.   76 templa] vel cruces *add. in marg.*

55   Tre 3:15.
56   Jer 8:18.
58–59 Is 38:17.
59   Sap 2:20.
60   Is 53:2–3.
62–63 Jo 10:32.

63–64 Osee 7:15.
65–66 Jo 7:46.
69–70 Heb 12:3.
73   1 Cor 3:17.
78   Gal 6:17.
82–83 Ecclus 29:20.

facere aut perire; sed ille qui neminem vult perire sed omnes salvos fieri   85
et ad agnitionem sui nominis venire, factus est homo et hominis fideiussor
aput Patrem et posuit pro eo animam suam. Pro hac inestimabili gratia, in
principio Misse canit Ecclesia hodie: "Misericordia Domini plena est terra,"
igitur gratiam fideiussoris tui ne obliviscaris in finem. Item, multum attendendum est quod Christus passus est. Si enim rex aliquis pro suo ribaldo   90
fugitivo maximas subiret penas ut ipsum doceret viam revertendi ad se ut
cum eo regnaret, quomodo non insaniret nisi attenderet redire ad dominum et sic intrare in regnum celorum?

   Christus hoc non solum verbis sed factis docuit: "relinquens exemplum
ut sequamini vestigia eius," unde He 12: "Accessisti ad testamenti novi   95
mediatorem nostrum et sanguinem aspersionis melius loquentem quam
Abel. Videte ne recusetis loquentem." Sanguis Abel bene loquebatur qui
de terris ad celum auditur, pro cuius effusione Chaym maledicitur; sic qui
Christum iterum peccando crucifigunt et eius sanguinem fundunt maledicti sunt et cum reprobis ibunt in supplicium eternum.   100

85–86 1 Tim 2:4.
88–89 This is the antiphon of the Office [Introit] of the Mass for the 1st Sunday
       after the Octave of, or 2nd Sunday after, Easter. See Appendix 8.
95–97 Heb 12:24–25.

Sermon 163: Sunday after Ascension

De Libro Rubeo Maiori, fol. 148b

1 Pe 4: Vigilate in orationibus

Hoc enim faciendum est multis rationibus, scilicet:

Vigilandum est in orationibus
— Ut Christum et sanctos eius imitemur. De Christo enim habetur in evangelio: "quod pernoctabat in oratione" et de sanctis eius ubique legitur in ecclesiis.
— Ut temptationes vitemus quia ecc 21: "Vigilia honestatis tabefaciet carnes," et mt 13: "Cum dormirent homines venit inimicus homo et superseminavit zizania," et ideo mt 21: "Vigilate et orate ne intretis in temptationem."
Ut periculum mortis vel magne iacture vitemus:

1   1 Pet 4:7.
4   Luc 6:12.
6–7   Ecclus 31:1.

7–8   Mt 13:25.
9   Mt 26:41.

10   Holofernes enim, et Cisara occisi sunt dormientes, Sampson dormiens viribus spoliatus est, sic et de multis testatur Scriptura.

Humiliter: ecc 34: "Oratio humiliantis se nubes penetrabit," illas scilicet
15 nubes de quibus tre 3: "Opposuisti tibi nubem," scilicet peccati, "ne transeat oratio"; et ideo ps.: "Subditus esto Domino, et ora eum."

Sapienter: ut non petamus superflua; ps.: "Unam petii a Domino hanc requiram," quia luc 8: "Unum est necessarium"; Bernardus: "O anima mea, quid vagaris per singula; quere unum in quo sunt omnia"; nimis enim
20 avarus est cui Deus non sufficit. Ut non petamus nociva sed utilia, non transitoria sed eterna, quia colo 3: "Que sursum sunt querite." Ista autem transitoria nociva non sunt; unde Bernardus: "Habere temporalia licitum est, non amare; habere enim aditum regni celestis facit difficilem, amare impossibilem." De primo, mc x: "Quam difficile est confidentem in pecuniis
25 introire in regnum celorum." De secundo, 1 thi.: "Qui volunt divites fieri incidunt in laqueum diaboli."

Confidenter: quia mc xi: "Omnia quecumque orantes petitis credite quia accipietis et fient vobis," et Ja 1: "Postulet autem in fide nichil hesitans."

Perseveranter: quia luc 18: "Oportet semper orare et non deficere."

30   ut Christum et sanctos eius imitemur
Orandum est ⟨ ut temptaciones vitemus
                    ut periculum mortis vitemus

                    humiliter   superflua
                   sapienter ut non petamus ⟨
35 Item orandum est ⟨   nociva
                  confidenter
                  perseveranter

17 sapienter *in marg.*   24 pecuniis *corr. ex* divitiis *in marg.*

11	*Holofernes*: cf. Judith 13;	21	Col 3:1.
	Cisara: cf. Judices 4.	22–24	*Bernardus*: cf. *Epistolae* 462.7
12	*Sampson*: cf. Judices 16.		(PL 182: 665–666).
14	Ecclus 35:21.	24–25	Cf. Mc 10:23.
15–16	Tre 3:44.	25–26	1 Tim 6:9.
16	Ps 36:7.	27–28	Mc 11:24.
17–18	Ps 26:4.	28	Jac 1:6.
18	Luc 10:42.	29	Luc 18:1.

18–19 *Bernardus*: not identified.
30–37 These distinctions are indicated by joining lines in the RHS margin; and are written out fully in the bottom margin.

Sermon 166: Sermo Fratris H. de Mordon: in die Pentecoste

fol. 150a

"Repleti sunt omnes Spiritu Sancto" [ACTUS 2:4].

Quando festum alicuius magnatis debet commendari oportet ut tria concurrant:
    Quod multi sint vocati,
5   Quod habundanter exhibiti,
    Quod de bono procurati.
Ista autem tria in dictis verbis notata in presenti Spiritus Sancti solemp-
nitate contigerunt, unde tria in dictis verbis notantur.
    Convivarum numerositas: *omnes*; qui omnes dicit nullum excipit: Ac
10 "In veritate comperi" etc. Sed "in omni gente" etc., ro x: "Omnis enim quicumque invocaverit nomen Domini salvus erit."
    Secundo, conferentis liberalitas: *repleti*; qualiter potuit liberalius de-
disse? Joel: "Effundam de spiritu meo super omnem carnem." Ps: "Aperis
tu manum tuam" etc. "Non enim ad mensuram dat Deus spiritum" etc.
15   Tertio, dati preciositas: *Spiritu Sancto*; quid Spiritu Sancto preciosius vel
utilius? "Unicuique enim datur manifestatio Spiritus ad utilitatem." Quid
dulcius? jud.: "Quid dulcius melle?" ecc: respondetur: "Spiritus meus super
mel dulcis." Repleti sunt ergo Spiritu Sancto ad consolationem, et ideo vocatur Paraclitus, id est Consolator. Unde ys.: "Ego ipse consolabor vos"; et
20 iterum: "In Jerusalem consolabimini." Item, ad communicationem, et ideo
dicitur Spiritus; Jo: "Spiritus ubi vult spirat." Item, ad amoris insinuationem, et ideo dicitur amor; prov.: "Qui dat munera aufert animas recipien-
tium." Sed qualiter melius amorem nostrum vendicare et allicere potuit
quam dare nobis quicquid habuit? Bernardus: "Quid est homo quia mag-
25 nificas eum?" Angelos committis, Filium mittis, Spiritum immittis, vultum
promittis. Jac.: "Omne datum optimum et omne donum perfectum" etc.

10	Actus 10:34–35.	19	Is 51:12.
10–11	Rom 10:13.	20	Is 66:13.
13	Joel 2:28.	21	Jo 3:8.
14	Ps 103:28.	22	Prov 22:9.
14	Jo 3:34.	24–25	*Bernardus*: cf. *De adventu Domini,*
16	1 Cor 12:7.		*Sermo* 1.7 (PL 183: 38–39); *Sermo-*
17	Judices 14:18.		*nes de diversis* 7.3 (PL 183: 560).
17–18	Ecclus 24:27.	26	Jac 1:17.

Appendix 10

An Analysis of Sermon Authorities

The following tables display the range of authorities from the Old and New Testaments as well as to other non-scriptural texts to be found in some eighty-four sermons from MS Laud Misc. 511.

Table 1 categorises these sermons according to liturgical season. The sermons were selected to give a representative liturgical sample from the whole manuscript. Paschaltide is over-represented because I chose to study in more detail all the sermons for the Second Sunday after Easter. The sermons for Easter Sunday as a group are not included.

The Old Testament authorities cited in the sermons can be found in Table 2. They follow the medieval order: the Pentatuech, the Histories, the Psalms together with Wisdom literature, and Prophets. The New Testament authorities, found in Table 3, follow the order of the Gospels, the Pauline epistles (including Hebews), the other epistles, James Peter John and Jude; and Apocalypse. Table 4 displays non-scriptural authorities, analysed according to various categories. While there is always a hope that all the authorities in a text have been recognised and identified, it is impossible to be sure. Subject to this reservation, the various totals in Tables 2, 3, and 4 are as complete as possible.

The results displayed in Table 2 are of particular interest, and perhaps raise questions. There is a very high use of the Psalms in Advent, together with a high use of Isaiah, both to be expected. There is the expected use and liturgical link of Isaiah, Jeremiah, and Lamentations in Lent. The exception here is the high use of these three books during Paschaltide. This seems to reflect a bias in the sermons preached during the Paschal season for the sufferings of Christ rather than his victory, and is exemplified in the study of the sermons for the Second Sunday after Easter. Of other books in the Old Testament the Wisdom literature is most highly used, particularly Ecclesiasticus and Proverbs. Sermons preached after Epiphany and after Trinity have a significantly high use of the Wisdom books. Is this because the bias of the liturgy in these seasons is the Christian life with an emphasis on right living, whereas the other seasons commemorate the principal events of salvation history? Of the prophets, Isaiah – the fifth evangelist – is consistently most used; Jeremiah, with or without Lamentations, comes second, followed by Osee.

Although the sample is relatively small, a few observations can be made about the number of New Testament citations. The total number is 1054, of which 562 (or 53%) are for gospel authorities. A closer look, reveals that the use of St John's gospel for authorities is standard in sermons preached at Advent, Epiphanytide and Septuagesimatide, is less frequent in those for Lent, but significantly more often cited in others for Paschaltide and Trinitytide.

Most of the interesting emphases which emerge underline this close relationship between the Scriptures and their liturgical use in the seasons of the Church's year. Paschaltide sees a higher use of the non-Pauline epistles than other liturgical seasons – again this correlates with the liturgy. Of the gospels Matthew is the most used, taking the lead in all liturgical seasons except Paschaltide. Mark is very rarely used, as thirteenth-century theologians saw it as a shorter version of Matthew and Luke.

A perusal of Tables 2 and 3 will show which parts of the Scripture were rarely used. In contrast, the lists of the most frequently used authorities from Scripture have their own interest: the emphasis on the creation of humankind in God's 'own image and likeness' (Gen 1:26), the 'plentiful redemption' (Ps 129:7), the division sin makes (Is 59:2) and the sorrow it causes, both to Our Lady and to the Church (Tre 1:12). In the New Testament the future joys of heaven (1 Cor 2:9), the life of the spirit contrasted with the life of the flesh (Rom 8:13), Christ the loving Redeemer (Apoc 1:5), who suffered for us (1 Pet 2:21) are the texts most often cited. Of the authorities used in these sermons, four-fifths come from the Bible: the preaching of the Word of God is done largely through the words of God in Scripture.

A summary of the non-scriptural authorities for a group of fifty-seven sermons is found in Table 4. The authorities are analysed in several categories: the Fathers and Doctors of the Church (*Patres*), including Bede and Rabanus Maurus; the Saints (*Sancti*), including Anselm and Bernard; the Teachers or Masters (*Magistri*), a group containing the famous twelfth-century masters Richard and Hugh of St. Victor as well as Peter Lombard; and the *Philosophi*, encompassing not only Aristotle and Boethius, but also Virgil and Horace, among others. Liturgical references, which make quite a sizeable total, references to the Gloss, to canon law and to etymologies are gathered at the end.

The total number of non-scriptural authorities is 579. Nearly half (273) come from just two authors, St. Augustine and St. Bernard. This proportion reflects the overwhelming influence of St Augustine down the centuries, and of St. Bernard as a recent power, in the Church of the mid-thirteenth century. St. Gregory comes third, but is not in the same league as the first two. Of particular interest are the references to St. John Chrysostom, an eastern Father. How far the works quoted are really his, or whether they belong to the writer known as Pseudo-Chrysostom, is not fully clear. By contrast with the Fathers and Doctors, the Masters are few. Perhaps the select group of thirty seven *Philosophi* carries a disproportionate interest. There are eleven references to Aristotle, and seven to 'philosophus,' generally held to be Aristotle; no other Greek philosopher is cited. The attempt to identify these sources has been as difficult as attempting to locate the patristic sources.

Table 1 □ Selected Sermons Classified According to Liturgical Season

---

Sermons 5, 8, 12–15 are Advent 'liturgical' sermons. *Sermons* 50, 53, 64, 72, 77, 78, 90, 100, 136, 153, and 207 are Elstow time-and-place dated sermons. *Sermons* 131–140, 147 are mostly on the theme 'Christus passus est' (1 Petr 2:21) for the Second Sunday in Easter. Named sermons are marked by n. 66 are by Simon of Hinton, OP; 82 by Richard Fishacre, OP; and 166 by fr. H. de Mordon. Sermons edited in Appendix 9 are marked with an asterisk (*); *Serm.* 82, by

Fishacre, can be found in Maura O'Carroll, SND "Two Versions of a Sermon by Richard Fishacre OP for the Fourth Sunday of Lent on the Theme 'Non enim heres erit filius ancille cum filio libere'" *AFP* 54 (1984), 113-141.

ADVENT
Serm. **3** (Schneyer T1) □ *Serm.* **5** (Schneyer T1) □ *Serm.* **8** (Schneyer T2) □ *Serm.* **12** (Schneyer T2) □ *Serm.* **13*** (Schneyer T3) □ *Serm.* **14** (Schneyer T3) □ *Serm.* **15** (Schneyer T3) □ *Serm.* **18** (Schneyer T4) □ *Serm.* **19** (Schneyer T4) □ *Total* 9

EPIPHANYTIDE
Serm. **23** (Schneyer T11) □ *Serm.* **25** (Schneyer T12) □ *Serm.* **26** (Schneyer T12) □ *Serm.* **27** (Schneyer T13) □ *Serm.* **29** (Schneyer T14) □ *Serm.* **30** (Schneyer T14) □ *Serm.* **31** (Schneyer T15) □ *Total* 7

SEPTUAGESIMATIDE
Serm. **32** (Schneyer T16) □ *Serm.* **39** (Schneyer T17) □ *Serm.* **41** (Schneyer T17) □ *Serm.* **46** (Schneyer T18) □ *Serm.* **47** (Schneyer T18) □ *Total* 5

LENT
Serm. **50** (Schneyer T19) □ *Serm.* **53** (Schneyer T19) □ *Serm.* **55, 56** (Schneyer T19) □ *Serm.* **57** (Schneyer T19) □ *Serm.* **64** (Schneyer T20) □ *Serm.* **66n*** (Schneyer T20) □ *Serm.* **69** (Schneyer T20) □ *Serm.* **72e** (Schneyer T21) □ *Serm.* **74** (Schneyer T21) □ *Serm.* **77** (Schneyer T22) □ *Serm.* **78** (Schneyer T22) □ *Serm.* **82n*** (Schneyer T22) □ *Serm.* **89** (Schneyer T23) □ *Serm.* **90** (Schneyer T23) □ *Serm.* **95** (Schneyer T23) □ *Serm.* **98** (Schneyer T23) □ *Serm.* **100** (Schneyer T24) □ *Total* 17

PASCHALTIDE
Serm. **114** (Schneyer T28) □ *Serm.* **118** (Schneyer T18) □ *Serm.* **119** (Schneyer T28) □ *Serm.* **130** (Schneyer T29) □ *Serm.* **131** (Schneyer T30) □ *Serm.* **132** (Schneyer T30) □ *Serm.* **133** (Schneyer T30) □ *Serm.* **134** (Schneyer T30) □ *Serm.* **135** (Schneyer T30) □ *Serm.* **136*** (Schneyer T30) □ *Serm.* **137** (Schneyer T30) □ *Serm.* **138** (Schneyer T30) □ *Serm.* **139** (Schneyer T30) □ *Serm.* **140** (Schneyer T30) □ *Serm.* **147** (Schneyer T30) □ *Serm.* **141** (Schneyer T31) □ *Serm.* **145** (Schneyer T32) □ *Serm.* **146** (Schneyer T32) □ *Serm.* **152** (Schneyer T33) □ *Serm.* **153** (Schneyer T33) □ *Serm.* **162** (Schneyer T36) □ *Serm.* **163*** (Schneyer T37) □ *Serm.* **164** (Schneyer T37) □ *Serm.* **166n*** (Schneyer T39) □ *Total* 24

TRINITYTIDE
Serm. **170** (Schneyer T42) □ *Serm.* **171** (Schneyer T43) □ *Serm.* **173** (Schneyer T43) □ *Serm.* **182** (Schneyer T44) □ *Serm.* **184** (Schneyer T44) □ *Serm.* **185** (Schneyer T45) □ *Serm.* **198** (Schneyer T46) □ *Serm.* **204** (Schneyer T47) □ *Serm.* **207** (Schneyer T47) □ *Serm.* **205** (Schneyer T48) □ *Serm.* **209** (Schneyer T49) □ *Serm.* **212** (Schneyer T50) □ *Serm.* **225** (Schneyer T50) □ *Serm.* **213** (Schneyer T51) □ *Serm.* **214** (Schneyer T51) □ *Serm.* **217** (Schneyer T51) □ *Serm.* **219** (Schneyer T52) □ *Serm.* **221** (Schneyer T53) □ *Serm.* **37** (Schneyer T59) □ *Serm.* **224** (Schneyer T60) □ *Serm.* **226** (Schneyer T63) □ *Serm.* **228** (Schneyer T64) □ *Total* 22

Table 2 □ An Analysis of Old Testament Authorities

Books	Advent	Epiphany	Septua	Lent	Paschal	Trinity	Total
Gen	4	7	18	15	12	14	70
Ex	2	1	8	13	5	4	33
Lev		1		1		5	7
Num		2		7			9
Deut		5	2	9	8	9	33
Subtotal	6	16	28	45	25	32	152
Jos				6	1	1	8
Jud	1	1	1	6	4	3	16
Ruth					1		1
1 Sam	2	2	3	2	3		12
2 Sam		1	1	7	3	2	14
3 Reg		2	1	3	4	1	10
4 Reg		1	2	2	5		10
2 Par					1	1	2
Neh				2			2
Tob		2	1	1	1	6	11
Judith				2	5		7
Esth		1	1	2		1	5
1 Mach					2	3	5
2 Mach				2		3	5
Subtotal	3	10	10	35	30	21	109
Ps	46	24	32	78	61	37	278
Job	1	11	10	30	21	13	86
Prov	7	10	10	32	7	20	86
Eccl	2	5	5	14	4	11	45
Cant		4	7	9	9	5	34
Sap	4	7	3	18	12	10	54
Ecli	7	21	14	31	26	30	129
Subtotal	21	58	49	134	83	89	434

Table 2 (continued)

Books	Advent	Epiph	Septua	Lent	Paschal	Trinity	Total
Is	21	10	17	23	49	24	159
Jer	1	6	7	16	21	8	59
Lam	1	2	6	10	14	4	37
Bar	1	2	4	3	1		11
Ez	1	3		6	2	3	15
Dan	1	1			1	1	4
Os		4	2	9	6	5	26
Joel			1	4	2	2	9
Am	1	1		1	2	1	6
Jon		2				1	3
Mich		1	1	2		1	5
Nah			2	3	1		6
Hab		3			1	3	7
Soph	1	1		2			4
Zach	1			1	2	2	6
Mal	2	1			2	1	6
Subtotal	31	37	40	95	104	56	363
TOTAL	106	145	159	388	303	235	1336

NOTES

The Old Testament authorities used four or more times in these sermons include: Genesis 1:26 (8), 3:19 (4); Exodus 8:27 (4); Psalmi 129:7 (7); Proverbia 8:31 (4), 28:13 (7); Ecclesiastes 11:6 (5); Sapientia 1:3 (4), 1:4 (6), 2:21 (5); Ecclesiasticus 3:20 (4); Isaias 1:6 (4); 9:6 (4); 53:12 (4); 59:2 (8); Jeremias 8:18 (6); 12:7 (6); Lam. 1:12 (8); Baruch 3:28 (5); Osee 2:19-20 (4), 11:4 (4).

Table 3 □ *An Analysis of New Testament Authorities*

Books	Advent	Epiph	Septua	Lent	Paschal	Trinity	Totals
Mt	21	28	16	67	48	62	242
Mc	2		4	2	5	3	16
Lc	12	12	14	36	36	42	152
John	16	17	12	30	62	15	152
Subtotal	51	57	46	135	141	122	562
Act	2	1	2	4	10	4	23
Rom	10	4	5	19	13	14	65
1 Cor	3	6	10	10	16	18	63
2 Cor	1	6	2	9	9	4	31
Gal	3	3	1	7	8	3	25
Eph	1	1	2	6	3	4	17
Phil	6	3	2	3	6	4	24
Col	1	3			5	2	11
1 Thess				3	3		6
1 Tim		5	2	3	3	2	15
2 Tim				1	4		5
Tit	2		1	1		1	5
Hebr	2	5		10	13	6	36
Subtotal	29	36	25	72	83	58	303
Jac	5	3	1	2	13	7	31
1 Petr	2	2	1	6	20	6	37
2 Petr				1	1	1	3
1 Jo	6	7	3	7	13	4	40
Judae	1					1	2
Subtotal	14	12	5	16	47	19	113
Apoc	6	9	3	11	16	8	53
TOTAL	**102**	**115**	**81**	**238**	**307**	**211**	**1054**

NOTES The New Testament authorities used four or more times include: Matthaeum 2:11 (4), 3:2 (6), 4:1 (4), 4:17 (4), 5:16 (4), 22:13 (4), 25:34 (4), 28:20 (5); Lucam 1:38 (4), 8:2 (4), 16:19-30, esp. 24-25 (4), 22:34 (4); Joannem 3:16 (4), 5:22 (4), 8:34 (4), 15:13 (5), 16:28 (4); Actus 14:21 (4); ad Romanos 6:23 (4), 8:13 (8); 1 ad Cor 2:9 (11); ad Galatas 6:8 (5); ad Phil.3:20 (5); ad Hebraeos 4:3 (4), 12:3 (6); 1 Petri 1:12 (4), 2:21 (12; the high number reflects the fact that all sermons on 1 Petr 2:21 were transcribed), 2:22 (7); 2:23 (4); 3:18 (4); Apocalypsis 1:5 (10), 19:16 (6).

Table 4 □ *An Analysis of Non-Scriptural Authorities*

SERMONS Type Number	Named sermon 3	Ox Quat. 2	Other Advent 3	Epiph 7	Septua 5	Lent 5	Pasch 10	Trin 18	Sanct 4	All 57
Patres										
Ambrosius				1	1	3	1			6
Augustinus	5	4	1	21	28	39	23	19	2	142
Basilius			1		2			1		4
Beda					1					1
Cassiodorus					3		3	1		7
Chrysostomus		8			1	1	4	5		19
Damascenus					1	2	6			9
Gregorius I	1		6	16	12	12	9	14		70
Isidorus				2	1	2	10			15
Isaac				1						1
Jeronimus				4	3	7	12	3	2	31
Rabanus			1				1			2
Subtotal	6	12	9	45	53	66	69	43	4	307
Sancti										
Anselmus					2					2
Bernardus	2	1		17	26	19	31	14	1	111
Saints' Lives								1	2	3
Subtotal	2	1		17	28	19	31	15	3	116
Philosophi										
Albimines			1							1
Algazel				1						1
Astronomi			1							1
Aristotle	1		1	4	3			1	1	11
'Philosophus'			3			4				7
Averroes					2					2
Boethius	1				1					2
Epicurus							2			2
Horace					1					1
Josephus					1					1
Seneca		1			2	1	1			5
Tullius						1				1
Virgil								2		2
Subtotal	2	1	6	5	10	6	3	3	1	37

Table 4 (continued)

SERMONS Type Number	Named sermon 3	Ox Quat. 2	Other Advent 3	Epiph 7	Septua 5	Lent 5	Pasch 10	Trin 18	Sanct 4	All 57
Magistri										
Haymo				1						1
Hugh St. Vict.				1	1			2		4
Pet. Comestor				1	2		1	1	5	10
Pet. Lombard				1	1					2
Pet. Ravensis								7		7
Richard St.Vic						1				1
Subtotal				4	4	1	1	10	5	25
Canon Law								2		2
Etymolgies		3	3			2	1	3		12
Liturgical		2	1	6	2	1	10	15	6	43
Glosses	1	6	2	1	6	8	6	6	1	37
TOTAL	11	25	21	78	103	103	121	97	20	579

Appendix 11

Summaries of Selected Sermons

The following list contains English summaries of the sermons discussed in the text: (A) the sermons preached at Elstow (see Chapter 5); (B) sermons for Easter Sunday; (C) for those of the Second Sunday after Easter on the theme "Christus passus est," together with five sermons from other sources on the same theme (see Chapter 7); and (D) the sermons on Advent made on liturgical themes (see Chapter 8). The analysis here has benefited from Nicole Bériou's studies of sermons: see *La prédication au béguinage de Paris pendant année liturgique, 1272–1273* (Paris, 1978), pp. 123 seq.

The summaries adapt the format of the Catalogue in Appendix 1. Each entry contains the principal elements: number, folio, source book, and, where appropriate, running title, place/date (where relevant) and the sermon theme. The precis is divided into two parts: the Antitheme, where it exists; and the main body of the sermon. Other facts of interest are included in the notes. For example, a preachers' failure to treat the division he has indicated at the outset of the sermon is recorded. It is worth noting that such omissions were not necessarily made by the preacher but could have been the work of a scribe.

A □ Sermons Preached at Elstow

Sermon 78
Folios 94a–94vb □ *Source Book* Liber Proprius □ *Date/Place* Lent, Sunday IV □ *Preached* at Elstow, 24 March 1275 □ *Notes* The third, fourth and fifth "loaves" (fasting, almsgiving, and prayer respectively) are mentioned but not developed. This sermon is similar to the one by Hugh of St. Cher found in Schneyer, *Repertorium* 2: 760, no. 30.

Theme Erat proximum pascha dies festus Iudeorum (Jo 6:4) □ *Antitheme* none
Body The five loaves symbolise the food of penance that brings us to Christ. The first loaf is contrition of heart, which is aroused by recollection of sins committed, by the prospect of judgement, by the prospect of eternal punishment and by the remembrance of the sufferings of Christ. The second loaf is verbal confession, which should be short and quick. Confession also rejuvenates sinners, as the deer is rejuvenated. Confession should also be resolute, as shown by the actions of Mary Magdalene and Judith. Confession should be direct.

Sermon 153
Folios 141a–142b □ *Source Book* Liber Proprius □ *Date/Place* Easter, Sunday V □ *Preached* at Elstow, 19 May 1275 □ *Theme* Si quid petieritis Patrem in nomine meo ... (Jo 16:23) □
Antitheme This sermon will be about prayer; so, "Let us pray."

Body Firstly prayer is supernaturally powerful and excellent. Through it God's presence is reached. As Augustine says: "God is far more anxious to give than man is to receive." The power of prayer is seen in Scripture: Moses, Joshua, Elijah, and Daniel, in the Old Testament; Christ himself, the apostles, Mary Magdalene in the New. Secondly, the Lord teaches what should be asked for: the kingdom of God: that is, salvation. All prayer is to be made in the name of Jesus. Thirdly, many things hinder the effectiveness of prayer: sin, anger, and envy – especially against one's neighbour – pride, a sinful tongue given to detraction, lies, defamation, quarrelling, cursing. Our Lady's example is important for effective prayer.

Sermon 230

Folios 198vb- 200a □ *Source Book* none □ *Date/Place* Nearest Sunday after the feast of St. John the Baptist □ *Preached* at Elstow, 30 June 1275 □ *Theme* Quodcumque solveris super terram ... (Mt 16:19)

Antitheme The Lord Jesus Christ, King, God, Maker of all creatures, became man for man's salvation. Desiring to give all men salvation from sin, he said to Peter, "Whatever you loose ..."

Body Christ desires to make salvation easily available to all. No one should despair, because the Judge of all men is also their brother. He is only too anxious to cheat the adversary. So, all should have great trust in the mercy of God. To rescue everyone from sin, Christ gave his power of forgiveness to the prelates. This is the significance of confession. The Lord entrusted the keys of the Church to Peter and to the other prelates to give to all people the chance of entering the kingdom. The key is penance. If penance is accepted, it will bring delight after difficulty.

Sermon 100

Folios 106vb- 107va □ *Source Book* □ Liber Conf. Aug □ *Date/Place* Palm Sunday □ *Preached* "up to "Cantandum est" at Elstow, 21 March 1277 □ *Theme* Noli timere filia Syon, ecce rex tuus ... . (Jo 12:15)

Antitheme none

Body First, Jesus is a king more powerful than earthly kings. He is called king of men because he became a man to redeem mankind and give his love. This is seen above all in his humble acceptance of suffering. Secondly, Jesus the king is seated on an ass. The ass means many things: it is weak, stubborn, uncooperative. Man is like the ass: the old man is like the ass, the young man like the colt. In man there is conflict about doing good. The meaning of the palm in the hand is victory over the enemy. There are many false palmers about. A man who makes no confession, or makes confession without amendment, is a false palmer. Such men betray Christ.

Sermon 207

Folios 170vb- 171vb □ *Source Book* Liber Proprius □ *Date/Place* Trinity VI □ *Preached* on 4 July 1277; no place given □ *Theme* Misereor super turbam ... (Mc

8:2) □ *Notes* The written sermon gives instructions for expanding the invective against false tithers.

   Antitheme Travellers and pilgrims pray daily for suitable leadership and safe journeys. All of us are travellers on life's journey, following the path indicated by the Word of God. Therefore let us ask ... .

   Body The compassionate Lord fed the great crowd with seven loaves and a few fish. The crowd represents all sinners who recognise their sinfulness. So God shows three kinds of mercy. First, he waits for the sinner to repent, and he waits with tenderness. The grace of sorrow, confession and satisfaction is a mercy from God. This should inspire all with gratitude. The second way is God's compassionate pardoning of the penitent sinner. The third is saving those who abandon sin, offering them love, friendship and happiness. When the day of judgement comes, God's justice will be experienced by all, especially the false tithers.

Sermon 50

Folios 53va–54b □ *Source Book* none □ *Date/Place* Lent, Sunday I □ *Preached* at Elstow, 6 March 1278 □ *Theme* "Ductus est Jesus ... (Mt 4:1) □ *Notes* The "third day" was not written up

   Antitheme none

   Body There is a desert of guilt and a desert of penance. Only the latter will be preached. The desert of penance is austere. Penance is a way of great austerity. Few people live in the desert of penance, as it is hard for young and old alike. The desert is a place of frequent attacks from the devil. Jesus went into the desert as an example for us all. For men, this is a journey like that of Moses and the Chosen People, a journey of three days. The first day is that of contrition, sorrow at having sinned, and a determination by God's grace not to repeat sin. The second day is that of confession. Confession should be prompt, frequent, and made to God; it should also be without pretence.

Sermon 72

Folios 83vb–84va □ *Source Book* Liber Proprius □ *Date/Place* Lent, Sunday II; preached at Elstow, 20 March 1278 □ *Theme* Cum eicisset Jesus demonium ... (Luc 11:14).

   Antitheme If S. Peter were preaching now at Bedford, all in the neighbourhood would hasten there to receive his blessing. But the saint of saints, Jesus Christ, speaks in today's gospel saying, "Blessed are those who hear the word of God and keep it". Doing this brings down the blessing of the Lord. Let us pray for the grace so to do ... .

   Body Christ performed three miracles against the enemy of mankind: the blind man sees; the deaf man hears; the possessed man is set free. The sinner is a slave to evil, is blind and is dumb. The Lord casts out the demon when by grace the sinner repents, examines his conscience honestly and thoroughly and, resolving to sin no more, makes undisguised, and sincere confession to

God and man. Confession must be true, clear, complete, undisguised not concealing anything through shame.

Sermon 136

Folios 127a–127vb □ *Source Book* Liber Niger Maior □ *Date/Place* Easter, Sunday II preached at Elstow, 16 April 1279 □ *Theme* Christus passus est pro nobis ... (1 Pet 2:21)

Antitheme In the season of the Lord's passion we heard much about it. Having celebrated the paschal season, there is once again a solemn commemoration of Christ's passion. Christ, like the quarry in the hunt, is to be followed with great eagerness by all who want to be with him in eternity. The alternative is condemnation and hell. Let us pray to God for the grace really to follow Christ: Pater noster...

Body Christ suffered; he suffered for us; he suffered to give us an example; God, the Son of God, suffered. Angels, prophets marvel. Peter, Christ himself, the whole created universe, even the dead, wonder at this suffering. Yet insensitive man does not marvel. Christ's suffering was most pitiable, most bitter, most shameful, most unmerited: particularly as he had done nothing but good to all people. Consider this suffering further. Everywhere we see a reminder in the cross. All churches have a crucifix; they also have consecration crosses. We should bear in ourselves the cross of Christ through penance. □ Christ suffered for us. Whoever heard of a judge suffering in place of the guilty? Yet Christ did this, making himself a surety for us with the Father. He laid down his life for us, instead of Adam whose responsibility it was. Whoever heard of a king suffering for a rascally fugitive? □ Christ taught us not only with words, but with actions, leaving his suffering as an example. His blood is more powerful than Abel's. Let us not, Cain-like, refuse it, and so earn eternal punishment.

Sermon 231

Folios 200va–201va □ *Source Book* none □ *Date/Place* Feast of the Assumption; □ *Preached* on 15 August 1279; no place given □ *Theme* Que est ista que ascendit quasi aurora consurgens, ... (Cant 6:9).

Antitheme Today's sermon commemorates the glories of Mary. All of us should pray to her Son for the grace to praise the Blessed Virgin to his honour and hers: Ave Maria ... .

Body There are three questions – Where does she ascend.? How does she ascend? Why is she compared to the dawn? Firstly, she ascends from earth to heaven, from toil to repose, from sorrow to intense happiness. She, like Bathsheba, is the mother of the king. There is great joy in heaven at her coming thence. There ought to be here on earth, as she is its Lady. On earth she protected the world through her goodness; how much more does she not do it in heaven? There is symbol of all this in the Old Testament: Assuerus the King = Christ; Esther = the Blessed Virgin; by Haman understand the devil. The people were saved from the death planned by Haman through Esther's intercession with Assuerus. This woman who is the cause of our salvation should be greatly loved and especially by women, for in her Eve's transgression, which has brought women much insult, has been redressed. So the allegations against women should end. In the Old Testament, God held out an avenging hand; in the New Testament he holds out great mercy. It was through Mary that God became man, so we should give practical expression of our devotion to her. Let us always turn to Mary, the most excellent of all saints.

Sermon 53

Folios 55b–56b □ *Source Book* Liber Proprius □ *Date/Place* Lent, Sunday I □ *Preached* at Elstow, 2 March 1281 □ *Theme* Ductus est Jesus in desertum (Mt 4:1).

Antitheme Just hearing the word of God is useless. Only by acting on what is heard will reward be merited.

Body The desert was the battle-ground of Christ and the devil. Lent is the time of spiritual battle, when Christ's example is followed. True penance is prompt; constant not ephemeral; upright: that is, genuine and interiorly honest; prudent. Penance is practised in the desert, for there the devil is beaten at his own game. There is a three-day journey into the desert of penance. This three-day journey consists of contrition, confession, satisfaction. Each of these is exemplified by the actions of a woman of the Old Testament: the woman who slew Abimelech; Judith who slew Holofernes; Jael who slew Sisara.

Sermon 90

Folios 101a–101vb □ *Source Book* Liber Proprius □ *Date/Place* Passion Sunday □ *Preached* at Elstow, 15 March 1282 □ *Theme* Christus per proprium sanguinem semel introivit in Sancta sua (Heb 9:12).

Antitheme In love, Christ has purchased mankind by nothing less than his own blood, sharing his delights with those who do penance. Yet man's ingratitude still drives Christ away so that he is homeless. Rogemus ... .

Body In Lent, the Church has used many examples to rouse her members to penance. Now, at the end of Lent, she uses the example of Christ's passion. First, Christ wants to enkindle in all the fire of love; second, by his suffering he offers abundant healing to men; third, from his sufferings Christ has made for men a refuge impregnable and well-supplied with good. Christ also wants to soften the hearts of men through sorrowful meditation and bring them to genuine contrition.

Sermon 64

Folios 69va–70vb □ *Source Book* Liber Proprius □ *Date/Place* Lent, Sunday II □ *Preached* on 14 March 1283; no place given □ *Theme* Hec est voluntas Dei sanctificatio vestra ... (1 Thess 4:3).

Antitheme Lent is a time of penance for confessing, fleeing away from, and being cured of, sin. For this, understanding the word of God in Scripture is of great help, as it heals those infected by the leprosy of sin, those blinded by wickedness, those living in the darkness of sin and ignorance. Pater noster ...

Body The soul is purified from original sin by baptism, and from actual sin by penance. Holiness consists in contrition of heart, confession from the mouth, and satisfaction by works. Contrition belongs to the mind and the heart, and involves real suffering, like that of childbirth. Confession is a remedy for sin – spiritual leprosy – and is a means of reconciliation. Confession should be voluntary, pure in intention, prudent, self-accusing only, not in any way accusing others or excusing self. Moreover, confession should be honest, calling sin by its name, not by pleasant circumlocutions.

Sermon 77

Folios 93vb, 93a–93vb □ *Source Book* Liber Proprius □ *Date/Place* Lent IV □ *Preached* at Elstow, 28 March 1283 □ *Theme* Illa que sursum est Jerusalem libera est que est mater nostra (Gal 4:26) □ *Notes* In MS Laud Misc. 511 the *antitheme* of this sermon was copied after the main *body* of the sermon.

Antitheme Sacred Scripture teaches us that the Lord is a powerful helper especially to those weakened by sin. Invocemus ... .

Body Those called to take the cross would be heartened to hear good news of the Holy Land. Lent is a time for taking the cross of penance, and going on pilgrimage to the heavenly Jerusalem, about which many good and reassuring things are heard. The cross is true penance: shown by sorrow for sin, honest confession, readiness to make satisfaction. The time of Christ taking his cross begins at the end of this week. He went to suffering and death, so doing mortal combat with the devil. Anyone who goes to confession out of ecclesiastical routine or human respect, is bearing the devil's cross rather than Christ's □ The sinner has powerful enemies. God's sword of justice hangs over him, held back only by God's mercy. All that stands between himself and destruction is the sinner's frail body. Already the one in mortal sin is standing at the gate of hell. The one who postpones repentance and the making of confession is preparing his own mansion in hell.

Sermon 100

Folios 106vb–107vb): see above □ *Date/Place* Palm Sunday □ *Preached* at Elstow a second time, 11 April 1283 □ *Theme* Noli timere filia syon, ecce rex tuus" (Jo 12:15) □ *Notes* After the part of the sermon already preached – of which there is a summary above – the preacher completed his preaching by taking the rest of the text available in MS Laud Misc. 511. The precis of this last portion of the sermon follows: The Hebrew children sing. Christ is the teacher. Christ is to be brought into the Jerusalem of the faithful soul. May all of us come to the throne of grace, Mary.

B □ Sermons for Paschaltide: Easter Sunday

Sermon 114

Folios 113a- 115b □ *Source Book* Liber Parvus Rubeus □ *Theme* Numquid qui dormit non adiciet ut resurgat (Ps 40:9) □ *Notes* The "courage of him who rose" is omitted.

Antitheme none

Body The certain death of Christ is the first part - he who lies asleep. First is the suitability of Christ's death about which three things are to be considered: at what time or season the battle happened, the place and manner of the fighting. Christ died and overcame the same month, day and hour as when Adam was overcome by the devil in paradise; but while the time was similar, the place was different. Man was overcome by the devil in paradise, but the devil was overcome in the midst of his own world. As for the means, the devil overcame Adam offering the tree; so the devil was overcome by the wood, tree, of the cross. The death of Christ is the medicine and healing of the death we incur by sin. The Church sings of the kingdom of Christ from the cross in its passiontide hymns.

The death of Christ is called sleep: a sleeper will waken, so Christ yielded up his spirit and resumed it. This sleep is very useful, of double benefit to us: it sets us free - this we will speak of elsewhere - and is for our instruction. Christ's passion teaches us to be humble, to be charitable and to be patient. Christ was the richest of all, yet he gave everything for us; he had great pain and healed us; he, the most righteous, never committed sin but he recovered God's dominion over creation. On earth Christ was a poor man who humbled himself to become the lowest, to teach us humility. Let us be taught by him.

Concerning being charitable: there are three human goods - money, time or leisure, and life itself. It is good to give others money, greater to spend time on others, but greatest of all to lay down one's life for them. Christ showed this supreme love, not only for friends, but for enemies too. Thirdly, when a person puts up with another's persecution he is patient; greater patience is shown by a good master who is persecuted by a bad servant; but the greatest patience is shown by God ending human corruption. Christ accepted all the suffering of the cross, the insults, the pain and the dreadful death, and prayed to the Father to forgive those who inflicted them on him. And this is to teach us patience in our sufferings.

The resurrection of Christ, "he shall rise up no more," is the second part of our sermon. We have three points: the question now that he lieth/sleepeth; resurrection; and the courage of him who rose. The question can express two emotions, either longing or doubting. If it is the longing, it is the voice of the glorious Virgin who remained constant in faith, longing for the speedy resurrection of her Son - that is why Saturday is her special day. If the feeling is doubt, then it is the voice of Christ's apostles and disciples who saw him only as a man and who were terrified and uncertain, though also joyful, when they saw him risen.

On the second point, of resurrection, we note two things: suitability and blessing. The suitability of the third day of resurrection is seen by its comparison with three periods of the world: before the law, under the Law, and the period of grace. As for the blessing of Christ's resurrection, three things are noted: he rose to strengthen our belief in being set free, to give us hope of future atonement, to refresh us as we journey along the way. At the supper, when he spoke of his body given and his blood shed, he was telling us that his death would destroy sin and death and set us free. The fact of his resurrection gives us hope that this freedom will lead us to a new life in Christ, as he is the first fruits of our nature and hence a pledge of our resurrection. Lastly, Christ knew we could not reach resurrection with faith and hope alone. We need works of charity, which we cannot do without being fed by his body and blood. This food strengthens us to walk in the way of good works. About this waybread, eucharist, we note two things briefly: the importance of faith in the bread and wine becoming the flesh and blood of Christ by his word, and so hiding the real humanity and divinity of Christ. To those with faith and good intentions this food brings great benefit; but to those of sinful intention it is very damaging. When the soul has spiritual life, this gift brings power and life and forgiveness of sin through the heat of love: when the soul is dead in sin it does not contain life. So it is important to be cleansed by contrition and confession to ascend to such great food. Just as a sick person makes careful preparation before taking bodily medicine, so much more should a person be prepared for this spiritual food when Christ, as it were, is eating with him. Let us honour him in all purity of mind and body.

Sermon 115
Folios 115b- 115va □ *Source Book* Liber Rubeus Minor □ *Theme* Si consurrexistis cum Christo ... (Col 3:1).

   Antitheme none

   Body If you have risen: Man is twofold, body and soul; he has a twofold death and so a twofold resurrection – the soul first then the body. As bodily death is twofold, internally by disease, externally by wounds; so is the death of the soul twofold: by spiritual interior sins and external carnal sins. But man should recover and rise from sin □ *With Christ*: there is a threefold rising: Samuel, Lazarus, Christ. Samuel rose in a vision; Lazarus really rose but only to die again. Those who rise from their sins with sorrow but fall into sin again are like Lazarus. But Christ's was the real resurrection, never to die again. Those who relinquish sin thoroughly and do not commit sin again really rise with Christ. □ *Seek the things that are above*: Leave behind the emptiness of earth and seek first the kingdom of God: those who do not find have not abandoned their sin. They are like Saul and Jeroboam. Those who seek and find meet the risen Christ like the women did, and they hold firmly to him □ So four things advise us to seek Christ: the nature of the soul, the quality of the body, the resurrection of Christ, and our own profession.

Sermon 116
Folios 115va- 115vb □ *Source Book* Liber Rubeus Minor □ *Theme* Christus resurgens ex mortuis ... (Rom 6:9).
    Antitheme none
    Body Death is in our very nature. We must all die; we leave behind nothing of ourselves. The death of the sinner is fearful, all the senses are attacked - blindness, stench, fire and brimstone. For the sinner this happens before judgement. At the judgement it will be worse, when further suffering is inflicted; after the judgement the punishment is undying death.

Sermon 117
Folios 115vb- 116a □ *Source Book* Liber Rubeus Minor □ *Theme* Pascha nostrum ... (1 Cor 5:7) □ *Notes* This is a sermon of Petrus de Remis OP. The fuller text is in MS Arundel 206. The text in MS Laud Misc 511 is not complete: a section of eight to nine lines is omitted at the beginning, as is most of the third division to give about three fifths of the Arundel text.
    Antitheme none
    Body The Israelites celebrated a triple pasch: their departure from Egypt; their sojourn in the desert; their time in Galgal. □ The departure from Egypt is a move from sin to grace. For those who in darkness do not see Christ, and who are unmindful of God's works of creation, redemption and glorification, there is a triple bitterness in Hell: conscience, remorse and pain. The Israelites had the lamb as food for the journey, its blood as defence against the destroying angel, a cloud to lead them, and a staff to divide the sea for them. In the pasch we have the flesh of Christ as food for our journey, his blood - grace - for our protection, and the cross or passion to lead us. So in daily life we practise chastity, follow the example of the saints, do works of repentance and have great desire □ The sojourn in the desert, the second pasch, is the change from vice to virtue, from fear to love, which comes from the desert of repentance. It is also the place where enemies who impede progress are met, such as the weakness of the flesh and the temptation to sin. We need to go straight through the desert □ The third pasch comes after the crossing of the Jordan into the land of promise, where the manna - acquiring knowledge - fades; so does hope. And charity will be complete.

Sermon 118
Folios 116b- 117vb □ *Source Book* Liber Confessiones Augustini □ *Theme* Transi hospes orna mensam" (Eccli 29:33) □ *Notes* The third and fourth divisions are reversed, contrary to the initial division of the theme.
    Antitheme none
    Body There are four points to be noted: who the guest is; whence he comes; what the table is; what is its preparation □ The guest is Christ. Christ, who delights to be with the children of men, is received in holy communion. Christ can be received unworthily through lack of faith, the recipient being

in persistent mortal sin; and by those who fall back into a state of mortal sin [recidivandi]. Neither mercenaries, that is, those in a state of mortal sin; nor foreigners, that is, those who have no belief in Christ, should eat of the paschal lamb. But the good Christian receives Christ in humility and obedience, welcomes Christ; and, in the future, will be welcomed by Christ.

Christ's host who is inconstant, and who after Easter falls back into sin, provokes God against himself. The sinner by returning to sin and death becomes the exact opposite of the rest of creation, which is full of new life and growth, nature celebrating the resurrection. Such wicked ones, like Adam and Judas, have no rest.

From whence does the guest come? Christ comes from this world to the Father. He has trodden the wine press alone. The sinner wants to reign with Christ, but does not want to labour in Christ's footsteps.

What is the table's preparation? The adornments of the table of Christ and his disciples are spiritual dishes, such as the exquisite humility of Christ in washing the disciples' feet. All his life Christ loved humility: in his birth is poverty; in his public life he is so different from the proud men in the gospel who chose the best seats at table and the synagogue; in his passion, accepting the greatest humiliation, he carried his own cross and was hung between two thieves. At the last supper he showed the greatest love, giving himself to his betrayer. As Gregory notes: Christ gave his flesh for food, his blood for drink, his life for a price, his clothing to the soldiers, his mother to John, and paradise to the thief.

What is the table? There are five tables: that of the devil, that of gluttons, that of the teacher, that of Christ's disciples, that of the blessed saints. The devil's table is luxurious and sinful. The table of gluttons leads to greed, sin and damnation. There are numerous courses: retributions against the rich, meanness towards the poor, excessive talking, detraction, grumbling and quarrelling, even killing, forgetfulness of God. The table of teachers is the sacred Scriptures: they minister to us in four courses - the historical sense, the allegorical sense, the moral and the anagogical senses. This is the table of Catholics, at which we are refreshed with the body and blood of Christ. Finally there is the table of the kingdom of heaven. May God lead us to this table.

Sermon 119

Folios 118a- 118vb □ *Source Book* Quaternus Oxoniensis □ *Theme* Hec est dies quam fecit Dominus ... (Ps 117:24; Easter Sunday Responsory)

Antitheme If we had, all of us, been condemned to death for our iniquity and, on the way to the gallows, were freed by an innocent man dying instead, we would congratulate ourselves. But if he rose from that death, we would not only rejoice but gladly listen. This is what Christ has done for us and for all those who by the sin of Adam were condemned to death. We should rejoice in Christ's resurrection and listen to those who speak, who ourselves cannot speak without his help.

Body *This is the day* which is very special in time because Christ who died harrowed hell, defeated its pains and led out his chosen ones, imprisoned for over 5,000 years, to the gate of heaven.

This is the day when Christ through his priests distributed his body and blood to his faithful. It is the day made by the Lord. Christ the sun of justice made daylight – the light of grace – where before was the night of sinners. As it were, there was one day from his birth to his passion; the sun set and he was in the sepulchre; but today he has risen.

This is the day, Easter. There are three feasts: Christmas, Easter, Ascension. Easter is the most splendid: the feast of God, of men, of angels, of all living creatures. Christmas is the special feast of man when Christ became man to redeem us. The Ascension is a special feast for heaven, of the angels. But the feast of the Resurrection is the feast of God, because he passed over and came into his own kingdom. But it is also our feast, because we share in his resurrection and he has taught us to rise from the death of sin.

But woe to those who fall back into sin after this feast! Such a person is two-faced, repenting in Lent, sinning again now. In Lent he is in the Church militant through repentance; after Easter he is in the devil's house through sin. What madness to prepare a house for your guest, clean it, decorate it, and then bludgeon your guest when he arrives! That is the sinner who repented through contrition, confession and satisfaction, but sank back into idleness, gluttony and luxurious living. Let those who have been made holy remain holier yet because of being incorporated into Christ.

Sermon 120

Folios 118vb– 119b and fol. 1a □ *Source Book* Liber Proprius □ *Theme* Christus resurgens ex mortuis ... (Rom 6:9).

Antitheme none

Body Christ died, but today has risen, never to die hereafter. Death is threefold: of nature; of guilt; of Gehenna. Christ redeemed the human race by suffering this death for us. All people, without exception, suffer this death. Moreover, we leave nothing behind us; like water, we slip away into the ground.

The second death – of guilt – Jesus never suffered because he never committed any sin. We, as sinners, suffer this death. How lamentable it is that many people, now that the Saviour's resurrection has come, fall back into sin; and so crucify Christ again! Such people are like a captive who attacks the one who rescued him from the Saracens; or like someone who gives away a precious jewel for a cake or a flagon of beer.

The third and most bitter death is that of Gehenna, the unending prepared fire of sulphur in hell.

Christ died on the cross that sin might be crucified with him; and he suffered in his body to teach us to suffer spiritually and to die to sin. Christ rose physically from the dead so that we might rise spiritually to virtue and the good works of repentance; but Christ is not going to die again, so let us not lapse again into sin. The sweet Lord who died is ever present with us, and he gives his body and blood to the faithful. Let us beware of approaching his table in mortal sin.

Sermon 121

Folios 119va– 120b □ *Source Book* Liber Proprius □ *Theme* Si consurrexistis cum Christo que sursum sunt querite (Col 3:1)

Antitheme The word of the Lord must be listened to and understood by the faithful, at least because of the reward God gives to those who hear and believe. This can only happen through the gift of God's mercy.

Body Christ died in the flesh, was buried, and rose again from the dead. The one who rises with Christ must die to sins and crush his spirit with abundant grief, soften the heart with tears, before he can rise spiritually. Three things working together bring about spiritual death: grief for the many sins he has committed; hatred for sin so as not to follow temptation; revulsion from sin and determination not to commit it again.

What does the sinner lose and find by sin? He loses the life of Christ and gains death from the devil; he loses light but finds darkness; loses the company of angels but finds the torment of demons; loses the suffrages of the Church but finds the destruction of hell. But anyone going to confession is led away from the devil and hidden from him to be restored to God.

Ultimately resurrection is spelled out in works of repentance and satisfaction. Just as Christ rose from death never to die again, so each one should so rise again as never more to commit sin. If a criminal were pardoned by the king, invited to the king's banquet, royally entertained; and then attacked the king with sword and knife he would deserve death. But this is what a man does when he relapses into sin after receiving the body and blood of Christ.

We can only rise truly with Christ, not with Samuel or Lazarus. Those who rise with Samuel are like hypocrites who only appear to be good; those who rise with Lazarus have repented in Lent, but die again in sin after Easter. It is important to approach the sacrament free of mortal sin. Those who come in sin condemn themselves to judgement. The one who wants to approach that table should have faith in the sacrament and be clean from sin.

Sermon 122

Folios 120b– 120vb □ *Source Book* Liber Niger Minor □ *Theme* Qui comederit de sanctificatis per ignorantiam addet quintam (Lev 22:14)

Antitheme none

Body The mystery of Christ's body and blood is the meaning of "holy" in the "gifts." Ignorance is shown by the one who has no idea of the virtue, dignity and quality of the sacrament. There is the need to use the five senses interiorly to gain spiritual self-knowledge, and so to feel the divine and the heavenly.

There are many reasons for receiving this sacrament: (i) A sharing in Christ's passion by the commemoration of his love for us in his passion; by the commemoration of our being freed; by our imitation of Christ in imitating his patience, humility and other virtues. (ii) A cause of its institution is the reward of faith, for faith has no merit when human reason proves our experience. The merit and glory of faith lie in "not seeing, yet believing" all the more, especially in what is set before us. (iii) O mighty uplifter, you are said to be with us bodily; let us hope the more earnestly that we can resist our enemies! (iv) The instruction the Lord gives us that in the bread and wine which our eyes see is the Lord's flesh and blood. So let us believe and obey his will. (v) Not to eat the leaven of malice towards our neighbour or evil towards self; but to eat the unleavened bread of sincerity and truth. We eat the bread of angels; every delight: the light of Christ, hearing his words, being anointed with his fragrance, tasting his sweet savour and being touched by him. (vi) This bread is as it were the new tree of life which gives us eternal life. (vii) This daily commemoration is a remedy for venial sins. (viii) It is the source of spiritual strength. (ix) Those who eat this food worthily become one bread, one body, one in the unity of the body of Christ. (x) Surmounting of the threefold evil of pain, the weakness of the body and death itself.

SERMONS FOR PASCHALTIDE: THE SECOND SUNDAY AFTER EASTER
Sermon 131
Folios 125a □ *Source Book* Liber Minimus □ *Theme* Eratis aliquando sicut oves errantes sed nunc conversi estis ad pastorem et episcopum animarum vestrarum (1 Pet 2:25).

Antitheme none

Body These words describe two kinds of men: sinners and penitents. First, consider why the sinner is compared to a "sheep gone astray"; second, consider what kind of conversion is right for the penitent. In the first the sinner has two things, nature and fault. He is a sheep in his nature by comparison with the simplicity, meekness and unity of the sheep. In his fault a sinner is like a straying sheep, for going astray is a turning from truth – created and uncreated. In conversion the repentant man turns away from sin through penitence. How, and for whom, should conversion take place? Conversion should be speedy, total, persevering.

Sermon 132
Folios 125b □ *Source Book* Liber Parvus Rubeus □ *Theme* Christus semel pro peccatis nostris mortuus est ... (1 Petr 3:18) □ *Notes* This sermon is incomplete; the last distinction is missing.

Antitheme none

Body "Christ" shows the dignity of the sufferer; "died" shows the advantage of the Passion; "for our sins" shows the removal of sin; "that he should offer us to God" shows the plenitude of reasons ☐ The advantage of the Passion is seen by comparison with someone being freed from prison, or from oppressive servitude. He who is king of kings died to take away our sins. Those who refuse to abandon sin or refuse to do penance offend Christ. Exemplum about a king

Sermon 133

Folios 125b– 126a ☐ *Source Book* Liber Parvus Rubeus ☐ *Theme* Christus passus est pro nobis relinquens exemplum ... (1 Pet 2:21).

Antitheme none

Body Condemned by an unjust judge for unjust reasons, Christ died for the unjust, in the company of the unjust, at the hands of the unjust. He suffered to take away our guilt and punishment; to offer us to God as a priest offers hostiam (host or victim); to arm us; to instruct us. Thus we are enabled to follow Christ's ways: to avoid the way of pride that forges ahead;the circular way of cupidity; the backwards way of voluptuousness; the standing stock-still way of sloth.

We have to follow Christ's footsteps. The martyrs follow his prints of blood, while confessors follow traces of Christ's perfume. His passion made a powerful way, being followed in the perfumes of wisdom, justification, sanctification, redemption. The traces of Christ's steps can also be interpreted as mercy and truth. His right foot of mercy rests on the sea, which represents sinners moved to humble repentance. His left foot of truth and justice rests on land, which is the image of the perverse. Behind and before and above Christ's head is the rainbow, a sign of the covenant.

Christ suffered to redeem us from the prison of ignorance and sin. He suffered to redeem us from our enemies. He suffered in order to possess us as a servant possesses his wages. We must not deprive God of his wages; in part – by sloth or lip-service; or in whole – by dying in sin. Christ suffered to lead us to heaven; he suffered so bitterly to give us an example; he suffered to lead us by the right paths; he suffered to bring us to the highest.

Sermon 134

Folios 126b ☐ *Source Book* Liber Parvus Rubeus ☐ *Theme* Christus passus ... (1 Pet 2:21).

Antitheme It is usual for heirs, after their father's death, to ask what he has left them in his will. We have been left Christ's footsteps. But we may renounce this inheritance. Remembrance of his passion stimulates reflection, as the saying goes: "Woe is shown outwardly, lest it be forgotten inwardly".

Body Christ who suffers has a fourfold dignity: he is the anointed one; he is king; he is priest; he is full of grace. If one so noble suffered for base man, then we should suffer for Christ. His suffering is indescribable in its abasement, shame, excessiveness and grief. He left us an example leading us to suffer willingly with him, so that we should share his glory, his kingdom.

The manner of this suffering with him is indicated by following his footsteps, especially by the spiritual foot of love.

Sermon 135

Folios 126va–126vb □ *Source Book* Liber Parvus Rubeus □ *Theme* Christus passus est pro nobis vobis relinquens exemplum (1 Pet 2:21).

Antitheme none

Body Three things are to be touched: the passion of Christ; our imitation of it; the manner of imitation □ With regard to the first: in his passion Christ entered the road of utmost poverty, having nothing to wear, eat, or drink, nowhere to lodge. He entered upon the road of utmost humility and abasement, putting aside his equality with God, to become the most despised and forsaken of men, condemned to the basest death. He entered upon the road of utmost disfigurement, being wounded, tortured and insulted so that he seemed a leper. He entered upon the road of utmost punishment. He, the immutable God, suffered nature's last punishment, death. Moreover, it was the long drawn out agony of the cross □ Secondly, we follow Christ's example, patiently imitating him by the road of poverty; by the road of humility; by the road of abasement; by the road of disfigurement, for sin has distorted us; by the road of punishment, because we are sinners □ Thirdly, the method of imitation is to do that of which Christ gave us an example; like the servant following the lord who freely accepted all these pains. Eventually we shall follow him to heaven.

Sermon 136

Folios 127a–127b) □ *Date/Place* preached at Elstow, 16th April, 1279; see under A above.

Sermon 137

Folios 128a–128b □ *Source Book* Liber Rubeus Maior □ *Theme* Christus passus est … (1 Pet 2:21) □ *Notes* Further points, other than the initial divisions, are found in this sermon. Unlike the avaricious, Christ in his passion suffered great poverty in having no home; greater poverty in his nakedness; the greatest poverty in having neither foot on earth. □ Unlike the proud, Christ in his passion suffered great abasement from blows; greater abasement from being spat upon; and the greatest abasement in being hung between two thieves.

Antitheme none

Body First, we remember the passion of Christ, by abandoning our ingratitude, by mortifying our flesh, by strengthening our spirit. "Sea" means the bitterness of Christ's passion, while "Sidon" means hunting, and is a sign of a pleasure-loving man hunting worldly joys □ Second, Christ's suffering is a proof of his charity; the friend laying down his life; the warmth of love drawing us □ Third, Christ's suffering is an influence in our lives. We follow Christ by turning from sin, by interior joy, by obtaining the kingdom.

Sermon 138

Folios 128b, fol. 129a–129vb; replacement folios □ *Source Book* Liber Proprius □ *Theme* Christus passus est" (1 Pet 2:21).

Antitheme "By the word of the Lord the heavens were made strong". You are inhabitants of the heavenly Jerusalem; our way of life ought to be in heaven. The word of the Lord can make it strong. Let us pray to the Lord, in whom is all wisdom.

Body First, Christ suffered for us: second, we should follow in his footsteps □ The memory of Christ's bitter passion is celebrated again after an interval of Easter blessings and joys. Christ's passion is a reproach to our ingratitude. The memory of a friend is very precious, and is enhanced by a keepsake. Christ our friend and counsellor has left a remembrance in his flesh and blood. He has laid down his life not only for his friends but for his enemies too. He has suffered, taking on himself our weakness to heal us of all weakness, leaving his blood to heal us □ We should follow in his steps. By the cross of penance Christ is followed. Let us look at and ponder on the sufferings of Christ: his back scourged, his head crowned with thorns, his feet transfixed, his hands pierced, in pain from head to toe. He has no rest for his head, no earth for his foot, no clothing for his body, no drink for his mouth, no friend for his comfort. Looking on the face of Christ, let us crucify our head, eyes, ears, tongue, mouth, heart, hands and feet, by repudiating sins of thought, hearing, word, touch, deeds. Let us hold out our hands in almsgiving and healing, and use our feet to lead us into good deeds. S. Peter gives us as the key to goodness, the remembrance of Christ's passion. In the past forty days we were following Christ by our penance. We received him in Easter communion. Let us reflect on the purity we need, thinking of Mary Magdalene, John the Baptist, and the woman healed of a haemorrhage.

Sermon 139

Folios 128va–128vb □ *Source Book* Liber Augustinus □ *Theme* Ego sum pastor bonus (Jo 10:11).

Antitheme none *Body* The Lord our God had a hundred sheep: one strayed from paradise to this world and to another master, who captured it. So the Lord our God sent his Son, disguised as the Lamb of God, to search for the lost sheep. He found his Father's sheep imprisoned and in need of redemption and pasture □ In the first part of this gospel Christ is the good shepherd redeeming the sheep; the price he paid was his own dear life. But the devil could not hold the price. By his own blood Christ turned wolves into lambs. Why did Christ give such great things for my sake when I make no return? Christ had as his own that which man, in Adam, had forfeited: life. He gave it up freely. We should meditate on the life of Christ, the price paid for us; then we will have rightful respect for ourselves and for one another, and will not easily enslave ourselves to sin □ Secondly, Christ the good shepherd, as well as redeeming the sheep, gives them pasture. He reinvigorates each sense: eyes by the sight of the Lord; ears through the Holy Spirit; nostrils by the perfume of the holy Name; touch by his wounds; the hungry palate by his body. That is why Christ is the good shepherd, pasturing his sheep with himself. Because they grasp him with their senses, he revivifies his sheep in the present life and will do so in the heavenly future.

Sermon 140

Folios 129a □ *Source Book* Liber Parvus Rubeus □ *Theme* Sequamini vestigia eius (1 Pet 2:21)

>*Antitheme* none

>*Body* We should follow: □ in purity of heart in what regards contrition. You have adhered to Christ through baptism and then despised him and gone to the devil. Through contrition the soul is purified from sin: □ in the truth of what we say; making honest confession, neither adding nor subtracting; □ in vigorously setting to work by satisfaction, manfully atoning for past sin, and resisting present temptation.

Sermon 147

Folios 137a– 137b □ *Source Book* Liber Niger Minor □ *Theme* Cum maledicere-tur non maledicebat ... (1 Pet 2:23).

>*Antitheme* none

>*Body* Patience is tried in two ways: by words and by blows. Christ experienced both ways: by words of hate and insult; by blows – attack and torture. Why did Christ endure such great sufferings? To leave us an example of patience, like Job and Tobit before him. We must not prevent his mighty efforts by our impatience. If so, we shall be accused on judgement day. We have another reason for being patient. By the law of equity, whatever is done to us we may do in self-defence. But how have we been treated when we have sinned? We killed ourselves, God's sons, by sin. Yet God has borne this loss patiently and many times, because his unending mercy has been given to us. If we have received such mercy and patience from God, should we not extend mercy and patience to one another? □ By our mortal sins we have deserved eternal punishment. In comparison, all temporal punishment is as nothing. But the Lord has changed this eternal punishment into one that ends. We should accept all this in patience □ Similarly, let us endure insult and falsehood, knowing that the Lord endured both and we, the servants, are not greater than our master.

C □ SERMONS FOR THE SECOND SUNDAY AFTER EASTER ON THE THEME "CHRISTUS PASSUS EST"

Sermon by Aldobrandinus de Cavalcantibus OP □ Dominica I post oct' Pasce □ Wroclaw MS I.Q. 427 □ *Folios* 135v– 137r)

Theme Christus passus est pro nobis, vobis relinquens exemplum ut sequamini vestigia eius (1 Pet 2:21).

Antitheme none

Body After the joy of the resurrection the Church reminds us of the suffering of the Passion for four reasons: lest like schoolboys after holidays we forget; lest we relapse; that our love be stimulated; that we may imitate Christ. Sadly, Christ's passion has been made cause and matter for sin: by forgetting, by relapsing, by growing tepid, by not imitating Christ □ Christ suffered for us. The person is Christ, anointed in a threefold way: as a warrior for battle, as a king, and as a priest. Peter writes of this threefold anointing: given by God as the "oil of gladness"; anointed by the Holy Spirit with strength to suffer; anointed pastor and bishop. □ Second, Christ suffered in three ways: in the manner, that is cruelty, being cursed, being scourged; by the minister, that is from the iniquity of an unjust judge; in the instrument used, that is the disgrace of the gibbet, the most shameful death □ Third, there is the cause of Christ's sufferings: us. Christ's passion has a threefold effect on us: it is satisfaction for our sins; it is for the healing of spiritual diseases, being anointed by his blood; it gives life to the dead, for we were dead in sin □ Peter shows the threefold intention for which Christ suffered, that we should follow his steps. Christ's way is the steps of innocence, the steps of patience, and the steps of penance. Let us ask ... .

Sermon by Guilielmus Peraldus OP (printed under William of Auvergne), page 67- 68 □ Dominica Secunda post Pascha: Sermo Primus □ *Theme* Christus passus est pro nobis, vobis relinquens exemplum ut sequamini vestigia eius" (1 Pet 2:21).

Antitheme none

Body The passion of Christ is to be remembered all the time, particularly in the Eucharist. His death is specially recalled at Eastertime. That is why Christ showed the apostles his wounds. At this time the Church celebrates the Finding of the Cross. Today's epistle recalls the passion. At Paschaltime spiritual combat is more hazardous; it is the season when things tend to decay. The memory of the Lord's passion is preservative from spiritual corruption. In summer choleric humours are prevalent, the bitterness of the Lord's passion restrains spiritual bad temper. When the season is hot, shade is pleasing; Paschaltide is a season of heats in which the shade of the Lord's cross is necessary □ Christ is the tree of life. People have five reasons for needing a tree: to protect the complexion by the tree's shade; to shelter from heat; to shelter from rain; when fatigued, to rest beneath it; to be refreshed with its fruit. We all need Christ our tree: his passion is the protection of our spiritual beauty, given us daily in his blood through the Mass. In times of oppression Christ's passion is a source of patience and comfort, of readiness to suffer. If the rains of temptation fall, Christ the tree provides shelter with the memory of his passion. The devil is afraid of this tree by which he was conquered. Again, Christ our tree is solace when we are overburdened by labour in his service. The memory of his passion will revive love. Love, as Jacob found, makes light of labour. Similarly, if we love Christ, the labour is easy and becomes repose beneath Christ the tree of life. Lastly, whoever comes to this tree will be refreshed with its fruit through meditating on Christ's Passion and on the virtues of humility, meekness, patience, charity and tender love; all of which Christ exemplified, and particularly in his passion.

Sermon by Guilielmus Peraldus OP (printed under William of Auvergne), pages 68– 69: De eadem Dominica: Sermo Secundus □ *Theme* Christus passus est pro nobis ... (1 Pet 2:21).

Antitheme Christ's sufferings are brought to mind in several epistles in the year.

Body Peter did not describe the things Christ suffered for us, since they are in a sense indescribable. But Christ suffered much for us, and suffers still for us, especially in us his members. As Christ suffered for us, we ought to desire to suffer something for him.

Many things make Christ's sufferings more grievous. First, the sheer greatness of the one who suffers. Any insult is measured by the dignity of the one offended: peasant, knight, count, king, infinite Lord. Second, Christ's sufferings were more grievous because he suffered for the unworthy. Third, he suffered many things at the hands of the unworthy. Fourth, he suffered in the company of criminals. Fifth, he was punished without cause. Sixth, his sufferings came from would-be friends. Surely this is enough suffering. We should not further heap grief upon grief.

Christ by suffering left us an example to follow. Following is threefold: by traces of footsteps, by traces of scent, by traces of blood. The first way is followed by beginners, by not being unkind to neighbours and being zealous in works of mercy. The second way is followed by those making progress, by taking pleasure in the perfume of Christ's example. The third way is followed by the perfect. They are ready to die for Christ, as he did for them. In the past, many have followed Christ's traces, but today those traces are being obliterated by the flooding waters of wealth and pleasure.

Sermon by an Italian Dominican, xiii c. *Source* printed under the name of Thomas Aquinas in the edition by Vives, 29: 234 □ *Date/Place* De Dominica Prima post octavam Paschae ex Epistola □ *Theme* Christus passus est pro nobis, vobis relinquens exemplum, ut sequamini vestigia eius (1 Pet 2:21).

Antitheme none

Body There are four points: the innocence of the Lord; his very great patience; his indescribable charity; the manifold profit to us of the foregoing. □ His innocence is shown in three ways: he did not sin; he never deceived anyone; he never harmed anyone.

His great patience is seen in three ways: he freely offered himself in his passion; having been unjustly condemned, he endured patiently, even happily; he hurled no threats against his executioners, rather he prayed for them. The greatness of his charity is seen in three ways: he took away our sins; he bore the punishment of our sins in his own body; he endured so cruel a death to take away our sins.

The death of Christ has brought us three kinds of advantage: he has freed us from the evil of guilt; he has restored us to the benefit of grace; he has preserved us from corruption.

There are three footprints of his that we should follow: in the purity of innocence for holiness to grow; in the strength of his patience; in charity.

May Christ who is life and light lead us to it. Amen

"Christ suffered for us": the great patience of Christ: *Christ suffered*, Palm Sunday the advantage of his passion *for us*: Passion Sunday.

Sermon by Hugh of Hartlepool OFM, preached at Greyfriars, Oxford on Good Friday, 20 April 1291 (printed by Little and Pelster in *Oxford Theology and Theologians*, App. 1.) □ *Theme* Christus passus est pro nobis (1 Pet 2:21) □ *Notes* The end of the sermon does not mention at this point the Reproaches, part of the Good Friday liturgy, but does paraphrase them.

Antitheme Let the word of Christ dwell in you. The intransitive exposition "of Christ" gives the meaning, "the word of Christ". The work of the preacher, the task of the hearer. The word of Christ dwelling in you implies three qualities of the heart: the reflection of the truth, the satisfaction of the will, the primacy in the heart. The word of Christ is true, satisfying, and has primacy. Its author triumphs, sets in order, sheds light. Let us pray to this author so that he may direct us.

Body Christ suffered for us: [1] Christ the Sacrifice prefigured in the sacrifices of the old law, six kinds of animals: turtle-doves, sparrows, pigeons, sheep, oxen, goats. These in their natural qualities prefigure Christ the sacrifice. The number six is a perfect number: Christ suffered on the sixth day.

[2] Christ suffered for us (i) Brief word about the Word who made himself brief. (ii) In these words Peter describes the twofold passion of Christ as costly and as fruitful: costly, because of Christ's nobility, fruitful because of the profit for the flock. (iii) In these words Peter touches on three things: the nobility of the sacrifice, *Christ*; the bitterness of the torment *he suffered*; the effectiveness of the remedy *for us*. (iv) Another way of looking at the theme. Four things are emphasised: the authority of the person; the death of the body; the permanence of the long-suffering patience; the intensity of the generosity.

[3] "Christ" (i) The authority of the person, Christ, the anointed one. Kings and priests are anointed. Christ's authority is spiritual. His dignity therefore excels that of all created things, power, authority. Christ is lord of all. Consider the shame of the sinner who gives the honour due to Christ to his adversary instead. In fact the sinner becomes a slave. (ii) The dignity of Christ excels

all who are wise in interior matters – a wisdom hidden in the Crucified. Those who are unwise are compared to the beetle and the pig. The splendour of eternal light does not shine for them. The eternal Sun, Christ, is eclipsed by the interposition of worldly things. Those who are wise hold themselves aloof from wrong sexuality, from folly in action, from love of money. They give of their learning, which remains undiminished, though given. Those who refuse to teach are greedy; those who use knowledge to score a triumph make little progress. (iii) The dignity of Christ excels all who are rising from lower things. He rose from death to life. We must rise from sin and never fall back into it. That is vain following of Christ. If we are happy to be called Christians, we must perform the actions of Christ. Sin makes us images of the devil. Therefore, we must not come to terms with sin. Knowledge of Christ is like sunlight enjoyed by healthy eyes – the good man: but a torment to diseased eyes – the sinner. (iv) The dignity of Christ excels all who rejoice in higher things. Christ is the splendour of eternal glory, is on the throne of majesty, transcending all joy and bliss. In time we do not have sufficient joy in Christ, because we see him only as in a mirror. When the end of time comes and the opportunity comes, we shall have joy seeing him as he really is. So let the soul always be held fast to Christ.

[4] "Suffered": We celebrate Christ's passion with mourning, and yet the passions of the Saints with rejoicing. The former, because the crown of our head perished on account of the injustices and insults he received; the latter because they gained something, in fact were reborn, so that the passion of a saint is a birthday party. Of the many things which made the passion of Christ oppressive, four only are considered. (i) The innocence of Christ's way of life. He was totally righteous, and so the intensity of his pain was increased. Yet his courage, his love for us, should arouse some response from us; not just in words, like minstrels who praise war but do not follow their lords into battle; nor like the countryman whose donkey was too unwell to fly; nor like the priest who could never fulfil his vow of pilgrimage as the time was never right; but in acts of sacrificing love. (ii) The injustice of the condemnation. The innocent was handed over, insults were heaped on him. Why did he redeem us with such great difficulty when one drop of blood would have sufficed? Because he wished to move us to love. We might be made from nothing: we were not redeemed for nothing. The Passion of Christ should arouse our compassion and our gratitude. It should help us to eschew avarice, accept poverty, wholeheartedly seek God. (iii) The lack of dignity in his position. □ He was driven out of the city, treated as a leper, condemned to death on the cross – at that time considered as the most degrading death – treated with great irreverence, scourged, shamed. His body, nailed by four nails, is like a book, for on it is written the song of his lamentations and tears. He chose to be wounded in his right hand to strengthen us in doing good; in his left hand to teach us to turn away from evil; in his right foot, that we

might love our friend; in his left foot, that we might love our enemy; in his side to teach us to love him personally. He was even more shamed, being hung between two thieves. By his loud cry as he died he attracted the attention of all around, like the fowler who by his cries attracts birds. But while the fowler slays what he catches, Christ brings life and salvation to those whom he knows as sharers in his passion. The elements - sky, sea, earth, sun - know the death of Christ. The remembrance of Christ's passion is the best remedy for temptation. (iv) The way in which he breathed his last □ Death is the extreme of what we fear, nothing is more serious. Yet Christ was obedient to the point of death. We were finally healed by that death. Sometimes healing is done by opposites, sometimes by similarities. Christ applies humility to our pride, poverty to our greed. But his death really destroyed our spiritual death of sin. So we should recall his passion with much devotion, for by it we are freed from death, purified from sin, made happy. By his passion, mercy and justice are harmonised; the Lord died to set the servant free, the supreme king was condemned to save an outsider. Listen to the Reproaches*. Can we repay his love with love? As the four parts of the cross meet in one point, so the four parts of the world ought to come together in Christ. As there were four points to the cross, showing four directions, so these ought to be in us. One should go upwards to show we love God above all; one should go down, showing that we love our neighbour; one should go to the left showing that we fear the judgements of Christ; one should go right, to show that we may enjoy eternal life.

D □ ADVENT SERMONS ON LITURGICAL THEMES
Sermon 5
Folios 7va- 8a □ *Source Book* Liber Niger Maior □ *Date/Place* Advent, Sunday I, II □ *Theme* Regem venturum Dominum, venite adoremus. (Advent, ferial Invitatory)

Antitheme As Advent has begun, we will say something about the coming of the king.

Body There are five kinds of king: of earth, of the world, of the flesh, of the devil, of heaven. The king of heaven has three comings. In his first coming, in humility, he came to redeem man. In his second coming, secretly in grace, he wants to turn man away from sin. In his third coming, as judge, he will come openly. Let us come back from vice to virtue; adore God not just by words, but by good deeds, especially prayer and almsgiving, and so prepare for the heavenly supper.

Sermon 8
Folios 9vb- 10b □ *Source Book* none □ *Date/Place* Advent, Sunday II □ *Theme* Surgite vigilemus, quia venit Rex, (Advent, Sunday Invitatory)

Antitheme God's writ deserves a short sermon. Let us listen, and let us pray for the grace to hear and keep his word.

Body Who is the king? The king of kings, king of creation, but especially king of men. For men he exercised all the king's duties: proclaiming the peace of God, defeating Satan. He did this by assuming our nature, dying to redeem us, showing his love for us. Our response should be proved by a real, practical love of our neighbour. Our Lady will help us in this.

Sermon 12

Folios 13va–14vb □ *Source Book* Liber Proprius □ *Date/Place* Advent, Sunday II □ *Theme* Rex noster adveniet quam Johannes predicavit Agnum esse venturum" (Advent, Sunday Invitatory

Antitheme In Advent the Lord comes to dwell in our hearts through grace. How pure such a dwelling should be! Like the patriarchs and the prophets, we should yearn to see Christ. Let us pray to Christ and his mother.

Body The ills of blindness, lameness, deafness, dumbness, run through Adam's deeds and those of his offspring. The task of Christ as physician was to heal these ills. To follow Christ is the middle way. It is like the return of the ark (an image of the Church) from the Philistines. The deer is an example of healing from sin. The coming of Christ has brought healing. We have lost the blindness of infidelity, but we are sometimes deaf in listening to and so serving the word of God; and we are dumb by not going to confession. We need to prepare, as for the coming of a special guest.

Sermon 13

Folios 14vb–15vb □ *Source Book* 1251 Liber Proprius □ *Date/Place* Advent, Sunday III □ *Theme* Veniet Dominus et non tardabit. (Breviary)

Antitheme Two things need to be said about this text: the coming of the Lord, the things which delay his coming.

Body The Lord is coming. The sun is an image of this, indeed, of the whole of the life of Christ. To prepare for this great feast we need to be purified from sin. We must not delay. The Church gives example of yearning through prayer, contemplation, and worship for the coming of her spouse. Christ was born as man to live on earth 1251 years ago. At this feast he will come by grace, not to live as man with men but within the soul. So the soul must be clean and decorated for his coming, as one prepares for the coming of a special guest. Nothing prevents this coming of Christ, except sin, which divides us from God, unites us with the devil, and makes us devils. To be full of sin is an insult to Christ, and mocks his coming. Moreover, sin cuts us off from the living Church. The uncertainty of the time of our death should encourage us to seek forgiveness now.

Sermon 14

Folios 15vb–16vb □ *Source Book* Liber Proprius □ *Date/Place* Advent, Sunday III □ *Theme* Veniet Dominus et non tardabit (Breviary).

Antitheme Let us invoke the Lord, who will soon be with us, to grant us the fullness of his grace, confident in his promise that our prayer will be heard, to his and his mother's honour, our profit and Satan's dismay.

Body The Lord who is coming is God, Lord of all, maker of creation, omnipotent Wisdom. He is king of all. He is expecially king of men because he became one of us, redeemed us, and loves us deeply. Moreover, man is as it were the favourite among the king's sons. Christ came to us visible as man; but now he comes spiritually and invisibly; while at the end of time he will come visibly and eternally. Therefore his present dwelling of the soul must be cleansed, prepared and decorated for his coming by casting away all sin. Sin makes a son of God a son of the devil; makes man a devil; makes man even more evil than the devil. There is no time on a short day to say why he comes swiftly. Let us pray that we will be ready to receive him.

Sermon 15

Folios 17a–18a □ *Source Book* Liber Proprius □ *Date/Place* Advent, III, IV □ *Theme* Rex noster adveniet quem Johannes predicavit (Advent Invitatory).

Antitheme Seldom is the word of God preached to you. Therefore it is necessary to listen with the inward ear, so that the word may be understood and practised. Let us pray for this grace.

Body Our king is lord of all and judge of all without exception. He is especially entitled king of men. His first coming was in meekness and tenderness; his second coming as judge will be terrible to sinners. The Church sings constantly of his coming, with joy at his birthday-coming in grace. The patriarchs, prophets and Simeon represent the time of Advent. As we would have a spring cleaning of the house before the arrival of a special guest, so we need to clean, decorate, and prepare our souls carefully for Christ's coming. He is called king of men because he made war on the devil and immediately established his peace. Peace-makers are sons of God and heirs with Christ. The unpeaceful are children of the devil. Through Christ's death on the cross we have our charter, and with it the right to possess heaven. Our confreres have gone before us so we have nothing to fear.

Advent IV The birthday of the king is approaching. We rejoice in the Lord, but very specially in his mother, mother of God-become-man. He drove sinners away. Mary made him tender and gentle. So he cared for sinners, eating with them and living with them. So many blessings have come through Mary. We should practise devotions in her honour [of which many examples are given].

Appendix 12

Index of Manuscripts

The following list includes all manuscripts used in researching this book. Some were used for content, others for codicological information for a contextual study of MS Laud Misc. 511. The list is organized conventionally by city, library, and manuscript collection. Parenthetical annotations provide information regarding medieval provenance, according to Ker's *Medieval Libraries*. Other codicological details, where relevant, are also included in abbreviated form: 'arabic num.' indicates arabic numerals are used for folios, pages, sections, columns, or lines; the use of Grosseteste's indexing symbols is signalled by 'Grosst. sym.'; the English scribal practice of using mostly blue initial letters flourished red is indicated by 'blue.' Of some three hundred and fifty manuscripts consulted to provide a wide-ranging and detailed context for the study of MS Laud Misc. 511, one hundred and fifteen are included in this index: they are marked below with an asterisk (*).

CAMBRIDGE
Corpus Christi 299; *306 (London OP; Grosst. sym.; arabic num.: folios); 315; *316 (London OP; Grosst. sym.; arabic num.: folios) □ *Gonville and Caius* *297 (Oseney Abbey); 348; *403 (Oxford and Cambridge OFM; arabic num.: sections); 481 □ *Magdalene* 4. 15 □ *St. John's* D.15 / 90; F. 6 / 91; *F. 7 / 144 (Bristol OFM; arabic num.: sections); F.20 / 157; G. 1 / 169 □ *Sidney Sussex* 49 □ *Trinity* B.15.38 / 373 (includes several sermons of Richard Fishacre OP); R. 7.11 / 749; *R.14.49 / 919 (Babwell OFM); R.15.16 / 940; O. 3.37 / 952; 993; 1209 □ *University Library* *Add 2991 (London OP; arabic num.: folios 1–56); *6886 (Babwell OFM); *Dd. 2. 5. (Abingdon Abbey; blue); *Ff. 4.11. (Balliol; blue; arabic num.: folios); *Ff. 6.10. (Jesus); Gg. 4.15.; *Ii. 1. 1. (Babwell OFM; arabic num.: folios; blue); *Ii. 2.10. (Balliol; Grosst. sym.); *Kk. 1.21. (Sudbury OP; arabic num.: sections); Kk. 1.22.; Ll. 2. 9. □ *Peterhouse* *(lat) 89 (Lincoln OFM; blue; arabic num.: columns) □ *Fitzwilliam Museum* 330 (formerly Dyson Perrins 3; William de Brailles)

HEREFORD
Cathedral Library *O i 1 (Hereford OFM; arabic num.: sections); *O i 4 (Hereford OFM; arabic num.: sections); O ii 11; O iii 3; O iii 6; O iv 1; *O iv 10 (Hereford OP; blue; ; arabic num.: folios 1–124); *O iv 11 (Ilchester OP; blue); *O v 5 (Gloucester OFM; arabic num.: folios); O v 12; O vi 3; O vii 3; O vii 7; O viii 12; P i 15; P iii 10; *P iii 12. (Hereford OFM; Grosst. sym.; arabic num.: columns and lines [ff. 1–67]); P iv 4; P v 6; P v 10; P v 13; P v 15; P vi 9; *P viii 11 (Hereford Cathedral; blue)

IPSWICH
Town Library MS 6 (since November 1982 MSS are kept in Ipswich School)

LONDON
British Library **Additional** 11283 (English); 11862 (Roman Missal, Netherlands); 14793 (Roman Missal); 15608; 17355 (Roman Missal, German); 17431 (Missal); 17742 (Roman Missal, French); 18031 and 18032 (Roman Missal, vols 1 and 2 from Stavelot); 18210; 23935 (Dominican Master General's copy of revised liturgy and Constitutions, sometimes called the *Portiforium*) Paris; 25104 (*Florilegium Anglicanum*); 25439 (exemplar with *pecia* marks); 27589; 29886; 30508 (contains Simon of Hinton OP, *Summa Juniorum*); 32446 (C.F.R. Palmer OP, transcript of Dominican Registers); 32579 (misc. Dominican writings, *Vitae fratrum*; cf. 23935); 35085 (Bible with Dominican *Temporale* pericope references); 35167 (English); 35285 (Lectionary); 37399 (Breviary, Hiemalis – Paris use); 37487 (portable Latin Vulgate Bible, Dominican *Temporale* pericope references); 37519 (Missal, Sarum use); 38723 (Missal, Paris use); 39675 (Missal, Hereford); 39924 (Sacramentary, Roman use, Spanish); 42555 (English?); 46919; 47214; 49622; 49999 (formerly Dyson Perrins MS 4; Book of Hours, Sarum use; work by William de Brailles □ **Arundel** 15 (interesting for book-trade); 52; 157 (stylistic similarities to William de Brailles' work); 165; 282 (*Summa Penitentia* of Raymund of Penaforte); 326; *332 (Grosseteste – Durham OSB; arabic num.: folios 1–169); 435 (book-trade, *pecia* marks) □ **Burney** 1, 5, 325 (these three manuscripts belonged to Franciscans in medieval times) □ **Cotton** Appendix xiii; Claud. A iii; Claud. C ix (Abingdon Abbey) ; *Cleo. C ix (Magdalen, Oxford, OFM; blue portion; Jul. A xi ; Nero A ix ; Otho A xiv; Tib. A iii (English); Tib. A ix (Oseney Abbey); Tib. A xii (Eynsham Abbey) □ Tib. B vi (Abingdon Abbey); Titus A xiv (Oseney Abbey); Vesp. A ii ; Vesp. B vi (Oseney Abbey); Vit. A i; Vit. A xiii (Abingdon Abbey); Vit. E xv (Oseney Abbey) □ **Egerton** 655 (some early OP sermons, with one by Alard OP); 2676; 2867 Bible with calendar, saints of Canterbury); 3036 (Italian Missal, c 1240); 3037 Dominican Missal, c 1340); 3133 (*De Adventu Fratrum Minorum*); 3153 Missal owned by OP nuns of Prouille, use not certain) □ **Harley** 76 (Roman Lectionary, English); 209; 493; 586; 632 (Grosseteste's *Templum Dei*); 876; 979 (theological miscellany); *1034 (Norwich OFM; blue); 1298 (contains *Templum Dei*); 1751; 1897; 1924; 3061; *3096 (Worcester OFM; arabic num.: sections [ff. 1–147]); 3241; *3244 (preacher's handbook, very likely Dominican; blue; English; contains *Templum Dei*); 3249; 3256; 3753; 4725; 4751 (English); 4987; *5116 (Coventry OFM; blue); 5294 (English); 5393 (Mass lectionary) □ **Lansdowne** *338 (Raymund of Penaforte's *Summa*, very small portable – Crowland Abbey; blue) □ **Royal** *1 A viii (Bible; arabic. num.: lines); 1 B vii (English); 1 C i (Vulgate Bible, tables); 1 D x (like de Brailles' work; cf Arundel 157); 2 B vi (English); 2 D xxiv; 2 E iii (Gospels, glossed); 3 A xi; *3 A xiv

(Robert Holcot OP – Reading Abbey; arabic num.: columns and folios); 3 C vi; 3 C ix; 3 D ii; 3 D iv; 3 D viii; 3 E i; 3 E ii; 3 E iii; 3 E iv; 3 E vii; 3 E viii; 3 E ix; 4 B vi (English); 4 C i; *4 C v (Canterbury OFM; arabic num.: sections); *4 D iv (London OFM; arabic num.: pages); 4 D vii; 4 E vi; *5 B v (Worcester OFM; arabic num.: folios 1- 196); 5 C iii; 5 C iv (Grosseteste); *5 C vii (London OP; blue; ; arabic num.: lines [ff. 102 seq], sections [ff. 1- 101]); 5 E iv; 5 F xv (contains Grosseteste's *Templum Dei*); *6 C ix (Warwick OP; arabic num.: sections, lines); 6 D iii; *6 E v (Grosseteste *Sermons* – Merton; blue; faces); 7 A iv; 7 A ix; 7 A x; 7 D i; 7 D xv; *7 E ii (Grosseteste – Brasenose; blue); *7 F ii (Westminster Abbey; Grosseteste texts; faces; blue); 7 F iii (Peter Comestor, *Historia* – Elstow Abbey); *7 F vii (Hereford OFM); 7 F viii (exemplar, identified by Destrez); 8 B xvii; 8 C iv; 8 E xvii; 8 G iv; 9 A iii (contains Grosseteste, *Templum Dei* and Simon Hinton *Summa juniorum*); *9 A xiv (Hinton's *Summa*; arabic num.: folios); 9 B x; *9 E xi Alexander of Hales (Rochester; arabic num.: folios; blue); *10 B vii (Richard Fishacre OP, *In 4Sent* – Cambridge OP; arabic num.: columns and lines); *10 C vi (Robert Holcot OP; blue; arabic num.: sections); 10 D vi; *11 B iii (Grosseteste; arabic num.: folio 29 seq.); 11 B v; 12 B iii; *12 E xxv (Merton; arabic num.: folios); 12 F xiii (English); 13 A v; *13 B vi (Lincoln OP; arabic num.: pages; blue); 13 B viii (English); 13 C vi; 13 D viii; 19 C v □ **Sloane** 278 (English); 1615; *1726 (Cambridge OFM; blue); 1975 (English) □ **Stowe** 15 (Gospel pericopes); 944 (Lectionary) □ *Dr. William's Library* MS Anc 1 (Bible) □ *Gray's Inn Library* 1; *2 (Chester OFM; arabic num.: folios 14 to end; blue); 5; * 7 (Chester OFM; arabic num.: folios 1- 171; blue portion); *11 (Chester OFM; arabic num.: pages); 12; 13; *20 (Sudbury OP; arabic num.: folios; faces); 24 □ *Lambeth Palace Library*; *57 (London OFM; arabic num.: sections); 116 (part of Fishacre *In 4Sent.*: ff. 123- 7) ; *151 (Gloucester OFM); *399 (Raymund of Penaforte, *Summa*; arabic num.: sections)

OXFORD

Blackfriars MS 1 (Dominican *Graduale*, c 1263; probably Spanish) □ *Bodleian Library* □ **Ashmole** 748 (Bible, Oxford); 757 (Sermons, possibly OFM, probably University); 1290 (Sermons of Guilelmus Peraldus OP) □ **MSS Auct** D.1.2, D.1.5, D.1.7, D.1.9, D.1.13 (Bible, NT: Gospels, Pauline Epistles, Peter I and II; glossed); D. 2. 6 ; D. 2. 11; D. 3. 2 (Bible); D. 3. 7 (Bible, annotated for preaching); D. 4. 9 (Bible, Oxford); D. 4. 11 (Bible); D. 4. 12 (Peter of Rheims OP, Sermons); D. 4. 13; D. 4. 18; D. 5. 9 (very small Bible); D. 5. 11; F. 5. 18; F. 5. 28; F. 5. 29; *F. 6. 4 (Oseney Abbey; blue) □ **Bodley** *4 (Merton; arabic num.: folios 104- 363; blue); 25 (sermons: English, Dominican); 35 (Peraldus, *Summa virtutum*); * 36 (pocket book, Franciscan); 62; *140 (Leicester OP; blue portion); 153 (Peraldus, *Summa vitiorum*); 157 (Hugh St. Caro OP, *Distinctiones*); *198 Grosseteste – Oxford OFM; many Grosst. sym.; arabic num.: folios 2- 129; blue); 200 (fol. 216- 224: *pecia* marks); 238; 252; 269; 275 (St. Jacques Paris, Con cordance, 3rd version); 310; 312; 333 (Robert Kilwardby OP); 355; *365 (Merton); *383 (Robert Holcot OP – Crediton; arabic num.: sections; blue); 397; 406 (Peter of Rheims OP 1291, Sermons – English); 435; 457 (Peraldus, *Summa vitiorum*); 477; 631 (contains good text of Grosseteste, *Templum Dei*); 655 (English); *681 (R. Rufus of Cornwall OFM, part of *In 4Sent.*); *685 (*Tabula Septem Cust'* OFM; arabic num.: folios; blue); 689; 696; 700; 722 (Robert Holcot OP); *745 (contains Robert Bacon's commentary on the Psalter; arabic num.: folios); 751 and 752 (both contain works of Ambrose; similar scribal style); 771; 786 (English); 809; 830 (Grosseteste – Exeter; blue); 859; 897 □ **Canon. Pat. lat.** 7 (Concordance, first version) □ **Digby** (a collection of largely mathematical and scientific manuscripts); 10; 11; 37; 39; 40; 67; 76; * 77 (Grosseteste – Meaux; arabic num.: sections; blue portion); 90; 93; 153; 155; 168; 176; 190; 191; *204 (Robert Kilwardby OP, *De Ortu Scientiarum*); *212 (Merton; arabic num.: folios 2–129); 218 (John Pecham, treatise on *Optics*) □ **Gough Liturgical** 2 (writing 'above top-line'; pictures said to be fourteenth-century) □ **Hatton** *102 (Hereford OFM; Grosst. sym.); 107 (portable preacher's note book, Dominican) □ **James** 26, 31 (both have *exempla*, probably Odo of Cheriton, copied from Oxford, Corpus Christi College MS 32) □ **Latin** Bibl. d. 9 (thirteenth-century French Bible, transferred to Oxford Dominicans in the fourteenth century); Bibl.e. 7 (formerly Dyson Perrins MS 5 made for Oxford Dominicans, illuminated by William de Brailles); *Misc.c.75 (Thomas of Eccleston OFM; blue portion); Misc.d.74; Misc.f.37; th. e 16 (Peraldus OP, Sermons); th. e 17 (Peraldus OP, Sermons); th. e 39; th. e 46 (John of Abbeville, Sermons) □ **Laudian: Laud lat.** 12 (Bible); Laud lat. 13 (Bible, illuminated by William de Brailles); Laud lat. 31; Laud lat.114 (fols.7–174: work by William de Brailles) □ **Laud Miscellaneous** 2 (contains Simon Hinton OP, *Summa Juniorum*); 71; 128 (contains some of Robert Kilwardby OP, *Capitula*); 166 (contains Simon Hinton OP, *Summa Juniorum*); 172; 176; 209; 318 (Hugh St. Caro OP, Sermons); 323 (Peter of Rheims OP, Sermons); 357 (John of Abbeville, Sermons); 369 (Peraldus, *Summa vitiorum*); 374; 376; 380; 397 (contains Hinton's *Excepciones*); 439; 453; 504 (Hugh St. Caro OP, Sermons); 506 (Hugh St. Caro OP, Sermons; Peter of Rheims OP, Sermons); 511 (preacher's handbook OP; arabic num.: columns and Lines; few faces; blue); 530 (Peraldus, *Summa virtutum*); 544 (Peraldus, *Summae virtutum ac vitiorum*); 604 (*pecia* marks); 728; 746; 750 □ **Lyell** 6 (John of Abbeville, Sermons); 8; 11 □ **e Museo** 19; *29 (Simon Hinton OP, commentary on Minor Prophets; arabic num.: folios; blue); 121 □ **Rawlinson** A. 373 (Peraldus, sermons); C. 308; *C. 780 (Worcester OP; blue portion); C. 900; *C. 939 (Oseney Abbey; blue); C. 940 (Psalter – Abingdon Abbey); D. 235; D. 238; *G. 14 (small Oxford Bible – Lincoln College; blue portion); G. 26 (example of first Dominican biblical concordance) □ **Savile** 19; 20; * 21 (Grosseteste; blue portion) □ **Tanner** *165 (*Registrum Anglie de Libris Doctorum Auctorem Veterum*, Franciscan)

Manuscripts of Oxford Colleges Deposited in the Bodleian

Corpus Christi College 32 E; 43 (has Grosseteste's hand); *138 D (Robert Holcot OP; arabic num.: sections); 155; 182 C; *225 E (Beverley OP; arabic num.: sections [ff. 158- 252]) □ *Lincoln College* Gk. 33 C; *Lat. 33 C (Oxford OFM; arabic num.: pages); Lat. 45 D; Lat. 54 D; Lat. 79; Lat. 98 E; Lat. 113 (Guy of Evreux OP, sermons) □ *Magdalen College* 14; 33 (Peraldus OP, sermons); *54 (Warwick OP; blue); 87 (*Manipulus florum*) □ 122- 132 (all glossed biblical books; MSS 124, 129, 131, 132 form the 'Oseney Bible'); 145; 174; 179; 195; 226 (Missal, Dominican use) □ *New College* 14; 70 F (example of the second Dominican Biblical concordance); *112 E (Richard Fishacre OP, *In 4Sent.*; arabic num.: folios and lines); 116 C (*pecia* marks, Destrez); 190 B; 285 D; 322 (Psalter, some illuminations by William de Brailles) □ *Oriel College* *15 (folios 1- 112: R. Armagh; arabic num.: lines; folios 113ff.: Robert Holcot OP, *In 4Sent.* - [part]; arabic num.: sections); 16 (*Manipulus florum*); * 43 (Richard Fishacre OP, *In 4Sent.*) □ *St. John's College* * 65 (Warwick OP; arabic num.: folios; faces; blue); *198 (three Dominican priories; arabic num.: folios [f. 25 to end]) □ *Trinity College* 17 E; 37 D; 50 C (fine ruling of bottom margin lines); 59 C □ *University College* * 6 (Beverley OP); *21 (Raymund of Penaforte - St. Augustine Cant.; arabic num.: columns); 41 D; *67 D (Beverley OP; blue); 77 C; *113 B (Beverley OP; arabic num.: folios); 143 D; *190 C (Beverley OP; arabic num.: columns; running titles) □ *Balliol College* * 27 (Robert Holcot OP, *Wisdom*, possible *exemplar*; arabic num.: sections ; blue); * 57 (Richard Fishacre OP, *In 4Sent.*; arabic num.: sections); * 62 (R. Rufus of Cornwall OFM, *In 4Sent.*; arabic num.: columns and lines); * 71 (Robert Holcot OP, *In 4Sent.*; arabic num.: page; blue); *133 (Cambridge OFM; blue portion); 193; 196 (R. Rufus of Cornwall OFM, *In 4Sent.*); *214 (Cambridge OFM; arabic num.: folios 1- 306); *215 (Robert Kilwardby OP, *Tabulae* of Augustine; arabic num.: folios 1- 121); 219 (Simon Hinton, *Summa Juniorum*) □ *Merton College* 22 (John of Abbeville, sermons); 96 (John Pecham OFM, *Quodlibets*); *111 (Robert Kilwardby OP, *Tabula super sententia*; blue); *113 (Robert Holcot OP, *In 4Sent.*; blue); 131 (Kilwardby); *132 (Oxford OP; arabic num.: folios 1- 56); 138 (Thomas of Sutton OP, *Quodlibets*); 197 (Robert Kilwardby OP, *Intentiones*); 202 (Simon Hinton OP, *Summa Juniorum*); 237 (H.2.4) (cf. Ashmole 757)

ROME

Santa Sabina Archivium Generale Ordinis Praedicatorum MS XIV L. 1 □ *Biblioteca Apostolica Vaticana* Ottobuoni *69 (Cambridge OFM; arabic num.: folios); *71 (Cambridge OFM; *pecia* marks in part of MS; arabic num.: folios); *96 (Cambridge OFM; arabic num.: folios 1- 60, 70- 141); *99 (Cambridge OP; arabic num.: folios); 101; *150 (Cambridge OP; arabic num.: folios 1- 40); *159 (Cambridge OP); *271 (Cambridge OP; arabic num.: columns); 277; *325 (Cambridge OFM; arabic num.: columns); 352; *442 (Cambridge OP; arabic num.: folios 1- 60); *611 (Cambridge OFM; arabic num.: sections); 623; 640; *758 (Cambridge OP; 'English' hand; blue); *862 (London OP); 2048; *2055 (Cambridge OP; arabic num.: folios 1- 58, lines [ff. 57- 68]); 2058

WORCESTER
Worcester Cathedral MS F. 5: cf MS Ashmole 757; Merton 237

Manuscripts Consulted in Microfilm

COLMAR
Bibliotheque Municipale MS 34 fol. 52a–52vb
MILAN
Ambrosiana MS O. 1. fol. 95r–97v

PARIS
Arsenal MS 857 (2e serie) fol. 74a–76a □ *Bibliothèque Nationale* lat. MS 15971: fol. 83vb–84a, fol.181va–181vb; lat. MS 16501: fol. 39a–40a

ROUEN MS A 571 (Cat. 634) fol. 92v–96v

VENDOME MS 218 fol. 107r–107v

VENICE
Biblioteca dei Redentoristi di S.Maria della Fava MS La Fava 29 (cols. 569–574: sermons of Aldobrandinus de Cavalcantibus OP Cols AN; MS La Fava 30: fol.126va–129va; MS La Fava 39: fol.74r–76v

WROCLAW
Biblioteka Uniwersyteka MS I.Q. 427: fol.135v–137r

Bibliography

ABBREVIATIONS

ACTA	*Acta Capitulorum Generalium Ordinis Praedicatorum*, ed. B.M. Reichert OP
AFP	*Archivum Fratrum Praedicatorum*
AHDLMA	*Archives d'histoire doctrinale et littéraire du moyen age*
ALKG	*Archiv für Litteratur und Kirchengeschichte des Mittelalters*
BLR	*Bodleian Library Record*
BQR	*Bodleian Quarterly Record*
BRUC	*Biographical Register of the University of Cambridge to 1500*, ed. A. Basil Emden
BRUO	*A Biographical Register of the University of Oxford to 1500*, ed. A. Basil Emden
CPR	*Calendar of Patent Rolls, Henry III to Edward III 1216–1292*, ed. J.G. Black, et al.
EETS	The Early English Text Society
EHR	*English Historical Review*
IMSS	International Medieval Sermons Symposium
JEH	*Journal of Ecclesiastical History*
MARS	*Medieval and Renaissance Studies*
Med.St.	*Mediaeval Studies* (Toronto)
MEFRM	*Mélanges de l'École Française de Rome*
MEH	*Medievalia et Humanistica*
MOPH	Monumenta Ordinis Fratrum Praedicatorum Historica
NS	New Series
OHS	Oxford Historical Society
PBA	*Proceedings of the British Academy*
PG	*Patrologiae Cursus Completus, series Graeca*, ed. J.P. Migne, 162 volumes (Paris, 1857–1866)
PIMS	Pontifical Institute of Mediaeval Studies, Toronto
PL	*Patrologiae Cursus Completus, series Latina*, ed. J.P. Migne, 221 volumes (Paris, 1844–1864)
RB	*Revue Bénédictine*
RS	Rolls Series
RTAM	*Recherches de théologie ancienne et médiévale*
SCH	*Studies in Church History*
SOPMA	*Scriptores Ordinis Praedicatorum Medii Aevi*, ed. T. Kaeppeli
TRHS	*Transactions of the Royal Historical Society*

Acta Canonizationis S. Dominici. In *Monumenta Historica Sancti Patris nostri Dominici* 2. Ed. M.-H. Laurent. MOPH 16. Rome: S. Sabina, 1935.

Acta Capitulorum Generalium Ordinis Praedicatorum. Ed. Benedikt Maria Reichert. 9 vols. MOPH 3-4, 8-14. Rome: In domo generalitia; Stuttgart: apud J. Roth, 1898-1904 .

Alfred, King. "The Proverbs of Alfred." Ed. R. Morris. In *An Old English Miscellany*. EETS 49. London: Early English Text Society, 1872.

Annales Monastici. Vol. 3: *Annales prioratus de Dunstaplia (AD 1-1297); Annales Monasterii de Bermundeseia (AD 1042-1432)*. Ed. Henry Richards Luard. Rerum Brittannicarum Medii Aevi Scriptores 36. London: Longmans, Green, 1866.

Anselm, Saint. *Basic Writings: Proslogium; Monologium; Gaunilon's 'On behalf of the fools'; Cur Deus homo*. 2nd ed. La Salle, IL: Open Court Publishing. 1962.

Aron, Marguerite. *St Dominic's Successor: The Life of Blessed Jordan of Saxony, Master-General of the Dominican Order 1222-37*. London: Blackfriars, 1955.

Ashton, T.H., ed. *The Early Oxford Schools*. Vol. 1 in *The History of the University of Oxford*, ed. R.J.A.I. Catto. Oxford: Clarendon Press, 1984.

Aubert, Marcel. *High Gothic Art*. London: Methuen, 1964.

Augustine of Hippo, Saint. *De Doctrina Christiana*. PL 34: 15-122. Trans. D.W. Robertson as *On Christian Doctrine*. New York: Bobbs-Merrill, 1958.

Aulen, Gustav. *Christus Victor: An Historical Study of the Three Main Types of the Idea of the Atonement*. Trans. A.G. Hebert. London: SPCK, 1931.

Baker, David. *Excavations at Elstow Abbey, 1965-1970*. Bedford: Bedforshire Archaeological Council, 1970.

Baker, Derek, ed. *Medieval Women*. SCH Subsidia 1. Oxford: Basil Blackwell 1978.

Baldwin, C.S. *Mediaeval Rhetoric and Poetic to 1400*. New York, 1929.

Baldwin, John W. *Masters, Princes and Merchants: The Social Views of Peter the Chanter and His Circle*. 2 vols. Princeton: University Press 1970.

Banks, M.M., ed. *An Alphabet of Tales*. [BL MS Add. 25719]. EETS 126-127. 2 vols. London: Early English Text Society, 1904-1905.

Barraclough, Geoffrey. *The Medieval Papacy*. London: Thames & Hudson, 1968.

Bartlett, Robert. *The Making of Europe: Conquest, Colonization and Cultural Change 950-1350*. London: Penguin/BCA, 1993.

Bataillon, Louis-J. *La prédication au xiiie siècle en France et Italie*. Variorum Collected Series 402. Aldershot: Variorum, 1993.

—. "Sur quelques Sermons de Saint Bonaventura." In *S. Bonaventura, 1274-1974* (Grottaferrata: Collegio S. Bonaventura, 1973), 495-515.

—. "Les Sermons de Saint Thomas et la 'Catena Aurea.'" In *St.Thomas Aquinas, 1274-1974 (qv)*, 67-75.

—. "La predicazione dei religiosi mendicanti del secolo xiii nell'Italia centrale."
    MEFRM 89 (1977), 691–694.
—. "Les Instruments de travail des prédicateurs au xiiie siècle." In *Culture et
    travail intellectuel dans l'occident médiéval*, ed. G. Hasenor and J. Longère
    (Paris: Centre National de la Recherche Scientifique, 1978), 197–209.
—. "Classifying Medieval Sermons." Paper given at IMSS Conference 1979.
    Published as "Approaches to the Study of Medieval Sermons." *Leeds
    Studies in English*, NS 11 (1980), 19–35.
—. "L'emploi du langage philosophique dans les sermons du treizième siècle."
    In *Sprache und Erkenntnis im Mittelalter*, ed. A. Zimmermann, Miscellanea
    Mediaevalia 13.2 (Berlin–New York: de Gruyter, 1981), 983–991.
—. "'Similitudines' et 'exempla' dans les sermons du xiiie siècle." In *The Bible
    in the Medieval World: Essays in Memory of Beryl Smalley*, ed. Katharine
    Walsh and Diana Wood, SCH Subsidia 4 (Oxford: Basil Blackwell, 1985),
    191–205.
—. "Les Images dans les sermons du xiiie siècle." *Freiburger Zeitschrift für
    Philosophie und Theologie* 37 (1990), 327–395.
—. "Intermediaires entre les traites de morale pratiques et les sermons: les
    distinctions bibliques alphabetiques." In *Les genres littéraires dans les sources
    théologiques et philosophiques médiévales: définition, critique et exploitation*
    (Louvain la Neuve: Université Catholique de Louvain, 1982), 213–226.
—. "L'Agir Humain d'àpres les distinctions bibliques du xiiie siècle." In
    L'Homme et son Univers au Moyen Age (Louvain la Neuve, 1986), 776–790.
—. "Les 'Exempla' dans les sermons universitaires." Unpublished paper,
    courtesty of author.
Beck, Hans-George; Karl August Fink; Josef Glazik; Erwin Iserloh; and Hans
    Wolter. *From the High Middle Ages to the Eve of the Reformation.* Vol 4 in *The
    History of the Church*, ed. Hubert Jedin and trans. Anselm Biggs. London:
    Burns Oates, 1980.
Berg, Dieter. *Armut und Wissenschaft: Beitrage zur Geschichte des Studienwesens
    der Bettelorden im 13.Jahrhundert.* Geschichte und Gesellschaft 15.
    Dusseldorf, 1977.
Bériou, Nicole. *La Prédication au béguinage de Paris pendant l'année liturgique
    1272–73.* Paris: Etudes Augustiniennes 1978.
—. *Sermons aux clercs et sermons aux 'simple gens': La prédication de Ranulph de
    la Houblonnière à Paris au xiiie siècle.* Paris: Etudes Augustiniennes 1980.
Berlioz, Jacques and M.A. Polo de Beaulieu. *Exempla médiévaux: Introduction à
    la recherche, suivi des tables critiques de l''Index exemplorum' de Frederic C.
    Tubach.* Classiques de la littérature orale. Garae/Carcassonne: Hésiode,
    1992.
Bernard, Saint. *Sermons on the Canticle of Canticles.* 2 vols. Dublin: Browne &
    Nolan, 1920).

Bernard of Clairvaux. *Opera genuina.* 3 vols. Paris: Gauthier Fratres, 1836.

Berthier, Joachim Joseph, ed.: *see* Humbert of Romans.

Bolton, Brenda. "Innocent III's Treatment of the *Humiliati.*" *SCH* 8 (1972): 73–82.

Bonniwell, William R. OP. *A History of the Dominican Liturgy 1215–1945.* New York: J.F. Wagner, 1945.

Bougerol, Jacques-G. "Les sermons dans les 'studia' des mendiants." In *Le scuole degli ordini mendicanti (secoli xiii–xiv),* Convegni del Centro di studi sulla spiritualità medievale 17 (Todi: Presso l'Accademia Tudertina, 1978), 251–280.

Boyle, Leonard E. *A Study of the Works Attributed to William of Pagula.* Unpublished DPhil thesis. Oxford, 1956. [Bodleian Library MS PhD d. 1710, 1711.]

—. "Three English Pastoral *Summae.*" *Studia Gratiana* 11 (1969), 114–144.

—. "The Constitution 'Cum ex eo' of Boniface VIII: Education of Parochial Clergy." *Med.St.* 24 (1962), 263–302.

—. "The *Summa confessorum* of John of Freiburg and the Popularization of the Moral Teaching of St. Thomas and Some of His Contemporaries." In *St. Thomas Aquinas, 1274–1974 (qv),* 2: 245–268.

—. "Aspects of Clerical Education in Fourteenth-Century England." In *The Fourteenth Century,* ed. Paul E. Szarmach and Bernard S. Levy, *Acta* [Binghamton, NY] 4 (1977), 19–32.

—. "Notes on the Education of the 'Fratres Communes' in the Dominican Order in the Thirteenth Century." In *Xenia medii aevi historiam illustrantia oblata Thomae Kaeppeli, OP,* ed. Raymond Creytens (Rome: Edizioni di Storia e Letteratura, 1978), 249–267.

—. "The Setting of the *Summa Theologiae* of Saint Thomas." The Etienne Gilson Series 5. Toronto: PIMS, 1982.

—. "Summae confessorum." In *Les genres litteraires dans les sources théologiques et philosophiques médiévales: définition, critique, et exploitation* (Louvain la Neuve: Université Catholique de Louvain, 1982), 227–237.

—. "The Fourth Lateran Council and Manuals of Popular Theology." In *The Popular Literature of Medieval England,* ed. Thomas J. Heffernan (Knoxville: University of Tennessee Press, 1985), 30–43.

Bremond, Claude; Jacques Le Goff; and Jean Claude Schmitt. *L'"Exemplum.'* Turnhout: Brepols 1982.

Breviarium Sacri Ordinis Praedicatorum. 2 vols. Mechlin: H. Dessain; P.J. Hanicq, 1865–1893.

Brooke, Rosalind and Christopher. *Popular Religion in the Middle Ages, 1000–1300.* London: Thames & Hudson 1984.

Brown, Carleton. *English Lyrics of the XIII Century.* Oxford: Clarendon Press, 1932.

Brown, William, ed. *The Register of Walter Giffard, Lord Archbishop of York, 1266–1279*. Surtees Society 109. Durham: Andrews, 1904.

Bund, J.W. Willis, ed. *Register of Bishop Godfrey Giffard, 1268–1301*. Worcester Historical Society. 2 vols. Oxford: James Parker & Co., 1902.

Burch, V. "The 'Excepciones' from Simon of Hinton's *Summa*." *MEH* 3 (1948), 69–80.

Calendar of the Patent Rolls and others under the superintendence of the deputy Keeper of the Records, M.C. Maxwell-Lyte. London, 1891– .

Callus, Daniel A. *Robert Grosseteste, Scholar and Bishop*. Oxford: Clarendon Press, 1955.

—. "Introduction of Aristotelian Learning to Oxford." *PBA* 19 (1943), 229–281.

—. "The Tabulae Super Originalia Patrum of Robert Kilwardby OP." In *Studia mediaevalia in honorem admodum Reverendi Patris Raymundi Josephi Martin, OP* (Brugis Flandorum: De Tempel, [1948]), 243–270.

—. "New Manuscripts of Kilwardby's *Tabulae super Originalia Patrum*." *Dominican Studies* 2 (1949), 38–45.

—. "The Contribution to the Study of the Fathers Made by the Thirteenth Century Oxford Schools." *JEH* 5 (1954), 139–148.

Cannon, Joanna. "Inghilterra." "Panorama degli studia degli ordini mendicanti." In *Le scuole degli ordini mendicanti (secoli xiii–xiv)*, Convegni del Centro di studi sulla spiritualità medievale 17 (Todi: presso l'Accademia Tudertina, 1978), 93–116.

Caplan, Harry. "Bibliography of the Writings of Harry Caplan." In *Of Eloquence: Studies in Ancient and Mediaeval Rhetoric*, ed. Anne King and Helen North (Ithaca and London: Cornell University Press, 1970), 271–276.

—. "A Late Mediaeval Tractate on Preaching." In *Of Eloquence*, 40–78. *See also* Pseudo-Thomas of Aquinas.

—. "'Henry of Hesse' on the Art of Preaching." In *Of Eloquence*, 135–159.

Cappelli, A. *Cronologia, cronografia e calendario perpetuo*, 3rd ed. Milan: Hoepli, 1969.

Catalogue of Romances in the Department of Manuscripts in the British Museum, ed. H.L.D. Ward and J.A. Herbert, 3 vols. London: Printed by the order of the Trustees, British Museum, 1883–1910.

Charland, Th.M. *Artes Praedicandi. Contribution à l'histoire de la rhétorique au moyen âge*. Ottawa: Institut d'études médiévales, 1936

Cheney, Christopher R. *English Synodalia of the Thirteenth Century*. 1941. 2nd imp. with new introduction. London: Oxford University Press, 1968.

—. *Episcopal Visitation of Monasteries in the Thirteenth Century*. Manchester: Manchester University Press, 1931.

—. *Handbook of Dates for Students of English History*. London: Offices of the Royal Historical Society, 1945.

—. "The Earliest English Diocesan Statutes." *EHR* 75 (1960), 1-29.

—. "Statute-Making in the English Church in the Thirteenth Century." In *Proceedings of the Second International Congress of Medieval Canon Law*, ed. Stephen Kuttner and J. Joseph Ryan, Monumenta Juris Canonici: series C, Subsidia 1 (E. Civitate Vaticana: S. Congregatio de Seminariis et Studiorum Universitatibus, 1965), 399-414. Reprinted in Cheney, *Medieval Texts and Studies* (Oxford: Clarendon Press, 1973), 138-157.

Chenu, Marie-Dominique. *La Théologie au douzième siècle*. Paris, 1957. Trans. J. Taylor and L.K. Little as *Nature, Man and Society in the Twelfth Century*. Chicago: Chicago University Press, 1968.

—. *La Théologie comme science au xiiie siècle*. Paris: Vrin, 1957. Trans. A.H.H. Green-Armytage as *Is Theology a Science?* London: Hawthorn Books, 1959.

—. "Moines, clercs, laics au carrefour de la vie evangélique." *Revue d'Histoire Ecclésiastique* 49 (1954), 59-89.

Cockerell, Sydney C. *The Work of W. de Brailes, an English Illuminator of the Thirteenth Century*. Cambridge: Roxburghe Club, 1930.

Congar, Yves M.J. *La Tradition et les Traditions*. Paris: A. Fayard, 1960-1963. Trans. M. Naseby and T. Rainborough as *Tradition and Traditions: An Historical and a Theological Essay*. London: Burns & Oates, 1966.

Corrigan, Felicitas. *Benedictine Tapestry*. London: Darton, Longman, Todd, 1991.

Coxe, H.O. *Catalogus Codicum MSS qui in Collegiis Aulisque Oxoniensibus hodie adseverantur*. 2 vols. Oxford, 1852.

Crane, T.F., ed.: *see* Jacques de Vitry.

Creytens, Raymond. "Les Constitutions des frères prêcheurs dans la rédaction de St. Raymond de Penafort (1241)." *AFP* 18 (1948), 5-68.

Cross, F.L.; and E.A. Livingstone. *The Oxford Dictionary of the Christian Church*, 2nd ed. London: Oxford University Press, 1964.

Cruel, Rudolf. *Geschichte der Deutschen Predigt im Mittelalter*. Detmold, 1879. Reprinted, Hildesheim: Olms, 1966.

Daniélou, Jean; A.H. Courtain; and John Kent. *Historical Theology*. The Pelican Guide to Modern Theology 2. Harmondsworth, Middlesex: Penguin Books, 1971.

Daniélou, Jean. *The Origins of Latin Christianity*. A History of Early Christian Doctrine Before the Council of Nicea 3. Trans. David Smith and John Austin Baker. London: Darton, Longman, Todd, 1977.

Davis, F.N. ed. *Dioecesis Lincolniensis, Rotuli Roberti Grosseteste*. Canterbury and York Society 10. Horncastle: Issued for the Lincoln Record Society, 1913.

d'Avray, David. *The Transformation of the Medieval Sermon*. Unpublished DPhil thesis. Oxford, 1976. [Bodleian Library, MS D.Phil. c 2088.]

—. *The Preaching of the Friars*. Oxford: Clarendon Press, 1985.

Davy, Marie-M. *Les sermons universitaires Parisiens de 1230-1231*. Paris: Vrin, 1931.

Delhaye, Philippe, ed.: *see Florilegium Morale Oxoniense*

Delcorno, Carlo. *Giordano da Pisa e l'antica predicazione volgere*. Florence: Biblioteca di 'Lettere italiane' 14. Firenze: Olschki, 1975.

Denifle, Henri, ed. *Constitutiones antique ordinis fratrum predicatorum*. In *Archiv für Literatur und Kirchen Geschichte des Mittelalters* 1 (Berlin, 1885), 193–227.

—; and A. Chatelain, ed. *Chartularium Universitatis Parisiensis*. 4 vols. Paris: Delalain, 1889–1897.

Destrez, Jean. *La 'pecia' dans les manuscrits universitaires du xiiie et xive siècles*. Paris: Jacques Vautrain, 1935.

Destrez, Jean; and Marie-Dominique Chenu. "Exemplaria universitaires des xiiie et xive siècles." *Scriptorium* 7 (1953), 68–80.

Dickinson, Francis Henry, ed. *Missale ad Usum insignis et praeclarae Ecclesiae Sarum*. Oxford and London: Cambridge University Press, 1861–1883. Repr. Farnborough, Hants.: Gregg International, 1970.

Dondaine, Antoine. "La Somme de Simon de Hinton." *RTAM* 9 (1937), 5–22, 204–218.

—. "Guillaume Peyraut: vie et oeuvres." *AFP* 18 (1948), 162–236.

Douais, Celestin, ed. *Acta Capitulorum Provincialium Ordinis Fratrum Praedicatorum, 1239–1302*. Toulouse: Éditions Privat, 1894.

Drane, Augusta T. *The History of St. Dominic, Founder of the Friars Preachers*. London and New York: Longmans, Green, 1891.

Duby, Georges, ed. *A History of Private Life*. Vol 2: *Revelations of the Medieval World*. Trans. Arthur Goldhammer. Cambridge, MA: Belknap Press; Harvard University Press, 1988.

Dugdale, W. *Monasticon Anglicanum: A History of the Abbies and Other Monasteries ...* . 6 vols. London, 1655–1673, 1622–1723. Ed. R. Dodsworth, 3 vols. London: Bohn, 1846.

Eadmer, d. 1124. *The Life of St. Anselm by Eadmer*. Ed. with an introduction, notes and translation by R.W. Southern. London: T. Nelson, 1962.

Ekwall, Eilert. *The Concise Oxford Dictionary of English Place-Names*. London: Oxford University Press, 1974.

Emden, A. Basil. *A Biographical Register of the University of Oxford to 1500*. 3 vols. Oxford: Clarendon Press, 1957–1959.

—. *A Biographical Register of the University of Cambridge to 1500*. Cambridge: Cambridge University Press, 1963.

—. "Dominican Confessors and Preachers." *AFP* 32 (1962), 180–210.

—. *A Survey of Dominicans in England*. Institutum historicam fratrum praedicatorum dissertationes historicae 17. Rome: S. Sabina, 1967.

Étienne de Bourbon. *Anecdotes historiques, legendes et Applogues tirés du receuil inédit d'Étienne de Bourbon, dominicain du xiiie, siècle*. Ed. Albert Lecoy de la Marche. Paris: Renouard, 1877.

Evans, Gillian R. *Anselm and Talking about God.* Oxford: Clarendon Press, 1978.
—. *Anselm and a New Generation.* Oxford: Clarendon Press, 1980.
—. *Anselm.* London: Geoffrey Chapman 1989.

Florilegium Morale Oxoniense (MS Bodl. 633): Prima pars: Flores philosophorum, ed. Philippe Delhaye; *Secunda pars: Flores auctorem,* ed. C.H. Talbot. Analecta Mediaevalia Namurcensia 5, 6. Louvain-Lille: Nauwelaerts, 1955-1956.
Forshaw, Helen P. *The Pastoral Ministry of the Priest Confessor in the Early Middle Ages, 600-1100.* Unpublished Ph.D.thesis. London, 1976.
—, ed. *Speculum Religiosorum* and *Speculum Ecclesie* in *Auctores Brittanici Medii Aevi.* London: British Academy, 1973.
Forte, Stephen L. OP. "Th. Hopeman OP: An unknown Biblical Commentator." *AFP* 25 (1955), 311-344.
—, ed. "A Cambridge Dominican Collector of 'Exempla' in the Thirteenth Century" [part of MS Roy 7 D i]. *AFP* 28 (1958), 115-148.
Frere, William Howard, ed. *Graduale Sarisburiense: A Reproduction in Facsimile of a Manuscript of the Thirteenth Century ... .* London: B. Quaritch, 1894.

Galbraith, G.R. *The Constitution of the Dominican Order 1216-1360.* Manchester: Manchester University Press, 1925.
de Ghellinck, Joseph. *Le Mouvement théologique du xiie siècle.* 2nd ed. Bruges: Éditions 'De Tempel,' 1948.
Gibbs, Marion; and Jane Lang. *Bishops and Reform, 1215-1272.* London: Oxford University Press, 1934.
Gibson, Strickland. *Early Oxford Bindings,* London Bibliographical Society Illustrated Monographs 10. Oxford: Printed for the Bibliographical Society, 1903.
—, ed. *Statuata Antiqua Universitatis Oxoniensis.* Oxford: Clarendon Press, 1931.
Gilson, Etienne. "Michel Menot et la technique du sermon médiéval." *Revue d'Histoire Franciscaine* 2 (1925), 301-350. Reprinted in Gilson, *Les Idées et les Lettres* (Paris: Vrin, 1932).
Gleeson, Philip, OP. "Dominican Liturgical Manuscripts from Before 1254." *AFP* 42 (1972), 81-135.
Glorieux, Palémon. *Répertoire des maîtres en théologie de Paris au xiiie siècle.* 2 vols. Paris: Vrin, 1933-1934.
—. "Les 'Deflorationes' de Werner de Saint Blaise." In *Melanges Joseph de Ghellinck, SJ* (Gembloux: J. Duculot, 1951), 699-721.
[*Glossa ordinaria; glossa interlinearis.*] *Biblia sacra cum glossa ordinaria et glossa interlinearis ... et postilla Nicolai Lyriani.* Lyons, 1545, 1590; Paris 1590; Venice, 1603; Antwerp, 1617.
Grensted, L.W. *A Short History of the Doctrine of Atonement.* Manchester: Manchester University Press, 1920.

Griffiths, R.G., ed.: *see* Thomas de Cantilupe.

Grosseteste, Robert. *Templum Dei.* Ed. Joseph Goering and Frank Mantello. Toronto Medieval Latin Texts. Toronto: Centre for Medieval Studies, 1984.

—. *Epistolae.* Ed. Henry Richard Luard. Rerum Britannicarum Medii Aevi Scriptores 25. London: Longman, Green, 1861.

Guerrini, Francesco, ed. *Ordinarium juxta Sacri Ordinis Fratrum Praedicatorum.* Iussu L. Theissling. Rome: apud Collegium Angelicum, 1921.

Guilelmus Peraldus [printed under the name of William+ of Auvergne or William of Paris]. *Guilielmi Alverni episcopi. 3. Parisiensis mathematici perfectissimi eximii philosophi ac theologi praestantissimi Opera Omnia tomis duobus contenta.* Paris: F. Hotot, 1674.

—. *Sermones eximii praestantesque, super Epistolas Dominicales totius anni.* Lyons, 1576.

—. *Homilia sive Sermones super Epistola et Evangelia.* Lyons, 1576.

—. *Summae Virtutum ac Vitiorum.* Antwerp, 1588.

Gumbley, Walter. "Provincial Priors and Vicars of the English Dominicans." *EHR* 33 (1918), 243–251.

de Hamel, Christopher F.R. *The Production and Circulation of Glossed Books of the Bible in the Twelfth and Early Thirteenth Centuries.* Unpublished DPhil. thesis. Oxford, 1978. [Bodleian Library, MS D.Phil.c. 2678.]

Haskins, Charles H. *The Renaissance of the Twelfth Century.* Cambridge, MA: Harvard University Press, 1927.

Heer, Friedrich. *The Medieval World: Europe 1100–1350.* London: Weidenfeld 1962.

Henderson, W.G., ed. *Missale as usum insignis Ecclesiae eboracensis.* 2 vols. Surtees Society 59, 60. Durham–London–Edinburgh: Published for the Surtees Society, 1874.

—. *Manuale et Processionale ad Usum insignis Ecclesiae eboracensis.* Surtees Society 63. Durham–London–Edinburgh: Published for the Surtees Society, 1875.

Herbert, J.A., ed.: *see Catalogue of Romances.*

Hervieux, Léopold, ed. *Les Fabulistes depuis le siècle d'Auguste jusqu'à la fin du moyen age.* Tome IV: *Etudes de Cheriton et ses derivés, ('Fabulae' et 'Parabolae' d'Odo de Cheriton).* Paris: Firmin-Didot, 1896.

Hill, Rosalind T., ed. *The Rolls and Register of Bishop Oliver Sutton 1280–99.* 8 vols. Hereford: Printed for the Lincoln Record Society, 1948–1986.

Hinnebusch, William A. *The History of the Dominican Order.* 2 vols. New York: Alba House, 1966–1973.

—. "Foreign Dominican Students and Professors at the Oxford Blackfriars." In *Oxford Studies Presented to Daniel A. Callus,* Oxford Historical Society, NS 16 (Oxford: Clarendon Press, 1964), 101–134.

—. *The Early English Friars Preachers.* Institutum fratres praedicatorum, dissertationes historicae, fasc. 14. Rome: S. Sabina, 1951.

Horwood, A.J., ed. *A Catalogue of the Ancient Manuscripts Belonging to the Honourable Society of Gray's Inn.* London: Spottiswoode, 1869.

Humbert of Romans. *De eruditione religiosorum praedicatorum.* Ed. Marguerinde de la Bigne. In *Bibliothece Veterum Patrum,* vol 25 (Lyons, 1677), 426–567.

—. *De vita regulari.* Ed. Joachim Joseph Berthier. 2vols. Turin: Marietti, 1956.

—. *Treatise on Preaching.* Trans. W.M. Conlon. Westminster, MD: Newman Press, 1951.

Humphreys, K.W. *The Book Provisions of the Mediaeval Friars, 1215–1400.* Amsterdam: Erasmus Booksellers, 1964.

Hunt, Richard W. "Manuscripts Containing the Indexing Symbols of Robert Grosseteste" *BLR* 4 (1953), 241–244.

—. [Bodleian Library]. *An Exhibition to Commemorate the 750th Anniversary of the Coming of the Grey Friars to Oxford, 1224–1974.* Oxford: Bodleian Library, 1974.

See also Medieval Learning and Literature.

International Medieval Sermon Studies Symposium. Report from the 1978 Symposium. *Reports.* Oxford: Linacre College, 1979.

Jacques de Vitry. *The 'Exempla' or Illustrative Stories from the 'Sermones Vulgares' of Jacques de Vitry.* Ed. T.F. Crane. London: for the Folklore Society, 1890.

James, Montague R. "Description of the Ancient Manuscripts in the Ipswich Public Libraries." *Proceedings of the Suffolk Institute of Archaeology and Natural History* 22 (1936), 86–103.

Jones, L.W. "Pricking Manuscripts: The Instruments and Their Significance." *Speculum* 21 (1946), 389–403.

Jordan of Saxony. *Beati Jordani de Saxonia Epistulae.* Ed. Angelus Walz. MOPH 23. Rome: Institutum historicum fratrum praedicatorum, 1951.

Jungmann, Josef A. *The Mass of the Roman Rite: Its Origins and Development..* 2 vols. New York: Benziger Brothers, 1951–1955.

—. *The Early Liturgy to the Time of Gregory the Great.* London: Darton, Longman & Todd 1960.

Kaeppeli, Thomas, ed. *Scriptores Ordinis Praedicatorum medii aevi.* 3 vols. Rome: S. Sabina, 1970–1980.

—; and Antoine Dondaine, ed. *Acta Capitulorum Provincialium Provinciae Romanae, 1234–1344.* MOPH 20. Rome: S. Sabina, 1941.

Kemp, Eric. *Canonization and Authority in the Western Church.* London: Oxford University Press, 1948.

—. "The Attempted Canonization of Robert Grosseteste." In *Robert Grosseteste, Scholar and Bishop,* ed. D.A. Callus (Oxford: Clarendon Press, 1955), 241–246.

Kennedy, V.L. "The Franciscan 'Ordo Missae' in the Thirteenth Century."
    Med.St. 2 (1940), 204–222.
—. "The Handbook of Master Peter Chancellor of Chartres." Med.St. 5 (1943),
    1–38.
—. "The Lateran Missal and Some Allied Documents." Med.St. 15 (1952), 61–78.
—. "The Calendar of the Early Thirteenth-Century Curial Missal." Med.St. 20
    (1958), 113–126.
Ker, Neil R. Medieval Libraries of Great Britain: A List of Surviving Books. 2nd ed.
    London: Royal Historical Society, 1964.
—. Medieval Manuscripts in British Libraries. Vol. 1: London; Vol. 2: Abbotsford to
    Keele; Vol. 3: Lampeter to Oxford; Vol. 4: Paisley to York (with A.J. Piper).
    Oxford: Clarendon Press, 1969, 1977, 1983, 1992.
—. "Cardinal Cervini's Manuscripts from the Cambridge Friars." In Xenia Medii
    Aevi Historiam Illustrantia oblata Thomae Kaeppeli OP (Rome: Edizioni di
    storia e letteratura, 1978), 51–80.
—. "From 'above Top Line' to 'below Top Line': A Change in Scribal Practice."
    Celtica 5 (1960), 13–16.
    See also [Oxford, Bodleian Library.] "The Sequence of Medieval Bookbinding".
Knowles, David M.; and R. Neville Hadcock. Medieval Religious Houses of Eng-
    land and Wales. 2nd ed. London: Longman, 1971.

Ladurie, Emmanuel Le Roy. Montaillou. Trans. Barbara Bray. London: Scolar
    Press, 1978.
Lattey, C., ed. The Atonement. Cambridge: Heffer, 1928.
Lawley S.W., ed. Breviarium ad Usum insignis Ecclesiae Eboracensis. Surtees
    Society 71, 75. 2 vols. Durham–London–Edinburgh: Andrews, 1880–1883.
Lawrence, C. Hugh. Medieval Monasticism. 2nd ed. London: Longman, 1989.
—. The Friars: The Impact of the Early Mendicant Movement on Western Society.
    London: Longman, 1994.
—. St. Edmund of Abingdon. Oxford: Clarendon Press, 1960.
—. "The University of Oxford and the Chronicle of the Barons' War." EHR 95
    (1980), 99–113.
—. "St. Richard of Chichester." In Studies in Sussex Church History. ed. M.J.
    Kitch (London: Leopard's Head Press, 1981), 35–55.
—. "The University in State and Church." In The Early Oxford Schools, ed. T.H.
    Ashton, 97–150.
Leclercq, Jean. L'idée de la royauté du Christ au Moyen Âge. Paris: Éditions du
    Cerf, 1959.
Lecoy de la Marche, Albert. La Chaire française au Moyen Âge. 2nd ed. Paris:
    Renouard, 1886.
Legg, J. Wickham. Three Coronation Orders. Henry Bradshaw Society 19.
    London: Henry Bradshaw Society, 1900.

—, ed. *The Sarum Missal*. Oxford: Clarendon Press, 1916.

Le Goff, Jacques. *L'Uomo medievale*. Rome: Bari, 1987. Trans. Lydia G. Cochrane as *The Medieval World*. London: Collins and Brown, 1990.

Lenfant, David, OP. *Concordantiae Augustinianae* (1656, 1665). Brussels: [Bruxelles Culture et Civilisation, 1963].

Lewry, P. Osmund. "A Passiontide Sermon of Robert Kilwardby OP [includes: Robert de Kilwardby, "Sermo in Dominica in Passione" (Cambridge, Trinity College MS 373, ff. 212v–215v)]." *AFP*, 52 (1982), 89–113].

Little, Andrew G. *The Grey Friars in Oxford*. Oxford: Clarendon Press, 1892.

—. *'Liber Exemplorum' ad Usum Praedicantium*. British Society of Franciscan Studies 1. Aberdoniae: Typis academicis, 1908.

—. *Studies in English Franciscan History*. University of Manchester, Historical Series 29. Manchester: Manchester University Press, 1917.

—. "A Record of the English Dominicans, 1314" *EHR* 5 (1890), 107–112; *EHR* 6 (1891), 752–753.

—. "The Educational Organisation of the Mendicant Friars in England." *TRHS* NS 8 (1894), 49–70.

—. "Provincial Priors and Vicars of the English Dominicans." *EHR* 33 (1918), 496–497.

—. "The Administrative Divisions of the Mendicant Orders in England." *EHR* 35 (1919), 205–209.

—. "The Franciscan School at Oxford." *Archivum Franciscanum Historicum* 19 (1926), 803–874.

—. "The Friars and the Foundation of the Faculty of Theology in the University of Cambridge." In *Melanges Mandonnet: Études d'histoire litteraire et doctrinale du Moyen Age*, Bibliothèque thomiste 13–14, 2 vols. (Paris: Vrin, 1930), 2: 389–401.

—; and R.C. Easterling. *The Franciscans and Dominicans at Exeter*. Exeter: A. Wheaton & Co., 1927.

—; and Franz Pelster. *Oxford Theology and Theologians, c. AD 1282–1302*. OHS 96. Oxford: Clarendon Press, 1934.

Long, R.James. "The Science of Theology according to Richard Fishacre." *Med.St.* 34 (1972), 79–98.

—. "Richard Fishacre and the Problem of the Soul." *The Modern Schoolman* 52 (1975), 263–70.

—. "Richard Fishacre's 'Quaestio' on the Ascension of Christ: An Edition." *Med.St.* 40 (1978), 30–55.

—. "The Virgin as Olive Tree: A Marian Sermon of Richard Fishacre and Science at Oxford." *AFP* 52 (1982), 77–87.

—. "Richard Fishacre." In *Dictionnaire de spiritualité, ascetique et mystique; doctrine et histoire*, ed. Marcel Viller et al., 16 vols. (Paris: Beauchesne, 1937–1994) 13 [1988]: 563–565.

Longère, Jean. *Oeuvres oratoires de maîtres parisiens au xiie siècle*. 2 vols. Paris, Études Augustiniennes, 1975.

—. *La Prédication médiévale*. Paris: Etudes Augustiniennes, 1983.

Lopez, R.S. "Concerning Surnames and Places of Origin." *MEH* 8 (1954), 6–17.

Lottin, Odon. *Psychologie et morale au xiie et xiiie siècles*. 6 vols. Louvain: Abbaye du Mont César, 1942–1960.

Luard, Henry Richards, ed.: *see Annales Monastici; Grosseteste; Matthew Paris*.

de Lubac, Henri. *Exégèse médiévale: Les quatre sens de l'Écriture*. 4 vols. Paris: Aubier, 1959–1964.

McDonnell, E.W. *The Beguines and Beghards in Medieval Culture, with Special Emphasis on the Belgian Scene*. New Brunswick, NJ: Rutgers University Press, 1954.

McEvoy, James. *The Philosophy of Robert Grosseteste*. Oxford: Clarendon Press, 1982.

McGuire, Brian P. *The History of St. Anselm's Theology of Redemption in the Twelfth and Thirteenth Centuries*. Unpublished DPhil thesis. Oxford, 1970. [Bodleian Library, MS D Phil d 4990.]

McIntyre, J. *St. Anselm and his Critics: A Reinterpretation of the Cur Deus Homo*. Edinburgh and London: Oliver and Boyd, 1954.

Mansi, Giovanni Domenico, ed. *Sacrorum conciliorum nova et amplissima collectio* ... . 31 volumes. Florence and Venice: A. Zatta, 1759–1798.

Matthew Paris. *Chronica Majora* [*Mattaei Parisiensis, monachi Sancti Albani, Chronica majora*]. Ed. Henry Richards Luard. Rerum britannicarum medii aevi scriptores 57. 7 vols. London: Longman, 1872–1883.

Medieval Learning and Literature: Essays Presented to Richard William Hunt. Ed. J.J.G Alexander and Margaret T. Gibson. Oxford: Clarendon Press, 1976.

Meersseman, Gilles. "Les 'Nations' dans l'ancienne province dominicaine de France." *AFP* 8 (1938), 231–252.

Missale Romanum. Antwerp: Ex typographia Plantiniana, 1711.

Mollat, Michel. *The Poor in the Middle Ages*. Trans. Arthur Goldhammer. New Haven and London: Yale University Press, 1986.

Mone, Franz J., ed. *Hymni Latini Medii Aevi*. 3 vols. Freiburg: Herder, 1853–1855.

Morawski, J. *Les proverbes français anterieurs au xve siècle*. Paris: Champion, 1925.

Morin, Dom G. "Les plus ancien 'Comes' ou lectionnaire de l'église romaine." *RB* 27 (1910), 41–74.

—. "Liturgie et Basiliques de Rome au milieu du viie siècle d'après les listes d'évangiles de Wurzburg." *RB* 28 (1911), 298–330.

Morris, Colin. *The Papal Monarchy: The Western Church from 1050–1250*. Oxford: Clarendon Press, 1989.

Mulcahey, Michele. "The Dominican 'Studium' System and the Universities of Europe in the Thirteenth Century: A Relationship Redefined." In *Manuels, programmes de cours et techniques d'enseignement dans les universités médiévales* (Louvain-la-Neuve: Institut d'Études Médiévales de l'Université Catholique de Louvain, 1994), 277-324.

Murphy, J.J. *Three Medieval Rhetorical Arts*. Berkeley and London: University of California Press, 1971.

Murray, Alexander. "Confession as a Historical Source in the Thirteenth Century." In *The Writing of History in the Middle Ages: Essays Presented to Richard William Southern*, ed. R.H.C. Davis and J.M. Wallace-Hadrill (Oxford: Clarendon Press, 1981), 275-322.

Murray, Mary Charles, SND. *Rebirth and Afterlife: A Study of the Transmutation of Some Pagan Imagery in Early Christian Funerary Art*. BAR International Series 100. Oxford: BAR, 1981.

Newman, John Henry. *An Essay on the Development of the Christian Doctrine*. 1878. Reprinted, London: Longmans, Green, 1903.

O'Carroll, Mary E. SND. "The Lectionary for the Proper of the Year in the Dominican and Franciscan Rites of the Thirteenth Century." *AFP* 49 (1979), 79-103.

—. "The Educational Organisation of the Dominicans in England and Wales 1221-1348: A Multidisciplinary Approach." *AFP* 50 (1980), 23-62.

—. "Notes on some Vernacular Phrases found in MS Laud Misc. 511" *Notes & Queries* 29 (1982), 301-303.

—. "Two Versions of a Sermon by Richard Fishacre OP for the Fourth Sunday of Lent on the Theme 'Non enim heres erit filius ancille cum filio libere.'" *AFP* 54 (1984), 113-141.

Orme, Nicholas. *English Schools in the Middle Ages*. London: Methuen, 1973.

[Oxford, Bodleian Library.] *"The Sequence of Medieval Bookbinding" in 12th Century Manuscripts Written in England*. An Exhibition in Honour of N.R. Ker. Unpublished catalogue.

—. *Summary Catalogue of the Western Manuscripts in the Bodleian Library at Oxford*. Ed. R.W. Hunt, F. Madan, and H.H.E. Craster. 7 vols. Oxford: Clarendon Press, 1895-1953.

—. *Laudian Manuscripts*. Ed. H.O. Coxe. Reprinted from the edition of 1858-1885, with corrections and an historical introduction by R.W. Hunt. Bodleian Library, Quarto Catalogues 2. Oxford: [Bodleian] Library, 1973.

Pantin, William A. *The English Church in the Fourteenth Century*. Cambridge: Cambridge University Press, 1955.

Patterson, Sonia. "Paris and Oxford Manuscripts in the Thirteenth Century." Unpublished BLitt thesis. Oxford, 1969. [Bodleian Library, MS B.Litt.d 1457.]

Paul of Hungary. *Summa de Casibus Tractatis de Vitiis et Virtutibus*, In *Bibliotheca Casinensis*, Series 4 (2nd ed., Monte Cassino: Ex typographia Casinensi, 1880), 191–215.

Pelikan, Jaroslav. *Historical Theology: Continuity and Change in Christian Doctrine.* New York: Corpus, 1971.

—. *The Growth of Medieval Theology.* Vol. 3 in *The Christian Tradition: A History of the Development of Doctrine.* Chicago and London: University of Chicago Press, 1978.

Pelster, Franz. "An Oxford Collection of Sermons." *BQR* 6 (1929–1931), 168–172.

Petrus Comestor. *Historia scolastica.* PL 198: 1049–1722.

Petrus Lombardus. *Magistri Petri Lombardi Parisiensis Sententiae in IV Libris Distinctae.* Ed. I. Brady OFM. 3 vols. Grottaferrata: Editiones Collegii S. Bonaventurae ad Claras Aquas, 1971–1981.

Peultier, Etienne; and Gantois, PP. *Concordantiarum universae Scripturae Sacrae thesaurus.* Paris: P. Lethielleux, 1896.

Pignon, Laurent. *Laurentii Pignon Catalogi et Chronica.* Ed. Gilles Meersseman. MOPH 18. Rome: Institutum historicum Fratrum Praedicatorum, 1936.

Pfander, H.G. *The Popular Sermon of the Medieval Friars in England.* New York: [New York University], 1937.

Pollard, H. Graham. *Notes for a Directory of Cat Street, Oxford, Before AD 1500.* Typescript. Oxford: Bodleian Library, 1937. [Bodleian Library MS 010368 i 88.]

—. "Notes on the Size of the Sheet." *The Library* 22 (1941–1942), 105–137.

—. "William de Brailles." *BLR* 5 (1954–1956), 202–209.

—. "The Construction of English Twelfth-Century Bindings." *The Library*, 5th Series, 17 (1962), 1–22.

—. "The University and the Book Trade in Mediaeval Oxford." In *Beiträge zum Berufsbewusstsein des mittelalterlichen Menschen*, ed. Paul Wilpert, Miscellanea Mediaevalia 3 (Berlin– New York: de Gruyter, 1964), 336–344.

—. "The Names of Some English Fifteenth-Century Binders." *The Library*, 5th Series, 25 (1970), 193–218.

—. "Some Anglo-Saxon Bookbindings." *The Book Collector* 24 (1975), 130–159.

—. "Describing Medieval Bookbindings." In *Medieval Learning and Literature: Essays Presented to R.W. Hunt*, 50–65.

—. "The 'pecia' System in the Medieval Universities." In *Medieval Scribes, Manuscripts and Libraries: Essays Presented to N.R. Ker*, ed. Malcolm B. Parkes and A.G. Watson (London: Scolar Press, 1978), 145–161.

See also *Studies in the Book Trade: In Honour of Graham Pollard.*

Power, Eileen. *Medieval English Nunneries.* Cambridge: Cambridge University Press, 1922.

—. *Medieval Women.* Ed. M.M. Postan. Cambridge: University Press 1975.

Powicke, Frederick M. *The Thirteenth Century*. 2nd ed. Oxford: Clarendon Press, 1962.

—. *King Henry III and the Lord Edward: The Community of the Realm in the Thirteenth Century*. 2 vols. Oxford: Clarendon Press, 1947.

—. *Ways of Medieval Life and Thought*. London: Odhams, 1949.

—; and Christopher R. Cheney. *Councils and Synods with Other Documents Relating to the English Church, 1205-1313*. 2 vols. Oxford: Clarendon Press, 1964.

Proctor, Francis; and Christopher Wordsworth, ed. *Breviarium ad usum insignis ecclesiae Sarum*. 3 vols. [Cantabrigiae]: typis atque impensis almae matris Academiae Cantabrigiensis, 1882-1886.

Raymundus de Penafort. *Summa de Poenitentia, et Matrimonio cum glossis, Joannis de Friburgo*. Rome, 1603. Facsimile edtion. Farnborough, Hants.: Gregg Press, 1967.

Reichert, Benedikt Maria, ed. *Acta Capitulorum Generalium Ordinis Praedicatorum*. MOPH 3-4, 5 (*Litterae encyclicae magistri ordinis*), 8-14. 10 vols. Rome: In domo generalitia; Stuttgart: Roth, 1898-1904.

—. *Vitae Fratrum Ordinis Praedicatorum*. MOPH 1. Louvain: Charpentier, 1897. Trans. Placid Conway, ed. Bede Jarrett as *The Lives of the Brethren of the Order of Preachers, 1206-1259*. London: Burns, Oates and Washbourne, 1924.

Renard, J.P. *La formation et la destination des prédicateurs au début de l'Ordre des Prêcheurs, 1215-1237*. Fribourg: Imprimerie St. Canisius, 1977.

Riley-Smith, Jonathan. *What Were the Crusades?* 1977. 2nd ed. London: Macmillan, 1992.

Rivière, Jean. *Le dogme de la rédemption: Étude théologique*. Paris: Victor Lecouffre, 1905. Trans. Luigi Cappadelta as *The Doctrine of the Atonement: A Historical Essay*. London: Kegan Paul, Trench, 1909.

—. *Le dogme de la rédemption au début du Moyen Age*. Paris: Vrin, 1934.

Robbins, R.H.; and John Cutler. *Supplement to the Index of Middle English Verse*. Lexington: University of Kentucky Press, 1965.

Roberts, Phyllis Barzillay. "The Pope and the Preachers: Perceptions of the Religious Role of the Papacy in the Preaching Tradition of the Thirteenth-Century English Church." In *The Religious Roles of the Papacy: Ideals and Realities, 1150-1300*, ed. Christopher J. Ryan (Toronto: PIMS, 1989), 277-297.

—. *Studies in the Sermons of Stephen Langton*. Studies and Texts 16. Toronto: PIMS, 1968.

Rouse, Richard H.; and Mary A. *Preachers, Florilegia and Sermons: studies on the 'Manipulus Florum' of Thomas of Ireland*. Toronto: PIMS, 1979.

—. "The Verbal Concordances to the Scriptures." *AFP* 44 (1974), 5-30.

—. "Biblical Distinctions in the Thirteenth Century." *AHDLMA* 41 (1975), 27-37.
—. "Biblical 'Distinctiones,' the Thematic Sermon and Peter of Capua." Paper given at the IMSS Symposium, Oxford, July 1982.
—, ed. *Registrum Anglie de Libris Doctorum et Auctorem Veterum*. Latin text established by R.A.B. Mynors. Corpus of British Medieval Library Catalogues. London: British Library, in association with the British Academy, 1991.

Salter, H.E. *Medieval Oxford*. OHS 100. Oxford: Oxford Historical Society, 1936.
—. *Survey of Oxford*. Ed. William A. Pantin and W.T. Mitchell. 2 vols. OHS, NS 20. Oxford: Clarendon Press, 1969.
Sayers, Jane. *Innocent III Leader of Europe 1198-1216*. The Medieval World. London: Longman, 1994.
Scheeben, H.C. "Prediger und Generalprediger im Dominikanerorden des 13 Jahrhunderts." *AFP* 21 (1961), 112-141.
Schmitt, Jean-Claud. "Receuils franciscains d'*exempla* et perfectionnement des techniques intellectuelles du xiiie au xve siècles." *Bibliothéque de l'École des Chartes* 135 (1977), 5-21.
Schneyer, Johannes B. *Wegweiser zu Lateinischen Predigtreihen des Mittelalters*. Munchen, 1965.
—. *Repertorium der Lateinischen Sermones des Mittelalters für die Zeit von 1150-1350*. 11 vols. Munster: Aschendorff, 1969-1990.
Schnurnan, J.C. "Studies in the Medieval Book Trade from the Late 12th to the Middle of the 14th Century, with Special Reference to the Copying of Bibles." Unpublished BLitt thesis. Oxford, 1960. [Bodleian Library MS B.Litt d 815.]
Schroeder, H.J. *Disciplinary Decrees of the General Councils*. St Louis: , 1937.
Sheehan, M.W. "The Religious Orders, 1220-1370." In *The Early Oxford Schools*, ed. T.H. Ashton, 204-205.
Sheils, W.J.; and Diana Wood, ed. *Women in the Church*. SCH 27. Oxford: Basil Blackwell 1990.
Shirley, Walter Waddington, ed. *Royal and Other Historical Letters Illustrative of the Reign of Henry III*. RS 27. 2 vols. London: Longmans, Green, 1862-1866.
Smalley, Beryl. *The Study of the Bible in the Middle Ages*. 3rd ed. Oxford: Basil Blackwell, 1983.
—. *English Friars and Antiquity*. Oxford: Basil Blackwell, 1960.
—. *The Beckett Conflict and the Schools: A Study of the Intellectual in Politics*. Oxford: Basil Blackwell, 1973.
—. *The Gospels in the Schools, c1100-c1280*. London and Ronceverte: Hambledon Press, 1985.
—. "Studies on the Commentaries of Cardinal Stephen Langton." *AHDLMA* 5 (1930), 152-220.

—. "Stephen Langton and the Four Senses of Scripture." *Speculum* 5 (1931), 60–76.

—. "'Exempla' in the Commentaries of Stephen Langton." *Bulletin of the John Rylands Library* 17, no 1 (January 1933).

—. "Two Biblical Commentaries of Simon of Hinton." *RTAM* 13 (1946), 57–85.

—. "Some More Exegetical Works of Simon of Hinton." *RTAM* 15 (1948), 97–106.

—. "The *Quaestiones* of Simon of Hinton." In *Studies in Medieval History Presented to Frederick Maurice Powicke*, ed. R.W. Hunt, W.A. Pantin, and R.W. Southern (Oxford: Clarendon Press, 1948), 209–222.

—. "Robert Bacon and the Early Dominican School at Oxford." *TRHS* 4th Series (1948), 1–19.

—. "Some Latin Commentaries on the Sapiential Books in the Late Thirteenth and Early Fourteenth Centuries." *AHDLMA* 18 (1951), 103–128.

—. "Thomas Waleys OP." *AFP* 24 (1954), 50–107.

—. "Which William of Nottingham." *MARS* 3 (1954), 200–238.

—. "Robert Holcot OP." *AFP* 26 (1956), 5–97.

—. "Oxford University Sermons, 1290–1293." In *Medieval Learning and Literature: Essays Presented to R.W. Hunt*, 307–327.

Southern, Richard W. *Robert Grosseteste: The Growth of an English Mind in Medieval Europe.* Oxford: Clarendon Press, 1986.

—. "From Schools to University." In *The Early Oxford Schools*, ed. T.H. Ashton, 1–36.

—. "The English Origins of the 'Miracles of the Virgin.'" *MARS* 4 (1958), 176–216.

—. *Saint Anselm and His Biographer.* The Birkbeck Lectures 1959. Cambridge: Cambridge University Press, 1963.

—. *Saint Anselm: A Portait in a Landscape.* Cambridge: Cambridge University Press, 1990.

—, ed.: *see* Eadmer.

Steele, R. "The Pecia." *The Library* 4th Series 11 (1931), 230–234.

Stegmüller, Friedrich, ed. *Repertorium Commentariorum in Sententias Petri Lombardi.* 2 vols. Wurzburg: Schoning, 1947.

Studies in the Book Trade: In Honour of Graham Pollard. Ed. R.W. Hunt, I.G. Philip, and R.J. Roberts]. Oxford Bibliographical Society Publications NS 18. Oxford: Oxford Bibliographical Society, 1975.

Sweet, Jennifer. *English Preaching 1221–1293.* Unpublished B.Litt thesis, Oxford, 1950. Bodleian Library MS B.Litt d. 107.

—. "Some Thirteenth-century Sermons and their Authors." *JEH* 4 (1953), 27–36.

Talbot, C.H., ed: *see Florilegium Morale Oxoniense.*

Tanner, Norman, ed. *Decrees of the Ecumenical Councils.* 2 vols. London and Georgetown: Sheed and Ward; Washington, DC: Georgetown University Press, 1990.

Taxatio Ecclesiastica Angliae et Walliae auctoritate P. Nicholai IV, circa AD *1291*. Ed.
    T. Astle, S. Ayscough, and J. Caley. London: Record Commission; printed
    by G. Eyre and A. Strahan, 1802.
Thomas Aquinas, Saint. *Opera Omnia*. Ed. Eduard Fretté et Paul Maré. 34 vols.
    Paris: Vives, 1870–1880.
—. *Summa contra Gentiles*. Book 4: *Salvation*. Trans. Charles J. O'Neill. Notre
    Dame, IN: University of Notre Dame Press, 1975.
—. *Theological Texts*. Selected and translated with notes and an introduction by
    Thomas Gilby. London: Oxford University Press, 1955.
St. Thomas Aquinas, 1274–1974: Commemorative Studies. Ed. Armand A. Maurer.
    2 vols. Toronto: PIMS, 1974.
Pseudo-Thomas of Aquinas [unknown 13th-century Italian Dominican]. ["Trac-
    tatus solemnis de arte et vero modo predicandi]. Trans. Harry Caplan in
    his "A Late Mediaeval Tractate on Preaching," in his *Of Eloquence*, 52–78.
Thomas de Cantilupe. *Registrum Thome de Cantilupo, Episcopi Herefordensis* / *The
    Register of Thomas de Cantilupe, Bishop of Hereford* AD MCCLXXV-MCCLXXXII.
    Ed. R.G. Griffiths and W.W. Capes. Canterbury and York Society 2. 2 vols.
    Hereford: Wilson & Phillips, 1906–1907.
Thomas de Chobham. *Summa confessorum; cum Miserationes Dominus*. Ed. F.
    Broomfield. Analecta Mediaevalia Namurcensis 25. Louvain: Éditions
    Nauwelaerts, [1968].
Thomas of Eccleston. "De adventu Fratrum Minorum in Anglicam." In *Monu-
    menta Franciscana*, ed. J.S. Brewer, Rerum Britannicarum medii aevi scrip-
    tores 4, 2 vols. (London: Longman, Brown, Green, 1858–1882), 1: 3–72.
Thomson, Samuel Harrison. *The Writings of Robert Grosseteste, Bishop of Lincoln,
    1235–1253*. Cambridge: Cambridge University Press, 1940.
Thompson, Sally. *Women Religious: The Founding of English Nunneries after the
    Norman Conquest*. Oxford: Clarendon Press, 1991.
Tibber, Peter H. *The Origins of the Scholastic Sermon c1100–c 1210*, Unpublished
    DPhil thesis. Oxford, 1983. [Bodleian Library MS D Phil c 5001.]
Tillich, Paul *A History of Christian Thought*. Ed. Carl E. Braaten. Revision of 2nd
    edition. London: SCM Press, 1968.
Tixeront, Joseph. *Histoire des dogmes*. 3 vols. Paris: Lecoffre, 1905–1912. Trans.
    from the 5th edition by H.L.B. as *History of Dogmas*. London, 1910–1916.
    Reprinted, London: B. Herder, 1923–1930.
Torrell, J.P. *Initiation à saint Thomas d'Aquin, sa personne et son oeuvre*. Paris:
    Cerf, 1993.
Trivet, Nicholas. *N. Trevet: Annales Sex Regum Anglie 1126–1307*. Ed. Thomas
    Hog. London: English Historical Society, 1845. Selection translated by
    Bede Jarrett in *The English Dominicans, 1221–1921*, revised and abridged
    by Walter Gumbley (London: Burns, Oates and Washbourne, 1937), 209.

Tubach, F.C. *Index Exemplorum: A Handbook of Medieval Religious Tales.* FF Communications 86,204. Helsinki: Suomalainen Tiedeakatemia, 1969.

Tugwell, Simon OP, trans. and ed. *The Nine Ways of Prayer of Saint Dominic.* Dublin: Dominican Publications, 1978. [Author unknown; probably written between 1260 ... and 1288; trans. is based on the text of Codex Rossianus ed. Innocenzio Taurisano, OP in *Analecta sacri ordinis fratrum Praedicatorum* 15 (1922): 93ff.]

—, ed. *Early Dominicans: Selected Writings.* The Classics of Western Spirituality. London: SPCK, 1982.

Turner, Henry Ernest William. *The Patristic Doctrine of Redemption.* London: A.R. Mowbray, 1952.

Van Dijk, Stephen J.P. "The Lateran Missal." *Sacris Erudiri* 6 (1954), 125–179.

—. "Some Manuscripts of the Earlier Franciscan Liturgy." *Franciscan Studies* 14 (1954), 225–264.

—. "The Old Roman Rite." *Studia Patristica* 5 (1960), 185–205.

—. "Sources of the Roman Gradual." *Scriptorium* 14 (1960), 98–100.

—. "The Authentic Missal of the Papal Chapel." *Scriptorium* 14 (1960), 257–314.

—. "The Urban Rite and the Papal Rites in Seventh and Eighth Century Rome." *Sacris Erudiri* 12 (1961) 411–487.

—. *Sources of the Modern Roman Liturgy.* Studia et documenta franciscana 1–2. 2 vols. Leiden: Brill, 1963.

Van Dijk, Stephen J.P.; and Joan H. Walker. *The Origins of the Modern Roman Liturgy: The Liturgy of the Papal Court and the Franciscan Order in the Thirteenth Century.* Westminster, MD: Newman Press. 1960.

Vicaire, Marie-Humbert. *Histoire de saint Dominique.* Paris: Cerf, 1957. Trans. Kathleen Pond as *St. Dominic and His Times.* London: Darton, Longman & Todd, 1964.

Walther, Hans. *Proverbia sententiaeque latinitatis Medii Aevi. Lateinische Sprichwörter und Sentenzen des Mittelalters in alphabetischer Anordnung.* Carmina Medii Aevi posterioris Latina II.1–9. 9 vols. Göttingen: Vandenhoeck & Ruprecht, 1963–1986.

Walz, P.A. "The 'excepciones' from the *Summa* of Simon of Hinton." *Angelicum* 13 (1936), 283–368.

Ward, Benedicta. *The Prayers and Meditations of St. Anselm.* London: Penguin, 1973.

Ward, H.L., ed.: *see Catalogue of Romances.*

Watson, Andrew G., ed. *Catalogue of the Dated and Dateable Manuscripts c. 700–1600 in the Department of Manuscripts, the British Library.* 2 vols. London: British Museum Publications, 1979.

Weisheipl, James A. "Curriculum of the Faculty of Arts at Oxford in the Early Fourteenth Century." *Med.St.* 26 (1964), 143–185.

—. "Classification of the Sciences in Mediaeval Thought." *Med.St.* 27 (1965), 54–90.

—. "Developments in the Arts Course at Oxford in the Early Fourteenth century." *Med.St.* 28 (1966), 151–175.

Welter, Jean-Th. *Le 'Speculum Laicorum' édition d'une collection d"exempla' composée en Angleterre à la fin du xiiie siècle.* Paris: Picard, 1914.

—. *La 'Tabula Exemplorum' secundum ordinem alphabeti: receuil d"exempla' compilé en France à la fin du xiiie siècle.* Thesaurus exemplorum 3. Paris: Occitania, 1926.

Wenzel, Siegfried. *Verses in Sermons: 'Fasciculus Morum' and Its Middle English Poems.* Cambridge, MA: Medieval Academy of America, 1978.

—. "Macaronic Sermons in Medieval England: Some Observations." Paper given at IMSS Symposium, Oxford, 1982.

—. *Macaronic Sermons: Bilingualism and Preaching in Late-Medieval England.* Ann Arbor: University of Michigan Press, 1994.

Whiting, B.J. and H.W. *Proverbs, Sentences and Proverbial Phrases from English Writings Mainly Before 1500.* Cambridge, MA: Belknap Press; Harvard University Press, 1968.

Wigram, S.R. *Chronicles of the Abbey of Elstow.* Oxford: Parker, 1885.

Wilmart, André. "Un répertoire d'exégèse composé en Angleterre vers le début du xiiie siècle." In *Memorial Lagrange* (Paris: Gabalda, 1940), 307–346.

—. "Le 'Comes' de Murbach." *RB* 30 (1913), 35–53.

Woolf, Rosemary. *The English Religious Lyric in the Middle Ages.* Oxford: Clarendon Press, 1968.

Zink, Michel. *La prédication en langue romane avant 1300.* Nouvelle Bibliothèque du Moyen Âge 4. Paris: Champion, 1976.

Index

This index includes both names and subjects. Readers are encouraged to consult the principal entries (and the relevant subentries and cross references) first. These are organized under the following headings: *Church; Dominicans; MS Laud Misc. 511; preaching; sermon(s);* and *sermons in MS Laud Misc. 511.* Numbers in **bold** type refer to the items (sermons or sermon material) in the Catalogue of MS Laud Misc. 511 found in Appendix 1.

Adam Marsh 18, 20

Albertus Magnus 44, 46, 52, 57

Aldobrandinus de Cavalcantibus OP 215, 217, 220, 243, 246

Alexander the Great 80, 193, 344, 347, 352

Alexander of Hales 238

Alexander Stavensby, bishop 12, 19

Ambrose, St. 204, 238, 241

Anselm, St., of Bec 204, 236; soteriology 217, 229, 236-241, 245-247, 253; *Cur Deus Homo* 237, 240, 253

Antiochus 193, 343, 352

Aquinas: *see* Thomas Aquinas, St.

Assisi 6, 121-122

Athanasius, St. 241

Augustine of Canterbury, St. 120-121

Augustine of Hippo, St. 1, 4, 22, 27, 32, 35, 54, 73, 140, 162, 204-208, 217, 229, 238-241, 248-250, 259, 273; rule of 35, 208

Bacon: *see* Robert Bacon OP

Basevorn: *see* Robert Basevorn

Basil, St. 241

Bede, St., the Venerable 204, 239

Beguines 6, 34, 118, 133

Benedict, St. 133

Bernard, St. 7, 27, 140, 162, 166, 204, 206, 217, 236-237, 248, 259

Bible 30, 38, 44-45, 49, 51-52, 54-57, 106-107, 114, 127, 238; commentaries 57, 188; concordance, 31-32, 57, 95; *Correctorium* 30; imagery 171-173, 194, 233 (esp. n64); manuscripts 106-107, 114, 431-434

Bologna 5, 35, 43-45, 47-48, 58, 116

books 19, 38, 45, 51-58, 81-88, 101-108, 113, 121, 127, 140-141, 181, 205-206, 238-241; book trade 86-87, 113-115, 127-128; *quaterni* 86, 87; stationers 86, 127, 186

Cambridge 61, 63, 67, 71-72, 93, 103, 105, 117, 125, 126, 191, 193; college libraries 103

Canons Regular 3-5

Cassiodorus 162, 204, 241

Cathars 7, 8, 35

Clare, St. 133

Charlemagne 193, 347

Church: 148; apostolic life, *vita apostolica* 4-8, 35, 102, 132-133, 146, 212; benefice 5-6; Crusade 7-8, 112, 166-167, 349, 411; Fourth Lateran Council 1, 2, 8-10, 14-16, 19-20, 23, 34 n114, 35, 41-42, 75, 118, 121, 155 n95, 229-230; heresy 7, 148; Our

Lady 86, 124, 144, 147, 151, 158–
161, 174, 203, 210, 226, 235, 358,
373–375, 354, 407, 409–410, 428,
429; patristic teaching 155, 234,
238, 240–241, 245, 247, 255, 267;
prayer 12, 13, 23, 25–26, 28, 38,
43, 98, 101, 147, 149, 161, 168,
172, 174, 207–208, 210–212, 232,
234, 236–238, 258, 406–407, 427–
429; religious devotion 225–226,
232, 236–237, 241–242, 249, 254;
religious movements 4, 6–8 (see
also vita apostolica); tradition in
2, 22, 24, 43, 91, 121, 131, 144,
168, 171, 174, 208, 229, 232, 234,
236, 238, 242, 247, 254, 255
Constantine 193, 345
Cyprian, St. 241

Diana d'Andalo, Bl. 133
Dominic, St. 7, 9–10, 35–39, 43–44,
58, 72, 74, 95, 211, 273
Dominicans 2, 16, 17–20, 30, 31,
34–74, 117–120, 127–128, 131–
133, 143, 145, 148–149, 153, 174,
213–215, 221, 238–239, 243, 250,
257, 265, 272, 273; Acta 39–43;
Constitutions 35–43; convents
38–39, 41, 58–62, 65, 74, 272;
diffinitors 39, 41–42, 44, 57, 74;
fratres communes 46–47, 56;
General Chapter 35, 39–48, 57–
58, 63, 73, 91, 116; liturgy 116,
120, 122–124, 260–261, 355–370,
380–381; and pastoral care 118,
132–133; pastoral care of women 57, 118–120, 133, 149, 155,
161, 174; poverty 4, 6, 35, 56,
102, 107, 136, 140–141, 148, 212,
225, 248–249, 263, 415, 420, 426,
427 (and the poor) 194, 198, 200,
210, 412, 415; preachers 35, 37–
38, 41–43, 46, 51–52, 57–58, 70–

71, 73–74, 116, 213–215, 221,
250, 256, 260–261, 271–272;
preachers general 38, 41, 57;
preaching and study 36–46, 51,
55, 68; provinces 35, 39, 40–44,
46–48, 56, 57; provincial chapter 39, 41, 44, 63, 67; and secular clergy 15, 41–42; sermons
57, 71, 73, 75, 79, 81, 84–98,
213–215, 221, 250; theologians
57, 72–74, 88, 91, 94–95, 238–
239; usefulness,' spirit of 130,
202; visitation (practice of annual visits) 38, 47, 52, 57; vicariates or visitations (division of a
province into) 47, 60, 62–64, 67
–, education of 37–39, 42–51, 57–
58, 60–70, 126; arts (liberal) 38,
44, 47–54, 67, 69, 177; degrees
in arts and theology 48–49; disputatio and quaestiones 51, 54–
55, 90; lectors 39, 44, 46–56, 71,
74; and literacy 139–140, 141,
155; logic 45, 48, 53, 54; master
and students 38, 45, 48, 55, 57;
philosophy 38, 44–45, 49–50,
52–55, 57, 67, 74, 89, 237; St.
Jacques priory, Paris 30–31, 48,
57, 95; and scholastic method
161, 177, 185, 237; schools or
studia 38, 40, 44–49, 51–52, 54,
57–58, 60, 61, 63–67, 71, 74, 101,
126–127, 129, 261; theology 35,
37–38, 41–42, 44–58, 60–61, 63,
66, 71, 72–74, 89–92, 144, 155–
156, 160–161, 168, 229–231, 234–
237, 239–240, 256, 263, 265–268,
274; trivium 44, 51–52
– in England and Wales 14–20,
58–74, 89–92, 125–126, 130–174;
divisions of province (visitations) 62–67; eminent English
friars 69, 71–73, 88–92, 223, 239,

241, 250, 257, 265; schools in the province 63-67, 126-127, 261; visitors 38, 47-48, 52, 57
Dunstable 69, 112, 125-126, 132
Didymus 241

Ecclesia Anglicana 1, 8-20, 61-63, 74; assistance of the friars 15-18; councils and synods 10-11; implementation of Lateran IV 10-15, 75; thirteenth century bishops 8, 118; canonized bishops 10 (see also Robert Grosseteste); educational level of the clergy 15-16, 70; parish clergy 6, 14, 18-20, 41, 70, 137; Synods 10-11, 119; diocesan and synodal statutes 9-15, 19, 34
Elstow 80, 108-113, 115, 118-120, 125-126, 129, 130-174, 259, 271, 273; abbesses 137-143; church holdings 137; community 133-143; disputed election 142-143; economy 136-138, 141; excavations 134-136; foundation 136; and Giffard family 142; land holdings 126, 136; learning 139-141; plan of the site 134; preachers of 108-113, 119-120, 131-132, 143, 217, 219, 222; school 141-142
England (and Wales): relationship of church and king in 263-265; road system 59, 61-62, 64-6, 126; social conditions in mid-thirteenth-century 164-168, 174, 193-201, 259, 272. See also Ecclesia Anglicana
Etienne de Bourbon OP 191, 201
Eusebius 204, 241

Fishacre: see Richard Fishacre
Francis, St. 6, 9, 35, 133

Franciscans 6, 16-20, 30, 35, 38, 60, 70, 95, 101-103, 116-119, 120, 122-124, 203, 211, 214, 221, 238-239, 241, 260, 263; liturgical reforms 116, 120, 122-123, 356-358; Mass pericopes of the Temporale 360-370, 380; Registrum Anglie 241
Fulk of Neuilly 5

Gregory the Great, St. 27, 33 n114, 155, 162, 204, 206, 217, 238, 255
Gregory Nazianzus, St. 241
Grosseteste: see Robert Grosseteste
Guilelmus Malliaco: see William of Mailly
Guilelmus Peraldus OP 34, 46, 57, 92, 93-98, 118, 156, 215, 217, 219-220, 223-224, 243, 246, 250-251, Sermons 10, 165, 198; sermon collections 34, 57, 117, 222-223; summa 46, 95, 202, 209

H. de Mordon 86, 88, 223, 397 Sermon 166
Haymo of Faversham OFM 116, 120, 357-358
Hilary, St. 238, 241
Hinton: see Simon Hinton
Historia Scholastica 44, 56, 140, 239. See also Peter Comestor
Honorius III 9, 35, 122
Hugh of Hartlepool OFM 214, 217-221, 242-243 n94, 246, 250
Hugh of Manchester OP 72, 115
Hugh of Mistretune OP 91
Hugh of St. Cher OP/Hugo de S. Caro OP 18, 30-32, 54, 57, 93-95, 97-98, 118, 163, 214 n3, 222-224, 239-240; Sermons 78, 171, 229 (?); and the biblical concordance 31-32, 57, 95
Hugh Sneyth OP 72, 115
Hugh of St. Victor 93, 140, 237

Humbert of Romans OP/Humbert-
us Romanis OP 1, 25, 32, 56–57,
68, 72, 116, 120, 123, 127, 130–
131, 202 n35, 207–208, 222; liturgical reforms 116, 120, 123, 355–
356
Humiliati 6, 35

Innocent III 5–9, 32–33, 35, 121–122
Innocent IV 48
Isidore, St. 162, 239

Jacques de Vitry 191, 193, 201
Jerome, St. 162, 204, 217, 241
Johannes Halgrinus de Abbatisvil-
lata/John of Abbeville 93–97,
118, 214 n3, 223 **98**
John Bromyard OP 73
John of Cesterlade OP 72
John Chrysostom, St. 204, 206, 217,
241, 259. *See also* pseudo- Chry-
sostom
John Damascene, St. 217, 227, 235,
239
John of Darlington OP 200
John of Freiburg OP 52, 55
John Mauntel 193, 354
John of Newport OP 119, 132
John of Parma OFM 116
John Pecham OFM 50, 139 n32
John of St. Giles OP 17, 20, 48, 71,
257
Jordan of Saxony OP, second mas-
ter general 36, 60, 93, 130
Julian 193, 351

Leo the Great, St. 204, 255
Liber Exemplorum 191, 193, 343
Lincoln 17, 63, 67, 69, 71, 119, 125,
132, 141, 204
liturgy: *see* MS Laud Misc. 511: liturgical context
London 43, 45–46, 57, 60, 62–63,

67–69, 103, 105, 114, 117, 126,
129
Lord Edward 267, 345
Luke de Wodeford OP 72

Manipulus Florum 204–205
manuscripts 75, 86, 90, 93, 97–98,
102–108, 140–141, 143, 191, 205,
214 n3, 239 n83, 241 n93, 342,
356, 358–359, 381, 430–435; monastic manuscripts 103, 104,
106, 113, 140–141, 430, 431, 433
MS Laud Misc. 511:
–, description and purpose: binding 79, 81–84, 114–115; codicological construct 221–224; dating 108–116, 257–258; palaeographical description 76–84;
provenance 117–129, 260–261;
as a preacher's handbook 175,
212, 273
–, characteristics: 'above/below
top line' 78, 113; annotation
79–82 (list of marks), 109–111,
131–132, 178, 182, 188, 191–92,
201–202, 296, 312, 342; alphabetical order 77, 84, 92-93, 106–
107, 205; cross references 80,
107; enumeration and numbering systems 84, 88, 96, 103–107;
arabic numerals 76, 78, 80, 87-
88, 103–106, 117, 126–127, 181–
182; roman numerals 103; line-
numbering 76, 88, 105–106;
flourishing 76, 81, 101, 103, 107;
histograms 99–100
–, compilation: and compiler of
85, 87–88, 98, 101, 108, 111–112,
114–115, 128, 159, 162, 175, 191–
192, 201–206, 208, 213, 215, 223,
225, 243, 254–255, 257, 261, 271,
273; scribes 78–81, 86, 110–112,
113–114, 126–128, 178, 182, 188,

190-192, 201-202, 205, 222-223, 257; source books 85-88, 92, 96-98, 100-101, 111, 158-162, 175, 182, 188, 206, 213, 221-224, 255, 257, 340-341

-, contents 78-80, 84-85, 87-96, 98-101, 108, 110, 115, 117-18, 130, 145-168; catalogue of the MS 275-321; concordance with Schneyer's *Reportium* 323-328; 343-354 (exempla); florilegia 84, 117, 162, 175, 204-206, 211, 240-241; 'missing sermons' 322; rejected folios 76-77, 222-223, 321; sermon material 84, 85, 86, 101, 203-212; theme, incipit and thema (alphabetical list) 332-339; the time-place-dated sermons 191-193, 178-210, 225-230, 242-254, 263-271

-, distinctions: 175-191, 201-202; and sermon development 27, 161-162, 175; collections of 176-177; marginal distinctions that are sermon summaries 178, 180-185, 188-190, 255, 268; methodology of 176-277, 238-239; specific distinctions 207 (on humility and *Pax*), 238 (division of Lombard's *Sentences*) 255, 268, 391 (on humility)

-, editions of sermon texts 382-397

-, exempla: description and sources 27, 90, 164-168, 191-201, 220-221, 245, 247, 256-257, 259, 263, 264; list of 342-354; allusions to specific exempla 193-200; particular exempla 97, 115, 145 nn45-46, n48, 146 nn51-52, n58, 147 n60, 148 n66, n68, 149 n71, 150 n72, nn75-76, 151-152 nn80-82, 153 n90, 154 n93, 157 n100, 158 n103, 159 n107, 164 n122, n124, nn126-127, 165 nn130-132, 166 nn135-136, 167 n137, 169 n147, 170 n152, 171 nn167-168, 220 n26, 245 n102, 246 n107, 247 n109, 257 n7, 258 n10, 259 n14, 264 n27, 266 n37, 267 nn38-39, 268 n43, 270 n58

- liturgical context 79, 87, 96, 115-116, 120-134, 139, 163, 232, 258-261, 358-359, 370-381; and calendar or liturgical year 79, 107, 116, 122, 161, 201, 260-262, 359, 379; Advent liturgy 375-377, 379; Breviary/Divine Office 51, 116, 120-124, 139-140, 162-163, 219, 240-241, 254, 258-261, 271, 373-379; Dominican, Franciscan, Paris, Sarum, York breviaries 116, 260-261, 373; Missal 121, 261-262, 355-358, 371-372, 375-381; Dominican, Franciscan, Paris, Sarum, York missals 122-124, 355-356, 359-360, 371-372; Mass pericopes (Gospel and Epistle readings) for the Temporale 261-262, 360-370, 380; and reform of liturgy (Humbert and Haymo) 116, 120, 122-123, 356-358; Roman liturgy 120-123, 261-262, 355-359, 380-381; Temporale 79, 101, 114, 122-124, 201, 203-204, 222, 260-262, 358-372, 377-379; Uses 120-124, 260-261

-, vernacular phrases in: 292 **78**, 293 **82**, 295 **95**, 295-296 **96**, 297 **106a**, 301-302 **130**, **134**

Mariscoes 193, 256-257 n7, 344
Mary of Oignies 133
Matthew Paris 257
Maurice of Provins 176-177, 186-189

monastic order: monks 136–137, 140–141; nuns 112, 119–120, 132–133, 136–138, 141, 143, 149, 154–155, 159, 161, 163–164, 166, 168, 174; reforms of 3, 4; tradition 237. *See also* Elstow

Nicholas, St. 193, 347, 354
Nicholas Biard 177, 186–187
Nicholas of Langetoft OP 119, 132
Nicholas Trevet OP 60, 72–73
Northampton 61, 67, 125–126, 129, 132

Odo of Cheriton 191–193, 201
Order of Friars Minor: *see* Franciscans
Order of Preachers: *see* Dominicans
Origen 241, 259
Oxford 1, 5, 11, 35, 47, 54, 56, 60–61, 67–68, 71–73, 76, 86, 88–89, 91–93, 103–104, 115, 117, 119, 124–129, 132, 214–215, 238, 261; Blackfriars 60, 63, 68, 89, 126, 127–129, regent masters at 88–89, 91, 115; studium generale 40, 44, 48, 63, 89, 91, 126; visitation 63, 67, 125; college libraries 103; Franciscans 60, 89, 93, 95, 101–105, 116; university 49–51 (disputes with), 126

Papal court, 5, 48, 73, 121; chapel 116, 120–121; power 263–64; studium 48
Paris 5, 30, 32, 34–35, 43–44, 47–50, 54, 56, 72, 89, 94–95, 106, 115, 122–124, 143, 177, 186, 193–194, 238, 260–261, 264, 346
parish clergy 6, 14, 18–20, 41, 70, 137; and preaching 15–16, 70. *See also* Dominicans

Paul of Hungary OP 44
Pecia 86, 107, 113
Peraldus: *see* Guilelmus Peraldus
Peter, St. 26, 135, 148–149, 152, 164, 171
Peter Abelard 5
Peter the Chanter: *lectio/disputatio/praedicatio* 5, 16, 90–91
Peter Comestor 44, 52, 56, 140, 239
Peter the Hermit 4
Peter of Limoges (Pierre de Limoges), 34
Peter Lombard (Petrus Lombardus) 5, 54, 238; *Sentences* 49, 54, 56, 74, 238, 247; commentaries on the *Sentences* 54, 74, 89–91, 103–106, 210, 239, 247
Peter Manners OP 91
Peter of Poitiers 5
Peter of Ravenna 204
Petrus de Remis OP/Peter of Rheims OP 34, 93–98, 118, 161, 217, 221, 223; Sermons 60, **83, 108, 117, 127, 133**
Poor Men of Lyons 6
preaching: aids 30–34, 57 (*see also* sermon(s): aids); and *artes praedicandi* 11, 21–24, 28–31, 75, 130, 161–162; audience of mendicant preaching 112, 130–132, 143–154, 161, 166, 168, 174, 203, 221, 260, 271–272; catechetical 13–14; at Elstow 145–146; exempla in 193–200; itinerant 6, 28, 35, 37, 46, 61; language of 29–30, 139–140, 163–164, 255–256 (*see also* vernacular); Lateran IV on 9; Lenten 46, 132, 145–154, 156–157, 213, 225–227, 359, 406, 407–411; macaronic 30; and oral/aural culture, 28, 55, 131, 181, 184, 222–223; mendicant pocket-books 87, 107; and

parish clergy 15-16, 70; and pastoralia 19, 20, 75; popular 4, 6-8, 30, 70, 107-108, 155, 174, 272; revival and practice of 1, 2-9, 13-15, 17-18, 24-28, 32, 43, 46, 51, 55, 68-71, 73, 109-113, 161-162, 175; and priests' - manuals 19, 20, 51, 177; techniques, including use of verbal patterns 25, 28-29, 31, 179-181, 184; theory of 22-24, 28-29; university preaching 214-15, 221, 254; vernacular 29-30, 42, 125, 139-140, 163-164, 203, 219, 220, 256

preachers: instructions for, in sermons 26, 158; licence 68-69, 118, 119, 125, 132; licence to hear confessions 68-69, 70, 119, 125. *See also* Dominicans: education of; constitutions; poverty

pseudo-Chrysostom 206, 259 n13

Rabanus Maurus 204, 217

Raymund of Penaforte OP 36, 39, 43, 44, 46, 51, 156

Rex Anglie 125, 165-166, 171, 199-200, 256, 258-259, 264-266; Henry III 50, 71, 257-258, 265, 343-354; coronation oath 264 n28

Rex Francie 125, 165, 199, 347, 349; King Philip 350

Richard Fishacre, regent master at Oxford Blackfriars, 26, 72, 88-96, 105-106, 115, 118, 129, 199-201, 209, 223, 238-239, 247; Sermon **82**; Commentary on the *Sentences* 89-90, 106, 209, 238-239, 247; use of *affectus aspectus* distinction in sermons 239

Richard Knapwell OP 72-73, 115

Richard Rufus OFM 89, 105-106

Richard Stavensby 31

Richard of St. Victor 5, 237

Richard of Thetford 179

Richard de Winkley OP 72

Robert Bacon OP 60, 72, 88, 94, 106, 239 n82

Robert Basevorn 1, 24-26, 28, 29

Robert Bromyard OP 72

Robert Grosseteste, bishop of Lincoln, 1, 10, 12, 14, 16-20, 29, 33, 55, 71, 81, 89, 103, 105, 107, 118, 140, 177, 204, 238-239, 245, 263; as scholar 55, 204; master at Franciscan school in Oxford 238; *Templum Dei* 19, 177, 250, 245

Robert Holcot OP 69, 73, 192

Robert Kilwardby 27, 50, 73, 89, 115, 205, 241, 250

royal power 50, 138, 199−100, 263-265. *See also Rex Anglie*

Santa Sabina 73, 94, 95

Scholastica, St. 133

Scripture 1, 5, 13, 18-19, 22-24, 27, 31, 35, 38, 51-52, 54, 57, 90, 107, 112, 143-144, 149, 153, 157, 161, 171, 173, 176-177, 186-188, 192, 201, 215-217, 228, 232-234, 237, 254, 258-259; 'types' in Scripture 228, 233; four senses of Scripture 23, 27, 54, 153, 161, 176, 187, 226, 232-233, 415

sermon(s): *ad status* 130, 155, 174; aids 30-34, 175-212 (*see also* preaching aids); antitheme 25-26, 84, 94, 97-98, 112, 143, 152 n82, 157, 171, 218-220, 271; audience of 112, 130-132, 143-154, 161, 166, 168, 174, 221, 260, 271-272; collections 32-34, 57, 75, 85, 88, 93, 101, 115, 222; dating 115, 145-161, 256-258; model 32-34, 96, 221-222; repetition in 250, 256; repetition of texts 150–151; and *reportatio* 33–34, 84, 89–90, 96, 161, 176, 178, 185, 221–222, 257; structure 22–28, 178–179; theme 24, 89–90, 92–93, 109–110, 149, 161, 163, 168, 179, 188, 202, 213–214, 221, 243, 251, 261, 272, 329–332, 370–373, 378; thema 92, 338–339; types 130, 155, 174, 221, 272; transmission 101, 151–152, 176, 206, 221, 223–224, 255, 257–258; and visual representations 241–242, 265–266

sermons in MS Laud Misc. 511
–, identification: 89–94, 97–98, 223; 10, 60, 66 (Hinton), **77a-b**, **78**, **82** (Fishacre), **83**, **98**, **108**, **117**, **127**, **133**, **165**, **171**, **198**, **229**; summaries 178–191, 255 (in distinction form), 406–429 (in English); duplicated content of 76, 79, 85, 256; edited texts of 382–397; Elstow sermons 156–161; time-dated sermons 225–230; preached Easter Sunday 242–254; preached first Sunday after octave of Easter 255–272; Advent sermons 101, 115, 122, 124, 163, 189 (summary in distinction), 217, 255–272, 263 (and theology of Advent), 375–377 (and Advent liturgy), 382–386 (and Sermon 13), 427–429 (summaries in English of **5**, **8**, **12**, **13**, **14**, **15**)
– preached at Elstow: 108–111, 143–168, 287 **50** (summary 408), 287–288 **53** (summary 410), 291 **72** (summary 408–09), 292 **77a-b** (summary 411), 292–293 **78** (summary 406), 294 **90** (summary 410), 296 **100** (summary

407, 411), 303 **136**, 305–306 **153** (summay 406–07), 319 **230**; no place named 289–290 **64** (summary 410–411), 315 **207** (summary 407–408), 319–320 **231** (summary 409–410); Sermon **136** 392–395; summaries in English 406–411; first Elstow preacher 145–149; second Elstow preacher 149–156; preacher of the time-dated sermons 156–161
– Paschal sermons 144, 161, 213–254 (esp. 225–230), 242–254, 392–395; summaries in English: Easter Sunday **114**, **115**, **116**, **117**, **118**, **119**, **120**, **121**, **122**, 412–418; Second Sunday after Easter **131**, **132**, **133**, **134**, **135**, **136**, **137**, **138**, **139**, **140**, **147** 418–422; comparative sermons 422–427
– authorities 27, 54, 55, 97, 143–144, 162–163, 175, 186–188, 201, 203–204, 206, 212, 215–221, 258–259, 398–405; classical allusions 188, 193, 218, 345, 404; etymologies and interpretation of names 107, 153, 162–163, 217, 259, 405; patristic 162, 204–206, 217, 259, 404; gloss 162, 217, 405; liturgical 163, 218–219, 259, 374–375, 377–379, 405; masters and saints 162, 204, 206, 217, 259, 404–405; scriptural 162, 215–217, 258–259, 401–403
–, biblical figures and subjects: Adam (and Christ) 228, 235, 246, 247, 269, 409, 412, 415, 421, 428; coming of Christ 263, 268–271, 427–429; kingship of Christ 148–149, 165, 171, 245, 262, 264–269, 271, 412, 416–417, 419, 423,

425, 427-429; imitation or following of Christ 4, 167, 190, 244, 251-253, 409-410, 418-426, 428; John the Baptist 219, 263; Passion of Christ 149, 154, 225-226, 243, 246-250, 254, 409-410, 412, 414-416, 418-427, 429; Our Lady (and devotion to) 124, 147, 159-161, 354, 375, 407, 409-410, 428, 429

-, catechetical content of 12-13, 22, 143-144, 155-156, 168-174, 225-230, 232, 242-254, 256, 262-271, 273-274, 406-429

- images and tropes: general 144, 149, 153, 168-172, 194-195, 197, 218, 220, 228-229, 233, 243, 245, 247, 249, 268-269, 270; Christ 169-171, 197, 233 n64, 243, 245, 247, 266-267, 269; *diaphonum* and *tenebrosa* 92, 348; God 168-169, 268; hell and devils 173, 194; sin 171-173, 270; soteriological tropes: 'devil's rights/ ransom' 233-235, 237-238, 240, 245-246, 348, 408-412, 415-417, 421-422, 424, 426-429

- sacramental references: baptism 11, 12-13, 172 n173, 219, 229, 241, 250, 411, 422; Eucharist 2, 20, 218-219, 225-429, 232, 250-251, 261-262, 413-415, 417-418, 423; penance or confession 1, 9, 11-20, 41-42, 46, 51, 68-70, 95, 112, 118-120, 145-147, 150-157, 189-190, 209-210, 225, 227-230, 251, 263, 270-271, 406-411, 413, 416-417, 422, 428; critique of the practice 155-156; sacraments 9, 11, 14, 19, 28, 118, 144, 161, 190, 208, 210, 212, 226-230, 244, 250-251, 263-264, 271-272, 417-418; preaching on confession 145,

146, 150-153, 155-156, 225, 251, 270-271; and penance 145-146, 149, 152-153, 156, 251, 263, 268, 270-271, 406-411, 413, 416, 417, 422, 428

- topics (other): almsgiving 198, 200, 208-210, 212, 406, 421, 427; contrition 145, 153, 156-157, 172, 189-190, 209-211, 229, 251, 406-408, 410-411, 413, 416, 422; forgiveness 146, 148, 154, 168, 208-209, 230, 407, 413, 428; hell 144-145, 172-173, 228, 253, 409, 411, 414, 416-417; and demons 150-151 n76, 152 n83, n86, 173, 201, 212, 346, 352, 417; humility 147, 150, 207-208, 211, 225, 248, 268, 412, 415, 419-420, 424, 427; mercy 101, 156-161, 168-169, 174, 201, 208-210, 212, 230, 249-253, 271, 407, 410-411, 417, 419, 422, 424, 427; penance 145-146, 149, 152-153, 156, 251, 263, 268, 270-271, 406-411, 413, 416-417, 422, 428; penitence 149, 155-156, 229, 418; prayer 12, 13, 23, 25, 26, 28, 38, 43, 98, 101, 147, 149, 161, 168, 172, 174, 207-208, 210-212, 232, 234, 236-238, 258, 395-396 **163**, 406-407, 427-429; and recidivism (*recidivandi*) 145 n49, 151-152, 153 n90, 180, 225, 227, 229-230, 244, 415; resurrection 225-226, 228, 243, 250, 412-413, 415-417, 423; redemption 263, 266-267, 407, 409, 416, 419, 421-422, 426-429; soteriology 231-240, 244-247, 253-254, 267-268; satisfaction 151, 153, 156, 189-190, 210, 229, 235, 237, 240, 245-247, 251, 408, 410-411, 416, 417, 422, 425; sin 147-149, 151-152, 154, 156, 171-172, 207-212,

225-230, 234-235, 237, 246-247, 249, 251-253, 263, 266-271
Simon Boraston OP 73
Simon Hinton OP 20, 40, 46, 52, 72, 88, 89, 91-94, 115, 118, 129, 208, 223, 239, 290 66 386-390; *Summa juniorum* 20, 46, 52, 91, 208, 239
Stavensby: *see* Alexander Stavensby; Richard Stavensby
Stephen Langton 5, 130, 191
Summa de casibus 44, 46, 52, 103. *See also* Paul of Hungary; Raymund of Penaforte
Summa confessorum 55, 75
summae 75, 190, 202, 204, 208-209
Summae de virtutibus et vitiis 46, 57, 95, 202, 209

Theophilus 193, 351, 354
Thomas Aquinas, St. 33, 44-46, 48, 50, 52, 55, 57, 73, 89, 190, 204, 215, 239-240, 264-265, 268-271; pseudo-Aquinas sermon 215, 230
Thomas de Cantilupe 10, 119
Thomas Hopeman OP 73
Thomas Jorz OP 72-73
Thomas of Ireland: *see Manipulus Florum*
Thomas de Lisle OP 73
Thomas of Sutton OP 50, 72-73

Thomas Ryngestede OP 73
Thomas Waleys OP 1, 24, 28, 72-73, 179, 185-186
Thomas of York OFM 50

universities: Cambridge 48, 63, 71; Northampton 67, 126; Oxford 48-51, 60; Paris 44, 47-50, 54, 56, 177, 186, 193-194; and the friars 49-51;

Victorines 5, 93, 237
Vincent of Beauvais OP 57
virtues and vices: *see Summae virtutum et vitiis*
Vitae Fratrum 193
Vitae Patrum 201, 211

Waldensians 6
William de Brailles 127
William of Hotham OP 72, 115
William of Macclesfield OP 72
William of Mailly 186-189
William de Montibus 93
William Peraldus OP: *see* Guilelmus Peraldus
William of St. Amour 50
William Rothwell OP 72
women 6, 7, 118-119, 132-133, 136-143, 149, 153-156, 160-161, 174, 198, 201, 343, 346, 348-351, 354, 409-410, 413, 421; pastoral care of: *see* Dominicans